A. F. Grundy · D. Köhler · V. Oechtering · U. Petersen (Eds.)

Women, Work and Computerization

Springer
Berlin
Heidelberg
New York
Barcelona
Budapest
Hong Kong
London
Milan
Paris
Santa Clara
Singapore
Tokyo

A. F. Grundy · D. Köhler · V. Oechtering · U. Petersen (Eds.)

Women, Work and Computerization

Spinning a Web from Past to Future

Proceedings of the 6th International IFIP-Conference
Bonn, Germany, May 24-27, 1997

Springer

A. Frances Grundy
University of Keele
Department of Computer Science
Keele
Staffordshire ST5 5BG
United Kingdom

Veronika Oechtering
Universität Bremen
Fachbereich Mathematik/Informatik
Postfach 33 04 40
D-28334 Bremen
Germany

Doris Köhler
Regionales Rechenzentrum
der Universität Hamburg
Schlüterstr. 70
D-20146 Hamburg
Germany

Ulrike Petersen
FIT-KI, GMD-Forschungszentrum
Informationstechnik GmbH
Schloss Birlinghoven
D-53754 St. Augustin
Germany

ISBN 3-540-62610-7 Springer-Verlag Berlin Heidelberg New York

Library of Congress Cataloging-in-Publication Data applied for

Die Deutsche Bibliothek – CIP-Einheitsaufnahme

International Federation for Information Processing: Proceedings of the ... international IFIP-conference. - Berlin ; Heidelberg ; New York ; Barcelona ; Budapest ; Hong Kong ; London ; Milan ; Paris ; Santa Clara ; Singapore ; Tokyo : Springer.
Women, work, and computerization: spinning a web from past to future ; Bonn, Germany, May 24 - 27, 1997 / A. F. Grundy ... (ed.). - Berlin ; Heidelberg ; New York ; Barcelona ; Budapest ; Hong Kong ; London ; Milan ; Paris ; Santa Clara ; Singapore ; Tokyo : Springer, 1997 (Proceedings of the ... international IFIP-conference ; 6)
ISBN 3-540-62610-7

This work is subject to copyright. All rights are reserved, whether the whole or part of the material is concerned, specifically of translation, reprinting, reuse of illustrations, recitation, broadcasting, reproduction on microfilm or in any other way, and storage in data banks. Duplication of this publication or parts thereof is permitted only under the provisions of the German Copyright Law of September 9, 1965, in its current version, and permission for use must always be obtained from Springer-Verlag. Violations are liable for prosecution under the German Copyright Law.

© IFIP 1997
Printed in Germany

The use of general descriptive names, registered names, trademarks, etc. in this publication does not imply, even in the absence of a specific statement, that such names are excempt from relevant protective laws and regulations and therefore free for general use.

Production: PRO EDIT GmbH, D-69126 Heidelberg
Typesetting: Schreibbüro Börding, D-53229 Bonn
Cover Design: design & production GmbH, D-69121 Heidelberg

SPIN: 10570510 33/3142-5 4 3 2 1 0 - Printed on acid-free paper

International Programme Committee and Referees

Alison Adam (GB)
Andrew Clement (CDN)
Barbara Becker (D)
Susanne Bødker (DK)
Cecile K. M. Crutzen (NL)
Steffi Engert (D)
Ulrike Erb (D)
Jutta Eusterbrock (D)
Christiane Funken (D)
Eileen Green (GB)
Joan Greenbaum (USA)
Frances Grundy (GB)
Ileana Hamburg (D)
Hanja Hansen (CH)
Maritta Heisel (D)
Ute Hoffmann (D)
Eva Hüttenhain (D)
Vivi Katsa (GR)
Doris Köhler (D)
Vitalina Koval (RUS)
Bettina Kuhlmann (D)
Christel Kumbruck (D)
Gloria Mark (D, USA)
Cecilia Ng (MAL)
Veronika Oechtering (D)
Uta Pankoke-Babatz (D)
Ulrike Petersen (D)
Bente Rasmussen (N)
Fanny-Michaela Reisin (D)
Gabriele Schade (D)
Heidi Schelhowe (D)
Britta Schinzel (D)
Bettina Schmitt (D)
Angela Scollary (AUS)
Heike Stach (D)
Lucy Suchman (USA)
Marja Vehvilaïnen (FIN)
Ina Wagner (A)
Gabriele Winker (D)

Conference Committee

Organising Co-Chairs
Doris Köhler, Veronika Oechtering, Ulrike Petersen

Tutorials Chair
Jutta Eusterbrock, Doris Köhler

Posters Chair
Ileana Hamburg

Demonstrations Chairs
Jutta Eusterbrock, Uta Pankoke-Babatz

Proceedings Chair
Doris Köhler, Veronika Oechtering

Local Arrangements
Barbara Becker, Eva Hüttenhain, Uta Pankoke-Babatz, Ulrike Petersen

Main Organizer Contact and Treasurer
Ute Claussen, Veronika Oechtering

Conference Management
Christine Harms -ccHa-

Design
Maike Kaluscha

Introduction

This book brings together all those submissions selected for presentation at the 6th International IFIP-Conference on Women, Work and Computerization. IFIP-WWC 97 is organised by the *Fachausschuß 'Frauenarbeit und Informatik'* (Special Interest Group on 'Women's Work and Informatics') of the German *'Gesellschaft für Informatik' (GI)*. The conference is being held under the auspices of the Working Group 9.1 'Computers and Work' of the *International Federation for Information Processing (IFIP)* and is co-sponsored by the *GMD-Forschungszentrum Informationstechnik GmbH* (German National Research Center for Information Technology).

The series of conferences provides an international forum for researchers, practitioners and users in the field of information technology. In addition, it provides an opportunity for women studying or working in computing to meet and share experiences.

Scope and Objectives of IFIP-WWC ´97

This year's theme is 'Spinning a Web from Past to Future'. At the conference we will be discussing how different areas of society are being transformed by computer technology, but with particular emphasis on changes in women's work and life and how these have come about. Such transformations include the transition from women's traditional work to work based on modern technology; from communicating within personal communities to communicating within virtual communities; from traditional job gendering to new perspectives on 'who does what'.

These conferences now have a tradition of interpreting the word 'computerization' not just in the narrow sense of computing systems, but also in a broader sense which includes the organisational and social context in which computer systems are designed and used. Both empirical and theoretical research will be presented from international perspectives. Discourses are to be linked to the following topics:

1. Information Society, Multimedia and Networking
Can women's request for interpersonal networking be realised by new information technology? How can multimedia and telecooperation be used successfully in order to improve women's living and working conditions? What is the impact of the transiency and changeability of electronic artefacts? What implicit strategies in the information society can be identified which exclude women from important political, cultural and social contexts?

2. Creating Models and Tools
Which aspects of feminist perspectives, such as epistemological criticism, can be integrated into informatics? Which paradigms and metaphors have contributed to the construction of computer (software) and the theory of computer science? Do they exclude women? How should computer systems be designed which consider the requirements of women, e.g. user interfaces? What happens to a gendered language in human-computer-interaction and in computer-mediated communication?

3. Not without a Body? Bodily Functions in Cyberspace
(How) Is the body represented in cyberspace/virtual reality and to what end? The body as interface. Transgressing the gendered body? Incorporating software agents.

4. Labour and Living: apart or together?
Do public and private space merge? Technical and social/political opportunities for flexible time-management; what are the restrictions? No more jobs without IT-knowledge? The global division of labour: are we on the way to equality?

5. Education
What should be the elements of an informatics curriculum which represents informatics as a node in the web of other disciplines? How can the subjectivity of modelling and designing be taught in informatics? Will information technology remove the distinction between public and private education?

6. History - Herstory
Herstory of feminist criticism of information technology. Has feminist criticism changed women's strategies for gaining access to and influencing new technologies? Can women's influence be recognised in the formative processes of informatics?

The Conference Programme

The international programme committee met on two occasions and all have worked hard to make this conference a success. A 'call for contributions' was issued in July 1996 and, in October, 59 submissions were submitted to a blind refereeing process in which each paper was reviewed anonymously by two referees. The programme committee, assisted by international referees, accepted 37 papers, 7 discussion notes and 6 posters. The number of papers submitted for each of the conference topics reflects the importance of 'labour' and 'education' as central themes of this conference series. There were far fewer submissions relating to the newly emerging topic of virtual representations of people's lives. A panel has been established by the programme committee to examine these issues.

We are especially happy to have seven keynote speakers focusing on current political, cultural and technical topics relating to computerization and women's work and lives: Rita Süssmuth - President of the German Bundestag, Heike Kahlert (D) - sociologist on political theory and sociology of science, Anke Burkhardt (D) - scientific researcher into higher education, Carolyn Guyer (USA) - artist in hyperfiction work, Allucquère Roseanne Stone (USA) - cultural theorist on transgender and cyberspace, Karin Junker (D) - Member of the European Parliament, and Marsha Woodbury (USA) - Chair of Computer Professionals for Social Responsibility.

This is the first time in this series of conferences that the conference proceedings have been published before the conference. All previous proceedings have been published after the conference has taken place and, in each case, only a selection of the presentations have been included.[1] We wish to thank Springer-Verlag for making pre-conference publication possible.

This book includes *all* the accepted papers. Discussion notes and those posters whose authors agreed to present their work at the conference, are each outlined on one page. Descriptions of some of the software demonstrations which will be part of the conference programme are also included. IFIP-WWC'97 will also offer five tutorials which give participants the opportunity to learn about theoretical and practical aspects of the conference themes and to enable interdisciplinary discussions during the conference; you will find abstracts of those tutorials in the proceedings. We hope that this book provides the reader with a comprehensive overview of the conference.

Acknowledgements

The editors wish to thank the members of the organizing committee, the members of the programme committee, and the referees for all their work in preparing for the conference. There are many, many other persons to thank for their considerable efforts. These include staff at IFIP, GI, and Springer-Verlag. We would also like to thank Christine Harms for her considerable administrative support. Many thanks also to all our colleagues at our home institutions for their patience and support. The support of the GMD-Forschungszentrum Informationstechnik GmbH is gratefully acknowledged. We also wish to thank the Federal Ministry for Education, Science, Research and Technology, and the universities of Hamburg and Bremen for financial, organisational and technical support. We acknowledge the sponsorship of IBM.

When in April 1995 the GI-Fachausschuß 'Frauenarbeit und Informatik' obtained approval from the IFIP Working Group 9.1 'Computers and Work' to organise the next conference on 'Women, Work and Computerization' in Germany, a great deal of information was already available from the previous WWC organisers in the United Kingdom. Their continuous helpful support has made the whole organising process much easier, has broken many language barriers - we hope this will serve as an example of successful interpersonal networking and telecooperation. Another very successful cooperation has been established between the GI-Fachausschuß and the

---

[1] These conferences took place for five times in different European countries: in Italy (1984), Ireland (1986), the Netherlands (1988), Finland (1991), United Kingdom (1994):

- A. Olerup, I. Schneider, E. Monod (Eds.): *Women, Work and Computerization: Opportunities and Disadvantages. First Working Conference Sept. 1984 in Italy*. Amsterdam, 1985.
- K. Tijdens, M. Jennings, I. Wagner, M. Weggelaar (Eds.): *Women, Work and Computerization: Forming New Alliances. Third Conference April 1988 in The Netherlands*. Amsterdam, 1989. (As appendix: Results of the 2nd Conference Women, Work and Computerization 1986 in Irland)
- I. Eriksson, B. Kitchenham, K. Tijdens (Eds.): *Women, Work and Computerization: Understanding and Overcoming Bias in Work and Education. Fourth Conference June 1991 in Finland.* Amsterdam, 1991.
- A. Adam, J. Emms, E. Green and J. Owen (Eds.): *Women, Work and Computerization: Breaking Old Boundaries - Building New Forms. Fifth Conference June 1994 in the United Kingdom.* Amsterdam, 1994.

women's group in the GMD-Forschungszentrum Informationstechnik GmbH. A web of new friends has been created throughout these months of preparation. We wish all participants at the conference and readers of this book success in spinning this web a little bit further.

March 1997

A. Frances Grundy, Doris Köhler, Veronika Oechtering, Ulrike Petersen

Table of Contents

Introduction

Welcome Addresses

Invited Talks

Accepted Papers and Discussion Notes

Topic 4: Labour and Living: apart or together?
– Part 4: Technological Innovations and Gendered Experiences

Topic 5: Education
– Part 1: From School to Informatics: Inclusion or Exclusion?

Topic 5: Education
– Part 2: Quality of Education with IT

Topic 6: History - Herstory

Posters

Tutorials

Software-Demonstrations

Information on IFIP, GI, and GMD

Welcome Addresses

Opening and Welcome Address

Prof. Dr. Dr. h.c. Wilfried Brauer

Vice President of IFIP
Technical University Munich, Germany

The International Federation for Information Processing (IFIP) is the multinational federation of professional and technical societies in the field of informatics representing the informatics communities of 56 countries. Its mission is to be the leading, truly international, apolitical organisation which encourages and assists in the development, exploitation and application of information technology for the benefit of all people. Technical work within IFIP is mainly done in its 12 Technical Committees with 70 Working Groups and one Specialist Group.

The German IFIP member is the Gesellschaft für Informatik (GI) which, via its IFIP Advisory Board, also represents societies from related fields, namely physics (DPG), mathematics (GAMM), electrical engineering (ITG), medical informatics (GMDS).

This conference is organized under the auspices of Working Group 9.1 „Computers and Work" of IFIP´s Technical Committee 9 „Relationship between Computers and Society" and is the 6th in a series that started in 1984. It is unusual for IFIP that all these conferences took place only in Europe.

As chairman of IFIP's Technical Assembly, the forum for strategic discussions between the TC chairs, the Executive Board and representatives from affiliate societies, I am particularly happy to open this conference and express IFIP´s thanks to all people involved in preparing and running this conference.

I am convinced that the topic of this conference series is very important for the further development of the ways we will work and live with computers and information technology. It even seems to me that in view of the current trends in technological developments it is particularly timely and appropriate to reflect more deeply on

Women, Work and Computerization

And since I think that everybody should participate in this process of thinking and discussion, I will start doing so by making some comments and raising some questions.

Let us look at the three pairs of words which can be formed by the nouns in the conference title.

1 Computerization and Work

There are two important trends concerning the relation of computers to work.

Computers become invisible, they are embedded in all sorts and parts of working environments; people need not learn to use a computer but only to operate an interface to a system which does a certain type of work. Already now using a telephone, a car, a teller machine etc. means using several computers without thinking of them.

The natural touch-on contact between people and reality will be more and more replaced by a relation mediated by computerized systems. There will be less physical contact to natural or technical systems and to other people, instead sensors and actuators, audio and visual aids, together with intelligent input data analysis, information processing capabilities and output presentation techniques, will be used when knowledge about reality is needed. Moreover this indirect contact will often be avoided by a computerized simulation of real processes, i.e. by creating a virtual reality.

These two observations lead to three questions

- Will we continue to be able to distinguish reality from a simulation, artifacts of system behaviour from effects in reality, virtual from a natural reality?
- How much direct contact to / confrontation with natural reality do we need?
- Are there differences between men and women concerning these two questions?

A closer look at the last question brings us to the next pair.

2 Women and Work

Work goes on within a working environment, which does not simply consist only of the tools to be used but also of the „ambiente“. From my personal experience I got the impression that women are more influenced by the character of the working environment and that they try to create their personal ambiente if ever possible, while men are less sensitive to the environment and do not change it so much in order to create a specific athmosphere.

- Is this a correct observation?
- How should working environments be designed such that a transformation to a personal style is easy?
- To what extend may also working procedures and information organisation be styled individually without affecting negatively the quality of the work - and are there gender differences concerning the way this is done?

The last two questions are related to the third pair.

3 Women and Computerization

- Would it not be better if women themselves (instead of men) design and shape the working environments for women - from the hardware over the software to the working procedures and the embedding in the organisation?
- Will the interfaces to reality designed by women be different than those designed by men? In what respect? For which types of interfaces?

If at least one of the two questions admits the answer yes then many more female informaticians are needed. And it should also be possible to interest them in the challenge to create their own individual types of systems.

Here however another problem comes up. To interest girls to studying informatics one should start rather early in school. But if girls and boys at school and in university are educated in the same way (mostly by men) concerning the design of informatics systems (including working environments), how may female graduates, after leaving university, all of a sudden be able to design other systems than male graduates.

In Germany there is, since some time a discussion about the question whether joint education in informatics for girls and boys at school level is really good for girls. In preparing this address I made an informal inquiry to IFIP General Assembly members concerning school and university education in informatics and gender issues. What astonished me most was that seemingly in no other country this problem has been discussed widely and that some people considered my question about separate informatics courses for girls and boys as politically incorrect or bilarious. Is this issue really only a German speciality, i.e. a secondary effect related to some other cause? Or is there really a need to think more deeply about the relationship between informatics, cognition, psychology and gender, i.e. is it necessary to admit that informatics is not only a formalistic, engineering discipline but also a very strong human science component?

Maybe since this conference takes place in Germany these thoughts and questions will stir up some discussions. I am sure that WWC'97 will be very successful in Spinning a Web from Past to Future.

Welcome Address

W. Stucky

President of the German Informatics Society

Dear conference participants,

on behalf of the "Gesellschaft fuer Informatik (GI)" – the German Informatics Society – I am very pleased to welcome you to this year's Conference on Women, Work and Computerization and I want to thank the "Fachausschuss Frauenarbeit und Informatik" of the GI – the "Committee for women's employment and computer science" – for taking over the organization of this event.

Reflecting upon the conference's motto – "Spinning a web from past to future" – two thoughts came to my mind: Firstly, we should be spinning rather quickly if we consider how fast information technology (IT) and computerization is evolving, and how soon future will turn into past. Secondly, a wide-spanning, strong web needs to be firmly attached to several different points – multiple nations, cultures, generations and genders should take part in its construction.

Let me explain these thoughts a bit closer:

Computerization has made vast changes to all aspects of our lives – home, work, education and leisure. Although there is nothing in the nature of computing that makes this industry more suitable for men than for women, the latter are still not represented adequately in the world of computing. Our world is rapidly growing together through the building of a global information and communication infrastructure. But how, after all, can we succeed in breaking down social, cultural and ethnic barriers if we do not manage to involve a large part of the western society appropriately?

This is a troublesome situation for both women and the IT and computing community: too many women miss a good chance to benefit from the – compared to other areas – extensive employment opportunities in IT and computing, and they also miss the chance to lay down their own terms in a quickly evolving area.

On the other hand, IT and computing simply cannot afford to lose 50 % of potential human capital in a world where human knowledge and skills become more and more the key sources of wealth and innovation. Furthermore, more and more companies produce for a world wide market, and the diversity of skills will soon be a crucial success factor – this involves computing skills as well as cross-cultural competence. Women can contribute to both fields and should be encouraged to do so.

Therefore, computer organizations have very good reasons to support female participation in computing, and I am pleased that the GI added "the support of women in computing" as an explicit goal to its new statutes last year.

Of course, such statements must be accompanied by concrete measures. At this point, once again, I want to thank the "Fachausschuss Frauenarbeit und Informatik" ("Committee for women's employment and computer science") for multiple activities. As I already mentioned at the symposium which was held in Göttingen last year to celebrate the 10th anniversary of this committee, the committee's efforts focus on various issues – including the motivation of girls and young women to start computer related studies, the situation of women occupied in computing and the status of women within the GI.

As far as the last point is concerned, I am glad to say that many women in the GI play an active part in the organization and do not hesitate to take over responsibility: Currently, around 12 % of the approximately 20000 GI members are female – and so are 50 % (six out of twelve) elected members in the GI presidium.

Looking at all these women who bring good ideas and valuable skills into the world of computing, it becomes apparent that it is a real loss if we fail to motivate more women to join us. Motivation and information about computing related studies is of course most effective if it starts early – in our schools. For this reason, it is important that one part of this conference deals with gender related educational issues like

- what barriers in school do discourage girls from science and mathematics?
- what can be done to encourage young women to pursue IT and computing related studies?
- what factors do affect the career opportunities of women in IT and computing ?

Another important topic that will be discussed on this conference deals with the challenges involved in building up and living in a so-called "Information Society". How do new information and communication technologies, like, e.g., multimedia and networking, influence our lives? What are the main chances, and what risks are involved – for society and for women in particular?

In some cases, chances and risks are different sides of the very same medal. Take, for example, telework. Of course telework and flexible working hours can, at least in some cases, increase the chances of women to maintain a career/family balance. It can also help to stay in touch with one's working area during a family break.

On the other hand, we must be aware that the opportunity to work at home does certainly not make child-care services obsolete and that telework should not be misused as an argument to reduce governmental and institutional efforts in increasing the number of available (and affordable) child-care facilities.

Moreover, if we ask for better opportunities to balance work and family, we must make sure that this does not contribute to a further cementation of traditional role models and gender stereotypes, and that we find ways for a better balanced sharing of domestic and family responsibility between the sexes. Therefore, it is necessary that flexible work patterns become a realistic option for both women and men.

Telework, of course, is only one example where we must carefully weigh up potential benefits and risks. In my opinion, whether a new technology is beneficent or not often does not depend so much on the technology itself but on the way we make use of it. This is a good reason why all – women and men of different nations and professions – should contribute to the discussion and share responsibility for our future.

I am looking forward to a stimulating conference which hopefully can help to break down old barriers and find new ways to bring more women into computing.

Welcome Address

Dr. Ute Claussen

On behalf of the special interest group "Women's Work and Informatics" of the German Society for Informatics (GI), I want to welcome you all to Bonn, the former German capital and international meeting place.

Like my predecessors, I want to tell you about the context of this conference, especially about the group that is the main organizer. "Women's Work and Informatics" is an association founded in 1986 as a working group of the GI. Nowadays, it would be comparable to a working group in the British Computer Society or a special interest group in the Association for Computing Machinery. For the meanwhile, we have decided to be part of the Society for Informatics to communicate and reach our goals inside the official community.

At the time being, our group has about 450 members and contacts to many interested institutions like archives for women's studies, universities, etc. About 40 women meet twice a year for workshops that last a whole weekend. During these meetings, presentations are made about topics in informatics and about topics from women's studies in or about informatics, e.g. educational issues or feminist research. Every now and then, we invite women from other countries to give us a more international perspective.

Inbetween meetings of the whole group, nine regional working groups meet monthly or bi-monthly. Many women, who don't want to participate in the national events, regularly meet in these regional groups.

To communicate our results, we founded a newsletter in 1989, and this appears twice a year. Every issue sets a focus on a certain topic, i.e. co-education, international comparisons, history, or women's studies. Beneath this main topic, book discussions, information for members, articles, conference announcements and reviews are fixed parts of the newsletter.

Our goal is to look at computer science from a women's perspective. We are using this technology, our jobs are dominated by this technology, and, furthermore, we know about the details of technology and hence have the opportunity to "create" and "design" it. We want to do this in a way, where we take over responsibility for our work and its results. We try to reach these goals by working inside and outside the GI, for example as a member of the so-called German lobby for women's interests (Frauenrat), which is a political instance of high influence.

During ten and a half year of activities, "Women's Work and Informatics" has reached some milestones, that are worthy of mention. The continuous activities of members every half year during the workshop and inside the issues of our newsletter is remarkable. A first conference titled "Frauenwelt - Computerräume" (something like "women's world - computer spaces") in 1989 was a big success with about 400 participants from several disciplines. Just one year later, our group moderated a workshop called "What are female users expecting from informatics?" during the main conference of the GI.

Though it sometimes was a difficult process, today, our group is an established part of the GI. The speaker is a member of the presidium of the society and the new statutes proclaim the goal of supporting women in the field until equality is reached.

1993, we issued a brochure to promote informatics to young women. It was distributed to every high school in Germany. Unfortunately, the percentage of women studying informatics still decreases. It was about 20% in the late seventies and now actually amounts to 6-7%. One of the regional working groups issued the results of a questionnaire about the jobs of women working in the field. We have started to be present at the important fairs, e.g. CeBiT, to get into contact with new potential members and to promote our ideas to a wider public. Nowadays, we are using the World Wide Web to communicate ourselves. Hence, we take part in spinning the web...

Networking our ideas with others was and still is a main part of our work. We are presenting political statements, that are signed and supported by politicians, we are working closely together with other national and federal organisations in the area of "women and techniques", and we try to keep in contact with international societies.

During the long history of the conference "Women, Work, and Computerization", members of our group have visited it, presented their own ideas, and worked in the program committee. Because we have so many women active in our group we decided to put forward a proposal to host the next conference here in Germany. And here we are!

Three years ago, Veronika first told us about her idea of organizing this conference. She, together with Doris Köhler, the women from GMD and a lots of women in the organizational group and the program committee, did a lot of work to render this conference a success. I want to thank all of them for their efforts.

I am convinced, that "Spinning a Web from Past to Future" will be an interesting conference in a friendly atmosphere and I wish you a pleasant stay.

Computer Science – A Chance for Women

Prof. Dr. Dennis Tsichritzis

Chairman of the Executive Board
GMD — German National Research Center for Information Technology
Sankt Augustin, Germany

Today, men still dominate natural sciences and engineering. While approximately 50% of the male students at German universities take up natural sciences or engineering, these are only 20% of the female students. For computer science, this figure is even worse. In Germany, the number of females starting in computer science has been decreasing since several years to a rate which is today considerably below 10%. Also in the higher academic degrees, the share of females is extremely low. Only some 30% of doctoral students at German universities (all subjects) are females and even only 13% of the graduates admitted for habilitation. The fact that only 6% of German university professors are females illustrates perfectly the situation of academic careers of women.

There is a broad discussion in Germany on the reasons for this situation and on the potential and desirable measurements to improve it. Traditional role behavior reinforced by an overly conventional school education seems to make many women somewhat shy about technology. At higher career levels, it is often the incompatibility of family and job which cuts short a woman's career or even makes her to give it up.

Industry and society and - with respect to a career in research - in particular universities and research institutes have to investigate the problem of how to facilitate and to improve education and career opportunities in technical disciplines for women. There is a wide range of possible measures: special classes for girls, special offers for women at universities, flexible schedule of work, part-time jobs, some sabbatical for the "family pause" etc. Some of these measures are currently being tested, some of them are already embodied in the law.

The small and decreasing share of women in scientific and engineering disciplines is all the more deplorable since today's industry and society are considerably influenced by these disciplines and their specific way of thinking. Today, shaping technology also means shaping society and this is a task to be accomplished equally by females and males.

With the emerging information society, computer science will play the leading role in a development process affecting and changing all areas of life and work. Computer science will combine with other disciplines from natural sciences, but also with social sciences, arts, and humanities. The creation of the information society is a comprehensive task requiring interdisciplinary and networked thinking. For accomplishing this task, computer science needs the participation of women and it offers a wide range of activities far beyond a mere orientation towards technology or engineering.

This year's IFIP conference on "Women, Work and Computerization" focuses on the participation of women in the development and utilization of information and communication technology. I am very happy that women from GMD contribute to the organization of this conference and I really hope that the conference will be successful and will get a good response in the scientific community and the general public.

Invited Talks

Welcome Address

Prof. Dr. Rita Süssmuth

President of the German Bundestag

"Spinning a Web from Past to Future": that is the motto of this year´s 6th International IFIP Conference on on "Women, Work and Computerization". The conference will focus on the changes which computer technology has brought about in many different areas and also on the need for networks.

Our entire economic and working environment is undergoing a period of fundamental structural change which might possibly be termed a second industrial revolution. New technologies and computer technology in particular are central to this process. The changes involved represent an exciting challenge for our society as a whole, for men and women alike. However, it is women in particular who need to prepare themselves for these pioneering changes.

In the working environment these changes involve the following: the automization of routine tasks in production and in the office; greater flexibility of production and services; the decentralization of production and services; moving away from large-scale technology; reversal of previous trends towards the division of labour, i.e. towards jobs which involve a variety of different duties; the separation of man and machine in time and space , i.e. the separation of the business or factory from the place of work, as well as the separation of working hours, machine operating hours and business opening times; and, last but not least, more flexible working hours.

Women must be quick to adapt to these changes so that they do not find themselves having to take a back seat again. First of all, this means that we need more women in technical and scientific occupations, in industry, in higher education and in research - and not just at lower levels but also in managerial positions. In this respect, it is particularly important for us to ensure that the number of women studying computer science, which has fallen dramatically, starts to rise once again. Of first year undergraduates who study this subject only 5 per cent are women - a figure which is appallingly low.

To improve the situation women face, we urgently need to do the following: remove gender-specific barriers to technology which are already evident at school; improve information on training, study and career opportunites for women in technology-oriented occupations; improve access for girls and women to technology-oriented occupations; overcome gender-specific structures of division of labour; lend new impetus to the shaping of technology by involving women and their specific range of experience.

In this area in particular we need to establish networks. These will serve as a basis for the exchange of experience and information, will provide points of contact for women, and will enable women across the world to join forces and work for the network itself and for the benefit of other women. In the past we have learned time and again that only organized groups at grass roots level usually succeed in making their concerns public and are thus able to intensify political pressure for change.

I am certain that the 6th International IFIP Conference on "Women, Work and Computerization" will serve as an interdisciplinary forum and as a motivating force in the field of information technology. Women must finally begin to participate in the public debate on the developments which are imminent and use their influence and above all their specific skills to help shape the course of these developments.

Feminist Perspectives on Democratization

Heike Kahlert

Hamburg, Germany

Since the beginning of modern democracy the women's movement, as one of the big emancipation movements of the 19th and 20th centuries, struggles for a different democracy. In western societies different social groups criticize the slogans of the French Revolution: *freedom* as maturity of the individual, *equality* as a universal principle of justice, *fraternity* as a public solidarity and as a social consciousness. Women in particular question the universality and rationality of these slogans: these slogans are discovered to be androcentric. Feminist social scientists show that the dominant orientation of the modern age is based on a middle-class, white and male mentality and on middle-class, white and male subject constructions that define universality for a minority and exclude a majority. They analyze the dominant construction of the social contract as a sexual contract which is based on and reproduces male power (e.g. Pateman 1988 und 1989). In terms of *female freedom, equality and justice between the sexes* and *sisterhood* as a public solidarity the democracy still is *unfinished* (Kahlert 1996).

Political theorists discuss different dimensions where democracy can be put into action: democracy is

1) a *political principle* of the development of an informed opinion "from the bottom to the top", which is combined with public elections and the establishment of a state under the rule of law;
2) a *type of state*, which is often oriented to liberalism and is combined with capitalism as the economic system because capitalism is seen to complete the political freedom of liberalism with the equality of the market laws in the best way (moderate forms are the welfare state and the social market economy);
3) a *way of life*, because politics cannot be limited to state politics but also means a special way to live one's life (Barber 1994). Politics are always there, where in society equality and freedom shall be guaranteed or restricted by power. Because of this, democracy is a basic political principle which structures society. Democratization aims to get rid of the contradiction between political equality and social-economic inequality.

Since the student's movement in the sixties and early seventies democratization means the process of abolishing hierarchical conditions of leadership and commands in parties, organizations and social institutions. To reach this aim the structures of decision shall be changed through the elements of grass-roots and direct democracy. These changes depend on participation on all levels. Therefore, democratization means a process of enlarging power from the bottom to the top. Democratization expands more and more from the realm of *political* relationships to the realm of *social* relationships. Political democracy is expanded and completed to a democracy in all social areas (Bobbio 1988), but this still is a traditional understanding of political theory which excludes or marginalizes the women's movement and feminist thinking.

If political theorists talk of democratization and democratic changes in politics and society they do not (want to) look at the democratization processes in *private* relationships. The relationships between the sexes have been set under great democratization pressure by the women's movement since the sixties. More and more women cancel undemocratic sexual contracts and urge men to (new) negotiations, where women have equal rights to negotiate. These changes are uncomfortable - for many men and for some women, too. Therefore, I suppose, male political theorists do not look at women or they assign them to the private realm, which does not belong to the public and that is why the private realm and women are excluded from traditional political thinking.

The inclusion of sexual difference in tradional political theory is uncomfortable and is not wanted by a lot of political philosophers. Anne Phillips claims, that the consideration of sexual difference will change all of our traditional political perspectives, because we will be forced to rethink each position and idea in a different manner. She writes, that politics has to be reconceptualized without the white patch of gender, and that democracy has to be rethought under conditions of equality between the sexes. All terms must get a new content (Phillips 1995, 10). If this work is to be done, political philosophy and practice will probably look quite different from now. Then the democratic values of freedom and equality would be interpreted differently, and fraternity maybe would be completed by sisterhood or by the term of difference (see Gutheil et al. 1996, 8).

In modern societies the question of democratization is still mainly is a question of establishing and re-establishing a political realm. Also for a democratic feminism the term and re-visioning of the public realm is the main task. This requires feminist work on *two* levels: On the *theoretical* level we have to renew the category of the public to make it more women- and difference-friendly (Cohen 1994), on the *practical* level we have to develop a political practice which knows how to handle difference (also among women) in a democratic manner.

The thinking of the Jewish philosopher Hannah Arendt, who left Germany in 1933, gives stimulating impulses for this theoretical and political work. Since the anti-communist revolutions and their consequences for the development of world politics, Hannah Arendt's political philosophy is often discussed in Germany (see e.g. Kemper 1993; Kubes-Hoffmann 1994). Though Arendt offers a lot of links and stimulating ideas for feminist theorizing and politics (see e.g. Honig 1995), the feminist reception of her writings has hardly started in Germany. One reason for this distancing of feminists from Hannah Arendt may be, that she herself did not write explicit about sexual difference and that she was at a distance to the women's movement. While feminist scientists consider gender a social construction and have begun to analyze the political from a perspective of gender, Arendt considers gender a fact and social inequalities and injustices a social question. In her opinion the consideration of social questions has led to the failure of political revolutions so that she stands for a clear separation between the private, the social and the political realms. That Arendt excludes sexual difference from the public realm cannot be accepted from a feminist perspective and needs to be criticized.

Before I come to this point, I will discuss Arendt's understanding of politics as "speaking and acting of the different". Like Arendt, feminists also stress speaking as a political act: speaking and the development of women's different voice(s) is a central aspect in the process of constituting a feminist politics as an alternative politics. Opposite to Arendt, who considers *difference* a basic principle for politics, the early attempts to constitute a feminist political realm were dominated in particular by the assumption of *equality* among women - and paralyzed. Meanwhile what theoretically is feminist consent - the differences among women - now also ends up in changed strategies of political action amongst women. In conclusion I will ask which impulses Hannah Arendt gives for a feminist re-vision of the political.

The Meaning of Politics is Freedom

For Hannah Arendt, both speaking and acting both are the two activities she considers politically most important for human beings. Their basic conditions are natality and plurality, that means the being-born and being-different of human beings. For her the fact of natality is the specific human ability to set new starting points and to institutionalize new meanings. She says, that men (and women - whom she does not mention) are born "to start something new" (Arendt 1981, 242; transl. H.K.). To start something new, that means to act, is for Arendt the political action par excellence: acting as starting something new corresponds with birth and puts the individual fact of being born into action. Speaking corresponds with the absolute difference given by birth; speaking puts the specific plurality into action (Arendt 1981, 167).

While people speak and act they differ actively from each other instead of purely being different (Arendt 1981, 165). They interpret and change the reality all together and bring new things again and again to the world. In this dialogue understanding politics is something which goes beyond the individual. Politics comes into being *among* people, that means *outside* of people. Politics means the cooperation and community of the *different* (Arendt 1993, 9). For Arendt, politics is established as the relation among individuals and is carried out in a network of communication among people which has come into being by speaking and acting. This network of communication of human affairs goes on ahead in all individual acting and speaking. Therefore the subjectivities of individuals, their interests, thoughts and aims are like threads which change still existing patterns and network of communication, and still existing patterns and network of communication, at the same time, stimulate all of the individual's life threads in an exclusive manner (Arendt 1981, 174). In Arendt's thinking there is no individual outside networks of communication and relationships. This thinking criticizes the traditional understanding of the subject as an autonomous being and stresses the necessity of relationships and communication among people.

These explanations make clear why postmodern thinkers like to go back to Arendt's understanding of politics. Hannah Arendt, of course, would not have named herself a postmodern thinker, but her reflections on the network of communication which goes ahead of the individuals, and her stress on speaking as a political act can be connected with poststructuralist thinking. Poststructuralists stress the meaning of language and of symbolic orders which go ahead of the subjects and produce them. As in poststructuralist theory politics is for Arendt *performative*, too (see Honig 1992):

Arendt (1993,11) stresses, that there is no real political substance in the individual, but that the political is produced in interaction among different people while they speak and act together. Therefore politics produces something that has not existed before, e.g. new meanings and a new symbolic order, and politics produces new relationships and realities. Politics requests of the individual the courage to start which Arendt (1994, 208) considers the "cardinal virtue of the political".

Arendt's approach to the plurality of human beings and her understanding of politics as speaking and acting difference can be used for feminist politics. Then politics means the speaking and acting of different *women*. This symbolic politics is based on the differences among women. It does not start from a "female" *identity* as a basis of the political community. In this understanding "female" identity first is produced "episodically" (Honig 1992, 223) and always only for a certain time in political relationships among women, because identity changes through the processes of speaking and acting. Arendt's performative understanding of politics makes it possible not to cancel the differences among women in favour of equality or identity but to think equality and difference together, to enlarge differences and to make them the starting-point of politics. Therefore Arendt can be considered a representative of a *politics of difference*.

Hannah Arendt (1993, 12) considers freedom the meaning of politics. Freedom in her opinion only exists in the open space among speaking and interacting people. For her, political freedom is not only the freedom to express one's opinion, the right to listen to the opinions of other people and to be heard, but also is in existence in the spontaneity that each human being is able to exert by him- or herself (Arendt 1993, 49). The freedom of speaking and acting is similar to the starting of something new, which for her can only be fulfilled in political community.

Meanwhile freedom means, in modern understanding, first the autonomy and sovereignty of the individual. For Arendt (1994, 214f), freedom can only be reached in relationships and therefore is connected with dependence on other people. This dependence starts with the birth which is the first relationship an individual has. The birth is already a relationship where at least two people are involved: the mother and the child. If human beings want to be free, they have to give up sovereignty and they have to talk to each other and to argue (Arendt 1993, 59). These forms of communication are only possible in community. Arendt (1994, 201) writes that people can only be free in relationships, that means only in the political sphere and in political action. Political relationships are the only locations where people positively experience what freedom is and where freedom is more than not being forced into doing something.

Freedom is a central cornerstone in the modern understanding of emancipation of civil societies and is also a democratic value. Freedom is as well a central cornerstone for the women's movements that try to put individual and collective self-determination and economic independence into action. For Carole Pateman (1992, 67), the freedom of women is the main issue in the problem of reconciling democracy with difference. According to Arendt's performative understanding of freedom, female freedom is not something that women can sue for with reference to contemporary masculine legal system, but female freedom is something which women can produce by themselves in political relationships with other women. Only these relationships make possible the expression of female difference and the female self (Libreria 1988; see List 1989,

460). Female freedom comes into being through the ability to change oneself which is a product of negotiations with oneself and of negotiations between oneself and the world. The ability to negotiate possesses a political character, especially in conflict, which often only can be solved by a "masterly circle of political action and changings of the self" (Libreria 1996, 56; transl. H.K.). According to this thinking a woman becomes free if she turns to another woman or to other womenwho can find in her or them a measure of her own thinking, acting, will and desire:

> "Just in a relationship among two women the free interpretation of the female difference comes into being, otherwise there would only be a reflection in the Other, and we could not speak of female freedom." (Libreria 1996, 32; transl. H.K.)

In this understanding female freedom is a *relational* value which comes into being, gets space and meaning in political relationships among women, which produces a female political realm and makes a self-determined and self-confident existence and participation possible for women. So female freedom does not have a boundary or a space which becomes smaller through the freedom of other women. Rather female freedom can be thought of as an expansion of the possibilities of political action and of spaces for participation of one‘s own. This politics of female freedom supports the processes of womens‘ individualization, and at the same time it tries not to fulfill female freedom at the expense of other people (women and/or men). More: this politics requires women to show their solidarities with other women in their difference, to support each other and to open up individual and collective scope for action in community. The central part of this symbolic politics is the willingness to communicate, that means the willingness to speak and listen.

Female Speaking and the Search for Women‘s Voice(s)

The history of feminist science can be read as the history of female speaking and as the history of the search for women‘s female voice(s). Gaining a voice is of great significance for all groups that are excluded from or marginalised by dominant universality. To find a voice of one‘s own means to find a way, to become or to be a subject, to express the experiences of oneself, and to make use of the democratic right of free speech and by this to make use of the democratic right of political participation. The female voice is a sign for female power and agency. Female speaking is a very important part of feminist activities in order to transform social representations and the symbolic order. By developing their voices and by beginning to represent their individual and collective experiences, women change the symbolic order. Even "poststructuralist" feminists have been unwilling to abandon the word "voice" as a signifier of female power, for women have not possessed the *logos* that deconstruction deconstructs (Lanser 1992, 3). Female speaking is an important part of powerful transformations to change social representations and the symbolic order. Female speaking produces a female political sphere, a feminist political.

During the seventies the feminist political realm was constituted in a double opposition: as an alternative political realm to (traditional) middle-class, male politics *and* to the patriarchal left politics of the students‘ movement (Dackweiler/Holland-Cunz 1991, 106). Feminists tried to put direct and grass-roots democratic principles into action; self-presentation and self-representation were at the centre of women‘s alternative political practices. As in the US-American west, feminist consciousness-raising-groups were also constituted in Western European countries. In these groups women talked about their lives and about their experiences. While they declared the personal to be political they wanted to deconstruct or to dissolve the traditional boundaries between the private and the public. These groups were locations where women searched for a self-determined identity and where they constituted an individual and collective self, a political identity in the women's movement. In this performed public sphere relationships among women could be developed and be taken seriously.

These consciousness-raising-groups were at the same time a structure of organization, a method of analyzing the (patriarchal) conditions of women's lives and a specific process of producing a feminist political sphere. These groups constituted a specific public where women criticized and reformulated sexual identities, where they developed interests and voices of their own and where they developed and discussed their political opinions. The political programme of these groups was to form an inclusive public realm that should be open to all women and where women could present themselves. The foreground was formed by questions of an inner democracy and by the assumption of equality among women. No voice should be entitled to have more weight than another. No woman was allowed to seize the most important and influential tasks. Knowledge and authority should be separated and shared by all women. Democracy was not understood as a question of representation or legitimation, but as a "really" equal distribution of power (Phillips 1995, 197).

The stress on meetings face-to-face should support the active and equal participation of all women. The dealings with differences among women were unsolved and often not named: Not all of the women had equally time to participate in the different activities, not all of the women were equally eloquent or competent for the different tasks and actions. Particularly in the first years the feminist groups assumed an equality (of interest) of all women, a common strength and a universal sisterhood. They created the feminist trap that women only are common in equality. The method of consciousness-raising is based on the assumption that women can recognize common grounds in the experiences of other women. This method excludes everything which cannot be identified as common ground (Dackweiler/Holland-Cunz 1991, 113). The methods lacked forms to deal with the differences and conflicts among women.

This universality of sisterhood was wrong and put pressure on women to produce a common consent which is not always consistent with the feminist stress on autonomy and self-determination taken from liberalism. The assumed universal sisterhood and equality of all women was a misapprehension and contradicted the different individual desires of freedom. The tension between freedom and equality and the necessary balance between both values is grounded in the liberal democratic tradition. Questions of social equality and inequality are another affair (Phillips 1992, 72). The "democratic dilemma" (Phillips 1992, 79) between a postulated liberal-democratic equality and real existing differences also dominated feminist groups.

Regina Dackweiler and Barbara Holland-Cunz (1991, 113) discuss in their reflections on the changes of the feminist public that the experiences, how and why the forms of producing a feminist public sphere failed, and were not taken into account in re-visioning the understanding and uses of the term "feminist public sphere". This term is still filled with claims like accessibility, comprehensibility and possibilities of active participation for every woman. The break with the claims and standardizations of a public politicized private realm and an inclusive public realm of self-representation is still not understood, not worked through and not finished.

In the political practices of women the claim of inclusive self-presentation and self-representation has now given way to more exclusive forms of political representation also among women: women's politics are delegated, institutionalized and professionalized. This institutionalized monopolization of a feminist political sphere is thematically and strategically dominated by professional female speakers (Dackweiler/Holland-Cunz 1991, 119). This can be seen e.g. in women's studies or in affirmative action politics which have been established in the traditional institutions since the eighties. The production of equality between the sexes is left to a politics of rights, struggles for equality often take place in the jungle of sections. Under conditions of individualization in postmodern societies the search for freedom is left to the individual herself and pushed into the private sphere. Feminist politics seem to decay and to lose democracy: the public places of the women's movement are put into hierarchies; power and competence become independent, information becomes exclusive and the possibilities to communicate among women from different institutions and spaces are reduced. These changes are accompanied by growing power relations among women which seem to paralyze the movement instead of supporting it. Many women still hesitate to name the inequal power relations among women and to discuss them in a female public sphere.

Some feminists point out that there is not only difference between the sexes but among women as well. These feminists criticize the way that feminist discourse universalizes women by talking of *a* female voice and that it excludes and marginalizes a lot of women, for example women of colour. "Black" feminists point out that women speak with many voices. They argue that dominant feminism is not democratic and reproduces the traditional model of western democracy, which promises to create equality for men and women without paying attention to the other differences among people in a democratic manner. Who is able to speak, for whom and with which voice is controversial among feminists (see Roof/Wiegman 1995). The feminist "we" now seems to become more and more suspicious. Feminism seems to have an "identity crisis" (Alcoff 1988).

For this reason, some feminist theorists now ask, if gender can be kept as a category for analysis and critique. However, to look at the difference among women does not abolish gender because homosexuality affirms gender as a continuing separating principle (see Hagemann-White 1988, 57). In our society gender still is politically important and (re-)produces social and political inequality between the sexes. Instead of disolving the category of gender we can try to develop an understanding of sexual difference that makes thinking about different levels of difference possible: difference between the sexes, inside each sex and inside individuals (Kahlert 1996). From this perspective the feminist subject must not be given up as Seyla Benhabib (1995, 239) fears. Instead of giving up the struggles for (feminist) solidarity and political action in a community of women we can also ask how other dealings with power relations among women could look like.

Female Authority and Political Relationships Among Women

For a long time in the women's movement power was associated with the structure of male relationships, where women were oppressed, or with the power of mothers which also has not been a positive experience to many women. This critical distance of feminists against traditionally experienced power as oppression did not prevent power relations becoming established among women. To name these power relations is necessary to put the political aim of the women's movement into action, namely to express sexual difference by language, to make it important and visible everywhere (Longobardi 1989, 128).

To form networks of relationships is a traditional feminist political strategy. The image of the horizontal net - in contradiction to male vertical mentorships - covers up the way that power relations among women are formed in the networks, too. If we take a closer look at a network we can see, that it is formed by a lot of dual relationships between women. Network-relationships serve less for friendships but more as political and vertical relationships that women form to reach a certain aim - that does not exclude the way, that political relationships can change into friendships. The appreciation of the authority of the other woman is very important for these political relationships between women. Italian feminists from Milan and Verona call this political practice of appreciation, judging and confidence in political relationships between women *affidamento* (entrustment).

So far there have been only a few reflections on authority and gender in the feminist discussion. Among women, authority or, above all, female authority has been up to now more or less taboo, maybe because the dominant associations regarding authority almost are connected with androcentric power and with the symbolic authority of the father. Political authority traditionally is hierarchical and conceptualized in a manner that excludes female voice (Jones 1987). Authority may as well be seen as a relationship, as a process and product of communication and bonding with other people. Authority may be the expression and the possibility of political action in communities. It can work for enrichment and productivity. This kind of positive and productive authority is dynamically constituted between interacting people. Such an understanding of authority can be found in the thinking of Hannah Arendt (1994), who considers authority the decisive category of human living together, an elementary form of relationship and one of the most elementary functions of all communities.

> "What constitutes authority for women is exactly what is most feared by men: sustained connections" (Jones 1987, 159). Kathleen Jones suggests discussing female authority in a context of the ethics of care which Carol Gilligan (1984) has developed. Gilligan found out that women prefer relationships more than rules and abstract rights. By prefering relationships women modify the forms how authority is traditionally practiced: as a connection of rules, hierarchy and masculinity. Jones (1987, 161) shows that relationships of authority must not follow a structure of power and oppression but can also be contexts of and can satisfy needs for supportive care (see Sennett 1990, 148). Kathleen Jones (1987; 1993) calls this kind of authority "compassionate authority".

In the Italian politics of difference authority is seen as a "symbolic quality of relationships, as a figure of exchange" (Libreria 1996, 42) and as a figure of mediation, which is necessary for communication. In this understanding, authority is the process of interpretation which gives meaning to relationships (Jones 1991, 123). Italian philosophers of difference say that female authority does not exist, but first has to be produced in political relationships among women. In this understanding, authority is performative and only exists if it is appreciated by another woman. Without the appreciation of the difference among women female authority cannot be developed. In this political practice the appreciated difference is a productive element which is based on the recognition of the value of what partial different knowledge or the partial different experience of another woman has for a woman. The appreciation of female authority is necessary to make qualitative differentiations among women possible. To appreciate female authority also makes the growing of each single woman and of the female political subject possible. The appreciation of female authority supports the establishment of a strong women's network which is constituted by many dual political relationships among women. Following Italian philosophers of difference, only a strong women's network provides women a fully social existence *as women* in the world.

This political strategy does not want to transfer androcentric dialectics of power and oppression which is based on hierarchical gender relations and only functions on this basis in political relationships between women. Rather it wants women to see political relationships among themselves as a space for female freedom where strength, power and productivity can be discovered and cultivated. And it wants women to recognize the greater partial (!) value of another woman as a mirror of her own desire. That does not mean to devalue the other woman if she is able to do something better but to see her value as an incentive for one's own development and growing. In this understanding, authority is productive. If a woman is willing to reflect on her own desire authority can strengthen her and can help her to find an own location in the world. That women are strengthened and authorized by other women is the product and at the same time the condition of this political practice of education in relationships. This political practice of appreciation is in the feminist context still a beginning.

In spite of the partly polemical critique in the German feminist discourse I want to insist on the necessity of this political practice. The problems the Italian women deal with also need to be discussed and to be solved in the German women's movement, e.g. the tensions between cooperation and concurrence or the lack of desire in political relations among women. If women want to transform gender hierarchies in their own interests and if they want to shape the social and political realms by themselves then women need to discuss and to deal with questions of power and authority of women as well as questions of power and authority among women. Feminist politics are speaking and acting in dissent: "Who takes on authority also takes on the conflict" (Libreria 1996, 55; transl. H.K.) - with a lot of men and with other women, too.

Feminist Re-Visioning of the Political

The speaking and acting of difference is not only at the heart of Hannah Arendt's understanding of politics but also at the heart of the development of the western women's movements. Important elements in the contemporary history of female speaking are the consciousness-raising-groups of the sixties and the early seventies, the critique of language by feminist linguists and the theory of the "different voice" (Gilligan 1984), which has been discussed up to now. Female speaking is always bound to the female body. To speak about female experiences means to speak about the body and to speak about the desire which is bound to the body and which is still more or less out of language in the traditional symbolic order. Female desire is very important for feminist politics and means a desire for symbolic, political and social appreciation of women as women.

Arendt herself surely would not have produced this connection between the body and politics: she put everything which concerned the body and sexual difference to the social sphere of necessity but not to the political where she excluded the (sexually differentiated) body - as the political thinking of antiquity, which she very often quotes in her writings, and in harmony with modern male political thinkers. She did not analyze that politics was in the Greek polis a privilege by birth only for a few men of the ruling class, while women, children and slaves were excluded from the political by definition. Her understanding of politics as participation and perfomance is very stimulating but it also has to be criticized: Arendt reproduces the traditional separation between the private and the public sphere and she reproduces the traditional division of labour which is gendered. She does not criticize the hierarchical relations between the sexes.

In fact she does not refuse women their political ability to act, but she excludes women‘s bodies from political action. Therefore she excludes central points of feminist politics from the political itself, e.g. women‘s rights for self-determination about bodies or the abolition of the gendered division of labour. Her understanding of freedom also shows this problem: in Arendt‘s opinion freedom starts where the care for life has stopped forcing human beings to act in a specific manner (Arendt 1994, 210). I want to ask how realistic such an understanding of freedom is in the contemporary changes of modern societies where especially the emancipation of women in the labour market suffers from backlash - not only in the eastern states of Germany. Nowadays we can see that care for the economic basis of life grows after times of relative prosperity of many social classes - in fact more so and in a different way for women than for men.

Otherwise one can argue, that Arendt‘s plea for the re-establishment of a strong and independent political sphere is quite important in the contemporary crisis of the political system, because, as Ulrich Beck (1996) writes, modern society does not have a future without the protection of democracy. As I have argued in the beginning of this paper, the democratization of modern societies is a question of the (re-)establishment of a political sphere which is produced by the speaking and acting of difference. Therefore Arendt‘s attempt to provoke the political with her affirmation of difference and plurality can be read as the fulfilling of the postmodern vision of democracy which is based on the *appreciation of difference* and on *justice for heterogenity*. "Arendt empties the public realm of almost all content." (Honig 1992, 224) In her public realm everything can be symbolically negotiated without giving up the struggles for a real *inclusive universality*. This new symbolic order is an arrangement without any exclusion because its existence depends on the multiplication of political relationships:

"The position of a world which is defined by outer signs (...) now is taken by the language which makes the world fluent and agile and which makes possible to negotiate permanently the meaning of things. The reality is namely not at all fixed - except we lose the hope to be able to participate in the adventure of interpreting and changing the world." (Libreria 1996, 42f, transl. H.K.)

Social scientists always emphasize that women are more talented in speaking than men and that women like to speak. Therefore there is no reason to let men speak and act by themselves, but there are a lot of reasons to bring women's voices very loudly to language everywhere. Language is the instrument which we use to produce and to mediate female knowledge and which we use to establish a female tradition of knowledge, for knowledge is the most important realm in modern knowledge societies (see Bell 1975; Stehr 1994). And language also is the instrument, which we use to spin a web from past to future and to change the world while we speak and act in a political community of women.

Bibliography

1. Alcoff, Linda (1988): Cultural Feminism versus Poststructuralism: The Identity Crisis in Feminist Theory. In: *Signs* 13 (3), S. 405-436.
2. Arendt, Hannah (1981): *Vita Activa oder Vom tätigen Leben.* München/Zürich: Piper.
3. Arendt, Hannah (1993): *Was ist Politik?* Aus dem Nachlaß herausgegeben von Ursula Ludz. München/Zürich: Piper.
4. Arendt, Hannah (1994): *Zwischen Vergangenheit und Zukunft.* Übungen im politischen Denken I. München/Zürich: Piper.
5. Barber, Benjamin (1994): *Starke Demokratie.* Über die Teilhabe am Politischen. Berlin: Rotbuch.
6. Beck, Ulrich (1996): Kapitalismus ohne Arbeit. In: *Der Spiegel* 20, S. 140-146.
7. Bell, Daniel (1975): *Die nachindustrielle Gesellschaft.* Frankfurt am Main/New York: Campus.
8. Benhabib, Seyla (1995): Von der "Politik der Differenz" zum "sozialen Feminismus" in der US-Frauenbewegung: Ein Plädoyer für die 90er Jahre. In: Huber, Jörg/Alois Martin Müller (eds.): *Instanzen/Perspektiven/Imaginationen.* Interventionen 4. Basel/Frankfurt am Main: Stroemfeld/Roter Stern, S. 225-248.
9. Bobbio, Norberto (1988): *Die Zukunft der Demokratie.* Berlin: Rotbuch.
10. Cohen, Jean L. (1994): Das Öffentliche und das Private neu denken. In: Brückner, Margrit/Birgit Meyer (eds.): *Die sichtbare Frau.* Die Aneignung der gesellschaftlichen Räume. Freiburg i. Br.: Kore, S. 300-326.
11. Dackweiler, Regina/Barbara Holland-Cunz (1991): Strukturwandel feministischer Öffentlichkeit. In: *beiträge zur feministischen theorie und praxis* 14 (30/31), S. 105-122.
12. Gilligan, Carol (1984): *Die andere Stimme.* Lebenskonflikte und Moral der Frau. München/Zürich: Piper.
13. Gutheil, Monika/Barbara Rendtorff/Barbara Köster (1996): Vorwort. In: Frankfurter Frauenschule (ed): *Freiheit, Gleichheit, Differenz.* Facetten feministischer Theoriebildung (Materialienband 16), S. 7-8.

14. Hagemann-White, Carol (1988): Geschlecht und Erziehung - Versuch einer theoretischen Orientierung im Problemfeld der Koedukationsdebatte. In: Pfister, Gertrud (ed.): *Zurück zur Mädchenschule?* Beiträge zur Koedukation. Pfaffenweiler: Centaurus, S. 41-60.
15. Honig, Bonnie (1992): Toward an Agonistic Feminism: Hannah Arendt and the Politics of Identity. In: Butler, Judith/Joan W. Scott (eds.): *Feminists Theorize the Political.* New York/London: Routledge, S. 215-235.
16. Honig, Bonnie (ed.) (1995): *Feminist Interpretations of Hannah Arendt.* The Pennsylvania State University Press.
17. Jones, Kathleen (1987): On Authority: Or, Why Women Are Not Entitled To Speak. In: Pennock, J. Roland/John W. Chapman (eds.): Authority Revisited. New York/London: New York University Press (NOMOS XXIX), S. 152-168.
18. Jones, Kathleen B. (1991): The Trouble with Authority. In: *differences* 3 (1), S. 104-127.
19. Jones, Kathleen B. (1993): *Compassionate Authority.* Democracy and the Representation of Women. New York/London: Routledge.
20. Kahlert, Heike (1996): *Weibliche Subjektivität.* Geschlechterdifferenz und Demokratie in der Diskussion. Frankfurt am Main/New York: Campus.
21. Kemper, Peter (1993): *Die Zukunft des Politischen.* Ausblicke auf Hannah Arendt. Frankfurt am Main: Fischer.
22. Kubes-Hoffmann, Ursula (ed.) (1994): *Sagen, was ist.* Zur Aktualität Hannah Arendts. Wien: Verlag für Gesellschaftskritik.
23. Lanser, Susan Sniader (1992): *Fictions of Authority.* Women Writers and Narrative Voice. Ithaca/London: Cornell University Press.
24. Libreria delle donne di Milano (1988): *Wie weibliche Freiheit entsteht.* Eine neue politische Praxis. Berlin: Orlanda.
25. Libreria delle donne di Milano (1996): *Das Patriarchat ist zu Ende.* Es ist passiert - nicht aus Zufall. Rüsselsheim: Göttert.
26. List, Elisabeth (1989): Ein Zimmer für sich allein genügt nicht. Anmerkungen zu den Perspektiven feministischer Politik. In: *Die Neue Gesellschaft/Frankfurter Hefte* 36 (5), S. 455-461.
27. Longobardi, Giannina (1989): Frauen und Macht. In: DIOTIMA: *Der Mensch ist Zwei.* Das Denken der Geschlechterdifferenz. Wien: Wiener Frauenverlag, S. 127-132.
28. Love, Nancy S. (1991): Politics and Voice(s): An Empowerment/Knowledge Regime. In: *differences* 3 (1), S, 85-103.
29. Pateman, Carole (1988): *The Sexual Contract.* Cambridge: Polity Press.
30. Pateman, Carole (1989): *The Disorder of Women.* Democracy, Feminism and Political Theory. Cambridge: Polity Press.
31. Pateman, Carole (1992): Gleichheit, Differenz, Unterordnung. Die Mutterschaftspolitik und die Frauen in ihrer Rolle als Staatsbürgerinnen. In: *Feministische Studien* 10 (1), S. 54-69.
32. Phillips, Anne (1992): Must Feminists Give Up on Liberal Democracy? In: *Political Studies* XL, Special Issue, S. 62-82.
33. Phillips, Anne (1995): *Geschlecht und Demokratie.* Hamburg: Rotbuch.

34. Roof, Judith/Robyn Wiegman (eds.) (1995): *Who Can Speak?* Authority and Critical Identity. Urbana and Chicago: University of Illinois Press.
35. Sennett, Richard (1990): *Autorität.* Frankfurt am Main: Fischer.
36. Stehr, Nico (1994): *Arbeit, Eigentum und Wissen.* Zur Theorie von Wissensgesellschaften. Frankfurt am Main: Suhrkamp.

New Professors – Old Structures: Results of Personnel Replacement in East German Universities from Women's Point of View

Dr. Anke Burkhardt

Berlin, Germany

The political changes, which started in November 1989 in the German Democratic Republic (GDR), set in motion intensive discussions about the function of the university system, its position in the research scene, about principles of conduct and models of financing, about educational innovations and so on[1]. Characteristic of the first months after the fall of the wall, when the reform of the GDR system was still on the agenda, was on the one hand an unusually fertile growth and exchange of political and scientific ideas. The 'round table' opened up the right of codetermination especially to minorities. At the same time, the development of a considerable creative potential led to a flood of projects and publications. East German scientists, who were already liberated from restricting dogmas and the restrictive influence of the state, but not yet hindered by the pressure of competition for advancement in their careers, developed a new level of co-operation in education and research. The period up to reunification was filled by a lively, and sometimes heated, debate about renewal and about the creation of corresponding institutional structures.[2].

The consequences for personnel remained marginal for the moment. Despite the dismissal of professorial staff in the field of Marxism-Leninism, the abandonment of compulsory education (at university) in sports and foreign languages, and the exchange of personnel in management positions, the staff as a whole changed only insignificantly.

Women and men expected a reform of the university educational system from German reunification which would combine the advantages of both systems: topics ceasing to be taboo, free choice of contents in research and teaching, integration into the scientific community, diverse possibilities of communication and publication, autonomy of educational institutions on the one side - social security, guaranteed

---

[1] An insight into the discussion at that time offers the following material:
Die Universitäten und Hochschulen in der Erneuerung des Sozialismus - Vorschläge und Überlegungen zu einer grundlegenden Hochschulreform / Ministerium für Bildung, Arbeitsgruppe Hochschulreform. - Berlin, Dezember 1989.
Burkhardt, A.: Parteien und Organisationen zu Bildung und Wissenschaft. Programmaussagen / Zentralinstitut für Hochschulbildung. - Berlin, März 1990.
Lehre, Forschung und Weiterbildung im Hochschulwesen der DDR. Ausgangspunkte und Wandel / Gutachten des Zentralinstituts für Hochschulbildung zum Prozeß der Vereinigung Deutschlands. - Berlin, Juni 1990.

[2] One of the new foundations at that time was for example the Centre for Interdisciplinary Women´s Studies at Humboldt-University at Berlin, which could stand its ground in the reunified Germany as well.

employment, co-operation and the possibility for all scientists - not only for professorial staff - of autonomous work in research and teaching on the other side. A look at today's all-German university scene shows that these ideas of reform, developed during the euphoria of unification, have remained Utopian.

Designing the process that became known as `the renewal of higher education', the Federal state and the German Länder followed the principle of adaptation to the higher educational system of the former Federal Republic (West Germany). This functioned as an (almost) unchallengeable reference system. Whether it was about the network of universities, university entrance, the contents of teaching and research, the support of the new generation of academics or staffing - in each case the adaptation required changes whose dimensions by far surpassed all previous university reforms since the beginning of the Federal Republic. On the one hand, the GDR university system showed a degree of similarity to its West German counterpart that made the continued operation of the university system, especially teaching and studies, possible during this period of change. On the other hand, over the course of the forty years of separate university development, peculiarities were formed whose removal - in accordance with higher education policy - had to lead to enormous interventions in the numbers, structure and function of the university staff. The scale of the reduction in the number of posts and personnel can be made clear with a few examples: the number of scientists' posts in East German universities was reduced from 37.800 to 22.800 over the period 1989 to 1995, ie by 40% [Burkhardt, Scherer, Weegen]. Considering the personnel replacement which occurred in the course of the university renewal (for example, only half of the new professors appointed before the beginning of 1996 came from the new Länder), it can be assumed that in year 6 of German reunification much less than half of the 1989 university staff remained in the East German university system. For thousands of GDR scientists who approached the renewal from the grassroots with great expectations, the new dawn ended in the social insecurity of temporary employment, loss of jobs and often permanent exclusion from scientific and professional life. And here I am not talking about those scientists who had to leave the universities due to lack of professional or personal aptitude.

The Federal Government, the Federal Ministries and political higher education committees appointed by the Federal Government played a more decisive part in the development of the process than is usual in the case of the old Länder. Deviating from the principle that the German Länder are independent in matters of culture and education, several essential premises were set 'centralistly'. The unification treaty, with its explicit orientation towards the federal 'Hochschulrahmengesetz' (HRG) (law setting the federal framework of higher education), the virtually obligatory advice given by the 'Wissenschaftsrat' (Federal Academic Council), the planning estimates provided by the 'Kultusministerkonferenz' (National Conference of the Ministries of Education and the Arts) and by the 'Bund-Länder-Kommission für Bildungsplanung und Forschungsförderung' (Commission of the Federal Government and the Länder for Educational Planning and Research), and the 'Hochschulerneuerungsprogramm' (HEP) (Programme for University Renewal) developed by the Federal Government and the Länder, pointed the way for the East German renewal process.

The Federal Government and the Länder have to face the question whether and how they have acknowledged and acted on their responsibility as laid down in paragraph 3 of the German constitution:

"*Der Staat fördert die tatsächliche Durchsetzung der Gleichberechtigung von Frauen und Männern und wirkt auf die Beseitigung bestehender Nachteile hin.*" [Gesetz zur Änderung] (The State promotes the enforcement of equal rights for women and men and works for the removal of existing disadvantages.)

A critical review of what 'promotion of women' has actually been achieved in the new appointments to all chairs in East German universities justifies the comment that only marginal advantage was taken of the historically unique opportunity to establish - unhindered by personnel structures which were not yet rigid - a new level of co-operation between women and men in academia.

The Working Woman and Mother

If we digress for a moment and look back at the GDR of the 1980s, we find that, in view of the reservoir of female academics available for work, reform from women's point of view was both necessary and possible. The GDR was no eldorado of equal opportunities, but a patriarchy still bearing the old 'colours' of the GDR. Although the constitution conceded women equal rights, in practice they didn't get equal opportunities. The role model of a socialist woman which had been propagated by the SED (Socialist United Party) the party of the state, put the working woman, mother and comrade-in-arms at the centre of politics. [Programm, pp. 53-54]. Women were expected to shoulder the multiple roles of caring for their families, doing a paid job and being actively involved in society, all this supported by a close-knit network of state-run measures for child care.

In spite of pronouncements about equal rights, there still existed stable patriarchal structures in the GDR. Unlike men, women could, and would, engage in professional life but only insofar as it did not conflict with family interests. This had negative effects on careers and qualification-oriented employment. The higher you looked within a profession, the lower the proportion of women. A truly classic example of the gradual exclusion of women was the gender-specific qualification requirements and the professional pyramid which characterised the higher education system and which was typical of the GDR. While for university entrance, studying and final examinations there was almost equal representation of men and women, in 1989 the proportion of women in 'promotion A' (doctoral thesis) reached only 34 percent and in 'promotion B' (the equivalent to the West German 'habilitation' a second thesis obligatory for a professorial career) the proportion of women reached only 17 percent [Burkhardt, Scherer 1995, p. 74 and p.81]. One third of the scientists, most of whom were employed on permanent contracts, were female but only 17 percent of these worked at the level of 'research assistant' - posts which were better paid and gave them more decision making powers [Hildebrandt, p. 50]. In the group of professors and lecturers the ratio of men to women was 10:1. Amongst the professors the proportion of women was only 5 percent (1989: 183 female professors) [Burkhardt 1992, p. 44]. The highest management level in GDR universities was almost without women as only just 3 percent of the chancellors, vice chancellors and heads of departments were female [Radtke, p 923].

Subjects	Professors		Lecturers		Professoral staff (total)		
	total	female	total	female	total	female	proportion (in %)
mechanical engineering/ chemical engineering	219	4	283	11	502	15	2,9
electrical engineering/ electronics	184	5	222	5	406	10	2,5
civil engineering	84	-	109	2	193	2	1,0
architecture	24	-	29	1	53	1	1,9
mining/ metallurgy	9	-	11	-	20	-	0
marine engineering / ship building	73	-	100	1	173	1	0,6
development planning/ logistics	7	-	12	-	19	-	0
land surveying	5	-	10	-	15	-	0
general engineering	18	1	21	2	39	3	7,7
engineering (total)	**223**	**10**	**797**	**22**	**1.420**	**32**	**2,3**
informatics (total)	40	-	44	2	84	2	2,4
engineering/informatics (total)	663	10	841	24	1.504	34	2,3
		proportion of women 1,5%		proportion of women 2,9%			

Figure 1: Professorial staff in engineering / informatics at GDR universities 1989 (number of persons)

In the GDR the traditional 'male domains', such as engineering, were also totally male preserves. Among 1.420 professors of engineering there were only 32 women in 1989. The situation was similar in informatics, and this in spite of the fact that 42 percent of the students taking this subject were female [Statistisches Jahrbuch].

However, it would be an over-simplification to suggest that women's politics in the GDR could be reduced to the enactment of an equality policy prescribed by government and primarily reduced to the point that women work - politics born out of the permanent shortage of workers in an inefficient economy. Looking back, East German women judge their equal rights as *the* superior characteristic of the GDR compared to the FRG [Schlegel, p. 20]. Women reached a level of economic independence which was unique in German history. They had opened up many professions which had been male dominated in the past. The working woman was more than a norm set by society. It was now possible for women to lead independent and self-determining lives.

In spite of the discrimination at work and the unequal domestic workloads, work had a very high status in the lives of women in the GDR [Frauenreport. p. 63; Frauen in den neuen Bundesländern].

Signs of Change

Women went through the political changes in the GDR aware that their status in the workplace was fixed. But very soon doubts began to emerge, doubts about taking the existence of state-supported work for granted. In view of the growing competition for the increasingly rare jobs in academia, co-operation between women and men in universities began to fade. 'Abwicklung' (non-reappointment), political reviewing, professional evaluation, change from permanent to temporary contracts and so on established an increasingly sexist climate in universities. Although shortly after reunification, the women's representatives as established in the old Länder started work, the replacement of women, especially of those female academics in permanent jobs, could not be stopped.

It is only a small success that the proportion of women professorial staff increased in East Germany after reunification, compared to the former GDR and to the old Länder. And the reduction of academic staff with middle level qualifications between 1989 and 1993/94 by 9.500 included the removal of 3.700 women - approximately one third.

Already in the period before reunification it had become obvious in Germany that women's promotion would not become one of the high priority topics in the politics of higher education. The twelve recommendations called 'Perspectives for Science and Research on the Way to German Unification' developed by the 'Wissenschaftsrat' on behalf of the Federal Government in July 1990 made no reference to the politics of women's promotion [Empfehlungen und Stellungnahmen, pp. 7-28]. Also the aims and measures formulated by the Federal Government in November 1990 to reach a 'harmonious *rapprochement* of the German higher education systems', give no hint of women's promotion [Hochschulpolitische Zielsetzungen, pp.33-34].

The trend to undermine women's position continued during the following years. In all the commissions which developed the higher education structures for each of the new Länder, there was no female member or, as in the Länder Berlin and Brandenburg, only the occasional woman. Appointment committees were predominantly filled with men - the reason given being men's scientific competence and ability to stand stress.

Politics consciously pushed women's promotion to the fringe of the renewal process. One instance of this is the 'Hochschulerneuerungsprogramm' (HEP), passed in July 1991, which concentrates on the topics of personnel renewal and support of a new generation of academics, the maintenance of academic personnel in non-university research and improvement of the infrastructure. The Federal Government and the new Länder had to spend around 2.4 thousand millions with 75% coming from the Federal Government and 25% from the new Länder.

On the point of women's promotion it included non-binding statements which lagged behind the 'Hochschulsonderprogramm' (HSP II) - a specific program for universities and polytechnics in the old Länder passed in 1990 [Vereinbarung zwischen Bund und Ländern]. For example, the amount of money and specific area of use dedicated to women's promotion wasn't fixed in the HEP even though this had been done in HSP II.

Consequently, the results of the HEP were unsatisfactory. In 1994 only 24 women (11%) could be found out of 216 university professors appointed to newly created chairs (those who founded new departments etc). To support the strengthening of the polytechnics HEP-money was provided to fund 169 new chairs or vice-chancellorships; 13 of these appointees are women. Altogether 348 men, but only 37 women were given the opportunity to assist in the foundation work with financial support. Compared with this the proportion of women who gave lectures, were made visiting professors or other less prestigious tasks was much higher [Hochschulerneuerungsprogramm].

The HEP gives convincing proof that women's promotion has to be covered by obligatory and strict rules. Non-binding statements - like the description of university tasks outlined in the higher education laws of the new Länder - are not enough to make lasting changes in university life. Without doubt the following analyses of the appointments made in East German universities would have turned out much more positively if universities had declared job quotas for appointments.

The Balance of Appointments

The announcement of and appointment to chairs according to new university laws was one of the main features of the personnel renewal of East German universities. During a very short space of time - compared to the normal West German situation - the number and form of future chairs had to be decided and thousands of personnel decisions had to be made. The universities had to complete these tasks, while at the same time keeping up teaching and mastering the ongoing political review and professional evaluation of staff. According to the unification treaty this had to be managed over a period of only three years and included, for example, extremely short schedules for appointing people.

By the middle of 1990 nearly 40 percent of the chairs had been appointed [Stand der personellen Erneuerung]. Three quarters of these appointments came from the new

Länder. This relatively high proportion resulted from specific rules governing the employment of personnel and often slow negotiations with applicants from the old Länder and from foreign countries.[3] In the second quarter of 1994 - almost one year later - 68 percent of the chairs had been appointed. The academies of art were the most advanced in this process while the polytechnics had reached only 63 percent.

At that time two thirds of the appointed chairs came from the East German area (including East Berlin), nearly one third from the West German area and three percent from foreign countries.[4] A survey conducted by the Project Team 'Hochschulforschung' Berlin-Karlshorst at the end of 1995 showed an appointment rate of 75 percent.[5] The ranking of the various types of institutions remained the same, however the polytechnics had clearly made up ground compared to 1994.

The different subject areas revealed different results. In language and cultural sciences, as in arts, the appointment rate at the end of 1995 was more than 80 percent. In subject areas like mathematics / natural sciences, engineering and medicine only 7 out of 10 chairs had been appointed. Problems arose especially with the appointment of chairs in law, economics and social sciences at polytechnics. Only two thirds of the chairs had been appointed at that time. Compared to the year before, the proportion of professors from West Germany had increased to 41 percent. Fifty-six percent of the new professors came from East Germany and three percent of the appointed chairs came from foreign countries. Again, the categories of institution show differences. The universities had the highest proportion of new West German professors (45%), followed by the polytechnics with 41 percent. At the academies of arts only two out of ten professors came from the old Länder, but 7 percent from foreign countries.

Type of institution	Proportion (in %)			Total
	West Germany	East Germany	foreign countries	
Universities	52	45	3	100
Academy of Arts	71	22	7	100
Polytechnics	58	41	1	100
Total	**56**	**41**	**3**	**100**

Figure 2: Professors at East German Universities/Polytechnics and their region of origin

[3] The survey carried out by the Project Team 'Hochschulforschung' Berlin-Karlshorst included 92 percent of existing university jobs that had been decreed in the new Länder calculations of the 'Wissenschaftsrat' [Burkhardt, Scherer 1994].

[4] see Burkhardt, A.: Besser als befürchtet - schlechter als erhofft. Zum Stand des Berufungsgeschehens an ostdeutschen Hochschulen aus Frauensicht. - In: Hochschule Ost: politisch-akademisches Journal aus Ostdeutschland. - Leipzig 4 (1995) 2. - pp. 107-121.
Burkhardt, A.; Scherer, D.: Zur Alters- und Fächerstruktur des Professoren an ostdeutschen Hochschulen. Personal- und Stellenanalyse/ Projektgruppe Hochschulforschung Berlin-Karlshorst. - Berlin, 1994.

[5] In that survey 62 institutions were asked and 50 replied: 14 universities, 12 academies of arts and 24 polytechnics. These are 83 percent of all positions at East German higher education institutions. In 20 polytechnics and 10 universities new professors were appointed to engineering and/or informatics.

The East-West relation showed subject-specific features. In several subjects, like language and cultural science, law, economics and social sciences where there was a high need for reform, 60 percent of decisions were made in favour of a West German person. In subjects with less reference to the State or to ideological aspects like mathematics/natural sciences, engineering and medicine that proportion was under 30 percent.

The results of this survey are similar to results of another survey published by the journal 'Nature' in 1994. So West German academics are dominant in the ideologically sensitive subjects like the humanities and social sciences: in the social sciences they make up two thirds, in economics around one half and in law 90 percent of the professors [Lindner; Nature: Deutsche Akademiker].

subjects	proportion of West German professors	hereof	
	total (in%)	male	female
languages, cultural sciences, sports	62	66	48
law, economics, social sciences	63	65	49
mathematics, natural sciences	26	27	17
medicine	28	30	7
agriculture, forestry, food science, veterinary medicine	53	54	44
engineering	28	28	29
arts	32	34	26
central institutions	29	33	0
total	**41**	**42**	**36**

Figure 3: Proportion of professors at East German universities, coming from West Germany, grouped by discipline and sex

The age distribution of the new appointed professors is pyramidal in shape. Nearly half of them were younger than 50. Only 10 percent were 60 or older. The results of the survey show the rejuvenation which took place in the process of university reform compared to the GDR. And it differs markedly from the situation in the old Länder where a wave of retirements is approaching.

subjects	Polytechnics				Universities			
	new Länder		old Länder/ foreign countries		new Länder		old Länder/ foreign countries	
	men	women	men	women	men	women	men	women
mechanical engineering/ chemical engineering	82	96	18	4	69	43	31	57
electrical engineering/ electronics	83	75	17	25	91	100	9	0
civil engineering	57	44	43	56	68	100	32	0
architecture	22	17	78	83	33	0	67	100
other engineering subjects	75	91	25	9	78	100	22	0
engineering (total)	**73**	**74**	**27**	**26**	**69**	**50**	**31**	**50**
informatics (total)	86	100	14	0	58	100	42	0
engineering/ informatics (total)	**74**	**77**	**24**	**23**	**66**	**58**	**34**	**42**

Figure 4: Region of origin of professors at East German universities in engineering and informatics (in percentages)[6]

The proportion of new chairs to which women were appointed was 11.7 percent by the end of 1995. This figure was nearly twice as high as the proportion of female professors in the old Federal Republic (1993: 6.4%; of which 3.7% were C4-positions [Grund- und Strukturdaten 1995/96]). It also surpassed the corresponding proportion in GDR universities (1989: 9.3%, of which 5.3% were in the highest category [Burkhardt, 1992, p.144]).

Nearly 40 percent of the women appointed came from West Germany. Their proportion at polytechnics was higher than the average, at academies of arts it was only one fifth. The proportion of West German female professors was especially high in language and cultural studies, in law, economics and social sciences. In these subjects they comprise nearly half of the female professors. In no science subjects were more West than East German females appointed, this was unlike the situation for men.

If the proportion of females continued to be 12 percent, by the end of the process of first appointments there would be 820 female professors in the higher education institutions of East Germany. This would represent nearly one third of all female professors in Germany. At least that would be a positive result, since a repetition of the even worse situation in West German universities wouldn't have occurred.

But, in view of the equal representation of women and men in university entrance in the new Länder, the appointment of almost 12 percent women is an unsatisfactory result. Female professors are still only a small minority in East German universities.

[6] The total numbers of appointed professors to engineering / informatics are: Polytechnics = 1.013 men, 65 women; universities = 596 men, 19 women.

The enormous gender differences in appointments according to type of institution, subject and level of salary proves the discriminatory tendencies and the perpetuation of hierarchical structures. Several structural effects of marginalization intensified each other: the combination of <university> (renowned university in a popular place), <C4-professor> and <traditional male subject> (e.g. engineering) led to a nearly total exclusion of women.

Subjects	Proportion of women (in %)		
	C3-Professor	C2-Professor	Professors (total)
mechanical engineering/ chemical engineering	3.8	12.5	7.1
electrical engineering/ electronics	2.6	25.9	3.8
civil engineering	2.9	5.8	4.0
architecture	0	31.6	10.5
marine engineering/ ship building	14.3	0	8.0
development planning/ logistics	23.1	25.0	24.2
land surveying	0	10.0	4.2
engineering (total)	**3.6**	**15.0**	**6.1**
informatics (total)	0	10.0	6.1
engineering/ informatics (total)	**3.3**	**10.2**	**6.0**

Figure 5: Female professors at East German polytechnics in the different engineering subjects and in informatics in 1995/96

At the end of 1995 each newly appointed woman in the universities was confronted with 12 male colleagues; in polytechnics with seven. In the academies of arts the situation was better, every fourth person appointed to a chair was a woman.

In the old Länder and the former GDR, the proportion of female professors was the lowest in engineering at 5 percent. No better was the proportion of women appointed in medical and mathematical / science subjects. In the arts women constituted a quarter of the professorial staff. In languages and cultural sciences the number was higher than the average. Consequently women were under-represented in university institutions with well known engineering faculties, and over-represented in universities with big humanities faculties.

The polytechnics give the impression of being the same. There were polytechnics with only one women appointed at the end of 1995 and others with proportions of around or over 20 percent. At polytechnics women were appointed especially in the fields of social sciences, education, arts and economics. Engineering remained a male domain. Engineering faculties without a single female professor are still the rule.

Subject	Proportion of women (in %)		
	C3-Professor	C2-Professor	Professors (total)
mechanical engineering/ chemical engineering	2.5	3.0	2.7
electrical engineering/ electronics	1.7	2.8	2.1
civil engineering	0	11.1	4.7
architecture	4.2	7.7	5.4
other engineering subjects	0	9.1	4.2
engineering (total)	**2.3**	**4.7**	**3.2**
informatics (total)	0	6.7	2.5
engineering/ informatics (total)	**1.9**	**5.1**	**3.1**

Figure 6: Female professors at East German universities in the different engineering subjects and in informatics in 1995/96

Within the professorial categories, as the level of salary increased the proportion of women decreased. Women in C4-positions were only half the number of women in C3-positions.[7] Similar observations can be made about polytechnics if we compare C3- and C2-positions.[8] While 35 percent of men were appointed to C4-positions, only 17 percent of women reached this grade. One third of the female professors were at C2-level, but only 18 percent of male professors.

There has been no change in the gender ratio of professors to students in the higher education system in East Germany. In 1989 the relation of female students to female professors was 81:1, the relation of male students to male professors was 9:1.[9] In 1995 a female professor had 140 female students, a male professor only 21 male students.

While male students see the university as a natural male professional field, female students see the female professor as fighting the fight single-handed. Deciding whether to start a career at university is already more difficult for women. We can only hope for real change if reforms of higher education incorporate women's promotion.

[7] In Germany the professorial salary range is divided into three categories called C4, C3, C2. C4 is the best paid category and includes several positions of authority within the universities.

[8] At polytechnics there are no C4-positions.

[9] Students from Germany and from foreign countries at GDR universities 1989: 58.282 men, 56.077 women [Hochschulstatistik 1989].

Subject	Proportion of women (in %)		
	Professors GDR 1989	Professors Old Länder 1993	Professors New Länder 1995/96
languages, cultural sciences, sports	17.1	10.8	21.1
law, economics, social sciences	12.7	8.5	14.8
mathematics, natural sciences	3.5	2.8	6.4
medicine	8.6	4.6	5.4
agriculture, forestry, food science, veterinary medicine	7.2	6.4	9.6
engineering	2.3	1.9	5.3
arts	17.2	17.1	25.9
central institutions	5.6	7.4	14.3
total	**9.3**	**6.4**	**11.7**

Figure 7: Proportion of female professors in East German institutions of higher education grouped by subject. Taken from: Berichterstattung deer Hochschulen an das Ministerium für Hoch- und Fachschulwesen deer DDR; Grund- und Strukturdaten 1995/6; Erhebung deer Projektgruppe Hochschulforschung Berlin-Karlshorst 1995

Type of institution	Proportion of women (in %)			
	C4	C3	C2	total
Universities	5.3	13.1	35.3	8.8
Academy of Arts	12.2	34.1	34.3	26.2
Polytechnics	-	7.6	18.4	12.0
Total	**5.9**	**11.8**	**20.8**	**11.7**

Figure 8: Proportion of female professors at East German institutions of higher education grouped by salary grade

Women are no minority - on the contrary: they now constitute the majority of students in Germany. Women have the right to equal opportunities. The upholding of that right should be one of the central tasks of the politics of higher education.

[Translated by A.Frances Grundy and Veronika Oechtering.]

References

1. Benz, W.: Die Zukunft des wissenschaftlichen Nachwuchses. - In: Forschung & Lehre. Mitteilungen des Deutschen Hochschulverbandes. - Bonn 1 (1994) 5. - S. 167.
2. Burkhardt, A.: Frauen an den Hochschulen. In: Klemm, K.; Böttcher, W.; Weegen, M.: Bildungsplanung in den neuen Bundesländern. Entwicklungstrends, Perspektiven und Vergleiche. - Weinheim und München: Juventa Verlag, 1992. - S. 138 - 149.
3. Burkhardt, A.; Scherer, D.: Zur Alters- und Fächergruppenstruktur der Professoren an ostdeutschen Hochschulen. Personal- und Stellenanalyse/Projektgruppe Hochschulforschung Berlin-Karlshorst. - Berlin, 1994
4. Burkhardt, A.; Scherer, D.: Förderung des wissenschaftlichen Nachwuchses an DDR-Hochschulen in den 80er Jahren - gesetzliche Grundlagen, hochschulpolitischer Kontext, statischer Überblick/Projektgruppe Hochschulforschung Berlin-Karlshorst. - Berlin, 1995. - (Projektberichte 3/1995)
5. Burkhardt, A.; Scherer, D.; Weegen, M.: Datenservice Wissenschaft '95/Hans-Böckler-Stiftung. - Frankfurt/M., 1995
6. Erste vorläufige Ergebnisse. Studenten und Studienanfänger an deutschen Hochschulen im Wintersemester 1995/96. - In: Mitteilung für die Presse Nr. 347/95/Statistisches Bundesamt. - Wiesbaden, 27.11.1995
7. Frauen in den neuen Bundesländern im Prozeß der deutschen Einigung. - Materialien zur Frauenpolitik. - Nr. 11/1991. - Zitiert in: Ostdeutschland: Hausfrau nur für drei Prozent der Ostdeutschen Traumjob. - In: BiB-Mitteilungen. - Berlin, 28.8.1991
8. Frauenreport '90. - Berlin: Verlag Die Wirtschaft GmbH, 1990
9. Gesetz zur Änderung des Grundgesetzes vom 27.10.1994. - In: Bundesgesetzblatt. Teil I Nr. 75. - Bonn, 3.11.1994
10. Grund- und Strukturdaten 1995/96/Bundesministerium für Bildung, Wissenschaft, Forschung und Technologie Bonn, 1995
11. Hildebrandt, K.: ZurNotwendigkeit von Untersuchungen der wissenschaftlichen Leistungsfähigkeit der Frauen im Hochschulwesen. - In: Frauen in der Wissenschaft. Wissenschaftspotential-Kolloquium VII am 26. März 1987 in Berlin/Akademie der Wissenschaft. - Berlin, 1987. - (Kolloquien Heft 60). - S. 49-54.
12. Hochschulerneuerungsprogramm (HEP). Maßnahmen und Ausgaben im Jahr 1994. Bericht der Ausschüsse „Bildungsplanung" und „Forschungsförderung"/Bund-Länder-Kommission für Bildungsplanung und Forschungsförderung. - Bonn, 1995. - (Entwurf, unveröffentlichtes Material)
13. Hochschulpolitische Zielsetzungen der Bundesregierung. Unterrichtung durch die Bundesregierung. Drucksache 11/8506 vom 29.11.1990. - Bonn, 1995. - (Entwurf, unveröffentlichtes Material)
14. Hochschulstatistik 1989. Studierende und wissenschaftlicher Nachwuchs/Ministerium für Bildung, TU Magdeburg. - Magdeburg, 1990.

15. Lindner, A.: Lehrstühle besetzt, Nachwuchs vergessen? - In: Deutsche Universitätszeitung: DUZ. Das Hochschulmagazin. - Stuttgart 50 (1994) 22. - S. 14-15.
16. Nature: Deutsche Akademiker finden Karriereboom im Osten. - In: Hochschule Ost: politisch-akademisches Journal aus Ostdeutschland. Leipzig 3 (1994) Juli/August. - S. 44-46.
17. Perspektiven für Wissenschaft und Forschung auf dem Weg zur deutschen Einheit. Zwölf Empfehlungen. - In: Empfehlungen und Stellungnahmen 1990/Wissenschaftsrat. - Köln, 1991. - S. 7-28.
18. Programm der Sozialistischen Einheitspartei Deutschlands. - Berlin: Dietz Verlag, 1976
19. Theorie und Praxis des wissenschaftlichen Sozialismus. - Berlin 43 (1988) 10. S. 930-936.
20. Schlegel, U.: Ostdeutsche Frauen. Rückblick auf die DDR und die deutsche Vereinigung. - In: Die Frau in unserer Zeit. - Sankt Augustin 22 (1993) 2. - S. 15-23.
21. Stand der personellen Erneuerung in den neuen Ländern - eine Zwischenbilanz (Umfrage DHV). - In: Mitteilungen des Deutschen Hochschulverbandes. - Bonn 41 (1993) 5. - S. 308-310.
22. Statistisches Jahrbuch des Hochschulwesens der DDR 1989/Ministerium für Hoch- und Fachschulwesen. - Berlin, 1989
23. Vereinbarung zwischen Bund und Ländern über ein gemeinsames Erneuerungsprogramm für Hochschulen und Forschung in den Ländern Brandenburg, Mecklenburg-Vorpommern, Sachsen, Sachsen-Anhalt und Thüringen sowie in dem Teil Berlin, in dem das Grundgesetz bisher nicht galt, vom 11.Juli 1991/Bund-Länder-Kommission für Bildungsplanung- und Forschungsförderung. - Bonn, 1991 sowie in der Fassung vom 9. Juli 1992/Bund- Länder-Kommission für Bildungsplanung- und Forschungsförderung. - Bonn, 1992
24. Verfassung der Deutschen Demokratischen Republik vom 6.4.1968 in der Fassung des Gesetzes zur Änderung der Verfassung der Deutschen Demokratischen Republik vom 7.10.1974. - In: Gesetzblatt der Deutschen Demokratischen Republik. - Teil 1 Nr. 47. - Berlin, 27.9.1974
25. Zur Situation des wissenschaftlichen Nachwuchses. KMK zur 269. Plenarsitzung am 6./7.10.1994 in Bremen. - In: Forschung & Lehre. Mitteilungen des Deutschen Hochschulverbandes. - Bonn 1 (1994) 12. - S. 532.

Along the Estuary[1]

Carolyn Guyer

... isn't it what always happens when you're with other people? that's when things get complicated... - "Buzz-Daze"

I live these days on the banks of a river that was once called water flowing two ways. Or at least, favored lore claims that Native Americans named it so. At any moment the Hudson contains some proportion of both salt water and fresh, mingled north then south then north again by the ebb and flood of Atlantic tides. Right here is where I am. On these gentle, ancient banks, extravagant swag of hills still called mountains for what they were, I know this to be a heart's place, because I have known others. One of those - a different estuary - is the Potomac, just where it touches the Chesapeake before breathing ocean. But I have also lived for a vast horizonal time on a Kansas prairie, where sky and earth mirror each other in a delirium of opposition.

It is easy to see that I measure things, the earth itself, with my body. Insisting on a swag and a delirium, turning geography to my own physical style, making landscape intimate, its presence more present. I anthropomorphize because when it comes to what we really know, our bodies are what we have to understand being alive. The present is a place as much as it is a moment, and all things cross here, at my body, at yours. It is where I consider the past, and worry about the future. Indeed, this present place is where I actually create the past and the future. Not alone, of course. Which is always the snag. There is no way to know who I am, without also some way to understand where it is not me anymore. There must be an Other in order for there to be a Me. Bodies bump, both in the night and in the street, colliding across the impasses, rivers, oceans, and continents. The proximity of yours and mine is the situation of difference and influence. It is how history is versioned, parceled and joined, invented as much as lived. And just the same in the other direction. We dream our future by incremental passes, carom into the unknown by tangent and gap.

As a girl on the Potomac, my concerns were rarely so high-flown and abstract. I didn't even know that my river was an estuary, or that not all rivers have tides. Instead, I was interested in learning to feel heavy so I could swim underwater. How to place a too bouyant self into that other world of seaweed tendrils, jellyfish, and fractured green light. Good practice, I think now. How better to understand a tidal mix than to swim in it? Under the water not far from the pier in front of my aunt's house, I knew something, and can easily recall some forty years later the pleasure of moving throughÐor trying to move through - a not entirely welcoming milieu. (Oh, milieu. The perfect word for underwater. A word without end, open and softly waving like the seaweed itself holding hidden dangers.)

or sometimes ... the tallgrass which billows along her flanks, viridian swell of skirt in the wind - Quibbling

[1] This essay first appeared in the anthology, *Tolstoy's Dictaphone: Technology and the Muse*. Graywolf Form I. Minneapolis: Graywolf Press. October 1996.

Specific attractions drew me to the use of computers. The first and easiest, and indeed, the seduction for most people, was mutable text. Just the words themselves become fluid, more on a beam (motes on a beam) with the way language is in me. Word processing is a dry distance of a label for what is, more accurately, writing with light. But once that became possible, once I found I could think better when the words reforming on the screen in front of my eyes began to approach the speed of the ones behind them, I found myself wanting the synchrony to increase. My growing ease with electronic text catalyzed a desire to be able to write in dimensions that reflect a more complicated human experience. Nothing new in that really. The truth is that people have always had this same wish about language, needing more than past and future tenses to indicate how we actually know and create such abstractions of time. We have all sorts of literary and storytelling devices to try to achieve the effect of simultaneity. But what I wanted was to be able to spatialize text; I wanted a changing, changeable form. Not the animated march of Holzer marquee aphorisms, though I like those very much. No, something further, a way to instantiate the temporal leaps and slides we make just getting through a day. I wanted hypertext. An electronic medium which theoretically can include and allow everything, and so finally allows only that we find our own perspective. Hypertext works tend to be so multiple, they reveal what is individual, ourselves, writers of our own story. When I discovered that this possibility existed, I hoped I had found the perfect medium for the creative process I had always known, the yielding, waving, pushing taction of form and formlessness. The way we can know that holding the paradox of existence is to be the cathexis, be the synapse. Human creativity is the dynamic of change, where difference is meaning, and where Self and Other are in tensional momentum. Beyond survival, and perhaps even as part of survival, this may be the most primal human impulse.

> Mother and Father. Earth and Sky. Like children, we try to make bridges between them, bind them together, never understanding the inextricable bond of difference. We sigh with relief and pleasure when they hold hands. We sigh. The comfort of rain, joy of glintingpond. - Quibbling

During my first decade of living in the wide spaces of prairie, I was still young and didn't notice what happens there. When I finally awakened, it was to the breathtaking swoop and curve of grass hills, called Flint Hills, continuing forever, rhythm on rhyme, matched in scope only by the sky itself. Matched and opposed, this was the first way - dramatic and clear as bones - that I began to understand the importance of difference. Recently, a friend told me the story of young nieces and nephews from the Midwest visiting his home here in the Catskills. They complained that they couldn't see anything here because "the hills and trees are in the way." And just so, the tidewater child of the Potomac, swimmer under water, foreigner to the Midwest till she married, began finally in her late twenties to look up and out, to see that it wasn't empty there, and to see that horizon was not just dividing line but also connection. A kind of fitting marriage, if you will. I began to observe how extremes turn into their opposites, and so beginnings and endings, firsts and lasts, the things we believe so specific and significant, are always refusing to be just themselves. Instead, in changing, they point to the real significance, the shoreless variety of mixtures of difference.

> Power ceases in the instant of repose.... - Emerson

The great cultural question of our time is how to accommodate our growing recognition of multiplicity. It is easy enough for any of us to make weary, snide remarks about "being P.C.," but the weariness is really due to the frustration of being expected to provide equal significance and respect for a seemingly infinite number of segments of society. It is a frustration resulting from our self-induced illusion of standing still. We may long for the simplicity of generalized core values, of a mainstream more important than its streams and creeks, but the reality is clearly not that way, never so singular as the perspective of a rationalized hegemony. We think we believe in the individual. The solitary soul, self-reliant, removed from pedestrian life, a singular voice rising above the rabble. Yet we know that even our beloved Thoreau could not escape persistent visitors by the pond. It's a strange vision, this heroic separateness. For there is no human momentum which is purely self-generated; we are and must be connected to others. Which does not mean there is no such thing as a distinctly identifiable individual. Great personalities will continue, and perhaps this is what we have meant all along. Every person is a conglomerate of influences, aspects, and conflicting notions, the coherence of which is personality. This kind of individual, a teeming culture unto herself, should actually be quite prepared for the leap to a vast multiplicity in the larger society, where a constant shifting among perspectives is necessary and enforces the need for a strong, flexible psyche, an individual who retains identity while recognizing that the sources of her own development are never singular or completely separate from herself. This is not easy to do, or even to say. The energy required to stay actively engaged, heart and mind creating without cease, makes the temptation of simplicity great. But the truth is as ordinary as a river metaphor and, because of that, as needful of reminder. We so easily forget that the only real simplicity is some ultimate balance among all things, a "quietude" that comes, not when directly sought, but of its own accord when we experience the most profound creative instant, everything at once and in equilibrium. The only way to keep my balance is to keep moving.

murmuring along the ridge a lip a line a brink of marriage
soft spoken meet and heard our edge - Izme Pass

It turns out that the boundaries between people, between groups of people, are permeable. There is no completely solitary individual and no homogeneous group. Each opposition is made of the other. The way we generally accommodate this wholly ungraspable reality, I believe, is the very essence of human creativity. We do it by the largely unexamined means of interiorizing disjuncture. That is, we gather the scraps and shards of interrupted conversations, overheard gossip, sound bytes, photo ops, advertisements flowing by right through everything else, and we manage to arrive at a coherence of some sort. Yesterday was this way, last week was so, and then, spring and creek, a river of days, changeful and cyclic, but eventually a life, all made of mixtures that "don't belong" together. This nearly invisible and indecipherable meshing of differences may be the most creative thing humans do. And we do it all the time. Might it be useful to become more aware of such a pervasive process? What if we were to turn an inundation of multiplicity deliberately to the grace of tides, to the waltz of a fitting marriage? By multiplicity, of course, I don't mean something like an ethnic street fair. But I do mean all the kinds of human dimensions and factors, all the most difficult, personal things. How to assess the quality of someone's work when everything can be considered valuable from some perspective or other. How to collaborate with someone with whom I simply cannot agree. How to live morally and ethically, really believing in my own principles, and still not assume they are also the best principles for everyone else. This is the hard stuff. But if we can imagine a way of doing these things, we can do them. Indeed, we have already in our electronic realm a medium where we can rehearse the leap and slide, where we can begin to work out the perverse problems of creating ourselves in a necessary paradox.

When I first began using hypertext almost ten years ago, I believed it was "natural," designed to work associatively, as the human braindoes. I still believe something like that, but amplified, and with the plentiful hitches of a young technology thrown in. From those first days till now, I have continued to see this medium as very life-like. I see it in the form of a quotidian stream. The gossip, family discussions, letters, passing fancies, and daydreams that we tell ourselves every day in order to make sense of things. The unconscious rhythms we incorporate - literally embody - as a reliable backbeat to our self-narratives provide familiar comfort as well as essential contrast for the changing turns of disjuncture. We live and make our stories in a line of time that wraps and loops on itself, trying to contend with the geometries of space we also inhabit. Affected by nearby hues we cannot or will not understand, we follow our influences, oppose, match, and continue, even in an electronic milieu, to measure with our bodies.

Some people have done things with hypertext that cause me to ache. The best have been the worst writers, the ones who have joined collaborative ventures with undeveloped skills and plunked what they felt right in the middle of someone else's sinuous prose. These I am grateful to for revealing to me my own biases, and for showing me the perspectival quickstep. Value is a contextual element, and contexts overlap. The worst, however, have probably been the best logicians in some world. They can take a living web of ideas and press it firmly into notched hierarchies, clearly linking exactly the path one is to follow. No straying, no trouble, this way to the castle. Let go the leash, I want to yelp. It is very hard for me to find the angle of vision by which I can see the value of this authoritarian approach. In the effort to get to such a perspective, I can, perhaps, grant that there may be times when guides are useful, and indeed, that most of us are so accustomed to being herded about that there is often a high preference for direction over finding one's own way. But oh, doesn't our best future swirl about somewhere beyond this scrim? I keep hoping that we may look up, or out.

> Dual channels give way to something more like the permeable flow of meaning between sometimes veering, sometimes nearing, banks of a single river. - Michael Joyce

The tiny river hamlet where I live is situated right at the place where a creek enters the Hudson. At this juncture, Wappinger's Creek appears to be misnamed, for it is as broad as a small river itself, and there at its wide mouth, it too is an estuary where the local citizenry sometimes fish for Atlantic blue crab, dropping baited lines straight down from the short curve of a bridge. In the autumn, white swans enter here from the Hudson, I suppose to live in the more protected reaches of water they know, swimming in a mile or more to dot themselves picturesquely about on a slender lake formed by the creek. This tributary extends for miles inland, gradually becoming more like its name. Away from the river, where it meanders steeply, people have built homes near it, and their lives inevitably take on something of the creek's character.

Something more of sudden delight, or intimate celebration, dappled and quick. Whether trickling between high banks and dense trees, or fanning broadly to meet the flux of the Hudson, it is a beautiful body in all ist parts and changing nature. For all its complexity, it has a particularity I crave. Each of the creeks and streams along the river has this effect on me. Like personalities to learn or invent, each its own neighborhood, arrangement and trajectory. Where does it go by the time it moves into the larger stream? No longer traceable as it flows south and north, then south again, day by day the tidal promenade to the sea.

> You can't tell me this isn't significant. You can't tell me anything. Ask the people who know me. It's true. This was all under water once. - Izme Pass

When I walk down the slope of my backyard, past the black walnut trees, and the old tool shed, down to the rocky garden now blooming in the late season of asters and mums, down to where I can see the river best, there I stand with my hills and stream in the same green tradition as anyone. They are for me a way of directly understanding my soul, gleam on water, blue of distance. From that same yard I can look back up at the house and see the window of the room where I use my computer, the site of a similar kind of exploration of existence. There is a difference between these two ways, but there is no reason for them to be anything other than an integrated process. Nature is what we are, and so cannot be opposed to, or separate from, humans and their technologies, even when we push our inventions to the point of self-destruction. Our newest and possibly most powerful technology, this electronic, known mostly as Computer, a word both comforting and spitting in its sound, promising the ease of things we do together (collaborate, cooperate, congregate, collect), and at the same time sharply forcing the challenge of individuality to find its center, this newest great invention is not yet at the point of self-destruct and still holds the potential for encouraging and supporting full human multiplicity and creativity. Of course there is no certainty, nor even a strong likelihood, that computer technology will fulfill that potential. Because of cultural realities surrounding its use, a patriarchal, white hegemony, and an economic system that has come to represent greed far better than social connection and responsibility, these and other factors will probably have their predictable influence. It takes little to realize for instance, that those of us who are already subordinated - women, people of color, developing countries - are the ones less likely to be participating in technology, and that as computers influence human society more and more powerfully, those same groups will be even more reduced in status than they are now. It is quite possible that all the inroads made in recent decades for social justice could be simply wiped away. Knowing that to be true is precisely the reason for more of us, concerned with the human condition, to become involved. I believe that this is indeed the most powerful and affecting technology we have ever contrived, and that there is no denying its hold on our lives and consciousness. As we form it, we are being formed. This is true for all of us, whether we use a computer or not. In the largest and most genuine sense, this is our future. Right here is where we are.

Notes

Hypertext is a category of software intended to allow links to be made among various kinds of information, including text, graphics, video, and sound. As a generic term, hypertext does not refer to writing alone, but rather to the linguistic and associative nature of human thinking processes. (Frequently, the word hypermedia is used instead, with an idea of reducing emphasis on text.) Hypertext is intended to allow information to be put together in such a way that a reader or user can move around in it however she likes. This has obvious and much utilized applications in orientation, training, and education, but hypertext is also employed to make many different kinds of interactive art.

There are two types of hypertexts, defined by Michael Joyce as: Exploratory, in which the reader explores a body of information and discovers the connections placed there by the author; and Constructive, in which the reader can enter the work and change or add to it herself, thereby becoming a co-author. The most densely populated portion of the Internet, the World Wide Web, is designed as a hypertext, though almost completely of the Exploratory type thus far.

References

1. Emerson, Ralph Waldo. "Self-Reliance" in Essays: First Series. Cambridge: Riverside Press. 1903
2. Guyer, Carolyn and Martha Petry. Izme Pass . Hypertext fiction in Writing On the Edge, Vol. 2, No. 2. University of California-Davis. 1991.
3. Guyer, Carolyn. Quibbling Hypertext fiction. Eastgate Systems, Inc. Boston: 1992.
4. Guyer, Carolyn. "Buzz-Daze Jazz and the Quotidian Stream." Panel on Hypertext, Hypermedia: Defining a Fictional Form, MLA Convention. New York, 28 Dec. 1992.
5. Joyce, Michael. Of Two Minds: Hypertext Pedagogy and Poetics . Ann Arbor: The University of Michigan Press. 1995.

Remembering the Future: Language, Webs, and the Power of the Invisible

Allucquère Rosanne Stone

Advanced Communication Technologies Laboratory
Department of Radio-TV-Film
The University of Texas at Austin
Austin, TX 78712, USA
http://www.actlab.utexas.edu/~sandy

Assistant Prof in the Radio-TV-Film Department (University of Texas), cultural theorist, performance artist, director of the ACTLab, and spiritual leader of the cadre of mad, brilliant cybercrazies who inhabit it.

Author of the book „The War of Desire and Technology at the Close of the Mechanical Age“.

The Social and Cultural Challenges of the Politics of the Information Society in the European Union

Karin Junker

Düsseldorf, Germany
Member of the European Parliament
Committee on Culture, Youth, Education and the Media

Saving our Children?
The Promise of the Internet and the Perils of Censorship

Marsha Woodbury, Ph.D.

Chair, Computer Professionals for Social Responsibility
and
Director of Information Technology
Graduate School of Library and Information Science
University of Illinois, Urbana-Champaign
http://alexia.lis.uiuc.edu/~woodbury/
Work: 217-244-4643
FAX: 217-244-3302
marsha-w@uiuc.edu

1 Preface

This quote comes from an editorial in an American newspaper:

"As the name implies, the Boston Public Library is a public institution. As such it has a responsibility to the children who come from all over the region to use it. That responsibility includes doing everything a responsible parent would do to block their access to on line pornography.

"Parents and city officials were shocked to learn that children as young as 10 were cruising the Internet for smut.

"A library is supposed to be a safe haven for our children.", says Boston City Councilor Maureen Feeney, who has filed an order with the council's Committee on City and Neighborhood Services to find ways to regulate library computers.

"The library's response is discouraging. 'We have children's librarians but we don't have Internet police,' sniffed spokesman Arthur Dunphy." (Boston Herald, 1997)

2 Introduction

What is the promise of the Internet and what are the perils of Internet censorship? Those are the questions that we are gathered here to explore. We want to examine our own values, and with the merits of censoring "offensive" material against the virtues of universal open access to information.

I will begin by defining censorship, the basic issue on our agenda. I will be emphasizing that censorship has many faces, and that censorship springs originally from subjects that are "taboo," another word that we have to define.

Then we will talk about the Internet and its structure, and finally, reflect on whether it is possible at all to censor the Internet, and if it is, what might happen to the Internet as a result.

Many people call the Internet a "new frontier," which some people would want to "tame." Historically, we have always been conquering frontiers: the colonies, the West, the oceans, outer space, and now cyberspace. Without a grand plan, the pattern is that we we colonize new territories, and then, according to some scholars, we turn them over to business interests to loot. (Ziauddin, 1996, p. 15) Bringing government and regulations and censorship to the Internet would be one way of civilizing the frontier, getting the Internet "under control."

3 Censorship

What is censorship?

Censorship is as old as civilization. You can find references to it in the Bible, and in China centuries ago members of a Dynasty burned the works of Confucius. Socrates suffered the ultimate censorship--the Athenian Assembly found him guilty of corrupting the young, and condemned him to death.

The modern English word comes from the Latin, "censor'-- the title of two magistrates in ancient Rome, who drew up the register or census of the citizens, and had the supervision of public morals. (Oxford English Dictionary). Many think of the word in terms of a person who exercises official supervision over morals and conduct. The positive view of censorship is that the government censors material for the good of the people, under the guidance of the people, and for the sole benefit of the people.

If a person or thing is censored, that means a voice is stilled, data or a news item, or lewd pictures, or hate speech are cut out so that other people can't have access. You can picture a newspaper with holes where stories have been removed, or redaction, the crossing out of certain words, or no newspaper at all. For example, there has been censorship of music, the Nazis censored Kurt Weill and Bertold Brecht; the USSR censored Dmitri Shostakovich; the singing group called the Weavers was censored by US radio stations during the McCarthy era.

Parents and religious leaders have also censored materials to "protect" others. This brings us to the issue of what is "taboo." A taboo is a ban or an inhibition resulting from social custom or emotional aversion. (Oxford English Dictionary) If something is "taboo," it is excluded or forbidden from use, approach, or mention. No culture is without its taboos, although they alter with time. But this paper does not end at the level of censoring subjects that are taboo.

Moving along with our definition of censorship, even a broader description includes an official whose duty it is to censor private correspondence in time of war, to prevent the transmission of military secrets.

We then move out of the sphere of morality and war secrets, and expand the definition to include government censors examining communications for anything offensive to the government, or as we saw in the case of TASS and the old Soviet Union, news withheld because it would weaken the government. Censorship silences opposition.

We all saw the fall of the Iron Curtain countries, largely due to the collapse of censorship, when governments could no longer control the information that the citizens could hear and see. The free flow of information is potentially destabilizing to autocratic regimes. As an aside, will the free flow be destabilizing to any regime?

Let's sum up this list: censorship is tied in our minds to music, the arts, to military secrets, to freedom of speech, and the First Amendment in the U.S.A. We also have a mental model of a person or appointed persons acting as censors.

What people tend to forget is that censorship--the removing of information--can result from lack of access to the means of transmitting information, or the muzzling of journalists by seemingly benign means. If the mutual agreement or outside threat is great enough, people will censor themselves--you don't need to do anything.

The factor missing from my previous list is commercial interests. In the U.S.A. we are in the dangerous position of having several large multi-national firms control the bulk of our communications media. No government-appointed officials, no religious group, no conservative politicians will be the censors--the large businesses will do it. The Internet has up until now been a way to get around commercial censorship. Perhaps control of everything from book reviews to investigative reporting about big business will be under the eye of commercial interests.

At the heart of the censorship debate up until now is the question of government regulation. I think we ought to be concerned also about telecommunications conglomerates and their powers of censorship.

4 The Internet, a living organism

Let us turn our attention to the Internet, the vast network of networks. Organically, it is decentralized and spread out, built to withstand attack. If one node goes out, information is routed around the damage. This territory is also called "Cyberspace." The Internet is growing fast. Although the nature of the Internet makes it impossible to determine its size, approximately 5,000,000 host computers worldwide are linked to the Internet, and over 50 million individuals around the world can access it. Two hundred million users are expected by the year 1999. (ACLU vs. Reno, 1996)

Unfortunately, many millions of people, for reasons of technology, infrastructure, or socio-economic status do not have access to the Internet or to electronic information. My experience in Europe is that only a small number of homes have computers that are connected to the Internet.

In the U.S.A., the Internet initially was an academic and research network serving the military, government, and university communities. Access was cheap for people involved in those institutions. The atmosphere has been one of fostering many voices. If you participated in the early days, you remember that censorship occurred organically. If someone made an offensive post, others would bombard him or her, and users would set up a "kill file," so that person "disappeared." The Internet took care of itself, establishing its own norms. This phenomenon is called self-regulation.

Incidentally, the organization that I represent, CPSR (Computer Professionals for Social Responsibility), grew up during the spread of the Internet. We have always taken the position that computer technology has a social impact, and that we must use our knowledge of the technology to make certain that computers are used responsibly.

We wrote a very influential NII report in the early 1990's, and the reach and content of the Internet are of vast concern to us. Also, I founded the listserv called cpsr-global so we could learn what the international repercussions of the Internet would be, and what international laws and interference would do to the Internet.

At any rate, with the Internet, digital information flows across boundaries and barriers despite attempts by individuals, governments, and private entities to channel or control it. (ALA, 1996) It is not tied to geography. On the other hand, it is a "place" where people "go". As one author said, "Crossing into Cyberspace is a meaningful act that would make application of a distinct "law of Cyberspace" fair to those who pass over the electronic boundary" (Johnson and Post, 1996)

As you may be aware, times have changed. Today, there are more computers from the commercial sector on the Internet than from the academic world. We may end up with a consumer-oriented network. In the year 2000, at our current rate of growth, there will be from 100 to 125 million computers connected to the Internet.

5 Censorship of the Internet

Is there any censorship of the Internet? That will be quite surprising, given the structure of the Internet.

5.1 Self-censorship

Censorship has already occurred, but not the way you might think. Private Internet content-providers have chosen to avoid the risk of criminal prosecution and incarceration, and have self-censored expression that might be deemed "offensive." For example, CompuServe, a large Internet access provider, shut off admission to a number of news groups that violated German pornography laws (The Economist, Jan. 6, 1996). The ban was worldwide, because there was no way to isolate CompuServe in Germany. The choice appeared to be whether to cut off service to Germany or to censor newsgroups.

Is it justifiable to impose the laws of Germany on people who live in Belgium? On the people who live in the United States? Will the Internet be "dumbed down" to the laws of the most puritanical nations? Those are the questions on the table before us.

Prodigy, an American company, censored public postings on its service. If private providers are going censor, then where can the population turn for free and open communication? The more the Internet is in the hands of private companies, the less freedom we may all enjoy.

5.2 Government Censorship

Some governments censor by denying Internet access to entire segments of their populations, either through very high charges or by restricting access to select populations, such as universities. These governments want it both ways, for they see the benefits to commerce and research and technology, but also recognize the disadvantage of having Cyberspace available to economically, socially, and politically disadvantaged groups. (Human Rights Watch, 1996)

Let me list for you some current examples of government censorship:

- China, which requires users and Internet Service Providers (ISPs) to register with authorities;
- Vietnam and Saudi Arabia, which permit only a single, government-controlled gateway for Internet service;
- India, which charges exorbitant rates for international access through the state-owned phone company;
- Germany, which has cut off access to particular host computers or Internet sites;
- Singapore, which has chosen to regulate the Internet as if it were a broadcast medium, and requires political and religious content providers to register with the state. (Human Rights Watch, 1996)

The Chinese Government recently loosened controls on accessing foreign news sources such as CNN and the Wall Street Journal, though it continues keeping watch for politically suspect content, and of course it still licenses providers. Let us look at Singapore as an example of the difficulties of censorship.

In Singapore, censorship is justified on historical and socio-political grounds--the people and the government elect to live within certain boundaries. (Ang, & Nadarajan, 1995)

The government hands out annual licenses to Singapore's three Independent Service Providers (ISPs), as well as to political parties that maintain Web sites, those who run discussion sites on politics and religion, and online newspapers. These groups are responsible for blocking out material deemed objectionable by the government, i.e. which "undermine public security, national defense, racial and religious harmony, and public morals." Violations will result in licenses being revoked. About ten Singapore Broadcast Authority officials will surf the Net daily for objectionable material. The rules are somewhat vague, and offer little in the way of specific do's and don'ts -- raising fears that discussions in cyberspace would be stifled by self-censorship. (Asian Wall Street Journal,1996)

One of the factors that weigh heavily on attempts to censor in Singapore is keeping up with the information--the amount of data dumped into the Internet every day would consume thousands of hours of censoring time--the ten officials will be struggling to keep up! Secondly, Singapore differentiates between censorship of the private and commercial sectors. With the Internet you can't make that distinction. The National University of Singapore has different servers for staff and students, so staff suffers less censorship than students. The local communications provider for the country has even more censorship. What is more, all USENET groups go first to the private provider before traveling to the universities.

Singapore classifies the Internet as a broadcast medium, rather than a communications (e-mail) system. However, Singapore does not historically censor mail, so stepping into the email realm is going against the historical grain. Also, Singapore tried to use technology to search for censored words--that method is bypassed by encryption and counter-technology.

Singapore is going to keep on trying. They hope to succeed through controlling access, so only the most determined user can find the materials. Yet, oddly enough, they are trying to counter Internet misinformation with their own Internet presence, and they use the Internet forums to rebut information that might show up in a group like soc.culture.singapore.

5.3 The CDA

Now let us turn to the United States and the Communications Decency Act (CDA), an attempt by Congress to get involved in censoring the content of the Internet. When the Telecommunications Act of 1996 was passed in February of this year, it included the language of the Communications Decency Act. The CDA made it illegal to transmit certain types of materials to minors over a telecommunications network. The Act had overly-broad language and attempted to block online materials that are easily and widely found elsewhere.

In essence, it made it a criminal act to send constitutionally protected communications among the adult population whenever those communications might be deemed "indecent" or "patently offensive" for minors.

"The challenged provisions violate the bedrock First Amendment principle that government cannot "reduce the adult population ... to reading only what is fit for children." (ACLU vs. Reno) You may have heard that last year CPSR and the American Library Association (ALA) and the American Civil Liberties Union (ACLU) and many other non-profit organizations led the fight against the CDA.

So far the Act fared poorly in our judicial system; the Federal court in Philadelphia found the CDA to be unconstitutional. That decision will be reviewed by the Supreme Court. However, these battles to keep our freedoms are costly and taxing for non-profit organizations such as ours.

What is a realistic solution to controlling access to online pornograpy?The ALA advises librarians that they should treat online information just as they do hardcopy information in their libraries. According to the ALA, all information is to be considered constitutionally protected speech unless decided otherwise by a court of law--only the courts can decide to remove materials from library shelves. The ALA policy is to treat young people as they would treat adults, thus young library users have the same rights to information as do adults.

In opposing the CDA, we all discovered that tremendous ignorance exists about email, and about the Internet. Most of our time and energy consisted of educating people about the technology of the Internet.

In my opinion, this is battle to preserve the open access to information is easy to explain and defend. Censorship that is overt at least can be identified and singled out. Because we in America have the First Amendment and a tradition of freedom, we could make logical arguments for keeping the Internet open. That battle is not so easily engaged when dealing with control of access done by big business.

5.4 Points Made in Educating the Legislators

The following points are taken from a report written by Karen Coyle:

- The Internet is not the same as television. Many people have these two confused. On the Internet, information or programming is not broadcast to you. You don't view anything on the Internet unless you have asked for it, and asked for it in a fair amount of detail. The CDA treats the Internet like a broadcast medium.
- The Internet is a global system. About one third of the computers connected to the Internet are outside of the United States. U.S. law isn't going to do much to regulate content that resides on computers in other countries, yet that content is

easily retrievable from computers in this country. We will have a very hard time defining community standards for a world-wide system.

- The Internet includes a wide variety of types of communication, from publicly available information on the Web to public and less-than-public discussion groups, to private one-to-one email. No law regulating content could be applied to all of those types of communication.
- Content providers have no control over who accesses their data. Any computer on the Internet is able to retrieve Web information, and you don't know the age of the person using that computer at that time. In general, the courts consider it a bad idea to make people liable for something over which they have no control. (Coyle, 1996)

5.5 Commercial Censorship

To the giant telecommunications companies, the model of the future is not a commercially built infrastructure that is letting people contact each other cheaply--there isn't much profit in that.

In a recent article, an author described NBC apologizing to China because a news announcer referred to China's problems with human and property rights...and to the threat posed by Taiwan. Yes, NBC apologized because a TV announcer told the truth. (Hickey, 1997). NBC is owned by General Electric, a company with millions of dollars of business tied up in China. Tough documentaries about China are few and far between. The majority of Cable TV in the United States is controlled by two large companies. That control means that an alternative news station may never appear, and the public won't miss what it doesn't know it could have. Self-censorship by broadcast and print journalists is happening now, as we sit here. The stage is set, more so than ever in U.S. media history, for corporate bosses to suppress unwelcome news and otherwise meddle in editorial decisions." (Ibid, p. 28)

Here is some current news from China. In a portent of things to come, newspaper magnate Rupert Murdoch's News Corporation has joined in partnership with People's Daily and the Communist Party is now offering ChinaByte, a Web-based service in China. Murdoch hopes his investment will be recouped from advertising. No doubt this will be a service that sifts out objectionable material, some of which may violate community standards, but also other news that the government does not approve of.

Make no mistake, large multinational telecommunications companies have reached out and taken control of the pathways.

In the United States, the NII program is being managed under the auspices of the Department of Commerce, of all places, and the Internet will not be built by the government but by the commercial sector. You are no doubt familiar with the dealings of companies like Disney, Time/Warner, and Microsoft as they form alliances and mold the Internet. They see it as a gold mine.

>From the beginning, one of the stated goals of the NII was that of universal access, but the Federal government is not planning on funding universal access. Instead, we will have something like Web TV providing games, infotainment, and entertainment to households world wide. Rather than being subversive, the Net of the future will be tamed and mined for profit.

Today the Internet is a gateway to libraries and to research papers like this one, to meeting schedules and to government information. Those who have access to these treasures have money or well-situated jobs or libraries and schools that are equipped with Internet access. This access has to be preserved by law, for unless we can provide universal access, and profit motives drive the enterprise, we will have censored people out of the equation.

5.6 Alternatives to Outside Censorship

The easiest place to control the Internet is at the receiver's end--the best solution is private censorship.

If you want to protect your children from harmful materials, you must take a strong parental stand. You should accompany your child to the library and guide her or him through the search process.

Also, we have programs such as Net Nanny, Surfwatch, and Cyberpatrol that are effective means of blocking web sites from all over the world that would bring unsuitable material to the eyes of children. Of course, sometimes these programs err. The filtering used by these programs filters whole Internet sites, not single documents. They thus deny access to some appropriate materials at sites that may have a small amount of harmful content

You can also subscribe to a server (sometimes called a proxy server) that pre-censors material for your children. Many church communities may wish to do that. Businesses may follow this route, so their employees don't waste time at work reading Playboy online.

5.7 Ways to Circumvent Censorship

These are many ways to get around a censor on the Net:

- Encryption: Encoding messages so that only people with a "key" can read what you write.
- Anonymous remailers: Take the headers off an email message and resend it,
- so it is untraceable.
- Opening up a new newsgroup the minute another one closes down
- Changing providers
- Changing sign-ons
- Using radio waves and satellite broadcasts to bypass the infrastructure.

6 Summary

This article began with a quote from an editorial about the Boston Public Library. On the same day that the editorial appeared, the Mayor of Boston pulled the plug on Internet pornography at the city's public libraries.

Because of reports that Boston schoolchildren were surfing for X-rated pictures on library computers, the Mayor ordered on-line restrictions for kids as well as adults in all municipal buildings.

"I am not going to use city money for pornography. If you want to use it, go look at the Internet at home," the Mayor said. (Mulvihill, 1997)

As you can see, we will probably be dealing with more censorship decisions rather than less. At any rate, I hope that I have answered as many questions as I have raised. We have seen that the Internet is a "new frontier" which some people would want to "tame." We have reviewed the history of censorship and skimmed over the history of the Internet, only staying there long enough to note its phenomenal growth. Then we have explored various permutations of censorship, and other solutions. I hope it has become evident to you that governments ought to keep out of the business of censoring the Internet, and that citizens ought to be empowered to take control of their use of the Internet, so that we can have responsible parents and teachers looking after the welfare of our young. We ought to support government efforts to allocate bandwidth for schools and libraries at a cheap price.

We do need to engage in battles over legislation, but not without keeping our eyes fixed on the real gatekeepers of the channels of communications. For I fear that our ultimate censors are not governments, but commercial providers.

References:

1. ALA–American Library Association (1996) Access to Electronic Information, Services, and Networks: an Interpretation of the LIBRARY BILL OF RIGHTS
2. Ang, Peng Hwa and Nadarajan, Berlinda (1995) Censorship and the Internet: A Singapore Perspective http://info.isoc.org/HMP/PAPER/132/txt/paper.txt
3. Asian Wall Street Journal, Singapore Business Times (1996 July 11) Associated Press.
4. Boston Herald (1997). Editorials: "Herald's view." February 13, p. 40
5. Coyle, Karen (1996) Libraries on the Information Highway: The Problems and the Promise. http://www.dla.ucop.edu/~kec/infopeop.htm
6. Financial Times. (1997) January 1997.
7. Hickey, Neil (1997) Columbia Journalism Review, January/February, pp. 23-28.
8. Human Rights Watch (1996, May) SILENCING THE NET http://www.eff.org/~declan/global/g7/hrw.report.051096.txt Vol. 8, No. 2 .
9. Johnson, David and Post, David (1996). Law And Borders–The Rise of Law in Cyberspace, CyberSpace Law,IN Issue One - November 1996, http://www.cli.org/X0025_LBFIN.html
10. Mulvihill, Maggie(1997). "Mayor cuts access to Internet." The Boston Herald February 13, 1997 third edition, News section: p. 1.
11. Oxford English Dictionary (1989) 2nd Ed. Oxford University Press.
12. Ziauddin, S. (1996) alt.civilizations.fac: cyberspace as the Darker Side of the West, in Cyberfutures, Edited by Ziauddin Sardar and Jerome R. Ravetz, 1996, New York University Press, NY. pp. 14-41.

Accepted Papers and Discussion Notes

Topic 1: Information Society, Multimedia and Networking

Part 1: Internet, Communication and Gender

Privacy and the Internet: Only a Woman's Concern?* **

Martina Schollmeyer[1], Linda Janz and Urs Gattiker[2]

[1] Research Institute for Applied Software Technology (FAST e.V.), Arabellastr. 17, 81925 Munich, Germany
[2] University of Lethbridge, Faculty of Management Lethdridge, Alberta T1K 3M4, Canada

Abstract. The Internet, which links computers worldwide into a global network, makes previously inaccessible information available and easier to acquire than before, when interaction between remote computers was limited. In this study, Internet users were asked to fill out a survey on privacy and safety issues concerning computer use and the Internet. Special emphasis was given to recruit women respondents. Answers to privacy-related questions from the survey are examined using quantitative methods. Differences in attitudes about Internet privacy between men and women are discussed.

1 Introduction

In 1989, actress Rebecca Schaeffer was killed by a stalker who found out her address through the driver's license database of the State of California [7]. This could only happen because electronic media make the acquisition of personal information easier, thus increasing the potential for its abuse. In response, the need for protecting personal information has become more and more accepted and there are laws governing the unauthorized access or sale of personal information.

Today, the widespread use of electronic media has also increased the amount of personal information that can be collected and stored. Whereas in the past, when access to the physical computer unit containing the information was restricted to very few, the advent of networking now makes it easy to remotely access computers that may be located on different continents. This also means that it has become easier to access information about others. By hacking into a computer system or by using tools such as network sniffers, it is possible to monitor electronic message transfer and consequently, collect data on the senders and receivers of messages, providing an opportunity for abuse of this data. This means that security and privacy are intimately linked.

* This work was performed while the authors were at the University of the Federal Armed Forces at Hamburg, Germany.

** Funding for this project was provided by the University of the German Federal Armed Forces at Hamburg and the Burns Endowment Fund, The University of Lethbridge.

When it comes to information privacy, one of the current issues is the privacy of electronic mail. As more and more companies switch from the traditional form of communication via paper office memos to computer and electronic memos, new laws have to be written to address how electronic information transfer and exchange of information may be different from traditional information exchanges. In contrast to mail sent via the post office in the United States, e-mail has not yet been declared 'private', i.e., it is not illegal for a supervisor to read his/her employees' e-mail messages. Thus, whatever is said in an e-mail message may have no protection of privacy [4]. For additional examples and references, see [5].

In this paper, we briefly examine the history of privacy and discuss the different categories of invasion of privacy. We then use our study on Internet and privacy to determine how Internet users feel about privacy and security issues. We especially look for gender-specific responses to determine if attitudes of men and women regarding privacy issues vary.

2 Definition of Privacy

The earliest legal definition of privacy was provided in 1890 by Brandeis and Warren [14] as "The right of determining to what extent one's thought, sentiments, and emotions shall be communicated by others." As early as 1769 [15], American courts confronted the issue of privacy protection: "It is certain every man has a right to keep his own sentiments, if he pleases. He has certainly a right to judge whether he will make them public, or commit them only to the sight of his friends." However, [10] state that the real issue when it comes to privacy may not always be the attitude of people towards invasion of privacy, but rather the effects a perceived invasion of privacy may have. This means that even though a violation of one's privacy may be unintentional, once personal information is revealed, the effects of that information may be hard to undo.

Several existing models to regulate privacy are described by [8]. The models go from a "hands-off" position by governments, where all control over privacy is in the hands of the individual, to a strictly regulated model where governments assume authority to regulate and license all corporate use of personal data. However, as van Swaay [13] points out, privacy cannot be a right. If it were a right, one could demand protection for it. Ironically, the need to monitor for an invasion of privacy may already be a violation of the right of privacy of those being monitored.

3 Literature Review

3.1 Gender Differences

The question of behavioral differences of the sexes has been addressed at length by researchers. Some research reports significant differences. For example, Dawson's [1] study of moral and ethical differences of men and women found that womens' behavior varied significantly from men. Women did what was the "right thing" to do, even if it was not in the best interest of their employers.

Eagly [3] states in a review of the literature on gender differences that "the importance of a difference depends on the consequences of the behavior in natural settings." [9] state that preferences for privacy are determined by both individual characteristics and by the factors of a given situation. [9] found that women tend to use mechanisms for privacy regulation within a given social context, whereas men escape the social context. Regarding privacy issues, however, there is unfortunately little research that examines differences in attitudes between men and women toward privacy protection and violation.

3.2 Attitudes Toward Privacy Protection and Privacy Violations

The Internet is a medium where users have very little control about who has access to data stored about them (e.g., [7] contains discussion on how much information the Lexis Nexis database contains on residents of North America). Individuals participating in this medium have to be concerned about what they say on the Internet, which, after all, is a public forum. Messages posted to Usenet news, for example, are archived in the data bases of powerful search engines, and unless a user explicitly indicates that data should not be archived, any other user on the Internet with access to the search engine may be able to obtain a list of all messages posted by a particular individual. This allows access to personal information that was difficult to obtain before the Internet and search engines were available.

In this study performed on the Internet, attitudes of men and women toward privacy protection and privacy violation issues were examined. The survey questions were asked to determine attitudes of men and women regarding privacy on the Internet, third-party monitoring of e-mail, and collection and use of personal information in data banks.

The research question to be addressed is: Are there differences between women and men in attitudes toward these privacy-related issues? Quantitative methods are used to examine the data collected.

The results from the survey questions are used to examine attitudes toward privacy protection and violation. We use van Swaay's [13] four categories (export beyond intended domain of information supplied by owner; misuse by persons or organizations inside the intended domain; acquisition of information without cooperation or approval of owner; and acquisition of information without knowledge of the owner) to classify the questions about privacy violations.

4 Method

The central component of the study consists of a survey that was placed on the World Wide Web (WWW) and which could be filled out using a WWW browser. Background data on Internet and e-mail use, opinions on current Internet issues and demographic data on respondents was collected. To examine attitudes toward privacy protection and privacy violations, several privacy-related questions were embedded into a series of sixteen questions on Internet-related topics.

The questions were scored using the Likert scale (1-7), with 1 representing "strongly disagree" and 7 representing "strongly agree". The t-test (which evaluates differences in means and variances of responses) was performed on the data obtained to determine whether gender-related differences existed in the responses provided. This method was selected because it helps find differences in groups of respondents that can be clearly divided into two separate categories (in this case: women and men). It provides the most reliable results if the two categories are of similar size (in this case: 60%-40% which fulfills this criterion) and if the sample of respondents for each group is greater than 100.

Quantitative methods were used in this survey to allow the evaluation of the responses without any bias. In contrast to some other research performed using the t-test, we only accepted a statistical significance for a two-tailed distribution. This means that we did not assume ahead of time that women would be more concerned than men about privacy issues, but we assumed that they would be differently concerned than men.

The survey was advertised on various Usenet news groups that discuss computer privacy and security issues. In addition, the survey was advertised on several mailing lists, including mailing lists that are read predominantly by women (e.g., WISENET - Women in Science and Engineering - and Systers - a women-only mailing list for computer scientists). The survey itself was located on servers in two different countries: Germany (Hamburg) and the United States (Corpus Christi, Texas) to allow for redundancy as well as a quicker response time for Internet users in different geographic regions.

The survey web site had three components: an introductory page, the survey questions, and a 'thank-you' page that was displayed to participants who submitted a survey. A total of 1575 accesses to the introductory page describing the survey were registered (811 in Texas and 764 in Hamburg). The survey questions themselves were examined 1034 times (563 in Texas and 471 in Hamburg). A total of 456 surveys was returned via the web pages (295 in Texas and 161 in Hamburg). After eliminating duplicates and incomplete surveys and adding the surveys that had been submitted by e-mail, fax, or postal mail, 471 filled out surveys were obtained, indicating a response rate of about 45% based on the number of accesses to the survey page. We assume that the response rate was lower in Germany (34%) than in Texas (52%) because respondents were concerned about the location of the survey on a server at the University of the German Federal Armed Forces. This impression was verified by e-mail from several individuals who indicated that they would not participate in such a study if it might be monitored by the German military.

5 Results

A total of 471 surveys are part of the study. Of these, 183 (38.9%) of the respondents were female, 278 (59.0%) were male, and 10 individuals did not indicate a gender. Compared to other studies performed on the Internet [6], this is a higher than average percentage of female participants. Of the female respondents, 26.8% were students, compared to 33.1% of the male respondents. Most of the respondents found out about the survey through mailing lists (142 - 30.1%), news groups (129 - 27.4%) and e-mail from a friend/colleague (57 - 12.1%).

The majority of respondents indicated the United States as their current residence (255 - 54.1%), followed by Germany (95 - 20.2%), Canada (42 - 8.9%) and several other countries with less than 5% each. The median age of the participants was 32 (31 for men, 33 for women), the median years of education were 16 years (i.e., bachelor's degree or equivalent). The median individual income was given as US $ 37,000 with the median household income slightly less than US $ 60,000. Income given in currencies other than US dollars were converted to US dollars using purchasing power parities provided by [12].

The values obtained match the ones collected by [6] over the course of several studies for the "average" Internet population. We can therefore assume that our sample of respondents is a representative sample for Internet-literate users - our target group.

Internet access at home was available for 359 of the respondents (76.2%). The median usage time was 24 months. The average user at home sent 20 messages per week and received 10. Only 83 (17.6%) of the participants indicated that their provider reserved the right to monitor e-mail on the system. A total of 186 (39.5%) respondents indicated that their provider had a code of conduct for accessing the Internet, but only 81 (17.2%) had read it within the past four months.

At work, 420 (89.2%) of the respondents indicated that they had access to e-mail, and 409 indicated Internet access (86.9%). The median usage time was 36 months. The average time per week on e-mail at work was 150 minutes, with 30 minutes being spent on private e-mail. The average user at work received 60 messages a week and sent out 20. The employer reserved a right to monitor e-mail for 94 (20%) of the respondents and 146 (31%) additional respondents indicated that they were not sure whether such a policy existed. However, 141 participants (29.9%) indicated that their employer had a policy on the private use of e-mail.

5.1 Attitudes Toward Privacy Protection

The first privacy protection question asked participants to indicate how they felt about protecting other people's privacy on the Internet:

> (1) As a user of the Internet/Information Highway I feel that it is my responsibility not to violate anyone's privacy on the Internet (i.e., their right to determine for themselves, where to, when, how and to what extent information about them is communicated to others).

Protection 1	Number of Cases	Response Mean	SD	SE of Mean
female	183	6.55	1.08	0.08
male	275	6.36	1.22	0.07

The $\underline{t}$-test indicates no gender-specific difference ($\underline{t}$=1.61, 2-tail significance = 0.11), and therefore the conclusion is that men and women felt similarly about this question. The response mean for both genders represents a value above "agree" on the scale provided in the questionnaire.

The second question on attitudes toward privacy protection dealt with the role that an appointed privacy commissioner should play when it comes to privacy and electronic media:

> (2) I feel that, to protect privacy, data-security/privacy-commissioners must have the right to check the accuracy of content in police data banks on behalf of citizens.

Protection 2	Number of Cases	Response Mean	SD	SE of Mean
female	179	5.27	1.83	0.14
male	274	5.72	1.80	0.11

The $\underline{t}$-test clearly indicates a gender-specific difference ($\underline{t}$=-2.46, 2-tail significance < 0.05 (p=0.01)). For the second question, men appear to feel more strongly than women that a privacy commissioner should have access to personal data in police data bases.

5.2 Attitudes Toward Privacy Violations

The first category of possible privacy violations according to [13], is "export of information supplied by owner beyond intended domain." The following survey question was used to address this concern:

> (1) I believe that the exchange/matching of government maintained central records on health, employment and income/tax records is important for protecting the collective good/interest (e.g., against various frauds such as collecting more than one unemployment or social welfare check).

Category 1	Number of Cases	Response Mean	SD	SE of Mean
female	181	3.88	2.00	0.15
male	275	3.83	2.11	0.13

The $\underline{t}$-test indicates no gender-specific difference ($\underline{t}$=0.30, 2-tail significance = 0.77), indicating that both men and women have a similarly neutral attitudes towards this type of possible privacy violation.

The second category is the "misuse of provided information by persons or organizations inside the intended domain." Several questions were used to test this concept:

> (2-1) I feel that, to facilitate law enforcement, the police should always have the right to collect personal data (such as gender, religion, sexual preference) in a central data bank about witnesses to a crime.

Category 2-1	Number of Cases	Response Mean	SD	SE of Mean
female	182	1.87	1.39	0.10
male	277	2.15	1.70	0.10

The $\underline{t}$-test indicates no gender-specific difference ($\underline{t}$=-1.92, 2-tail significance = 0.06), indicating that there are no significant differences in attitudes of men and women about this classification of privacy violation. Both men and women disagreed with the statement made.

(2-2) I feel that, to facilitate law enforcement, the police should always have the right to collect personal data (such as gender, religion, sexual preference) in a central data bank about alleged victims of a crime.

Category 2-2	Number of Cases	Response Mean	SD	SE of Mean
female	182	2.05	1.64	0.12
male	274	2.28	1.70	0.10

The $\underline{t}$-test again indicates no gender-specific difference ($\underline{t}$=-1.49, 2-tail significance = 0.14).

(2-3) I feel that, to facilitate law enforcement, the police should always have the right to collect personal data (such as gender, religion, sexual preference) in a central data bank about suspects to a crime.

Category 2-3	Number of Cases	Response Mean	SD	SE of Mean
female	181	2.98	2.01	0.15
male	276	2.86	1.99	0.12

The $\underline{t}$-test indicates again no gender-specific difference ($\underline{t}$=0.65, 2-tail significance = 0.52).

Although there are no gender-specific differences in this series of questions, it is interesting to see that respondents felt less and less opposed to collecting data in a central data bank the more a person was involved with a crime. This indicates that in addition to the degree of privacy violation, other value judgements were used.

The third category of van Swaay [13] refers to the acquisition of information without cooperation or approval of owner. One survey question examined this category:

(3) I feel that it is unacceptable for a supervisor to access employees' computer files and/or computer accounts at work without prior authorization.

Category 3	Number of Cases	Response Mean	SD	SE of Mean
female	182	5.70	1.68	0.13
male	276	5.35	2.07	0.13

The $\underline{t}$-test indicates a gender-specific difference ($\underline{t}$=1.99, 2-tail significance < 0.05 (p=0.048)).

In this case, women appear to be more strongly concerned than men about unauthorized access to the information they store on their computer at work.

The last of the categories deals with "acquisition of information without knowledge of the owner." Two survey questions addressed this category:

(4-1) I feel that an organization, for its own protection, should reserve the right to randomly monitor e-mail traffic on its computer system (e.g., every 20th message).

Category 4-1	Number of Cases	Response Mean	SD	SE of Mean
female	183	2.72	1.81	0.13
male	277	2.77	1.95	0.12

The *t*-test indicates no gender-specific difference (*t*=-0.29, 2-tail significance = 0.77). Both men and women disagree somewhat with the statement made.

(4-2) I feel that the government should always have the right to gain access to financial data of individuals from financial institutions without a court order.

Category 4-2	Number of Cases	Response Mean	SD	SE of Mean
female	182	1.42	1.11	0.08
male	277	1.53	1.26	0.08

The *t*-test indicates no gender-specific difference (*t*=-0.97, 2-tail significance = 0.334). Clearly, from the results in this category, both men and women are equally opposed to the acquisition of information without their prior knowledge and consent.

6 Discussion

From the results of the tests it can be seen that both men and women are concerned about privacy issues. There are a few differences between the attitudes of men and women in regard to the questions evaluated in this survey. The first privacy protection question indicates that, at least for the respondents to this survey, people are aware of the need to protect the privacy of others on the Internet. The mean answer on the Likert scale was above "strongly agree," making it the question with the highest level of agreement of all questions asked. However, many individuals who responded to this survey found out about it through privacy-related or professional news groups and mailing lists and were therefore possibly more aware of and concerned about privacy issues than the average Internet user.

The position of a privacy commissioner received a positive response from survey participants. The median answer for this question was "somewhat agree." Since no specific job description was provided for this commissioner, many respondents may have agreed to a certain degree but were not able to indicate what alternative to privacy enforcement they might have preferred. It is, however, interesting to see that women are clearly less in favor of privacy commissioners than men. This may be related to the privacy violation question in which women indicated, stronger than men, that they did not want their supervisors accessing their computers. The need to protect their own privacy may cause women to reject the privacy commissioner since that person would have access to their data, even if it is only to determine accuracy.

A summary of the privacy violations in van Swaay's [13] four categories, indicates that women and men are equally concerned when it comes to most issues:

The respondents felt neutral about the export of information supplied by owners beyond the intended domain, if it helped society in general. This suggests that it is acceptable for the organizations to examine information already provided by its clients to prevent fraud and abuse.

For category two, addressing the (possible) misuse of information provided by persons or organizations inside the intended domain, the involvement of government authorities triggered a negative response. The median answer to these questions was in the general area of "disagree." This is probably caused by a certain lack of trust in the police forces in countries such as the United States, where a large portion of the survey participants came from. It is, however, interesting to note that it is more acceptable to collect data about suspects than it is to collect data about witnesses or victims. The statement about "innocent until proven guilty" apparently does not apply to the acceptability of data collection (and its possible misuse by the authorities).

An interesting observation can also be made about the collection of information on victims. Had we assumed a directional hypothesis, stating that women are more concerned than men about protecting victims' privacy, we would have clearly observed a gender-related difference. This may be due to the fact that women, more than men, being afraid of becoming a victim of a crime.

Category three, addressing the acquisition of information without cooperation or approval of the owner, and using the example of a supervisor at work, again triggered a gender-specific response. Women, more than men, were concerned with the invasion of their privacy through that means. One explanation for this may be that men may have less personal information stored on their computers at work, or it may be caused by women feeling more concerned about revealing too much personal information to their supervisors [10]. In this case, additional analyses should be performed to link potential computer ownership at home with privacy concerns at work.

Finally, in category four, dealing with the acquisition of information without the knowledge of the owner, both men and women appear equally concerned about their employer, or the government, obtaining information about them or others.

7 Conclusion

In this paper, we examine the question of the difference in concerns of women and men regarding privacy-related issues. From the results, it is obvious that both men and women are very concerned about privacy protection. However, there are some issues where women indicate more concern than men. Women are more opposed to their supervisors examining information stored on their computers without prior authorization. This may be related to the result that they, less than men, feel that a privacy commissioner can guarantee that the information stored about them in data bases will be accurate. We conjecture that the reasoning here is that personal data should not be examined at all rather than allowing someone access it who might be able to misuse the data.

Men and women are obviously concerned about their privacy on the Internet and with other electronic media. In some areas, women are clearly more concerned than men about an invasion of their privacy. It is important to address these issues so that women can feel as comfortable as men using the Internet and other electronic media for job-related and private purposes. Possible solutions to this problem may include better user training and the emphasis of ethical behavior by all users of the Internet.

References

1. Dawson, L.M.: Women and Men, Morality and Ethics. Business Horizons, July/August, (1995) 61–68. (1995).
2. Doss, E., and Loui, M.: Ethics and the privacy of electronic mail. The Information Society, **11**, 223–235. (1995).
3. Eagly, A.H.: The science and politics of comparing women and men. America Psychologist, **50**, 145–158. (1995).
4. Eskow, D.: Your e-mail can be used against you. Corporate Computing, January, **7**, 171. (1993).
5. Gattiker, U.E., Janz, L., Kelley, H., Schollmeyer, M.: The Internet and privacy: Do you know who's watching? Business Quarterly, **60**, 79–84. (1996).
6. Kehoe, C.M. and Pitkow, J.E.: Surveying the territory: GVU's five WWW user surveys. The World Wide Web Journal, 1(3). (1996).
7. Lefrevre, G.: Guarding privacy tougher as Internet expands. CNN Interactive, Sci-Tech Story Page, September 19. (1996).
8. Milberg, S.J., Burke, S. , Smith, H.J., and Kallman, E.A.: Values, Personal Information Privacy, and Regulatory Approaches. Communications of the ACM, **38**, 65–74. (1995).
9. Pedersen, D.M. and Frances, S.: Regional differences in privacy preferences. Psychological Reports, **66**, 731–736. (1990).
10. Tolchinsky, P.D., McCuddy, M.K., Adams, J., Ganster, D., Woodman, R.W., and Fromkin, H.: Employee perception of invasion of privacy: A field simulation experiment. Journal of Applied Psychology, **66**, 308–311. (1981).
11. Türkheimer, F.: Privacy and the Internet: The next step. Computer Networks and ISDN Systems, **27**, 395–401. (1995).
12. Union Bank of Switzerland: Prices and Earnings around the Globe. (1994).
13. van Swaay, M.: The Value and Protection of Privacy. Computer Networks and ISDN Systems, **26** (Suppl 4), 149–155. (1995).
14. Warren S. and Brandeis L.: The Right to Privacy. Harvard Law Review, **4**, 193–220. (1890).
15. Yates, J. in Millar v. Taylor: 4, Burr, 2303, 2379. (1769).

This article was processed using the LaTeX macro package with LLNCS style

A Woman's or Worm's-Eye View of the Information Society

Dr. Christel Kumbruck

Abstract. From a global, bird's-eye view people are euphoric about the information society. In this paper I shall look at the information society from with a worm's-eye view and will highlight small changes in everyday life gleaned from empirical studies. These small changes are indications of a cultural change concerning the human-machine interface and the socio-cultural structures of interaction between human and machine - and their boundaries. I will concentrate on necessary technical framework measures allowing the use of the data highway. These are digital signatures for the protection of "privacy", copyright and (financial) obligations. The worm's-eye view is a methodical way to discover the "invisibilities" or "soft factors" of communication and cooperation, which are normally forgotten in the design of information and communication technology. Women complain about the absence of these factors.

1 Introduction

Women place much hope in the information society and the potential offered by the new media, especially the "freedom of information" and the possible egalitarian and emancipatory potential of networks. What is particularly welcomed is the possibility of interconnecting women[1] - and in this context the connections which were established at the Women's Conference in Beijing are mentioned - as well as the opportunity of creating an opposing public. The role of the Internet within the framework of the war in the former Yugoslavia is emphasized in this connection.

Apart from the justified hope of promoting "communication from bottom up" and "communication from everybody to everybody" there will be a number of obstacles on the data highway.

Electronic communications and cooperation are immaterial and incorporeal; they are a virtual manifestation of human communication. No trace of the act of cooperation refers back to an individual; no results of these acts remain and or are visible. This aspect is especially important where financial transactions or copyright are concerned. But also in the case of the receipt of information, it is problematic if, due to the lack of material traces, it is not possible to recognise the well-known writing of a friend and to find proof of the authenticity of the document's contents, of the time it was prepared, of the author etc. No fading of the paper or celluloid stripe indicates the date of authoring. There is no scratch, cut or variation of the pencil or typewriter ribbon which might help to discover any alterations. There is no clumsy writing which might be a hint that information in the document or the signature has been falsified.

[1]See Strossen 1995, 12 ff.

There is no envelope, which protects the document from unwelcome scrutiny and ensures the privacy of the communication.

These aspects are not obvious. During the R&D-process of designing information and communication technology they are normally not considered. In my investigations of the psychosocial affects of telecommunication and telecooperation technology I used ethnographic research methods. They deliver a worm eye's view not a bird-eye's view in that I am looking for the small things in every day life.[2]

2 A Feminist Perspective

With regard to the design of technology identifying the invisibilities and soft factors is a matter of concern for women, as the literature shows.

Feminist researchers show shortcomings in the design of communication and cooperation technology, which mostly concern women in their working and their everyday lives.

Microcosm: Special emphasis is given to the "invisibility of women's work".[3] Specialists responsible for the development of technical systems consider office work, for instance, as a collection of trivial tasks which can be accelerated at any time by providing machine support. The variety of necessary context-related activities connecting the different tasks is simply ignored.[4]

Only if these supposedly invisible aspects or other everyday peculiarities are made visible, will the benefit and usefulness of a procedure for the completion of these tasks show. Since the invisible work elements often contain interactive elements, they are of special importance in the evaluation of electronic media.

Everyday life: Technological systems are designed largely to support the workplace. The interests of other people such as the clients are often forgotten. As women identify themselves much less with their work than men do and are concerned with all aspects of everyday life they refer to this lack.[5]

Social skills: In firms activities like caring, communicating and organizing are practiced at the higher levels of the hierarchy by managers, and at the lower levels of the hierarchy by women such as secretaries. These activities aren't recorded by system-analytic design approaches[6], but are part of cooperation and communication. And they are characterized as feminine.

Using technology in a different way: The new electronic technology is not the most suitable for all situations. For example, the advavtages of using paper cannot be simply replaced by the benefits of television and computers. Suchman emphasizes that women have a different attitude towards technology and, therefore, their answers are also different when questions about the design of technical systems arise.[7] Female design criteria for technical systems are particularly connected to the question of the usefulness of a technical solution. Women compare the practical benefits of a new

[2]See Geertz 1973 and Suchman 1987.
[3]See Star 1991, 81 ff.
[4]Bødker / Greenbaum 1993, 57.
[5]See Hülsmeier / Winker 1992, 129 ff.
[6]See Pain et.al. 1993, 22f.
[7]Suchman 1994a, 47.

technology to those of the existing one. They prefer the differentiated use of technology to the imperialistic use: The new media are not intended to replace traditional ones but to offer people the possibility of selecting between them depending on the purpose in hand and the possibility of cooperating with people using other (traditional) media. This approach is based on the idea that technical objects are not context-free, floating objects but that each technique has its field of application with respect to certain work procedures. Suchman emphasizes the importance of investigating the situated action.[8] This approach, which implies that the use of technology is bound to the requirements of a certain situation, is opposed to the approach which favours the use and development of technical systems giving way to the instinct of playing in an unreflected manner.[9]

This feminist design perspective is characterized by:

- The maintenance or even the extension of different working and interactive procedures, including all invisible elements requiring various capabilities.
- The reflected orientation towards a purpose or an everyday problem, which also includes the use of various media for different activities.
- The importance of communication and cooperation with others.

This perspective compares the solution of the problem to traditional solutions and solutions at another level. The question is asked whether the technical innovation possibly makes a new definition of everyday activities necessary. For this purpose, attention is paid to the little things of everyday life. Especially important is the microscopic perspective, the "worm's-eye view", i.e. that comprehensive interpretations and abstract analyses are based on a thorough knowledge of the small things of everyday life.[10]

3 A Worms's-Eye View of the Data Highway

With respect to their usefulness in everyday life the microscopic nearly invisible elements of the technical potential of the data highway are being studied.[11] Electronic communication and cooperation is characterized, on the one hand, by facelessness, incorporeality, having a virtual manifestation and, on the other hand, by immateriality, particularly paperlessness.

The lack of face-to-face communication, for instance, leads to anonymity. Changes in the field of social psychology towards face-to-face communication, such as

---

[8]Suchman 1987.

[9]In contrast to men, the pattern of behaviour of women with respect to spare time activities is not only characterized by the idea of the benefit of their activities, but also by a limited use of resources and technical means; see Kirkup 1992.

[10]This microscopic perspective corresponds to the ethno-graphical procedure, see Geertz 1973 and Suchman 1987.

[11]The empirical bases are one field and two simulation studies in the area of justice administration and office work. The context for these studies was a research project. Its purpose was to understand how people in open telecommunication contact cooperate together and deciding how the technology should be designed. See Kumbruck / Schneider 1996 and Kumbruck 1996.

impersonality, but also no effects of visible status symbols and thereby more balanced participation rates in group discourses were described in detail by Hiltz/Turoff[12] and Kiesler et.al.[13]. These results refer to a central aspect of communication and cooperation on the data highway, i.e. the lack of visual control of the partner and his or her activities. There are no indications to the user which would help him or her to get an idea of his/her partner. Communication and cooperation, however, depend on commitment and confidence. Confidence helps to make the physical presence of the partner superfluous and to accept his or her absence.[14] For this purpose, the sociologist Giddens[15] distinguishes between facework commitments and faceless commitments. Commitments are experience and communication modes established at the physical level. Personal confidence based on personally negotiated commitments (facework commitments) can be replaced by an action based on the commitment to generally recognized rules (faceless commitments). If facework commitments are, however, not sufficient, it is possible to negotiate new commitments and responsibilities under the condition of physical presence. The personal signature is such a socially negotiated mechanism which makes the presence of the cooperating partner superfluous. It is a physically stored biometric sample which can be used for the definite identification of a person.

The link between facelessness and immateriality deeply influences the act of cooperation. Therefore, faceless commitments have to be concluded.

Compared to paper transmission the major problems in connecting through the transmission of electronic documents are: There is no longer the possibility of recognizing individual features as their is with paper. Because of this the recipient of a document is no longer able to locate it at the cognitive level with the sender simply on account of its individual traces, especially the personal signature, or by means of the written context and physical medium (letterhead, letter paper). Electronic documents can be easily modified without any trace being left and without the opportunity of providing evidence of the modifications. Therefore, so-called originals, copies and amended versions cannot be distinguished from each other. It is no longer possible to determine the chronological order of the various versions or to classify them on the basis of the modifications performed. Statements can be made under a false name without this being visually recognized. Transmitted data can be accessed by third parties and used as data traces or for profile creation.

These deficiencies of the electronic media will be eliminated in future by means of electronic security procedures.[16] The intention is to introduce public coding procedures and to use chip cards as safe hardware components. There are plans for these procedures to be supported by the appropriate organizational measures which will help to encrypt texts, to recognize any kind of manipulation of the contents, to protect copyright and to ensure "privacy".

Digital signatures are not only intended to provide evidence of the authenticity of a document, but also of its ownership of the public code and, thus, of the copyright.

---

[12]See Hiltz / Turoff 1978.

[13]See Kiesler et.al. 1984. The aspects referring to social psychology are not pursued further.

[14]Ses Luhmann 1989 and Kumbruck 1996.

[15]See Giddens 1990.

[16]Security problems and technical solutions, see Hammer / Schneider 1995.

However, the authentication of the certificates belonging to the signature only means that their contents have not been changed. At the organizational and technical level it must be ensured that it is in fact only the indicated user and no one else who has access to the appropriate secret code. To ensure this a so-called trustworthy third party has to issue the secret keys and to guarantee the connection between key-owner and key. It is also necessary to protect the chip cards as the carrier medium against unauthorized access, for example, by means of a personal identification number (PIN). This measure guarantees that only the authorized person, i.e. the owner of the code, can use it.

From a bird's-eye view these cryptological measures for the digital signature correspond to the procedure used with a personal signature.[17] However, from the worm's-eye-view, i.e. use in everyday life, the two procedures are different in important respects.[18] The results of my empirical studies considering this question are as follows:[19]

- *"Hand-made subscription is so easy"*
  The digital signature is not an individual, physical activity, so to speak "à la main". On the contrary, in order to use it people need tools such as the chip card and the PIN. These are not "a natural part of people", but can get lost, can be forgotten or given to someone else. Moreover, they can be stolen or spied on. The digital signature can be automated so that a conscious decision to sign a document is no longer necessary.

- *"It's a black box"*
  Users cannot rely on the correct functioning of the equipment (computers) which they use for the signing of documents. A hidden text can, for instance, be included in the document which they also sign without knowing it. Finally, the user has no visual control whether he or she signs the intended document. For this reason, it is recommended that users use only their own equipment and their own software.

- *"That's typical bureaucracy, that's powering"*[20]
  A security infrastructure is necessary to ensure the allocation of the code to only one person in open user groups. The user becomes dependent on this so-called trustworthy third party.

- *"I miss the physiognomy of my communication partner"*
  The personal signature is a biometric sample definitely belonging to a certain person. The personal signature can also be examined with relatively high accuracy by non-experts with the naked eye. In contrast to this, machine control is required

[17] See Seidel 1990, 315 ff.

[18] See Kumbruck 1994a and Kumbruck 1995 too.

[19] The investigation was made by non-structured interviews and observations and hermeneutic evaluation. The following headers are characteristic statements from my inteviews. See the results from simulation studies and field trials in the area of justice administration and office work: see provet / GMD 1993, provet-PB 8, provet / GMD 1994, Kumbruck 1993, provet-AP 84, Kumbruck 1993, provet-AP 105, Kumbruck 1993, provet-AP 119, Bizer et.al. 1995.

[20] The trustworthy third party could block the secret key without informing the user. This statement is a reaction to such a situation.

for a digital signature. The user does not receive any individual traces of the author of the document, but only a machine reference to a person. This reference is not easy for non-experts to understand.

- *"If the systems says 'the proof is okay' it has to be"*
  Another impediment for handling the digital signature according to security reqirements is that the electronic verification does not always offer reliable information about the correctness of the signature. In addition to the global test result displayed on the screen, e.g. "correct signature", users have to deal with particulars in the certificate, e.g. the set-up of certificate sequences or to compare the name in the certificate with the name in the address.

It becomes obvious that face-to-face communication and paper possess qualities necessary for communication and cooperation which have no parallel at the electronic level. The differences are only seen regarding the soft factors. These results from the worm's-eye view show that the data highway does not only ensure enhanced interconnection possibilities according to the bird's-eye perspective, but that it is accompanied by a fundamental restructuring of everyday life, which I would like to call a cultural change.

4 Conclusion: Cultural Change

What is especially important is that people no longer have the opportunity to ascertain visually whether a message is correct or whether they can trust a person and they are no longer able to assume responsibility by means of an individual act. Psychological and corporeal activities experience a technological embodiment.[21] This implies two cultural aspects:
Technology of accountability: With regard to trust people and to take responsibility machines and institutions of the digital signature take over human tasks. People have to depend on the correct proof of this security technology and they do it. In this way it's a technology of accountability.

> By technologies of accountability, I mean systems aimed at the inscription and documentation of actions to which parties are accountable not only in the ethnomethodological sense of that term[22] but in the sense represented by the bookkeeper's ledger, the record of accounts paid and those still outstanding.[23]

Boundary object: The machine is a prothesis to perception. Human and machine have to interact. Hard and soft factors are unseparably bounded. The human body is come into being as a boundary figure belonging to two previously incompatible systems of meaning - "the organic/natural" and "the technological/cultural".[24] In using such technology people have difficulties in separating human and machine. For them the

---

[21]See Balsamo 1996, 215 ff.
[22]Suchman refers to Garfinkel / Sacks 1970.
[23]Suchman 1994b, 188.
[24]See Balsamo 1995, 213..

technology has become a "boundary object"[25]. The cultural phenomenon crossing this border is called a 'cyborg' by Haraway.[26]
The cultural changes are shown by the details in interacting - in the worm's eye view. They are relevant to the development of society. Woman's perspective on interacting, to the activities in everyday life uncovers these small but affective aspects and helps to negotiate about them concerning to design telecommunication and telecooperation technology in a human (male *and* female) manner.

References

1. Balsamo, A. (1995): Forms of Technological Embodiment: Reading the Body in Contemporary Culture, in: Featherstone, M. / Burrows, R. (Eds.): Cyberspace / Cyberbodies / Cyberpunk, London, 213 ff.
2. Bizer, J. / Grimm, R. / Hammer, V. / Kumbruck, C. / Pordesch, U. / Roßnagel, A. / Sarbinowski, H. / Schneider, M. / Schneider, W. (1995): Rechtsverbindliche Telekooperation in der elektronischen Vorgangsbearbeitung, GMD-Studien Nr. 261, Sankt Augustin.
3. Bødker, S. / Greenbaum, J. (1993): Design of Information Systems: Things versus People, in: Green, E. / Owen, J. / Pain, D. : Gendered by Design? Information Technology and Office Systems, London, 53 ff.
4. Garfinkel, H. / Sacks, H. (1970): On Formal Structures of Practical Action, in: McKinney, J. / Tiryakin, E. (Eds.): Theoretical Sociology, New York, 337 ff.
5. Geertz, C. (1994): Thick Description: Toward an Interpretative Theory of Culture, in: Geertz, C.: The Interpretation of Cultures. Selected essays. New York, 3 ff.
6. Giddens, A. (1990): The Consequences of Modernity, Oxford.
7. Hammer, V. / Schneider, M. J. (1995): Szenario künftiger Sicherungsinfrastrukturen für Telekooperation, in: Hammer, V. (Hrsg.): Sicherungsinfrastrukturen - Gestaltungsvorschläge für Technik, Organisation und Recht, Berlin, Heidelberg 1 ff.
8. Haraway, D. (1985): "A Manifesto for Cyborgs: Science, Technology and Socialist Feminism in the 1980s", in: Socialist Review 15, 65 ff.
9. Hiltz, S. R. / Turoff, M. (1978): The Network Nation, Massachusetts.
10. Hülsmeier, D. / Winker, G. (1992): Sozialverträgliche Arbeits- und Technikgestaltung: Stabilisierung oder Aufhebung der geschlechtshierarchischen Arbeitsteilung?, in: Langenheder, W. / Müller, G. / Schinzel, B. (Hrsg.): Informatik cui bono?, GI-FB 8 Fachtagung Freiburg, 23.-26.9.1992, Berlin, 129.
11. Kiesler, S. / Siegel, J. / McGuire, T. W. (1984): Social Psychological Aspects of Computer-mediated Communication, in: American Psychologist 39, 1123 ff.
12. Kirkup, G. (1992): The Social Construction of Computers: Hammers or Harpsichords?, in: Kirkup, G. / Smith Keller, L. (Eds.): Inventing Woman. Science, Tchnology and Gender, Cambridge, 267 ff.

---

[25] See Turkle 1986 and Star 1989.

[26] Haraway 1985.

13. Kumbruck, C. (1993): Anwendergerechtheit in der Rechtspflege - eine empirische Studie, provet-Arbeitspapier 105, Darmstadt.
14. Kumbruck, C. (1993): Auswertung der Langzeitstudie "Elektronische Urlaubskarte", Technikversion DISCO2, unter dem Kriterium der Anwendergerechtheit, provet-Arbeitspapier 119, Darmstadt.
15. Kumbruck, C. (1993): Die elektronische Urlaubskarte, provet-Arbeitspapier 84, Darmstadt.
16. Kumbruck, C. (1994a): Der "unsichere Anwender" - vom Umgang mit Signaturverfahren, in: Datenschutz und Datensicherung 1, 20 ff.
17. Kumbruck, C. (1995): Digitale Sicherung und Sicherheitskultur, in: Hammer, V. (Hrsg.): Die Sicherungsinfrastruktur für offene Telekooperation - Gestaltungsvorschläge für Technik, Organisation und Recht, Berlin, 217 ff.
18. Kumbruck, C. / Schneider, M. J. : Simulation Studies, a New Method of Prospective Technology Assessment and Design, Beitrag zur Konferenz Computers in Context - Joining Forces in Design am 14. - 18.8.95 in Aarhus, Dänemark, Provet-Arbeitspapier 190, Darmstadt.
19. Kumbruck, C. : "Angemessenheit für situierte Kooperation" ein Kriterium arbeitswissenschaftlicher Technikforschung und -gestaltung", Habilitationsschrift, Kassel Dezember 1996.
20. Luhmann, N. (1989): Vertrauen - Ein Mechanismus der Reduktion sozialer Komplexität, Stuttgart.
21. Pain, D. / Owen, J. / Franklin, I. / Green, E. (1993): Human-centred Systems Design: A Review of Trends within the Broader Systems Development Context, in: Green, E. / Owen, J. / Pain, D. (Eds.): Gendered by Design? Information Technology and Office Systems, London, 11 ff.
22. Provet / GMD (1993): Die Simulationsstudie elektronische Vorgangsbearbeitung, provet-Projektbericht 8, Darmstadt.
23. Provet / GMD (1994): Die Simulationsstudie Rechtspflege - Eine neue Methode zur Technikgestaltung für Telekooperation, Berlin.
24. Seidel, U. (1990): Sicherer als Unterschriften: Elektronische Signatur, in: KES 5/1990, 315 ff.
25. Star, S.L. (1989): The Structure of Ill-structured Solutions: Boundary Objects and Heterogeneous Distributed Problem Solving, in: Gasser, L. / Huhns, M. (Eds.): Distributed Artificial Intelligence, London, Vol. 2., 37 ff.
26. Star, S.L. (1991): Invisible Work and Silenced Dialoques in Knowledge Representation, in: Eriksson, I. / Kitchenham, B. / Tijdens,K. (Eds.): Woman, Work and Computerisation: Understanding Bias in Work and Education, Amsterdam, 81 ff.
27. Strossen, N. (1995): Menschenrechte und Frauenrechte im Neuen Informationszeitalter, in: Auf dem Weg in die 'Kabeldemokratie'?, Frauen in der Medien und Informationsgesellschaft, Dokumentation der Frauenpolitischen Konferenz 17.-19.11.1995, Hamburg, Hrsg. von der Frauenanstiftung e.V., Hamburg.
28. Suchman, L. (1987): Plans and Situated Actions. The Problem of Human-machine Communication, Cambridge.

29. Suchman, L. (1994a): Supporting Articulation Work. Aspects of a Feminist Practice of Technology Production, in: Adam, A. / Owen, J. (Eds.): Proceedings of the 5th IFIP International Conference on Woman, Work and Computerization, Manchester, 46 ff.
30. Suchman, L. (1994b): Do Categories have Politics? The Language / Action Perspective Reconsidered, in: Computer Supported Cooperative Work 2, 177 ff.
31. Turkle, S. (1986): Die Wunschmaschine. Der Computer als zweites Ich, Reinbek 1986.

"I don't think that's an interesting dialogue": Computer-Mediated Communication and Gender

Margit Pohl[1] and Greg Michaelson[2]

[1] Inst für Gestaltungs- & Wirkungsforschung
Technische Universität Wien, Möllwaldplatz 5, A-1040 Wien; Austria
phone: +43 1 504 11 86 13, FAX: +43 1 504 11 88
email margit@iguwnext.tuwien.ac.at

[2] Dept of Computing & Electrical Engineering
Heriot-Watt University, Riccarton, Scotland EH14 4AS
phone: +44 131 451 3422, FAX: +44 131 451 3431
email: greg@cee.hw.ac.uk

Abstract. An experiment to investigate gender differences in email mediated co-operative working is presented, involving Austrian/Scottish pairs acting as domain experts for each other's tasks. While gender and culture are not overall predictors of the effort a subject expends on their own and their partner's task, classic gender stereotypes are found in individuals' co-operation strategies.

1 Introduction

There is much empirical evidence that there are gender differences in face-to-face communication but it is an open question whether these differences can also be observed in computer-mediated communication (CMC). Gender as such tends to disappear in CMC because identity is not stable in electronic communication. On the other hand, it is well documented that the participation rate of women on the Internet is relatively low (Shade 1994). Problems which might account for this include broad social inequities based in financial, institutional and educational barriers, socialisation and gender stereotypes. Even where women have Internet access, their active participation may be affected by the forms of interaction they encounter.

Internet interaction forms are, to some extent, male dominated. This probably reflects the social marking of all technology as male and the strong influence of male forms of behaviour on computer culture. For example, there is evidence that some women are frightened away from the Internet by strategies like flaming (Herring 1994, Spender 1995) which are mostly used by men. Sutton (1996) points out that netiquette usually prescribes extreme politeness to avoid conflicts. Flaming is the only exception to this rule.

Nonetheless, the Internet is a fluid medium which is, in principle, open to different forms of use by different social groups. For example, Sherry Turkle (Turkle 1995) thinks that the Internet provides new opportunities for women. She posits that the Internet supports a style of interaction which is more feminine than traditional programming (Turkle 1990). She calls this style "soft mastery" or "bricolage". It is characterised by a bottom-up approach and more intuitive and holistic behaviour. Bricoleurs play around with objects on the screen rather than use predefined and structured strategies. Simulations and virtual worlds are their favourites. Turkle states that this style of behaviour is more similar to a female style of interacting with the world.

At the other end of the spectrum, cyberfeminists like Sadie Plant (Plant 1996) see opportunities for the dissolution of all forms of identity on the Internet. The Internet is a medium where an individual may construct actively their own persona, free from social stereotypes which are reinforced by physical appearance. Whether this is in itself revolutionary seems moot. Such escapist role play may serve instead to palliate the day to day oppressions and exploitations of actually existing reality, which is the ultimate basis of all human activity. None the less, it is undoubtedly the case that people need not be constrained by their gender identities in cyberspace, which could have significant effects on Internet expectations and behaviours.

It has often been argued that CMC is the modern form of the telephone. Spender (Spender 1995) states that the telephone is one of the most commonly reported "non-work" activities of women. CMC might provide women with the opportunity to chat even more easily over the Internet. It must be noted, however, that it is difficult to detect such opportunities in actual empirical material, especially in quantitative studies. Case studies of atypical subjects can overcome this to a certain extent. Kaplan and Farrel (1994) investigated the attitudes of young women who spend much of their time surfing the Internet. They found out that there are many aspects of the Internet of interest to young women as well as young men.

2 Gender Differences and Email

Gender differences in face to face communication strategies have been thoroughly investigated. Tannen (Tannen 1991) distinguishes the male favoured public "report" talk, to do with negotiating and maintaining status, from the female favoured private "rapport" talk, for establishing and maintaining relationships. She provides a useful overview of women's and men's different styles in and uses of questioning, interruption, making suggestions and giving opinions. In public "report" communication between men and women these differences tend to favour a male agenda. Gender stereotyped extra-linguistic cues, for example tone of voice, accent, clothing and body language, also reinforce the expectation of such differences in conversation.

Email's fundamental differences from face to face communication might be expected to modify some of these factors. Email messages are neither "spoken" nor "written" in the traditional sense (Herring 1996). Therefore, it can be seen as an entirely new form of communication. It reduces the awareness of personal and social standards and the awareness of the social context of communication (Matheson 1992). Visual cues like clothing or auditory cues like accent do not play any role. It is not possible to interrupt anybody. Therefore, some researchers conclude that email breaks down socio-economic, racial or other traditional barriers (Herring et al 1992). For example, Kiesler and collaborators (Sproull & Kiesler 1991) found that while participation rates in face to face communication are determined by group status, this is far less significant in computer conferencing and email. However, despite this democratic potential, many traditional barriers are apparently not broken down.

There is empirical evidence (Hesse, Garsoffky & Hron 1995) which indicates that the mutual commitment in email is less strong than in face-to-face communication. There are no rules governing email which force anybody to answer an email message. This regulation makes email very flexible but rather noncommittal as well. This lack of obligation for communicative reciprocation might have a negative influence on women participating in email conversations: it might be argued that women behave more co-operatively (because of their socialisation) and therefore feel uneasy in the absence of such obligation.

Another difference between face-to-face communication and email is the disorderly character of the latter. In email conversation, there is no well-understood turn-taking process. It is always everybody's turn. This makes it sometimes difficult to keep track of an argument. Quoting the other's messages is a possibie way to overcome this problem. It might also be argued that this affects women differently. In face-to-face communication men often take their turn by force by interrupting women (Trömel-Plötz 1984). In email force is not necessary any more. It is always the men's turn. This might distort the ratio between participation of women and men in communication even more than in face-to-face communication.

This agrees with empirical results reported by Susan Herring (1994, 1996). She posits that women and men use different styles when posting to the Internet although these styles are not exclusively used by women or men:

"By characteristic styles, I do not mean that all or even the majority of users of each sex exhibit the behaviors of each style, but rather that the styles are recognizably -- even stereotypically -- gendered. The male style is characterized by adversariality: put-downs, strong, often contentious assertions, lengthy and/or frequent postings, self-promotion, and sarcasm.... The female-gendered style , in contrast, has two aspects which typically co-occur: supportiveness and attenuation." (Herring 1994)

We found this definition of styles very useful for our study.

On the other hand, there is evidence that women feel comfortable in Cyberspace. Gladys We (1993) conducted a study to find out how people feel when they communicate online. Her respondents mostly think that women are allowed to behave more actively and that gender considerations do not play such an important role as in face-to-face communication. These results to a certain extent contradict the assumption that women are frightened away from the Internet because of aggressive interaction forms.

The empirical study described in the following sections tries to clarify some of these questions through an experiment in co-operative task solving.

3 The Experiment

We decided to investigate the use of email in mediating co-operative problem solving between pairs of subjects, where each subject has their own task but needs help from the other to carry it out. Here, each pair consisted of one subject in Vienna and one in Edinburgh, and each was asked to describe an afternoon visit to the other's city, visiting four places of interest. Note that our concern was not with the outcomes of the tasks but rather with the strategies employed in carrying them out. None of the Edinburgh subjects had been to Vienna. Only one of the Vienna subjects had been to Edinburgh, but some years ago and only briefly. While each subject was given a map and guidebook for the other's city, they were expected to treat each other as task domain experts. Thus each subject needed to find some balance between satisfying their own task, helping their pair and getting assistance from their partner.

The experiment was conducted twice during afternoon sessions lasting around 3 hours where the subjects were seated continuously at keyboards, focused on the tasks. In each session, four Edinburgh subjects were paired with four Vienna subjects to give balanced gender and cultural pairs i.e. Edinburgh woman/Vienna woman, Edinburgh woman/Vienna man, Edinburgh man/Vienna woman, Edinburgh man/Vienna man. The subjects were told that their opposite had to solve a similar task and that they were expected to help each other. They were given no personal information whatsoever about each other. With the subjects' permissions, all email exchanges during the sessions were recorded for subsequent analysis.

The subjects were final year undergraduate and/or MSc students from Heriot Watt University and the Vienna University of Technology, all of similar age and computer use experience. The sessions were conducted in English: all the Vienna subjects were happy to use English and thought their English competency was adequate. After the sessions, none of the subjects indicated that language had been a source of communication problems.

4 Analysis

4.1 Quantitative Analysis

We wished to analyse each entire email exchange to see how much effort each subject put into their own and their partner's task: it is here that we might expect to find gender stereotyped behaviour reproduced from face to face co-operation. In face to face communication, topics brought up by men are usually given more prominence than those introduced by women (Trömel-Plötz 1984). Thus, for quantitative purposes, within a message we distinguish between task, meta and personal utterances.

A task utterance may either be to do with the sender's task (e.g. How do I get from the station to the castle? I want to visit the cathedral.) or the recipient's task (e.g. You need to get a bus from the station. The cathedral is closed from 2.). A meta utterance is about how the tasks are being approached rather than task content. These are predominantly opening and closing greetings (e.g. Dear Megan... Ciao Gerda), discussion about email frequencies and response times (e.g. I haven't heard from you for a while and I've sent you 7 messages so far.), to do with making an explicit focus on one or other person's task (e.g. Time's getting on so I'd like to concentrate on my visit.) and, rarely, about how to organise the whole exchange (e.g. We could take it in turns to ask each other questions.). Personal utterances are usually about the subjects themselves and again may either be about the sender or the recipient (e.g. Are you from Edinburgh? I don't like going to pubs much.). Note that these are not hard and fast distinctions; for example, personal utterances may also serve to fuel task discussion (e.g. Please suggest another location as I don't like museums.). There is empirical evidence that women talk about personal relationships to a greater extent and men are more task oriented in face to face communication (Aries 1984). We might, therefore, expect that women's scores for personal utterances and mens' for meta utterances would be higher.

Based on these categories, entire email exchanges were coded sentence by sentence to record the type of each utterance and the number of words it contained. For each subject, gender group and culture group we divide the number of words spent on the own task with that spent on the other's task to give a measure of co-operative effort. We call this the "own/other" ratio. A value less than one suggests "altruism". A value greater than 1 suggests "selfishness". These are not intended as hard definitions: rather as a shorthand terminology. A value near one suggests a balance of focus on the own and the other's task. Note that this measure compensates for differences in the overall number of words used by each subject by focusing on the balance of word purpose within that use. With only 16 subjects we cannot expect to find representative results. Nonetheless, these summaries are useful in clarifying the very different strategies employed by the subjects and in looking for gross differences between subjects by gender, culture and gender/culture combination.

4.2 Qualitative Analysis

In addition to quantitative analysis we also used qualitative methods to analyse the interaction processes between the students from Edinburgh and Vienna. Conversation analysis, which studies the order and organisation of everyday interactions (Psathas 1995), has often been used to assess gender differences in verbal behaviour. In this context, question/answer sequences play a major role. It was mentioned above that email tends to weaken the coherence of successive utterances. In our study, we analysed this phenomenon and its possible consequences for women and men. One of these consequences is a lack of feedback which could affect women and men differently.

In addition, we analysed typical individual conversations. As Herring mentions (Herring 1994), a gender specific style frequently cannot be observed in a "pure" form. Nevertheless, we assume that in some cases a gender specific style is more pronounced than in others.

5 Results

5.1 "Altruism", "Selfishness" and Co-operation Strategy

The gross categories show no marked gender or cultural effect in the ratio of words on one's own and the other's tasks:

female	0.6	male	0.7
Edin.	0.6	Vienna	0.6
Edin. female	0.4	Vienna female	0.7
Edin. male	0.8	Vienna male	0.5

All categories display some "altruism". Overall, women display slightly more "altruism" than men, showing a very weak correspondence to the gender stereotype. There are some mixed gender/cultural effects in the ratio of words on one's own and the other's tasks so Edinburgh females and Vienna males are both more "altruistic" than Edinburgh males and Vienna females. Again, this could be an artefact of the small sample size.

However, for individuals, the own/other ratios taken in pair groups correspond to a variety of co-operative strategies. In the following summaries, each person's name (changed to protect the innocent...) is followed by city and sex codes (E = Edinburgh, V = Vienna, F = female, M = male), and their own/other task word count ratio.

Pair 1: Craig (EM) 0.8 Herbert (VM) 0.3

Here, Craig sent Herbert an almost complete suggestion for the latter's task in an early message. The rest of the exchange tended to focus on Craig's task, displaying overall co-operation despite the apparent emphasis on Herbert helping Craig. Note that due to a bizarre misunderstanding, Craig sent some email to Paul (see below) whom he called "Susanna". Paul both answered Craig and sent Craig's email on to Herbert. This is an interesting example of the apparent unconscious dissolution of gender and individual identities in Internet group working. This exchange was subject to email delays but not apparently affected by them.

Pair 2: Victoria (EF) 1.7 Edith (VF) 7.2

This exchange was also affected by email delays, resulting in poor feedback and only one true co-operative exchange. Furthermore, in an unresolved early misunderstanding, Victoria proposed that they take turns and Edith that they concentrate on one task and then the other. The result was no overall co-operation.

Pair 3: Michael (EM) 0.5 Gerda (VF) 0.4

This exchange displays balanced overall "altruism" with a weak tendency to more female than male "altruism". The exchange was well structured and systematic. They were polite and took turns as if in a face to face task. Gerda drove the exchange which still showed equal positive co-operation. Gerda pretended that she was actually in Edinburgh.

Pair 4: Graeme 0.9 (EM) Paul 0.9 (VM)

This typically "macho" exchange never the less demonstrated a high degree of balanced co-operation. They adopted similar approaches, displaying supportive criticism. Paul used a high proportion of questions and an advanced "smiley" vocabulary. This exchange had the highest proportion of personal messages. Graeme attempted to introduce an explicit split screen protocol, to divide each exchange into a focus on his own and the other's tasks, but Paul explicitly declined this. Graeme surreptitiously introduced this split which Paul then followed due to whole message quoting. Initially, Paul mistakenly addressed Graeme with the female marked version of the name about which Graeme never complained.

Pair 5: Morna (EF) 2.2 Chris (VM) 2.0

This was the most "selfish" mixed sex exchange with Morna displaying slightly more focus on her own task. There was no co-operation and no personal identification with the task. Thus, Morna refers to her task as if she is doing it for a third party, and

Chris to his as if he is doing it for Morna. This exchange was also subject to poor email response with no noticeable effect.

Pair 6: Muriel (EF) 0.2 Phillip (VM) 0.4

This is the most "altruistic" exchange with Muriel displaying higher "altruism" than Phillip. There was much personal exchange, displaying some mild flirtation. Phillip dominated the exchange, asking many questions and deploying "smiley"s. Muriel generally accepted Phillip's suggestions.

Pair 7: Megan (EF) 0.4 Cecilia (VF) 0.5

This exchange was again marred by email failures but none the less shows overall "altruism", with Megan slightly more "altruistic" than Cecilia. Cecilia dominated the exchange, making many suggestions for Megan, which is more typical of a stereotyped male strategy. Megan attempts to split the screen twice (see above) which Cecilia ignores. Overall, this was a moderately co-operative exchange.

Pair 8: Charles 1.5 (EM) Susanna 0.6 (VF)

This was the most stereotypical exchange in that Charles gave Susanna no help and received much help from her. Susanna dominates the exchange but still does much of Charles' task for him. Some co-operation was displayed. Susanna assumes explicitly that Charles always receives her email. The pair did not appear to like each other.

Five distinct forms of co-operation are present with stereotypical "male" and "female" behaviour displayed by both men and women. In pairs 1,3 6 and 7, both subjects have a balanced "altruistic" approach. Pair 1 is male/male and pair 7 is female/female. However, in the female/male pairs 3 and 6, the women are slightly more "altruistic" than the men. The female/female pair 2 shows unbalanced "selfishness". In the female/male pair 5 there is a balance of "selfishness" but with the woman slightly more "selfish", once again a normally male stereotyped behaviour. In the male/male pair 4 there is a balance of "altruism" and "selfishness", effected by a traditional male mix of competition driven co-operation. Only in the male/female pair 8 is there the usual face to face stereotype of the man receiving help from the woman without reciprocation.

Overall, in 3 out of 4 mixed pairs, women could be interpreted as slightly more "altruistic" than men, which appears to confirm the gender stereotype.

5.2 Gender and Message sizes

In total, 158 messages were sent with a total of 11,139 words or an average of 70.5 words to a message. Thus, each exchange consisted of an average of around 20 messages.

Overall, men sent more messages than women (87 to 71) but this result is not significant ($t = 0.97 < t\ (0.05; 14)$). There is a significant difference in the number of words which were sent by either women or men ($t = 2.3 > t\ (0.05; 14)$). All in all, women sent 5073 words and men 6066. Men's messages are not visibly shorter (average 69.7 and 71.5 words). There is no consistent pattern in the mixed pairs: in pair 3, Michael sends more and longer messages (8, 62.5) than Gerda (7, 52.0); in pair 5, Morna sends less but longer messages (4, 71.0) than Christian (5, 36.8); in pair 6, Muriel sends less but longer messages (10, 122.3) than Paul (12, 116.0); in pair 8, Charles sends less but longer messages (12, 48.7) than Susanna (14,38.4).

Similarly, there is no pattern in the same sex pairs: in pair 1, Craig sends the same number of messages as but slightly shorter messages (9, 90.7) than Herbert (9,101.1); in pair 2 Edith sends more longer messages (7, 80.1) than Victoria (5, 31.8); in pair 4, Paul sends more longer messages (18, 58.3) than Graeme (14,43.3); in pair 7, Megan (8, 93.1) sends less longer messages than Cecilia (16, 74.9).

5.3 Gender Stereotyping in Communication Styles

A minority of the men show typical macho behaviour (see Paul/Graeme) manifested as a collection of symptoms: pornographic allusions; remarks about girls; long and frequent messages; remarks which show a strong competitive orientation; ironic and abusive remarks. This behaviour is probably produced as a joint effort: thus two men may be necessary for such an interaction and they reinforce each other.

There were a few cases of "typical" gendered conversations. The conversation between Graeme and Paul (described above) shows a typical male style. The conversation between Edith and Victoria, on the other hand, can be described in terms of a female style. They exchange only few and short messages. In contrast to Graeme and Paul, their interaction is severely affected by the timelags, and lack of feedback disturbed at least one of the women deeply. The interaction between Muriel and Phillip shows some of the typical features of mixed conversations. Phillip was friendly and at the same time so overwhelming that he dominated the conversation with his topic. Muriel was very helpful towards Phillip and, as a consequence, had difficulties getting her task done. The other conversations had similar elements but not to the same extent. This supports the view that female or male style are prototypes rather than clear-cut categories. There are a few typical prototypes, and all the other cases only show a few typical features.

5.4 Identity and Personal Communication

No explicit gender issues were raised by the subjects. In particular, Graeme did not complain when repeatedly addressed as a woman though some of the subsequent banter with Paul may have been to reinforce heterosexual male identities. While there was some interaction between people who were not supposed to interact, due to email address confusion, nobody complained. It is perhaps significant that all these phenomena only happened in the male/male pairs. When a confusion about a name occurred in a mixed group the misunderstanding was immediately solved.

Overall, only 3.8% of words in all message content was concerned with explicit personal matters. Men talked more about themselves (3.5%) than women (1.6%). Men and women talked roughly equally (1.3% & 1.2%) about the other. The Viennese talked more about themselves (3.0%) and their pair (1.2%) than the Scots (2.1% & 0.6%).

There are no apparent patterns in either same sex or mixed sex pairs. There is especially no evidence for the hypothesis that women talk more about personal matters.

5.5 Communication Protocols and Metacommunication

Generally the question/answer orientation of face-to-face communication is preserved. Apparently, this orientation is very strong because it is one of the most important rules which makes conversation keep going. Questions were usually answered in all the conversations. The only exception was the conversation between Graeme and Paul which became confused because the high volume of messages resulted in both participants losing track of which they had sent and received. One of the major differences between face-to-face communication and email is that there is no immediate feedback or sometimes no feedback at all. On the emotional level, the lack or delay of feedback can be frustrating. This especially applies to women who tend to reply to the other person's requests and interests to a larger extent than men. Men tend to go on sending messages even if there is no immediate answer whereas the women in our task tended to wait for an answer.

Metacommunication formed a significant proportion (19.8%) of all messages with men having a slightly higher proportion of meta words (20.6%) than women (18.9%), and Viennese more (22.1%) than Scots (17.0%). Not surprisingly, those pairs that experienced email delays had higher proportions of meta words. Most meta utterances took the letter writing form of greeting and parting phrases.

6 Conclusions

These results show no overall discernible differences in female and male email communication styles. Thus, there were no gross differences in average message size, "altruism" and "selfishness", amount of personal communication and meta communication. This agrees with the findings of Evard (1996) who investigated the participation of girls and boys in computer-mediated communication during a project dedicated to the development of educational video games. She found out that many of the gender stereotypes which are related to online communication did not apply. The boys were generally helpful and the girls did not confine themselves to the social sphere but also discussed technical questions. Still, there were a few differences between girls and boys. The girls tended to use a feminine style in phrasing their messages (making suggestions, using apologetic tones) whereas the boys were more direct. Evard argues that a reason for this phenomenon might be that the children had not reached adolescence yet and were therefore more open in their world view. Birkenes and Fjuk (1994) argue that women feel more comfortable in the more private situation of email communication. This might be another reason for the fact that in some investigations gender differences are not very pronounced.

However, the individual exchanges in our study confirm Herring's concept of a continuum of gendered styles with "pure" forms only found in a minority of the corresponding gender. Thus, Graeme and Paul show "typical" male competitive style at one extreme. At the other, Edith's and Victoria's inability to cooperate may be due to excessive deference to each other. All the other exchanges show a mix of correspondence of gendered style with gendered persona. However, where there was a dominant partner in an exchange they tended to adopt a male style.

We now wish to repeat the experiment to acquire more representative results. We also intend to analyse the exchanges for gendered question use, personal communication and meta-communication.

Acknowledgements

This work was co-ordinated entirely by email between August 1994 and September 1996: the only occasions on which the authors have met in person. The experiments were conducted in June 1995, necessitating some recourse to telephonic communication.

We wish to thank all the participants in our experiment. We also wish to thank Nancy Falchikov for helpful comments on this paper.

References

1. E. Aries: Zwischenmenschliches Verhalten in eingeschlechtlichen und gemischtgeschlechtlichen Gruppen. In: S. Trömel-Plötz (ed.): Gewalt durch Sprache. Die Vergewaltigung von Frauen in Gesprächen, Frankfurt am Main: Fischer 1984, 114-126
2. T. Birkenes, A. Fjuk: The Troublesome Issue of Co-operation Seen from a Women's Perspective. In: A. Adam, J. Emms, E.Green, J. Owen (eds.): Women, Work and Computerization. Breaking NewBoundaries - Building New Forms. Amsterdam, Lausanne, New York: Elsevier 1994, 75-89
3. M. Evard: "So Please Stop, Thank You": Girls Online. In: L.Cherny, E.R. Weise (eds.): wired_women. Gender and New Realities in Cyberspace. Seattle: Seal Press 1996, 188-204
4. S. Herring, D. Johnson, T. DiBenedetto: Participation in Electronic Discourse in a Feminist Field. In: K. Hall, M. Buchholz, B. Moonwoman (eds.): Proceedings of the Second Berkeley Women and Language Conference. University of California, Berkeley 1992
5. S. Herring: Gender Differences in Computer-Mediated Communication: Bringing Familiar Baggage to the New Frontier. Keynote talk at panel entitled "Making the Net *Work*: Is there a Z39.50 in gender communication?", American Library Association annual convention, Miami, June 27, 1994, unpublished manuscript
6. S. Herring (ed.): Computer-Mediated Communication. Linguistic, social, and cross-cultural perspectives. Amsterdam: John Benjamins 1996
7. F.W. Hesse, B. Garsoffky, A. Hron: Interface-Design für computerunterstütztes kooperatives Lernen. In: L.J. Issing, P. Klimsa (eds.): Information und Lernen mit Multimedia. Weinheim: Psychologie Verlags Union 1995, 253-267
8. N. Kaplan, E. Farrell: Weavers of the Web: A Portrait of Young Women on the Net. In: The Arachnet Electronic Journal on Virtual Culture, July 26, 1994, Vol.2 Issue 3

9. K.Matheson: Women and Computer Technology. Communicating for herself. In: M. Lea (ed.): Contexts of Computer-Mediated Communication. New York, London, Toronto: Harverster and Wheatsheaf 1992, 66-88
10. S. Plant: On the Matrix: Cyberfeminist Simulations. In: R.Shields (ed): Cultures of Internet. Sage 1996, 170-183
11. G. Psathas: Conversation Analysis. The Study of Talk-in-Interaction.Thousand Oaks, London, New Delhi: Sage 1995
12. L. R. Shade: Gender Issues in Computer Networking. In: A. Adam, J. Emms, E.Green, J. Owen (eds.): Women, Work and Computerization. Breaking NewBoundaries - Building New Forms. Amsterdam, Lausanne, New York: Elsevier 1994, 91-105
13. D. Spender: Nattering on the Net. Women, Power and Cyberspace. North Melbourne: Spinifex 1995
14. L. Sproull, S. Kiesler: Connections, MIT Press, 1991
15. L.A. Sutton: Cocktails and Thumbtacks in the Old West: What Would Emiliy Post Say. In: L.Cherny, E.R. Weise (eds.): wired_women. Gender and New Realities in Cyberspace. Seattle: Seal Press 1996, 169-187
16. D. Tannen: You just don't understand. Virago, 1991
17. S. Trömel-Plötz (ed.): Gewalt durch Sprache. Die Vergewaltigung von Frauen in Gespr (chen Frankfurt am Main: Fischer 1984
18. S. Turkle: Style as Substance in Educational Computing. In: J. Berleur, A.Clement, R. Sizer, D. Whitehouse (eds.): The Information Society: Evolving Landscapes. Berlin, Heidelberg, New York: Springer 1990, 145-160
19. S. Turkle: Life on the Screen. Identity in the Age of the Internet. New York, London, Toronto: Simon and Schuster 1995
20. G. We: Cross-Gender Communication in Cyberspace. A graduate research paper done in the Department of Communication, Simon Fraser University, 1993

Sex, Age and the Desirability of Computers

David Foreman[1], Frances Grundy[2], Sue Lees[2]

[1] Dept. of Psychiatry, Keele University, Keele, Staffordshire, ST5 5BG, UK
[2] Dept. of Computer Science, Keele University, Keele, Staffordshire, ST5 5BG, UK

Abstract. Rather than focus on computing as an academic subject, in this paper we take a step 'back' and ask how women value the computers themselves, for example a PC and the software that goes with it. We report on a survey of undergraduates in which they were asked how they would spend £1500.
This survey shows that men of all ages ranked computers higher than women. However, there is an interesting change in attitude amongst women of 21 and older who showed a higher preference for computers than younger women.

1 Women Don't Like Computers?

There is plenty of evidence that by the time they reach the age of 18 girls have already opted out of computing. 'A' level[3] figures show that in 1992 women represented only 17.3% of those attempting this examination at school [8] and in UK universities in 1992 women represented only 12.2% of those studying computer science [12].

Girls, by and large, don't play computer games and when they do play them there is evidence that by the time they reach 12 to 14, they have much less confidence than the boys in handling these entertainments [5]. But we don't know whether this is because they don't like the games, which are mainly violent, or because of the context in which they are played, with boys dominating the physical environment, or if it is the machines themselves which influence their behaviour. While the first two factors have been studied, the third, that women may not like the machines themselves, seems to have received scant attention in connection with gender. One author who does raise this possibility is Róisín Ní Mháille Battel [1]. And it is the last factor – the computers themselves – on which we concentrate in the study reported here.

There is one survey which gives a glimpse of attitudes to computers. This was conducted by the computer magazine *PC Home* of its, overwhelmingly male (98%), readership. It shows that 61.6% of respondents (87% of whom were men) would opt for spending money on more computer equipment. 14% would spend money on home improvements, 13.2% would buy presents for their children,

[3] Schoolchildren in England, Wales and Northern Ireland normally start 'A' or Advanced level studies at 16 and take the examination at 18. Normally, three 'A' levels are needed to qualify for university entrance.

11.6% would spend it on a romantic week-end and just 2% would spend it on a present for their 'girlfriend or wife' [*sic*]. This survey, while certainly large - the first 1000 responses were used - is no use for our present purposes because of the very few women respondents.[4]

So rather than focus on computing as an academic subject and why women choose not to study it or why they don't get heavily involved in computer games, in this paper we take a step 'back' and ask how women value the computers themselves - a PC, for example, and the software that goes with it? And does their view differ from that of men? The initial hypothesis for our study was in fact that men like computers more than women do.

2 Method

2.1 Our Sample Population

To test our hypothesis we asked questions of a set of undergraduates at Keele University. As well as taking two major, or as they are known at Keele *principal*, subjects for an honours degree, students are required to take one year subsidiary courses and one of the subjects offered at subsidiary level is computing. Subsidiary subjects can be taken either beforestudents start their degree proper (that is in a special introductory year, known as the Foundation Year or FY) or in either the first or second year of their degree course.

These students had opted for a course on computing, but one with an emphasis on computer applications or using computers to assist in other subjects rather than studying computing *per se*, that is how the software is designed and so on. There were no computing prerequisites for this course and all computing equipment was provided.

In the first semester students have to choose between computer programming and IT, and one out of five further options in the second semester. They were taught to use electronic mail and were expected to read their mail regularly for announcements about the course. All 501 students enrolled on the subsidiary course for 1995/96 were approached to answer a questionnaire, in the first instance by email three weeks into the second semester in February 1996. The majority of replies to this first mailing were received within 12 days. A second approach was made at the beginning of March to those who had not responded asking them to complete a paper version.

2.2 Measures

The questionnaire assessed the students' estimation of a computer's value in their lives. Eight other items, all of approximately the same financial value as a computer, were identified between the three authors as being of equivalent potential attractiveness to at least some students. Items were chosen such that

[4] The results of this survey conducted by Cape Cowley Associates were received in a private communication to one of the authors in March 1996

some would be attractive to women, some to men and some to both sexes. The students were asked to imagine they had been given £1500 (approximately $2250) and then order the items according to their wish to buy it. Thus, the students ranked each item on a 9-point ordinal scale against all the others. 1 represented the most preferred item and 9 the least preferred item. This was a 'forced choice procedure' which means that they were not allowed to give items equal ranking; in other words, it was ranking without ties. The full questionnaire, together with the instructions given to the students, is given in the Appendix.

We were able to collect data on the students' age, sex and principal subjects. We were also able to obtain the year of entry to the University for the subset of students who replied by email.

3 Analysis

3.1 Re-coding of Data

The principal subjects offered at Keele at undergraduate level were grouped into three types according to the descriptions of the courses given in the 1995/96 undergraduate prospectus. These categories are sciences, arts and social sciences. This allowed the students' areas of study for joint honours to be collapsed into six categories: two arts subjects, two social sciences, two sciences, an arts and a social science subject, a social science and a science, and an arts and a science. This variable was called Study Category.

3.2 Methods Used for Analysis

Apart from chi-square tests which were used to ascertain whether categorical variables (like Sex and Study Category) are independent of one another, Kruskal-Wallis analysis of variance [9, Chap 6] (ANOVA) was used. This is an analysis of variance operating on ranked data and, as usual for analysis of variance, tests if the samples come from the same or different distributions. So, for example, it was used to test if the women ranked computers significantly differently from the men irrespective of other variables.

A non-parametric regression technique known as logistic regression [11, Chap 12] was employed. This method allows the use of an ordinal variable for the predicted, or dependent, variable. For this study it is the ranking of a computer which was used for the dependent variable. Variables other than the rankings, namely Age, Sex, Study Category and Year of Entry were potentially independent, or predictor, variables used for regression.

A graphical technique known as correspondence analysis which displays many dimensional data in 2 dimensions was used to illustrate relationships between variables ([4, pp 239–42] and [3, pp 579–94]).

4 Results

4.1 General Characteristics of Sample

The gender breakdown for the population sampled was 301 females and 200 males. Of these 134 responded to the initial electronic 'mail shot', 3 of which were discarded because the respondents indicated no preferences. And 66 responded to the subsequent paper mailing. This gave a total of 197 responses. Of these 197 respondents, 121 were female and 76 were male.

While the age range was from 18-59 years, 78% of the sample was of 20 years or less. Therefore all students of 21 or over were collapsed into a single group and age was analysed as a set of ordered categories (table 1).

Table 1. Age Distribution

Age	Count	Probability	Cum Prob
18	46	0.24468	0.24468
19	76	0.40426	0.64894
20	25	0.13298	0.78191
21+	41	0.21809	1.00000
Total	188	9 Missing	

*Checking for Possible Influence of Missing Checks were made for the possible influence of missing data. Where there is more than 5% of data missing for any variable it is conventional to check to see if this missing data has any relationship with other variables used in the analysis. The distribution for Study Category is shown in table 2. There were 39 items missing for this variable out of the 197; this represents 19.8%. And for Year of Entry to University the proportion of missing data was 33.5%. However, the missing data for both these variables did not relate to computer ranking. Nor did it relate to age[5] or sex[6]. Therefore, in spite of their missing data, both Study Category and Year of Entry could be included in the analysis where appropriate.

4.2 What Are the Significant Predictor Variables for Computer Ranking?

It is the ranking of computer that we are primarily interested in predicting. And figure 1 shows the distribution of computer ranking for the whole data set, ie men and women taken together. The median ranking for this variable was 4 with

[5] A Kruskal-Wallis ANOVA gave a statistic $H < 1.19$ with 1 degree of freedom (DF) which was not significant (NS)

[6] Chi-square < 0.21, DF $= 1$, NS

Table 2. Distribution Amongst Study Categories

Study Category	Count	Probability	Cum Prob
Arts	74	0.46835	0.46835
Arts/Science	6	0.03797	0.50633
Arts/Social Science	41	0.25949	0.76582
Science	4	0.02532	0.79114
Social Science	19	0.12025	0.91139
Social Science/Science	14	0.08861	1.00000
Total	158	39 Missing	

the higher quartile at 2 and the lower quartile at 5 (a score of 1 indicates the highest preference).

This figure illustrates how the rankings for this variable are distributed and shows the variation which we shall try to explain statistically.

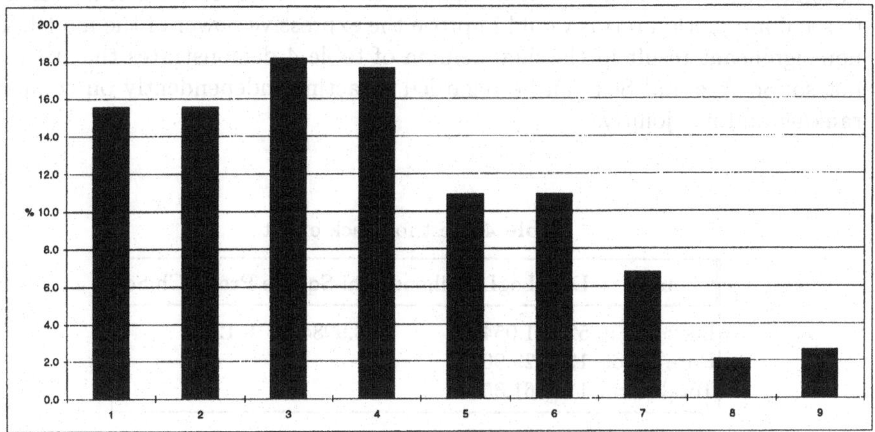

Fig. 1. Distribution of Computer Rankings – All Data

Each of the independent variables – Age, Sex, Year of Entry and Study Category – was tested separately (using Kruskal-Wallis ANOVA) against computer ranking. Only two were significantly associated with this variable, namely Age and Sex. These two were therefore used as the independent variables in an ordinal regression using them together to predict computer ranking. After missing data was excluded 'casewise', 184 cases remained for analysis. The results are shown in table 3 in what we call the 'whole model equation'. The low Rsquare in this table shows that, taken together, these two variables explain only a small proportion of the probability of choosing a particular rank for a computer.

Adding each of the other individually non-significant independent variables,

Study Category and Year of Entry, in turn produced no change in Rsquare and so did not improve the model's explanatory power. These latter variables were therefore discarded.

Table 3. Whole Model Equation

Model	-LogLikelihood	DF	Chi-Square	Prob>ChiSq
Difference	10.94885	4	21.89769	0.0002
Full	361. 85904			
Reduced	372.80788			
Rsquare	0.0294			
Observations	184			

What about the interaction effect of Age and Sex? Do they operate together in some way over and above their separate effects? A test for lack of fit was used to see if interaction terms would improve the expressive power of the model. The non-significant result in the final column of table 4 demonstrates that this was not so. So Age and Sex can be regarded as acting independently on computer ranking and not jointly.

Table 4. Test for Lack of Fit

Source	DF	-LogLikelihood	Chi-Square	Prob>ChiSq
Lack of Fit	52	31.95422	63.90845	0.1244
Pure Error	120	329.90481		
Total Error	172	361.85904		

Table 5 shows how both Age and Sex were individually significant in the 'whole model equation'. The low probabilities in the final column, which are both less than 0.05, indicate the individual significance of these variables. These regression coefficients are shown in table 6.

Table 5. Separate Effects

Source	No parameters	DF	Wald Chi-Square	Prob>ChiSq
Agecat	3	3	8.35888	0.0391
Sex	1	1	9.50398	0.0021

Table 6. Parameter Estimates

Term	Estimate	Std Error	Chi-Square	Prob>ChiSq
Agecat[19]	0.29072	0.33110	0.77	0.3799
Agecat[20]	-0.12560	0.40594	0.10	0.7570
Agecat[21]	0.92426	0.45613	4.11	0.0427
Sex[F-M]	-0.42837	0.13895	9.50	0.0021

These show that while students aged 19 and 20 are n ot significantly different from those aged 18, those of 21 and over are significantly different from 18 year-olds (Prob = 0.0427). Also male students are significantly more likely to give a computer a high ranking than women (Prob = 0.0021).

These relationships are further illustrated by the correspondence analysis shown in figure 2. A contingency table with all combinations of Age and Sex (8 categories) called 'agesexcat' as one dimension and computer ranking (9 categories) as the other is the basis for this analysis. Each category in this contingency table is shown as one data point: a double X for agesexcat and a double □ for computer ranking. Correspondence analysis works with probabilities derived from the raw data in such a way that we can use the same pair of axes, or 2 dimensions, to show different categorical variables for the same individuals. But it is probabilities, derived from the contingency table, we are using - not the raw data. So, for example, 'M18' represents the cell containing the 18 year old males. And the double square marked '1' is the highest rank for computers.

In this figure we have, first, a cluster consisting of male students and the oldest female students in the lower half of the scattergram; this is associated with high computer rankings. Secondly, it shows another cluster of younger females associated with lower rankings. Finally a smaller age effect is also apparent within the male students; the oldest and the youngest are shown close to high rankings.

5 Some Observations on the Statistical Model

There are two points to discuss here. The first point concerns one possible implication of the forced choice procedure allowing no ties. There is the possibility that the gender bias of other items in the list contributed to the gender bias we have seen towards computers. We have already noted that the overall median for computer ranking was 4. Figure 3 shows the distribution of computer ranking for females and for males. The median for females was 4 with an upper quartile of 2 and a lower quartile of 6. The median for males was 3 with an upper quartile of 1 and a lower quartile of 4. For both sexes it is clear that computers were ranked moderately and not extremely, therefore there was both an upward and a downward bias operating for both genders. This suggests that bias from the other items has been minimised within the research design.

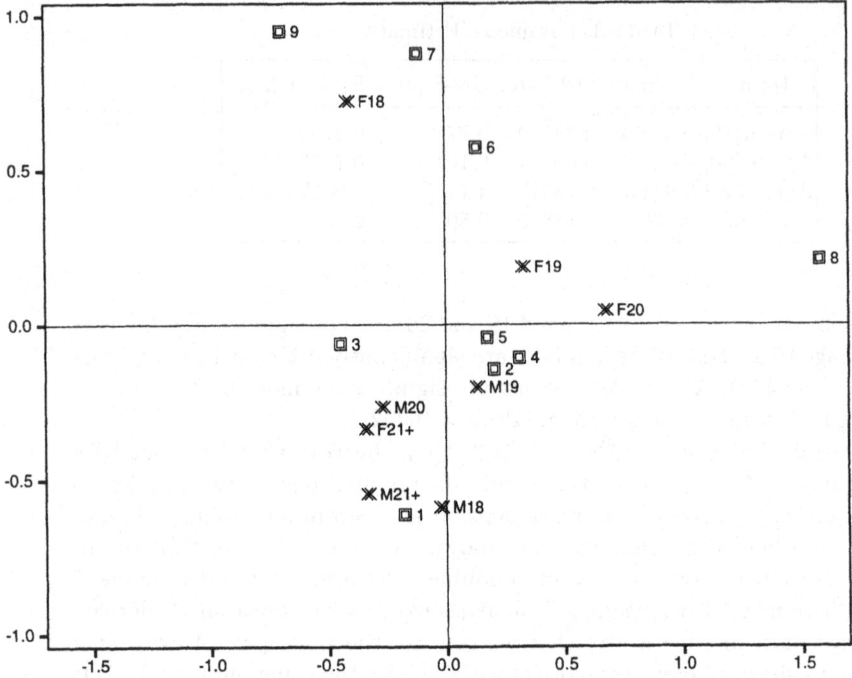

Fig. 2. Correspondence Analysis

The second point for discussion here is the low Rsquare in the regression, or the low explanatory power of the 'whole model equation'. The computer rankings are dependent on the rankings of the other items in the questionnaire; if respondents rank computer as 1 nothing else can be ranked as 1. The apparently poor explanatory power of the model, suggested by the low Rsquare in the 'whole model equation', is probably due to this feature of the questionnaire. This view is supported by the non-significant interaction effect of age and sex and the failure to obtain any improvement in explanatory power by the addition of the other independent variables. Taken together, these factors suggest that the model is explaining that small portion of the variability in computer ranking that does not result from the structure of the questionnaire. The small size of this portion means we are at risk of making a Type II error (of assuming something isn't there when it is) rather than a Type I error (assuming something is there when it isn't). In other words, since the amount of variability to be explained is so small, the model will give us a conservative error. It cannot therefore be said that it is lack of power in the model that explains these results; the explanation is due to the variability in sex and age that we have discussed earlier.

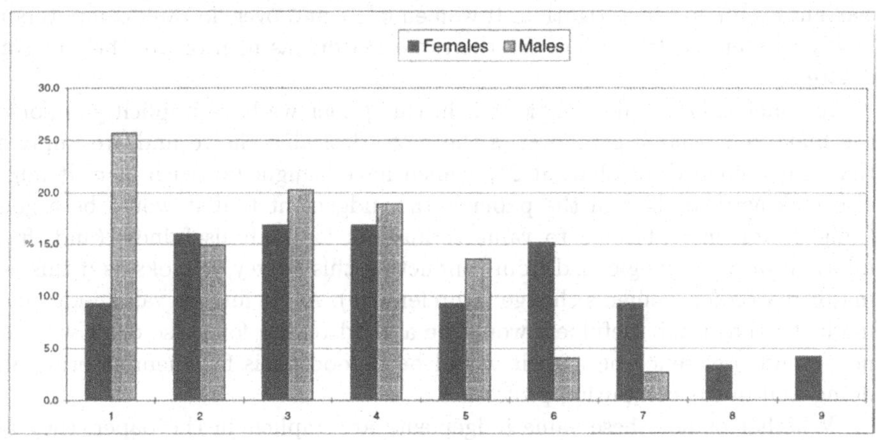

Fig. 3. Distribution of Computer Rankings – Females & Males

6 What Do These Results Point to?

For girls, socialisation against computers starts well before eighteen. Straker [10] reports that twice as many boys as girls have access to a computer at home and Matthew Maurer [6] lists a number of studies which also found this. Lorraine Culley reported in 1986 that whereas 56% of boys said there was a computer at home this was true of only 22% of girls. She also reports how girls get 'pushed off the computers ... the boys think they own them ... The boys said they should use them before us' [2]. She further reports how girls-only computer clubs in mixed schools proved difficult to sustain. Teachers do not do all that could be done to counteract this phenomenon of boys dominating the use of computers. Sanders [7] reports how teachers are likely to make more eye contact with boys than girls when referring to technology in general and computers in particular. Computer games are designed with boys' interests in mind; there are very few games which satisfy the traditional interests of girls.

The fact that we have shown that men show a higher preference for computers than do eighteen year old women reinforces this idea that, before they reach eighteen, girls have little affinity for them. Women of 21 and over show an interest similar to men of all ages.

One possible explanation for this change in attitude is that, as they become older, girls' social confidence improves. With this comes a growing realisation that the boys have been, albeit unconsciously but certainly with society's tacit approval, using the machines as part of the process of forming friendships and bonds with their male peers. This process places the girls outside the male sphere within which machines, including computers, are retained. To start with, girls respect the conventional view that 'Girls can't do it', but once they start to 'do it' they realize they can.

Further detailed examination of why this change takes place is one area warranting further investigation. If women of 21 and over do rank computers as highly as men, do they do so for the same reasons as men or are their reasons different?

In conclusion, it might look as if in this paper we have implicitly endorsed the male view that a computer is the most desirable choice and are implying that it is a good thing that, at 21, women have 'caught up' with men. It might also look as if implicit in the paper is the judgement that it would be a good thing if women had come to value computers for their usefulness (and, from information we have gleaned from conducting this survey, it looks as if this is a major reason for women's change in preference). A yet further value judgement might be that their usefulness would be a good reason for these older women's new-found preference because it would be a good basis for them entering and doing well in the computing profession.

Whether or not these value judgements are implicit in the paper, they are ones which we should want to make at some point. However, we are not saying women should catch up and join computing in as large numbers as men regardless of the costs, any more than we would want to say that third world countries should catch up economically with first world countries regardless of the social and moral costs. In other words women must be careful not to compromise themselves and should take care not to pay too high a price for catching up.

Appendix: Questionnaire

We are interested in students' attitudes to different aspects of their lifestyles, and completing this questionnaire will help us clarify the kind of questions we will need to ask as we develop our research.

To help our analysis please indicate your principal study subjects (intended if you are an FY student) here
( )
and age here ( )
and male or female (M or F) here ( )

Imagine you have just been given £1500 to spend on one of the items listed below. Please rank the items according to your desire to buy them. For example, if you consider you would most like to buy a horse to ride, and then a computer system, put a (1) next to 'a horse to ride', and a (2) next to 'a new computer system.' Please rank ALL the items listed. When you have completed your questionnaire, it should look something like

A second hand car (1)
A musical instrument (5)
A set of new clothes (3)
etc.

ITEMS TO CHOOSE:
A. A second hand car ( )

B. A musical instrument ( )
C. A set of new clothes ( )
D. A holiday abroad ( )
E. A new computer system ( )
F. New hi-fi equipment ( )
G. Sports equipment ( )
H. A weekend at a health farm ( )
I. A horse to ride ( )

You can assume that the running costs for the horse and the second hand car are taken care of.

Please fill in the questionnaire by replying to this message (using r, including the message and editing it with your answers). Thank you for taking part in our study.

If you do not wish to take part, just do not return the questionnaire.

Your answers will not be analysed individually, and we are happy to make the results of our study available to you on request.

Please add any additional comments you might wish to make here.

Please put an x in the brackets here ( ) if you do NOT wish to be mailed again about this research.

References

1. Róisín Ní Mháille Battel. 'Women and Technology: A Place for Hardware'. In Alison Adam and Jenny Owen, editors, *Proceedings of the 5th IFIP International Conference on Women, Work and Computerization 'Breaking Old Boundaries Building New Forms'*, pages 397–404. Conference Papers, 1994.
2. Lorraine Culley. Gender Differences and Computing in Secondary Schools. Technical report, Department of Education, Loughborough University, Leicestershire, UK, 1986.
3. John C. Davis. *Statistics and Data Analysis in Geology.* Wiley, New York, 2nd edition, 1986.
4. George H. Dunteman. 'Principal Components Analysis'. In Micheal S. Lewis-Beck, editor, *Factor Analysis and Related Techniques*, pages 157–245. Sage Publications Toppan Publishing, 1994.
5. Marcia C. Linn. 'Gender Equity in Computer Learning Environments'. *Computers and the Social Sciences*, 1(1):19–27, 1985.
6. Matthew M. Maurer. 'Computer Anxiety Correlates and What They Tell Us: A Literature Review'. *Computers in Human Behavior*, 10(3):369–76, 1994.
7. J. Sanders. 'Computer Equity for Girls: What Keeps It From Happening?'. In *Proceedings of the IFIP, TC3 Fifth World Conference on Computers in Education*, pages 181–5, 1990.
8. SOE. Statistics of Education 1991/92. Schools Examinations GCSE and GCE. Department for Education, 1993.

9. Peter Sprent. *Applied Nonparametric Statistical Methods.* Chapman and Hall, London, 1989.
10. A. Straker. MEP Primary Project Progress Report No.4, 1985.
11. Barbara G. Tabachink and Linda S. Fidell. *Using Multivariate Statistics.* Harper-Collins, New York, 3rd edition, 1996.
12. USR. University Statistics 1992-3; vol 1, Students and Staff, 1993.

This article was processed using the LaTeX macro package with LLNCS style

Accepted Papers and Discussion Notes

Topic 1: Information Society, Multimedia and Networking

Part 2: Exploring the Internet

Access to the Internet for Women's Groups Across Canada

Leslie Regan Shade

Research Affiliate, Information Policy Research Program,
Faculty of Information Studies, University of Toronto, and Constructive Advice, Ottawa
ac900@freenet.carleton.ca

Abstract. This paper summarizes a project sponsored by Status of Woman Canada which investigated access issues to the Internet by women's organizations across Canada.

1 Introduction

In the Winter of 1996 the Women's Program, Status of Women Canada (SWC)[1] requested that a project be conducted which would investigate the use of the Internet in women's organizations across Canada[2]. Specifically, the project's aims and goals were to provide: an overview of equity issues regarding the Interent for women; a brief overview of technical issues and costs associated with connecting to the Internet; an inventory of funding possibilities for the Internet at the provincial and federal level; and, an inventory of current Internet projects in Canada specific to anglophone and francophone women.

The project also specified that a survey regarding access to the Internet by Canadian women's groups be conducted, facilitated by contact with regional SWC coordinators. One of the purposes of the survey was to better ascertain the types of women's groups that were not connected to the Internet, any common funding requests, and the particular needs of francophone women with respect to connecting to the Internet. This paper will briefly examine the issue of access, particularly as it relates to gender; report on the specific results of the survey which identified access barriers for women's groups; and suggest future directions that women's groups

[1] Status of Women Canada is a federal agency which ensures that the federal government carries out its commitment to women's equality in all spheres of Canadian life. Status of Women Canada, Women's Program, 360 Albert St., 7th Fl., Ottawa, ON,Canada, K1A 1C3. URL: *http://www.swc-cfc.gc.ca*. The full report is Report on the Use of the Internet in Canadian Women's Organizations, Leslie Regan Shade, August, 1996.

[2] Women's organizations are varied in both focus and scope. They include: shelters for battered and homeless women; telephone crisis lines; rape crisis centres; education and political advocacy agencies; cultural groups; student associations; research centres; professional and business organizations; health organizations; agencies serving disabled women; legal advocacy organizations; social and arts organizations; housing advocacy groups; self-help organizations; unions; publications and publishing; and childcare organizations.

should pursue as Canada works on a national access strategy for their information infrastructure.

2 Access Issues

Ensuring universal access to basic network services is an urgent issue that public policymakers internationally are currently deliberating[3]. Public policy statements with respect to gender equity for the information infrastructure have emphasized the need for women to become integrally involved as users, creators, and policymakers. For instance, the final Beijing Declaration and Platform for Action from the Fourth World Conference on Women reiterated the need for women, especially in developing countries, to enhance their skills, knowledge and access to information technology[4].

Canada has been one of the few countries to publicly consider the issue of gender equity to the information infrastructure in their public policy deliberations. With the release of Building the Information Society: Moving Canada into the 21st Century, the Information Highway Advisory Council (IHAC) reiterated their commitment to ensuring universal access to all, including an examination of gender as one factor affecting access[5]. Several passages in The Federal Plan for Gender Equality, Setting the Stage for the Next Century, are also concerned specifically with information technology[6].

---

[3] Most governments have formally recognized the need to increase access to the information infrastructure by advocating a deregulatory, competitive and liberalised market. See: Leslie Regan Shade, Universal Access: The Next Killer App, A Discussion Paper for Defining and Maintaining Universal Access to Basic Network Services: Canadian Directions in an International Context. Invitational Workshop Sponsored by Industry Canada and the Faculty of Information Studies, University of Toronto, 14- 16 March, 1996. URL: *http://www.fis.utoronto.ca/research/iprp/ua*

[4] Beijing Declaration and Platform for Action, 1995. URL: *http://women.usia.gov/usia/beijpg.htm*. For another look at the case in developing countries, see IDRC Gender and Information Working Group, Information as a Transformative Tool, pp. 267-293 in Missing Links: Gender Equity in Science and Technology for Development. (Gender Working Group, United Nations Commission on Science and Technology for Development. Ottawa: International Development Research Centre, 1995).

[5] The passage read: Affordable access for all: Measures to ensure that the Information Highway fully reflects Canada's linguistic duality and supports the French language and services in French will be essential. The strategy will also involve steps to ensure that the Information Highway reflects the diversity of Canada's multicultural society. Equally important, the strategy will take into account the need for analysis to identify how gender, age and other social factors create differences in participating in and benefiting from the Information Highway. Canada, Information Highway Advisory Council, Industry Canada, Building the Information Society: Moving Canada into the 21st Century, May 1996. URL*: http://info.ic.gc.ca/info-highway/society/toc_e.html.*

[6] This report, Setting the Stage for the Next Century: The Federal Plan for Gender Equality, was developed and coordinated by Status of Women in collaboration with 24 federal departments and agencies, and approved by Cabinet in 1995. In particular, the Federal Plan emphasized that "...the absence of equity and access-related research [to the information infrastructure] is of growing concern. For example, it appears that women do not use the Internet or Freenet to the same extent as do men. This is of concern, given that much of the

Access to the information infrastructure is multifaceted, and encompasses physical, technical, economic, and social factors. Public policy examinations on access mainly consider the technical barriers towards access; for instance, the hardware and software to support communication, resource discovery tools and issues surrounding interoperability. The myriad factors that comprise the social infrastructure need to be considered as a holistic component affecting the access triumvirate of equity, affordability, and ubiquity. These include an ongoing examination of the many facets of network literacy; and of the diverse social variables affecting geographic, linguistic, income and class-based barriers[7].

Some of the particularities of gender which can influence access include: mundane economic factors; access to the hardware and software to support communications; user-centered designs; the creation of online gender issue information services; workplace issues; and the domestication of cyberspace.[8]

3 Status of Women Canada Survey

In April and May, 1996, a representative survey of women's organizations across Canada was conducted to assess how they are using the Internet. For those groups not connected to the Internet, the survey asked what specific Internet resources they were interested in; and for those groups on the Internet, the survey asked specific questions regarding the types of Internet services they use. The survey asked questions regarding the organization's anticipated use of the Internet, as well as some of the possible barriers to adoption of Internet services. Finally, the survey asked about funding and grants for Internet adoption that the group had either applied for and received; and for the types of funding the organization anticipated it would need to facilitate use of the Internet within their organization.

Names of national women's organizations to survey were received from the Women's Program and SWC Regional Coordinators. The survey was conducted through the telephone. The survey was also sent off to two mailing lists, Par-l and Women-l, and approximately 25 responses were received through e-mail. A total of 70 groups was consulted, and approximately ten were not included in the survey results

---

information needed to make informed decisions in today's world, and even the decision-making process itself, is being conducted along the cables of cyberspace. Those without access to this new technology that is rapidly transforming the way business is done, will be left out of the mainstream." (para. 270). The Federal Plan also questioned the effect of competition and market-driven scenarios to developing the information infrastructure: "Rapid global expansion of telecommunications and the deregulation of markets may reverse gains women have made in achieving equality of access to participation in all forms of cultural expression" (Ibid).

[7] To account for the intricate relationship between the social/technical architecture of the information infrastructure, a seven-layer model for analysing and discussing access to network services has been conceptualized. See Andrew Clement and Leslie Regan Shade, What Do We Mean By 'Universal Access'?: Social Perspectives in a Canadian Context, Proceedings of INET96, Montreal, June 25-28, 1996.URL: *http://info.isoc.org/isoc/whatis/conferences/inet/96/proce edings/f2/f2_1.htm*

[8] These ideas are further explored in Leslie Regan Shade, Gender and Community in the Social Constitution of the Internet, forthcoming Ph.D thesis, McGill University, Graduate Program in Communications, 1997.

because of no contact (telephone tag, out of office, fax not received, etc.). Although this survey is by no means a definitive overview of all the women's organizations in Canada, it does present, at this time, a fairly accurate portrait of how women's organizations are using the Internet, and what their barriers to access are.[9] Overall, the survey identified the following trends:

Familiarity With the Internet Most women's organizations are familiar with the Internet, and recognize that their organizations will need, in the near future, access to e-mail and the implementation of a homepage on the World Wide Web for outreach purposes. 21 out of the 70 groups surveyed were not on the Internet; and of those 21, 19 were in the process of either getting tangibly online or exploring the possibility. Only 2 groups indicated they were not sure if they wanted to get online; both cited a need for more knowledge concerning the Internet in order to make an informed decision about its adoption.

Most organizations recognized that, just as they adopted fax communication, e-mail is the next communications tool they will need to implement for cost- efficient and timely communications. Most, however, are excited, rather than daunted, about the possibilities. A woman at the Victoria Women's Sexual Assault Centre summed it up when she wrote:

> We have been online for one year now and really love the flexibility if gives us in so many ways. For us the Internet didn't seem like something inaccessible but rather as something interesting and useful which we love to explore and use in providing better services for our clients! ... I truly believe that the Internet is a wonderful tool and am very excited by all the opportunities it will give us to extend our services to women, recruit volunteers, establish and maintain relationships with donors, inform ourselves of the services provided by others and reach out to the world.

Barriers to Access-Technical Repeatedly, women's organizations cited the need for funding for computer hardware and software (usually for upgrades); modems; Internet Service Provider (ISP) costs; and funds for the creation and maintenance of World Wide Web pages. Although many women's organizations have found the money within their budgets to purchase the necessary equipment or services to get online, most cited the need for targeted financial support to continue their endeavors.

Barriers to Access-Organizational A common barrier to widespread access to e-mail for women's organizations is ensuring that organizations with diffuse memberships (including Board members, volunteers, and users) who are located in geographically dispersed areas, can all have access to e-mail within their community (through domestic or workplace access, at community access points such as libraries, and through freenets). Women's organizations therefore find that, until the widespread diffusion of e-mail, a variety of media must be used to communicate with their membership, including e-mail, faxes, and postal mail. Pat Webb of the CCLOW (Canadian Congress on Learning Opp- ortunities for Women) reiterated the concerns of many women's organizations when she wrote:

[9] Several women consultants answered the survey, but their comments were not included, as they were not traditional women's groups. Given the trend towards home- based knowledge work, a study of how these women are using the Internet would be timely.

> There is already a gap between have and have-not volunteers in terms of frequency of communication (e-mail) and immediacy of access to useful information. Because of our feminist principles, including our belief in equitable access, we could not make effective use of the technology a standard, without providing all Board members or all committee members access. Currently most board members have some access to a fax, with any costs covered by CCLOW. Public access to email and the WWW is simply not available in corner stores, yet, so home equipment would be needed.

Likewise, Madeline Bosco and Carla Marcelis of the Canadian Women's Health Network (CWHN) wrote that:

> A very important point for the organizations that are part of the network is the issue of accessibility: many women do not have access to computers or providers (i.e., in rural areas, in isolated regions) or they have other access barriers such as language and literacy levels.One of the main reasons that the CWHN have gone ahead with electronic communications is cost reduction (re. long-distance charges), however, we are trying to keep a close evaluation of whether we eliminate participation (and how that can be remedied) by doing most of our comm- unications electronically.

Barriers to Access-Training Access to training was repeatedly cited by women's organizations as being a necessary requisite for successful Internet access. Both onsite training and training packages developed for Internet dissemination were cited as attractive options. Madeline Bosco and Carla Marcelis of the Canadian Women's Health Network (CWHN) wrote that:

> A remark regarding training needs: it is true that getting training in Internet use would be very helpful for many groups that participate in the CWHN, however, these groups are mostly women's groups that operate on small budgets, doing an amazing amount of work. For them, taking the time to take training, is taking time away from other immediate and often pressing tasks – a hard choice to make. They will need to see the content there as well. Therefore training should include this component.
>
> Most training programs and trainers are useless for women. I have watched a variety fail. I think we need mentoring programs, specific women friendly educational materials and programs that work specifically with the equipment, programs and service providers that the women have available. We also need to show them how to use the technology to distribute their materials.

Barriers to Access-Philosophical Susan Simmons of WebSisters wrote that the male-domination of the Internet profession is a barrier to access for many of the women's groups she works with:

> One of the main barriers I experience is the perception by many women's organizations that the Internet is a boy toy. I am also limited by the amount of money they do not have to pay for my services. The other main problem is the difficulty I experience with this male dominated profession. Many people do not realize that women work in this area as well. Instinctively, many people turn to males for help.

Barriers to Access-Francophone Groups Francophone women's groups repeatedly cited as one of the main barriers to access the overwhelming anglophone content of the Internet. More francophone content needs to be developed before the majority of francophone women's organizations will find the Internet a useful tool.As well, many francophone women's groups did not perceive the Internet a being a valuable communications tool. Knowledge of the Internet was lower here than in other

Provinces surveyed (notably, compared to urban centres in British Columbia and Ontario).

Barriers to Access-Aboriginal and Native Women's Groups Aboriginal and Native women's associations are ill represented on the Internet. Of those groups that were surveyed, most had little to say because of a lack of knowledge about the Internet. Clearly, these groups need to have more education about the Internet in order to make informed choices about how access could effect and possibly enhance their everyday communication.

Barriers to Access-Disabled Women's Groups Disabled groups are also not well represented on the Internet. More research needs to be conducted on the specific technical mechanisms and design elements that would enhance access for these individuals and groups.

Barriers to Access-Geographical Access to the Internet is difficult for many organizations located in rural and remote communities. Although a specific federal funding program, the Community Access program (CAP) is addressing this issue, several women's organizations remain frustrated at CAP's designation of women's organizations as 'special interest groups' and therefore ineligible for funding. As well, CAP does not lend much support for the development of training programs, which women's groups have identified as being a necessary requisite for getting more women online[10].

4 Eliminating Barriers

Eliminating barriers primarily involves ameliorating the financial constraints of the organizations so that they may purchase various equipment to get online; provide access for the necessary training; and devote the appropriate time towards the development of online content. Most women's organizations are grappling with funding cutbacks from federal, provincial, and municipal entities; a consequent reduction in staff; and, in many instances, waning memberships.

Access Barriers-Lack of Funding Repeatedly, women's organizations surveyed cited the need for funding for computer hardware and software (usually for upgrades); modems; Internet Service Provider (ISP) costs; and funds for the creation and maintenance of World Wide Web pages. Although many women's organizations have found the money within their budgets to purchase the necessary equipment or services to get online, most cited the need for financial support to continue their endeavors. Women's groups surveyed expressed frustration at the lack of viable funding support for their information infrastructure projects at many levels, including provincially and federally. The surveyed groups welcomed the opportunity to work together to

[10] The Community Access Program objectives are to provide program funding for rural communities to get connected to the Internet, and "to raise awareness about its potential for creating jobs and growth; to stimulate the development of new electronic learning tools and services; [and] to provide Internet training facilities for local entrepreneurs, employees, educators and students." See URL: *http://cnet.unb.ca/cap/*.

ensure that their common goals of attaining widespread accessibility to the Internet could be met. Scarlett Pollock and Jo Sutton of Women'space [an online and print magazine on issues related to Canadian women on the Internet] wrote, with respect to their activities to secure funding:

> ...Very frustrating- [funding entities have] no mandate for funding technology training for women; unfamiliarity of funders with Internet. We're doing what we can with the limited resources we have, which basically means working for nothing. Still the need is there. Women'space magazine has taken off and is encouraging organizations, Advisory Councils and women's groups to get online.

Sharon Reiner of the Alberta Status of Women Action Committee commented that:

> There is a much bigger issue here than just needing funding to get active in this technology. Women's organizations such as ASWAC are struggling to survive. I personally think the Internet and electronic communication is an excellent (and overall affordable and accessible) means of creating social change and furthering the goals of women's organizations, but there is no way this will happen without the commitment of the Federal government towards women's equality. The gov- ernment has a respon- sibility towards ensuring the voice of all women are heard in this country and without that, the organizations will fold and only the elite will have a say. Simply providing funding for specific projects and not ongoing support will only further isolate women.

One of the active funding programs for access to the Internet for women has been implemented by the British Columbia Ministry of Woman's Equality. Their Community Internet Training Program will give funds in the range of $1,000-3,000 for Internet projects, to include: the purchase of hardware and software, including computer upgrades, memory, modems, and miscellaneous software; the purchase of an Internet Service Provider for a year; payment of an extra phone line for dedicated use; payment for storage space on a server for World Wide Web; creation and maintenance of a homepage on the World Wide Web; and training for staff (who would then be required to train other staff in a train-the-trainer approach)[11]. Women's groups surveyed felt that this was an excellent idea for a grant program, as it allocated monies for both technical and training resources. If this program is successful, it could be a model for adoption for other grant programs. Another area to investigate is potential partnerships with industry and the private-sector.

Access Barriers-Content & Women's Resources The development of World Wide Web content for and by Canadian women's groups is imperative. By building a critical mass of women's content, access and interest in the Internet will be accelerated. Specific areas of Internet development that women's groups identified as necessary components in ensuring widespread access included a directory of women's organizations and Internet information. This would involve the creation of a dynamic directory of Canadian women's organizations online, with contact information, including links to World Wide Web sites; a list of ISPs, community networks, and funding opportunities for information infrastructure projects; and the creation of an online list of international women's organizations and resources on the Internet, grouped by sector, so that groups looking for content, ideas, and resources to create their own Web sites could see what resources are there for emulation, outreach, or

---

[11] For more information on the B.C. Ministry of Woman's Equality Community Internet Training Program see URL: *http://www.weq.gov.bc.ca/.*

coordination. (i.e., feminist magazines, women's studies resources, health, international development, business, etc.).

Access Barriers-Training Access to Internet training was repeatedly cited as a necessary component towards ensuring successful access by women's groups. Several researchers have commented that training for women must be contextualized.For instance, Akman[12] in describing the experiences of training methods from the Women's Networking Support Program (WNSP) of the Association for Progressive Communication (APC),relates how WNSP training and outreach is altered according to the specific needs of the users. Since the APC attracts a diverse range of international, and especially developing country users, trainees are consulted about their needs and concerns, and individual trainers strive then to meet the needs of these diverse users.

However, the question has been raised repeatedly amongst women's groups as to whether or not 'women- centered' training is necessary, and, if so, what this would consist of. Many women and women's groups believe that women-centered training, which would be training conducted by a women instructor, and emphasizing the content needs of women and women's groups, helps to demystify the technology by providing a more conducive learning environment. Certainly the argument can be made that women-centered training could produce a convivial environment for some women, but this argument also veers perilously close to essentialist arguments.

A cost-effective way of disseminating training material would be to make available a combination of online information pertinent to gaining familiarity with the Internet; and developing online mentoring programs. Several already exist through World Wide Web sites and listservs. For instance, the creation of training resources (on e-mail packages, World Wide Web searching, HTML coding, CGI scripting, etc.) which can be taken through online delivery is a cost-efficient method for training. Train- the-trainer programs are another cost-efficient method. It was further suggested that successful training programs should be identified as to their strengths and weaknesses.

Access Barriers-Francophone Women's Groups Barriers to access were more pronounced for francophone groups, primarily due to linguistic and geographic barriers. A more thorough survey of the Internet barriers and needs from a much larger sample of francophone women's groups needs to be conducted. As well, public information and awareness materials regarding the Internet ahould be developed for francophone women's groups, and enquiries be made into possible funding for programs through the Quebec Secretariat de l'Autoroute de l'Information.[13]

---

[12] See Justine Akman, Increasing Women's Use of Electronic Networks: The Women's Networking and Support Program of the Association for Progressive Communications. Feminist Collections: "Women's Studies and Information Technology: Reports From the Field" (Winter 1996): 24-26.

[13] The Secretariat de l'autoroute de l'information is particularly trying to address the pervasive anglophone content of the Internet. Areas for support include the modernization and development of infrastructures; support and partnering with private sector projects; support for experimental projects; and development of francophone resources. See URL: *http://www.gouv.qc.ca/francais/minorg/sai/index.html*

5 Survey Conclusions

The results of the Status of Women Canada survey indicated that women's groups were enthusiastic about gaining access to the Internet. However, they were very concerned about their financial viability (particularly in a 'deficit-busting' climate where the funding base for social change groups is being increasingly eroded) in attaining access to specific tools--both technical and social, such as training--for their wider membership. As the debates continue about the trajectory of national information infrastructures, it has become clear that the task of ensuring that the needs of a diverse citizenry can be met will be an ongoing struggle. In Canada, explorations on how to assess and subsidize universal service to basic network services is underway; the Infor- mation Highway Advisory Council (IHAC) is currently undertaking studies as the nature of essential services, the concept of a 'public lane', and the effects of competition. Left to its own devices, and encouraged by a free and unfettered regulatory regime, there is every fear that the marketplace will simply not protect the public interest; and every reason to believe that such forces would increase substantially the rift between the information rich and the information poor.

6 Future Directions

Canada is currently formulating their National Access Strategy to the Information Highway, as delineated in Building the Information Society. Focal policy research issues that affect women and women's groups with respect to access include:

1) defining universal access to essential services;
2) proposing support mechanisms to ensure essential services are universally accessible; and,
3) elaborating conceptions of 'electronic public space'.[14] [14]

Essential Services: What should be the technical 'core services' provided: single-party telephone service, access to operator and emergency services, Internet access? What sorts of constituency oriented information services for the women's community should be considered as part of the 'essential basket' of services? What sorts of information should be deemed to be essential for education, public health, or public safety? How can more francophone and multicultural content be created to meet the diverse needs of the citizenry?

Support Mechanisms: What sorts of information 'safety nets' could be designed and established so that all citizens, regardless of their ability to pay, can partake of services? There are a variety of funding options available for support mechanisms. Questions raised include: should telecommunication carriers be required to contribute to a universal access fund? should tax credits be made available for telecommunication carriers that contribute to a universal access fund? should the telecommunications and computer industries be encouraged to develop a standard 'information

[14] These research areas will be the focus of a workshop, Developing a Canadian Access Strategy: Universal Access to Essential Network Services, to be held February 6-8, 1997 at the Faculty of Information Studies, University of Toronto.The workshop proceedings and other background material will be available at URL: *http://www.fis.utoronto.ca/research/iprp/ua*.

appliance' (akin to a device attached to the television, or a Minitel/videotex box) which would allow low-income users to access the Internet?

The Concept of a Public Lane: Given the commercial trajectory of the information infrastructure, there is an essential need to ensure that a vigorous public sphere is maintained. The creation and sustenance of a public sphere can allow for a broad range of citizens to participate in the benefits of the information infrastructure, thereby, potentially ameliorating the distinction between the information 'have's and have-not's'; and also extend and enhance democratic practices.

The creation of community access points (CAPS) has been pushed by governments and public interest groups as a way for the public to gain access to the information infrastructure. While such a goal is laudable and necessary, the rhetoric tends to be wildly uninformed; i.e., a band-aid solution to a deeper access problem. While it is true that until domestic access is ubiquitous, CAPS serve a useful function, salient issues related to their pervasiveness, management, affordability, and usefulness need to be examined. Therefore, the needs of women and women's groups with respect to CAPS needs to be considered in the ongoing policy process.

IT EQUATE Through the Web and Internet

Christine Whitehouse, Gillian Lovegrove and Sue Williams

School of Computing, Staffordshire University
Beaconside, Stafford, ST18 0DG, United Kingdom

Abstract. The web which has been spun in the last twenty years in respect of computing, gender and education has been a complex one. It has involved the inter-weaving of many facets of our culture to produce a female gender imbalance within computing at higher education in 1996, which was not as strongly marked in 1976. Today the proportion of women on typical computing-related courses is around 12%, whilst during the 1970s the figure was of the order of 25% (Lovegrove 1995).

The IT EQUATE action research project at Staffordshire University is nearing completion. It has been running for three years and has been an intensive study involving Staffordshire University, girls at three local schools, teachers, careers advisors and parents. Its aim has been to examine the computing/gender issues and to develop strategies to improve the image of careers in computing amongst schoolgirls.

The research has so far shown that the perceptions and attitudes of girls are influenced by the use and teaching of IT in schools, their peers' and parents' viewpoints, career literature, industry, media, government and the information explosion. These areas need to be addressed in the future to help bring about change with respect to the dwindling numbers of females entering computing: "only 23% of IT employees in the UK are women, compared with 39% in France, 45% in the US and 55% in Singapore" (Acey 1995). The IT EQUATE research also appears to indicate that in order to stimulate girls' interest in computing in the future, the "Web", the Internet and multimedia may hold the key.

1 Introduction

It is generally accepted that PCs and the internet in homes will have a great effect. No one is quite sure by just how much or in what way. More information will be readily available for everyone; security is a hot topic; the dark side of implications such as easily available pornography has to be of national importance.

However the theme of this paper is around a more specialist question: when we have more PCs and the internet is available to all, what will be the implications for women and their possible careers within the information technology areas? Can we hope to see more or less women working in these vital fields? By implication, the authors of this paper believe this to be an important question with significance for society in general. The nation needs women as well as men forming and making decisions in the design of future computer systems (Green et al 1993). The number of women taking up careers in the IT area is relatively small considering the aptitude and capability of women for these careers. This means that the influence of women on the design of all aspects of the new internet technology is relatively weak. The implications of some of these decisions may not have been seen early enough. Apart from this aesthetic and practical aspect, there is also one of wealth creation; there simply are not enough skilled people in the workforce and women are a valuable resource in this respect (Lambeth 1996).

The IT EQUATE project has been working with schools to try to encourage young women to take up careers in IT. The project attempted to give a number of girls a very positive experience in several aspects over a time period which we expected would have had a positive effect on their decisions about future careers and choice of degree. However the effect was quite seriously qualified. A description is given of some critical factors which affect girls in this respect, the greatest of which appear to be sociological: deeply based in UK society attitudes.

The paper continues by considering the current influences and possible changes, affecting all areas of society, which might have a future impact. This is followed by a summary of the current technological developments around the internet. The big question is then posed: will the internet accessibility alter the critical factors which have influenced young women to take up careers in IT? Can we hope to see more women in this vital area or do we need to resign ourselves to seeing the continuing slide of computing into the realm of the male-dominated science and engineering professions?

2 Evolution of the Staffordshire IT EQUATE Project

Staffordshire IT EQUATE was established in 1993 by the School of Computing at Staffordshire University, to continue the work of a pilot project commenced by the University of Southampton. Full details of the results of this pilot project can be found in (Lovegrove et al 1994).

The aims were to:

- increase the awareness of girls to careers involving computing;
- develop strategies for encouraging girls to enter computing related courses;
- raise awareness within schools and in the home to computing careers and related issues.

The plan was to:

- work with two or three schools intensively;
- start with committed schools who would actively support the programme;
- work the programme over a three year period;
- continually try to support a "pro-IT" careers environment around the girls, including a range of careers involving information systems;
- provide a programme for curricula materials, computer club materials, management ideas, industrial liaison/mentoring/visits/role models, parent involvement and parent workshops, careers videos, self-discovery/equal opportunities/workshops for girls, university visits and workshops.

In short, the plan was to force a "success" story by weighting every effort and choice towards a positive influence. Three schools were chosen in October 1993 to work intensively with the Staffordshire IT EQUATE team over a three year period. They were from different backgrounds and geographical areas, using co-educational schools and a single sex school and from the private as well as state systems. All three schools were selected because they were very enthusiastic about the objectives of the Staffordshire IT EQUATE project.

Two groups of girls were targeted at the three schools. One was around 14 to 15 years when option choice and peer group pressure are important, the other was 15 to 17 years when pupils are considering their future prospects. The IT EQUATE events were then aimed at three contingents of girls:

- a total of 33 girls from the three schools, aged 14-16, who volunteered to be involved with the IT EQUATE project for a three year period until they left school;
- 60 girls from the three schools aged 14-15, chosen according to predefined criteria each year of the IT EQUATE project;
- pupils identified by the schools as requiring careers talks - this included the 15-17 age group.

3 Staffordshire IT EQUATE Past Action

The planned action was to take place at three different venues; these were the three schools, Staffordshire University and local industries involved with computing.

The IT EQUATE team first investigated the schools' resources for computing and the teaching of the subject. They examined the hardware and software used, the kinds of teaching staff involved and the timetabling of classes including the elapsed time, frequency and pupils taught. The investigation covered the various computing courses which were being studied, how computers were used within other subject teaching and the computer literature and career material available to the pupils. Further details of this study can be found in (Williams et al 1996). All schools were visited by the IT EQUATE team and University students to provide careers talks, as and when requested, by the schools themselves.

The events which took place at Staffordshire University were many and varied. They involved demonstrations of multimedia by staff and students, demonstrations of image processing involving morphing (the changing of one image to that of another) and fractals (colour representation of graph samples). There were demonstrations of the Internet and its use within video conferencing and links were made to talk to people in America and Australia. Hands-on experience on the computers was given in the area of graphics, Internet searching and Internet page creation and business advert production using people's computerised images. Facilities were also provided for the design and creation of cartoons, teaching material and icons on the computers.

Demonstrations and hands-on involvement were provided in the area of computer control, where simulations were given of production lines, washing machines, sorting by colours and control of the speed of motors, calculators, buzzers and fans. The importance of teamwork, adhering to a specification and problem solving (required by the computing industry) were explained with the exercise to build a six foot paper tower using only A4 paper. In contrast, career videos, talks by students from Staffordshire University and role models from industry clarified the reality and overcame some of the myths of what a career in computing involves.

The 33 girls from the three schools over the three year period, had the opportunity to experience all the above events at the University, whilst a further 168 girls were involved with a subset of these events. A total of some 100 teachers, parents, pupils (including boys) and LEA careers personnel associated with the three schools have also had experience of such events at the University. For the 33 girls, visits were made to the brewing industry to see computer control within the canning and packaging department and to the ceramics industry to see computer aided design and the processing of sales orders, from receipt to despatch of the product. Finally these girls visited a computer component manufacturer to view the creation of computer circuit boards.

4 Staffordshire IT EQUATE Findings

Statistical details from the IT EQUATE research, pertaining to perceptions and attitudes, may be found in (Whitehouse et al 1996). To summarise the statistics, the events within IT EQUATE were successful in that the girls enjoyed the computing experiences and understood the possibilities offered to them by computing careers. However the numbers wishing to commit early to this as a career choice, by choosing to study a degree related to computing, were disappointing. It is worth looking at this more closely.

Of the 200 girls who have been involved with the IT EQUATE project at Staffordshire University, due to age, it is only from the contingent of 33 girls that members are progressing to higher education in 1996. It is therefore not possible to gain a full picture of the influence that the IT EQUATE programme has had on the girls. Only one girl from the 33 has applied to study computing at University as a result of our action research; however all girls are now aware of the significance of computers and the importance to them as a tool in their future careers. All expressed their willingness to study a computing module if it was offered within their chosen degree or career programme.

Staffordshire University's IT EQUATE work with respect to gender and computing is unique in the UK, in that the work has involved a small number of girls participating in many computing activities. This is in contrast to the worthy efforts of other Universities in the UK who have involved a large number of girls generally within a single event. We had weighted our efforts expecting to find success.

Contrary to our expectations, this lack of influence by the IT EQUATE team on the initial direction the girls have taken with regard to a choice of careers, has led us to speculate about the reasons for "failure".

As a result of the IT EQUATE team's observations and findings, the following hypothesis is put forward as to why there is non take-up of careers by girls into the computing profession: *"it is the combination of such criteria as parental influence, teacher influence, self-esteem, stereotyping, peer pressure, employers' attitudes, image of the working environment, the perception of working in groups and the overall perception of the work itself"*. Despite the very positive experiences gained by the girls, they hold reservations about the pleasure and therefore the suitability of the career.

In order to identify strategies for the future for encouraging girls to consider computing, the IT EQUATE team examined the situation from each angle that could influence girls to reject a career in this field. These covered: IT in schools; the girls' peers' and parents' viewpoints; the available career literature; the industry, media and government viewpoints and the effect of the information explosion. Further background information on these influences can be found in the IT EQUATE work (Whitehouse et al 1996) and in a reflection of the situation at IBM (Gill 1996). The following paragraphs give a summary and suggested strategies.

5 Current Influences and Possible Strategies

IT in Schools: despite the fact that the appreciation and practice of Information Technology appears in the National Curriculum at all levels, it became clear during our research that pupils held some misconceptions; they failed to understand the problem solving capabilities of IT, were confused about the application of IT in the real world and within other subject areas. Any interest fostered in IT as a subject for further study at an early age was sometimes lost, as there was not always the opportunity to study IT at higher levels for staffing reasons. Changes to the National Curriculum with respect to IT also led to staffing problems, due to the broadening of the study area to be taught throughout all subjects. There were few female role models teaching IT in the schools and staff and technicians were frequently male.
On the positive side, the teachers recognised the use of computers in their subjects areas and educational software systems are becoming more widely available. This is an area for further development as long as training and support for teachers are provided, children "need to be taught by teachers who are themselves confident, who do not have high anxiety levels about computing and who enjoy it" (Grundy 1996). It is encouraging to note that with the changes to the IT curriculum in 1995, since our project began, the emphasis has been placed more on the application of IT and this may go some way to rectify the perceptions of IT and introduce the students to take a more problem solving approach.

Peers' Viewpoint: many of the girls encountered during the project were found to be lacking in confidence when confronted with new hardware and software and seemed to be afraid of being teased if they did not know what to do. When questioned about why this was so, they implied that computing was boring and that they would rather talk to their friends than to a machine. Thus the girls' and their peers' perceptions are important. Girls require further practice in IT skills, working at their own pace either in a class situation or at home, each with their own machine and worksheet, or at a computer club where fun is the main aim. Teachers and parents are needed to encourage and participate and be aware of the particular difficulties that girls have. The boring aspect of IT was addressed within the University workshops; the Internet and multimedia sessions proved very popular and investigation into progression and development in these areas is a possible solution. Production of games and virtual reality software can be aimed at girls by being more creative, problem solving and educational.

Parents' Viewpoint: children naturally turn to their parents/guardians, together with teachers and careers advisors for advice concerning their future career paths. It is therefore imperative that these sources are supplied with as much information as possible. By looking at what parents knew or thought they knew about computing as a career for girls, we discovered weaknesses. Parents' advice is often guidance towards a discipline that they know and understand. There is still the old adage that computing is not for girls (arguably not for the intelligent males either) and there is a typical view of male domination and the masculine image in the profession. This latter is not supposition but a fact. Office of Science and Technology (OST) statistics show that during the last two decades, the number of women studying computing and subsequently being employed as computer professionals in the Western world has declined drastically. Parents need to be informed of the potential within the profession. This message can only be spread by providing relevant material and running more workshops.

Careers Literature: there is widespread confusion concerning computer semantics and jargon used when explaining what is meant by a career in computing and when describing specific jobs. Does a career in computing only involve programming? If so, what is the difference between a computer programmer and a software engineer? Is the latter someone who uses engineering techniques such as designing and modelling a solution using a computer or is it an academic discipline dealing with theoretical methodologies? Job advertisements have a wide variety of titles for apparently similar occupations. Although adverts have to avoid gender specifics, they are written in male-oriented language, e.g. the word engineer has a negative effect on girls. Solutions to these problems are again far reaching and require changes within our social culture; however, it should be possible to produce career material which is not gender biased using a variety of media such as leaflets, video, multimedia presentations and televised educational programmes.

Industry Viewpoint: we invited role models and supporters from a cross-section of companies and organisations to attend our workshops. The girls were also given the chance to visit three companies to experience different views of computing in the workplace. During our investigations (both formal and informal) which included the companies, we found that there was a general lack of awareness of the shortage of female applicants, although some Government departments (e.g. OST) and companies (e.g. IBM, ICL D2D) have begun to realise this and are therefore more supportive in our aims and objectives. When we questioned the girls, we found that they are motivated into employment by subjects they enjoy rather than by salary levels, even though the latter were important. Many of the women we talked to who are currently employed within the computing profession entered it by accident rather than by design. It is difficult to suggest solutions to these problems, only to note that it is becoming recognised that the female style of management is more appropriate for the millennium (Gill 1996). The software engineering profession (BCS) recognises the need to cross cultural boundaries as well as technological divides. Industry must be more proactive in raising children's awareness of the computing industry and the future opportunities.

Media Viewpoint: the media have a tremendous influence on the public. Details of all our events were sent to editors of national and local papers, the local radio and television companies resulting in a certain amount of publicity. Valuable though this was for the project and the University, often the coverage was rather superficial, which is probably a reflection of the facts lacking media drama. Thus, the media does not help the general public's understanding and perspective of the computing as much as it could. It has been shown that children are influenced by television in their choice of career. TV dramas are not usually set in a computing company, but 'high tech' is used to provide excitement and glamour (e.g. Bugs). Portrayal of computer wizardry is not always balanced with a clear explanation of the problem the computer has solved, although this has been addressed recently by the programmes 'How do they do that?' and 'Does it really work?'.

Government Viewpoint: there are several issues involving the Government. Expenditure on hardware and software within schools has not generally been matched with expenditure on support for teachers and pupils in IT; this needs to be addressed in order to exploit the original investment to the full. The government-sponsored initiatives to promote women in technology, both in the universities and the workplace, need to be strengthened. It is suggested that lack of IT skills and funding will lead to the 'haves' and 'have nots' within society. Education of the general public concerning technology is required.

6 Current Developments: Technology and the Information Explosion

When the girls were questioned about the IT EQUATE events, the Internet searching, multimedia and video conferencing scored highest on their enjoyment level, hence the attention of the IT EQUATE team turned to why such an interest might lie in these fields and whether the Internet, which supports all these facilities, might hold the key to the future. To do this, it was initially found necessary to consider the girls' interests and social skills.

The girls had identified that they did not particularly enjoy learning how to use computer packages - word processors, spreadsheets or database management systems, to perform exercises set (Whitehouse et al 1996). On questioning the girls they did not appear to appreciate the application of the computers to the real world or identify that the computing industry is about communicating and solving problems collaboratively. The girls worried about their lack of machine skills, at the University events and at a computer club held at one of the schools they needed 'hand holding', they were aware of the speed reaction of the boys and felt this was not for them. This corresponds to other research findings: Lorraine Culley reports about how at a computer club the girls appeared uncomfortable and said that: *"The boys considered the computer room to be their 'territory'..."* (Culley 1986). Girls find it insular and anti-social; a father of two daughters, who attended an IT EQUATE event at the University for parents wrote:

"There is an antisocial impression given by a person sitting at a VDU, which makes it difficult for another person to break into. Girls often complain that those with skills on computers will not let them in to have a go - this feeling continues at all stages but could be critical in putting girls off at an early stage in their interest. I have found that a PC at home helps break this barrier."

Let us now consider in contrast, what girls are good at and where their interests lie. Girls generally are interested in communicating, solving problems and teamwork. They are interested in subjects other than computing, they like dealing with and processing information, information which is real or which they can relate to the real world. They generally like being creative and they are interested in the organisation and presentation of their work.

What then can the Internet offer girls? If girls enjoy communicating, the concept of electronic mail provides the ability not only to interact locally, but internationally with other schools and not only with users of the same learning levels but with experts in the field. This means of social interaction, allowing the extension of individuals to move beyond their capabilities, may not only take place remotely via the Internet, but may also take place locally within the classroom with children working in groups on a task which utilises the Internet. The computer then appears less insular and antisocial and provides the opportunity for girls to work in teams and solve problems collaboratively - communication can not only then occur within their own personal communities, but also within these virtual communities.

The processing of information to solve problems, that girls enjoy, is facilitated by the World Wide Web. Consider a user task model, set in the class environment, which requires pupils to find information from alternative sources, using different search strategies and then to subsequently sift the information returned (when excessive) to fit the problem set. The Internet provides the ideal medium such that students have access to resources beyond their physical reach and can utilise material from newspapers, museums or art galleries that otherwise might not be available to them. Large amounts of information can be accessed very quickly, whilst indexes and menu systems allow easy access to sophisticated materials or to references that permit traditional resources to be used more effectively.

Within the information age, it has been suggested, that traditional goals may change with the belief that in the future textbooks will not always dominate the curriculum and that "individual customisation and reorganisation becomes the goal, not the communication of fixed knowledge" (Cunningham et al 1993). If this is the case the Web provides for ideas, in the form of text, sound and images, to be cross-referenced, it allows for pupils to cut and paste material from the Internet with ease or to create links to relevant pages they have found. Since girls focus their attention on the format of their delivery, it reduces the workload of the written and presentational task and hence frees further time for the pupil to engage in constructive thinking.

The concept of working with real information or with material which could be related to the real world is also satisfied by the Web. The publishing of surveys, research and advertising material, the availability of museum, art gallery, media and scientific sites provide the opportunity of manipulation of real data. The Internet technology aids understanding by permitting audio-visual representation to provide links between difficult subject areas and the real world. Such can be achieved within mathematics, where interactive media can allow pupils to actually see the linkage between a mathematical model and its real world application, thus bringing a clearer understanding to a larger number of pupils than was previously possible (NCET 1994). In the field of modern languages "learning can often seem lifeless and uninteresting to many students" (Mitchell 1995). The Internet has provided the means for pupils from different countries, to communicate with each other via e-mail, in a language that is foreign to both parties in order "to bring new life to their studies".

Whatever the interest of the schoolchild, then material maybe found on that subject area on the World Wide Web. Given then that girls' interests generally appear to lie in areas other than computing, that interest may be further stimulated and extended by the material that may be found. This situation was identified at the IT EQUATE events, when such stimulation whilst searching the Internet appeared to overcome the computer as a barrier. If this then can become the general case, whereby the interest lies beyond the machine, then the computer may take its rightful place as a tool to be used in the learning process. The absence of such a barrier may then enable girls to see the potential of the machine as an aid to problem solving and thus of suitable interest to consider opportunities within the computing field.

7 The National Curriculum and the Internet

If the Internet can perhaps provide the key to the stimulation of girls' interest in computing, it becomes necessary to examine what role the Internet can play in the delivery of the National Curriculum. The educational value of the Internet and the potential to deliver the National curriculum is currently being explored by the UK Government's "Superhighways for Education" initiative (DFEE 1995) and the Department for Trade and Industries "Schools On Line" projects (DTI 1995). The IT capabilities required by the National curriculum (DFE 1995) cover:

- using information services and IT tools to solve problems;
- using IT tools and information sources, such as computer systems and software packages, to support learning in a variety of contexts;
- understanding the implications of IT for working life and society.

Furthermore, the National Curriculum for IT states that pupils should be given opportunities, where appropriate, to develop and apply their IT capability in their study of other National Curriculum subjects.

An initial consideration of whether the Internet might contribute to the goals of the National Curriculum, leaves little doubt that it ought to be able to do so. The Internet allows the access to a huge information source and in order to access this information, it presents itself as an IT tool, involving computer systems and software. The ability to solve problems using the information retrieved, whether in the context of electronic mail, information browsing, file transfer, newsgroups, publishing or from using others computers, has huge potential, although equally it is also accepted that it may create problems for the schoolchild. It is highly likely that users of such a system will become aware of the potential of the Internet for "working life and society", through the access of advertising material, visiting Internet sites which permit the ordering of goods, retrieving up-to-the-minute detail on research or products, or by almost instantaneous retrieval of information from the other side of the world. Finally, the range of information accessed and presented via the Internet covers every subject area within the National Curriculum and beyond, although its accuracy in parts may be questionable.

If the Internet then has the potential to satisfy the girls' interests and the requirements of the National Curriculum, then what of the boy/girl divide identified within the computing arena? It has already been suggested from our observations that use of the Internet appeared to overcome the barrier of the machine. With the possibility of lack of face-to-face interaction, social status, race, gender, age and even physical appearance and disabilities are lacking. This can lead to greater equality and thus may encourage participation between group members as a positive outcome.

Whilst the Internet may help to change girls overall outlook to computing, it does not provide the panacea to all the problems. Its application may lead to challenges to the social and organisational cultures of a school and to the teaching strategies used, however this paper does not provide the forum for discussion in this area, only its consideration. Similarly recognition is given to the Web's lack of good search mechanisms and problems of accuracy, availability and control.

8 Conclusions: Will This Alter the IT EQUATE Critical Factors?

The IT EQUATE three year action research has identified many problem areas which are interwoven; there is a need to address the different strands of our society, the teaching of IT in schools, peers' and parents' viewpoints, the career literature available, the industry, media and government viewpoints to bring about the culture change necessary to enable girls to feel differently about careers in IT.

The availability of more computers in schools and in the home, together with more training for teachers would create an environment where girls would feel more comfortable and less threatened by computers. The current National Curriculum now places less emphasis on hardware and programming skills and more onus on application software and problem solving, whilst CD ROMs and the Internet provide information, such that technology can move into more subject areas. Both these latter instances provide for a more female friendly computing environment.

Thus our prediction for the future for women using technology is a bright and hopeful one; careers which involve technology but do not focus on it, should attract women more in the future.

For careers focusing on computing, our outlook is one of realism rather than optimism. We have observed the number of females entering computing courses at higher education dropping both nationally and internationally. The Staffordshire IT EQUATE project was believed to be a good strategy for change; however we were disturbed to find that the social forces are so great within UK society that our strategies have not worked in the short term and we have not facilitated an increase into computing higher education. Whilst we concede that the Internet and multimedia may increase the 'comfort' factor with respect to girls and computers, such that girls will consider the machine to be less of a barrier and more of a tool, we do not believe that this will much affect the numbers of girls in the 18+ age group studying computing at University in the future.

Only with the 25+ age group is there likely to be any significant increase. Hopefully in about 10 years time, when the current 13-14 year old girls have experienced a 'comfortable' computing environment at school and, once post 18, have become aware of the implications of IT to society and the opportunities available to them in careers in the computing field, they may move to take up computing at age 25+.

References

1. M. Acey: Bill to Promote Women in IT. Computer Weekly March 16, (1995)
2. L. Culley: Gender Differences and Computing in Secondary Schools. Technical report, Department of Education, Loughborough University, UK (1986)
3. D.J. Cunningham, T.M Duffy and R.A Knuth: The textbook of the future. In: McKnight et al, (eds). Hypertext a psychological perspective, Ellis Horwood (1993)
4. Department for Education: Information technology in the National Curriculum. HMSO publication (1995), 1/95
5. Department for Education and Employment: Superhighways for education, the way forward. HMSO publication (1995), 11/95
6. Department for Trade and Industry: Schools on line to the Internet - Tim Eggar. Press notice March 21 (1995)
7. H Gill: Who holds the Key to the Glass Door?. Conference on Professional Awareness in Software Engineering, London, UK (1996)
8. E. Green, J. Owen and D. Pain: Gendered by Design. Taylor and Francis (1993)
9. F. Grundy: Women and Computers, Intellect (1996)
10. J. Lambeth: IT graduates in demand as skills shortage strikes. Computer Weekly, July 18, 1996
11. G. Lovegrove, M. Fletcher, C. Johnson and C. Mayer: Staffordshire IT EQUATE: Project and Plans. IFIP Conference on Women, Work and Computerization, Manchester, UK. 511-518 (1994)
12. G. Lovegrove, Women in Computing. In: C. Myers (eds.): Professional Awareness in Software Engineering, McGraw Hill. 110-133 (1995)
13. A. Mitchell: Learning Online. Internet and Comms Today, 5/95, 46-47 (1995)
14. National Council for Educational Technology: Teaching and learning with Interactive media (1994)
15. C. Whitehouse, G. Lovegrove and S. Williams: But Isn't Computing Boring? Conference on Professional Awareness in Software Engineering, London, UK (1996)
16. S. Williams, G. Lovegrove and C. Whitehouse: Working Towards Equality in IT in the Year 2000. GASAT Conference on Towards Sustainable Development: Achieving the 4E's: Education, Employment, Equality and Empowerment, Gujarat, India (1996)

Women's Online Media (WOM) and Women's Internetwork Shuttle (WIS) – A Pioneering Project in Japan

Yayoi Taguchi[1] and Junko Yoshimura[2]

[1] Women's Online Media
1411-1131 Shiomidai, Isogo-ku, Yokohama, Japan 235
phone/fax:+81-45-758-0572
e-mail:yayoit@suehiro.nakano.tokyo.jp

[2] Women's Internetwork Shuttle
2-2-18-805 Kita-karasuyama, Setagaya-ku, Tokyo, Japan 157
phone:+81-3-5384-7020, fax:+81-3-5384-8587
e-mail:junkoy@po.iijnet.or.jp

Abstract. Women's Online Media (WOM) was the first WWW server set up in Japan exclusively by, for, and on women. In this paper the motivation for WOM's establishment, the efforts made since the Beijing Conference to ensure that WOM expands and receives social recognition, as well as the main interests by members of each mailing list, are discussed. Finally, the recent establishment of WOM of Women's Internetwork Shuttle (WIS), a limited company run by and for women, which disseminates computer and Internet-related know-how and technology, will be explained.

1 Introduction

A year and a half has passed since five members of Women's Online Media (WOM) established the first women exclusive WWW server in Japan. In the world of computerization, the technology of six months ago is said to be out-of-date, so a year and a half has brought a great change in the world of computerization. Japan has also undergone the same changes and growth in this field. Here we would like to reflect on WOM's experiences during this period and present the future prospects of Women's Internetwork Shuttle (WIS) which was started by several members of WOM.

2 History

2.1 The Establishment of WOM

WOM (Women's Online Media) was established in May 1995 under the Keio University Consortium VCOM Project. VCOM is the successor of InterVnet, a network which was developed as an information pool and networking tool for relief volunteers after the Hanshin Earthquake which hit Kobe in January 1995.[1] Four months after the earthquake, when the need for information in the Hanshin Area decreased and uploaded information became scarcer, some volunteers got together and used tools and the Internet connections donated at the time of the disaster by various companies and organizations to establish VCOM. VCOM is an NGO which provides virtual space for other NGOs to promote their activities over the Internet.

Under the auspices of the VCOM project, five Japanese women jointly established WOM and produced the first WWW home page for, by and about Japanese women, using these same Internet servers and computers. WOM later established the first women's server, as well.

2.2 The Motivation Behind WOM

Some of the founding members of WOM experienced sexual harassment in the original computer network to which they belonged. From this experience we realized that in order to create a comfortable atmosphere where all women can speak freely without being harrassed by men, it was necessary for us to create a women-only network of our own.

In addition there were six other motives for establishing WOM, as follows:

1) Concern about Issues Related to Japanese Women's Status The majority of our members are deeply concerned with the status of Japanese women, the rank of Japanese women's status compared to that of women of other developed countries[2], and the way the Equal Employment Opportunity Law has been applied in workplaces in Japan[3]. Many Japanese women are not aware of these issues. In order to inform Japanese women about such issues, we decided to establish our own alternative media where essential information on these topics could be accessed twenty-four hours a day. We can not rely on the mainstream media as it is often controlled by men, and because it often selects news from a male-biased point of view. For example, the short news broadcast which covered the disaster in Kobe from a male-biased perspective have been criticized[4]. Also, facts which are considered very important to women may be ignored by the mass media.

2) Networking and the Empowerment of Women via E-mail It is said that "Information is Power." Yayoi Taguchi participated in an international conference,

---

[1] VCOM's URL: http://www.suehiro.nakano.tokyo.jp/c-s/

[2] The status of Japanese women according to the UNGDI (Gender Development Indices) is 0.896, or 8th in the world. However, when Japan's GDI is subtracted from the HDI (Human Development Indeces) a negative balance is obtained, indicating a lower level of gender equality given over-all national human development. See Ryokichi Hirono et. al. eds. *Ningen kaihatsu repooto.* by UNDP. (*Human Development Report 1995*). Trans. UNDP (Tokyo [Japanese]: Kokon-shoin, 1996), p.86.

[3] The Equal Employment Opportunity Law was enacted in 1986 in Japan. However, it does not call for punishment for violations so it has been criticized internationally for its lack of effectiveness.

[4] Midori Suzuki, et.al., *TV Programs and the Hanshin Earthquake: Using the Approach of Media Literacy.* (Hayama [Japanese]: Kawamura-Insatsu, 1995)

called "Women, Information and the Future" sponsored by the Schlesinger Library and held at Radcliffe College in June, 1994[5]. She learned about the existence of a public list called WMST-Listserv (wmst-L@UMDD) organized by the Department of Women's Studies, University of Maryland.[6] From her experience in subscribing to the listserv she realized that a mailing list, when it is well organized and members participate constructively, is almost like having a vast top-class database. If you throw out a question or a problem, first class specialists in this particular field will answer you and you can, for example, assemble a bibliography for a university course within a week or so.

It will take time to build such a listserv in Japan, however, at least by sharing information, Japanese women will be able to support each other despite distance and other barriers.

3) Providing Access to Information Related to the Fourth World Conference on Women and the NGO Forum Gathering and disseminating information on what was happening at the Beijing Conference was the main motivation for establishing WOM's WWW server. Since Japanese is not an official UN language, it has been very difficult for Japanese women to learn about issues discussed at UN conferences and the concurrent NGO Forums. We did not know whether or not the opinions of NGOs were actually taken into account by governmental delegates. Nor did Japanese women know where to get this type of information. The need for this kind of information was attested to during the Beijing Conference, when the Yokohama Women's Association for Communication and Networking (YWACN) received many telephone and fax inquiries from all over Japan asking about ways to access WOM's home page and other news sources related to the Beijing Conference.

4) Interest in Women and Technology In Japan, traditionally, science and technology have been considered fields almost inaccessible to women. Since we insist on women-only membership in WOM, and the people who make our home pages and do maintenance are women, the very existence of our WWW site is a symbolic example of the fact that women are capable of acquiring technological skills and know-how. Computer skills are becoming essential in Japanese society. In fact home pages made by women are already no longer very rare these days in Japan. One of WOM's goals was to support women's empowerment in the area of high-technology. Women have limited access to this area, mainly because they lack the money to buy computers and because of the myth that women are not capable in the fields of science and technology.

[5] See Eva Steiner Mosely, ed., *Women, Information and the Future: Collecting and Sharing Resources Worldwide.* (Fort Atkinson: Highsmith, 1995)

[6] See Judith Hudson and Kathleen A. Turek, *Electronic Access to Research on Women: A Short Guide.* (Albany: Institute for Research on Women, 1994) p.7.

5) Providing Support for Women Interested in Networking and Communication via the Internet The percentage of female networkers is said to be around 10% in Japan. The number of women networkers in K-net in Kanagawa Prefecture is 14%. We hope to increase the number of women networkers so that the ratio of women and men in networking will be balanced in future. Accordingly, WOM tries to establish supportive relationships with women's centers and institutions all over Japan, such as the above mentioned YWACN in Yokohama, the National Women's Education Center in Saitama, Dawn Center in Osaka, and the Tokyo Women's Plaza. WOM members provide workshops and seminars for women in these organizations.

6) Dissemination of Information on Japanese Women to the World Japan has long been eager to receive information from the outside world. However, there is an imbalance between information received by Japan and that disseminated from Japan, mainly due to the language barrier. Therefore, WOM tries to improve the balance by providing information in English on Japanese women through our WWW server. However, despite our desire, this is the most difficult activity, because translation takes time and energy and not all the members are capable of doing it. The lack of adequate translation software further contributes to this problem. Japan is not alone in this regard, as people in many non-English speaking countries are currently facing difficult choices about language and internationalization.

In accordance with this initial goal, WOM helped YWACN – a women's NPO, subsidized by the City of Yokohama, at which one of WOM's members is employed – to launch a temporary WWW home page, in exchange for receiving information related to women worldwide via the Internet.

2.3 Three Members of WOM Help Out at the NGO Forum on Women's Communication Center

Three members of WOM, Ayako Shimatani, Junko Yoshimura and Yayoi Taguchi, joined the staff of the Communication Center of the NGO Forum Site in Huairou, China, organized by APC (Association for Progressive Communications)[7]. This was the first time Japanese women participated in the establishment of a Communication Center for a UN-related international conference.

As mentioned above previously, there had been some concern over the scarcity of information in Japanese from major UN conferences. From the Forum Communication Center, using our own computers equipped with Japanese word-processing software, we disseminated information, not only in English, but also in Japanese. With the cooperation of the Apple Computer Co., and the APC Communication Center, we succeeded in transmitting information in Japanese to a server standing by in Tokyo. The quantity of Japanese-language information disseminated during the Beijing

[7] APC has its headquarters in Rio de Janeiro, Brasil and a North American regional office in San Francisco. It represents more than 133 member and partner networks from more than 50 countries.

Conference was considered to be the highest of all recent UN-related international conferences[8].

2.4 WOM Attracts Media Attention

The fact that three Japanese women joined the APC Communication Center caught the attention of several major nation-wide newspapers, such as *Yomiuri*[9], *Asahi*[10], and *Nikkei*[11] as well as local newspapers in Tokyo[12]. Later on, feminist newspapers in Japan such as "*I*" started writing about WOM[13]. Then we received attention from a computer- and Internet-related magazine[14]. We also caught the attention of a TV producer after the Beijing Conference[15], and the Japan Broadcasting Company (NHK) also broadcasted WOM's activities all over the world via its English short-wave program[16].

In a way, we have been lucky, because the time that we set up our WWW site for women in Japan happened to coincide with the Beijing Conference, and also with a period of rapid expansion of the WWW in Japan. Our women-only WWW server was not only a very rare thing at that time, but our home page was said to have some of the best links for sites related to women in Japan, as well as internationally[17].

2.5 WOM Expands: Post-Beijing Changes

After the Beijing Conference our Steering Committee began discussing possibilities for WOM's future activities. As the number of members increased, the flow of e-mail also increased and it started to become a burden for each member to read all the e-mail received each day. In order to solve this problem, we created mailing lists according to the interests of our members. We also increased the number of Steering Committee members by adding the leaders of each of our mailing lists to the Steering Committee. These changes made our network more level, or less hierarchical, and more flexible in dealing with the needs of members.

---

[8] The number of e-mail account issued for Japanese women was 19, out of a total of 1129 according to the final statistics provided by APC Communication Center in Huairou, September 1995.

[9] "Using the Internet: Preparation towards World Conference on Women,"*Yomiuri*, [Japanese] July 3, 1995.

[10] "Women's Group Teaches Internet Technics" *Asahi Evening News*, September 11, 1995.

[11] "The High Seas of Media, Part II: Global Citizens Dance in the Free Zones" *Nikkei*, [Japanese] February 11, 1996.

[12] "Following-up the FWCW in Beijing: NGOs Work to Implement the Platform of Action." *Tokyo*, [Japanese] November 4, 1995, p.15.

[13] "Women's Information on the Internet: Information Dissemination to the World during Beijing Conference." *Women's Newspaper "I"*, [Japanese] February 25, 1996.

[14] "Women's Online Media: Working toward Electronic Media for Women," *Internet Magazine*. [Japanese] December 1995, p.208.

[15] "Multimedia Special: Multimedia and Women," dir. Ryoji Toba. Asahi Newstar Cable TV., Tokyo, [Japanese] Dec. 1, 1995.

[16] "Internet: Connecting Women of the World," dir. Noriaki Taira, NHK Radio Japan, March 2, 1996.

[17] WOM's URL:http://www.suehiro.nakano.tokyo.jp/WOM/

3 Membership

WOM's only membership qualifications are that applicants are women and approve of WOM's motives on our home page. We now number over sixty in all. However, at the time of a survey taken in January 1996, there were forty-seven members. The ages of members span from twenties to fifties, however, the majority of our members are in their late-twenties to late-thirties.

3.1 Occupations

The occupation of forty-five members who answered the questionnaire are indicated in the following table. Two members did not reply to the questionnaire.

Occupation	# (%)
system's related fields	17 (38%)
researchers at universities or institutions	12 (27%)
university graduates & undergraduates	9 (20%)
women's center staff	3 (7%)
publication company staff	1 (2%)
freelance journalist	1 (2%)
part-time worker	1 (2%)
full-time homemaker	1 (2%)
Total	45 (100%)

Table 1. Occupation of WOM Members

If we add the percentages of researchers (27%) and students (20%), the sum is 47%. From this table we can see that the members of WOM are primarily highly educated women.[18]

3.2 Areas of Interest

The areas of interest of WOM members are indicated in the following table.[19] Members were free to name any issue.

[18] The ratio of female students who enter four-year universities in Japan is 21%. See Prime Minister's Office. ed. *Current Situation and Policy for Women.* (Tokyo [Japanese]: Ministry of Finance Printing Bureau. 1995) p.65.

[19] According to Item 750, Paragraph 2, Chapter 2, Volume 4 of Japanese Civil Law, one party of a married couple must abandon his/her original family name at the time of marriage and be entered into the family register of his/her partner. In practice it is almost always the woman who has to change her name.

Areas of interest (Total 19)	#
women & work	17
childcare	6
sexuality	4
gender discrimination	4
WID	4
reproductive health	4
marriage registration	4
women & education	3
women & media	2
women's movement	2
prostitution in Asia	1
care of the elderly	1
sexual harassment	1
women & war	1
women & science	1
immigration of women	1
women's studies	1
single women's rights	1
women's ways of living	1

Table 2. Area of Interest of WOM Members

From this brief survey, we came to know that the interests of our members cover a variety of women's issues. However, the issue of working women seems to be the central focus, which is not surprising, given that all members except one are working women. Also, the recent media interest in the difficulties female university graduates face in trying to find jobs in recession-hit Japan, called the "super-glacial period," might also have had an influence.

4 Activities

In order to realize our goals, we have initiated the following activities:

1) Providing information on the WWW home page
2) Public education: Internet demonstrations, workshops and seminars
3) Discussions via mailing lists
4) Periodical advertisement via Netnews
5) Group work by the Steering Committee
6) Public relations using paper media and mass media

Below we provide a brief explanation of a few of these activities.

4.1 Discussions via Mailing Lists

enables us to communicate with each other and to share information from various fields. The use of mailing lists is thus a strategy to further women's networking and empowerment.

In the above section we introduced WMST Listserv as a powerful example of using e-mail for information sharing and dissemination among list subscribers. WOM's mailing lists perform an equivalent role. Here we would like to discuss some of the topics taken up in WOM'S various mailing lists. Because of limited space, we will just present four major mailing lists:

1) "wom-tech": Technical discussions on topics such as systems planning, authoring tools, hardware, and advise on the use of CGI are found in this mailing list. Technical advice on computers and using the Internet is also available from WOM's technicians. When a member has difficulty either sending or receiving messages, such as truncated letters, she can write to this mailing list for advice from our technicians.

During the "Networkers' Japan '96: Off-line Festival" held in Yokohama in August 1996, WOM and two other women's groups set up a booth. WOM designed a project "CU See-Me", which was a composite of multimedia – moving image and voice-based mutual transmission of information – by connecting three sites: WOM's Booth at the Yokohama Exhibition Hall, the "Kids' Room" for mothers participating in the festival, and the "WID Seminar Site" at the National Women's Education Center in Saitama. During the project's preparatory stage, questions such as what kind of free software can be retrieved from which ftp site, and which type of cables must be purchased in order to set up a "CU See-Me" station, were discussed here.

2) "wom-kids": This mailing list focuses on the problems of working mothers and on sharing information on child-rearing. The group received 380,000 yen (US$3,800.00) in funding from a YWACN fund which supports grassroots activities. With this funding the members of this mailing list made a home page listing of the day-care centers in the region. This page is highly appreciated by working mothers.

3) "wom-labor": This mailing list provides a space for sharing information about working, and providing support for fellow women networkers who have experienced sexual harassment in their workplaces. For example, recently a report on a sexual harassment court case was uploaded. It was a rather traditional example of such cases between a Member of Parliament and his secretary. It was pointed out in the mailing list that the way the defendant's lawyer tried to expose the scene of sexual harassment for the judge was another example of sexual harassment in itself.

4) "wom-marriage": Topics such as marriage, divorce, co-habitation and retaining one's last name after marriage are discussed here. Most of the participants of this mailing list, whether single or married, are working women who are interested in having a baby in the near future, or working mothers. Some discussants are working women wondering whether their career is compatible with married life and a family. However, none of the members are inclined to abandon their careers in favor of marriage. WOM members seem to give priority to achieving economic independence rather than marrying.

Other discussants describe their struggle with their mothers-in-law who hold traditional ideas about women and marriage and who insist that their daughters-in law abandon their work after marriage or when they give birth.

4.2 Group Work by the Steering Committee

WOM places importance on group work. Before the Steering Commitee makes any decisions, a proposal is placed in the mailing list for all members to see. All opinions are considered and the final decision is then made by the Steering Committee. This flexible way of decision-making is considered to be one of the reasons why WOM has been so well-publicized by the Japanese mass media and related women's organizations.

4.3 Public Relations via Paper Media and Mass Media

To disseminate information on our workshops and seminars, as well as provide technical consultation to individual women and women's organizations who do not have access to the Internet, we use paper media and mass media. The participants of WOM's free workshops receive a manual for easy access to e-mail and the Internet.

Since women are a minority in networking and computer technology and WOM's novel activities have attracted favorable attention from various media in Japan, we are becoming better known to the public as a reliable alternative media source exclusively for women.

5 Heading toward the Future: Refining the Goals of WOM and Establishing Women's Internetwork Shuttle (WIS)

After having conducted various activities, some Steering Committee members came to realize the limitations of being a voluntary organization. WIS was established in response to these problems, which are outlined below.

5.1 Problems with Japanese Legislation

Japanese legislation does not allow non-commercial voluntary organizations to be juridical persons, because of the lack of recognition of the important roles such organizations play. For this reason, no voluntary organizations can register as a legal body, nor can they legally have their own resources under the organization's name, rent offices under their name, borrow money from the bank, or undertake any commercial activities, whatsoever.

In order to continue our volunteer activities we needed money. For example, it costs a lot of money to set up a LAN in places where there are no computers nor Ethernet equipment. Transport is very expensive in Japan. And the burden of paying these fees fell to those members who were working most actively in WOM. Worse yet, Japanese legislation does not even allow individuals to make tax deductions for such charitable donations.

We came to realize that there are many services which you cannot afford to provide for free. If WOM remained unable to accept money as an organization, or to issue an invoice or a receipt for money received from outside organizations, our future prospects would be grim. WOM is currently using the resources of the VCOM·project. However, we cannot rely on donations from outside companies forever. The Internet connections are offered to VCOM by several companies but only for a limited period of time. Accordingly, each project under VCOM auspices is expected to be economically independent within few years. WOM's desperate need for economic independence and social recognition could not be met as long as WOM remained a volunteer organization under current Japanese law.

That means that in order to carry out the goal of becoming economically independent, we had to establish a limited company. Thus, we will be able to avoid having to do so much skilled work for no money. Earning some necessary money in WIS and doing a volunteer work in WOM, WIS and WOM will work like two wheels of the same cart. This is the main reason we set up WIS as a limited company.

5.2 Launching WIS

In September 1996 eight women from WOM collected 8 million yen (US$80,000.00). In order to set up a limited company, Junko Yoshimura assumed the Presidency and two other members of WOM became Director Generals. WIS has finally gained legal status.[20]

5.3 Future Plans

Services which were originally provided by WOM free-of-charge, will now be provided by WIS at reasonable fees. In other words, WIS will provide technical support services in order to promote the use of the Internet and computers among women. We will also make computer repairs. WIS members will thus be empowered economically and technically by doing their work.

In the near future WIS plans to gather old computers and donate them to welfare institutions, especially for the use of children who are hospitalized for long periods. Old computers have yet to be donated to charitable causes in Japan.

WIS also plans to upload a database of women resource persons in our home page, in order to let people know which female engineers can do what.

Incorporation has enabled us to expand. However, we view the establishment of a company as a transitional process. When the Japanese Parliament finally passes the pending law which will allow voluntary organizations to have legal status, WIS hopes to become a non-profit organization, where all investors will have equal status, and staff will be paid.

After establishing WIS, a limited liability company, we are now redefining WOM's goals using Peter Drucker's *Self-Assessment Tool for Nonprofit Organizations*.[21]

6 Conclusion

The Beijing Platform of Action addresses twelve cirtical areas of concern regarding women's status.[22](22) "Women and Media" is one of the critical areas of concern. In

---

[20] WIS's URL: http://www.iijnet.or.jp/wis/junko/

[21] Yayoi Tanaka. trans. *Hieirisoshikino jiko-hyouka shuhou.* by Peter Drucker. (*The Drucker Foundation Self-Assessment Tool for Non-profit Organizations*). (Tokyo: [Japanese] Diamond-sha, 1995), pp.58-119.

Japan WOM, as an alternative media for women, will be a powerful tool in advancing women's status and gender equality. We would like to use this tool not only for networking and information dissemination but also for changing the attitude of our government, and changing our unequal society and the world.

Other Resources

1. Kole, Ellen. The Benefits of Electronic Networking for Women: The Case of the *Fourth UN-World Conference on Women, Beijing 1995.* Amsterdam: University of Amsterdam, 1996.

I would like to express my hearty thankfulness to Debbie Lunny for proofreading.

[22] United Nations. *Beijing Declaration and Platform of Action 1995*. (Beijing: UN/DPCSD. 1995) p.116.

What You See is What You Get: Cyberchix and Virtual Systers

Susan Myburgh

University of South Australia, St Bernard's Road, Magill SA 5072Adelaide, Australia

Abstract. The metadiscourse of the Internet phenomenon could reveal as gendered a culture as the real world that created it, which would impede its use by women. However, the Internet is seen to have assumed a life of its own. It is being claimed as a territory uniquely useful for women, providing new opportunities. Women are boldly defining new personas and cultures in Cyberspace.

1 Introduction

Technology is often regarded as being remote or hostile to women. The Net is a unique, complex technology that acts and has meaning beyond the intentions of its creators. It should be the epitome of a rationalist, empiricist, scientific mode of thought. Instead, it is like a bastard, enjoying an existential freedom that scorns its heritage. This fractured identity creates new opportunities for women.

In Cyberspace, everything is digitised, reduced to bits that are on or off. To the computer, the meaning of these bits is irrelevant, and they make meaning for us only when reassembled. Filtered through the matrix, all reality becomes patterns of information. We become information. One's being is machine mediated. There is no body, and there is a lack of engagement of all the senses.

2 Representation

Women commonly assume a range of roles and, for them, realities are multiple and simultaneous. Women therefore are easily able create new identities, to deconstruct and reconstruct personalities in cyberspace. As information agents, women appear to be as confident, capable, articulate, assertive and knowledgable as any men on the Net. (Myburgh: 1994).

There are discussion groups, Web pages and MU's where women assume the characteristics of new persona – Cyberchix, or Wolves, or Systers. The binary acceptance of gender clearly does not exploit the full range of opportunities with which we are already familiar, and which are possible on the Net. Social and biological roles do not always intersect. This is demonstrated in these communities. Haraway (1991) has a different, equally powerful, view. She claims that through the use of technology, a women (in the guise of a cyborg - part person, part mechanism) can escape the oppressive boundaries imposed by both society and technology. The cyborg, though, is not a representation of a woman. It encapsulates the satisfactory, successful merging of machine and person, creating a new social force.

3 Conclusion

Cyberculture is still in the process of emerging. We can go with the flow of technological determinism, and later lick our wounds and call ourselves victims; or we can act, and using the power of semiotics and linguistics, and construct a new amenable society, either through joining forces with the new technology, or through exploiting its capbilities.

References

1. Haraway, Donna. (1991). Simians, Cyborgs and Women: The Reinvention of Nature. London: Free Association.
2. Myburgh, Sue. (1994) "Women on the Internet: Female Participation in Discussion Groups". In: Women and computing: proceedings on a one-day conference held by the Centre for Gender Studies, April 1994. Adelaide: University of South Australia.

Accepted Papers and Discussion Notes

Topic 2: Creating Models and Tools

The Moral Order of an Information System

Sarah Willis

Department of Computation, UMIST
Manchester M60 1QD

Abstract. This paper discusses how it is possible to 'see' gender relations in the organisation of information systems. It analyses how gender relations are constituted within the discursive space of a clinical information system currently under development. The paper illustrates how concepts from the sociology of technology (3, 4, 6, 7, 8, 20, 21, 22, 26, 32) can be used to research the distribution of gender relations inscribed in an information system. It explores how the development of a technology effects a series of 'translations' or 'transformations' (6, 20) - and then attempts to sanction these translations or transformations. I focus on three of them - the construction of information as a conceptual key, the management of information, and the organisation of reasoning through information - and suggest how they strive to constitute a 'world order' (32). The paper is concerned with the way a 'world order' represents an historical interpretation of medicine and information which is founded on a rationalist philosophy that excludes alternative ways of knowing (1, 2, 25).

1 Introduction

This paper argues that gender relations are constituted within the discursive space of a clinical information system. The aim of the paper is therefore to explore how computerised information systems are organised by and inscribed with (gendered) relations. The kinds of questions that I am trying to address do not ask if it's possible to have a (or some) feminist theory of information systems. Rather, I am concerned with how concepts such as 'rationality', 'information', 'medicine' etc. are played out in the context of an information system and how these ideas may be used in both contingent and specific ways (29). In addition to researching how some concepts are made present in a context (and in textual representations of that context) I am also interested in those concepts which may be left out of accounts of the activities describing the development of an information system. It is through an analysis of the absence or presence of concepts that it is possible to see how both the content and context of an information system incorporate and sanction particular representations, or discursive accounts, of the system. Thus inscriptions - and especially textual inscriptions - enfranchise (or make present) some things, and disenfranchise others (by absenting them from accounts) (6). Enfranchisement works to organise a boundary between inside and outside, and is a necessary strategy in the (hopeful) constitution of a stable, effective technology. Enfranchisement is therefore a procedure which strives to manage exclusion and inclusion, and can be considered as contributing to the constitution of a project or world.

2 The Empirical Focus

In what follows I illustrate my arguments with examples from an empirical study of a clinical information system that is currently under development. The study was undertaken as part of my PhD research. My study focused on one partner in an international project which I shall call Hippocrates, after the ancient Greek philosopher-physician. The partner was located at a university in the North West of England, and it acted as the co-ordinator of the project which actually involved around a dozen European collaborators.

The expressed aim of Hippocrates is to provide terminological services 'which will allow clinical information to be captured, represented, manipulated and displayed in a radically more powerful way'. Web pages about Hippocrates viewed in February 1994 suggest that this radicalism can be achieved by employing a particular methodological approach to representing medical information. It is an approach which assumes that 'there is a terminological - or more properly, a conceptual - component of clinical language which can be usefully separated from other aspects of medical natural language processing, information modelling, Knowledge-Based systems, and user interface design...[Hippocrates] contends that this conceptual component can be made largely independent of surface natural language characteristics'.

In this paper I examine how Hippocrates' approach to developing clinical information systems creates a particular 'presence' (3) for the system. I consider the creation of a presence to constitute an act of enfranchisement, a marking of a boundary to and for the system. Creating a presence also institutes a particular way of knowing the project. As the above quotation suggests, Hippocrates' methodological approach to knowledge representation is framed in terms of a distinction between terminological medical information (referred to as 'concepts') and other, less important, types of medical information which rely on natural language expressions to have meaning. Thus we are introduced to Hippocrates as a system which sets out to solve particular problems, and from this introduction we come to know a particular presence of version of what Hippocrates is. The next section introduces some general issues related to researching the presence of an information system.

3 Some Research Questions

The initial problem that this paper addresses is how it is possible to research and describe something which, on first reading, may appear absent, disenfranchised, or unspoken (and hence irrelevant or unspeakable). If there are no obvious instances of gender relations in a research situation then does this mean that feminist sociological research is, at best, inappropriate, and may in fact prove impossible? Or does it mean that feminist sociological research is limited to commenting on the absence of women working in technologically-defined employment? With such an interpretative framework in mind, and applying it to my empirical study, an analysis of the gender division of labour would produce the (perhaps unstartling) observation that there was only one female member of staff based at the local Hippocrates site. And since I believe that it is methodologically and analytically unacceptable to move from the experiences of a single woman to making generalised claims about the relationship between women and information sytems, I would picture an extremely constrained research report emerging .

Given the under-representation of women in my case study, what research strategy is best suited for an exploration of the ways that gender is constituted in relation to a clinical information system? I see a workable solution if gender is imagined to be some thing, or set of relations, or condition that makes it possible for that particular system to be developed (19). While gender can be considered as some thing that makes a system possible, it is also a political consequence of the socio-technical world in which the system is developed. The purpose of my research is therefore to discover these conditions and consequences. Thus my engagement with the absence and presence of gender relations is not simply with whether they are the consequence of a sexist or non-sexist context of development of an information system. And my concern is not simply with whether gender relations pre-exist the development and are therefore 'built into' a system as a condition of its development. Rather, applying the concept of absence as theorised by Mannheim (27)- as 'not only the absence of certain points of view, but also the absence of a definite drive to come to grips with certain life-problems' (27: 246) - I understand that an absence or presence can operate in more that one way: as *both* a condition ('the absence of certain points of view') and a consequence ('the absence of a definite drive to come to grips with certain life-problems') of that context (K & M).

But if absence and presence are created as both a condition and a consequence of a technology then it may prove difficult to decide just how or where the ordering of absence and presence takes place. For example, as I suggest in in a later section, conventional descriptions of systems legitimate and sanction the goals and activities of a project. Textual practices, work as 'framing devices' (3) priviledging particular visions and versions of a world or project. The vision or version which I concentrate on in this paper authorises a reading of the information system which acts to suppress debate about how information could be otherwise configured (that is, defined, enabled and constrained (32)), thus working as a condition of the system, and consolidating one particular world view and making alternatives to it unthinkable or unspeakable, and hence working as a consequence of the system.

Of course, there may be ways of detecting the presence of an absence. These are instances when the privileged version of the project is questioned or undermined: they are instances where the absence of certain points of view is acknowledged but unchallenged. Such moments can be understood as representing dis-ease or insecurity in relation to the legitimate version of the project, and they may suggest a failure of knowing how to act in relation to the political project they are configured within (19). Or perhaps they are times when the actors are attempting to move outside the bounded, constrained configurations of a project in order to discount or deny the politics present in an account of the organisation . During my field work, those working on Hippocrates knew that one of the expressed aims of my research was to investigate relations between gender and information systems. A software designer asked me about my role as participant observer. "What do you write in your notebook?" he enquired. I answered that I tried to report conversations, activities and practices taking place at the meeting we were attending. He laughed and said "I bet you write comments like 'fat misogynist in the corner is trying to dominate the debate'". Of course, I denied this. (In fact, I had been transcribing an exchange between two project workers where they were arguing about the relative merits of modelling methodologies.) This example is a very rare instance of someone raising what they considered to be a gender issue for my benefit. Upon reflection I considered it an attempt to flag to me, as a researcher, that he knew that the practices of developing an information system are gendered and political.

Yet as I have just commented, such self-consciously political statements scarcely ever occurred. As disruptions or contradictions of the conventional narrative (where information systems development is described as a rational, politically neutral practice) they present problems for a researcher trying to construct a coherent account of the organisation of a clinical information system. In order to try to situate such glimpses of engendering, I shall now (briefly) turn to consider how other feminists have accounted for the presence of gender in relationships with technologies.

4 Some Questions for Feminism

Recent feminist constructivist studies of technology have been concerned with addressing issues of how gender relations are enrolled within what they describe as 'technology-relations'(10, 11, 12, 31). The hyphen implies that technology can only be understood *in relation* to other things. For example, Cynthia Cockburn (10, 11) has examined how technologies are socially and historically constructed in relation to masculinity; Wajcman (31: 22; 17) has argued that 'technologies bear the imprint of the people and social context in which they develop' and as such embody 'patriarchal values' positioning them as essential to the construction of masculine identity. Technologies therefore act to mark out the boundary of masculinity in relation to femininity. Thus an absence of women from the context of the development and use of technology is theorised as being managed by the exclusive relations of a masculine culture of technology. For instance, Wajcman suggests that technical competence can be seen as performing masculinity: she states that 'it is evident that men identify with technology and through their identification with technology form bonds with one another' (31: 141). In contrast to this co-construction of masculinity and technological ability, she asserts that a lack of technical know-how 'does indeed become part of feminine identity' (31:155).

The problem with accounts describing technology as constitutive of gendered identities (and vice versa) is that they tend to produce arguments that detail how technology functions in the social construction of a gendered identity; or how gendered identities function to construct relationships with technologies, but they are unable to address how that ordering is constituted (16). Instead, functionalist arguments are limited to describing the interests of masculinity as if these interests are able to act outside of, and independent to, the relationships in which they occur. Feminist constructivist accounts fail to account for how technologies may take on different roles: and they fail to 'see' how gender is translated and transformed as the conditions and consequences of the organisation of an information system. What happens in these accounts is that the technology seems to become a tool for analysing a type of engendered interrelationships, activities and practices, a tool for satisfying the agenda of the research in its description and deconstruction of the instruments of patriarchy.

Feminist constructivist accounts assume that gender-technology relations are present in interactions between subjects who are already constituted by their gender and objects which have already been defined as technological. Subjects and objects are therefore theorised as pre-determined to perform according to pre-scripted gender and technical roles. In contradistinction to these feminist constructivist theories of technology, I understand gender and technology relations as something to do with the 'moral' (32) practices of ordering. I shall now turn to expand on this concept of a 'moral' order.

5 Some Questions of Order

In a previous section I introduced the idea that accounts of any entity are committed to particular visions, world views or orderings. I suggested that accounts are replete with assumptions about the potentiality and boundedness of an entity, and with assumptions about the relationship of that entity to other entities (32). After Woolgar (32), and Bloomfield and Vurdubakis (3, 4), I consider accounts to represent ordering practices: that is, to be methods for arranging (and managing arrangements of) a world. Hence it is possible to read inscribed relations of power and knowledge in accounts and in representations in general (3). This paper is moving towards such an analysis of Hippocrates' texts. But before I begin, I shall expand on the politics of order.

In other words, accounts are inscribed with a particular version of power and knowledge that can be considered as a particular 'moral order' (32). By moral order I am referring to a concept of 'a world view which embodies notions about the character and capacity of different entities, the relationship between them, their relative boundedness, and the associated patterns of rights and responsibilities. Linking all these are sanctioned procedures for representation' (22:66). The practices of representing, in other words, are sanctioned procedures that incorporate assumptions about how things may be put together, combined and (re)ordered. By using the word 'moral' to describe ordering practices I hope to convey the sense of an activity that makes distinctions and marks boundaries: I am not using the notion of morality to simply imply a prescriptive code of practice that acts to determine what is right from what is wrong. But I do imagine a 'moral order' as a method for regulating inclusion and exclusion, and in this sense, a 'moral' order suggests that representation, or enfranchisement, acts to sanction or support what it includes.

Describing an information system in terms of its moral order entails an analysis of how that system attempts to 'institute particular versions of the organisation, its members, and their activities' (3), creating a 'presence' for a group of facts, that can then be inscribed as known, relevant and significant to the members of the organisation. In what follows I question how representational practices attempt to manage presence and absence, creating discursive space for those things inscribed as relevant, necessary, conventional or standard. I consider how an information system acts as a 'framing device...(as a) means of inclusion and exclusion' (3) which attempts to make a world that is ordered, orderly and stable. I consider the politics of an information system as a set of sanctioning practices that are concerned with order, with what can be represented, how, and by whom (3).

It is my contention that the moral order of information systems is gendered, and that there is an inscribed presence for masculine rationality. I suggest that the interrelationship of absence and presence is discursively constituted through the grounding of information systems in rationalist, foundationalist philosophy. This interpretation of the world makes several critical assumptions about how it is possible to order and organise an information system. In addition, this interpretation makes assumptions about the *best* way to order and organise an information system, and can therefore be seen to make moral judgements about the world and the project.

The most important boundary that Hippocrates marks is between rationality and irrationality. In making distinctions between conceptual and other types of medical information, Hippocrates differentiates between 'real' medical knowledge (ie, that which can be separated from the body and represented formally in an information system as unviersally accepted facts about the clinical world) and general medical information which relies on context (and hence is not always real or true). That which can be represented - the conceptual, rational component of medicine - is privileged, and other types of knowledge are hidden because they go unrepresented (1, 2). Legitimate medical knowledge becomes that which is included within Hippocrates' representation formalism, and as such a presence is created for rationality. In the same move, an absence is created for anything which fails to conform to the discipline of the formalism.

In my discussion, I concentrate on the language deployed to constitute rationality as politically neutral, as a necessary condition of a clincial information system. The same accounts also describe a rational approach as morally constituting the best way to develop a system. I trace this constitution through the following constructions: information as the key to effective and efficient health care; the management of information; the organisation of reasoning through information. I analyse how these concepts have a logical, directional order that moves the discursive space from the particular (or the empirical), to the general (the theoretical or philosophical). Through these moves the individual information system can be seen to anchor itself in an external reality. And it is in these moves that a space is created through which the information system may be known.

5.1 Information is the Key to Providing Effective and Efficient Health Care

This is the opening statement of a document written in support of Hippocrates. It occurs within a funding application made to the European Union. It represents the first stage in constituting the discursive space for the Hippocrates project. It is a move to build a world, to privilege a particular view of that world. It constitutes a 'framing device' (3, 4), that works to join up a role for information with the provision of health care. But because it is written with a particular audience in mind, the text is also framed by the assumptions of the authors who are attempting to enrol the reader (in this case, the EU) into their way of thinking about health care provision. In making an appeal to the concepts of economy and efficiency, together with a reference to the emotional need for health care, the statement is trying to position a particular interpretation of the best way to service the demands for health care.

Hence the framing device brings together an interpretation of the concept of information with a vision of organising health care. This interpretation of information is inscribed in an 'investment of form' (8), where heterogeneous entities (information) and events (health care provision) are made more controllable - more homogeneous - so that they form 'a simplified but workable representation'. Investments in form constitute a kind of narrative shorthand, where many things are being translated and represented by a single term, such as 'information', 'efficiency' 'health care'. Investments in form do a lot of work, a lot of translating: they 'enframe' (3) or make visible the concept of information in relation to the problem of health care, and they make invisible the moves that have been made to translate information and health care so that they can appear in the same discursive space.

The definition or position of information as 'key' is a further investment in form which imagines information as having an objective, economic value (I discuss this more fully in the context of the second move of the transformation, that of 'the management of information'). The role for information in health care can therefore be seen as an 'obligatory point of passage' (7) or a necessary detail in the constitution of the Hippocrates project. But it has to be a particular construction of the role of 'information' in health care to distinguish Hippocrates' appeal for funding from others. This is acheived by describing Hippocrates' methodological approach to information systems development as representing a 'paradigm shift'.

Thus the account, as part of the system of representational practices, is attempting to perform the work of constituting, or enacting, Hippocrates. The quotations from both the Hippocrates proposal and the web pages strive to enact how Hippocrates, as a network, is conceptualised, understood, and represented. It's a way of trying to bring together - in some sort of stable form - what the facts of Hippocrates are, and how Hippocrates is a problem that is 'do-able' (15). The script works to articulate Hippocrates as recognised, established, and - critically - necessary to medical informatics actors.

Low and Woolgar suggest that 'the constitutive (technical) repertoire is not merely a disengaged set of words and descriptions for application to a state of affairs (actions, behaviour and so on). Rather... its usage is constitutive in the more profound sense of performing community' (26:38). Thus the constitutive attempts to have effects across time and space, to perform a community at a distance. As discursive devices, constitutive repertoires work to make something transportable that can translate interests and facilitate interaction (22). They must be able to work at a distance, because when something leaves the physical space of the local environment it is less controllable. In this sense, a local community strives to inscribe the constitutive with the quality of 'immutable mobility' (21). Immutable mobiles act to stabilise things, theories, other actors etc. Clarke and Fujimura (9:12) describe immutable mobiles as 'things that can travel without withering away (are mobile), that do not fundamentally alter on the trip (are immutable), that can be provided to and interpreted by others (are presentable and readable), and that can be linked to other things (are combinable)'. Thus it is possible to think of the proposal for Hippocrates project as acting as an attempt to inscribe a particular information system with the qualities of immutable mobility.

The successful writing of constitutive accounts requires representations to be highly managed or constrained: and in the constraining it is hoped that alternative readings or interpretations of the text can not be made. The successful writing of accounts therefore requires that textual inscriptions manage the concepts they mobilise. This is achieved through the next necessary detail of the information system's discursive space.

5.2 The Management of Information

Information needs to be managed. As I detailed above, Hippocrates has a particular methodological approach to the management of information. For example, as I described in section 5.2, to position information as the 'key' to a project takes a lot of work (it requires investments in form, the configuration of necessary details etc). But if Hippocrates' attempt to configure a script or role for information is accepted, then the concept of information can be performed as fundamental to the project. Thus if information is managed successfully, it can operate as the solution to the problem of efficient health care provision.

But information can take on other roles, too, within the project, including the following: information can operate as a unit that has a function; information can be mobile; and information can be made visible in representations (3: 11). I shall expand on each of these roles, starting with how information can operate as a functional unit. If information is to be an object, to be a unit that has a function, then it has to have an objective. If information is to have an objective, then it needs to be ascribed with the role of solving an information problem. Thus an information system can take on the objective of filling information gaps, and can operate as the solution to an information problem. This also enrols information as a thing which can solve the problem of users who have information needs (so that information needs can be managed as well). Thus the concept of information is constituted as addressing problems of content and context within one discursive move. It is this move that Bowker (5) describes as 'information mythology'.

Turning to the other ways that information is managed, it's possible to think of information as having an objective character, and as such information can be a thing that has economic - and hence exchange - value. If the content of information can be objective - can be characterised as an unambiguous, context-independent 'fact about the world' - then this information can be shared with others without losing its factual status, without the danger of those facts being polluted. Furthermore, if the content of information has an exchange value it follows that it can be commodified and can travel across time and space (that is, it can take on form of immutable mobility).

The practices of information mythologising therefore work to manage the discursive mobilisation of the concept of information. It is a theoretical interpretation and mobilisation of information: it marks another necessary detail in my journey to trace the moves from a particular project - Hippocrates - to the gendered philosophical grounding of information systems.

5.3 The Organisation of Reasoning Through Information

If information is disciplined - if it conforms to the practices of its ordering - then the concept of information can take on epistemological weight. Information can become the key for translating abstract knowledge into an object, or code, that can then be processed computationally. All knowledge can then be translated into information that is codifiable (and code can be translated back to knowledge), so that knowledge can transcend a context and become universally true.

This organisation of reasoning is a philosophical interpretation of the moral order for an information systems world. Hippocrates is therefore a system which has an inscribed way of knowing the world. It describes the organisation of this system for knowing in the following account: 'reality appears as concrete objects... or as abstract objects' which are stored as 'items of information that are characteristic of such objects. These items of information reflect the properties of objects. When we think about a particular object, concrete or abstract, we use these properties to form... constructs called concepts.' Concepts can be named, defined, and classified 'according to essential characteristics', and 'systems of concepts' can be 'built up' from these characteristics (Hippocrates' Concept Analysis page 21).

Through the moves described above, Hippocrates imagines a world that is organised and rational: it is a world that is constituted through a particular interpretation of the concept of information, and it is a world that imagines that knowledge can be represented as systems of concepts, which are themselves systems of items of information. This kind of interpretation of epistemology suggests that how knowledge is made is unimportant, and that who makes the knowledge is not relevant to the end product: it suggests that knowledge is a thing which can be added to in order to gain a more complete and more true and accurate representation of the world 'out there'. Yet as I suggested in section 5.2, reasoning, or rationality, are political interpretations which make absent the role of power in relation to knowledge. While the moral order of the system inscribes a concept of rationality as being outside of politics, it simultaneously works to deny the politics of its own constitution. It has been my aim in this paper to write the politics of this moral order back into my account of the development of a clinical information system.

6 Conclusion

This paper has addressed how discursive practices constitute a clinical information system as an object. It has discussed how those practices can be seen as incorporating a rationalist vision of the world. I have asked 'What lies behind this vision?', 'How does this vision manage absence and presence?', and, above all, 'What does this vision make absent and present?'. I have suggested that discursive practices work to manage gender relations, creating absence and presence as both a condition and a consequence of the development of a clinical information system. My conclusion illustrates how information systems are necessarily social and political phenomena (19). I have argued that this approach is able to understand how inscribing an absence of gender relations in accounts of information systems as 'rational','value free', or 'gender neutral' is a political strategy that makes it possible for political discourses to deny or manage their politicality (19).

References

1. Adam :Artifical Knowing: Gender and the Thinking Machine. London: Routledge (1997) (forthcoming)
2. P. Addelson Moral Passages: Toward a Collectivist Moral Theory. London: Routledge (1994)
3. P. Bloomfield& T. Vurdubakis: 'Visions of Organization and Organizations of Vision: the Representational Practices of Information Systems Development' paper presented at the EIASM Workshop on Writing, Rationality & Organisation: Brussels (1994)
4. P. Bloomfield & T. Vurdubakis: 'Paper Traces: Inscribing Organisations and IT' (1997) (forthcoming)
5. Bowker: 'Information Mythology: the World Of/As Information' in L. Bud-Frierman (ed.) Information Acumen: The Understanding and Use of Knowledge in Modern Business. London: Routledge (1994)
6. Callon: 'Some Elements of a Sociology of Translation: Domestication of the Scallops and Fishermen of St. Brieuc Bay' in J. Law (ed) Power, Action and Belief: ANew Sociology of Knowledge?. London: Routledge and Kegan Paul (1986a)
7. Callon, J. Law& A. Rip (eds.): Glossary to Mapping the Dynamics of Science and Technology: Sociology of Science in the Real World. Basingstoke: Macmillan Press (1986b)
8. Callon & J. Law: 'On the Construction of Sociotechnical Networks: Content and Context Revisited' Knowledge and Society: Studies in the Sociology of Science Past and Present 8 (1989)
9. E. Clarke & J. H. Fujimura, J. H. (eds.): The Right Tools for the Job: at Work in Twentieth Century Life Sciences. Princeton: Princeton University Press (1992)
10. Cockburn: Machinery of Dominance: Women, Men and Technical Know-How. London: Pluto Press (1985)
11. Cockburn:'Feminism/Constructivism in Technology Studies: Notes On Genealogy and recent Developments' CRICT Workshop on: European Perspectives on New Technology: Feminism, Constructivism and Utility, Brunel (1993)
12. Cockburn & R. Fürst Dilic (eds.): Bringing Technology Home: Gender and Technology in a Changing Europe. Buckingham: Open University Press (1994)
13. Cooper, C.Hine, J. Low, S. Woolgar:'Ethnography and Human Computer Interaction'. CRICT Discussion Paper No. 39, Brunel (1993)
14. Flax: 'Postmodernism and Gender Relations in Feminist Theory'. Signs 12 (1987)
15. H. Fujimura: 'Constructing Do-able Problems in Cancer Research: Where Social Worlds Meet'. Social Studies of Science 17: 257-93 (1987)
16. Gill:'Beyond Technological Determinism and Social Determinism: Theorising Gender-Technology Relations'. CRICT Discussion Paper No. 49: Brunel (1994)
17. Grint & R. Gill(eds.): The Gender-Technology Relation: Contemporary Research and Theory. London: Taylor & Francis (1995)

18. Knights: 'Technology, Knowledge and Masculinity'. Paper presented at the Rethymnon Seminar on Technology and Knowledge: Philosophical and Sociological Explorations (1996)
19. Knights & F. Murray: Managers Divided: Organisation Politics and Information Technology Management. Chichester: John Wiley & Sons (1994)
20. Law: 'Notes on the Theory of the Actor-Network: Ordering, Strategy, and Heterogeneity'. Systems Practice 5:4 (1992)
21. Latour: 'Visualisation and Cognition: Thinking With Eyes and Hands'. Knowledge and Society 6 (1986)
22. Latour: Science in Action. Milton Keynes: Open University Press (1987)23. B. Latour: 'Pragmatagonies: A Mythical Account of How Humans and Nonhumans Swap Properties'. American Behavioural Scientist 37:6 (1994)
23. Lennon: 'Gender and knowledge'. Journal of Gender Studies 4:2 (1995)
24. Lloyd: The Man of Reason: 'Male' and 'Female' in Western Philosophy. Minneapolis: University of Minneapolis Press (1984)
25. Low & S. Woolgar: 'Managing the Socio-Technical Divide: Some Aspects of the Discursive Structure of Information Systems Development' in P. Quintas (ed.) Social Dimensions of Systems Engineering: People, Processes, Policies and Software Development. Hemel Hempstead: Ellis Horwood (1993)
26. Mannheim: Ideology and Utopia: an Introduction to the Sociology of Knowledge. London: Routledge and Kegan Paul (1936)
27. Murray: 'A Separate Reality: Science, Technology, and Masculinity' in E. Green, J. Owen & D. Pain (eds.) Gendered By Design? Information Technology and Office Systems. London: Taylor & Francis (1993)
28. Ormrod: 'Feminist Sociology and Methodology: Leaky Black Boxes in Gender/Technology Relations' in G. Grint & R. Gill (eds.) op cit. (1995)
29. L. Star: "The Structure of Ill-Structured Solutions: Boundary Objects and Heterogeneous Distributed Problem Solving' in L. Gasser & M. N. Huhns (eds.) Distributed Artificial Intelligence Volume 2. London: Pitman (1989)
30. Wajcman: Feminism Confronts Technology. London: Polity Press (1991)
31. Woolgar: 'Configuring the User: the Case of Usability Trials' in J. Law (ed.) A Sociology of Monsters: Essays on Power, Technology, and Domination. London: Routledge (1991)

Sometimes Texts Speak Louder Than Users: Locating Invisible Work Through Textual Analysis

Ellen Balka

Associate Professor, School of Communication, Simon Fraser University, Canada

Abstract. In recent years, interest in identifying invisible work has increased within computing communities because of its relevance in the design of computer systems. Here I discuss the nature of invisible work, whether feminist organizational strategies contribute to the invisibility of women's work, and the use of textual analysis to identify organizational fissures that are bridged through invisible work. These issues are addressed through a personal reflection about the development of an administrative computer system for a university that failed to meet the needs of the university's women's studies program.

1 Introduction

Interest in identifying invisible work and making it visible so it can be accounted for in computer system design has grown in the last few years (Schmidt and Bannon, 1992; Suchman, 1994 and 1995; Star & Ruhleder 1996). In particular, articulation work "that gets things back 'on track' in the face of the unexpected, that modifies action to accommodate unanticipated contingencies" (Star p.84, 1991) has received considerable attention. Because articulation work is invisible to rationalized models of work (Star, 1991) it is often not accounted for in computer system design. The failure to account for this invisible work in system development can lead to system failure. In addition, because a great deal of articulation work is performed by women, failures to account for articulation work in computer system design also contribute to the invisibility of women's contributions to work (Star, 1991; Suchman, 1994; Wagner, 1994). Suchman (1994) has suggested that focusing on articulation work could provide the basis for an approach to system design that is consistent with feminist analyses.

In this paper I focus on invisible work through an example of a system design that failed to account for work performed by women workers. One consequence of this failure was an increase in the amount of articulation work and workarounds performed by women workers in their efforts to perform their jobs. Using as an example the development of a university administrative computing system that failed to acknowledge the non-standard work involved in supporting the university's women's studies program, I pursue questions posed by Star and Ruhleder (1996, p.112): "what is the relationship between large scale infrastructure and organizational change? Who (or what) is changer, and who is changed?" Through the example of a failed system design I explore the nature of invisible work, the process of system development, and the connections between invisible work and the exercise of power along gender lines.

Using this failed system design as an example, I suggest that Smith's (1990) approach to documentary analysis and an analysis of organizational materials as 'active texts' may give "voice to the traditionally invisible (Markussen, 1995 p. 173). Markussen suggests that giving voice to groups that have traditionally been invisible "requires a purposeful effort to understand work practices, currently not articulated within the dominant understanding."

2 The Development of an Administrative Computer System

2.1 Context and Background

Until recently, I was a faculty member in women's studies at a Canadian University. For two years (from 1991-1993) I ran (or 'coordinated') the university's women's studies program. The women's studies program is an interdisciplinary program of study, defined in the university calendar as a series of courses which, when completed, qualify a student for a degree. Students at the undergraduate level are able to pursue a minor in women's studies by taking a combination of specified classes offered by twelve departments from three different schools or faculties. Beginning in 1993, students could earn a master's degree in women's studies, which also involved combining course offerings in a number of departments and offered the possibility of taking classes outside of the faculty that housed the women's studies program.

2.2 Description of System

In 1992, the university began to redesign its administrative computing system. The university's administrative computing system serves a number of functions. The system is used to keep track of students and the courses they are taking. It restricts the number of students registering for courses, creates waiting lists for courses that are full and advises students of additional sections of courses they attempt to register for that are full. The system performs a number of 'control' functions. For example, it is supposed to check to make sure that a student registering for a course has completed the pre-requisites for that course. The administrative computer system is also used extensively to determine whether or not students have met the requirements to graduate (referred to as 'graduation audits').

The administrative computer system is also used for a number of reporting functions. These include generating end of semester reports of students' grades, as well as class lists for professors. The administrative computing system also includes access to a database which is supposed to allow data to be retrieved and analyzed in relation to a number of different variables. For example, a dean might request a report of the number of students who graduated in a given year from each of the departments in his or her faculty, or a department head might request a report detailing the number of students enrolled in his or her department over a ten year period. A vice president might want a report indicating enrollment levels in courses by department.

2.3 Development of the Administrative Computer System

Development of the new administrative computing system was completed by the fall of 1995. Students registering for courses offered in the winter of 1996 used the new administrative computer system to enroll in classes. Although it would be misleading to refer to the development of this new computer system as a participatory process (here meaning that users were engaged in an unmediated relationship with system designers), the system design process was widely consultative. A number of mechanisms were used to solicit input from system users. The process of designing the new administrative computer system was widely publicized in campus publications, and the campus community was invited to provide input into the design of the new system. In addition, the project manager (a university employee who held a joint faculty and senior staff appointment) held a series of meetings with system users across campus, soliciting information about problems with the administrative computer system that was being replaced, as well as input about additional features that should be included in the new system. Input was solicited from faculty, administrative and support staff about what the new administrative computer system should be able to do. Using input from the consultative process, the project manager developed specifications for the new system along with the help of a team. Actual coding was contracted out to an off campus agency.

In my capacity as the coordinator of the women's studies program, I participated in this system development process, particularly during the early stages of development. I attended meetings designed to elicit information about shortcomings of the administrative computer system that was being replaced, wrote memos about administrative computing problems particular to the smooth functioning of the women's studies program, and, when my tenure as the coordinator of the women's studies program ended, I regularly met with the program's administrative assistant and the new program coordinator to discuss issues related to design of the new computer system.

2.4 Administrative Computing Needs of the Women's Studies Program

My concerns about the new computer system revolved around three issues in particular. First, the administrative computer system that was being replaced had been unable to perform graduation audits for women's studies students. This meant that the coordinator of the women's studies program had to manually go through the academic record of each student who applied to graduate, to ensure that she met graduation requirements. It also meant that any graduation audits that were performed for a student prior to her application to graduate had to be performed manually. This was a labour intensive and time consuming process. My second concern had to do with pre-requisite checking for courses. One of the courses required for students completing a women's studies minor program was in high demand. The course had a pre-requisite that was used to ensure that the students had an adequate background for the course, but, in the face of high demand for entry into the course, also served to reserve spaces for students who needed the course to graduate. The administrative computer system that was being replaced had not been able to adequately check that students had the pre-requisites for this course. As a result, students had to obtain a series of signatures (from the professor teaching the course as well as the program coordinator) in order to register for the course.

My final concern had to do with the report generation functions of the new administrative computer system. On several occasions, when I had been coordinator of the women's studies program I had requested reports (e.g., detailing the number of students who had graduated each year with a minor in women's studies, outlining our course offerings and enrollments historically), and I had been told that the system simply would not generate the reports I had requested. On a few other occasions I determined that the reports I had received contained incorrect information (e.g., one report indicated that several students who had long ago graduated were currently enrolled). It was my hope that the new administrative computer system would accommodate accurate generation of a wide range of reports related to women's studies. This seemed particularly important as university budgets were reduced, and we were informed that budgetary decisions would increasingly be made on the basis of course enrollments and program popularity.

2.5 Project Outcome

Shortly after the new administrative computer system replaced the old, it became apparent that the new system was not any better at handling the peculiarities of the women's studies program than the old system had been. This first became apparent in relation to pre-requisite checking. It turned out that the new computer system had not been designed to accommodate a combination of pre-requisites like the combination we used to control entry into one of our courses. Faced with our pre-requisite request that they were unable to meet (which required that a student complete one required and five elective courses from a list of twenty courses offered by three faculties or schools prior to entry into a sixth course), system administrators entered an alternate criteria for course entry (completion of two years of university), which was inadequate. After a disastrous result (where students who didn't urgently need the course to graduate were able to register prior to those who met the 'real' pre-requisites, and students who didn't need the course urgently had to be persuaded to drop it), we returned to manually registering students for the course.

We soon discovered that the reporting functions of the new computer systems were unable to produce the full range of reports we had hoped for. Faced with enormous budget cuts, our dean instigated a process to deal with the allocation of declining resources. As the representative for interdisciplinary programs, I immediately noticed that the background materials provided for this process lacked data about women's studies (and, to a lesser degree, other interdisciplinary programs). When I requested additional data, I again found the limitation of the new administrative computer system. Although it could produce a wider range of reports than the system it replaced, the new system still did not accommodate the range of requests for information generated by the threat of budget cuts. Not surprisingly, the new system was unable to adequately perform graduation audits, and in the worst tradition of system design, this prompted a move to 'clarify' program requirements so they were more compatible with the limitations of the new system.

3 Discussion and Analyses

It would be easy to dismiss this tale as simply another instance of poor system design. However, recasting this flawed instance of system design provides fertile ground for consideration of invisible work, and further analyses of this example provides a context for a discussion about the nature of invisible work, the politics of system design, and the use of an organization's documentary reality as a resource for uncovering invisible work in system design. I begin this section with a discussion of the nature of invisible work.

3.1 The Nature of Invisible Work

In order to be accounted for in system design, work must be made visible. For the purposes of my discussion here, I will assume this is a desirable end, although clearly there are numerous issues (such as the possibility for surveillance) that can arise when work is made visible.[1] It is useful to consider when work is visible and when work is invisible prior to considering how to make work visible. There are at least three different kinds of invisible work. Work can be invisible because it is non-standard, because of the political consequences of acknowledging it, or because the configuration of technologies used to complete a constellation of tasks was unable to capture all aspects of the work, requiring that a worker complete either articulation work or a workaround in order to accomplish a set of tasks.

Non-standard work is often invisible simply because the reality of completing a constellation of tasks is not widely shared. For example, living for an extended period of time in a foreign country entails considerable labour (e.g., obtaining visas, work permits, a social insurance number, the proper forms for filing taxes as a 'temporary alien', permission to temporarily import a car) which is likely to remain invisible to the majority of people, simply because it is out of their realm of experience. In an organizational setting, if a department within the organization differs dramatically from the norm for that organization, work in an atypical unit is likely to remain invisible. This type of invisible work can become visible if norms switch. For example, if a government requires all residents (not just foreigners) to get a new social insurance number, the experience of the foreigner (in having to obtain a social insurance number) becomes the norm, and, widely experienced, becomes visible.

Some work remains invisible for political reasons. Several authors have suggested that one of the defining characteristics of work typically done by women (e.g., secretarial work, caring work) is its invisibility. Service work, often done by women, is least visible to those who depend upon it, the better it is done (Suchman, 1995; Clement, 1993; Star and Ruhleder, 1996). Others have suggested that because work typically done by women involves maintenance (e.g., of homes, of children) rather than the production of tangible products, it remains invisible. Suchman (1995, p. 58) has suggested that making some forms of work visible may "call into questions the grounds on which different forms of work are differently rewarded, both symbolically and materially." There are significant consequences involved in rendering some forms of work visible.

[1] Several of the contradictions of making work visible are addressed by Suchman, 1995, p. 60.

A third form of invisible work is the non-routine work one engages in to complete a set of tasks. This type of work takes at least two forms. Articulation work is non-routine work that one engages in that allows a technology to be used effectively in a given setting. In contrast, workarounds (Sachs, 1995) allow users to complete a set of tasks despite the inadequacies of a technology, by 'working around' them. Suchman (1994, p.7) suggests that articulation work "names the continuous efforts required in order to bring together discontinuous elements- of organization, of professional practices, of technologies- into working configurations" (Suchman, 1994, p.7). One of the characteristics of articulation work is that it is non-routine, and as such, cannot be rationalized and incorporated into system design (Star, 1991). Articulation work includes various forms of customization and configuration as well as a range of mundane activities required to incorporate a computer system into everyday practices in local settings (Suchman, 1994).

It is sometimes useful to make a distinction between articulation work and workarounds. Sachs (1995, p.43) describes a workaround as "a form of on-the-job innovation that reveals the tension between the standards for a job and the realities of doing the work." She suggests that generally knowledge about systemic problems and solutions to them is not often tapped in job design. Articulation work may be required to utilize a particular technology in a particular setting. In contrast, a workaround may enable a user to circumvent the limitations of a particular technology in a particular setting.

3.2 The Invisible Work of Running Women's Studies Programs

Although it is possible to identify many things that could have been done differently in the process of developing the administrative computer system described above, it is perhaps more fruitful to ask why verbal and written reports provided during the system development process described above did not result in a system that better met the needs of the women's studies program. As Star (1991) points out, there are always choices to made in formalizing work, which include choices about what work becomes the target for formalizations. Only routine work (or assemblages of routines) can be rationalized, and in being rationalized, protected from the need for articulation work (Star, 1991). The failure of the new administrative computer system to meet the needs of the women's studies program probably occurred both because of the non-standard nature of the women's studies program vis-à-vis departments within the university (and thus, the non-standard nature of work that occurred within the unit, which contributed to its invisibility), and because of the politics of making the work required to run the women's studies program visible through its formalization in the new administrative computer system.

One feature of women's studies programs in Canada is that in many instances, the organization of women's studies remains non-standard in relation to the organization of other academic units in universities (see Eichler, 1990, Eichler and Tite, 1990; Tite and Malone, 1990 and Balka, 1992), and the work required to run women's studies programs remains largely invisible, along with, in some instances, the programs themselves.[2] For example, course offerings in women's studies programs often consist

[2] The invisibility of women's studies programmes in Canada inspired the title of Tite and Malone's (1990) article "Our universities' best kept secret: Women's studies in Canada" which

of a majority of courses offered by other departments throughout the university, with only a few courses offered by the women's studies program per se. This deviates sharply from the norm of programs of study offered primarily by a single department (e.g., sociology) with the occasional supporting course (e.g., statistics) offered by another department. This seemingly simple difference becomes complex when tracking a student's progress towards completion of graduation requirements.[3]

Although it is quite possible to design a computer system that can track the greater number of contingencies presented by the women's studies requirements,[4] (although differing from the norm, the greater range of contingencies can be captured computationally), in this case, the non-standard nature of the work combined with the political implications of recognizing it meant that it remained outside of the domain of what was rendered visible in the new system design. Recognizing the work required to administer the women's studies program (or more generally, any non-standard unit) would almost certainty lend legitimacy to the program. Such legitimacy might in turn lead to demands for new resources (space, more support staff, more faculty members), or demands to standardize (and hence anchor) women's studies within the university structure. The failure to accommodate non-standard work in system design tends to reinforce rather than remove the need for articulation work in the non-standard units. At the same time the non-standard units have a tendency to become more marginal as the new systems are adapted and new organizational norms (e.g., new guidelines for reporting student enrollments) emerge from possibilities created by new systems. In this instance, improving service to standard units came at the expense of those units like women's studies that failed to conform to organizational norms at the start of the system development project.

The structural difference between women's studies programs and discipline based departments probably reflects an ideological rejection of established structures that dominate university workplaces, the demands of creating a 'non-standard' interdisciplinary academic program, as well as an inability to recreate 'standard' structures (such as departments) in the service of women's studies.[5] Women throughout the United States and Canada have overcome institutional and ideological

---

addressed, among other things the absence of information about otherwise vibrant women's studies programmes in Canadian universities.

[3] Although not an insurmountable problem, this difference leads to issues about how a computer system 'counts' a course (e.g., a course on the psychology of women could be counted as either a psychology course or a women's studies course), and, in the case of requirements in the programme described here, also led to more complicated pre-requisite checking. Pre-requisite checking became more complicated because the seemingly simple requirement that a student complete six women's studies courses prior to entry to her seventh course was difficult to track by computer because her six courses could be taken in any of twelve departments. In the case of other academic programmes (e.g., sociology) pre-requisites usually consisted of either a minimum number of courses all in one department, or a very specific combination of courses. Both situations resulted in fewer contingencies, which were easier to formalize during system development.

[4] Through a series of 'if...then' statements, e.g., if the student is a women's studies minor, then count the following list of courses (sociology 3314 and 4092, psychology 2240 etc.) as women's studies credits.

[5] One of the lores of workplace culture surrounding the formation of the women's studies programme described here was that a condition that accompanied its formation was that it would never cost the university any money.

barriers to women's studies by working around organizational and political resistance to the development of the feminist project in academia. However, along with the success of many of these programs has come an increased share of invisible or articulation work, required to maintain these programs in the face of larger systems that fail to acknowledge the realities of their existence.

The work required to run the women's studies program described here differed substantially from work required to run other administrative units in the university, precisely because the structure and organization of the program deviated so much from the departmental norm of the university structure. Star (1991) suggests that women as a group have developed a set of skills for juggling work that escape formal representation, but are essential to knowledge work. In a sense, the non-standard nature of the women's studies program can be seen as an extension of these skills. Feminist projects like women's studies programs, and feminist non-profit organizations[6] are at times like water, flowing along the path of least resistance, around (and over) obstacles as constraints warrant. They succeed in challenging processes through which power is exercised along gender lines partly because they are able to flow, like water around constraints, as warranted, rather than following well trodden paths. One consequence of defying norms in this way is that the work required to maintain feminist projects is likely to remain invisible to system developers. This in turn can result in a muting (e.g., an inability to produce reports that can be used to bolster one's existence), or can increase the need for articulation work or workarounds. Creating new organizational forms in this way may allow women to accomplish feminist projects in the short term, but may undermine our efforts to gain legitimacy in an increasingly computer-mediated world.

One of the qualities of invisible work, and particularly work that remains invisible because it is non-standard or invisible for political reasons, is that the boundaries that mark these forms of work as invisible are malleable and subject to change. For example, in efforts to address the impending budget cuts faced by the university, one of my colleagues proposed that departments increase their reliance on courses offered by other departments. Had this proposal been adapted, the previously non-standard combination of courses used as pre-requisites for women's studies courses would have become the norm. Similarly, if it became more politically expedient to acknowledge the existence of the women's studies program (for example, if 'documenting' a strong women's studies program meant an increase of funds to the university), the visibility of the work required to maintain the program would increase. As visibility and/or perceived importance of a set of work tasks expands, so too do the opportunities to increase the visibility of work required to accomplish these tasks.

3.3 Infrastructure and the Politics of the Invisible

Star and Ruhleder (1996) suggest that infrastructure is relational. Something "becomes infrastructure in relation to organized practices" (p. 113), and "infrastructure occurs when the tension between the local and the global is resolved" (p.114), and when local practices are accommodated by a larger scale technology, which can be used in a natural, ready-at-hand fashion. In the case of the new administrative computer system

[6] See Balka, in press and Balka and Doucette, 1994 for a discussion of issues that arise in implementing computer systems in feminist non-profit organizations.

and the women's studies program, a system that was clearly intended to be adapted as infrastructure resulted in an increased reliance on manual workarounds by the faculty and staff involved in maintaining the women's studies program (e.g., students had to be manually added to classes with pre-requisites, and graduation audits had to be performed manually), precisely because the system failed to resolve the tension between the global realities of the university and the local realities of the women's studies program.

Infrastructure, in addition to being relational, is political. Faced with a range of demands in system development, system designers typically are unable to accommodate the full range of characteristics users would like to see in a system. Some characteristics are included, and others are excluded. As Star (1995) points out, computer systems simplify, and make choices about voice, politics and knowledge that are often invisible. Such decisions embody power in their ability to encode some parts of human life while excluding others. These decisions have often not immediately apparent consequences. For example, one consequence of the failure to fully integrate the demands of the women's studies program into the new administrative computer system was that documenting the success of the women's studies program (through the generation of reports from the related database) was quite difficult, and in some cases impossible. However, based on how the new system performed for other units, there was an expectation that such reports would be produced, and the role of such reports gained importance in the face of budget cuts.

When participatory design takes place, although it may have the potential of meeting more user demands than other approaches to system development, its success rests in part upon who participates in the design process, as well as whose voices are heard, or whose demands are acknowledged by system designers. Most participation in participatory design projects remains representative, and, as such, could just as easily have neglected the demands of the women's studies program as the approach to design that was utilized. Some design methods (e.g., contextual inquiry) assume that speaking to more than a certain proportion of users during system design will not yield any new results.[7] As Birkenes and Fjuk (1994, p.75) pointed out, "the underlying perspective in CSCW [computer-supported cooperative work] oriented research has been that people involved in co-operative work (a 'group') is understood as a homogenous and harmonious ensemble of people." They suggest that this perspective neglects the individual group member, relations between people in groups, and differences between participating actors that may have implications for the design of computer systems or the utility of those systems.

Obviously, no approach to system design is perfect, and any one of several approaches might have failed to meet the somewhat unique demands of the women's studies program. Nonetheless, given the often invisible nature of women's work, and the increase in articulation work or workarounds necessitated by non-standard situations often adapted by women in efforts to overcome the restrictions imposed by constraints we face, we remain in need of strategies that will render invisible work

[7] For example, in the electronic newsletter Contextual connection v.9, Hugh Beyers writes "in Contextual Design...we build our understanding of the customer through interviews with relatively small numbers of customers-- 10-15 for a first round, usually less than 30 for a whole product version...We find that this is enough-- talking to more customers does not result in significant new data..."

visible so that it can be accounted for and accommodated in redesigned work environments. Smith's (1990) approach to textual analysis offers the possibility of finding clues to the existence of invisible work, where other methods (including those that emphasize participation) fail.

4 The Active Text

In his paper on the sociology of collective memory, Hjellbrekke (1996) suggests that control over the way people classify and remember the past is a relevant topic of research. He reminds us of Orwell's awareness of the significance of the past in sustaining power relations in the present in his utilization of the slogan "Who controls the past controls the future: who controls the present controls the past" (Orwell, 1949, p. 260) by the totalitarian party in his novel 1984. Hjellbrekke suggests that memory is a social fact, structured and sustained by social groups, and that history often becomes an arena of conflict. Following this reasoning, historical accounts should provide insights into past struggles, which have had significance in shaping relations between various groups in the present.

Just as Hjellbrekke suggests that historic accounts yield insights about social relations in the present, Smith (1990) suggests that texts are constituents of social relations. Indeed, textual practices coordinate, "order, provide continuity, monitor, and organize relations between different segments and phases of organizational courses of action" (p.217). For Smith, discourse is central to the development of the ideological currency of society. Textually mediated forms of social organization depend upon and exploit the textual capacity "to crystallize and preserve a definite form of words detached from their local historicity" (p. 210). She suggests that in its permanent material form, meaning (conveyed through text) is detached from the lived processes that led to its creation. Textual records, or the documentary reality of an organization represents a moment in the organization's collective memory, a snapshot of the organization's social relations at a particular moment in time. An organization's documentary reality is also central to the accomplishment of organizational rules and norms.

Smith (1990) suggests that the investigation of textual practices will allow us to see the extended 'social relations of ruling' and that recognizing documents or texts as constituents of social relations can lead to the social organization of the production of those texts as a prior phase in the social relation. For Smith, "texts speak in the absence of speakers" (p. 211). Smith suggests that the capacity of texts to transcend social processes and remain uniform across local settings is a distinctive form of social organization mediated by texts, and is key to their force. An organization's textual reality, like a map[8] or other forms of representation, is a negotiated accomplishment. By reading an organization's texts as 'active texts' we may be able to identify some of the social relations that led to the production of those texts, as well as identify fissures in organizational practices, that are obscured through the accomplishment of invisible work.

---

[8] See Wood's (1992) The Power of Maps. New York: Guilford.

4.1 Finding Clues to Invisible Work in Textual Reality

A return to the case of the inadequate administrative computer system helps illustrate how texts might be used in a purposeful effort to give voice to and understand traditionally invisible work practices (Markussen, 1995). Tite and Malone (1990) inspected official documents from all Canadian universities, including university calendars (the documents that contain the 'official' regulations students must follow to complete degrees, as well as course descriptions and descriptions of administrative units). They commented that in very few instances these programs were immediately visible. In the majority of instances, inspection of university calendars yielded a range of complex arrangements for inclusion of women's studies programs. Often faculty attached to women's studies programs were not identified in lists of faculty, and course descriptions for women's studies courses were included under departmental listings, rather than under the entry for the women's studies program.

In the case of the women's studies program I worked with, inspection of university documents would have yielded several indications of organizational fissures bridged through invisible work. These include

- the presence of a program coordinator (rather than a department head, or program supervisor) who is not listed as a faculty member in women's studies;
- the absence of course descriptions in the section of the calendar containing regulations (where this was otherwise the norm);
- the initial absence of women's studies faculty members from the list of all faculty members in the university listed by department, and the subsequent inclusion of women's studies faculty on this list, as the only 'program' with faculty;
- the absence of women's studies in the 'special divisions' section of the calendar, where most interdisciplinary units were included;
- no regulations or definitions in the faculty collective agreement pertaining to program coordinators or programs.

An examination of seemingly less significant textual artifacts from the workplace (such as faculty and staff pay stubs) would have yielded information about the anomalous nature of the unit, as faculty and staff received their pay via the dean's office, because payroll insisted all pay was disbursed through departments, and women's studies was not a department.

Each of these seemingly insignificant textual occurrences together represent textual evidence of organizational incongruencies. These incongruencies are anchored in sets of social relations, and are representations of conflicts, frozen in the organizational documentary reality. Each of these organizational fissures requires the performance of varying amounts of invisible work to correct. Through the performance of workarounds and articulation work the distance between the global dimensions assumed in the development of infrastructure, and local circumstances is bridged. Although I continue to pursue computer system design through participatory means, the above example reminds me that not all parties are represented or heard through participatory means, and an organization's documentary reality can speak as Smith (1990) suggests, in the absence of speakers. The adaptation of Smith's (1990) technique of analyzing active texts as a secondary method in system design is likely to yield valuable results, and may help render some invisible work performed by women more visible to system designers.

Participation in participatory design projects is most often representative. In situations where all participants in a given work setting are able to engage in system design, relations between individual participants as well as relations between groups within the organization may well render some organizational fissures and their underlying social relations invisible, despite participation. Smith (1990) suggests that the investigation of texts makes many phases of organizational and discursive practices that would otherwise be inaccessible visible. She goes on to suggest that successful analysis of textual materials for their properties as organizers of social relations requires a competent or active reading of the text. An analyst of text should be familiar with the interpretive schema used in a given setting. An active reading of text depends on membership within the community or society that has produced the texts. Thus Smith's approach could be easily adapted within a participatory design context.

Textual materials can be used in participatory design projects in a variety of ways. For example, participants can be introduced to the idea of organizational fissures, and asked to actively read taken for granted materials (such as university calendars) with an eye towards uncovering organizational fissures. In addition, analysis of textual materials from the workplace can be used as a tunnel into hidden social relations of the organization. Textual analysis can be used to supplement designers' understanding of underlying social relations, especially in circumstances where participation is limited. Workers can 'collect' and analyze documents that in some way are problematic, and in their analysis of such documents they may develop a keener sense of the social relations of work.

References

1. Balka, E. (1992). *"If you are hiring a co-ordinator..."* Co-ordinator's column, *Canadian Women's Studies Association Newsletter*, Fall Issue.
2. Balka, E. (In Press). Participatory design in women's organizations: The social world of organizational structure and the gendered nature of expertise. *Gender, Work and organizations*.
3. Balka, E., & Doucette, L. (1994). The accessibility of computers to organizations serving women in the province of Newfoundland: Preliminary study results. *Electronic Journal of Virtual Culture*, 2(3), 739 lines.
4. Birkenes, T., & Fjuk, A. (1994). the troublesome issue of co-operation seen from a women's perspective. In A. Adam, J. Emms, E. Green, & J. Owen (Eds.), *women, work and computerization: breaking old boundaries- building new forms* (pp. 75-90). Amsterdam: IFIP/North-Holland.
5. Clement, A. (1993). Looking for the designers: Transforming the "invisible" infrastructure of computerized office work. *Artificial Intelligence and Society*, *7*, 323-344.
6. Eichler, M. (1990). On doing the splits collectively: Introduction to the Canadian Women's Studies Project. *Atlantis*, *Fall*, 3-5.

7. Eichler, M., & Tite, R. (1990). Women's studies professors in Canada: A collective self- portrait. *Atlantis*, *Fall*, 6-24.
8. Hjellbrekke, J. (1996). The sociology of collective memory. Paper presented at the national conference in sociology, Voss, Norway, Sept. 1996.
9. Markussen, R. (1995). Constructing easiness- historical perspectives on work, computerization, and women. In S. L. Star (Ed.), *the cultures of computing* (pp. 159-180). Oxford: Blackwell.
10. Orwell, G. (1949). *1984*. London: Penguin.
11. Sachs, P. (1995, September). Transforming work: Collaboration, learning, and design. *Communications of the ACM*, *38*(9), 36-44.
12. Schmidt, K., & Bannon, L. (1992). Taking CSCW seriously: Supporting articulation work. *Computer supported cooperative work (CSCW): An international Journal*, *1*, 7-40.
13. Smith, D. E. (1990). textually mediated social organization. In *texts, facts and femininity* (pp. 209-224). New York: Routledge.
14. Star, S. L. (1991). Invisible work and silenced dialogues in knowledge representation. In I. V. Ericksson, B. A. Kitchenham, & K. J. Tijdens (Eds.), *Women, work and computerization: Understanding and overcoming bias in work and education* (pp. 81-91). Amsterdam: Elsevier Science Publishers (North Holland).
15. Star, S. L. (1995). introduction. In S. L. Star (Ed.), *The cultures of computing* (pp. 1-28). Oxford: Blackwell.
16. Star, S. L., & Ruhleder, K. (1996). Steps toward an ecology of infrastructure: Design and access for large information spaces. *Information systems research*, *7*(1), 111-134.
17. Suchman, L. (1994). Supporting articulation work: Aspects of a feminist practice of technology production. In A. Adam, J. Emms, E. Green, & J. Owen (Eds.), *Women, work and computerization: Breaking old boundaries- building new forms* (pp. 7-22). New York: IFIP/ North Holland.
18. Suchman, L. (1995, September). Making work visible. *Communications of the ACM*, *38*(9), 56-64.
19. Tite, R., & Malone, M. (1990). Our universities' best-kept secret: Women's studies in Canada. *Atlantis*, *Fall*, 25-39.
20. Wagner, I. (1994). Hard times: The politics of women's work in computerized environments. In A. Adam, J. Emms, E. Green, & J. Owen (Eds.), *women, work and computerization: breaking old boundaries- building new forms* (pp. 23-34). Amsterdam: IFIP/North-Holland.

Giving Room to Femininity in Informatics Education

Cecile K.M. Crutzen

Faculty of Technical Sciences, Open University of the Netherlands
P.O. Box 2960, 6401 DL Heerlen, The Netherlands
cecile.crutzen@ouh.nl

Abstract. Models of concepts in Informatics are mostly based on functionalism and objectivism. By giving alternatives for such models it is possible to give room in education to subjectivity and for instance the principles of social contructivism. This change is a necessary first step to be made for starting a discussion on gender aspects within Informatics education.

1 Introduction

From 1998 on the new optional subject Informatics will be introduced in the higher classes of Dutch high schools. Meanwhile a discussion has been started on the concepts that will be used in that subject. Out of the experience of designing basic courses on Informatics for the Open University of the Netherlands, I will discuss in this paper various models for the two crucial concepts in Informatics: "Information System" and "Communication" [1, 2, 3, 4].

A curriculum design should start with a critical view of concepts that are usually used in Informatics education, because the definition of the concepts is crucial for the room that will be given to femininity. As Hirschheim, Klein and Lyytinen have mentioned, textbooks promote mostly only one paradigm: Functionalism in Information System Design and objectivism in data modelling.

> "... So the academic community perpetuates, consciously or unconsciously, functionalism. We teach it to our students since only functionalist textbooks are available." [5, pp. 237].

2 The Relationship between Informatics and the Education of Informatics

Within a critical view on Informatics and the education of Informatics we can see a very strong impact of the products of the Informatics (industry) on education. The content of Informatics education is strongly influenced by any new representation of this technology. The effect is that introductory education of Informatics only gives attention to the physical and syntactical aspects of each new representation and little attention is given to the semantics and pragmatics of the new technology. The range of the possible meanings of technology is therefore pre-given. In this type of education a process of giving meaning, constructing meaning, and embedding meaning in already existing meanings and experiences of every individual student cannot take place. The meaning of Informatics will therefore be associated with "haste". For teachers and students Informatics seems to be a subject that is always changing. It seems to be impossible for them to catch up with the newest developments in that discipline. They cannot break through the physical external representation of the products of Informatics. Focusing on the semantic and pragmatic level of Informatics can take away the feeling of powerlessness. At the semantic and pragmatic level it is apparant that the changes in Informatics are much slower than commonly assumed, because the users (including students and teachers) construct the meaning of technology themselves.

3 The Relationship between Women Studies and Informatics

Technology generally and especially in Informatics is not gender-neutral. However the participation of more women in the design processes and use processes does not change technology at all [6 pp. 11-13, pp. 16-17]. Technology-use and technology-design will produce and reproduce cultural values, standards, and gender codes. Technology functions as a symbol for masculinity and therefore it seems that femininity does not participate in technology at all.

Murray formulated this as follows:

> "In arguing that technology is a core domain of a social constructed masculinity I want to suggest that it plays an important role as a boundary marker; what is perceived to be technological is perceived to be masculine. That is, masculinity claims for itself an exclusive control of the technological and when masculinity fails to control or loses control of technological practices those practices then lose their status as technological practices." [7, p. 67]

A process of socialization and participation of women in Informatics can be possible only if there is room for femininity, with all their differences and all their dynamics and change potentials. By creating and filling this kind of "room", it could be possible to disconnect the one-to-one relationship between masculinity and technology. Technology then will be no longer defined and structured by a dualism of femininity and masculinity. Informatics will lose the symbolic function for masculinity only if it starts this process of giving room to femininity. In designing an Informatics curriculum the focus should be: "What kinds of values do we want to communicate in that subject in high school education?"

The curriculum should be designed in such way that both female and male values are changeable. The deconstruction of the dualism femininity/masculinity can take place in Informatics, not by throwing away these values, but by breaking off specific connections between value classes. The starting point is that the female is present in Informatics; we only have to listen and give room to it and make it powerful [8, p.105 and p.122]. Giving room to femininity could have the effect that more woman will participate in Informatics, but such a quantitative criterion for judging a curriculum is useless, because the process of deconstruction and construction takes a long period of time. Giving room means that change in Informatics education is possible. An attitude of change offers chances for integrating the human interests' aspects of technology into technology-education as a subject and as a strategy in technology-education itself. Within that view it is not ethical to design education or an educational environment which will exclude the female systematically.

4 Education of Informatics is an Information System on Informatics

The lives of people consist of interaction with themselves and interaction with others: people, machines and other living beings (see figure 1). They are connected with physical and mental machines inside and outside their bodies. E.g., human beings can discover themselves by experimenting with several appearances in MUDs, representing themselves on home-pages, meditating and relaxing with the help of computer-adventures and simulations [9, pp. 173-174]. In the future people will live in webs of connections, in webs of information systems. Webs will be in the people and at the same time they will be a node in several webs of information and communication. People will become "Cyborgs" and live in "cyborg worlds" (10, pp. 149-182). This perspective of "affinities" and interactions should be the guide-book for the design of a curriculum.

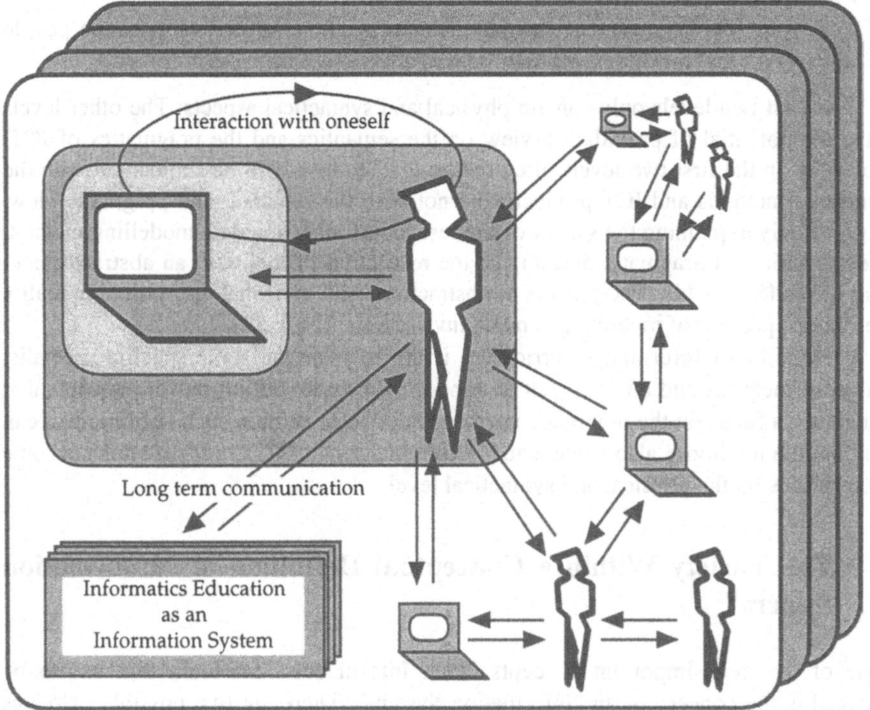

Figure 1: The web of interactions

Any kind of interaction will be influenced by information and communication technology (ICT). This influence is not a deterministic one because people themselves will construct the meaning of the technology. Giving meaning to technology is not an easy task, certainly not for students today, because they are overwhelmed with the phenomenon of ICT.

In schools, Informatics should be a subject with a universal educative character. Informatics is an information system with the domain "Informatics". Informatics should become a node in the webs of connections into which children will position themselves [1, 2, 4]. The dynamics of Informatics as an information system should be very flexible. The students should be able to use that system not only during their school time, but the concepts in that system should stay meaningful for a longer period of time.

Designing a curriculum for Informatics means making choices about on which level (physical, syntactical, semantic, pragmatic) we want to focus. The focuses could be (see figure 1):

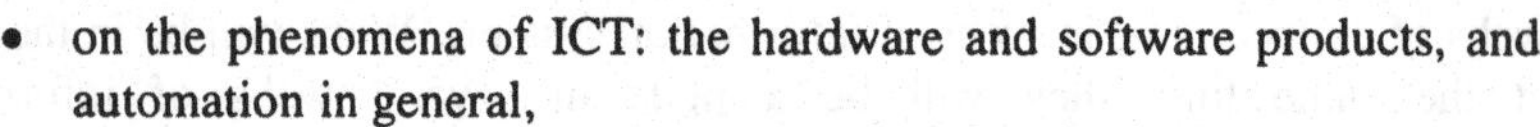

- on the phenomena of ICT: the hardware and software products, and automation in general,

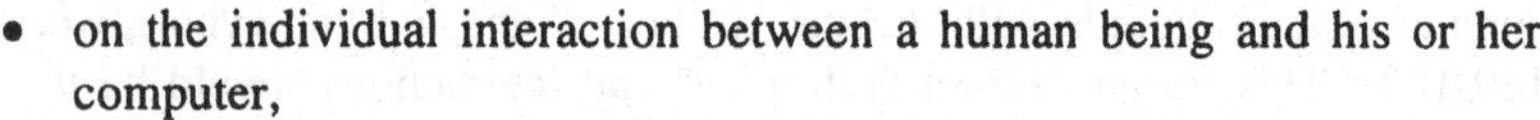

- on the individual interaction between a human being and his or her computer,

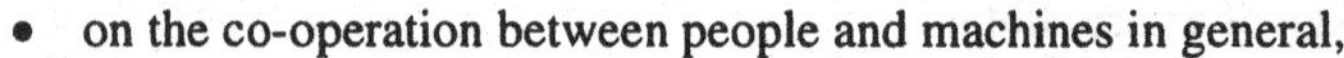

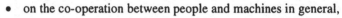

- on the co-operation between people and machines in general,

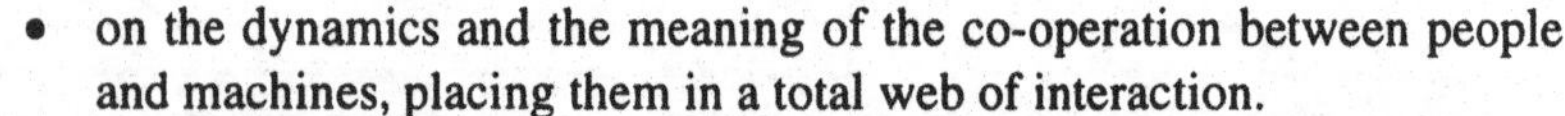

- on the dynamics and the meaning of the co-operation between people and machines, placing them in a total web of interaction.

The first two levels only contain physical and syntactical aspects. The other levels have the potential of providing a view on the semantics and the pragmatics of ICT. Focusing on the first two levels often means that students will be acquainted with the syntax of methods and ICT-products and not with the semantic and pragmatic view. E.g., by only explaining the syntax of the restriction rules of a data modelling method, the semantic and pragmatic meaning of the restriction of reality to an abstract model will be made invisible. The process of abstraction itself and what was visible in reality before this process of modelling is made invisible too [11, p.82].

Designing an Informatics curriculum is not to focus on some specific specialist subjects, methods and theories, but to choose for breadth definitions of concepts that guarantee a focus on the pragmatic and semantic levels. Within such definitions it can be possible to choose also some actual representations of ICT, to give students some experiences on the physical and syntactical level.

5 The Variety Within a Conceptual Definition of "Information System"

One of the most important concepts in an Informatics curriculum that has to be defined is the concept of an "Information System". There are two possible extremes (see figure 2):

E1: An "Information System" is a computer system or a software system which can process information; it is an input-output system; it is a technical system.

E2: An "Information System" is an interactive web of people and machines which together constitute a social system; an "Information System" is a social system in which the main interaction is "Communication" [5, p.1].

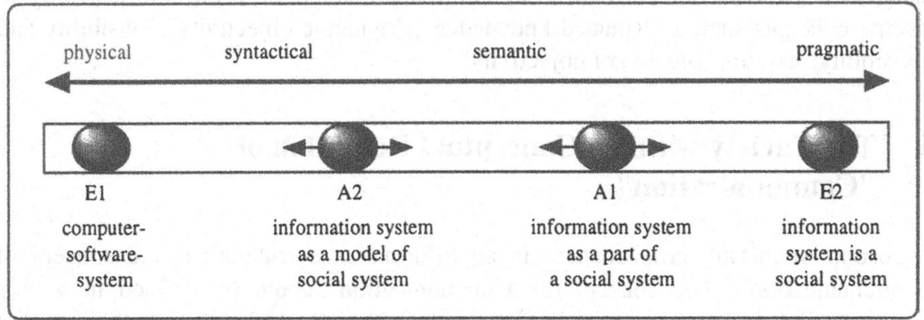

Figure 2: Definition extremes and alternatives of the concept "Information System"

The definition E2 is seen as too unspecific, because, if "an Informatics curriculum is an information system on Informatics itself", Informatics seems to be a subject concerning the whole lives of people. Furthermore, within this definition there is no difference between people and machines, by placing them as equal actors in a social web we remove any differences.

Between those two extreme definitions of an "Information System" there is a choice between two alternatives. One is: An "Information System" is always a part of a social system (A1). Information systems function in social systems. They are that part of the system in which communication takes place (A1, see figure 2). Within that definition there should be made the choice, which part of the social system. Excluding people out of that part means: moving towards the extreme E1. Saying that an information system is a system in which the interaction between its components is formal, informal, verbal, and non-verbal communication, will be a move to E2. The exchange of information is then seen as the most important activity in the social system.

Another aspect of information systems is that "an information system contains a model of a part of the world (of reality)" (A2). Choosing in this alternative A2 for a static character of the model (descriptive model) then "Information System" is defined in the line of E1. A more dynamic character, which includes an awareness of the prescriptive elements of a model will be oriented towards E2.

Strongly related to the definition of "Information System" is the choice what kind of information will be included in the Informatics curriculum. Should the curriculum include informal information, the relation between formal and informal information, communication and interaction or should Informatics be restricted to formal information: Rules, algorithms and data? This choice depends strongly on the definition of "Information System". If the choice is for the definition in which information systems are only software systems (E1) the discourse on information and communication will be reduced only to the formal part.

The definition of "Information System" will influence many themes, e.g., the discussion on the conception of "process" and "procedure". Do we want to focus only on automated processes and on routines or do we want to include the relationship between spontaneous and initiated processes? How can we explain in a restrictive definition of "Information System" the tension between the objectivity and subjectivity of information? At the extreme E1 this theme can only be placed in the margin. At the extreme E2 there is in Informatics education room and necessity to discuss concepts such as "situated knowledge", "dynamic objectivity", "visibility and invisibility" and the "illusion of objectivity".

6 The Variety within a Conceptual Definition of "Communication"

A second important basic concept in an Informatics curriculum is the concept of "Communication". The concept of "Communication" could be defined in a very technical and syntactical manner, but with a broad definition of the concept "Information System" there are possibilities for the definition of "Communication" which includes also the pragmatics and semantics of the communication process itself [see e.g., 12, 13, 14, and 15]. In most curricula the concept "Communication" is defined as the transmission of data between a sender and a receiver through a channel (see Communication Model C1, figure 3). This definition is based on the communication model of Shannon-Weaver. Such "transmissive" types of models of communication are strongly related to the extreme E1 for the concept of "Information System". These models of "Communication" reduce communication to its technical level: The syntactical representation of information and the transmission of data. The semantics and pragmatics of information are excluded. The role of sender and receiver are fixed and separated. The sender has the active role and the receiver has the passive role. Transmissive models of communication do not have "a message to the message". The meaning of a message is considered as fixed. Using within Informatics such model type of "Communication" leaves no room for a "meaning construction process" and consequently there is either room for an active role of information technology users, nor room for participatory design. The relation of the subjects and the objects in processes of knowledge representation and interpretation within the information system design processes depends only on the communication model chosen.

It is possible to widen these types of transmissive models by conceiving sender and receiver as information systems and opening the black box representation of the sender and receiver of model C1. Still it depends on the definition of "Information System" how we can elaborate the image of the sender and receiver in this enlarged model of "Communication" (see Communication Model C2, figure 3). E.g., if the conception is that every information system contains a model of its environmental world, it is possible to give sender and receiver separate memories with their own view on this world and their own language base. In this model the sender is more interested in the constitution of the receiver and has a responsibility for looking for communalities of interest.

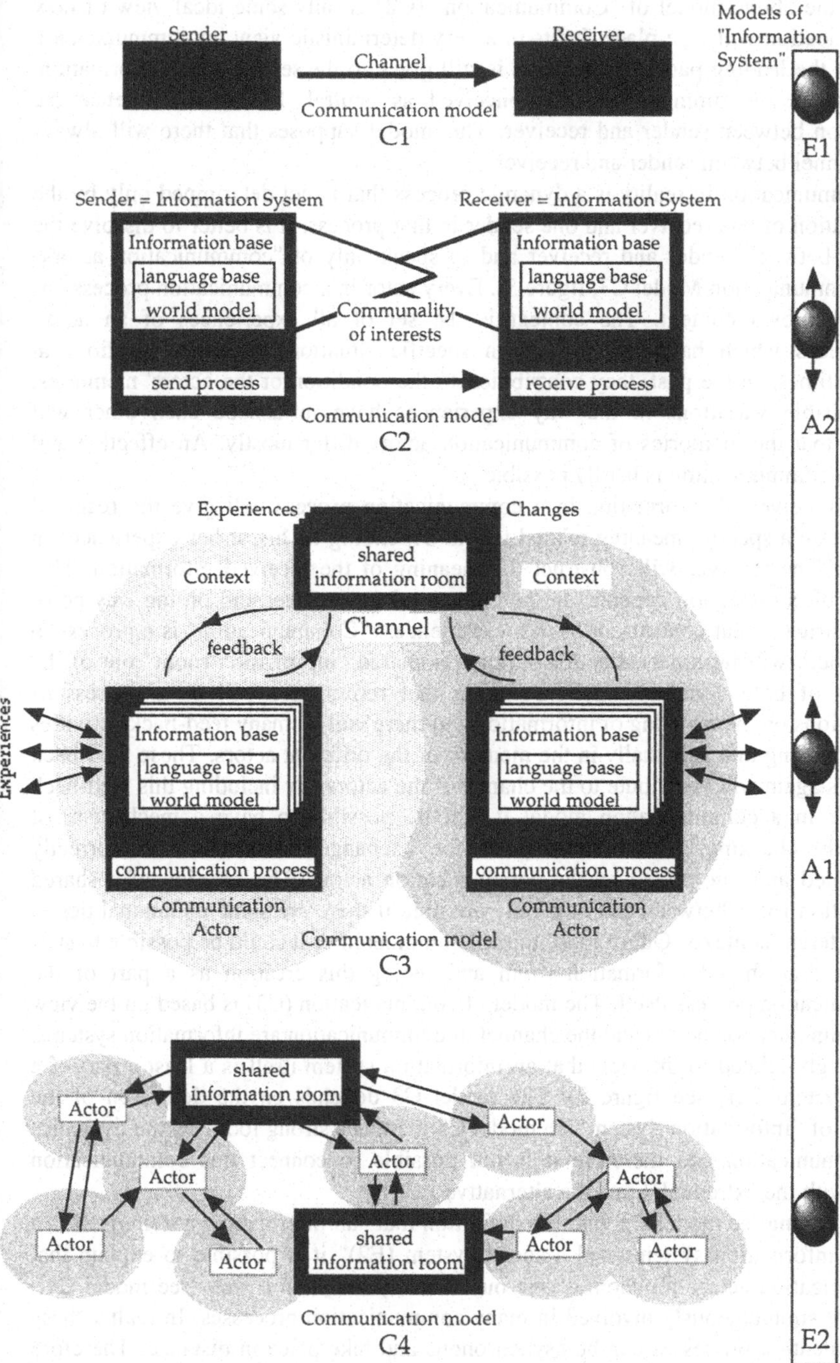

Figure 3: Models of the concept "Communication"

Still the above model of "Communication" (C2) is only some ideal view of how communication will take place. It fits in a very deterministic view on communication in which the leading part in the process is still given to the sender of the information. The channel of communication is conceived as neutral. It cannot influence the interaction between sender and receiver. This model supposes that there will always be a channel between sender and receiver.

Communication in reality is a dynamic process that is not determined only by the participation of one receiver and one sender in that process. It is better to dissolve the dualism between sender and receiver and to speak only of "communication actors" (see Communication Model C3, figure 3). Every actor in a communication process has her or his own context. The context is the set of all experiences of an actor. Experiences which have taken place in specific situations, cultures, locations at specific times. In the past, they contributed to the condition of the actors' memories. The possible variations in the way experiences have influenced each other will provide that the memories of communication actors differ mostly. An effective and efficient communication is hardly possible.

The receiver of information in a communication process will give the received information a specific meaning related to and depending on his or her experiences in the past. The receiver will construct the meaning of the received information. This process of construction depends on the context of the receiver and on the way he or she constructed that context out of past experiences. "Communication" is a process in which there will be a necessity for building a shared "information room" out of the contexts of both communication actors. In that room there will be a process of negotiations on the meaning of information and there will be many feed-back activities to the meaning that is actually in the memory of the different actors. These feed-back activities again will contribute to the change of the actors. By including this feed-back principle in a communication model it will be possible to have a mechanism of constantly checking, if the meaning of the exchanged information is correctly represented and interpreted by the communication actors. The creation of a shared information room between actors is only possible if there are some communalities in their different contexts. Out of those mutual communalities it could be possible to start building that shared information room and seeing this creation as a part of the communication process itself. The model of communication (C3) is based on the view that communication actors and the channel of communication are information systems, are strongly related to the view that an information system itself is a least a part of a social system (A1, see figure 2). The model C3 depends on the definition of the concept of "Information System". In model C3 there is a strong focus on the dynamics of communication and therefore it is not possible to connect this communication model with the extreme E1 and the alternative A2.

Combining the model C3 with the definition that "an information system itself is a web of information systems and a social system (E2)" it is possible to explain that communication actors function as one out of many nodes in a web (see model C4). They are simultaneously involved in many communication processes. In reality these communication processes can be asynchronous and take place in distance. Therefore in our model we have given room for harmony and conflict, for order and disorder, for subjectivism and objectivism, for participatory design of information systems, and for the different views on domains that can exist. In the model's C3 and C4 communication is equal with change.

7 Conclusion

Giving room to femininity can only take place if the concepts that will be taught in education are broad enough to integrate:

- discussions on objectivity/subjectivity of information,
- the effects of reduction and abstraction,
- differentiation between group building and classification within a technical
- implementation and the way group building can take place in social situations,
- focusing not only on hierarchical structures in design in the relationship between subject (designer) and object (user) but moving towards structures of communication and participation,
- focusing not only on formal languages and methods but exploring the relationship between the natural and the formal,
- breaking down the illusion of order and harmony and also discussing disorder and conflict.

Giving room to femininity can only start with an awareness of curriculum designers that chosen concepts in curricula are not neutral and cannot have an objective meaning. This awareness is a first move towards the deconstruction of the distance between subject and object, teacher and student, and will place the education of "Informatics as an information system" into the total web of relations and negotiations. An awareness and the concrete implementation of the variety of approaches that are possible can change the character of the models of the basic-concepts. Models of concepts are not absolute and formal representations of theory anymore, but can be seen as metaphors. A metaphorical view of concepts can enlighten also the differences and the similarities with real practice of Informatics. As Richard Coyne put it: "Metaphor makes obvious the process that is covert in all attempts to derive meaning, namely, the conflict between sameness and difference.,..It could be said that metaphor resides at the interstice between "is" and "is not" [18, p.298]."

The elaboration of the basic concepts of Informatics ("Information System" and "Communication") will start a negotiation process between femininity and masculinity and Informatics. This negotiation process will be the change and the break down of the one-to-one relation between masculinity and Informatics.

Acknowledgement

I want to thank Dr. Marjolijn Witte for her contributions to the discussion on the models of the concepts and for making possible the implementation of the ideas in a basic course Informatics of the Dutch Open University [17].

References

1. Crutzen, C. K. M. (1993): "A Female View on the Design of Information Systems". In S. Haggerty, A. Holmes (eds): "Transforming Science And Technology: Our Future depends on it", Contributions GASAT 7th International Conference, Ontario: The University of Waterloo, pp. 460-468.
2. Crutzen, C. K. M. (1994): "The Influence of Feminist Theory on Informatics Course Design". In A. Adam, J. Emms, E. Green, J. Owen (eds): "Women, Work and Computerization, Breaking Old Boundaries, Building New Forms", Amsterdam: Elsevier Science Publishers B.V., pp. 59-74.
3. Crutzen, C. K. M., e.a. (1994): "Oriëntatie op informatica: mens, machine en informatieverwerking". Heerlen: Open universiteit.
4. Crutzen, C. K. M. (1995): "Feministische Theorien: Eine Inspiration für Curriculum-Entwicklungen in der Informatik". Informatik-Kolloqium (18.01. 1995, Universität Bremen) und Kolloqium Frauen-Mathematik-Informatik, Zwischen Anspruch und Wirklichkeit (24.10.1995, FU Berlin, TU Berlin). Partly published in: Zeitschrift Frauenarbeit und Informatik, Organ des Fachausschusses "Frauenarbeit und Informatik" der Gesellschaft für Informatik e.V., Bonn, June 1995).
5. Hirschheim, R., Klein, H. K., Lyytinen K. (1995): "Information Systems Development and Data Modeling, Conceptual and Philosophical Foundations". Cambridge: Cambridge University Press.
6. Gill, R., Grint, K. (1995): "Introduction, The Gender-Technology Relation". In K. Grint, R. Gill (eds): "The Gender-Technology Relation, Contemporary Theory and Research", London: Taylor & Francis, pp.1-28.
7. Murray, F. (1992): "A Separate Reality: Science, Technology and Masculinity". In E. Green, J. Owen, D. Pain (eds): "Gendered by Design?", London/ Washington D.C: Taylor & Francis, pp. 64-80.
8. Haegen, R. van der (1989): "In het spoor van seksuele differentie". Nijmegen: Sun.
9. Turkle, S. (1996): "Live on the Screen, Identity in the Age of the Internet". New York: Simon & Schuster.
10. Haraway, D. J. (1991): "Simians, Cyborgs, and Women, The Reinvention of Nature". London: Free Association Books.
11. Star, L. S. (1991): "Invisible Work and Silenced Dialogues in Knowledge Representation:. In I. V. Eriksson, B. A. Kitchenham, K. G. Tijdens (eds): "IFIP TC9/WG 9.1 Conference on Women, Work and Computerization, Understanding and Overcoming Bias in Work and Education", Amsterdam: Elsevier Science Publishers B.V., pp. 81-92.
12. Zoonen, L. van (1994): "Feminist Media Studies", London: Sage.
13. Hall, S. (1994): "Encoding/Decoding", in D. Graddol O. Boyd-Barret (eds): "Media Texts: Authors and Readers", Clevedon, England: The Open University, p. 200-211.
14. Chandler, D. (1995): "The Act of Writing: A Media Theory Approach". Aberstwyth: University of Wales.

15. Graddol, D. (1994): "Three Models of Language Description". In D. Graddol, O. Boyd-Barret (eds): "Media Texts: Authors and Readers", Clevedon, England: The Open University, pp. 1-21.
16. Coyne R. (1995): "Designing Information Technology in the Postmodern Age, From Method to Metaphor". Massachusetts: The MIT Press
17. Crutzen, C. K. M., Witte M. e.a. [1997]: "Context van informatica". Heerlen (The Netherlands): Open Universiteit.

How to Prove it

Brigitte Pientka

Technical University of Darmstadt

In this note I compare the motivation of conventional theorem proving and proof planning and show that the methodology is influenced by gender. In conventional theorem proving the aim is to control technique by verifying programs. The method which is used is implied by this motivation. The theorem prover is applied to a random selection of theorems and the search for a proof is pruned by crude heuristics which prefer winning branches to losing ones. From the beginning of philosophical thought mathematics has been defined as the highest rational exercise. Conventional theorem proving builds upon this tradition and therefore I identify this as a male form of reasoning. As femaleness has been associated with what transcends male rationality, the concept of proof planning will be considered as female form of reasoning.

In contrast to conventional theorem provers proof planning is concerned with investigating the proof process and to make this transparent to the user. As proof enhances an understanding how it is possible to invent a proof, the final control comes back to the user. Using classical proof planning the complete proof plan for a conjecture is computed prior to executing any tactic. No information about the history of the proof and previous steps in the proof plan are available to the *uninformed* planner.

These drawbacks are obsolete for *incremental proof planning*. In *incremental proof planning* the knowledge about the domain of application, i.e. the strategy, and about tactics is declaratively represented by *meta-rules*. Within incremental structured proof planning, the history of the proof is exploited in order to determine the next applicable meta-rule. The heuristics build on the experiences of the user. The modeled knowledge is context-dependent. Meta-rules can be structured in *meta-rule sets* providing a further level of abstraction. For instance, techniques for certain proof situations may be collected in some meta-rule sets. Changing the meta-rule set adopts the strategy to the current proof situation. The declarative representation of strategy knowledge eases the maintenance and development of the meta-reasoning component, since the meta-knowledge is no longer scattered over the proof planner. The proof planner can explain why a certain tactic has been applied or why the results have been rejected by the persistence condition. Thus the user may infer the reason for a failure of the proof which may assist them in speculating about a lemma or it might be a hint for a modification of the set of meta-rules.

Feminist Computational Linguistics

Alison E. Adam and Maureen Scott

Department of Computation, UMIST, P.O. Box 88, Manchester M60 1QD, UK

Abstract. This paper reports the political considerations surrounding a technical AI project based on aspects of feminist theory. The project itself sought to add a gender dimension to software tools which model conversational analysis. This involved criticizing and augmenting an existing model of the repair of conversational misunderstandings and non-understandings to produce a model which could be used to predict the outcomes of inter-gender communications under certain circumstances. Rather than reporting the technical details of the project (although brief details are given in appendices), the paper focuses on our political concerns in framing the project.

1 Introduction

The aim of the project reported in this paper was to design an artificial intelligence (AI) system, based on aspects of feminist theory. In tackling this problem we wanted to avoid the kind of justifiable criticisms levelled at 'women into' approaches by writers who argue that they are based on a liberal feminism which does nothing to challenge the underlying structures of society which keep women in oppressive roles; where the status quo is left unchallenged; where women are the problem for not entering computing [1, 2]. Although, as we argue below, our project does not fall into such a category, thinking about the forms of political action taken in 'women into' type projects suggests that we may be able to steer a course between the Scylla of unbridled enthusiasm for liberal approaches and the Charybdis of an immobilizing theoretical feminism. We argue that it is possible to acknowledge the deficiencies of liberal feminism, especially in the way that it puts all the onus on women to change, but at the same time to applaud some of the effects of projects built on its foundations. On the positive side, projects to 'get more women in', provide a focus for women already within or entering the computing industry to network and support each other. Secondly, why shouldn't women have access to the well-paid and interesting careers available in computing? Thirdly, and most importantly, as both Rosemarie Tong [3] and Judy Wajcman [4] argue, feminism is a political project and the best research is where action proceeds from description. At least on the surface, the liberal feminist view provides a much clearer course for action than a more theoretically based feminism. We see this to be the most important message from 'women into' or liberal feminism which can inform the present research.

2 Theoretical Positions

We believe that there are alternatives which can work alongside the liberal view, which are at the same time informed by a more theoretical feminism, yet involve some level of action (eg. see [5]). For the present project this involves thinking through the ways in which AI research could be informed by feminist theory and then applying those considerations to a real project. The fact that AI projects consciously informed by feminist concepts are thin on the ground is hardly surprising [6]. Realistically, we do not expect to somehow 'convert' those who are unconvinced that it is important or interesting to examine the way in which gender is inscribed in information technology. But if such work is not undertaken in the spirit of conversion then we had to consider whether it belonged to the successor science project of the standpoint theorists [7, 8]. Feminist standpoint theory arose, at least to some extent, in response to the kind of liberal, empirical feminism described above. It has roots in Marxist theory and argues that women, as an oppressed group, have access to a truer description of their oppression than is available to men. We have some sympathy with this view; for instance it is hard to argue that a woman who has been raped does not have a truer picture of her condition than the legal system which will try the case if she presses charges. As Rose [8] points out, the realism of standpoint theory is more attractive than an unbridled postmodernism which struggles to give reasons for believing one 'story' over another.

Whatever the merits or demerits of standpoint theory, the political project that it offers is the idea of a successor science or technology i.e. a new science or technology built on feminist principles. Within AI, as an example, it is hard enough to uncover and make explicit, the masculine structures upon which the discipline rests, without conjuring up a feminist alternative [9, 10]. This means that, in this project at least, we were not laying claim to a feminist 'successor' AI, no matter how attractive such an idea might be. This piece of research makes little theoretical input into the heart of AI. It is, rather, and more modestly, showing ways in which AI can be informed by feminist theory and can be used for feminist projects. In itself, this requires some imagination and undeniably there are contradictions. We are reminded of the occasion at a gender and technology workshop, when a man asked the question 'How would a fighter plane designed by a feminist look any different from one designed by a man?' If our immediate response is that feminists do not design fighter planes then perhaps we should acknowledge that feminists do not design AI applications either. But this will not do as it loses sight of the political project. To hope for change is to show how change can be made no matter how modest the beginnings.

3 Background to the Linguistics Project

The project started with a consideration of the role of language in feminist theory. At least from the early 1980s onwards, there has been a growing awareness that natural language is never neutral with regard to gender [11]. In contrast with the Anglo-American feminist tradition which grew out of grass-roots equal rights movements, Continental feminism has laid particular emphasis on language [12].

The crucial question for the current project became: if feminist linguistic models challenge the models of traditional views of language then how might this challenge be incorporated into the design of an AI system which analyses language? The project itself (reported in detail in [13]) sought to add a gender dimension to software tools which model conversational analysis. This involved criticizing and augmenting a model of the repair of conversational misunderstandings and non-understandings [14, 15, 16]. This resulted in a formal (i.e. logic based) model which could be used to predict the outcomes of inter-gender miscommunications and which forms the basis for a design of a computer system to perform the same task.

Natural language understanding (NLU) has continued to be an important part of AI research throughout its history. Early NLU systems such as Winograd's [17] SHRDLU, a system which reasoned about a toy blocks world and Weizenbaum's [18] ELIZA, which acted as a non-directive psychoanalyst were hailed as successes by the AI community of the day. However it soon became clear that the reasons for their apparent successes lay in the severely restricted nature of their dialogues. In SHRDLU's case this was due to the sort of toy blocks 'micro-world' for which AI has since become notorious. In ELIZA's case it was because the kind of dialogue expected of that particular type of psychoanalyst was of a very artifical nature. The dialogue soon breaks down when attempts to inject common sense are made. Nevertheless there are still compelling reasons why the ability to represent natural language in a computer system would be desirable in interfaces to existing computers systems, eg. spreadsheets, databases, operating systems and also in automatic abstracting, automatic translation and intelligent language based searches for information.

An important part of the process of understanding language is to understand when there has been a misunderstanding between speakers and to repair that misunderstanding in a meaningful way when it occurs. Indeed Collins [19] suggests that the reason that machines do not, so far, share our culture or 'form of life' rests upon the interpretative asymmetry which exists in the interactions between humans and machines. We, as humans, are so good at repairing and making sense of the rudimentary, often fragmentary, signals which make up conversation that we can make sense of almost anything, that is if that something is meant to make sense and we are not being tricked in some way. But until machines can act in that way, the asymmetry in our relative powers of interpretation will remain. Even if it is never possible to build a full natural language understanding interface, and many believe that it is not, the understanding behind at least a partial natural language processing interface would be of considerable interest both in general for computer scientists and for feminists researching language.

4 Conversational Misunderstandings ñ Is Gender Missing?

The original inspiration for this work came from the feeling of unease with the 'finessing' away of social factors which is pervasive in AI work. This was very much in evidence when we began to look at the original material on conversational misunderstandings on which this project is based. It seemed to us that the authors had finessed away many of the 'social factors' which made their conversational excerpts misunderstandings in the first place. These inter-related factors include age, size, race, class and gender; subtle power relations are implied, connotations of body language are missed by the traditional account. For instance, take the following reported misunderstanding [15: p. 227].

Speaker A: Where's CSC1004 taught?
Speaker B: Sidney Smith Building, room 2118, but the class is full.
Speaker A: No, I teach it.

Hirst [15] describes that Speaker *B* assumes that *A*'s plan is to take course CSC104, when in fact her plan is to teach it. However there are a number of salient facts within this example which only emerged when one of us quizzed the author directly at a conference. *A* was at the time one of his graduate students and in her twenties (*B* is a male administrator) – the author agreed that age has something to do with the misunderstanding. But at the time of our conversation he pointed out that *A*, having reached her thirties was now going grey, and he felt would not now have the same problem. We can only speculate as to whether women, in a desperate attempt to be taken seriously, have somehow got hold of hair products which perform the inverse of those that promise to magic the grey away! In all fairness, subsequent correspondence with the author suggests that he is much more sympathetic to an incorporation of gender than the original encounter suggests, although perhaps not sympathetic enough to have gender included in the first place. But this only serves to underline the complexity of the relationship between gender and age. True, if *A* were a young man, he might have had the same problem. But we wonder if a middle-aged male *A* would fare differently, and what about a middle-aged female *A*? And what about the gender of *B*? The mantle of authority which men acquire as they grow older is much harder won by women. There are different ways of not taking a woman seriously which may vary according to her perceived stage in life. The point about this is that there is a rich sub-text in examples such as this one and it is this layer, we argue, which gives the example meaning and which probably causes the misunderstanding to occur in the first place.

There is now a wealth of literature on gender and language. This ranges from Spender's [20] and Lakoff's [21] work which has exerted considerable influence in the assertiveness industry of the 1980s, to Tannen's more recent work [22, 23] some of which is aimed at a more popular market, and which demonstrates the complexity of men's and women's linguistic interactions. Most pertinently, *You Just Don't Understand* [22] covered precisely the subject matter in this project. Tannen's [22] and Fishman's [24] researches suggest that there are several differences in the way that men and women approach a conversation. In particular Fishman [24] found that women work much harder than men in initiating and maintain a conversation and worked harder in repairing misunderstandings in mixed (i.e. between men and women) conversations. (See Appendix A, for the way in which this is illustrated in our model.) This suggests that there are important elements, relating to gender, which need to be incorporated to provide a rich enough picture for a model of misunderstanding and this could arguably help in the development of speech analysis, recognition and synthesis. Interpreting everyday communication is far from simple. Speech understanding applications need to resolve ambiguity without added information from acoustic stress, intonation and indeed without the information of the particular characteristics of the speakers.

5 Developing the Model

Tannen's [22, 23] research on men's and women's linguistic behaviours shows the way in which men seek to enhance status, while women seek to level out hierarchies. Independence is traditionally associated with male behaviour; intimacy with female. The complexities of these elements add extra layers of meaning to conversational misunderstandings which would be difficult to capture in a model which was gender blind. For instance Tannen [22] offers two examples of misunderstandings which can only be made understandable in the light of the genders of the participants. In the first, a woman asks her male partner what time the concert is, only to be told what time to be ready. In the second, a man asks his female partner if she is leaving, only to be told he can take a nap. On the surface these misunderstandings look to be the same. However when the man in the first example was asked his aim, he said he was trying to be protective. On the other hand, the woman in the second conversation intended to be helpful.

Hirst's research on the analysis of mis- and non-understandings includes a number of top-level action schemas which are used to describe the actions of the parties in a conversation. These include things like accept-plan(NameOfPlan) which signals the speaker's acceptance of the plan and reject-plan(NameOfPlan) which signals that the speaker is rejecting the plan which is being offered by the other speaker. These top-level schemas are decomposable into surface linguistic actions. Combining Tannen's [22] analyses with Hirst's research [15] suggests that there are a number of distinct patterns in female to female, male to male and mixed conversations to the extent that we have developed a predictive model (see Appendix A for the model and Appendix B for an application of it to an example conversation). In other words, we are arguing that it is possible, at least to some extent, to predict the response expected to each conversational turn following gender patterns described in the model. In particular, this suggests that a woman will avoid terminating a conversation using reject-plan as a man might do; instead she might use postpone, expand or replace to encourage another reponse from her conversant. With this augmented format we have been able to produce more exact analyses of a number of conversations. Using the new models as a basis for a conversation analysis tool, misunderstandings can be predicted: if a man responds with a form that is not expected by a woman, or *vice versa*, an analysis tool would recognize the beginnings of a misunderstanding possibly before the participants can. It is important to note that this does not constitute a claim that male and female conversational interactions will follow these proposals in every culture. This is very much a white, UK, middle-class model, something which, we believe, is not made explicit in the original linguistics research from which this project follows. We cannot even claim that it is Anglo-American, given that, for instance, New York Jewish conversation contains more interruptions than non-New Yorkers [23]. There is plenty of anthropological and ethnographical evidence [25] to show how men and women make different uses of language, which is often more apparent in non-European languages, some of which seem to support two separate vocabularies.

6 Conclusion

Our involvement in this research has made us aware of unresolved contradictions. It could be argued that we have actually made an example of a 'fighter plane designed by a feminist', in other words, were we to put together the software system based on the model described above, we may have something which does not look substantially different from a computer system designed along more traditional lines. At the nuts and bolts level of PROLOG predicates it might be hard to distinguish a PROLOG predicate written by a feminist from one written by a hard-line male misogynist, despite research on men's and women's different programming styles [26]. But to argue along these lines misses the point of the endeavour. In addition, although we are in sympathy with feminist writing which has been critical of the way in which modern linguistics is cast in the form of predicate logic, following Nye [27], we acknowledge that our project follows the logic of the original research albeit to suggest modifications and amendments.

We are aware of the limitations of our model in imposing a formal structure on the rich complexity and widely varying conversational interactions available to men and women in different cultural settings. We concede this project uses entirely conventional techniques of knowledge representation and programming which we have criticized elsewhere for being unable to capture all the important things about knowledge, especially women's knowledge [28, 9, 10]. The original could have been criticized without offering these alternatives but we suggest that then the critique would have lost much of its force; it is criticizing the original research both from the point of view of feminism and in its own terms to offer an alternative model, which is important. We hope that it is a beginning and may offer hope of subverting traditional areas of information technology towards more feminist ends. Even if it is perhaps not reasonable, as yet, to imagine a fully working system based on our model, we hope that it can lend support to work which challenges the notion that newer forms of computer mediated communication are *ab initio* gender neutral and democratic and which demonstrate that male dominance is often magnified in men's and women's networked linguistic interactions [29, 30].

References

1. F. Henwood: Establishing Gender Perspectives on Information Technology: Problems, Issues and Opportunities. In E.E. Green, J. Owen, D. Pain (eds.): Gendered by Design? Information Technology and Office Systems. London and Washington, D.C.: Taylor & Francis 1993, pp. 31–49
2. E.E. Green: Gender Perspectives, Office Systems and Organizational Change. In A. E. Adam, J.M. Emms, E.E. Green, J. Owen (eds.): IFIP Transactions A-57, Women, Work and Computerization: Breaking Old Boundaries – Building New Forms. Amsterdam: Elsevier 1994, pp. 365–377
3. R. Tong: Feminist Thought: A Comprehensive Introduction, London: Routledge 1994
4. J. Wajcman: Feminism Confronts Technology. Cambridge: Polity Press 1991

5. F. Grundy: Women and Computers. Exeter, UK: Intellect Books 1996
6. C. Metselaar: Gender Issues in the Design of Knowledge Based Systems. In I. Eriksson, B. Kitchenham, K. Tijdens (eds.): Women, Work and Computerization 4, Amsterdam: Elsevier 1991, pp. 233-246
7. S. Harding: Whose Science? Whose Knowledge?: Thinking from Women's Lives. Milton Keynes: Open University Press 1991
8. H. Rose: Love, Power and Knowledge: Towards a Feminist Transformation of the Sciences. Cambridge: Polity Press 1994
9. A.E. Adam: Embodying Knowledge: A Feminist Critique of Artificial Intelligence. European Journal of Women's Studies 2, 355–77 (1995)
10. A.E. Adam: Constructions of Gender in the History of Artificial Intelligence. IEEE Annals of the History of Computing 18, 47–53 (1996)
11. S. Tromel Plotz: Languages of Oppression. Journal of Pragmatics 5, 67–80 (1981)
12. S. Sellers: Language and Sexual Difference: Feminist Writing in France. Basingstoke, UK and London: Macmillan Education 1991
13. M. Scott: Conversation Analysis Model to Incorporate Gender Differences. Unpublished Final Year Project Report, Department of Computation, UMIST 1996
14. P.A. Heeman, G. Hirst: Collaborating on Referring Expressions. Computational Linguistics 21, 351–382 (1995)
15. G. Hirst, S.W. McRoy, P. Heeman, P. Edmonds, D. Horton: Repairing Conversational Misunderstandings and Non-understandings. Speech Communication 15, 213–229 (1994)
16. S.W. McRoy, G. Hirst: The Repair of Speech Act Misunderstandings by Abductive Inference. Computational Linguistics 21, 435–478 (1995)
17. T. Winograd: Understanding Natural Language. New York: Academic Press 1972
18. J. Weizenbaum: ELIZA – A Computer Program for the Study of Natural Language Communication Between Man and Machine. Communications of the ACM 9, 36–45 (1966)
19. H. M. Collins: Artificial Experts: Social Knowledge and Intelligent Machines. Cambridge, MA.: MIT Press 1990
20. D. Spender: Man Made Language. London: Routledge & Kegan Paul 1980
21. R. Lakoff: Language and Woman's Place. New York: Harper & Row 1975
22. D. Tannen: You Just Don't Understand: Women and Men in Conversation. London: Virago 1992
23. D. Tannen: Gender and Discourse. Oxford: Oxford University Press 1994
24. P.M. Fishman: Interaction: The Work Women Do. In B. Thorne, C. Kramarae, N. Henley (eds.): Language, Gender and Society. Rowley, MA.: Newbury House 1983, pp. 89–101
25. J. Coates: Women, Men, and Language: A Sociolinguistics Account of Gender Differences in Language. London and New York: Longman 1986
26. S. Turkle, S. Papert: Epistemological Pluralism: Styles and Voices within the Computer Culture. Signs 16 128–157 (1990)

27. A. Nye: The Voice of the Serpent: French Feminism and Philosophy of Language. In A. Garry, M. Pearsall (eds.): Women, Knowledge and Reality: Explorations in Feminist Philosophy. New York and London: Routledge 1992, pp. 233–249
28. A.E. Adam: Who Knows How? Who Knows That? Feminist Epistemology and Artificial Intelligence. In A. E. Adam, J.M. Emms, E.E. Green, J. Owen (eds.): IFIP Transactions A-57, Women, Work and Computerization: Breaking Old Boundaries – Building New Forms. Amsterdam: Elsevier 1994, pp. 143–156
29. L. Cherny, E.R. Weise (eds.): wired_women: Gender and New Realities in Cyberspace. Seattle, Washington: Seal Press 1996
30. S. Herring: Posting in a Different Voice: Gender and Ethics in CMC. In C. Ess (ed.): Philosophical Perspectives on Computer-Mediated Communication. Albany, NY: State University of New York Press 1996, pp 115–145

Appendix A - Proposed Models of Linguistic Interaction

Note the relative simplicity (abruptness?) of male to male conversation where postpone, replace and expand are used less often than in female speech.

Female to Female Conversation

	may be followed by:
propose-plan	accept-plan, postpone-plan, replace-plan, expand-plan.
accept-plan	expand-plan, postpone-plan, replace-plan, nothing.
postpone-plan	expand-plan, replace-plan.
replace-plan	accept-plan, postpone-plan, expand-plan.
expand-plan	accept-plan, postpone-plan, replace-plan, expand-plan.

reject-plan is rarely found in female-female speech.

Male to Male Conversation

	may be followed by:
propose-plan	accept-plan, reject-plan.
accept-plan	nothing.
reject-plan	replace-plan, nothing.
postpone-plan	nothing.
replace-plan	accept-plan, reject-plan.
expand-plan	accept-plan, reject-plan

Mixed Conversations
Male to Female:

	may be followed by:
M_propose-plan	F_accept-plan, F_postpone-plan, F_replace plan, F_expand-plan.
M_accept-plan	F_expand-plan, F_postpone-plan, F_replace-plan, nothing.
M_reject-plan	F_expand-plan, F_postpone-plan, F_replace-plan, nothing.

M_postpone-plan	F_expand-plan, F_ replace-plan.
M_replace-plan	F_accept-plan, F_postpone-plan, F_expand-plan.
M_expand-plan	F_accept-plan, F_postpone-plan, F_replace-plan, F_expand-plan.

Female to Male:

	may be followed by:
F_propose-plan	M_accept-plan, M_reject-plan.
F_accept-plan	nothing.
F_postpone-plan	M_accept-plan, M_reject-plan.
F_replace-plan	M_accept-plan, M_reject-plan.
F_expand-plan	M_accept-plan, M_reject-plan

Appendix B

Example of conversation (from [22]) analyzed according to the augmented model proposed in [13]. In the original model [15], the problem in the conversation below begins with turn 2 which is intended as an expand-plan, but is interpreted as a reject-plan; this is not apparent, however until turn 8, allowing the misunderstanding to compound over several turns in between. Scott's [13] additions to Hirst's model include (1) a propose-plan to describe the introduction of a plan into conversation and (2) a classification of each speaker by gender at the beginning of the conversation, prior to analysis. Knowing the speaker's gender makes it possible to predict the response expected to each form according to patterns described by [22, 23, 24].

1. Female: 'The only weekend we seem to have free is October 10th.'
   F_propose-plan (p1)
2. Male: 'That's the opening of the hunting season.'
   M_expand-plan(p1) & surface-inform (M,F, p2)
   [expected to be M_reject-plan (p1)]
3. Female: 'Well, let's do it Saturday or Sunday evening.'
   F_replace-plan (p1) [to repair M_reject-plan (p1)]
4. Male: 'Okay, make it Saturday.'
   M-accept-plan (p1)
5. Female: 'Wouldn't you want to hunt later on the first day of hunting?'
   F_postpone-plan (p1, p2) [still trying to repair M_reject-plan (p1)]
6. Male: 'I said Saturday, so obviously, that's the day I prefer.'
   M_accept-plan (p1), repair of F_postpone-plan (p1)
7. Female: 'I was just trying to be considerate of you. You didn't give a reason for choosing Saturday.'
   surface-informref (F, M, surface-request (F, M))
8. Male: 'I'm taking off Thursday and Friday to hunt, so I figure I'll have had enough by Saturday night.'
   M_expand-plan (p2)
9. Female: 'Well, why didn't you say that?'
   surface-request (F,M)

10. Male: 'I didn't see why I had to. And I found your question very intrusive.'
surface-informref (M,F)

11. Female: 'And I found your response very offensive.'
surface-informref (F,M)

Exploring the Excluded. A Feminist Approach to Opening New Perspectives in Computer Science

Dr. Ulrike Erb,

Gneisenaustr. 90, D - 28201 Bremen

Abstract. This paper presents some results of my empirical study of the professional ways and experiences of female computer scientists in their discipline, and I draw some conclusions for further feminist research *inside* the discipline of computer science.

Among other things, my study shows that, to deconstruct the stereotype of a "women-specific distanced relation to technology", it is not only necessary to explicate exactly the kind of technology we are referring to, but it is also necessary for women themselves reflect upon their self-perception concerning their technical competences.

Furthermore, my empirical study shows that many of the women interviewed are missing need- and use-oriented research questions, and that many of them complain of the marginalization of "non-technical" skills and approaches in computer science. Finally, in this paper it is argued that by exploring "the excluded" feminist research could open new perspectives in computer science.

1 Introduction

My study of the professional ways and experiences of female computer scientists in their discipline (Erb 1996), is based on an inquiry among graduate women who are working as computer scientists. The empirical part was performed in 1991/1992. First, I sent questionnaries to all graduate female computer scientists working as assistant or professor in computer science faculties of German universities, altogether 77 women (46 in the eastern and 31 in the western part of Germany). 55 % of these women replied to my questionnaries, in which I asked for their biographical backgrounds, for their professional paths and for their main research fields. Based on these answers I had qualitative interviews with 22 of these women (5 from the eastern and 17 from the western part of Germany). The interviews showed more of their motives for studying computer science, of the experiences they made in this field, of the obstacles they had to cope with. Furthermore I asked for their research fields and their research preferences in computer science, I wanted to know if they were missing anything in computer science or in their research jobs, and if there was anything they disliked in their professional lives.

2 The Low Participation of Women in Computer Science

Until now, women have been almost excluded from computer science and they have had almost no chance to participate in building this discipline. When I performed my investigation, the proportion of women working in computer science faculties was about 8,7%. Previous studies of women in computer and engineering sciences asked above all for the reasons for the low participation rate of women in these sciences. The growing relevance of computer science professions, gendered division of labour and a closed association of men, power and technology, as well as the divergence of (socially constructed) stereotypes of experts in technology and of femininity are some of the reasons asserted by such studies (compare Janshen/Rudolph 1987, Roloff 1989, Wajcman 1991, Schmitt 1993). Furthermore, the Norwegian scientists Tove Håpnes and Bente Rasmussen (1991) show persuadingly that a certain hacker culture is one of the main reasons for the marginalization of women in computer science. They show that the "culture" of computer science at the Norwegian Institute of Technology is dominated by the values and interests of male computer freaks, especially by "their machine-fascination and -fixation, their work hours and their work-style". However, Håpnes and Rasmussen have found that the dominance of the freak culture is produced and reproduced by *all members* of the computer science department, that is not only by the computer freaks, other male students and the male staff but also by the *female students* of this subject.

In view of the results of those investigations, in my study I wanted to know more about female computer scientists, who, inspite of the hacker culture and women's marginalization, have successfully made their way in computer science. I was interested in the experiences of this female minority, and I wanted to know how these women managed to make a career in a professional field which typically is the domain of men. Especially, I turned my attention to *women's views* of computer science, which are the views of a nearly excluded minority. I wanted to find out, if the women's views open new perspectives on this discipline. For me, being a computer scientist myself, it was very important to present this study as a PhD thesis in a *computer science faculty*, because I wanted my results to have some influence on this discipline, and because I think from the women's perspectives we can learn how to open new perspectives on computer science, which would open new possibilities for women (and perhaps for men too).

3 Main Results of my Empirical Study

- **Theoretical Computer Science as an Access Path for Women to Computer Science**
  My empirical study shows that nearly all of my interviewees came into computer science because of an interest in mathematics and logic, some of them also because of an interest in natural sciences. Only two women (both from the former GDR) have come to computer science with a technical or engineering background.

  Many of the women interviewed changed the domain of their research subjects during their academic career. While at the beginning of their careers most of them specialized in theoretical domains of computer science, later on they changed to practical research and to application oriented subjects. Only two of my interviewees still feel that they are theoretical computer scientists. The others nearly all emphasize that (at the latest after their graduation) it is important for them to develop concrete applications or to research in a context with practical relevance. They often left theoretical computer science, because for them theoretical research was too abstract, or because they missed the possibility to identify a concrete problem of practical relevance which might be solved by their theoretical researches.

It becomes evident that their fascination in mathematics and logic is combined with the motivation to do use-oriented research. And it becomes evident as well that, though the women interviewed have multiple interests in computer science, for most of them *mathematical and theoretical domains served as an access path to computer science.*

I assume the following explanation for the women's start in theoretical computer science: It is much more difficult for women than for men to decide to study computer science, because until now, women have been marginalized in this discipline, and because there exists a 'common stereotype that technology is inherently masculinist'. So, for most of my interviewees, an important prerequisite for being encouraged to study computer science was to be successful in mathematics at school. (At that time informatics was not yet taught in schools, and computer science was supposed to be a discipline very close to logic and mathematics.) Consequently, for these interviewees the security of being competent in mathematics was an important factor influencing their primary orientation to theoretical fields of computer science. Another motive for their theoretical orientation was that they preferred the culture in theoretical working groups: In theoretical computer science competence is less a question of *competition*, and success is less a question of elbowing one's way than in other fields of computer science, because in theoretical computer science competence is well defined; it depends on the correct application of logical rules and on an ability to argue logically. For women, who typically are less socialised in competition and elbowing than men, the possibility of proving their competence without competing seems to be important in getting a footing in computer science (for more detail see Erb 1996).

- **Techno-centered Computer Culture as an Obstacle for Women**

  Further results from my inquiry call into question the often pretended distanced relationship between women and technology, and they especially call into question the underlying use of terms like "technology" and "technical".[1] The female computer scientists interviewed describe the main obstacles in their professional paths as being caused by a machine- and techno-centered culture in this discipline. Many of them have difficulties with the dominance of computer-centered attitudes and with the high estimation of computer freaks, who are in control of the latest technological innovations.

  The interviews show that even among computer scientists it remains vague what it means to be competent in computer technology or to be a "technical insider": Does it mean sitting all day and night in front of the computer? Does it

1 In the German language, I refer to the terms "Technik" and "technisch".

mean knowing every bit and byte or knowing the latest software? Or does it mean knowing how to construct blinking surfaces? In the interviews it became evident that in fact all this is associated with technical competence, while on the other hand knowledge on system design like requirements engineering, specification and design of algorithms is not thought to belong to technical competence.

Furthermore, looking at the interviews, it can be seen that the women interviewed describe only the competence of others as being technical competence, while they think of their own competence as being non-technical. This is especially remarkable, because their working practices described in the interviews prove of very competent technic-near occupations with computer technology. So, their professional activities consist in the development of diverse software systems, in constructing operating systems, in designing interfaces, in building expert systems and so on. But nevertheless, they do not feel as "technical insiders". Some of them describe their own approaches to computers as pragmatic and use-oriented approaches. Others consider themselves as using the computer only when they *need* it, and not for exploring it or playing with it. It would seem that these women do not want their working styles being identified with the techno-centered hacker-style or with computer-fixated approaches. So, in describing their occupations they distinguish their own approaches from computer-centered approaches. This means at the same time that they keep their distance from an image of "technical insiders". They keep this distance even though on the other hand they admire the know how of "technical insiders", and even though, in social contexts and in computer science, this image is held in higher estimation than need- and application-oriented approaches. As my study shows, the women's self-perception of not being "technical insiders" is to a great extent due to an indistinct notion of technical competence, which allows them to associate certain activities at one moment with technical competences and at the next with non-technical skills. I have found a similar indistinct use of terms like "technical" and "technology" in social science studies of the relation of women and men to technology. There is some evidence that, as these studies don't explain their use of the notion "technical" and as they don't differentiate between the various meanings of this notion, they tend to reproduce stereotypes of "technical competences" as being inherently masculinist and of a "distanced relationship to technology" as being inherently feminist. (See for more detail Erb 1994 and 1996).

- **Need-orientation versus Machine-centered Approaches**
  Common to many of my interviewees is the fact that they complain of the high estimation of machine-centered approaches in computer science while need-oriented approaches are neglected. For example, one of them reported of her experience that the development of a blinking prototype with amazing show effects was very much appreciated in her research group though the prototype did not work well and though it was not adaptable to the needs of the later users. In contrast to this, an approach, which designed a protoype *after* investigating the users' needs and requirements did not attract the same appreciation. Other computer scientists interviewed reported of being the only ones in their research groups who asked about the needs of the developed system in its later application context or who asked about the needs of the later users of the system. Another one complained

that criss-cross programming with quick results often gets more appreciation than the development of well structured and reusable software.

However, though many of the female computer scientists interviewed are missing need- or use-oriented approaches, this does not imply that their individual research practices already consist of need- and application-oriented approaches. Most of them do not see any possibility of pursuing such approaches within their research work. By the way, to prevent a misunderstanding, I do not think that need-oriented research is necessarily equivalent to social-oriented research. For example, it is possible to develop use-oriented information systems which have the aim of controlling the activities of persons, or of developing expert systems which are useful for military applications. Moreover, several of my interviewees had to admit that they were not sure whether their research might have undesirable social or ecological impacts.

Three conclusions I derive from these findings:

1. If we want to know more about the relation of women and men to (computer) technology, it is imperative to explicate exactly the kind of technology or the kind of technical competence we are referring to.
2. The fact that most of my interviewees describe their working practices as being non-technical and their approaches to computers as being pragmatic is not proof of their distanced relation to computer techniques. Rather it proves their distanced relation to techno-centered habits. So, if we want to deconstruct the stereotype of a "women-specific distanced relation to technology" it is not only necessary to distinguish between different kinds of technology, it is also necessary that women themselves reflect upon their self-perception concerning their technical competences.
3. From the women's perspectives, pragmatic, need- and application-oriented approaches often are considered as being excluded or marginalized in computer science, while techno-centered attitudes and approaches are dominating this discipline.

4 Women's Perspectives – the Excluded of Computer Science?

Though my investigation does not reveal the invention of a "female computer" or of a "female alternative to the binary logic", my investigation of the women's views of computer science reveals however some desire for changes in this discipline, changes which can be perceived in the research questions they are missing and in their discontent with several aspects concerning the "context of discovery". So, as mentioned above, many of the women interviewed are missing the need- and use-oriented research questions. Furthermore, many of them complain of the marginalization of "non-technical" skills and approaches in their research contexts.

In this context, it is notable that *consideration of the marginalized and excluded* seems to be a central concept of women's studies on "Women, Work and Computerization":

Cecile Crutzen states that modelling an information system is a gendered process because the man-made is assumed to be objective, while a possibly different female perspective is ignored (Crutzen 1995, p. 49). Lucy Suchman, who criticizes the missing accountability, the "view from nowhere" in systems design, proposes "a process of revealing multiple voices of design-in-use, which are often women's voices, as essential to the successful creation of working technical systems." (Suchman 1994, p. 130) In a quite similar way argues Alison Adam, who discusses the androcentric nature of Artificial Intelligence (AI): As traditional AI systems make "the knower at once invisible and universal" they exclude "alternative points of view where feminist epistemology emphasizes the standpoint of the observer which can include race and class as well as gender and also the role of the body in knowledge production. In this way AI systems, by the process of reifying knowledge, can be used to exclude the other, the different and inevitably women." (Adam 1994, p. 630) Though she cannot prove gender influence in the field of logic, the German philosopher Käthe Trettin, asks whether the radical formalization in logic is already *man-made* and whether the absence of subjectivity, the absence of qualities and of non-determination are already signs of a tacit, asymmetric valuation of gender. And she asks whether in consequence of this neutralisation, more values associated with female stereotypes are excluded from logic than "male" values. (Trettin 1991)

In these approaches "the female" is associated with the excluded perspective of the system users, with the "invisible work" of women (Star 1991), with the "invisible standpoint of the observer and knower" (Adam 1994), with the excluded subjectivity and variety (Crutzen 1995 and Trettin 1991). So, following Judy Wajcman (1991), who shows a certain association between men, power and technology, I assume a certain association between women, marginalization and the excluded aspects of technology. Evidently, the female computer scientists interviewed during my investigation would identify more with working in this discipline, if such excluded aspects were to be integrated into computer science. It can be assumed that a change of paradigms into computer science which integrated these excluded aspects would open up new chances for the participation of women in this discipline.

5 Conclusion

In my opinion, the purpose of studying women's perspectives is not only to support women's interests in computer science. In particular if we do feminist research inside the discipline of computer science, one main purpose of this research might be to explore forgotten and excluded aspects of computer science. As my study shows, investigating the perspectives of women in this discipline helps reveal potential for changes in computer science, that means for changes, which are not necessarily indicated in the working practices of the women interviewed, but changes which are described in the interviews as the excluded or neglected potential of computer science. I think, in this field there is a great need for women's research and in particular for women's research done by female computer scientists. In this way women's studies can help to reveal the excluded and *to integrate the excluded in order to enrich computer science by means of the forgotten perspectives.* Integration of the excluded and a corresponding change of the image and the paradigms of computer science could open new identification possibilities for women in this discipline, and it would also augment the possibilities for both women and men to realize their creative potentials in computer science.

References

1. Adam, Alison (1994): Who knows how? Who knows what? Feminist epistemology and artificial intelligence. In: Alison Adam; Judy Emms; Eileen Green; Jenny Owen (Eds.) (1994): Women, Work and Computerization "Breaking Old Boundaries: Building New Forms." Amsterdam, 143-156
2. Crutzen, Cecile K. M. (1995): Feministische Theorien: Eine Inspiration für Curriculum-Entwicklungen in der Informatik. In: Frauenarbeit und Informatik 11/1995, 45-54
3. Erb, Ulrike (1994): Technikmythos als Zugangsbarriere für Frauen zur Informatik. In: Zeitschrift für Frauenforschung 3/1994, 28-40
4. translated in Norwegian as: Teknologimyten – en barriere mellom kvinnene og informatikk-utdanningen? In: Nytt om kvinneforskning 4/1994, 23-33
5. Erb, Ulrike (1996): Frauenperspektiven auf die Informatik. Informatikerinnen im Spannungsfeld zwischen Distanz und Nähe zur Technik. Münster
6. Håpnes, Tove; Rasmussen, Bente (1991): The Production of Male Power in Computer Science. In: Inger V. Eriksson, Barbara A. Kitchenham, Kea G. Tijdens (Eds) (1991): Understanding and Overcoming Bias in Work and Education. Proceedings of the IFIP-Conference on Women, Work and Computerization 1991 in Helsinki, Finland. North-Holland, 395-406
7. Roloff, Christine (1989): Von der Schmiegsamkeit zur Einmischung. Professionalisierung der Chemikerinnen und Informatikerinnen. Pfaffenweiler
8. Schmitt, Bettina (1993): Neue Wege - alte Barrieren. Beteiligungschancen von Frauen in der Informatik, Berlin
9. Star, Susan Leigh (1991): Invisible Work and Silenced Dialogues in Knowledge Representation. In: Eriksson/Kitchenham/Tijdens (1991): Women, Work and Computerization. Understanding and Overcoming Bias in Work and Education. 81-92
10. Suchman, Lucy (1994): Located Accountability: Aspects of a feminist practice of technology production. In: Eberhart/Wächter (eds.): 2nd European Feminist Research Conference. Feminist Perspectives on Technology, Work and Ecology. Proceedings. July 5-9, 1994 Graz/Austria. 124-131
11. Trettin, Käthe (1991): Die Logik und das Schweigen - zur antiken und modernen Epistemotechnik. Weinheim
12. Wajcman, Judy (1991): Feminism Confronts Technology. Cambridge (UK)

Accepted Papers and Discussion Notes

Topic 3: Panel

"Not Without a Body? Bodily Functions in Cyberspace"

To be in Touch or not?
Some Remarks on Communication in Virtual Environments

Barbara Becker

German National Research Center for Information Technology
Schloss Birlinghoven, D-53754 Sankt Augustin, Germany
Barbara.Becker@gmd.de

At first glance, text-based communication in virtual environments, i.e. in MUDs and MOOs, is characterized by an absence of the physical body. In fact, the possibility to escape from the own body[1] seems to be one of the main motivational factors to participate in virtual spaces. Even if we agree that the body is still there as a social and discoursive construct[2], we have to admit, that the sense of embodiment in virtual environments is an entirely constructed feeling[3], coming mainly from our consciousness and not from our physical and sensual impressions.[4] We are in touch with our dialog partners only via text.

Looking at the implication of this, I would like to outline two arguments very briefly:

1) to show that the absence of the physical body may be seen as one important reason for misunderstanding in virtual environments;
2) to point out that the processes in virtual spaces should rather be regarded as production and reception of literature than communication in "real life".

1) It is obvious that the absence of the body in virtual spaces implies a lack of nonverbal communication strategies, i.e. gesture, facial expression, and other signs of the body. It is well known that these signs play an important role in understanding others. Furthermore, the body has become more and more an important guarantee for evaluating what has been said: signals and signs of the body are often interpreted as hints to decide whether the communication partner is speaking truthfully and authentically. The relevance of believing in trustful and authentic argumention for successful communication has been pointed out by Apel and Habermas very clearly. Therefore we may assume that the absence of sensorical and bodily impressions is a main reason of miscomprehension in virtual spaces.

---

[1] which sometimes is seen as a prison, see some remarks in Turkle, S. "Life on the Screen"
[2] Sandy Stone 1993
[3] Lynn Cherny, "´Objectifying` the body in the discourse of an object-oriented MUD"
[4] Being a body in cyberspace can be compared with the cartesian and idealistic tradition, where the idea of the body and its intellectual construction have been interpreted as more relevant than our primary sensoric impressions and our direct contact with the world via our body. There is a long tradition in phenomenology where this cartesian and idealistic tradition has been attacked very strongly by pointing out the relevance of our physical Being in the world

2) According to this, we may ask more generally: Can we describe the processes in virtual environments in terms of communication analog to real-life-interaction? What do we know about our dialog partners when we are only confronted with what they have written?

To put it radically, I suppose that we rather have contact with a fiction of ourselves than with a concrete person: We interact with a product of our imagination and projection. This applies especially to text-based communication in virtual spaces like MOOs or MUDs, where we have only very little information about our dialog partners because of the absence of the physical body and because of the possibility to construct the body in a desired way; i.e. we don´t know whether we are talking to a male or female or neutral persona or even a program[5]. In real life, there is a primary contact between me and the others through our bodies and our sensual impressions: We see our dialog partners, we feel something, we smell them, we hear their voices, we are aware of their physical presence, we are in touch and touched by them through our body without being totally aware of what happens between us and what we know already about the other one before and besides speaking to him or her.[6] Therefore, the space for projection and imagination is limited. Insofar, the processes in virtual spaces should not be compared to real life communication but rather with the production and reception of literature, where we project our desires, wishes and hopes in the fictional persons and literal heros in the same way as we seem to do it in these virtual environments.

[5] This explains the often described shock-effect in real-life contacts after having met in virtual spaces before.

[6] This has been shown very clearly by phenomenological tradition in philosophy, i.e. Merleau-Ponty, Waldenfels, Meyer-Drawe, Taylor, Madison.., see i.e. Metraux, A., Waldenfels, B., "Leibhaftige Vernunft", München 1986

The Physical Body in Cyberspace: At the Edge of Extinction?

Kerstin Dautenhahn

The University of Reading, Department of Cybernetics
Whiteknights, PO Box 225, Reading, RG6 6AY, United Kingdom
kd@cyber.reading.ac.uk
http://arti.vub.ac.be/~kerstin/home.html

My research is about embodied, "socially intelligent agents". I am interested in how autonomous agents (hardware agents, robots, as well as simulated or virtual agents) explore their environment and interact with the world, including interaction of agents of the same "matter" as well as "multi-species" interactions. As soon as a human is involved in these interactions (in the role of a user or just as a co-inhabitant of the same real or virtual environment), all interactions are "cross-species" (e.g. between humans and robots or between humans and intelligent agents). The question is whether for all these different agents, contexts, situations and modes of interaction different mechanisms for interaction and communication have to be realized, or whether a common "social interface" exists, which is applicable to interaction and communication situations in general. So, is there anything "universal" which makes up "successful" communication situations, "successful" in terms of being efficient, enjoyable and "natural"? (With respect to artifacts "natural" means "acceptable", i.e. whether humans like to become engaged in interactions or not. Humans cannot avoid contacts to other humans, but artifacts and new technology can, to some extent, be used or not.)

I assume that there is such a common basis underlying interaction, communication and "understanding". If we talk about interaction and communication, in an entertainment or business context, agents have to understand each other. And all what nature (and studies in natural sciences confirm this) tells us is that understanding cannot be separated from a "living body", an embodied mind. Understanding means re-experiencing and re-construction of past experiences on the basis of the current context and bodily state of an agent. The body is the point of reference for the reconstruction of old "stories" and the reinvention of new ones; it is the point of reference for a developing personality. Additionally, in human species we find the most elaborated forms of self-manipulation, using the body as a "social tool", as a means to express personality and social roles, also as a means to manipulate others.

In public, but also in the scientific community, "cyberspace" is often used as a metaphor for a world where the human body only plays a minor role, where we are in danger of becoming a creature without a body, getting experiences by direct stimulation of the nervous system, where we will lose the sense for reality and get lost as a virtual creature in a virtual world. A world where we become isolated, ending up as extremely individualized selfish beings. Some people in the artificial intelligence and virtual reality community are very enthuastic about this bodiless future; they are looking forward to "getting rid" of the ("imperfect", mortal) body, i.e. they like the idea of transmitting their personality and intelligence to a computer memory and leading an immortal and perfect life.

I do not believe in such a future, for the following reasons. 1) If we create inside a computer memory anything analogous to the dynamics of nervous activities in our brain, then we should not hope that this activation pattern "is me". If intelligence and personality is so tightly connected to an active body, then why should this representation be human, and why should it behave intelligently at all? Moreover, all what we know about how meaning comes into the world, e.g. when a child grows up, is linked to a physical body, to physical experiences, to the full variety of pain and pleasure felt with a body. Even if we could (hypothetically) extract the essence of our personality in computational terms and transfer it to a computer memory, then who or what should "enjoy" immortality and "admire" the computational beauty of ist "life". We as humans, are able to "feel" the beauty of algorithms or data structures; the data structure itself definitely cannot!

2) Social interactions in real and virtual life are not only necessary to "entertain" humans or for solving a specific task (business meetings). Social interactions are important for the feeling of being there (the presence effect), to have "social" reality, to be "real". Social interactions are important for the development and maintanance of a personality and for behaving intelligently. Cyberspace can potentially enlarge the social network of people; it increases dramatically the chances to find "related souls", to get feedback and reinforcement from other people. Technology can and should support this social networking aspect.

3) In my view one should not regard virtual environments and reality as two different "worlds". In the same way could we make the difference between "real worlds" and "fictional worlds" (which we know from novels, movies etc.), or "ideological worlds" (worlds of religion, politics, i.e. cultural constructions etc.). What matters are the ideas which are constructed in our embodied mind and which have an important meaning to us. A real person can have the same importance as a cartoon figure (e.g. to a child), or a football team (e.g. to adults). Technical devices which let humans enter virtual worlds manipulate the human body. They do not replace the body, they try to make virtual experiences (as we know them say, from watching TV) more realistic to us by allowing active exploration and interaction. This interactive aspect is the crucial difference to other media like TV or reading books. A movie or TV film tells a single story, we can re-experience according to a fixed timing, we are spatially and temporarily "enslaved", watching passively, consuming. Reading a novel is much more "powerful", but energy consuming. A "script" is given, but multiple potential realizations can be created inside or mind, we can re-write the story and choose the timing ourselves. But it is not "realistic", sensory-motor feeback is still missing. Since actively exploring the world is a crucial aspect in (animal) intelligent behavior and learning, virtual environments could potentially bridge this gap. Various metaphors in different languages show the strong interrelationshiop between understanding and physical activity, e.g. the German word "begreifen", touching with the mind requires touching with the hands. This "interactive" agent-environment coupling is the mechanism by which the world around us makes sense to us.

To conclude, in my view we are not in danger that the physical human body will become extinct in cyberspace. It will be re-interpreted, somehow re-invented. Its meaning and expression will be adapted to changing conceptions of (social) "reality". But it is the very same process which has been going on since members of the homo genus discovered themselves as embodied minds, as "I" and "you".

References (small selection)

1. Elliot Aronson (1994) The social animal, W.H. Freeman and Company, New York
2. Richard Byrne (1995) The thinking ape, evolutionary origins of intelligence, Oxford University Press
3. Kerstin Dautenhahn (1995) Getting to know each other - artificial social
4. intelligence for autonomous robots. Robotics and Autonomous systems
5. Kerstin Dautenhahn (1997) I could be you - the phenomenological dimension of social understanding, Cybernetics and Systems, special issue on epistemological issues of embodied artificial intelligence
6. Mark Johnson (1984) The body in the mind, University of Chicago Press, Chicago, London

Body Language Without the Body: Situating Social Cues in the Virtual World

Judith S. Donath

MIT Media Lab
20 Ames Street, E15-428, Cambridge, MA 02138
judith@media.mit.edu

The physical self is the locus for a wide range of social cues: gait, race, gender, hairstyle, gestures, etc. which all place the person in a particular location in society.

Such cues are sparse in the virtual world. In text-based environments, one's utterances emerge independent of any visible, palpable self. And graphical environments, while they hold out future promises of subtle gestures and virtual fashions, are still far from that stage; today's graphical environments with their simplisticly rendered avatars provide even fewer social cues than their textual counterparts, for they are missing the nuanced cadences of the written, conversational word.

This dearth of social cues is both good and bad. One of the most widely hailed features of on-line communication is its democratic leveling: one's thoughts and ideas, rather than one's age, race, gender, etc., are the first things known about one. Yet social cues are not simply vehicles for prejudice; they play an essential role in the formation of community and in our comprehension of social interactions. In particular, cues that reveal who one has become, that show one's affiliations, beliefs and interests, (as opposed to those based on one's genetic traits) are an integral part of commmunication.

Virtual worlds are synthetic spaces. Today's designers have the opportunity to create the foundation of new social structures. How social cues will evolve in these new worlds is in part a question of how the worlds are designed. Understanding the roles that such cues play in the physical world is necessary in order to build environments that draw from the best of the real world, without replicating its least desireable traits.

I will outline how social cues are embodied in the physical world and show ways that such cues are emerging in today's virtual world. I will then discuss how design affects this emergence and suggest some directions for future work.

Does Gender Still Matter?
Bodily Functions in Cyberspace: a Feminist Approach

Priska Gisler

University of Potsdam, Germany
gisler@rz.uni-potsdam.de

The gendered body theoretically does not play an important role anymore, considering for example the work at a computer screen -- nor does it in the world of the net where the decision for a gender is practically of free choice. So why do we have to think about bodies in Cyberspace?

In his concept of the *Domination Masculine*, French sociologist Pierre Bourdieu argues that the binarity of the category gender is a thousand-year old institution, inscribed into the objectivity of social structures and the subjectivity of mental structures (the thinking). As such, it is also integrated into the functioning of virtual reality as well as into the structures of Cyberspace.

Society is structured binarily by gender, says Bourdieu. This categorisation is considered being absolutely natural and normal. Gender difference is integrated into social relationships of domination and suppression as well as into our brains, our thinking and our thoughts. On a symbolic level all things in the world are classified according to this binarity as male or female. The classification of the world finally seems given as an objectivity. Gender functions as category arranging our thinking. How does that look in Cyberspace? In a virtual reality the possibility exists to abstract from two genders; it is possible to invent neutral figures, to play with binarities, categorisations, to deceive our expectations, or finally undo them. But nevertheless, gender has gone far beyond bodily characteristics, it is founded in our thinking, has gained its own existence, has become a factor structuring realities - virtual and real ones. So we will have to look carefully into gender play in Cyberspace.

Candace West and Don Zimmermann try an ethnomethodological approach to the understanding of gender. As a starting point, they consider gender as a routinely based, methodical and natural achievement. Gender is done by men and women, it contains socially based, interactive, micropolitical actions, their special conducts as expressions of the nature of male or female beings. West and Zimmermann argue to focus on interactive and institutional fields; actions are always based in social situations. Doing gender is fundamentally interactive and has institutional character, properties which aren't abolished in Cyberspace, where bodies are not as such present, but bodily signs are not forgotten. Even there exist requests of gender labeling (by "gender flags" for example), even if they do not necessarily have to do with the bodily gender of the real. Bodily representations reflect the possibilities of the "real world" but constitute an order of virtual reality. There is one important point which we should think about: the constituted social order seems to reflect "natural differences". But, by "doing gender", men do domination and women do give in. In this way, doing gender reinforces and legitimates hierarchical arrangements. Even if gender is not any more recognizable, is not any more evaluable, there exist symbolic meanings of opinions, properties, and actions connotated as male or female. Therefore, I propose to focus power processes in virtual worlds, how exclusions are functioning, how processes of hierarchisations are made possible, and how far they are played onto the backs of bodily representations and their symbolic meanings. As long as power structures are important in the net, gender will play an important role. And as long as it will not be possible to untie gender as a symbolic meaning from bodily ascriptions, body will be present in cyberspace.

References

1. Bourdieu, P. (1990): La domination masculine. In: Actes de la recherche en sciences sociales, No. 84, septembre 1990, Paris.
2. West, C., Zimmermann, D. (1991): Doing Gender. In: Lorber J., Farrell S.A.: The Social Construction of Gender. Sage, Newbury Park, Ca.

Flying Through Walls and Virtual Drunkenness: Disembodiment in Cyberspace?

Gloria Mark

German National Research Center for Information Technology
Schloss Birlinghoven, D-53754 Sankt Augustin, Germany
Gloria Mark@gmd.de

This panel is concerned with the question of what the body means in Cyberspace. Do we have the notion at all of physical disembodiment in Cyberspace? What form of representation do we actually experience, and how do we express ourselves and communicate through this? In contemplating this question, we must consider some basic points.

First, when we enter a virtual world, is it fair to say that our consciousness is separated from our bodies? When we consider this, we can refer to the mind-body problem in philosophy, where the relationship between the mind and the body has been interpreted in different ways: materialism vs. idealism, and the Cartesian tradition where a clear distinction between mind and body has influenced our point of view up to today. This distinction is exemplified by Daniel Dennett's (1982) point that people of a disembodied society would not get intoxicated, since it is the brain that gets drunk, and the blood supply of the body is not connected with the blood supply of the brain. On the other hand, although real grieving has been reported to occur when people's MUD characters are killed, death in a virtual world does not mean that our physical bodies have died. Should we really speak about disembodiment, or rather should we imagine a background-foreground relationship with our bodies where they exist more in the background as we enter a digital environment?

To what extent do we project our own bodies into a virtual world? Conventions and standards of bodies in the real world are too often carried over into virtual environments: the beauty myth is manifest in descriptions of bodies as sexy and beautiful; similarly there also exist many examples of virtual characters represented as strong and powerful bodies. Although in electronic worlds, status does not play a strong role in determining interactions, users have not completely escaped from the idea of status in many MUDs and MOOs. This holds true whether one chooses to be a wizard or when one is of lower status, in which case they generally treat a wizard with extreme deference and respect (Curtis, 1996). Are we too deeply infused with the notions of beauty, power, and status that our virtual characters must also represent these conventional ideas? Does the fact that we see so many examples of real world conventions about the body transported into the virtual world mean that we are really disembodied? Are we not portraying bodies of our virtual characters as those that we strive our own bodies to be like? How can we transcend the beauty myth in a virtual world and develop new ideas about attractivity of other individuals?

Our perception of a virtual world is still mediated through our senses in our physical bodies. However, the sensory information available in such a world is different and restricted, compared to our physical world experiences. Whereas in real life we receive sensory information through multiple perceptual channels, in a virtual world sensory information is restricted, either through a single or very few channels. In a text-based MUD, physical descriptions of ourselves and others, our gender, personalities, is all conveyed through a single channel. In a graphical virtual world, although visual information is present, it is often packaged into stereotypical representations. How does our use of different perceptual channels affect our ideas about our own and other actors' representations?

Although sensory information is different than our real world experience, technology is already providing us with new ways to explore movement in virtual environments. We can fly over landscapes, penetrate walls, enjoy multiple views simultaneously, move through all corners of Euclidean space, and step outside our portrayed representations, and back in again. Will these new experiences push our awareness of our body further into the background, will we feel completely disembodied, or will we be able to bring these bodily movement experiences back into our physical worlds to think anew about our own physical selves.

In this panel, we will explore the idea of the body experience in Cyberspace, through the perspectives of philosophy, sociology, psychology, social agent development, and virtual interface design.

References

1. Dennett, Daniel (1982). Where am I? In the Mind's I: Fantasies and Reflections on Self and Soul, D. R. Dennett and D. R. Hofstadter, eds. Harmondsworth, Eng: Penguin.
2. Curtis, Pavel (1996). Excerpt from „Mudding: Social Phenomena in Text-Based Virtual Realities. In M. Stefik, Internet Dreams: Archetypes, Myths, and Metaphors, Cambridge, MA: The MIT Press.

Between Deconstruction and Construction: Contradictory Body Experiences in the Development of Software

Christina Schachtner

Philipps-University of Marburg, Institut für Erziehungswissenschaft
Wilh.-Röpke Straße 6 B, D-35032 Marburg, Germany
+49 (06421) 28-47 75

This contribution is based on a study of computer-related thought processes, perceptions and actions in the development of software. Consultants on the study were software developers and researchers in the area of artificial intelligence. The empirical data are from qualitative interviews and body perceptions. The data evaluation indicates that there is a contradiction in body experiences in software production: A variety in bodily sensory stimulation contrasts with experiences of fragmentation and making functional of the body and its senses. Based on this result, I would like to pursue the idea more exactly of the decontruction and construction of body awareness in software production in preparation for the conference. I will analyze the data again with regard to their body-related contents and raise the questions: What new forms of bodily direction are shown in production and in action in virtual worlds? How successful are these direction attempts and what do they tell us about ideas of one's self? I will leave the decision as to whether to focus on the interviews with females or to include the statements made by male interview partners open at this point.

The verbal interpretation of the results will be expanded upon and differentiated by pictures drawn by the developers.

Accepted Papers and Discussion Notes

Topic 4: Labour and Living: Apart or Together?

Part 1: Local and Global Division of Labour: on the Way to Equality?

Formation of the "Global Office": Women and the Globalization of Information Labor

Stana B. Martin

Dept. of Radio/TV/Film, University of Texas at Austin
Austin, TX 78703

Abstract This paper defines and explores the phenomenon of the global office, or the international relocation of information work. It offers an explanation for why the global office is developing at this juncture in history, analyzes the skill patterns emerging with the transition to a global information labor market, and discusses the implications for women functioning therein.

1 Introduction

Trade journals now regularly report on the international relocation of information work.[1] "Global office,"[2] a term recently coined to describe this trend, is a play on the now familiar "global assembly line," or the international relocation of manufacturing labor. This paper defines and explores the phenomenon of the global office. It offers an explanation for why the global office is developing at this juncture in history, indicates the factors which facilitate and constrain growth in globalization, and discusses the implications for women functioning in an increasingly global information labor market.

2 Information Labor

Office work primarily involves the manipulation of information. Conceptually, then, office workers can be grouped under a larger heading known as "information workers," or workers who engage in the production distribution, and manipulation of information. Machlup[3] first defined and measured the number of workers in the United States engaged in the production, distribution, and manipulation of knowledge. He dubbed these workers "knowledge workers." His work was followed by that of

---

[1] The list is extensive. However to name a few: Condon, R (1991) "No Blarney: Irish Labor Costs Less' *Computerworld* Aug. 26, V25 N34 p62; Perera, J (1991) "Data Input Offshore" *World Press Review* Sept. V38 N9 p42; Strehlo, K (1994) "Round the Clock Off-sourcing" *Datamation* Dec. 1 V40 N23 p44.

[2] Barwick, S (1988) "Sleepy Castle Island Enjoys Home Comforts in the Global Office" *The Independent* (London) Aug. 20.

[3] Machlup, F (1962) *Production and Distribution of Knowledge in the United States*, Princeton: Princeton University Press.

Porat[4] who is credited with the current term "information workers." Porat's work was also adopted by the Organization for Economic Cooperation and Development (OECD),[5] and has since become the international standard for measuring participation in information work.

The definition of information work is sufficiently broad to include a wide variety of workers. A brief list is informative: clerical workers, artists, managerial personnel, engineers, draftsmen and architects, teachers, mail carriers, printing trades, etc. In short, an information worker is any occupation whose primary output is information; thus, all office work is information work.

Though all of the occupations listed above fit the definition of information work, it is important to note that they do not all deal with information in the same way. Some occupations primarily move information from one place to another (mail carriers, messengers, etc.), while other occupations transform and manipulate information (engineers, architects, etc.), and yet others primarily create new information (writers, researchers, etc.). A close scrutiny of information occupations would reveal that most of them perform some combination of these activities. Information occupations are thus similar in that they are conceptually differentiated from manufacturing or agricultural occupations. However, within this broad similarity there remains a great deal of variety. This variety is crucial to understanding the formation of the "global office," and I will return to it at length below.

3 Changing Patterns in Information Labor

When Machlup[6] first estimated the number of information workers in 1960, he judged that roughly 43% of the employed workforce in the U.S. was engaged in information work. Though surprising at the time he published, this finding has since become generally accepted and forms the foundation of theories about the "information society." Besides this rather widely known finding, however, he also noted two other interesting trends. First, he observed that the proportion of workers engaged in information work has steadily risen through mid-century. Second, within that general growth pattern, the trend in the U.S. appeared to be from routine information handling towards more skilled information handling. In other words, routine information handling occupations had lead the growth of the information sector, but as mid-century approached, jobs with more complex information handling had come to the fore. This suggests that growth, and by inference decline, in information occupations may happen in distinct patterns.

Though sustained growth in the information sector observed by Machlup has been substantiated,[7] work done by Katz[8] and Sinha[9] indicates that the trend may be

[4] Porat, M. (1977) *The Information Economy: Definition and Measurement*, Washington DC, Dept. of Commerce.

[5] OECD (1986) *Trends in the Information Economy*, Information, Computers, Communications and Policy Section (ICCP).

[6] Machlup (1962) *op cit.*

[7] Rubin, M (1986) *The Knowledge Industry in the United States*; Porat (1977) *op cit.*; and Schement, JR and Lievrouw, L (1984, Dec.) "A Behavioural Measure of Information work" in *Telecommunications Policy* pp. 321-334.

changing. Katz took a comparative look at information employment across several countries. He noted a marked decrease in the rate of growth for information work in the U.S. by 1986. Sinha's data in 1993 also documents a decline in growth rates for the information sector. According to a report by the OECD[10] on growth of the information sector, these results seem to be consonant across member countries:

> There has been continued growth, though at a slower pace, in those occupations primarily concerned with the creation and handling of information.... [I]nformation producers in the form of scientific and technical personnel, consultative services and market search and co-ordination specialists, are still in buoyant demand. [While] information processing occupations, especially the clerical and related grades, are growing much more slowly, being mainly responsible for the reduced growth rate noted for information occupations as a whole. (p. 19)

The pattern, then, appears to be that in most developed countries' economies information work is still large and growing, albeit slower recently. However, this pattern of growth is not steady across the full range of information occupations. It appears that routine information handling occupations are in decline in industrialized countries while complex information handling continues to be in demand. The question before us is, *why* are the routine-information occupations disappearing from occupational structures in developed countries?

The leading explanation is automation. Information technologies (IT), particularly digitally based, computerized information technologies, are eminently capable of performing routinized, rule-bounded information handling tasks. This argument is indeed difficult to refute. There is hardly any aspect of office work that has not been touched by the computer revolution. Back offices once filled with clerks bent over complicated accounting ledgers are now filled with quietly humming computers, and row upon row of telephone operators have given way to automated switching technologies. Automation has undoubtedly had an impact on information work.

However, to this powerful argument I submit an emendation: it is not possible, nor economically feasible, to automate *all* routine information handling. First of all, there are some routine information handling activities that still defy technological solution. Consider, for instance, sales. Though many sales procedures have gone a long way towards routinization, sales workers still abound. Quite simply, we have yet to produce an information technology which can approach all of the requisite skills for human interaction. When it comes to language and body language, the simplest IQ still far outstrips the most sophisticated computer. In short, for some routine-information handling, we have yet to devise a technological solution.

In the second instance, the technology may be available, but economics precludes its use. There may be situations where it is still far cheaper to hire human labor than to invest in expensive information handling equipment. As economists are quick to point out, it is the ratio of possible workers to available jobs that dictates wages. When the number of workers exceeds the number of jobs, wages drop; as wages drop, there comes a point where it is cheaper to rehire human labor than it is to continue to

---

[8] Katz, R (1986) "Measurement and Cross-national Comparisons of the Information Workforce," in *The Information Society* V4 N4 pp231-277.

[9] Sinha, N (1993) "Technological Unemployment in the Information Age," Paper presented at 43rd Annual conference of the International Communication Association -- May 27-31, 1993.

[10] OECD (1986) *op cit.*

invest in a technological solution. It is this last phenomenon that is of particular interest here. Indeed, it is that "ratio of possible workers to available jobs" that is being transformed mightily as the global economy emerges; it lies at the heart of the formation of the global office. Though automation is taking its toll, I submit that the decline in routine information handling occupation in industrialized countries may also be due to the transition to the global office.[11]

A working definition of the global office is the performance of certain types of information work within a global labor market. The definition is delimited by "certain types" because, as we shall see, not *all* information work is equally globally adaptable. There are limitations to the global migration of information work. These limitations mean there will be distinct patterns in the formation of the global office. However, before we explore those patterns, let us first address three reasons for the appearance of the global office at this juncture in history: (1) technological innovations, (2) shifting economic imperatives, and (3) changes in organizational culture.

3.1 The Importance of Information Technology

The importance of the recent advances in information technology cannot be overstated. The latter half of this century has seen the emergence of an international communication infrastructure (ICI). This infrastructure is composed of a mish-mash of private, semi-private, and public networks. These networks are comprised of a mix of fiber optic and satellite telecommunication systems which connect a vast number of mainframes, servers, and personal computers. The separate systems are not always interconnected or compatible, though frequently enough they are. Certainly enough networks are in international operation to substantiate concerns over trans-border data flow (TBDF).[12]

Indeed, growth in ICI seems to have been nearly exponential recently. If we take the Internet as a proxy for global interconnectedness,[13] we can estimate the current extent of global interconnectivity. Figure 1 shows over two-thirds of the occupied landmass as Internet capable. Those that are not fully Internet connected have at least

---

[11] This pattern of declining routine information handling occupations simultaneous to robust figures in highly skilled information handling in developed countries would not alone substantiate the argument presented here. However, Pearson and Mitter (1993. "Employment and Working Conditions of Low-skilled Information-processing Workers in Less Developed Countries" in *International Labour Review* V132, N1 p: 49-64) have noted growth in routine information handling occupations in less developed countries. Problematically, comparative data on a country-by-country basis is virtually unavailable. This analysis is, therefore, primarily deductive, but based on available data.

[12] The literature is large and growing. One that gives an international perspective is: United Nations Commission on Transnational Corporation, Secretariat (1987) *Transnational Corporations in the Service Sector, Including Transborder Data Flows: Report of the Secretary-General, Commission on Transnational Corporations*, 13th session, New York, 7-16 April 1987. United Nations, Economic and Social Council.

[13] Though the Internet is certainly not synonymous with an international communication infrastructure, there are several reasons it is a reasonable approximation. First, Internet connection embodies nearly all of the elements requisite to the ICI as a whole. Second, and more practically, actual data for the ICI is ferociously difficult to estimate, while data on the Internet is readily at hand.

email capabilities, barring, of course, the 20 countries with no connection. It is notable that the majority of the latter are on the African continent.[14]

Although the rate of growth in the Internet has been phenomenal in the last few years, there are still several obstacles to complete global connectivity. Until issues of standards, security of data transmission, and building/ownership of plant are resolved, the Internet will remain partial, occasionally unreliable, and somewhat maddening to use. Nevertheless, it is usable and the stumbling blocks, both large and small, are slowly but surely being resolved.

Fig. 1 Global Internet Connectivity

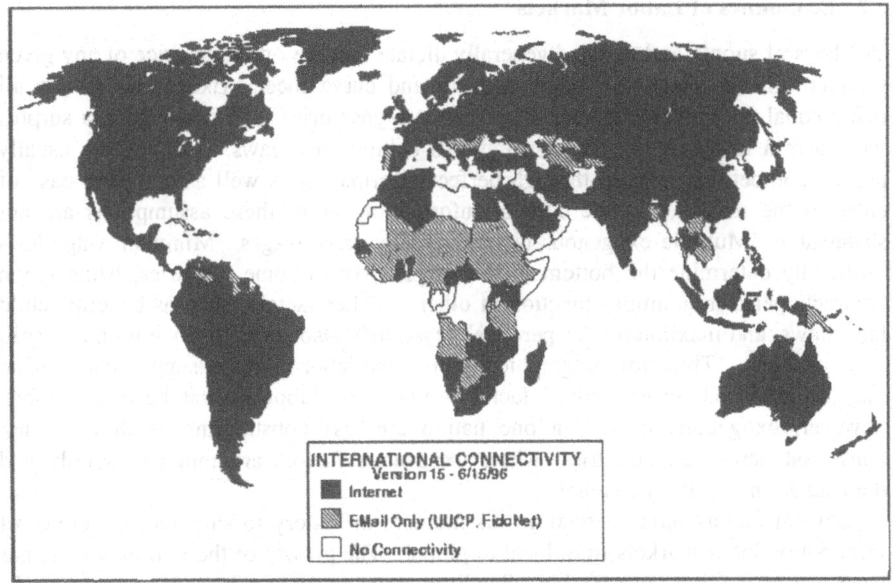

Source: Larry Landweber and the Internet Society[15]

It should also be noted that though the Internet may be a reasonable proxy for global interconnectedness, it may not be the best acid test for usability of the ICI for international relocation of information labor. The Internet is largely a public or semi-public network. Since a substantive amount of trans-border data flow occurs via private networks, it is reasonable to believe that firms using international information labor are most likely using private networks. These private networks, designed specifically for the international exchange of proprietary data, are less likely to suffer from security issues and incompatibility problems. Thus, though the Internet can stand as an estimate of international interconnectivity, it must be remembered that

[14] This, in combination with other factors, suggests that the global office may also have a geographic pattern to its emergence. If so, knowing the elements that drive the pattern would allow us predictability about *where* jobs may emerge. Due to length, however, this issue is left unexplored here.

[15] Available by anonymous FTP from ftp.cs.wisc.edu.connectivity_table directory. Original in color.

portions of the international communication infrastructure are privately held; for now, these portions are more likely to carry the bulk of data traffic associated with the global office.

It would be tidy to argue that the mere availability of the ICI is single-handedly producing the global office. Such technological determinism is insupportable when confronted by more critical perspectives; technologies do not exist autonomous of political, social and economic conditions. That technology exists which makes possible the global office does not mean that the global office is inevitable. Therefore, let us turn our attention to economics.

3.2 Economics of Labor Markets

The laws of supply and demand generally dictate that the optimum price of any given product will be where the supply and demand curve meet. Exogenous factors all being equal, an inadequate supply will mean higher price, and conversely, a surplus will mean a lower price. The assumptions behind these laws, however, are usually perfect competition insured through perfect information as well as complete ease of entry to the market. In the case of information labor, these assumptions are not sustainable. Multiple exogenous factors actually drive wages. Minimum wage laws artificially determine the bottom of the wage curve in some countries, while union contracts perform a similar function in others. Other factors, such as benefits, child labor laws, and maximum hour-per-week laws, may also serve to drive up the overall costs of labor. Thus, for geographically bounded labor markets, supply and demand may be modified by exogenous factors. Once the labor market becomes global, however, exogenous factors in one nation are less constraining as they are not consonant across all countries; where exogenous factors are minimal, supply and demand are more likely to reign.

Several factors have merged at this moment in history to shift the economics of information labor markets from local to global. The growth of the ICI, of course, has been one of the most remarkable. Satellites, trans-oceanic cables, microwave feeds, mainframes and personal computers are spinning a web across the globe. First and foremost, this growth makes the global office technically feasible. However, it has yet another benefit in that it is facilitating a reduction in the intermediate costs of data transfer. Instead of boxing and shipping hard copy and floppy disks of data in both directions, data can now be returned (or, in some cases sent and returned) via the ICI. In most cases this reduces not only shipping fees, but also turnaround time. For businesses where timely data represents money, this can be a significant savings. Furthermore, the intermediate cost of data exchange should continue to drop as economies of scale and/or competition in provision of services drive the price of digital data transfer down.

Yet another factor has been the establishment of Free Trade Zones (FTZs). FTZs are geographic areas designed specifically to attract foreign investment. Business located in these areas is effectively sheltered from, and thereby mostly exempt from, the national customs territory of the host country. Because of their desire to attract foreign investment, the FTZs provide unusually favorable conditions for conducting business. Most notable for the global office, FTZs are usually located in or near areas which can provide a steady supply of fairly well trained workers who work for low wages often under conditions which implicitly or explicitly bar union organization.

Last but not least, many countries possess a comparative advantage with regards to wages when assessed against developed countries. The exogenous factors listed earlier (minimum wages, child labor laws, etc.) are more common to industrialized countries. In combination with monetary exchange rates and generally lower wages in less-developed countries (LDCs), off-shore workers are often far more cost effective than local workers in industrialized countries. The net effect of these factors (the ICI, FTZs and comparative advantage) has been to make a global information labor force economically as well as technologically feasible for the first time in history. As the information labor supply extends to global dimensions, economic imperatives would suggest jobs migrate to where wages are cheapest.

The existence of the ICI and the economies achievable in a global labor market still would not necessarily dictate the formation of the global office. While technology provides the means and economics provides the motivation, organizational hierarchies need to be in place which can efficiently utilize such a dispersed workforce. Such is the role of transnational corporations.

3.3 Transnational Corporations

Galbraith[16] identified the symbiotic relationship between nation-states and large corporations that endured through most of this century. He argued that for industrialized capitalism to succeed, there was tacit governmental approval of, as well as general policy support for, large single-nation based corporations (like U.S. Steel). Reich[17] identifies a radical shift in this long-standing successful pattern. He argues that increasing global competition has contributed to the development of transnational corporations who owe allegiance to no nation-state (though often claim one when need arises). These corporations no longer function under the ideology of centralized, hierarchical control. Instead, these corporations, the "leaner and meaner" corporations of the 1980s and 1990s, function out of more web-like organizational structures. These web-like organizations increasingly rely on outsourcing to serve the immediate needs they cannot perform themselves. Outsourcing allows corporations to contract for only the amount of resources (human or material) needed on any given project. As projects change, they recontract for the new level of need. Corporations are thus able to cut waste, and thereby increase profit margins.

This web-like organizational structure is dependent for success on being largely transnational:

> The new organizational webs...are reaching across the globe.... As the world shrinks through efficiencies in telecommunications and transportation, such groups in one nation are able to combine their skills with those of people located in other nations in order to provide the greatest value to customers located almost anywhere. The threads of the global web are computers, facsimile machines, satellites, high-resolution monitors, and modems--all linking designers, engineers, contractors, licensees, and dealers worldwide. (pp. 110-111)

[16] Galbraith, JK (1978) *The New Industrial State* Boston: Houghton Mifflin.

[17] Reich, R (1991) *The Work of Nations* New York: Knopf.

Indeed, it is the global nature of their enterprise that allows these firms to maintain a competitive edge in the emerging global economy. As customers' needs are located around the globe, so must be the key personnel in the production-sales loop. A transnational labor force allows a firm to locate both potential sales opportunities and talented workers who solve problems and move product.

In short, these new web-like structures are quintessentially designed to take advantage of both the ICI and the economies achievable in global labor markets. Whatever the technological venue, the shift in managerial tactics from an hierarchical, rigid pyramid to a fluid, flexible, and global web-like structure means the creation of organizations ideally situated to take advantage of global information labor markets.

4 Patterns of the Global Office by Skill Level

Knowing that information work is increasingly performed in a global labor market and knowing how and why this is occurring now are but two legs on a three-legged stool. Given that we know the global office is forming, is it possible to determine any patterns? In particular, is it possible to know which information tasks are most mobile in a global information labor market?

As noted earlier, different information occupations deal with information in highly divergent ways. Some jobs simply move information from one place to another, others transform information from one form to another, and yet others create information from scratch. From this variation in skill requirements it is possible to deduce that routine information handling tasks (like data entry) will be the easiest and the earliest to be deployed in the global office. This is not to say that highly-skilled jobs (like software design) will not migrate. Quite the contrary. Highly skilled jobs already migrate. It is rather to say that highly-skilled jobs will be less likely than routine information jobs to migrate out of industrialized countries due to constraints imposed by skill requirements. A brief look at the match between specific skill requirements for each type of information handling task and the ability of the global labor market to provide those skills will explicate this deduction.

The skill match between routine information handling and the global labor supply is quite good. For most routine information handling tasks simple literacy will suffice. Indeed, for most data-entry, one need only read and write numbers. Though it is true that numbers can be depicted with different symbols, it is equally true that the western way of writing has become universal. For work that requires more sophisticated language, English has largely become the de facto standard. And for the next three most commonly used languages, the history of colonization has guaranteed portions of the globe whose educated population is fluent or semi-fluent.

Besides literacy and language fluency, it is also possible that familiarity with computers will be required. Data-entry, for instance, could conceivably require familiarity with programs, files, etc. Not long ago this might have proven a heavy skill barrier. However, computer programs have become vastly more sophisticated over the last fifteen years. For most routine information handling, the operator exists as a conduit, merely transferring data from a source to the computer as it runs automatically through pre-specified slots. Though the actual level of computer literacy may vary from task to task and technological system to technological system, in general computer skill requirements for routine information handling are quite low. A minimal training investment will usually result in even a novice worker grasping enough to perform adequately. Thus, the match between skill requirements and skill attainment in the global workforce means that potential information labor force on a global scale is quite large.

Such is not the case for highly-skilled information workers; the skill match is rather more geographically limiting. Language fluency, education requirements and even specific manual skills all serve to limit the potential global labor supply. Furthermore, several global patterns serve to favor the industrialized countries in producing highly-skilled information workers. The historic patterns of basic and advanced education (as well as curricular choices in each) serve to produce a workforce in industrialized countries that is fluent in the required language(s) and who have generally attained a high degree of education, including, in many instances, specific manual or intellectual skills. Furthermore, industrialized countries generally have a higher rate of adoption of information technologies, thus rendering the population at large more accustomed to and proficient with technology.[18] Taken *in toto*, this means western and northern countries still retain an advantage in producing highly skilled information workers.

This does not mean that LDCs will have no highly-skilled information workers. There has been a history of students turning to higher education in the west and north in order to gain just such skills. The logistics and financial drain of studying in a developed country, however, insure that few students from LDCs will be able to manage such education. Some highly-skilled information workers may participate in the global office while residing in LDCs. However, the probability is that industrialized nations will produce *most* of the global supply of highly-skilled information workers.

Having argued that routine information handling is more likely to be globally competitive than highly-skilled tasks, I should like to point out that not all routine information workers will be globally competitive. Some types of tasks will continue in the near future to be geographically bound regardless of an expanding global office. For example, in order to perform the task of moving information from local place to local place, mail carriers and messengers are geographically bound . As long as these tasks are not completely automated, there will be routine information labor that is not, because it need not, be internationally relocated. Nor is this to say that any and all types of highly skilled workers will be salable in a global labor market. Artists and writers, in particular, often create information which is culturally specific. If the symbol systems of a culture do not translate well cross-culturally, then those who primarily work to serve the culture-of-origin will not be particularly mobile within a global labor market.

---

[18] Though the computer is thought of first, let us not rule out menu driven phone systems, digital price scanners, swipe cards, semi-programmable VCRs, and etc. Continual exposure means one becomes accustomed to thinking of interactions as abstract. "Saving" the VCR program, "moving" through a menu driven system, and "storing" information on a dot the size of a pin head are all commonplace concepts and cultivate skills of intellectual abstraction. Thus, rather than the computer in isolation, it is the totality and ubiquity of IT that render populations technologically proficient.

What we can deduce from these practical considerations is that the vast majority of information jobs are potentially fodder for the global office. Information work will be performed in one location and purchased or contracted for by customers located nearly anywhere on the globe. Underlying this general pattern, however, are other trends. Routine information handling work will generally migrate from industrialized countries to LDCs--at least until exogenous factors, wages, or both become more internationally equal. The labor market for highly skilled information work will be primarily among industrialized countries--at least until education and/or technological diffusion become more internationally equal.[19]

5 Implications for Women

As with most changes, the global office is a mixed bag of opportunities and mishaps. For the vast majority of women workers in industrialized countries, the shift to a global office will undoubtedly mean more competition for fewer jobs. Due to historical and lingering sex segregated patterns of employment, women workers are more heavily employed in routine information handling positions. Since the global labor market is rather large for routine information handling, most women workers in industrialized countries will face stiff competition from other workers in LDCs. Exchange rates, cost of living disparities, and other external factors will give comparative advantage to workers in LDCs. Furthermore, there is every likelihood of a downward spiral on wages of routine information handling occupations in developed countries. Low wages elsewhere in the global market will serve to drive local wages down until they are again competitive.

The story is not entirely negative, however. Concerted efforts in many industrialized countries to "get women into technology" have not been entirely without fruit. Women have made small inroads into technologically heavy, highly skilled information jobs. The opening of a global market for these services means increased opportunities for women who have the requisite skills. These benefits, however, are bought for the few at the cost of the very many.

In those countries that acquire routine information handling work, women workers will receive a mixed blessing. On the one hand, it may mean steady employment--no mean achievement in a struggling economy. On the other hand, it will probably come with problems similar to the global assembly line: poor working conditions, long hours, low pay, no job security, and few or no rights to organize.

Highly skilled information handling jobs in LDCs for women will be fairly non-existent. If women's representation in highly skilled information work in developed countries is still fairly dismal, in LDCs, women's participation is virtually nil. There are many barriers to women's success in highly skilled information jobs, not the least of which are cultural attitudes about women, work and home; formal educational policies; and even lack of resources both technical and textual. If technological transfer is not occurring for the society at large, it certainly will not be happening for women in particular.

[19] Let me note that I do not imagine any of these conditions being met in the near future.

These outcomes should come as no surprise. Indeed, they follow closely patterns established in the transition to global assembly line production in manufacturing. The significant difference with the globalization of information work is gender specificity. Whereas the global assembly line transferred primarily male manufacturing jobs out of industrialized countries into LDCs, the global office render's women's office jobs in industrialized countries globally mobile and output from (primarily) men's highly-skilled jobs globally salable.

The global office, in short, represents opportunities for those workers (some women, but mostly men) who are in highly skilled information work. Though the labor market includes most industrialized nations, potential employers include the entire globe. For highly skilled information workers, continued demand for services will mean that a slight increase in competition will not cut significantly into their market niche. However, for the rest of the information workforce (primarily women), the global office represents highly geographically mobile information jobs and increasing competition in a growing global labor force. The more routine the information handling task is, the more true this becomes. As most women are still segregated into routine information handling tasks, the relevance to women workers cannot be overstated.

6 Conclusions

We are beginning to see a transformation in the way information handling is performed. Information work, once geographically bound, is being loosed from its fetters. The synergy of the development of the ICI, the economics of global labor markets, and the shift in corporate organizational strategies is fueling the transition to a global office. However, the development of the global office is and will probably remain uneven around the world. Due to inherent differences in skill requirements for information tasks, routine information tasks will be more amenable to true global migration. Highly skilled information tasks will be mobile among mostly developed countries.

For women workers, the global office represents both promise and misery. For the few women successful in highly-skilled information handling tasks, it will represent increased opportunities to sell their skills on a global basis. For women who inherit the migrating routine information handling tasks, it may represent steady employment. However, both of these pluses have a darker side. The increased opportunities for highly skilled women information workers are bought at the expense of increased competition and eventually lower wages for the vast majority of women information workers in developed countries. For women in LDCs that are hired in routine information handling, it will probably come with continued exploitation.

In closing let me end with a bit of prognostication of the not-so-difficult type. The ideology of the global office is that of capitalism. The search for ever lower wages and more talented personnel that give a firm its competitive edge are the essence of the global office. Issues of technological transfer and social or economic development are far to the edges at best. In spite of a surface appearance of spreading work more evenly around the globe, the global office has every probability of continuing the long-time disparity between economically (or information) wealthy and economically (or information) poor.

Women and Computer Technology in the Banking Industry: An Empirical Example from Nigeria

Bimbo Soriyan[1], Bisi Aina[2], and Tanwa Odebiyi[2]

[1] Computer Science & Engr.Dept.
Obafemi Awolowo University, Ile-Ife. Nigeria
hsoriyan@oauife.edu.ng

[2] Sociology & Anthropology Dept.
Obafemi Awolowo University, Ile-Ife, Nigeria

Abstract: The role of the banking institution in building a viable national economy cannot be over emphasized. However, a lot of problems, especially low technological capability, continue to hinder the effective performance of the banking sector in many of the developing countries, including Nigeria. One of the solutions to the African growth crisis is the acquisition of appropriate technological capability (Computer Technology in particular) for the banking sector. Thus, many banks are now investing in Computer Technology (CT) to improve their services and their overall operations. Using some of the preliminary findings from an ongoing research project in this sector, the present paper discusses the inherent implications of the presence of the Computer Technology in the Nigerian banking industry for men and women's career options and career development. The paper focuses on the role of the computer scientists in developing appropriate technology for banking operations in Nigeria, and specifically noting gender differences in the performance of these roles. On the whole, the growth of a 'masculine' ethic (which has negative implication for women's career development) remains visible in the Nigerian banking industry. This is made visible as the paper enumerates the existing opportunity structure offered men and women computer scientists within the Banking Industry in Nigeria.

The Nigerian Banking Sector

The banking sector is the most significant of the financial institutions in Nigeria. The sector is made up of the following components: The Central Bank of Nigeria (serving as the monetary authority but under the direct control of the Ministry of Finance); Merchant banks; Commercial Banks; Development Banks and the Federal Savings Banks. The Central Bank serves as the mother bank, performing the overall coordinating functions. The Development banks engage in medium and long-term lending loans with loans provided in both local and foreign currency. These banks include the Nigerian Industrial Development Bank (NIDB), the Nigerian Agricultural and Cooperative Bank (NACB), Federal Mortgage Bank (FMBN), Community Development Banks (CDBL), and Nigerian Bank of Commerce and Industry (NBCI). What distinguishes the Development banks from Commercial banks is that the former is responsible for furthering the nation's development and its development policies. Commercial banks on the other, lend large sums of money to industrial enterprises without knowing to what use these funds will be put, and in most cases, they need not be concerned with the ways in which the money is used, as long as they have sufficient security or collateral from their borrowers. It is often on a short- term basis and it is usually for commercial undertakings.

Government intervention at regulating the business of banking started in 1958 with the establishment of the Central Bank of Nigeria to stabilize the banking sector which witnessed massive failures in the 1950s. This resulted in the establishment of about 17 Commercial banks by 1972. This growth continued until recently. As at 1985, the number of commercial and merchant banks has increased to 40. However, this situation changed drastically after the introduction of the Structural Adjustment Programme (SAP) in 1986. The increase in the number of banks was envisaged to increase competition, and to create a more conducive atmosphere for the government implementation of its adjustment policies (e.g. privatization, the foreign exchange markets etc.). Added to these banks, are a number of finance houses and mortgage banks.

Unlike other banks, Commercial banks have branches all over the country even in rural areas where the roads and the communication systems are inadequate. However, the communication system in Nigeria as in most parts of the Less Developed Countries (LDCs) is plagued by numerous problems ranging from human to infrastructural.

Computerisation in the Nigerian Banks

It has been recognized that access to Information Technology (IT) is an important prerequisite for economic and social development (ITU, 1984). In the past few years, the importance of IT has been emphasized in Africa and other developing countries. In today's setting of diverse, interdependent, and competing organizational forms, improvement of productivity is a major concern to managers. The function of management is to plan the use of resources at its disposal, to motivate the workers and to co-ordinate and control the activities necessary to carry out the plans. These functions have not changed with the advent of IT, especially computers, but the ways in which they are carried out have changed. To carry out these functions effectively, managers need accurate and timely information. Information is the product of the processed data, the amount and variety of which keep increasing at an alarming rate.

Computerization in Africa started in the late 1950s and early 1960s in the government offices, the bigger Multinational Corporations and later by private financial organizations. In the late 1970s and early 1980s Nigeria witnessed the introduction of micro computers which are cheap and small in size (relative to the massive Mainframes). Computerization stopped being a myth to many organizations as computer networks expanded the scope of information transfer and resource sharing within and across these business organizations. The problem of the huge capital investment involved and the 'special' office space to house mainframes no longer exist with the introduction of new computer technology. Hence many organizations especially the financial institutions started to invest in computerization.

The financial sector is a complex of markets for financialassets. It has its own industries, the monetary system utilizing inputs of productive factors according to relevant technologies. The sector is unique in the degree to which its markets, prices, institutions, and policies impinge upon all other sectors. The most significant of the financial Institutions in any economy is the banking sector. Essentially, the roles of the banking system include that of financial intermediation, the supply of money, the activation of entrepreneurial talent and guidance for the economy as a whole. The decision to examine computerisation in banking automation is one of the relatively easier and earlier entry points for computers in the economy when compared with say the manufacturing as an example. Again the accounting, payroll and other such functions are fairly 'rational' processes with well established routines, and are thus easily computerised. Moreover, the computer plays a major role in the development process. In fact, computer spending as a percentage of GDP is now a measure of industrialization. For while computer spending in Africa (1988) averaged 0.34 percent of the GDP, that of the United States is 2.5 percent (Moussa & Schware 1992). New and advanced IT for telecommunications are having major impact on LDCs and in Nigeria in particular. Telematics or the introduction of computers into communications associated with digitization for transmission of data, including sound and pictures is becoming very popular. The empirical example provided in the subsequent sections provides an insight into the place of women in the Nigerian banking industry. The project - Computer Technology and the Banking Operations in Nigeria - is being sponsored by the Carnegie Corporation of New York, under the auspices of the African Technology Policy Studies with headquarters in Nairobi (the fieldwork started by July, 1996).

The Empirical Example

This study is being conducted in the 5 State capitals in SouthWest Nigeria i.e. Lagos - which is the commercial heart of Nigeria, and which until recently was the administrative capital of Nigeria; Abeokuta - capital of Ogun State; Ibadan - capital of Oyo State; Oshogbo - capital of Osun State and Akure - capital of Ondo State). Specific banks selected for study are: The First Bank, Cooperative Bank, Great Merchant Bank, Eko International Bank, Federal Mortgage Bank, and Eco Bank. From the 5 states in Southwest Nigeria, a total of 18 banks were surveyed using the case study approach, interview survey and in depth interviews to collect information from management staff; computer technical experts in the selected banks; and other bank workers.

Preliminary Findings

a. The Present State of Computerisation in the Surveyed Banks:

Although most of the surveyed banks have computers in place, the level of use differs from one bank to the other. The least computerised of the these banks have at least one PC in one of the main offices, and such is used mainly for document processing. Other banks, especially the old generation banks, use computers for internal office transactions only. In over 98% of cases, customer services are restricted to specific hours of the day (for example, 8 a.m. to 3.30 p.m. on Mondays, and 8 a.m. to 1.30 p.m. Tuesdays to Fridays), while in all cases, there is no use of credit cards. In most of the old generation banks, the effect of computerization is so insignificant that customers are hardly aware of the presence of computers. This is likely to be due to the sections of computer emphasis. For example, in such banks, computers are still used only for internal processing of data, while customer services are yet to be computerized, including authorization of cheques, and withdrawal procedures. The average transaction time spent on savings and withdrawals is still relatively the same as before computerization, and in some cases is even worse. For instance, when there is there is power failure, a customer may have to leave the bank unable to contact any business with the bank for that day.

The story is a little bit different in the new generation banks. Computerization is at the inception. Many of the new generation banks are highly computerized, with multi-user set up and/or standard network, both intra-city and nation-wide, and thus providing an on-line, real-time service. It is therefore possible in these banks to withdraw and/or save money from any part of the country where a branch office exists. One or two of the new generation banks have introduced electronic wallets which are based on smart card technology, although it is reportedly run at loss. The number of customers using this facility is less than 200, while only 5 of the merchant houses accept transactions based on the use of the smart card.

Interestingly, 75% of the computer personnel in one of the new generation banks surveyed are women. In fact this bank is the most computerized and it is quite progressive. It thus becomes interesting to ask the following questions. Is the introduction of computer technology offering women better opportunities in the present day banking industry in Nigeria? Are men and women computer scientists given the same opportunity for career development? For example, it was found that most banks develop their own software in-house. Is this software mainly developed by men or by women or by both? Do men and women have different career paths in the banking industry? Some of the answers to these questions are the focus of the subsequent section of this paper.

b. Women and Computer Technology and the Banking Operations in the Surveyed Banks:

The banking institution in Nigeria is diverse in its mode of operation, priorities and target customers. Hence the structure and administrative environment in each type of bank where computers are introduced has direct bearing on the effective use of the technology. Until recently, high school graduates were employed in banks, to be later trained in the different specialities in the banking operations. Such bank workers were expected to sit for different external banking examinations from time to time. Many bank workers therefore got their promotions based on whether or not they passed these examinations. Many of the old generation managers got to their present positions by these incremental promotions. Unfortunately, at that time most bankers were men, the few female bankers were mostly in the low income group, rather than in the mainstream banking operations. Women at the time, were found in the banks as typists or secretaries, and so could not eventually move up to the management positions.

Uche (1994) argues that the inferior social status accorded women, degradation of women's values and low aspiration contributed to the low percentage of women's participation. Another factor is the status of the women who are not encouraged to go to school but rather are specifically prepared for marriage. They are thought to be dependent, submissive, and passive while the boys are thought to face the issues of life.

Today, situations in the Nigerian banks have changed. With the growing economic crisis, and the attendant high rate of unemployment, university graduates now flood Nigerian banks. This in itself has implications for women's employment. First, many graduates (male and female) now take up appointments in the banks, even as mere clerical workers. This situation makes it more competitive for women to be employed in the banks, especially as technical experts. For example, computer technology is often seen as "a male system" which "requires a behaviour that women are not prepared for while at the same time female structures, abilities, and attitudes do not fit" (Sklorz-Weiner, 1991). This stereotyped assumption has increased the burden on women first in attracting jobs involving technical knowledge, and second in keeping such jobs. Aina and Soriyan (1996) argue that women in developing countries are subjected to double subordination, first as members of the peripheral economies, and secondly for being culturally treated as socially inferior to men. Thus, technology is therefore not only a symbol of maleness and a source for male identity, but also a symbol of power and dominance (Aina et. al, 1996). Since women traditionally have limited rights in the larger Nigerian society, including rights to education, they are therefore restricted in the choice of a profession. They experience restricted opportunities and have limited career progressions (Aina, 1992).

Although Nigeria has witnessed various national policies targetting women's empowerment and improvement of opportunities, many of these policies and programmes are mainly at the grassroots level, and women in the informal sector. Presently, no policies on women exist which target employers of labour, especially in the formal labour market. In most parts of Africa, women of the working class are believed to be working for extra money which became the measure of their worth and women's work is not as valuable as men's.

Computer technology is one of the socially attractive professions in the country, and unlike other engineering disciplines, it has, over the years, attracted a lot of female undergraduates (Soriyan and Aina, 1991). The impact of computer technology on women's lives in Nigeria creates aunique experience being seen as a relatively softer engineering discipline. The present study reported here finds that men still dominate the computer technology field. This is confirmed in the old generation banks where computer staff recruitment highly favours the men especially in the hardware section, where less than 10% of the staff are women.

The sample discussed in this paper subsequently are bank workers who either work in the computer departments of the surveyed banks, or those work in other departments with the aid of computers (i.e. bank cashiers, secretaries, and clerks etc.). Out of the total of 233 interviews already carried out in these banks, only 74 of these are women. These women have a mean age of 31.4 years compared to the total sample mean of 33.4 years and they are mostly married (58.9%), while 41.1% are single (i.e. have never been married). Although marriage within the Nigerian context is not necessarily a barrier to taking up modern paid employment, what determines a woman's job placement and career opportunities tends to be individual investment in human capital (e.g. education); ability to combine the demands of home and work; and being able to overcome traditional gender biases in modern work organisations (as these are presently dominated by men). Aina (1995:103) argued that the continuous disparity in education between gender groups in Nigeria means a disparity in access to lucrative employment.

Looking at the distribution of these female sample by their educational levels, 38.9% have university education or its equivalent, 21.2% have professional training in either banking or accountacy; while 38.9% have high school education or its equivalent. A critical look at the gender distribution for technical education in the country still shows that women are at a disadvantage. For example, only 6.1% of students in the Engineering/Technology Faculties of the Nigerian universities are females (NUC,1990). It is therefore not surprising to find in this study that only 4 out of the 74 women surveyed are computer scientists. The rest are typists/secretaries (14.3%); data entry operators (9.5%), clerical officers (52.4%); auditors/accountants (12.7%); and only 4.7% as managers. It is however important to note that the fact that women are now found as bank managers, or as senior officers in the banks is a great achievement and a of ray hope for the next century.

Another important aspect of the study is women's career advancement, and opportunities offered by the job. These women recorded a mean of 6years service with the present employer. This shows that an average person selected would have had enough experience to talk on training opportunities and career advancements offered by the surveyed banks.

Different types of computer training are presently offered professionals in these banks. These are: training on data processing; CT appreciation; and application software. The workers reported that such computer training is acquired through private arrangements; on-the-job-training; in-house training; or training in established institutions. Only 33.7% reported that they have acquired such training (compared to over 55% of male workers), while 64% of these women got the training through private efforts (compared to less that 25% of the male sample). This simple data shows some insights into the distribution of opportunities between the gender groups in the Nigerian banking system, for it could be deduced that:

- more men are given a better opportunity to train and to excel at work;
- the few women who are determined to have a fulfilling career path end up spending their money to acquire training which are of necessity given to men at work.

Data on salaries received by workers show that these are relatively high in banks compared to other sectors of the Nigerian economy. For example, the minimum wage for the country is about N2,500 per annum (i.e. U.S. $30 using the rate of N80 to a dollar), while the average salary for the female sample is N67816.10 (U.S. $847.70). The average salary for the total sample of male and female workers is N68861.73 ($860.77). For the female sample, the poorest paid is N87,00 ($108.75) per year, while the highest paid is N230,000 ($2,875.00), compared to men with the least average income of N69907.35 ($873.84), and the highest income of N708,000 ($8850.00). We can also deduce from these data that:

- Men occupy the highest positions in the Nigerian banks, and are therefore the highest paid;
- There is a gender disparity in education, hence, men who are more favoured by gaining access to more education tend to control the high paying jobs;
- Women in Nigeria are also struggling to penetrate modern paid employment including the technically based ones (e.g. computer technology), hence, they record in this study a salary average of N67,816.10 compared to N68,861.73 for the total sample.

However, it is also worth knowing that sex segregation of jobs still exists in the Nigerian banking industry. Even though a conscious effort was made to include both men and women in comparable jobs, it is a general pattern in all the banks for women to be concentrated in sex-typed jobs which attract lower pay compared to men's jobs. For example, women in the surveyed banks concentrate in such jobs like secretarial jobs, clerical jobs, and as data entry operators, whereas men dominate the managerial and the technical positions.

Many of these banks employed just computer personnel, who later trained other bank workers in- house. All banks which fell into the old generation banks (pre-SAP banks) employed male computer scientists as overall heads of their respective computer sections. Few women in highly placed positions in the new generation banks (post-SAP banks) (especially as heads of computer sections/Managers) shows that such banks have relatively more relaxed and flexible policies towards women. This also shows that the society itself is gradually relaxing its rules of gender role relations. The economic and technological changes that marked the transitions from the domestic economy to the consumer economy have resulted in a change of traditional belief of identifying the women with 'home', although these women continued to work both at home and in the public labour force.

Notably, only very few women have the advantage of holding prestigious and highly paid jobs offered by the computer profession, for within this profession, women are concentrated in the lower ranks and in less prestigious specialities. In Nigeria, the Sales Representative, for instance, is not as prestigious as the Sales Manager or the Engineer who does the actual repairs and maintenance. Yet in most cases, women Computer Engineers are often assigned sales jobs. So within the practice of the computing profession in the banks certain categories of jobs will only be done by men except when they are not available and even then the woman is usually under supervision of another man, and in fact sometimes under non computer personnel. Women are perpetually under pressure because of the need to impress the men who already have biased beliefs in male dominance.

The women in the managerial level in the banks surveyed tend to gain more control and this results in resentment among the other workers, including other female workers. The women are conscious of their marginalised positions and so seek ways to be heard within the office. Their attitude could be expressed in Kennedy and Piette's (1991) statement that "we were the submerged, the subordinate half of the human race, fighting the dominant group, men, for our proper recognised place in the world".

Conclusion

There is no doubt that there is a gradual move to integrate women into the formal labour processes in Nigeria. Employers of labour are opening their doors for young women to take advantage of new opportunities in the banking industry. However, many of these women still continue to struggle for full acceptance. This is obvious in the way that banks distribute men and women into positions of authority. Women professionals do not enjoy the same privileges, such as training opportunities that could eventually give them career advancement. Men are favoured in jobs requiring self-assertion, and control, whereas women are preferred where they are used as a "showpiece" either as personal secretaries, and as cashiers.

The application of IT in the banking system is unavoidable. Strategies for proper management should be embarked upon without gender biases. A good development plan with reference to socio-cultural implications in the society should be put in place. For example, even though the developed countries have automated their banking systems with the advantage of reducing drastically their staff strength while the customers increase, this strategy may not be employed in Nigeria where there is a population problem and a high percentage of unemployment. Actually the automation strategy should be modified so that automation will improve efficiency rather than lead to staff reduction. The old generation banks should adopt strategies that will enhance their automation processes.

The basic infrastructure and facilities for data communication should be improved. There is the need to build a lasting solution for the telecommunication problems if only within the financial institutions. The possibility of employing VSAT technology should be reviewed with the mind of collaborating within the financial sector.

References

1. Aina, Bisi and Soriyan, Bimbo (1996). "Technology: Women and Development". In: Cheris Kramarae, Dale Spender (eds.). Women Encyclopedia, U.K.
2. Aina, O.I (1992). "Gender differences in work attitudes and behavior among selected industrial workers in Lagos". Unpublished Ph.D. Thesis, Obafemi Awolowo University, Ile-Ife, Nigeria.
3. Kennedy, M. and Piette, B. (1991). "From the Margins to the Mainstream: Issues Around Women's Studies on Adult Education and Access Courses". In: J. Aaron and S. Walby (Eds.). Out of the Margins: Women's Studies for the Nineties, The Falmer Press, London, pp. 30-40.
4. National University Commission, Nigeria Annual Report, (1990).
5. Sklorz-Weiner, M. (1991). "Gender and Technology: A Psychological View". Preproceedings of the 4th Conference on Women, Work and Computerization. Tampere, Finland.
6. Soriyan,B. and Aina,O.I. (1991). "Women's work and Challenges of Computerization: the Nigerian Case".In Proceedings of the conference on Women, Work and Computerization held in Helsinki, Finland 30 June-2 July. Anna-Maija Lehto and Inger Eriksson(eds). p. 189.

What is our Worth?

Eva Turner

School of Computing Science, Middlesex University
Bounds Green Road, London N11 2NQ
eva1@mdx.ac.uk

Abstract. This paper was written on the basis of personal experience, observation and a small-scale (pilot) study and is designed to facilitate a discussion on increasing women's involvement in research in computer science in academia. The paper looks at the position of carers in general and women carers in particular, the relationship that exists between caring responsibilities and involvement in research, and argues that due to the extremely fast development of computing and computer technology, women as researchers have been at a greater disadvantage in relation to men and researchers in other academic disciplines. I suggest that women are only accepted into the academic research community if they have an established research record before becoming carers. Positive action needs to be taken to offer women equal opportunities and research needs to be conducted into the speed of development.

1 The Scenario

Until 1992 higher education in England consisted of two types of colleges, the universities and the polytechnics. The universities had a long-standing academic tradition of research while the polytechnics were primarily thought of as teaching institutions. Their research was based on the individual enthusiasms of staff.

In 1992 new government legislation enabled all polytechnics to become universities. With the change of title came a change of ethos. Research became the expected thing, a matter of academic standing, an issue of competition between the old and the new universities. The government supports all universities by financially contributing towards each student, but has decreased the amount with some later budgetary decisions. At the same time the government has taken upon itself to be the judge of the quality and the amount of the research output of each academic institution through its Research Assessment Exercise. Every four years the government financially rewards the quality of research output, the numbers of research students and completed research degrees, the number of publications and the amount of income generated through privately funded research.

The diminishing income from student numbers, government decisions on research funding and academic competition have placed the new universities under an enormous strain to produce as much visible research output as possible and to generate as much income from private sources (Research Councils, Industry, Local Governments, Charities, etc.) as possible. The question of pure survival as well as the question of attracting large research grants became of primary importance. This pressure has in turn reflected on individual members of staff. The staff that had for years put all their effort into good quality teaching, and were supported and valued for it by their institution, suddenly felt inadequate and undervalued, because they had produced insufficient publishable research. The institutions changed emphasis in their choice of staff promotions and new appointments biased towards those with an actual or potential research record.

I want to argue that, while the academic institutions do not provide equal opportunities for women lecturers, the above change of emphasis is particularly discriminatory towards women carers and women returners wanting to enter academic research.

In June 1996 I went to hear the Inaugural Lecture of the new Research Professor of the Faculty of Technology at my university. For the purposes of this paper I shall call him W. After welcoming, among others, W's immediate family the Academic Director of the university introduced W. with warm words and a long list of W's achievements: W. became at one time the youngest professor in computing science and to date has published 3 books, 80 refereed papers in distinguished journals, 210 articles, attracted over 2 million pounds in research grants, appeared on television and radio, organised and attended numerous conferences and has been active in other prominent walks of life. In the audience I noticed W's four young children and his wife. W. is about 40 years old.

Now, this paper is not about W., it is an immediate reflection that was born from the introduction to him. How, I wondered, can anyone with 4 young children find the time for all this? How long does it take to write a 10 page conference paper or a 20 page handout? When I have done my weekly teaching, preparation, marking and individual tutorials, why don't I have time to start writing articles? Could it be that I am a parent with two small children at home, who need to be picked up from school, fed, shopped for, washed, played with, cared for etc.? But W. is a parent, too! Could it have anything to do with the gender difference between me and W.? I have never asked W. about his family life, nor about the life and work of his wife. That is not the issue, though I am making a big assumption about his personal life arrangements.

The topic here is the fact that there is no question in the establishment's mind about the gender of the achiever. Would you feel that there was something funny if a woman with 4 small children achieved all that? How many women/mothers with such a distinguished record in the technology field do you know? Would such a man have really managed this if he were a woman with 4 young children?

Research, it can be argued, is a compulsion, an overriding interest, something that is stronger than the individual's other needs. That is the picture we have in mind when we think of the great figures in scientific research. But the overriding majority of the great minds were and still are either men or women without children.

2 Equal Opportunities?

In the 1970s the Sex Discrimination Act was passed in Parliament. It was very welcome at the time. Since then a lot of research has been conducted on the real equal opportunities for men and women and for carers and non-carers. Part-time work and its implications for children and mothers was examined as well as the reasons for its existence from the employers' and the employees' points of view. In the seventies the debate was about equal pay for equal work, in the eighties the debate shifted towards shattering the glass ceiling and towards the types of work women can and should perform. The approach to women's employment became more organised and gained a higher profile. The position of mothers in society, the traditions of motherhood, the expectations that society places on women as mothers and carers and in turn the effect these expectations have on women in employment, were all researched and investigated.

We now live in a society which claims to give women the freedom to choose their career, yet demands that they remain the main carers of their children and other dependants. The economic situation and the high levels of unemployment do not really support women in their choice to build a career, but even women who make it are still forced to make the sort of choices men are not expected to make.

There is limited legislation in Britain protecting the employment rights of carers. In 1990 a Ministerial Group On Women's Issues came up with a Five Point Plan which talked of guidance and encouragement to employers to employ parents. Other carers were not mentioned. However there is a great reluctance in the British government to be seen as actively supporting women in employment or promoting fathers as carers. The financial benefit of not losing skilled women through motherhood is so far the most powerful argument to employers. Actions like Opportunity 2000 highlighted the financial benefit to be gained from taking on board mothers' needs. The numbers of women in employment are rising world wide. 43% of the labour force in Britain are women. 12% of the workforce are women providing all of their household income , 19% provide about half. 42% of employed women regard their employment as a career as opposed to a job, of those only 34% are women with children (19).

With the economic predictions of the late eighties came also the vision of the society growing older. With numbers of young people diminishing the society will become desperate to employ more women. Many papers and books have been written on needs of women in employment, mainly predicting that if employers were to take full advantage of the women they will need to employ, they will have to enable them to perform their caring responsibilities.

The latest state of affairs was proudly published in a joint Department of Trade and Industry(DTI) and Opportunity 2000 publication in 1995 (22). Seven very large technological UK employers were presented as those best understanding the benefits they gain from supporting women/mothers and having therefore the best working conditions for them. They have long introduced part-time or job-share or flexible working hours, established nurseries for underschool-aged children, allowed parental leave and career breaks, introduced training (even single sex) and retraining programs. When I enquired into how these example companies were selected for the booklet, it appeared that they were judged as being the good practitioners of equal opportunities on the basis of material the companies themselves had presented to the DTI. No research, checks or comparisons were made by the booklet instigators. When I telephoned one of the companies to ask about women returners, I was informed that there is no problem with women returners, as all women wanted to return after the official 4 months maternity leave to attend retraining programs. When I probed further about those women who wanted to return later than 4 months, I was told that they would not be included on the retraining program and would have to start "from the beginning". When presented with a "real equal opportunity employer " in computing (a large bank), I was shown a large computer department encased in bullet proof glass, where workers worked 12 hour shifts. There were only 2 women out of many men employed at that time and I was told that jobshare and shorter or flexible working hours were out of the question, as the computer operation involving transfers of millions of pounds sterling could have been disastrously endangered by these working practices. There was no space for a nursery in this very new building devoted solely to the computer operation. However, in the cellar of the building there was an enormous hall with large conveyor belts and computers on either side of each one , used for processing of used cheques. There must have been 200 people working there, mostly women and there, I was told, women and men were allowed to work part-time and flexible working hours.

The Biotechnological and Biological Sciences Research Council (BBSRC) was mentioned as one of the most successful companies in the DTI-Opportunity 2000 booklet (15). In their Equal Opportunities Summary of Progress (23) they identify a rise of numbers of women and a rise of numbers of carers in their various management strata , however take-up of part-time work for women scientists was very low in comparison with women in administrative posts and almost non-existent in senior posts.

Some employers pay lip service to equal opportunities, some claim that women returners are welcome. What I have presented is not evidence just an impression. The discussion on the role of mothers (4) in society, the role of fathers in a family, the changes needed in attitudes and expectations is alive and, though it is taking place elsewhere, it should be affecting us in academia too.

This discussion is not taking place on academic soil. In 1990 Sue Lees and Maria Scott (8) analysed the equal opportunity situation in academia and came to the conclusion that, though equal opportunities is firmly on the agenda and is at least being officially monitored in terms of gender and minorities, the actual situation for academics has not really changed. The authors outlined a set of crucial prerequisites for change, which has, six years later, still not been taken up.

My own university's latest Equal Opportunity (EO) Policy and Code of Practice published in 1994 (18) goes as far as saying that the university "...will develop patterns of working consistent with EO policies and practices in relation to (among others) caring and parental responsibilities and career break and return to work". Further, under the heading of training it promises a "briefing program designed to increase awareness of the ways in which institutional discrimination operates and to raise awareness of any specific forms of discrimination that are identified". My experience suggests that these two policies, if implemented, have not really penetrated into practical dealings with academic staff. In terms of other EO measures, the university now operates three nurseries and a summer play scheme to cater for the needs of students and staff. I have been told that academic staff rarely use this service. Such statistics are, however, not collected.

3 Women Academics

Many women lecturers started working as part time (contract) lecturers. This form of employment gives them the opportunity to stay on academic soil, where they want to work, and yet enables them to perform their duties as carers. Most of them hope that when the children grow up, they will be able to gain full time employment at the university and start doing their chosen research. All part time workers I know work extremely hard, often performing duties and putting in time, which is comparable to the full timers. Writing from experience, it is assumed that academic women choose their career for two reasons:

Either they are very interested in their field, often fitting the stereotypical view of women making a conscious decision not to have children to allow themselves sufficient time and space for their working life. However I have heard a view which presented me with a different stereotype: most of these women are "brainy" but "unattractive" (whatever these terms may mean) and could not marry anyway.

Or it is a career where women can do only a few hours of teaching a week and get long holidays so they can comfortably fit their jobs around their caring responsibilities. The stereotypical view is that these women have a relatively easy ride, most of them work part time and get good money for it, they do their "brainy" work to satisfy that side of their needs and really have it both ways. I must admit that when my children were very small, this is what I did and how I looked at my job, too. Somehow I accepted that the nights and the weekends that I put into the job were part of the deal. Little did I imagine, that my long wanted and planned academic career is in reality a non starter.

3.1 Women Academics in Science and Technology

There seems to be very little research on women lecturers and researchers in general and none on women in the departments of computing. In 1975 Joan Abramson (12) published her own account of her fight against discrimination in a US university and Jessie Bernard (11) published a very interesting study of women academics (in technology) in the US. Much of her book is specific to the educational system in the States and much of it is now (30 years later) not applicable due to the feminist movement in general and equal opportunities legislation in particular. However there are some findings, which seem to ring a bell. For example the working relationship of men and women researchers, high numbers of women reporting children as career liability. A study of that size is needed in Britain today. I know of one woman lecturer in computing in Britain who has taken her university employer to an Industrial Tribunal alleging sex discrimination. She won her case. However, she tells me that although that was 20 years ago nothing has changed.

I started looking at women researchers in the technology field in general, as computing science is a technological subject. The Engineering and Physical Sciences Research Council (EPSRC), a government body that finances much of universities' research, published a special issue of their newsletter in May 1996 (14) on the lives of women who work in science, engineering and technology. There were 12 successful women researchers presented, working for the most part in universities, some in computing. They were presented by the EPSRC as an example of its commitment to encouraging women into research (21% of women students and 8% of women fellows are currently supported by EPSRC). Examining the history of these women from the point of view of their caring commitments I found a different picture to the success presented:

5 of the 12 women have no children and did not indicate other caring responsibilities.

Of the 7 women with children only one woman works outside academia and says that her employer allowed her flexible working hours and time off for her children. This women does not appear to have a PhD. The remaining 6 mothers all have PhDs and all completed it at least 5 years, most 7 to 10 years before they had children. So the picture presented here is one of a *well established research record before any caring responsibility occurred.* The EPSRC has now introduced five-year part-time PhD studentships for those returning to research after a career break. This is a very welcome breakthrough, though there is no indication of the criteria for the studentships' allocation.

4 Women Academics in Departments of Computing Science

What I described above can apply to any academic discipline, so why do I think that computing is different?

4.1 Speed of Development

Computer science is probably the fastest developing technological field. Just to stay in tune, to be able to perform their duties as lecturers competently and to keep pace with their chosen field of research, all computer scientists have to update their knowledge and skills constantly. The amount of material to be studied is potentially enormous. Women carers often have to put in nights and weekends to keep up.

Nowadays most computer development is industry led. It appears that large multinational companies, backed by their capital, are racing towards ever higher goals. Academia seems to trail behind and have little control over the speed of development. The reasons for the macho image of technological development in industry has to be investigated. Furthermore comprehensive and well-funded research into the influence of gender on the discipline is sorely needed.

It has been suggested that the rapid progress is a myth constructed by the male researchers to prevent interference and control from other members of society. Whether a myth, which is to be deconstructed, or a reality which is to be brought under control in order to prevent exclusion of women, the first step must be the understanding of the process through research.

I am certain that the speed of development in this discipline leaves women and carers behind much faster than it does in other scientific disciplines.

When I first started in computing the reality was punch cards and coding sheets, DEC10/PDP11 machines, Fortran 4, non-structured programming etc. That was only 17 years ago. We all know the enormous progress all computing disciplines have made since. As a non-research part-timer I was timetabled for teaching where the subject areas changed from term to term, depending on which of my colleagues was assigned to other duties. I gladly accepted all that was given to me, grateful for the work which I loved and always delivered well. Over the years I taught packages, languages, databases, graphics, hardware, systems analysis and more. All entailed a complete course of study for me, which had to be fitted in between my teaching and my small children, and I must say that over those years I must have passed successfully several university degrees. I was successful and proud of myself and I believed I had done well. However I became a Jack (sic) of all trades and master of none. No other academic discipline has developed and progressed so much and I believe that no other academic field expected as much of its lecturers as computing has done.

4.2 Some Numbers (The Pilot)

The Faculty of Technology had 16% female academic staff in 1993 and has 21% female academic staff now. There are no women amongst the pure research staff(24).

The total number of 105 academics employed in the faculty has remained constant over the last three years, but within this Faculty the *School of Computing Science had an increase of 15 new staff*. However the increase in the overall percentage in female staff has not projected into the School of Computing Science, where the 44% increase in staff meant a 3% decrease in the number of women academics.

In 1993 the School had 21% women academics (4 women and 15 men) and now the School has 18% women academics (7 women and 27 men - although in the university statistics these women appear as 7 bodies, 2 of them have 0.5 appointments, hence there has been a 3% decrease). One reason for such a large increase in numbers of staff in computing is the huge increase in students. There was a 118% increase in the number of students gaining first degrees in the 2 years between 1994 and 1996 and an additional 41.% increase in students gaining other qualification (MSc, HND etc.).

	first degree			MSc			HND/PGD			total
	m	f	%	m	f	%	m	f	%	% f
1994	42	17	29	22	10	31	33	17	34	31
1996	78	45	37	57	14	20	28	18	39	32

Student statistics *(obtained at my University)*

It is necessary to add that the School provides introductory IT courses for the whole University which has over 1300 students and that the above statistics do not include the many additional students who minor in the subject and for whom tuition is also provided. The data above only includes the students who completed their courses, it should be noted that the Faculty has over 40% failure rate. The representation of females in student numbers is much higher than it is in the numbers of staff (24).

I have carried out a small scale research among my colleagues and staff at other universities, trying to find how many of them were carers and whether they perceived caring as a drawback on their career. 16 colleagues returned my questionnaire (47%).

	total num. of academic staff	%	number responded	identified as carers	research before caring	research during caring
female	7	20.6	4	2	1	1
male	27	79.4	12	6	2	4

My University

2 women and 3 men carers have indicated that caring has made their job more stressful and/or difficult and that caring has slowed down and/or changed the course of their career. One woman said "I find it hard to work the 60-65 hours a week needed". Two men said that caring had made their work more difficult but had not prevented them from doing what they wanted. In terms of the institution taking the caring responsibilities into account, two men and one woman indicated that the University never took them into account, one woman and two men thought that the University was trying, "depending on individual understanding", one man thought that it was always taken on board. Two of the staff commented on the flexibly of hours in academia.

I sent the same questionnaire to Exeter University and to Heriot-Watt University. From *Exeter* I received 3 replies from one man and two women, all non-carers. From *Heriot-Watt University* came the following data:

	total num. of academic staff	%	number responded	identified as carers	research before caring	research during caring
female	3	9	0	0	0	0
male	29	81	10	5	4	1

Heriot-Watt University

3 men found that caring had not slowed down, postponed or changed their career, but one of them found that it made his job more stressful. Two carers felt that caring changed the direction of their career, for one it meant slowing it down , the other was not prevented from what he wanted to do. In terms of whether the institution took the caring responsibilities into account, all ticked "never" to the question, and commented: "do not see this as relevant to me", "my employer did not know about it", "as carer I take responsibility" and "the hours were flexible".

Over the e-mail I received the following quick responses from *Dundee university.*

	total num. of academic staff	%	number responded	identified as carers	research before caring	research during caring
female	3	20	3	0	3	1
male	11	80	10	8	6	2

Dundee university

A quick response came from *Edinburgh University* which has 2 female lecturers and 27 men and several other staff involved in research only. Of the 2 women lecturers one is not a carer the other works part-time and received her PhD during her caring years. The comment I got about the men in the department was that " ... many of them have children, but their wives are either at home or work part-time with one exception , where the wife is a lawyer, but they have a nanny.." The sender of this message was a woman.

Summary of the pilot study:

- 50% of respondents identified themselves as never being carers. This must be very different from the working population in general, and a comparison with other academic disciplines would be interesting. Further research needs to be undertaken to confirm this data and to establish what motivated people to reply.
- Majority of carers had established a research record (have either published work or completed their PhD) before they became carers.
- Most of them did not think that the academic institution had taken their caring into account as far as their workload, working hours or career was concerned, most did not appear to think that caring was relevant to their work.
- Seven out of the ten men carers did not feel that caring affected their careers, while both of the women and three men thought it did.
- There seems to be unquestioned acceptance of the fact that working hours in academic research are much longer than those in industry.

5 Conclusions and Recommendations

Academic institutions are limiting career opportunities for women carers and returners by not providing equal opportunity of access to research. Women in computer science are at a particular disadvantage because the rapid development of computer science is placing extreme expectations on academics working in this area, who are required to spend a disproportionate amount of time updating their skills and knowledge. Since an *established research record* is the main criterion for accepting new academics, women returners are, by implication, excluded.

Many men researchers still do not believe that their role of carers conflicts with their role as scientific researchers and would not, therefore, recognise the clash of priorities women researchers have to face. It is largely men who occupy the decision making positions in departments of computing science. It is men who are seen as the traditional researchers who attract the largest grants, both because there are too few women and because there is still inherent discrimination.

The criteria of equal opportunities which are acceptable to industry must be adopted by academic institutions. As there are financial benefits to be gained now from engaging in academic research, universities need to take on board that it may be financially rewarding to support women who want to engage in scientific research. Researchers must be seen as a long-term investment, not just a short-term benefit. The opportunity to postpone research output must be built into contracts of employment as must be the universities' commitment to pro-active continuous training for their staff.

Strategies for breaking the glass ceiling currently discussed in industry must also be adopted in academia (7).

There must be an active, coordinated program of awareness-raising through formal and informal groups and organisations. The discussion currently taking place in the UK between the pressure group Women into Computing and the body representing heads of departments Conference of Professors and Heads of Computing, is a good example.

A research program on the influence of the speed of development in computing science on women's academic careers should be undertaken.

Women students must be encouraged to enter research, rather than simply gain skills which guarantee employment. Ideally we should be in a situation where students see women engaged in research as role models, as women who will pass onto them the results of their research and their knowledge with confidence.

For myself I do want a different treatment from my male colleagues, I want to be valued for my real achievements, I do want the establishment to take on board the gender difference and, as long as society is arranged the way it is, I want to be given the time and the space to produce my articles and my research. I do not want to feel that I am permanently running just to stand still, and I want to say so.

References

1. Julia Brannen: Money, Marriage and Motherhood : Dual Earner Households after Maternity Leave, In: S.Arber and N.Gilbert (eds.) Women and Working Lives, Macmillan (1992)
2. Carole Truman: Demographic Change and 'New Opportunities' for Women : The Case of Employers' Career Break Schemes. In: S.Arber and N.Gilbert (eds.) Women and Working Lives, Macmillan (1992)
3a. Peggy Newton (1991), Computing: An Ideal Occupation for Women? In: J.Firth-Cozens and M.A.West (eds.) Women and Work, Open University Press (1991)
3b. Jenny Firth-Cozens and Michael A.West: Women at Work: reflections and perspectives. *In*: J.Firth-Cozens and M.A.West (eds.) Women and Work, Open University Press (1990)
4. Suzan Lewis: Motherhood and Employment: The Impact of Social and Organizational Values. *In*: A.Phoenix, A.Woolleett, E.Lloy, (eds.) Motherhood Meanings, Practices and Ideologies, SAGE Publications (1991)
5. Janet Webb: The Ivory Tower: Positive Action for Women in Higher Education. In: A.Coyle and J.Skinner(eds.), Women and Work, Macmillan Education (1988)

6a. Susannah Ginsberg: Women, Work and Conflict. In N.Fonda and P. Moss (eds.), Mothers in Employment, Conference Papers, Brunel University (1977)
6b. Sheila Green: The Employer's Attitude to Working Mothers. In N.Fonda and P. Moss (eds.), Mothers in Employment Conference Papers, Brunel University (1977)
7. The Times Higher Education Supplement: Chipping Away at the Glass Ceiling (July 26, 1996)
8. Sue Lees and Maria Scott: Equal Opportunities : Rhetoric and Action. In Gender and Education, Vol.2, no.3, CARFAX (1990)
9. Karen Mahony and Brett Van Toen: Mathematical Formalism as a Means of Occupational Closure in Computing - Why 'Hard' Computing Tends to Exclude Women. In: Gender and Education, Vol.2, no.3, CARFAX (1990)
10. Jackie West and Kate Lyon:The Trouble with Equal Opportunities : the Case of Women Academics. In: Gender and Education, Vol.7, no.1, CARFAX (1995)
11. Jessie Bernard: Academic Women, New American Library (1974)
12. Joan Abramson: The Invisible Woman: Discrimination in the Academic Profession, Jossey - Bass Publishers (1976)
13. Linda Sharp: Women in Engineering and Technology, the Business Benefits. In: IDPM Journal, February 1996.
14. EPSRC: The Distaff Side of Science. In Newsline Special Issue, May 1996
15. DTI and Opportunity 2000: Making The Most, HMSO (1996)
16. Michael Gibbons: The Changing Role of The Academic Research Systems. In: Gibbons M and Wittrock B (eds.), Science as a Commodity, Longman (1985)
17. Claudia B Douglass: Discrepancies Between Men and Women in Science : Results of a National Survey of Science Educators. In: Buttler Kahle Jane (eds.), Women in Science, The Falmer Press (1985)
18. Middlesex University: Equal Opportunities Policy and Codes of Practice (1994)
19. Whirlpool Foundation Study: Women: Setting New Priorities, Whirlpool (1996)
20. PM National Committee for Equal Opportunities and Pay and Employment Cond: Work and the Family, Carer-friendly Employment Practices, IPM (1990)
21. HESA: Academic Statistics (1994)
22. Department of Employment : Women & Work, A Review, HMSO (1975)
23. BBSRC: Equal opportunities in the BBSRC 1992 - 1995, Summary of Progress (1995)
24. Middlesex University: Own Data (1996)

Factors that Attract Women to Careers in Information Technology : A Case Study of Women in Ireland

Ms Thérèse Rafferty

University of Ulster at Jordanstown, Northern Ireland

1 Introduction

This study aimed to identify factors that attract women to work in a computing environment. It has three parts:

1. A background to the company, what it does and how it is organised.
2. A brief look at the educational influences on Women in Ireland.
3. Details of the study and how it was conducted .

2 Results

This study's initial aim was to investigate the factors that attract women to work in technology. The main factors identified will be discussed.

Two other aspects of women's working lives were also included. These cover issues of concern which apply solely to women working in technology and positive experiences which the women had due to working in technology. The responses will be considered.

3 Recommendations

The company needs to concern itself with

- the retention and career progression of women in technology
- the empowerment of management who subconsciously allocate work using a gender bias
- expanding women's talents to the full to avoid boredom and frustration.

The key issue in retaining women and attracting women is providing *challenging, stimulating work.* Women are concerned with

- long hours of work and expected overtime at times of production deadlines
- opportunities for flexible working and career breaks for family reasons
- the need to develop and publicise retainer and re-entry programmes for women
- the lack of career progression, and company promotion procedures.

From these facts three key factors emerge:

1. Women need technological updating and opportunities to progress into technical management.
2. Technical level women have the potential to move up to professional level in technology.
3. Women at the lower levels, as team members, could be developed to become senior team leaders and not necessarily in management positions.

All these suggestions require mentor support, informal advice and work-based learning. Often, however, in the technical fields there is a need for formal study for qualifications. Women need to plan their career progression pathways, and especially consider the opportunities to move into management positions at every level. An atmosphere of positive expectation concerning the desirability of career progression for women in technology must be generated.

Accepted Papers and Discussion Notes

Topic 4: Labour and Living: Apart or Together?

Part 2: (Dis-)Location of Workplaces?

"And it's a Generalisation. But no it's not": Women, Communicative Work and the Discourses of Technology Design

Toni Robertson

School of Information Systems, University of New South Wales
Sydney 2052 Australia

Abstract. This paper considers the importance of skilled communicative work in the utilisation of CSCW technology. It is based on a field study of a small company that uses computer systems and communication technology to support flexible work practices within a distributed work environment. The company is owned and managed by women, and most of the staff are women. Its successful functioning depends on the work done by its members to maintain the flow and quality of the communication between them. Strategies are examined for making communicative work visible within the discourses of technology design. The implications are considered both for the recognition of women's workplace skills, and for the design and implementation of CSCW technology.

1 Introduction

> For feminists working in philosophy - or any academic discipline - the most pressing difficulty in relation to affirming the presence of women is the theoretical exclusions implicit in the discourses with which we have to deal. Creating other modes of conceptualising human culture that do not involve the passivity or invisibility of women is obviously of the greatest importance (Gatens, 1996: 58).

This paper considers the difficulties and strategies for making visible, within the working environments of technology design, women's skilled use of computer systems and communication technology. Its empirical basis is a field study of a small distributed company that makes computer based training and educational software products. The context of the study was a Computer Supported Cooperative Work (CSCW) research project carried out within a technical department. The purpose was to understand how a small group of people coordinated a cooperative design process when they spent most of their time working in geographically separate places. This understanding would then inform the design of CSCW systems that could support designers working together over distance. The project was organised and realised from the perspective of technology design.

The company studied has been in existence for over seven years. It has been distributed since it began, with its members working at home and gathering together for a weekly meeting in the home of one of the directors. Computer systems and communication technologies were used to provide crucial infrastructure support as well as communication links between its various members. Over time, the company members had developed a range of skills and practices that enabled them to coordinate their work within a distributed work environment. This was an environment where there were major geographical constraints on the time when they could be physically together, and equally major physical and technical constraints on the ease and effectiveness of communication when they were not. The experiences and skills of the company members offered a valuable resource for CSCW researchers seeking greater knowledge of the work environments where their systems might be used in the future.

During a long-term field study of the design of a multimedia, educational computer game, it was possible to observe how the company members negotiated and achieved a cooperative design process without constant access to the communicative resources always implicitly available in same-site workplaces. Because co-presence was not an assumed resource for the organisation of their work, the company members had to explicitly work at ensuring the steady and robust flow of communication between them. This work enabled them to create and maintain the context for their individual activities and to successfully work together over distance. Communication between them, while they were working apart, was mediated and supported by telephones, faxes, overnight and normal postal services, couriers and an electronic bulletin board that supported the asynchronous exchange of computer files, including work in progress and electronic mail. Work practices had been developed that embedded communication work in the practices themselves. These included weekly meetings in a shared physical space, regular shared work, modularisation of work, file naming schemes and procedures to notify others about files that were available to them.

The company was owned and managed by women and seven of its eight members were women. It was established, in the first instance, when the two directors refused to work under the corporate culture imposed after a multi-national takeover of their previous employer. The agency of the company members, their control over their work, and their pleasure in its doing were central to the company's culture, organisational framework and work practices. Early in the study, I asked one of the directors, Susan, about the procedures and techniques the company had developed to enable them to work the way they did. She began her reply, paused in mid-sentence, looked at me for a few moments, then leant forward and said

Susan. I guess you know all the staff except Reg are female. Not everybody has children, and not everybody's married. I have found females, funnily enough, and it's a generalisation. But no it's not. We couldn't work this way if most of the staff weren't women. I have found that women, with this set up, that the women are much better at being part of the team and getting on with their tasks and responsibilities and looking across the network of people and understanding how what they are doing affects the rest of the network and vice versa. And thinking ahead. And thinking about relationships. And, like the Melbourne people are very isolated. And I'll talk about how we deal with that in a minute. But this team here are always very concerned, and they want to know about the Melbourne people, and how they are as people. And they often drop letters, just of their own volition down to Melbourne, to say "hullo" and cards and just things like that.

Toni. Things that women do?

Susan. Yes. Exactly. Yes. I've found that women work much better in this situation.

This paper does not report the empirical research that inspired it (see Robertson, 1996a, 1996b, 1994, for detailed accounts of the company's work practices). Instead, my focus is how it might be possible to take seriously Susan's statement and its implications within the environments of technology design. This focus is not intended to imply that there is necessarily any active prohibition, as such, to speaking specifically about women's work within those environments. But it is to recognise that already existing meanings, and the social processes that produce them, exclude or constrain consideration of that work as skilled and necessary to the successful use of the technology. I want strategies to ensure recognition of the specific technical workplace skills, that the company members used to enable them to work successfully over distance, within the context where technology intended to support that work might be designed.

The use of highly developed personal communication, coordination, and relationship building skills was the central factor in the successful operation of this distributed company. They were respected skills in the company culture. Yet differences in personal communication skills and style, and responsibility for communication and relationship building work, remain unnamed variables in studies of CSCW design and use. Indeed, they remain largely unnamed and undefined within the context of discussion and reward of skilled work in general, except interestingly, at management level. Skill and style in communication, and responsibility for its vitality, are practices that are highly gendered, culturally differentiated, and usually unrecognised and unacknowledged. Taking seriously Susan's claim, "We couldn't work this way if most of the staff weren't women", has important implications both for the design of CSCW technology and for feminist strategies to gain recognition and reward for women's workplace skills.

But identifying and naming particular workplace skills as women's risks being caught within the confines of essentialism. At the same time, those newly named and carefully-made-visible skills, risk being devalued simply because women's skills usually are. The remainder of this paper examines possible strategies for making communicative work visible within the discourses of technology design and for recognising that, at this point in time, women are more likely than men to have learnt skills necessary to accomplish this work. The implications of making communicative work visible are considered both in relation to the recognition of women's skills within distributed workplaces and to the design and implementation of CSCW technology.

2 Making Communicative Work Visible

It requires great care to speak about communication within the context of technology design. There, communication is something that computers can do when they are linked together by communication technology. They encode, transmit, receive, and decode information in the form of discrete symbols. Successful communication occurs when the decoded discrete symbols on the receiving end are the same as those on the sending end. The sender/receiver model of communication is assumed within the social processes of making and producing meaning within technology design. That communications technology can successfully implement this model in an increasing range of media is a considerable achievement in itself. Moreover, it is precisely what makes the development of CSCW technology viable in the first place.

But if the meaning of language is determined by its situation of use, then it is problematic within the context of technology design to speak of communication as a process that involves the negotiation of shared meaning among people. Communication *means* something else in that context. This is one of the major theoretical exclusions implicit in the discourses of technology design. I worked in a technical environment for some time before I realised that when I spoke of communication, if I meant the sort that people do, I had to explicitly say so, and then explicitly define what I meant. Otherwise my colleagues generally assumed I was talking about computers. At best I risked being interpreted as assuming the sender/receiver model as a metaphor for human communication. I mean communication where people constantly interact to create, negotiate, maintain, share and review meaning, understanding and knowledge, to enable cooperation, to build and maintain relationships, and use whatever options for achieving this that they can. It is precisely the work done to accomplish communication in this sense (the default meaning for the remainder of this paper) that Susan is articulating when she states "I've found that women work much better in this situation". The successful accomplishment of communicative work depended on skills that enabled the company members to exploit whatever options existed to support that work, even when they were working apart. But the question still remains, how can this work be made visible within the contexts where technology that might support that work is designed?

2.1 Disrupting Dualisms

The assumption of a sender/receiver model of communication renders invisible the work required to achieve a robust and flexible flow of communication between a group of people relying on communication technology. To consider the skills required for the successful accomplishment of this communicative work as gendered, requires the consideration of the excluded and the invisible. But we need to unpack these further if we want to avoid the pitfalls of essentialism. The excluded and invisible in rationalist models of human action, including the sender/receiver model of communication, is precisely the acting and perceiving embodied subject, the excluded middle of the mind/body dualism. Feminists have sought to disrupt this and other dualisms since the 1970's as a strategy to change the social practices, particularly patriarchy, but including here the discourses of technology design, that are produced by such oppositions (Cranny-Francis, 1995: 6; Gatens, 1996: 49-59; Wajcman, 1991: 5). This process has included rethinking human subjectivity using the subject's corporeality as a framework, instead of that provided by various dualisms, particularly those that define sex and gender (Grosz, 1995).

Situated cognition and action and distributed cognition challenge rationalist assumptions and both are visible within CSCW research and design. Both disrupt the inside the head/outside the head dualism of traditional cognitive science. Moreover, the acting and perceiving body also constitutes the excluded middle of the inside/outside dualism. This offers an important and useful point of convergence with feminist rethinking of corporeality as a tactic to disrupt the mind/body opposition. Situated cognition provides a way of making visible the role of interaction and context in organising behaviour. It recognises that human action is always situated, that is embodied action that always occurs within a context of particular, concrete circumstances (Suchman, 1987: viii). Distributed cognition assumes situated cognition and is concerned with the nature and properties of an entire functional system and its environment. Hutchins (1995) emphasised the importance of embodied communicative activity in distributed cognition and action. It is the means of connection between an embodied subject and her environment, including other people, technical systems and other physical objects. Hutchins argued that "the cognitive properties of a group may depend as much on the system of communication between individuals as on the cognitive properties of the individuals themselves" (p. 239). Viewed from this perspective, the communicative work achieved by the members of our distributed company is defining of the work of the company itself. The sender/receiver properties of the communication medium are merely the physical prerequisites for effective communication to occur. Moreover, the successful outcome of the process of cooperative design is directly determined by differences in personal communication, coordination and relationship building skills.

2.2 Communicative Work as a Requirement of Articulation Work

Supporting articulation work has been argued to be a key issue, if not *the* key issue in CSCW (Schmidt and Bannon, 1992). It is reasonable to assume that researchers and designers of CSCW systems would be familiar with the term. Articulation work (Strauss, 1985) is the work required to mesh the different elements, including tasks, artefacts, people and organisational structures into a coherent process. It is work that is situated (Gerson and Star, 1986) and invisible to rationalised models of work (Star 1991). Suchman (1994) linked the focus on articulation work in design discourse to the development of a system design practice that is consistent with some recent feminist analyses of technological production and use (Probert and Wilson, 1993; Green et al., 1993; Wajcman, 1991; Cockburn 1988). She argued that "Bringing it [articulation work] forward, and rendering visible the practical reasoning and action that it requires, challenges existing political economies of knowledge" (p. 51).

In the statement that forms the focus of this paper, Susan defined some of the kinds of articulation work required for the successful operation of a distributed company.

> Susan. . . . I have found that women, with this set up, that the women are much better at being part of the team and getting on with their tasks and responsibilities and looking across the network of people and understanding how what they are doing affects the rest of the network and vice versa. And thinking ahead. And thinking about relationships. . .

Moreover, she claimed that women are much better at it. If we follow Suchman's argument, and bring forward the practical reasoning and action that articulation work requires, then in distributed companies articulation work requires communicative work. Given that articulation work has been established as a visible concept in the discourses of CSCW, it potentially offers a way to render communicative work visible too. And if communicative work is a requirement of articulation work, and the skills utilised in communicative work are gendered, then we can make similar claims, as Susan does, about the accomplishment of the articulation work required to work successfully in a distributed company.

2.3 Naming Women's Workplace Skills

The extensive restructuring of Australian workplaces over recent years has included an increasing emphasis on skill audits as part of the process of award restructuring and the identification of training needs. Feminist researchers, concerned that the failure to identify and acknowledge the character and value of women's skills might further disadvantage women in the workplace, have sought to recognise and name women's skills. Cox and Leonard's (1991) project was to match unpaid community work skills with those in the paid workforce. Their argument was that many women develop technical, management, interpersonal and organisational expertise which is transferable into paid work situations (p. 5). But they found that the language of skills, abilities and learning is not gender neutral. It referred to those skills that are validated by formal training and certification, and that lend themselves to an assembly line paradigm rather than the more complex multi-skilled requirements of the modern work group. The activities that are most often seen as female, including communication, interpersonal relationships, the ability to do many things at the same time, to do emotional and physical caring are called "natural" or "gifts" rather than "skilled" (pp. 18-19). The study provided a list of some 15 skills ranging from mediation, conflict resolution, operating networks, and crisis management to managing invisibly, nurturing and making a friendly ambience (p. 39-40).

Poynton and Lazenby's What's in a Word? project (1992) emphasised the central role of language in the construction of feminine and masculine identities. The project used linguistic analysis to provide a way of defining as "technical" a range of "interpersonal" skills by recognising them as language skills. These were not limited to basic literacy or the ability to speak another language, but referred to all skills that involve spoken and written language. These are specific skills that are learned and finely honed by use (Poynton, 1993: 86). This understanding of language reflects feminist and post-structuralist arguments that language is not a general "thing" that we have, but more a resource that is always used by an embodied speaker in a concrete situation (p. 89).

> Neither "personality" nor "knowledge" can exist independently of language, or some form of communication. Language is not just the clothing we put on something else; language is the means by which knowledge, personality and relations between people are quite literally constructed. We *make* knowledge, ourselves and our relations with each other through the ways we learn to use language, particularly through talk. . . Learning to talk is also about learning when, where and how to talk in appropriate ways. And the evidence of the now substantial research on language and gender is that, to a considerable extent, girls and boys learn to talk in different ways (Poynton and Lazenby, 1992: 12, original emphasis).

From this perspective, the work the company members did to enable them to work together over distance was achieved by their use of specific workplace skills, namely language skills, to produce and shape their work environment. This process included not just the quality and flow of information between the people involved, but the planning and coordination of the company's work, the building and maintenance of interpersonal relationships, the negotiation of specific power relations, and the intertwining of all of these to maintain the company itself.

2.4 Language Skills are Embodied Skills

As girls and boys learn to use talk in different ways, then there are no such things as general, or neutral, language and communication skills; there are only embodied ones learnt through a socialisation process that produces girls and boys, and eventually women and men, who act, more or less, according to the expectations of their cultures and their position within it. The particular kind of "training" that girls receive in language use means that many more women than men are regarded as being good listeners, good communicators, interested in relationships. These labels render invisible the specific, active, moment-by-moment work that women do with language to achieve these qualities, leaving visible only what women are, as if skills in interpersonal communication were simply a matter of personal qualities or personality. Language skills, as embodied skills, belong to the acting and perceiving body that disrupts the mind/body dualism, the inside/outside dualism of cognitivism and the sender/receiver model of human communication.

At this particular point in time, the embodied language skills that women are more likely to have learnt, appear to give them a distinct advantage when they need to rely on the mediation of various kinds of technologies to work together over distance. Susan articulated the extent of the current difference between women's and men's workplace skills, within her particular work situation, by admitting she was making a generalisation and then immediately contradicting herself in order to make the claim she wanted to make.

> Susan. . . . and it's a generalisation. But no it's not. We couldn't work this way if most of the staff weren't women.

Articulation work might offer a strategy to make communicative work visible within the discourse surrounding CSCW research and design. But making visible gendered differences in skilled language use, in ways that work to the advantage of women, will require something else. The efforts of feminist researchers to provide names for women's workplace skills have provided some useful tactics for both the analysis of women's skilled use of technology and for its defence. But Poynton (1993) reminds us that "skill is historically best understood not in terms of what people actually do, and the real economic value of their activities, but rather as a product of workplace struggle" (p. 100).

2.5 Avoiding Essentialism

Hanson and Pratt (1995: 23), identified two meanings of essentialism used within feminist literature. The first grounds all women's common experience in the female body, the second refers to speaking about women as a category of beings. Both have been criticised by feminists as ahistorical and reductive. Both are implicit within the cultures of technology design and both have been used to silence or render invisible the activity and skill of specific women.

> However understandable the charges of essentialism may be . . . they presume that only anatomical, physiological, or biological accounts of bodies are possible, obscuring the possibilities of sociocultural conceptions of the body and ignoring the transformations and upheavals that may transform biological accounts. Nonbiologistic, nonreductive accounts of the body may entail quite different consequences and serve to reposition women's relations to the production of knowledges (Grosz, 1995: 31).

In patriarchal societies that constitute embodied subjects on the basis of sex, we have little choice but to work within those categories. But this is not to ignore or deny that they are constructed ones. On the contrary, recognition of women's workplace skills depends on our insisting that they are women's skills because of the position that women have been socialised into occupying in relation to men, and not because the skills themselves are in any sense inherently gendered (Poynton, 1993). It should be possible to speak of women as a group, in particular contexts like working within distributed companies, without being bound to a commitment that nature has determined the particular grouping. When Susan says ". . . and it's a generalisation. But no it isn't", perhaps she is not contradicting herself at all. The generalisation she wants to deny, might be her unwillingness to speak of all women as a single category. The "But no it isn't" an acknowledgment that the category of women is indeed a valid one, though not a "natural" one, within the specific historical and cultural context of her company's organisation and work practices. "I have found that women, *with this set up*, that the women are much better at . . ." (my emphasis).

This is not an easy, nor particularly welcome, distinction to make within the environments where technology is designed and where differences in communication skills and interests between the sexes are regarded as natural. Both the discourses that surround technology design and those that shape our workplaces, have a stake in the perpetuation of essentialist categories as the basis of claims about women's experiences and skills. Rendering the skilled nature of women's communicative work invisible, by disguising it as natural, means that the forces that perpetuate inequalities based on sex can be disguised as natural as well. In the discourses of technology design, the results are its practice as something that is naturally done by men and the perpetuation of the theoretical exclusions that render invisible women's skilled use of computer systems and communication technology.

3 Implications of Making Communicative Work Visible

When communicative work is visible then its contributions to the achievement of cooperative work, within distributed workplaces, can affect both the value placed on that work and the design of technology to support it. This is not to say that this work does not contribute to the achievement of cooperative work in same site workplaces. On the contrary, the ability to cooperate and communicate are becoming increasingly important to the effective functioning of any workgroup, whatever its physical organisation. Moreover, working in teams involves complex issues around negotiating power in terms of cooperativeness and responsibility and these require the skilled use of language to speak in appropriate ways (Poynton and Lazenby, 1992). But the difficulties of coordinating work, when the communicative resources of co-presence are not generally available, makes crucial the use of specific language skills to enable the productive utilisation of mediating technology. It also demands technology that is capable of being utilised by people skilled in communicative work.

3.1 Implications for the Recognition of Women's Skills in Distributed Workplaces

Cockburn (1988) argued for the need to dismantle the links between gender and jobs. "Anything short of this can be converted by men into a new source of power" (p. 249). Even with full industrial recognition of the specific language skills that women have and their full visibility within the discourses of technology design and use, their continued attribution as women's skills will merely see them devalued. Moreover, both Poynton and Lazenby (1992: 42-61) and Cox and Leonard (1991: 19) recognised that women have learnt to undervalue their workplace skills at the same time as they have learnt the skills themselves. They argued for strategies to encourage and enable women to identify and articulate their strengths and competencies.

Developments in computer systems and communications technology have increased the range of communicative support available to people working together over distance. These developments have been exploited by companies like Susan's, whose members already work this way, as well as by organisations and individuals altering their work practices so that some, or all of their work, can be done from home. More people, mostly women, are working from home (*Working From Home,* 1996: 3). But studies of home-based work that involves computer use have shown that the sexual division of labour is being extended into domestic workplaces. The advantages and disadvantages of home-based work are proving to be determined by what kind of work it is, as well as the gender of the worker (*Ibid*; Wajcman et al., 1989; Dawson and Turner, 1989). As more people work from home, their ability to coordinate their work with others will be shaped by how effectively they utilise the communicative options, including CSCW technology, available to them. The culture of the company studied ensured that communicative work was visible, valued and rewarded. Moreover, the company members were not clerical workers, but designers of multi-media software with skills that are in high demand in the Australian labour market (Wajcman et al., 1989). In other work environments and industries, failure to recognise and value the skills entailed in communicative work and their fundamental contribution to productivity, leaves women vulnerable to the appropriation of their competence in these areas by their employers and/or their clients.

An increasing number of women are running their own businesses. Those operated by women are more likely to employ women and they have a significantly higher survival rate due both to better preparation prior to startup as well as careful, skilled management (*Making It Work: Women and Small Business*, 1994). The creation of appropriate communication environments, and the planning and delivery of work in cooperative working groups, are management skills that are crucial to the survival of businesses. The recognition that many women already do the kind of interpersonal work these skills enable may represent the first step in a long-term strategy for gaining recognition and appropriate recompense for women's language skills (Poynton, 1993). But at the same time, it may also encourage more women to create their own work environments, including distributed workplaces that use CSCW technology, where the benefits of their communicative work skills accrue directly to them.

3.2 Implications for the Design and Implementation of CSCW Technology

The field study of cooperative work uncovered the interplay of organisational and technological solutions to the communication problems of distributed workplaces. The company members' skills in the use of language enabled them to exploit whatever communication options were available. In a distributed company a workforce valued and rewarded for their skill in communicative work can utilise appropriate technological support productively and effectively. A workforce whose communicative work is not recognised, or whose members lack the appropriate language skills, will *not* utilise technological support productively and effectively. This will be the case even if the technology itself is robust and/or expensive and/or impeccably designed. That is, technological solutions, irrespective of the environment where they are designed, will not solve the range of communication problems inherent in distributed workplaces without skilled communicative work by the people who use them. At the same time the value of CSCW technology, to a workforce of skilled and valued communicators, will be increased if it is designed to be sufficiently flexible to accommodate the highly specific ways that language is used to accomplish specific instances of communicative work.

A sobering implication of the importance of communicative work is the development of CSCW systems that embed the agency for achieving that work in the technology itself, by implementing the structuring and organisation of interpersonal communication. If communicative work remains invisible, or unvalued, or if the workforce lacks the language skills, or the collective will necessary to achieve it, then the coordination of work may be implemented by the technology. The history of CSCW design has already included the implementation of the language/action perspective in the structured coordination application COORDINATOR (Winograd and Flores, 1986). In Suchman's (1993) re-examination of the place of coordination technologies in CSCW research and development, she wrote that her "particular concern is the problem of how theories informing such systems conceptualise the structuring of everyday conversation and the dynamics of organisational interaction over time" (p. 2). Suchman's paper and the ensuing debate it created (e.g. Bannon, 1995) have placed the "contest over how our relations to each other are ordered and by whom" (Suchman, 1993: 12) in the centre of the politics of CSCW systems design. The analysis of women's skills in the use of computer systems and communication technology, developed in this paper, suggests that structured coordination systems disadvantage women by neutralising the advantages held by those who have learnt the necessary skills to effectively structure their own communicative work.

4 Conclusion

Taking seriously Susan's claim, "We couldn't work this way if most of the staff weren't women", has demanded a consideration of how women's skills in communicative work might be named and made visible within the environments where technology is designed and used. Despite the ubiquity of the sender/receiver model of communication and other rationalist oppositions within these environments, concepts like articulation work and the approaches of situated and distributed cognition, offer strategic resources for disrupting these dualisms by making communicative work visible. In turn, an understanding of communicative work can make visible the skills required for the successful use of computer systems and communication technology.

Feminist research, aimed at identifying and naming women's workplace skills, has provided resources for analysing the skills involved in communicative work as both gendered and embodied. And theories that stress cultural constructions of embodiment over essentialist explanations, enable us to argue that these skills are not themselves inherently gendered but available, with appropriate training, to both women and men. This is not to say, however, that women should not position themselves to benefit from the skills that their historical and cultural position makes them more likely to possess, particularly those involved in the use of communications technology to coordinate and accomplish distributed work. Strategies, that enable the inclusion and analysis of the communicative work involved in the successful use of CSCW technology, can be used to insist on both the recognition of that work in the workplace and its inclusion in the discourses of technology design.

> If discourse cannot be "deemed" outside, or apart from power relations, then their analysis becomes crucial to an analysis of power. This is why language, signifying practices and discourse have become central stakes in feminist struggles (Gatens, 1996: 70).

Acknowledgments

My thanks, again, to those whose work inspired this paper and to Catherine Blake Jaktman, Susan Newman, Lucy Suchman and Kay Vernon for comments on an earlier draft. This research was partly financed by an Internal Research Grant from the University of Technology, Sydney and by the Telstra Fund for Social and Policy Research in Telecommunications.

References

1. Bannon, L. (Ed). (1995). Commentaries and a Response in the Suchman-Winograd Debate. Special issue of *Computer Supported Cooperative Work (CSCW)*. Vol. 3, no 1. Kluwer Academic Publishers, The Netherlands.
2. Cockburn, C. (1988). *Machinery of Dominance: Women, men and technical know-how*. Northeastern University Press, Boston, USA.

3. Cox, E. and Leonard, H. (1991). *From Ummm . . . to Aha! Recognising Women's Skills.* Research report, Department of Employment, Education and Training. Australian Government Publishing Service, Canberra.
4. Cranny-Francis, A. (1995). *The Body in the Text.* Melbourne University Press, Victoria.
5. Dawson, W. and Turner, J. (1988). *When She Goes to Work She Stays at Home: Women, new technology and home-based work.* Department of Employment, Education and Training. Australian Government Publishing Service, Canberra.
6. Gatens, M. (1996). *Imaginary Bodies: Ethics, Power and Corporeality.* Routledge, UK.
7. Gerson, E. M. and Star, S. L. (1986). Analysing Due Process in the Workplace. *Transactions on Office Information Systems,* Volume 4, Number 3. ACM Press, NY. pp. 257-270.
8. Green, E., Owen, J. and Pain, D. (1993). *Gendered by Design?* Taylor & Francis Ltd, UK.
9. Grosz, E. (1995). *Space, Time and Perversion: The Politics of Bodies.* Allen & Unwin, Sydney.
10. Hanson, S. and Pratt, G. (1995). *Gender, Work, and Space.* Routledge. London.
11. Hutchins, E. (1995). *Cognition in the Wild.* MIT Press, USA.
12. *Making It Work: Women and Small Business.* (1994). Research report, National Board of Employment, Education and Training. Australian Government Publishing Service, Canberra.
13. Poynton, C. and Lazenby, K. (1992). *What's In a Word? Recognition of Women's Skills in Work Place Change.* Research report, South Australian Department of Labour, Adelaide.
14. Poynton, C. (1993). Naming women's workplace skills: linguistics and power. In B. Probert and D. Wilson. (Eds). *Pink Collar Blues: Work, Gender and Technology.* Melbourne University Press, Victoria. pp. 85-100.
15. Probert, B. and Wilson, D. (Eds). *Pink Collar Blues: Work, Gender and Technology.* Melbourne University Press. Victoria.
16. Robertson, T. (1996a). Embodied Actions in Time and Place: The Design of a Multimedia, Educational Computer Game. In *Computer Supported Cooperative Work: The Journal of Collaborative Computing,* vol 5, no ??, pp. 1-27.
17. Robertson, T. (1996b). The Constraints and Resources of a Distributed Workplace. In *Proceedings of Oz-CSCW 96.* August 30th, Brisbane, Queensland. DSTC, Brisbane. pp. 57-65.
18. Robertson, T. (1994). "We Can Do It Better": Communication and the Control of Work Practices. In *Proceedings of OZCHI '94.* Melbourne. pp. 295-300.
19. Schmidt, K. and Bannon, L. (1992). Taking CSCW Seriously. Supporting Articulation Work. In *Computer Supported Cooperative Work (CSCW)* 1, 1-2, pp. 7-40.
20. Star, S. L. (1991). Invisible Work and Silenced Dialogues in Knowledge Representation. In I. Eriksson, B. Kitchenham, and K. Tijdens. (Eds). *Women, Work and Computerisation: Understanding and Overcoming Bias in Work and Education.* North Holland, Amsterdam. pp. 81-92.

21. Strauss, A. L. (1985). Work and the Division of Labor. In *The Sociological Quarterly*, Vol. 26, No 1. JAI Press. pp. 1-19.
22. Suchman, L. (1994). Supporting Articulation Work. In Proceedings of the 5th IFIP WG 9.1 International Conference on Women, Work and Computerisation: Breaking Old Boundaries, Building New Forms. Elsevier, Amsterdam. pp. 46-60.
23. Suchman, L. (1993). Do Categories Have Politics? The Language/Action Perspective Reconsidered. In *Proceedings of the Third European Conference on Computer-Supported Cooperative Work.* Kluwer Academic Publishers, The Netherlands. pp. 1-14.
24. Suchman, L. (1987). *Plans and Situated Actions.* Cambridge University Press, NY.
25. Wajcman, J. (1991). *Feminism Confronts Technology.* Pennsylvania State University Press, USA.
26. Wajcman, J., Probert, B. and Tanter, R. (1989). Bringing It All Back Home: A study of new technology homework in Australia. In K. Tijdens, M. Jennings, I. Wagner and M. Weggelaar. (Eds). *Women, Work and Computerisation: Forming New Alliances.* North Holland, Amsterdam. pp. 37-43.
27. Winograd, T. and Flores, F. (1986). *Understanding Computers and Cognition.* Addison-Wesley, USA.
28. Working From Home. (1996). *Women & Work.* Volume 17, No 1, March. Women's Bureau, Department of Employment, Education and Training. Canberra.

The Resources of The Productive Office – Women's and Men's Opinions on Telematics and Intelligent Building Features

Mervi Lehto

VTT, Building Technology, Automation and Information Systems
PO Box 1804, 02044 VTT, Finland, email:mervi.lehto@vtt.fi

Abstract. Telematics and building features for intelligent offices are designed keeping in mind the comfort of the work environment and work efficiency. In this study different user groups in intelligent buildings (IB) and in other high quality offices have been evaluating the technology which they are using. The difference between these two types office speaks in favour of the intelligent building. Of the groups surveyed, female supervisors in the IBs consider telematics the most effective, more so than their male collegues, female and male, experts or office workers. Female experts in the IBs cannot employ telematics as well as their colleagues in the other type of office. Men seem to get more advantages out of technical and IB features and they have bigger rooms than their female co-workers. Low salary, not being promoted and frequent sick leave are some factors underlying lower work satisfaction of women than that of men, which is emphasized among female experts in the IBs.

1 Indroduction

The latest results of the studies on the use of telematics show that Finns are using a lot of use of telematic services in offices and at home. Finland and Sweden have the largest numbers of mobile phone users in Europe (Hienonen 1996), and Finns are accessing the Internet more frequently than any other people in Europe. According to the statistics from the Finnish Ministry of Labour a half of Finns employedneed computers in their work. Finland is one of the small information intensive nations.

In some countries the number of female IT students has decreased during the last few years (Klawe & Leveson 1995, Morell 1996), but in Finland women continue to make careers in IT business (Sutela 1997). Women are working longer with computers during the day than men, 43% of them spend half of the day at their computer, while only 23% of men work that long with a computer (Lehto A-M. 1989). This study, made in 1994, shows no difference between men and women in the hours spent working with a computer, but the supervisors use computers far less than the experts, and the workers in the IBs evidently work more time with computers than their colleagues in the other type of office. New statistical information on IT and gender will be available in March this year (Sutela 1997).

There are not many studies on intelligent offices, and that is why gender has not been an issue for scientific discussion in this context, unlike in IT science. However, the indoor air studies show similar results to female experts, while women are not satisfied with the air quality in their offices (Smith 1989). The clothing of women and men in the office is very different (Lehto M. 1978), and the physiological differences are well known facts. Both these issues may have a role in determining IT working conditions.

2 The Concept of an Intelligent Building

An intelligent building is a development process which brings an awareness of both the needs of the purchaser of a modern building or real estate developer and the possibilities of combining hi-tech building solutions. The aim of this process is to achieve an intelligent overall system of building solutions that will serve the building user, in either a residential or office context.

A long list of technical equipment is no guarantee that a building will be intelligent; however an intelligent building must include the characteristics of being:

- modifiable and flexible
- structurally active
- capable of structural and functional integration
- informative
- interactive
- secure
- comfortable and service-oriented
- healthy and therapeutic
- economic and productive
- based on correct fundamental solutions.

Typical Finnish intelligent building features are assembly floors, adjustable walls, special lighting, personally regulated indoor climate, advanced advice and security systems, automatically operated doors and windows, job-specific work sites, advanced office automation and telematics, green spaces and communal spaces promoting the free flow of information. These are all known in other countries as well.

In USA, Canada and Japan there are many IBs, and many European countries are active in this area too, like the United Kingdom, France, Scandinavian countries, the Netherlands, Italy, Switzerland and Spain. In Finland there are in Helsinki alone app. 25-30 office buildings which can be called intelligent and some have been built in other cities as well.

3 A Holistic Approach

The functionality of telematics and intelligent building features can be seen first-hand in buildings already constructed. Twelve offices have been studied by VTT in the greater Helsinki region in Finland. In order to be able to make comparisons half of the offices studies are of intelligent offices and the other half are of offices of high quality.

The study consists of a questionnaire about users' opinions, an economic survey, energy calculations and indoor air measurements. The questionnaire covers such subjects as: indoor air quality, lighting, intelligent building features (image of the building, space and structure, building automation), telematics, office automation. More than 500 answers to the questionnaire which contained 166 questions give a good idea how efficient the intelligent building concept is for office workers.

In the questionnaire the workers were asked to evaluate each variables (space, device, etc.) according to its importance for an efficient working environment. To draw a comparison, the users were divided into categories according to their occupation (supervisor, expert, office worker) and gender. In the statistical study several variables showed significant differences in respondents´view on the power of telematics and the intelligent building design. The female respondents gave rather lower responses than men, when evaluating with an index from 4 to 10 (best) the options of multiple choice questions. In general, the supervisors give higher responses than the experts, and the experts higher responses than the office workers.

The primary aim of the intelligent office building study has been to find the features that will best promote the competitive benefits of the construction industry and its customers. However, the analyses of users' opinions on telematic and office automation device offer a lot of information for the future of office work and computerization (automation).

4 Who Works in an Intelligent Office?

In the intelligent office, there are more male workers than in the other type of office. They are also better educated than workers in the other type of office. There are many employees with good educational background, and they hold supervisory positions more often than employees working for those companies located in the other kind of office buildings.

Although those who answered the questionnaire were selected according to the building they were working in, there were no special differences found in the sample compared to average Finns.

There are 9% more female experts and 16% more male clerks in Finnish offices than in offices in USA, according to the figures reported in the American BOSTI Office Survey carried out in the middle of the 80's by Michael Brill with Stephen T. Margulis.

The personnel of the companies located in the intelligent buildings work overtime more often for compelling reasons than workers in the other offices. However, the workers in the IB-offices are more satisfied with their work, that is, in respect of position, company, supervisors, co-workers, salary and occupation.

The IB-office workers take less sick leave, but they do have more symptoms relating to the quality of indoor air than those working in the other type of high quality offices. When it comes to the female experts, those who work in the IBs take sick leave most often (See Table 3). 56% of men report that they can work at home (flexi-work) due to the technical facilities available, but only 21% of women agree with this.

Amount of (percentage/%)	IB	Non-IB
Male	58	45
Age (average)	37	39
Education (academic degree)	58	45
Supervisor	24	13

Table 1. Office workers (IB=Intelligent Building)

Two of the intelligent offices studied are the headquarters of private companies in the telecommunications and the information service sector, one is a building belonging to the Ministry of Foreign Affairs, and the remaining two are multi-user buildings. For each intelligent building selected, one of the same size and with a corresponding number of companies using the building was selected for the Non-IB group. These buildings are used for the same kind of companies as the intelligent offices.

5 Productivity is Success Coming True

According to the study, from the users' point of view, one can make the most of office automation in the intelligent offices. There is all kind of high-technology, such as a LAN (local area network), personal computers, telecommunication systems and telematics on the desk tops, in the reception area and in the secretarial work environment and in information services. The technology is not very different from that of the modern office building. The integration of the devices and structures has a positive influence on the performance of the equipment too.

In every case, the advanced advice and security system is the only one not very highly valued. Its controlling nature might be the reason for this. Software design might solve the problems.

In addition to lowering real estate expenses, the revenue-generating potential of commercial properties will be improved due to telematics and the intelligent building features thereby increasing the incomes of both the owners of buildings and the firms that make use of them. For example it is the case shared space lowers rent costs, while tenants have no need to rent permanently. The shared space is at the same time, however, earning more money for the building owner, due to many users and high frequency of use, than when it is being rented out to a company permanently. Thus, having a house does not necessarily mean only costs for tenants, but a good office building can be considered as a source of income as labour, device and capital have been, and not only as a good investment. The intelligent building is a way of making information a source of income, just as the brainwork of the information era is in general. Productivity through user-oriented building technology observes the old wisdom: by helping others, such as your customers, in this case tenants, to succeed you are helping yourself most.

Efficiency improvements will also be felt by society as a whole, for instance, as a result of reduced commuting and traffic. In addition to economic productivity, enhancement of social and mental welfare in accordance with the objective of harmonious development is also an aim in the construction of smart houses and the information society.

6 Limitless Computerization and Information Efficiency

In Finland as in other industrial countries with high labour costs, automation has taken a leading role in business life, and this includes office automation, building automation and telecommunications. The need for computers, telefaxes and printers in offices is undisputed. The thing that matters is the quality; speed, capacity and user friendliness. According to this study, workers in Finnish offices prefer a person to a machine to answer the phone, in training and in building management, while in copying, in editing, in computer aided information services, in emailing and in teleconferencing machinery a computer aided service is good enough.

In every fourth Finnish home there is a computer, but 44% of office workers have a home office and 52% of them a home computer, 32% have a printer, 7% a telefax and 2% a copying machine. The attitude towards telematics is very positive in offices. Only 15% of those who answered the questionnaire like to minimize their usage of telematic services.

In the office, phone and video conferencing devices are communicating systems with very low frequency of use (in 1994). Few users leave buildings where there is a video conference room or companies where the use of teleconferencing is supported in other ways.

Can we take an advantage of this stock of ever-advancing technical equipment? It seems obvious that it would be good to pay attention to the human ability to learn new things like new versions of computer programs. In the study approximately 40% of the office workers report that they know how to use all the telematic services which they need daily in their work. On the other hand one third know only limited ways of employing the new technology available to them. 26% of female workers like to acquire more knowledge of the technology and only 15% of male empoyees feel the same. This difference is statistically significant.

It helps to know, however, that it is the supervisors who appreciate the office services and equipment most. In the intelligent offices there are more supervisors, i.e., people with good salaries, than in the other type of offices. This makes it possible to think that the investment in apparatus and services as well as in the other intelligent building features can be recouped by an increase in work efficiency.

7 Female Supervisors and Telematics

There were only a few female supervisors (≈ 10 women) in the intelligent offices, as not many exist. Their opinion of office automation was more positive than that of the others. Discussions with the real estate rental personnel confirm this conclusion.

The female supervisors seem to value telematics higher than any other group. They also like some devices which their colleagues do not like, and vice versa. (See Table 2).

	SUPERVISORS				EXPERTS			
	Male		Female		Male		Female	
	IB	Non-IB	IB	Non-IB	IB	Non-IB	IB	Non-IB
Mobile phone	8,4	8,0	**6,3**	8,4	7,6	7,4	**6,7**	7,5
Phone: central	7,8	7,2	**8,6**	7,6	7,1	7,1	7,6	7,3
Answering machine	7,0	6,6	**9,0**	7,0	6,7	6,4	6,5	7,8
Email	8,3	7,8	**10,0**	7,8	8,4	8,0	8,4	8,1
Portable PC	**8,2**	7,5	**8,5**	6,5	**8,2**	7,4	7,3	7,2
Security system	5,9	5,9	**6,8**	6,0	6,0	5,7	5,4	5,9
Worktime control	5,5	5,3	**7,0**	4,8	5,9	5,6	5,4	**6,3**
Paging	6,5	6,1	**4,0**	7,25	6,4	6,3	**5,5**	6,4

Table 2. The evaluation of the telematic services with a rating from 4 to 10 (best) by the office workers in the intelligent building (IB) and in the high quality office buildings (Non-IB)

8 Female Experts - a Lesson from the Exception

Workers in intelligent offices evaluate technical devices as being more useful for their work efficiency than workers in the other type of high quality office buildings. The only exceptiona are female experts in the IBs, who cannot employ intelligent devices as well as their colleagues in the other type of office (See Table 3). On the other hand, female supervisors in the intelligent offices evaluate the technology most positively of all (See Table 2). Is this due to the male-culture (Hemenway 1995) in the intelligent buildings where there is a majority of men, even through the female experts are as well educated as their male colleagues? Who are the female supervisors in the IBs? That they are their fathers' princesses, is a possible explanation.

Female experts in intelligent offices are most often on sick leave and have the lowest salaries than any other group, and their office rooms are the smallest (see Table 3).

The work satisfaction is generally good in all groups. Female supervisors in the high quality offices are not so satisfied with their work as their colleagues in intelligent offices. While the female supervisors like the technical devices in the office, they stay at their desk longer than others during working hours. Although, when comparing women and men in more detail a significant difference is found, the women are less satisfied with their position, salary, choice of occupation and supervisors than the men. The women are as satisfied with their co-workers and the company policy asthe men.

Women value all services (secretary, travel agency, information and conference services) more highly than men, especially receptionists and personnel helping with computers. Does this mean lack of support or does it prove they have good social skills?

	SUPERVISOR				EXPERT			
	Male		Female		Male		Female	
	IB	Non-IB	IB	Non-IB	IB	Non-IB	IB	Non-IB
Telematics	**8,1**	**7,6**	**8,4**	**7,1**	7,3	7,0	7,6	7,4
Device	7,8	7,2	**8,2**	7,2	7,6	7,1	**7,2**	7,7
Worksatisfaction	8,4	8,5	**8,5**	**7,8**	8,1	8,1	8,2	8,0
Roomsize [1]	3.3	3.4	3.7	3.6	2.7	3.1	**2.3**	2.6
Leave (days/year)	0.5	0	0	0	0.7	0.9	**3.8**	1.8
Time spent in office (min/day)	316	285	**356**	303	330	318	302	306
Salary FIM/month	22432	20654	20375	18500	15091	15357	**12130**	13129

1) index from 1 to 4, 1 smallest and 4 largest (1 ≡ under 5 m^2, 2 ≡ 5 - 9 m^2, 3 ≡ 9 - 13 m^2, 4 ≡ over 13 m^2)

Table 3. The evaluation of the telematic services and technical device with a rating from 4 to 10 (best) by the office workers in the intelligent building (IB) and in the high quality office buildings (Non-IB) and the background information of those who answered the questionnaire

With this questionnaire were gathered other variables which might give further information on the differences of the male and female workers. They are family relationships, work trips and work related trips, type of housing, type of work and working hours, but these will be analyzed later. Both the more detailed analyses of the variables of this study and the more careful study of the literature, might end up drawing valuable conclusions about the right way of employing modern technology, telematic services and building and office automation, while women and men using their female skills (animus/anima) are making the success come true. This paper is asummary of the results so far.

9 Working Space and Meeting Point

The size of the Finnish office work site is app. 9 - 13 m^2. Office space per person is 25 - 35 m^2. In intelligent offices less than the average working space is needed. In contrast, the meeting rooms and space for office services take double the space in the intelligent office buildings than in the other type of office.

In those offices studied, 15% of the working hours were spent out of the office, and 38% of the working time workers were not in their own rooms. In spite of the spacious conference and seminar rooms, workers in the IB-offices spend more time on their own work site. Workers do not consider working areas significantly good in intelligent offices. On the other hand, lobbies and reception, show rooms and meeting rooms, parking and green rooms are valued in profit making organisations.

10 Influencing One's Environment

The target in design is to allow as much personal freedom as possible. Also, due to flexibility and modification in the intelligent office, it is easy to have more room for extra people, to change places, to modify the office rooms for organizational reasons, or if there are changes in company size. That is not the case for offices in general.

The opportunities to intelligently modify each piece of furniture and the layout of furniture is judged significantly higher that the same opportunities in the other type of office.

Moreover, a result of the study is that moving into the intelligent building is easy, as expected, since it is an objective in the intelligent building design.

However, the female office workers consider that the possibilities for them to influence their working environment are not so good as the men. Their working space is less functional and comfortable than men's. The women are not as satisfied with the possibilities for altering the size of their working space or the fillers for moving the computer and for controlling indoor air temperature as the men. The women cannot as well as the men, change their position at the desk or move in the office space and find place for the temporary working groups. The small room size of female white collar workers might have an effect on this result.

The control and regulation of heating and air conditioning is not good for the men either. Balancing the human need to control one's own environment, and the human desire to have it made as easy as possible has proved to be not that simple. A reason for this might be the use of new integrated technology in many intelligent buildings, and designers and constructors are not yet mastering it well enough. Another reason could be the image that 'intelligence' implies high standards, which do not allow any kind of imperfection.

The possibility to work overtime in good conditions is an advantage gained through the flexibility of the office building. In this study, it was unfortunately impossible to gather information on the amount of overtime work done in the various companies. Thus, we cannot calculate the significance of overtime work in the overall performance of the intelligent building.

11 Conclusion

According to this study of over 500 office workers in the greater Helsinki region, it seems simply that the use of the intelligent building concept as a holistic approach to building design makes the difference between a high quality office building and an intelligent office. However, not only does the intelligent office differ from the high quality office building, but the various user groups in offices have different opinions of the new technology.

Consequently, the message is that the user oriented concept proves that work efficiency, reduction of traffic, energy efficiency and cost benefit ratio, all speak in favour of intelligent offices. The female supervisors especially seem to be able to get most out of the advantages of new technology.

However, the users are not only satisfied with the telematic services and the intelligent building features of the offices. Female experts evaluated the current office automation not as highly as the other user groups. There might be use of more advanced technology.

12 The Essence of the Concept

The intelligent building concept can be understood as a metaphor. Intelligence indicates a human being, and a building an artificial item. To understand the intelligence of the building, and in some cases even to accept the building as intelligent, it is helpful to understand human intelligence. It is important also to be aware of the results of artificial intelligence research. This issue is worth an article of its own, and I am mentioning it in this context only because of its importance in the definition of the intelligent building concept.

13 Office – the Academia of the Information Era

When the end users of the buildings were asked the most important reason for a company to move into an intelligent office building, they replied that the image of the building was essential, not its price. The price is dominant in the other type of high quality office building. Efficiency counts in the quality of the workplace. Efficiency is traditionally understood as the cost benefit ratio. One cannot deny that the office is the factory of the information society.

Finally, I would like to point to the next step. How long will mankind be interested only in becoming better off, with progress gained through the means which are the cause of the cost benefit ratio, or with that which the cost benefit ratio is describing? Technology carries with it various values. Could it be possible to think that the performance of office technology is described also by 'fun to knowledge ratio', 'positive experience to wisdom ratio'? Benefiting from the material good gained might lead to the office becoming a fertile place for creative knowledge and skills, multiculturalism, or an energetic place for satorian insight. Enjoying one's work is totally different from being a workaholic. Enjoyment is based on success gained by recognizing problems, not avoiding them.

Women are considered to take care of themselves. They are using their brains and feelings simultaneously, and they are the ones sitting in various learning courses and meditating. Are these the female themes to be discovered and discussed in the artificial intelligence as the means of getting all of us, also men, from the information era to the conscious era?

Network marketing, imaginary organizations, female leadership are utilizing the intelligent offices, hot desking, flexiwork showing positive thinking and using the harmonious, healed operations of everyone's own path and benefit.

References

1. Hemenway, Kathleen. 1995. Women in Computing. Human Nature and the Glass Ceiling in Industry. Communications of the ACM. Jan 95. Vol. 38 No. 1. p. 55-62.
2. Hienonen, Risto & Lehtinen A. 1996. Elektroniikka- ja sähköalan kehitysnäkymät 1995-2000. VTT Automaatio 1995. Espoo. 190 p. (in Finnish)

3. Klawe, Maria & Leveson, Nancy. 1995. Women in Computing. Where Are We Now? Communications of the ACM. Jan 95. Vol. 38 No. 1. p. 29-35.
4. Lehto, Anna-Maija. 1989. Information Technology at Work On Changes in the 1980's. (Tietotekniikka työssä - Muutoksista 1980-luvulla. Tilastokeskus.) Statistics Finland. Helsinki. 53 p.
5. Lehto, Mervi. The 'Intelligent Office' Concept Makes the Difference. Nordic Architectural Studies Review. Nordisk Arkitekturforskning 1996:1. pages. 61-72.
6. Lehto, Mervi, Flink, Selja, Pulakka, Sakari, Karjalainen, Sami. 1995. Intelligent Office Features in Finland. VTT Building Technology. Feasibility Study for Tekes, the Helsinki Telephone Co. and Puolimatka Oy. 187 p. (to be publiced in Finnish)
7. Lehto, Mervi. 1978. Polyesteri-selluloosakuitusekoitekankaiden soveltuvuus työvaatemateriaaliksi. Sairaalahenkilökunnan työpukujen käyttöominaisuudet. Espoo. HTKK Diplomityö, 1978. 119 s. (in Finnish)
8. Morell, Virginia. 1996. Computer Culture Deflects Women and Minorities. Science. Vol. 271. 29 March 1996. p. 1915-1916.
9. Smith, Phil. 1989. Docklands SKILLNET: A new Concept in Training. High Tech Buildings. Proceedings of the conference held in London, June 1989.
10. Interviewed:
11. Sutela, Hanna. Senior Statistian, Statistics Finland. 1997.
12. a writer of the study: "On the Way to Information Society" (Tiellä tietoyhteiskuntaan) Helsinki. 1997. (to be published)

Who is in Control?
Canadian Experiences in Teleworking

Crystal Fulton

Graduate School of Library & Information Science
The University of Western Ontario, London, Ontario, Canada

Abstract. An exploratory study revealed that while teleworkers choose this work option to improve their quality of life, they may not actually control work processes. Familial obligations, interruptions, potentially problematic work environments, work routines of others, and isolation from coworkers all contribute to the teleworker's lack of control. In fact, the teleworker can become susceptible to workaholism and find that distinctions between home and work times blur as the worker tries to juggle both. This situation is particularly dangerous for women who often function as primary child care givers.

1 Introduction: Telework in Canada

Telework is a form of home-based work in which the worker spends part or all or his/her work time at home, using telecommunications technologies to communicate with others. By the year 2001, Statistics Canada predicts that over 1 million Canadians will work at home. An increasing number of these home-based workers promise to be women.

Organizations have applauded telework as a means of increasing productivity and decreasing expenses. Researchers Duxbury and Higgins found that the flexibility of telework reduced stress for workers because teleworkers could control and absorb change in work and family settings – especially women. However, this study also revealed that teleworkers worked 2.4 more hours per day than did non-teleworkers.

Similarly, Hartling found that telecommuters worked 5 to 10 hours per week longer.

The public perceives telework as a situation in which people have full control over the work processes and product. What is the reality?

2 Studying Teleworkers and Their Work

During interviews teleworkers reported that this work arrangement offered them flexibility, but this flexibility required them to fit their work around other demands on their time. Home interruptions replaced office interruptions. Teleworkers often paid for expenses, such as their own computer equipment. The quality of the physical work environment often depended on an organization's involvement in arranging and maintaining home work spaces. Teleworkers reported higher productivity and long work hours. Frequent descriptions of blurred divisions between home and work seemed to be linked to workaholism. For some, the opportunity to work, even on one's own time, was omnipresent and compelling. For teleworking women, who tend to fill both mother and employee roles, this question of control is critical. These problematic control issues suggest the potential emergence of a new sweatshop: the home.

References

1. Lipovenko, D. (1996, March 14). More Canadians Work From Home. Globe & Mail, p. A12.
2. Duxbury, L. and Higgins, C.A. (1994). Telework: Enhancing The Quality of Life. Paper presented at Telework/T,l,travail 1994, Toronto, ON.
3. Hartling, D.E.J. (1985). Telecommuting: The Trend Towards Remote Worksites. A Canadian Sample. Unpublished master's thesis, Queen's University, Kingston, Ontario, Canada.

Support for this research is gratefully acknowledged from a grant to Roma Harris from the Social Sciences and Humanities Research Council, Grant Number 410-95-0185.

Telecommuting: A Woman's Friend or Foe

Caroline St.Clair

DePaul University, Chicago, IL

> "Telecommuting is the partial or total substitution of telecommunications technology for the trip to and from the primary workplace along with the associated changes in policy, organization, management, and work structure" [1].

In years past, most telecommuters have been women with low-paying clerical jobs. Many of these women tried to maintain a full-time telecommuting job along with housework/child-rearing responsibilities. Telecommuting was not beneficial for these women [2] [3]. The isolation these women experienced both physically and psychologically was compounded with the additional stress of trying to maintain a dual career. These women were often overlooked when business meetings were held or when promotions were handed out, since they were not physically present at the company. Of course telecommuting is not restricted to women, however in the past, jobs that used telecommuting as an alternative work environment were primarily held by women.

The ever increasing role of technology in business is changing the scope of telecommuting. Telecommuting is no longer restricted to jobs such as data entry. Many businesses are finding alternative ways of using telecommuting. and are embracing the benefits offered by telecommuting. In order for these businesses to avoid the pitfalls of the past it is important for a well written policy on telecommuting to be incorporated. I refer the reader to [1] for an important discussion of this policy. What does this mean for women today? First of all, telecommuting will no longer be restricted to data entry type jobs. Jobs of all types and all levels will have the opportunity to telecommute thus requiring businesses to incorporate a telecommuting policy. Second, solutions to the isolation and job advancement problems that telecommuters of the past have experienced can finally be addressed in the policy. Of course it will also be important that telecommuting not be viewed as a solution to choosing between a career and housework/child-rearing responsibilities. With its increasing popularity and policy enforcement, telecommuting will no longer isolate and restrict the advancement of many women's careers.

References

1. SMART Valley Telecommuting Information Guide, http://www.svi.org/PROJECTS /TCOMMUTE/TCGUIDE/telecmmtng_guide.txt.
2. Olson, Margrethe H., Primps, Sophia B., "Working at Home with Computers", Computers, Ethics, & Society, ed. Ermann, M. David, Williams, Mary B., Gutierrez, Claudio (New York: Oxford, 1990), 189-200.
3. Zimmerman, Jan, "Some Effects of the New Technology on Women." Computers, Ethics, & Society, ed. Ermann, M. David, Williams, Mary B., Gutierrez, Claudio (New York: Oxford, 1990), 201-213.

Accepted Papers and Discussion Notes

Topic 4: Labour and Living: Apart or Together?

Part 3: Engendering by Organizational Development?

Change and Continuity: Transformations in the Gendered Division of Labour in a Context of Technological and Organizational Change

Diane-Gabrielle Tremblay

Professor and Director of Research, Télé-université, Université du Québec
P.O. Box 670, Station C, Montréal, Québec, Canada, H2L 4L5

Abstract. Our paper presents some of the results of a research conducted in 10 firms in Canada. The object of the research was to analyze the transformations in the gendered division of labour in these firms following technological and organizational change. The research covered 4 firms in manufacturing and 6 in the service sector , and was based on a quantitative questionnaire (for a total of 118 women and 66 men as respondents) and more qualitative interviews (with 43 women and 35 men). The results presented here show some difference in the components of daily tasks of men and women, and present some results on the effects of technological and organizational change on these men and women. We observed that while technological and organizational changes could represent an ideal occasion to change the division of labour according to gender, it seems it is not often considered even. Thus, we conclude that hypotheses about "the end of the division of labour" should be re-examined in light of the reality experienced by women in the workplace.

1 Introduction

The literature on new forms of organization of work, production and the enterprise emphasizes globalization (of the economy, research and development and technology), the internationalization of markets, and the increasingly fierce competitive environment confronting firms, to explain the rise of new forms of work organization. These new forms of work organization include new norms related to quality of production (eg., just-in-time systems and total quality management practices), the emergence of new "multiskilled" occupations, as well as the transformation of work and authority relations (notably, increased employee participation in the labour process, in the organization of production and in quality control). (See Horst and Schumann.) Often associated with technological innovations, these organizational changes are considered by many scholars to be essential in the search for business competitiveness.

However, few studies include gender as a variable in their analysis and this was the point of departure for our study.[1] When problems or doubts are raised, these are most

[1]Amongst the few studies which do, let us mention Appay (1993), Kergoat (1992); Hirata (1991) and Schneider (1991).

often discussed in terms of the "male worker". We are therefore justified in asking if the "promises" of new models of production, such as the "end of the division of labour" (Kern and Schumann, 1989), job enrichment, the effort to make better use of workers' competencies and capabilities, the intensification of training, and a focus on treating workers as individuals, are relevant in the case of female jobs, even following technological and organizational changes. As most of the research done on these issues was done in male occupations in the manufacturing sector (paper, steel, auto industry), it appeared to us that some research should be done which would include female occupations, and ideally men and women in similar positions.[2] Are women and men equally affected by the type of flexibility that involves removal of barriers between job categories, the disappearance of traditional hierarchies and supervision, as well as by multi-skilling of the labour force? Similarly, are the new skill requirements and training related to the new forms of work organisation and the use of computer technologies the same for both sexes? The aim of this study, which was carried out from 1993 to 1995, is to provide some answers to these questions. Such questions, we would argue, are fundamental, not least because the issues currently being raised in relation to the degradation of work associated with Taylorist work organization can affect both women and men. Both men and women are affected by contemporary transformations of the labour process and production, but little research is done in a comparative perspective. To address these questions, this paper presents the results of a study which is exploratory in nature and was conducted in ten Quebec firms on the theme of human resource management (HRM) and training, and more particularly on the gendered division of labour, and its evolution in a context of technological and organizational change.

2 The Research Problem

As was pointed out in the introduction, few researchers have considered gender differences as a relevant variable in studies of new forms of work organization. As was revealed in our review of the literature for this research, only a few authors have dealt with this subject. According to Ellen Ruth Schneider, who studied German cases for example, a first phase of workplace change ("job control" and a greater control of work organization) can prove to be positive for women since it provides an opportunity to learn new tasks (maintenance, repairs, loading and changing programs, etc.). However, this positive impact will not necessarily last since this phase is often only transitory. As she goes on to say, "...the room for manoeuvre related to the integration of tasks will decrease with the following stage of technical evolution" (1991: 7). Thus, men are given the new operations in automated manufacturing systems, jobs which confer greater responsibilities and autonomy in the work carried out. Women are only given work of lesser importance (auxiliary and operational tasks) in mechanized or partially automated manufacturing workshops. The changing forms of the gendered division of labour are thus rapidly overshadowed by their enduring forms, that is, a reinforcement of the position of skilled male workers and a

[2] We say "similar" because it is difficult to find men and women in exactly the same positions in employment, as employment data indicate and as our research confirmed.

concentration of female workers in the least skilled jobs and at the lowest levels of the job hierarchy. As our own research will show, two key terms - enduring forms and changing forms of the gendered division of labour - in our view currently paint an accurate portrait of the many workplaces that have undergone a variety of forms of technological change.

Based on similar observations in France, Danièle Kergoat argues that the claim that the flexible model of work and production will improve the reality of work is a myth (Kergoat, 1992). She notes that in fact men are given new forms of cooperative autonomy while women only have access to training that is directly related to the job, a weaker form of multi-skilling (that is, *horizontal*[3]) including frequent mobility and limited-term contracts. Thus, for women, the Multiskilling, New Forms of Work Organization and the "new widening of skills" mean little more than the addition of new tasks to old tasks at the same level. In this way, female workers do not become real multi-skilled workers, nor do they benefit from accompanying advantages, i.e. a significant wage increase and the real possibility of promotion (Kergoat 1992). This further example demonstrates the way in which traditional forms of the gendered division of labour can be superimposed on its new forms.

All of these findings on the division between female and male tasks attest to the persistence of traditional forms of the gendered division of labour in a context of technological change. The de-skilling/re-skilling dynamic does not appear to work in the same way for women and men, making it a relevant subject of research. Considering little research had been done on this specific issue in Québec, we oriented our own research on this subject.

Thus, two contrasting propositions concerning the impact of new technologies and new production models on skills and work can be identified. Since the first approach, often referred to as the "High Performance Work Organization", which does not take gender into account, is dominant, we wanted to test these hypotheses in more detail by analyzing the experience of ten Quebec firms. This research process is all the more relevant since, as was previously observed, to our knowledge, the majority if not all studies that take gender into account from this precise analytical perspective on the "end of the division of labour" are European, and they are very few. Since situations may vary according to sociological, economic or institutional factors (state of industrial relations, employment equity legislation, etc.), research on Quebec/Canada is particularly relevant.

3 The Canadian Experience

Our research is based on quantitative and qualitative methods in order to try to obtain simultaneously some breadth, as well as some depth, and understanding of processes. We thus conducted interviews with a number of women (43) and men (35) in the 10 firms studied and also had questionnaires of a more quantitative nature filled in by women (118) and men (66) in the same firms; the persons interviewed also completed the questionnaire, so that their numbers are included in the second set. Both enduring and changing forms of the gendered division of labour in a context of technological

[3]Emphasis added.

and organizational change were observed in the Quebec firms studied. Four specific sets of themes were covered in the research in order to demonstrate that both enduring forms of and innovations in the gendered division of labour clearly do exist. We examined firstly, the job content of women and men's work in these firms; secondly, women and men's use of technologies in the workplace; thirdly, the effects of technological changes on their job content; and finally, training within the firm, since it can affect the possibilities of "benefiting" from new technologies (*cf.* Hirata 1991). In this paper, we will concentrate on the technological dimension, i.e. its relation with work, its impact on job content and the concerns associated with technological change, always keeping in perspective the gendered dimension.

3.1 The Firms Studied

Of the ten firms that make up the study sample, four are in the manufacturing sector, identified here by the letters, A, B, C and D. Firms A, B and C are in the food sector, while Firm D is in the pulp and paper sector. Among these firms, two from the food sector are highly innovative in work and production organization as well as in technology. The other six firms studied are in the service sector, identified here by the letters E, F, G, H, I and J. Firms E and F are in the restaurant and financial sectors respectively, while the four other firms - G, H, I and J - are in the communications sector. Of the six service-sector firms, four are performing well in general while two of the firms in the communications sector are experiencing some economic difficulties.

3.2 Profile of Respondents

Although the sociological profile of female and male respondents does not differ much between the manufacturing firms and the service-sector firms, there are nonetheless slight differences. In the manufacturing firms, the average age of women is 42 and men 36.5. In the service-sector firms, the average age of women (35.4) is lower than the average age of men (40). The seniority of employees within the service-sector firms is also lower than the seniority of respondents in the manufacturing firms, a reflection of both greater discontinuity of women's career paths and greater rigidity of internal markets in the manufacturing sector.[4] Women's seniority rises to 12.05 years in the service-sector firms and 19 years in the manufacturing firms. In these two categories of firms, men's seniority reaches 12.4 and 15 years respectively. The number of years in the labour market (as opposed to in the firm) is slightly higher but does not exceed 25 years.(All data presented in the article is based on detailed tables which can be obtained from the author.)

Several differences in educational levels can be observed between the two categories of firms, differences largely attributable to occupational differences between the two types of work forces. Thus, the educational level of women and men in the manufacturing firms is lower than that of respondents in the service-sector firms. On average, the educational level of respondents in the manufacturing firms

[4]With regard to internal labour markets, see D.-G. Tremblay, *Économie du travail: la réalité et les approches théoriques* (Montréal: Éditions St-Martin), Chapter 11. New edition 1997.

does not go beyond high school (in Quebec, Secondary V). In these firms, individuals occupy positions of temporary workers, labourers, mechanics and fork-lift truck drivers, which basically require a high school education. In service-sector firms, the educational level of respondents would appear to be more diversified. Some individuals have high school, but others have college and sometimes even university education. It must be said that in these firms, the range of occupations (including waitresses, cashiers, office workers, technicians and journalists) is also more diversified.

The respondents in our study therefore constitute a relatively young work force who still have many years of labour market activity ahead of them before reaching retirement. This underlines the importance of analyzing the internal job market of these firms, the adjustment of workers in a context of technological and organizational changes, as well as their perceptions in this regard, since the educational profile of the work forces reflects the composition of the labour pool on the contemporary labour market.

3.3 Changes in Work

During the last twenty years, the majority of respondents (both women and men) within the firms studied have experienced many changes in their work, such as the introduction of new technologies and the reorganization of their tasks, the two often being related. Some 70% experienced technological change and 50-58% experienced organizational change.

The most significant change in work involves the introduction of new technologies, followed closely by work reorganization. In the case of manufacturing firms, 69% of the female respondents and 72.4% of the male respondents have been affected by the introduction of new technologies. In these same firms, the reorganization of work affected 49% of the female respondents and 58.6% of the male respondents.

In the service-sector firms, 67.1% of female respondents and 64.9% of male respondents have been affected by technological changes. The proportion of women and men affected by work reorganization reached 66% and 43.2% respectively, again out of total respondents of each gender in these firms. There were more women in the service sector (66 %) and more men in the manufacturing sector(58 %) who experienced organizational change, while percentages are closer for technological change.

Both the manufacturing and service-sector firms also established quality circles and work teams, however these changes are clearly of less importance than those mentioned previously. Moreover, in some of the firms, quality circles and work teams had been introduced in the past but had disappeared by the time of the study.

Attention should be drawn to two characteristic features of both the manufacturing and the service-sector firms. First, in the majority of these firms, technological change is accompanied by work reorganization or by a new distribution of tasks. Secondly, most of the firms also eliminated jobs, which was associated with work reorganization. In recent years, for example, Firm A imported new technology from Germany that has accelerated the production of fruit juice through an automated, low energy-consuming process. In this case, work reorganization was the result of technological change in the sense that the elimination of jobs following the technological change spurred work reorganization. For example, before the reorganization, testing was carried out by quality-control staff. However, as a result of these changes, quality control was decentralized to a certain degree, with operators being made responsible for ensuring that they were meeting quality standards. After having implemented changes in technology, Firm A introduced multi-skilling and moved to set up work teams.

Multi-skilling is a rationalization measure that is often pursued in order to reduce labour costs. This was the case for one of the manufacturing firms, Firm D, which introduced multi-skilling as a result of the elimination of jobs following technological changes (new production lines, new paper machine, a "stacker", packer, etc.). The firm was thus able to economize on labour costs without decreasing the volume of work carried out. Several years ago, Firm F in the service sector, which specializes in financial services, introduced two major computer systems which resulted in the automation of many activities.These computer systems and related technological improvements allowed client data (account balances, loans, stop-payments and transfers) and authentication of certain information to be computerized. In this firm, the automation of work and the consequent disappearance of certain tasks also necessitated a reorganization of tasks.

Moreover, as we have just seen, the reorganization of work that frequently follows technological change demands not only a new way of working, but increasingly, a greater commitment of workers to their work. This explains the fact that a good number of firms studied had established continuous improvement committees in order to increase the involvement and participation of the work force in the work and production processes. These aspects of work reorganization are, of course, an integral part of the new human resource management theories.

The importance, the role, the content of meetings and the way in which these committees work vary according to the firms studied. In the manufacturing firms, there may be occasional meetings between supervisors and employees, at which the latter make various suggestions (safety, team spirit, etc.) to solve specific work problems (Firm A). Such meetings also provide the opportunity for supervisory staff to appreciate the importance of employees and for reinforcing this recognition through the process of joint problem-solving (Firm B). Finally, the committees represent a preferred tool for finding solutions to major problems, or any other aspect of work organization that needs improvement (Firms C and D).This is the case in all four manufacturing firms, but the degree of participation and the influence on decisions vary according to sector; also these committees seem to have more responsibility and influence when they are composed of men.

Much the same approach to committees, though in the context of a different perspective on work reorganization, was found in one of the service-sector firms that had established a semi-autonomous work team. The change was an integral part of new management practices in the firm. Two departments were merged, and multi-skilling and job rotation were introduced, but this represents a small percentage of the firm's workers. With the establishment of a semi-autonomous work team, employees' new jobs included some tasks usually carried out by managers, in particular, certain types of decisions, the organization of the work day, and the determination of the daily work load.

This overview of changes in technology and work organization has allowed us to identify elements of both change and continuity in the division of labour in the firms studied. In the next section, it will be shown that the effect of the changes, which in theory involve both gender groups, can vary and that there are particular differences between women and men.

4 Women and Men: Contrasting Experiences with Technological Change

Before examining the ways in which the gendered division of labour has or has not changed, we will describe the tasks carried out by men and women in order to draw a picture of the overall gendered division of labour.

4.1 Overview of the Gendered Division of Labour: The Task

We turn first therefore to an examination of the nature of respondents' tasks in order to bring out characteristic elements of the gendered division of labour. As was pointed out above, the introduction of new technologies and the reorganization of work are the two most significant changes within the firms studied. Nevertheless, not all of the groups of employees studied necessarily use technologies to carry out their daily tasks.

In the manufacturing firms, the majority of female and male respondents perform manual tasks. However, this applies to a much higher proportion of men (93.1%) than women (75.5%). Slightly more than half of the women (53.5%) carry out handling tasks, and again, the proportion of men is higher (69%). Slightly more than a third of the women (37.8%) make use of a technology in carrying out their work, compared to almost half of the men studied (44.8%). Women (37.8%) mainly carry out verifications or testing with the help of technologies. This is also the case for men (44.8%), who carry out machine control as well (41.4%); the percentage is only 20% for women.

In service-sector firms, the majority of female and male respondents perform tasks related to the use of a technology, however this applies to proportionately more women (72.6%) than men (59.4%). Compared to men (43.2%), a higher proportion of women (58.9%) say that they carry out data input with the help of technologies. They also perform the correction of operations and errors (56.2%) as well as verifications or testing (42.5%). A much greater proportion of men (67.6%) are engaged in testing; for women the percentage is only 42,5% . Finally, these workers also do other tasks such as word processing, archiving, filing, as well as a variety of technical operations.

These results indicate several differences between women and men, but also some similarities. For example, in manufacturing firms, women mainly perform manual tasks and the proportion of women doing so is higher than the proportion of women carrying out manual tasks in service-sector firms, but this is also true for men. Handling work (the physical moving of objects) ranks second for women, but this is also the case for men. Thus, although technologies have changed job content, there has not always been such a great change and many tasks remain quite traditional and manual.

In the service-sector firms, similarities in the type of tasks accomplished are slightly less apparent, but nevertheless, some do exist. Thus, tasks related to the use of a technology are at the top of the list of responses of both female and male respondents. However, the proportion of men (32.4%) carrying out diverse technical operations is higher than the proportion of women (23.3%) performing this type of work. Moreover, intellectual tasks occupy a greater place in both gender groups. Nevertheless, tasks of an "administrative" nature (administration, planning, accounting) and technical tasks (control, technical operations) show higher percentages for men.

4.2 Effects of Changes in Work on Skills

By studying the effects of changes in work on skills and other elements, the way in which certain components of the gendered division of labour both change and persist can be observed. The effects of changes in work on occupational skills, multi-skilling of tasks and occupational mobility of female and male respondents are particularly interesting in a context of technological and organizational change. In manufacturing firms, while only 26.6% of women respondents indicate that they have experienced an increase in their skill levels, 60% of them indicate greater multi-tasking in the work. Thus, the so-called "multi-skilling" that they have experienced in their work is mainly *horizontal*, that is, the addition of tasks at the same level, not an increase in responsibilities or skills associated with the task and this should therefore be called "multi-tasking". It is mainly related to jobs for which tasks are noticeably similar and at the same skill level. This finding corresponds to the situation observed by Danièle Kergoat (1992) in the case of France.

Moreover, less than half of the respondents (42.2%) mention that these changes increase the possibility of being employed in other jobs. In contrast, the situation of men is completely different. Some 62.1% of men (compared to 26.6% of women, as was seen above) have experienced an increase in their occupational skills following changes in their work. As in the case of women, these changes also bring about greater multi-skilling, but for men the proportion is higher (79.3%). Thus, the question is whether men, as opposed to women, have experienced greater multi-skilling of a "vertical" nature. The results of the study indicate a small trend in this direction since a slightly higher proportion of men (44.8%) experienced an increase in employment possibilities in other jobs. Moreover, the skills that they use on the job have increased even more. In our interviews, the perception was that men did benefit from an increase in skills and also somewhat more mobility, which is often associated to skills.

To summarize, in the manufacturing firms women and men have experienced an increase in their occupational skills, in what is generally called multi-skilling, and in access to other positions. However, the positive effects on skills and mobility have been proportionately greater for men, making the nature of their multi-skilling appear more "skill-enhancing". In light of these research results, it appears that in a context of technological change men seem to be more often directed preferentially to the more skilled jobs, while women benefit from a weaker form of multi-skilling which should be called "multi-tasking" (*cf.* D. Kergoat). As will be shown below, similar findings can be observed in the service-sector firms.

In service-sector firms, the increase in occupational skills and multi-skilling of tasks has been proportionately greater for men. Only 35.6% of women, compared to 54.1% of men, indicate that changes in work have translated into an increase in their occupational skills. In terms of the multi-skilling of tasks, the proportions are more comparable between women (63.01%) and men (67.6%) despite a slight advance for the latter. Since proportionately fewer women have experienced an increase in their occupational skills, they tend to experience a much more horizontal multi-skilling. These results resemble those presented above for the manufacturing firms.

Nevertheless, these results must be considered with a degree of caution since in the service-sector firms, a slightly lower proportion of men (24.3%) than women (27.4%) indicate an increase in access to other jobs following technological and organizational changes. This situation can be attributed to the negative effect of certain economic factors on service-sector firms (Firms H and J in particular). In these firms, a certain limit on expansion has been reached in terms of organization, structure, promotion and hiring. In Firms H and J, more than two-thirds of women (72.6%) and three quarters of men (78.4%) indicate a lack of opportunities for promotion. Similarly, more than half of the women (60%) and of the men (62.1%) within manufacturing firms indicate that opportunities for promotion are unfavourable.

5 Conclusion

The aim of our research was to examine the reskilling and "end of the division of labour"[5] thesis in terms of gender in a context of technological change; in this paper, we centered on the impact of technologies on work and tasks, and from there, on the gendered division of labour and tasks. This actually brought us to highlight a situation of simultaneous *change and continuity* in the gendered division of labour observed in a context of technological and organizational changes.

Based on specific elements, changing forms of the gendered division of labour were identified. Findings indicate that, confronted with the same technological and organizational upheavals, both women and men obviously must adjust to the new realities of their work. This occurs in a very similar way, through multi-skilling or multi-tasking, etc. Certain similarities in the content of their tasks related to the use of technologies were noted.

Beyond some changing elements that tend to bring the situation of men and women closer together, it was also found that for men, there are frequently slight discrepancies (just that "little bit more" or that "little bit less") that allow differences between the sexes to persist, or even increase. In a context of technological and organizational changes, men have seen their skills grow. Their tasks have been automated and have become more repetitive, however proportionately less so as compared to women. Moreover, women have had slightly less access to skill-enhancing jobs.

---

[5]The title of the well-known book by Kern and Schumann (1989), mentioned in the references.

Thus, it appears pertinent to call into question the theses on "the end of the division of labour", which are based principally on the Kern and Schumann book cited above[6]. Indeed, there is a need to examine in a more subtle way assertions that there has been a decentralization of control and responsibility, *re-skilling* of jobs in the context of new technologies and new productive models, and, consequently, a challenge to the traditional division of labour. Changes in the places assigned to women and men are often dependent on a series of transformations of the work process within firms, and these are not necessarily - if ever - aimed at the search for greater employment equity. As was seen above, practices aimed at increasing work force flexibility are an example of this. In some firms, the introduction of multi-skilling has been a port of entry for women into non-traditional occupations, while in other firms women remain confined to tasks of the same type.These changes are not based so much on a willingness to modify the places traditionally given to women and men, as on a specific human resource management strategy aimed at other objectives, such as the rationalization or reduction of the costs of production activities.

Thus, changing forms of the gendered division of labour are the consequence of both technological and organizational changes and of more general managerial strategies. In this study, it was observed that processes of re-skilling and multi-skilling tend to reflect concerns that are different from those of employment equity, and that the latter are rarely - if ever - considered in times of technological and organizational changes. While such technological and organizational changes could represent an ideal occasion to change the division of labour according to gender (Tremblay 1988), it seems it is not often even considered. Thus, it can be concluded that ideas and hypotheses about "the end of the division of labour" should be re-examined in the light of the reality experienced by women in the workplace. We hope that the research results presented in this article will contribute to this critical analysis.

References

1. Appay, Béatrice (1993) Individuel et collectif : Questions à la sociologie du travail et des professions. L'autonomie contrôlée. In *Cahiers du GEDISST*. No. 6. IRESCO, CNRS.
2. Gadrey, Nicole (1992) *Hommes et femmes au travail*, Paris, Editions de l'Harmattan
3. Hirata, Helena (1991) Nouvelles technologies, qualification et division sexuelle du travail. In *Cahiers du GEDDIST, Changements techniques et division sexuelle du travail*.1. IRESCO, CNRS.pp. 23-43.
4. Hirata, Helena and Rogerat Chantal (1988) Technologie, qualification et division sexuelle du travail. In *Revue française de sociologie*, XXIX. pp. 171-192.

[6] Some more recent work by the same authors apparently questions the thesis they popularized through previous work, but this latter work has not yet been translated from German to English, and to our knowledge, still does not explicitly take gender into account.

5. Kergoat, Danièle(1992). Les absentes de l'histoire. In *Autrement*, No 126.pp. 73-83.
6. Kern, H. et M. Schumann (1989) *La fin de la division du travail? La rationalisation dans la production industrielle l'état actuel, les tendances.* Paris: Editions des Sciences de l'homme.
7. Schneider , Ellen Ruth (1991) Progrès technique, stratégies d'adaptation et division sexuelle du travail dans l'entreprise : quelques résultats empiriques en République Fédérale d'Allemagne. In *Cahiers du GEDISST. Changements techniques et division sexuelle du travail.* No 1. IRESCO, CNRS. 3-21
8. Tremblay, Diane-Gabrielle (1992). L'emploi des femmes et la division sexuelle du travail. Dans D.-G.Tremblay (sous la dir.-1992). *Travail et société. une introduction à la sociologie du travail.* Montréal: Éditions Agence d'Arc/Téléuniversité. 351-402.
9. Tremblay, Diane-Gabrielle (1992b). Innovation et marchés internes du travail dans le secteur bancaire. Vers un modèle multidimensionnel de l'innovation. *Technologies de l'information et société.* Vol. 4, no 3. Paris: Dunod. 351-380.
10. Tremblay, Diane-Gabrielle (1991a). Computerization, Human Resources Management and Redirection of Women's Skills. In Eriksson, Kitchenham et Tijdens (1991). *"Women, Work and Computerization: Understanding and Overcoming Bias in Work and Education".* Amsterdam: Elsevier Science Publishers.
11. Tremblay, Diane-Gabrielle (1990, reedited in 1997) *Economie du travail : la réalité et les approches théoriques*, Montréal, Editions St-Martin.544p.
12. Tremblay, Diane-Gabrielle (1988). Stratégies de gestion de main-d'oeuvre : de nouveaux paravents à une gestion sexuée ou un défi pour les organisations? In *Interventions économiques*, 20/21.
13. Volst, Angelica, and Wagner, Ina. (1988) Inequality in the Automated Office : The Impact of computer on the Division of Labour. In *International Sociology*, 3, 2.

Engendered Systems Development: Ghettoization and Agency

Androniki Panteli[1], Harvie Ramsay[2], and Martin Beirne[1]

[1] University of Glasgow Business School, Glasgow G12 8LF, UK
[2] University of Strathclyde, Graham Hills Building, Glasgow G1 1XT, UK

Abstract. The available literature on gender and information systems (IS) has been content to present ghettoization in a narrow sense by considering merely its immediate dimension of sex segregation and regarding it as the outcome of an increasing rationalization and the masculine nature of computing work. We suggest in the paper that ghettoization needs to be understood in terms of the process in which it is produced and the values of the organisation in which it is embedded. Drawing upon a case study, the paper illuminates episodes of informality in systems development, the active agency of female low-level staff and notions of empowerment which contribute to a broader understanding of ghettoization.

1 Introduction

Available research on gender and information systems (IS) has reproduced the preoccupation with the glass ceiling in management literature, focusing on women's exclusion from higher status IS occupations and their segregation into lower levels of the IS industry. This is ghettoization, a phenomenon which often appears as the outcome of the male-dominated and masculine nature of computing work. However, an emerging assumption is that female staff passively and unreflectively accept their disadvantaged position in the IS workplace. The active agency of female IS staff has been a missing factor within this literature. Instead, management and male co-workers have been the central actors in shaping the nature and direction of software development.

This paper aims for an informed understanding of ghettoization in IS occupations, explicitly acknowledging key events that contribute towards this phenomenon. It presents a case where women actively position themselves within their workplace as competent, skilled and independent individuals.

2 Dimensions of Segregation in Information Systems - The Case of Ghettoization

The increasing representation of women in this male dominated area has been conceptualised as one of three levels of occupational segregation: genuine integration, resegregation and ghettoization [21]. Genuine integration is achieved when women share occupational and economic equity with men. In principle, the new and rapidly expanding IS occupations should be open and gender neutral, providing more opportunities for women than other sectors. In practice, although there has been an increase in the number of women entering IS since the seventies, women are still under-represented in this occupation in all member-states of the European Union [22]. In no member state is the share estimated to be above 30 per cent, and in most cases it is closer to 20 per cent. In the US, women account for just 37 per cent of IS staff, which although higher than the European statistics, is still 7 per cent lower than the national average of women in the total workforce of the country [6].

Resegregation, the second form of occupational segregation, occurs when an entire occupation or major occupational specialty switches from a predominantly male to a predominantly female work force. The statistics presented above do not support the emergence of resegregation of women in IS occupations.

The third form of segregation is ghettoization. This is the case when women and men in the same occupation hold different job titles and ranks, and as a result perform different tasks. From the three types of occupational segregation identified by Reskin and Roos [21] this is the one evident in this area. In addition to their low representation, there appears to be a segregation of male and female work in IS occupations. Empirical studies on gender careers in IS [1] have shown that women are mostly found in the non-managerial group of IS personnel, while men are predominantly in managerial positions. Men therefore are more likely than women to be project leaders, IS managers and consultants, while women are often found in roles such as systems analyst, designer and programmer. Also, based on the Computerworld's Salary Survey 1995 [6], it appears that only 17 percent of chief information officers in the US are women. In the UK, this percentage is even lower. Ordroyd [18] reports that since 1991, women constitute between 21 and 22 per cent of the UK IS workforce, while only 4 per cent were heads of IS departments.

Furthermore, even when male and female employees have the same job title and formal role in their organisations, they are not equally qualified [12] nor do they necessarily undertake same tasks and projects[19]. In a study in the UK, Grundy [10,11] reported that men get intensively involved with the 'pure', abstract software work which is challenging and prestigious, leaving the 'messy' type of work to their female colleagues. This latter type of job involves tasks such as merging and tidying up databases and writing summary report programs which although important for the effective functioning of every organisation are nevertheless considered as monotonous and less glamorous. Similarly, Sonnentag [23] who examined the work situation of female and male team leaders in software development in German and Swiss organisations, found that women in subteam and team leading positions experienced less complex work situations than their male colleagues. Therefore, when a man was promoted to a team or subteam leader he was more likely to deal with an increased amount of complexity in his work, and also to spend more time communicating with other people, whereas for women complexity and communication remained largely stable. Clearly then, the same job title does not imply the same job responsibilities and challenge.

On several occasions, ghettoization was related to an increasing amount of rationalization [3, 7, 9, 14, 15] whilst the masculine nature of computing work was also identified as a barrier to the entry and development of women in this field [13,

25]. Although such studies are significant because they attempt to identify potential factors (antecedents) that could contribute to the evolution of a ghettoized environment (outcome) they provide little understanding of the process of a gendered evolution in this ghettoized occupation. This limitation means that although several researchers within the area of sex segregation in computing occupations are interested in explaining ghettoization, they conceive of this in a rather narrow way. We suggest that the phenomenon of ghettoization needs to be understood in terms of the process in which it is produced and the values of the organisation in which it is embedded.

A process approach to understanding this phenomenon focuses specifically on sequences of events within the context in which it takes place. The point is to explain how and why outcomes are reached, how they are enabled or constrained by structured patterns within the organisation [8] and how and why actors relate to each other [16, 17]. With regard to the ghettoization phenomenon the approach is concerned with explaining how the relationships between male and female employees and managers are shaped with the introduction of a new information system and the establishment of an information systems department. Below we present a case to illustrate this approach. This is the case of an organisation that introduces a computer-based system for the first time. We will observe in the case a sequence of events that are used as explanatory devices to the phenomenon of ghettoization. It is found that ghettoization is considerably more complex than is suggested simply by reference to the segmentation of employment. The study took place at a tertiary education college designated in this article as FEC.

3 The FEC case

FEC is a tertiary education institute located in the northwest of the UK. The institute has been providing vocational and pre-university national diplomas for over 60 years. These qualifications are verified and assessed by the regional Accreditation and Awarding Council (AAC). FEC is mainly funded by the Local Authority (LA). In 1991, there were about 2000 students (both full time and part time students) at FEC.

Until 1991, the college administration, including students' records, were based on a manual, card-driven system for the storage and retrieval of information for internal and external evaluations. At the beginning of that year, LA decided to fund the development of a computer-based administrative system, called SADIS (Students Administrative Information System) for all tertiary educational institutes in its region. This was initially based upon a standard student enrolment software package designed to meet the administrative needs of secondary schools. The expressed intention was to adapt this to the needs of tertiary educational institutes.

SADIS was introduced at FEC in August 1991. The software was installed by the supplier organisation and Mike, a computing science lecturer, was assigned to be the systems manager on a secondment. Two female computing graduates, Maureen and Mary, who had successfully completed their HND (Higher National Diploma) course at FEC earlier that year were employed as casual workers at the lowest clerical grade to do the data entry in the new enrolment system:

"We were asked to do just data-entry ... we did not get any introduction, the day we arrived we were shown the students' application forms and we were shown the screens that we would enter the data in to and that was all the training we got".

Soon after the beginning of the new academic year, it was realised that SADIS could not meet college requirements. It could not produce student records sufficiently, nor present data for evaluation purposes as requested by AAC. At the same time, the SADIS supplier was not easily contactable, nor willing to respond effectively to user-colleges' queries and problems with the system. Maureen complained that the systems' supplier did not make sure that the users of the system knew what they were doing: *"they just dumped the package on you and just said: 'up and run it' "*.

The effective use of the system in coping with FEC requirements was further constrained by the system manager's unwillingness and incompetence in handling systems related problems.

"[Mike] was supposed to be the trouble shooter...He was supposed to write a user manual for us and for the lecturing and office staff ... but we never saw it. He was supposed to set up the back-up procedures, he was supposed to do any updates that came in [from the vendor] he was supposed to be there when it broke down which it did frequently".

With a system not running properly and a system manager who was not willing nor ready to undertake his responsibilities, *"... you either could wait several days for the supplier, or if you knew how to do it, which we both did, then you just go on and do it. There didn't seem to be much point hanging about waiting" [Mary].*

Maureen and Mary spent their first few weeks on the job inputting student records to the new system. With the beginning of the academic year, however, when the finance department as well as lecturers began demanding reports with students' records, the inefficiencies of the system became evident.

"Nobody was happy with the system...None of the reports met the departments' requirements...no department wanted some of the reports that were generated and yet there were constantly people [lecturers] coming up looking for the reports that weren't available to them [through the system]".

Lecturers then had to continue keeping manual records for students' attendance and assessments, while the finance department needed reports that had to be sent to AAC for evaluation. By that time, most of the data was loaded into SADIS but there was not a sufficient program to pull out information and create the required reports. Facing the pressures from the lecturers as well as from the finance department, Maureen and Mary began thinking of ways for extracting the data stored in the system to create the required reports outside SADIS.

"We did ask the systems manager if it was O.K., but he said that if anything went wrong, it was on our heads. Initially, we didn't change anything; you can imagine this data just sitting there in big columns, all we did was to go in and pull the information off, we didn't do any changes initially".

"We wanted to write new reports; so what we did was to tell Oracle to put a header in and select from the tables this information and lay it out in the required way. All that was done in Oracle... SADIS just didn't meet the requirements".

Even though they were not trained on Unix-operating systems, they were willing to dig through the manuals to acquire the needed knowledge. *"We started from scratch going through the basics [of Unix] and finding out from there how to do things...If we were really stuck we would go to another computing lecturer (Philip) who was the Unix specialist at FEC"*.Even though their own study of computing at FEC had not covered relevant areas, they both demonstrated flair, creativity and confidence.

This became a regular thing, especially after the lecturers and the office staff found out.

> "People would happen to mention and others would say 'Oh, how did you get that?', 'we asked them to produce that and they did it', so it just got so that there was no peace for us because there were people coming up and saying: 'I want this information but in that layout, I want this information but I want also that with that'; it just got to the point that SADIS was doing nothing and we were producing reports outside it...Afterwards ... we actually put a board up to stop the lecturers coming through and a sign on it saying 'SADIS - you can't come in, go away!'.

The systems manager never changed his password and this enabled them to get into the system and make the changes.

> "The people who were in charge [Peter and Mike]...knew what we were doing but said that it would be on our heads if it came to any grief: 'we don't want to know' was their line all the time. 'We don't want to know what you are doing, just do it, just get it done, get the reports produced on time'"

The two operators were finally sent on a four-day 'Introduction to Oracle SQL' course initiated by senior IS members of all the Regional colleges that adopted SADIS. However, *"all the stuff we learnt on the course, we had already used"*.

With the redesign of the system, the flow of work was supposed to involve lecturers passing student records (e.g. attendance, assessments marks) to the data entry operators who in turn installed the data in the system to produce the required reports for AAC. However, there were lecturers who could still not trust the system:

> "... we were asking them to give us input documents, standard input documents with proper control and procedures for entering the students data and they would still say: 'Here is a spreadsheet that I made earlier, why don't you use that? In fact, one lecturer wanted us to take his floppy disk, 'can you use the content of my floppy disk to update your database?" Lack of recognition and trust in the data-entry operators' attempts in redesigning the system were some of the consequences: "Some lecturers didn't appreciate the efforts we were making; it was taking us hours to get a report to work".

To redesign the system was their initiative, effort and responsibility. Besides, they could support of each other, they were acting as a group and not on an individual basis. As Mary explains:

> "...if it had been just ourselves we would have been more reluctant to do it. It wasn't a case of I'll say it was you if it goes wrong'...both of us had the attitude of ...what's the worst that could happen, we get the sack, and really we weren't bothered, neither of us at the time really cared because we were only getting paid the lowest office job wages and we just thought well if it doesn't work and we get into a lot of trouble it's too bad, but I think because we were the two of us, we were much more blasé about it...we did feed off each other 'well, should we do it, maybe not, oh come on, we will' ".

Effective systems development is usually accomplished by systems specialists and users who help each other by sharing knowledge [9]. By sharing knowledge and support, Maureen and Mary created the basis upon which they could gain power and control over their workplace, as well as an ability to tolerate the contradictions they faced every day on the job. Even though they did not like the stress-related to this responsibility, they did like the creative side of it: *"when you are sitting and just keying in all these forms all day long, you do get bored, so it broke up the day; it also let us use our programming* skills... , *it was a buzz to get things working...*".

Their efforts to redesign the system to meet college requirements made the system functional for the rest of the academic year. Yet our interviews with the two operators uncovered feelings of anxiety and considerable cynicism about their position. They would be penalised if they were caught by the supplier (the system had a copyright) yet pressurised and potentially sanctioned if suitable reports were not forthcoming. In their view, managers were protecting their own position and saving FEC considerable amounts of money by letting the operators redesign the system. During this period, although there had been apparent managerial approval for their efforts, there was no formal recognition and thus no change to the unofficial status or to salary levels for Maureen and Mary.

The actions and risks undertaken by Maureen and Mary had short and long term benefits for the college. Their persistence to make the system work enabled the college to continue functioning and meet its requirements to the external authority at low cost. Clearly, however, the SADIS experience as a system that could not meet users' requirements and which had threatened the functioning of the college, enabled management to realise the strategic importance of information systems to the institute. As a result, a systems department was established and a full-time IS manager recruited: *"I wanted somebody working from 9 to 5 [and not an academic on a secondment]. I've seen that game played before [in the case of Mike]"* (FEC Deputy Director). With the establishment of the systems department, Maureen was recruited as a full-time programmer (by that time, Mary had chosen a post elsewhere). Although this meant some career development for Maureen, the ghettoization issue persisted with a male IS officer being appointed to manage the newly established systems department.

4 Towards Building a Ghettoized Environment - A Process Perspective

In the case presented, antecedent conditions contributed to a new computerized system that could not meet users' requirements. They also revealed a lack of internal computing expertise. The outcome of the case was the ghettoization of systems management with female staff persistently in a disadvantaged position. Between the antecedent conditions and the outcome, and within several months, there was a sequence of episodes and phases which significantly contribute to our understanding of how and why male and female actors relate to each other within a ghettoized environment.

There are three main phases to the development of SADIS within FEC. The first phase shows the female workforce as users of the new computerised system and male lecturers as having the responsibility for managing the new environment. It seems that early on in this newly computerised environment, female staff were given low-status under a male systems manager. At a later stage we see the same female staff acting as informal designers of the system. Subsequently, we can identify an interesting shift in the roles formally allocated to the two female data entry operators.

This second phase highlights the active agency and creativity of low-level female staff in making their influence effective. By contrast to the conventional images of passive female workers, the case demonstrates the active agency of low-level staff in claiming space to assert themselves, taking the initiative and developing their own resources to secure viable systems. Maureen and Mary took significant steps in building an effective computerised system for their institute e.g. listening to lecturing and office staff's requirements, consulting senior IS specialists (e.g. Philip), and taking precautions for not losing their work (e.g. making back-ups keeping their own manuals/notes for later reference). Here we can see the ability, willingness and agency of low level users in initiating and actively participating in desperate attempts to improve the functioning of their computerized system and, by extension, the functioning of the whole organisation. These efforts were not directly undertaken for personal or status gains (e.g. increase in salary, promotion). It was rather *"...a buzz to make things work"*.

The third phase of the case reproduces the traditional male dominated environment within the college, reinforcing the ghettoization of IS occupations. It was because systems operations were initially viewed as tedious clerical work of low status that it was assigned to women. As the complex skills and value of programming and negotiating with vendors and users emerged, the management of the newly established systems department was assigned to men.

Following from the above sequence of events, the process approach illuminates episodes which would have been otherwise difficult to identify and appreciate. These are:

1) Informality in systems design:
Even though Maureen and Mary were not paid to design but only to key in data to the system, they chose to do so: *"it was too much of a job for the amount of money we got ... but we did enjoy the creative part of it"* [Maureen]. Even with inadequate training, moral and financial support, they managed to adequately develop databases which met user requirements. The SADIS case shows how users' interests in developing systems can be enhanced because of the everyday pressures and painful interactions with other members of staff, rather than in spite of them. Following from this point, this case presents a broader understanding of the patterns of communication between informal designers/participants and the other users, as well as the day to day work, its pressures and tensions. We are certainly aware and concerned that these interactions may also hinder and not always help user participation in systems development. These people, the informal participants in systems development, should be awarded with the appropriate status, payment and respect [4] and should not be led to self-exploitation and pseudo notions of empowerment. The notion of informality in systems design is discussed in some detail in Beirne, Ramsay and Panteli [2].

2) The active agency of female low level staff:
The literature has been content to assume that female IS developers passively and unreflectively accept the ghettoization of their workplace. Yet the SADIS case shows a different picture. The case is reflective of the active agency of low-level IS staff. It shows the ability and willingness of female and [not only] male agents to construct and reconstruct social reality within the workplace. This is not simply a matter of breaking through the glass-ceiling. It is more than recruitment or giving access to women to enter the IS field. It relates to the gendered nature of the process itself and the working out of gender and power relations in this specific context of IS

management and development. Even though these people are not as visible as those who manage organisations, this does not mean that they are unimportant or without influence in the framing of their working practices [24].

"When you are sitting and just keying in all these forms all day long, you do get bored, so it broke the day. It also let us use some programming skills; it was a buzz to get things working".

Clearly, female low-level staff are not invariably passive; they react to systems and gender constraints within their workplace, and even shape the further encounters with senior male colleagues. As a result, they are capable of making a positive contribution to systems development without the crutch of independent technical expertise. Indeed, the point is that they took the initiative themselves, in the absence of formal support systems and despite significant pressures and constraints. By sharing knowledge and support they created the basis upon which they could gain power and control over their workplace, as well as an ability to tolerate the contradictions that they faced every day on the job. Mary explained:

"..if it had been just ourselves we would have been more reluctant to do it. It wasn't a case of 'I will say it was you if it goes wrong' ... because we were two of us, we were much more blasé about it... 'Well, should we do it, maybe not, oh come on we will' ".

3) The shift from self empowerment to self exploitation.

Maureen and Mary managed to cope with the inefficiencies of the system in their workplace by informally redesigning it and therefore taking control over the system rather than be controlled by the conventions inscribed into it. As a result, they themselves created room for experimentation in their work, exercising choice and discretion which led to their self-empowerment.

However, because of the lack of official recognition, respect and adequate income, the development of this kind of empowerment to a democratic one is restricted. As Clement [5] explains, democratic empowerment emphasises not only the abilities but also the rights of people to participate as equals in decisions and actions about the conditions under which they work. Furthermore, the fact that Maureen and Mary were not given any official approval or support by the management of their organisation also inhibits the evolution of an authentic type of empowerment [5]. Clement has described examples of authentic empowerment in computer-based workplaces, where low level employees forced (often with union support) their management to formally work with them in undertaking changes within their workplace which were beneficial to both the employees and the organisation. The issues of formality and management support were missing in this case. Maureen and Mary gained a kind of empowerment which was not granted to them, but rather it was grasped, tacitly approved but never fully recognised. Consequently, satisfaction is found to be gradually reduced. Though this type of empowerment is user-initiated and developed, because it remains tacitly and not formally approved, it soon becomes puzzling and uncertain, leading to self-exploitation. Even though they both enjoyed the creative side of it, their group formally disintegrated with Maureen's decision to move from the department: *"it was too much work for the amount of money we received"*.

From the sequence of phases and episodes identified in the FEC case, the ghettoization of systems management appears as a phenomenon that reinforces traditional paternalistic structures within organisations. Most importantly, these events present ghettoization as a complex process, comprising of a variety of dimensions and not only the immediate dimension of occupational segregation as it tends to appear in the literature [21]. Ghettoization therefore relates to a process of status and formal power as it is also a process of job control, income and acknowledgements of skills. While this list of dimensions is impressive, what is most striking is not simply the accumulation of them. The observations in the SADIS case relate to the interaction and mutual reinforcement of these various dimensions.Thus, to limit the attention to the most immediate dimension of ghettoization, that of occupational segregation, would be to neglect the crucial way in which these are constructed and sustained through processes described under the other dimensions [20].

5 Conclusions

Clearly a process approach to the evolution of ghettoization can generate insights into areas where little theory has been developed (e.g. informality in systems design, active agency of female low level staff and experience of empowerment). This perspective has also led to a better understanding of the various dimensions of ghettoization revealing that this is a phenomenon which cannot be separated from the complex dynamics and power relations found in organizations.

The most confident outcome of the material presented in this paper is that of the active agency of female low-level staff. Given the growing number of women in IS occupations, as well as the efforts made by various associations (e.g. women associations, educational institutions and other public and private organisations) to encourage women to enter the field, more research is required to investigate the efforts that women themselves make to gain occupational identity and identify conditions that may contribute to their emergence as a privileged elite. We also advocate the need for similar and parallel studies to be carried out in a range of cultures in an attempt to identify how patterns vary across international boundaries.

Acknowledgements

We are grateful to Maureen and Mary and the managers of FEC who have given freely of their time to talk to us about the experiences with SADIS. We would also like to thank the reviewers of this paper for their helpful and encouraging comments. Thanks are also due to the ESRC for funding the project from which this research material has been drawn.

References:

1. Baroudi, J.J. and Igbaria, M. (1995), "An Examination of Gender Effects on Career Success of Information Systems Employees", Journal of Management Information Systems, 11, 3, 181-201

2. Beirne, M., Ramsay, H., and Panteli, A.(1996), "Participating Informally: Opportunities and Dilemmas in User-Driven Design", paper for the Fourth Biennial Conference on Participatory Design (PDC'96), Cambridge, Massachusetts, November 13-15, 1996
3. Burris, B.H. (1993), "Technocracy at Work" , SUNY Series, The New Inequalities, State University of New York Press, Albany
4. Clement, A. (1993) "Looking for the Designers: Transforming the 'Invisible' Infrastructure of Computerised Office Work", AI and Society, 7, 323-344.
5. Clement, A. (1994), "Computing at Work: Empowering Action at Low-Level Users", Communications of the ACM
6. Computerworld's 9th Annual Salary & Survey": Unequal Opportunities", Computerworld, September 4, pp 1/70-72,74,78
7. Donato, K.M. (1990), "Programming for Change? The Growing Demand for Women Systems Analysts", in Reskin, B.F. and Roos, P.A. (eds), Job Queues, Gender Queues: Explaining Women's Inroads into Male Occupations, Temple University Press, Philadelphia
8. Giddens, A. (1979), Central Problems in Social Theory: Action, Structure and Contradiction in Social Analysis, University of California Press, Berkeley, CA
9. Greenbaum, J. (1979), In the Name of Efficiency: Management Theory and Shopfloor Practice in Data-Processing Work, Temple University Press, Philadelphia
10. Grundy, F. (1994), "Women in the Computing Workplace: Some Impressions", in Adams, A, Emms, J, Green, E. Owen, J. (eds), Women, Work and Computerisation (A-57), Elsevier Science, B.V. (North-Holland), Amsterdam
11. Grundy, F (1996), Women and Computers, Intellect Books, Exeter
12. Halford, S. and Savage, M. (1995), Restructuring Organisations, Changing People: Gender and Restructuring in Banking and Local Government, Work, employment and Society, 9, 1, 97-122
13. Knights. D. and Murray, F., (1994), Managers Divided -Organisational Politics and Information Technology Management, Wiley Series in Information Systems, Wiley, London
14. Kraft, P. (1977), Programmers and Managers: The Routinization of Computer Programming in the United States, Springer-Verlag, NY
15. Kraft, P. (1983), "Computers and the Automation of Work", in Kraut, R.E. (ed), Technology and the Transformation of White-Collar Work, Lawrence Erlbaum Associates, NJ
16. Mohr, L.B. (1982), Explaining Organisational Theory, Jossey-Bass, San Francisco, CA
17. Newman, M. and Robey, D. (1992), "A Social Process Model of User-Analyst Relationships", MIS Quarterly, June, 249-265
18. Orldoyd, R. (1996), "Is the IS industry a turn-off for women?", Sunday Business (1996), May 26, page 9
19. Podmore, D. and Spencer, A. (1986), "Gender in the Labour Process - the Case of Women and Men Lawyers", in Knights, D. and Willmmott, H. (eds), Gender and the Labour Process, gower, Aldershot

20. Ramsay, H.E, (1996), "Engendering Participation", Occasional Paper: No. 8, Department of Human Resource Management, University of Strathclyde
21. Reskin, B.F. and Roos, P.A. (1990), Job Queues, Gender Queues: Explaining Women's Inroads into Male Occupations, Temple University Press, Philadelphia
22. Social Europe - Occupational Segregation of Women and Men in the European community - Supplement 3/93, 70-76
23. Sonnentag, S. (1994), "Team Leading in Software Development: A Comparison Between Women and Men", in Adams, A, Emms, J, Green, E. Owen, J. (eds), Women, Work and Computerisation (A-57), Elsevier Science, B.V. (North-Holland), Amsterdam
24. Thomas. R. (1994), What Machines Can't Do: Politics and Technology in the Industrial Enterprise, University of California Press, Berkeley
25. Wright, R. (1996), "The Occupational Masculinity of Computing", in Cheng, C. (ed) Masculinities in Organizations - Research on Men and Masculinities, Sage, London

Technology Structuration: A Research Paradigma for a Gender Perspective on Technology?

Sigrid Wübker, Stuttgart and Zürich
Beatrice Sigrist, Zürich

ABSTRACT. In the following paper we suggest a possible framework and new research questions in order to study the impact of information and communication technologies (ICT) on women's work. Since the impact on organization structure and the workplace is of a new qualitative dimension, we wish to stress the relevance of new frameworks supplementing the already existing research on 'Women in technology' as well as 'Women and technology'.

1 Introduction

In recent years the capabilities of information and communication technologies (ICTs) has increased dramatically. The OECD Report on Technology, Productivity and Job Creation shows how the application of ICTs affects skills, employment, organization, as well as the development of new services.[1] Most significant however is the emergence of the knowledge-based economy. The advanced use of ICT goes hand in hand with structural changes that have contradictory consequences for women's employment and sex segregation.[2] The many facets of the impact of ICT on women's job opportunities and working conditions still need to be examined. In this paper we try to develop a theoretical framework for this examination.

In the second section we are going to review some research on the issues of gender and information technology (IT). In contrast to IT, ICTs are general-purpose media, hence may facilitate a range of possible interactions.[3] Therefore we focus on the shortcomings in the existing concepts for analyzing the relationship between ICT and women's work. In the third section of our paper we will introduce the technology structuration perspective. Based on this framework we sketch out the relationship between ICT and gender and suggest three issues for further research.

---

[1]OECD: Technology, Productivity and Job Creation. Vol.1 and Vol. 2, Paris 1996

[2]The recently published survey „Trends and Prospects for Women's Employment in the 1990s." of the European Commission's Network of Experts on the Situation of Women in the Labour Market, n.p. 1996, shows for example that despite high levels of unemployment more women move into higher level jobs.

[3]ICT include electronic messaging systems, executive information systems, collaborative systems, group decision support systems, and other technologies that enable multiparty participation in organization activities.

2 Gender and Information Technology

2.1 Important Research Issues on Gender and Information Technology

Henwood (1993) identified two approaches to the development of a gender perspective of IT. She termed them: 'Women in technology' and 'Women and technology'. The '*Women in technology*' approach focuses on women's exclusion from technological work and on the effects of IT on women's jobs.[4] Results of this research are that the introduction of IT „does not substantially undermine sexual division in the labour market, the gendering of occupations allocated to men and women, or the social construction of skill."[5] The problem with the 'Women in technology' research is that it takes technology as given and therefore unproblematic (technological determinism). Also gender segregation is viewed as given. It seems to be an object rather than an factor that influences the change brought about through the introduction of IT.

In the '*Women and technology*' approach the social shaping or social construction of IT is taken into account.[6] Influences of the social context as well as social economic factors are here integrated in the examination of the nature of technological work, its development over time and its articulation with changing gender relations. The gendered division of labour is regarded as having a profound effect on the pace and the direction of technological change in the workplace: Men are more likely to be reponsible for the conception, installation, management and servicing of systems, whereas women are users of IT and often perveiced as technically low skilled.

Human-centred systems design is a possibility to empower women to take part in the process of system design and to develop IT systems that meet their needs.[7] These design methods are more 'woman-centered', because they concentrate on the people using the systems rather than upon the artefacts ultimately created in the design process. Shared knowledge of office workers about the working process is considered to be more important than the authoritative knowledge of systems developers. One of the frequently used human-centred design methods is the sociotechnical approach.[8] Here people of different job-grades are integrated in a participating design group.

---

[4]Flis Henwood: Establishing Gender Perspectives on Information Technology: Problems, Issues and Opportunities. In Eileen Green et. al. (eds.): Gendered by Design?, London, Washington 1993, pp. 31-49

[5]Juliet Webster: What Do We Know About Gender and Information Technology at Work? In: The European Journal of Women's Studies 2, 315-334 (1995, 322)

[6]The ‚social shaping of technology' perspective and the ‚Social construction of Technology' school contend that technological change is a complex social activity and not a linear process. It involves struggle, interest articulation and learning. Different actors possess socially defined interests and differential levels of expertise. They interact in networks and define in an iterative way the form of the emerging technologies. Examples for these research traditions are: Donald MacKenzie; Judith Wajcman (eds.): The Social Shaping of Technology. How the Refrigerator Got its Hum. Milton Keynes 1985 and Bruno Latour: Science in Action: How to follow Scientists and Engineers Through Society. Cambridge 1987

[7]See for example Susanne Bødker, Joan Greenbaum: Design of Information Systems: Things versus People. In Eileen Green u.a. (1993) op. cit., pp. 53-63

[8]F. E. Emery: Characteristics of Socio-Technical Systems. London, Tavistock Document No. 527 1959

They develop the IT system together with the organizational structures and working processes.

2.2 Shortcomings of the Gender and IT-Research

The existing concepts like 'Social shaping of technology', 'Social construction of technology' or human-centred design methods are not able to describe and analyse the potential influence of ICT on organization structure. So the shortcomings of gender and IT research are more precisely shortcomings of the frameworks this research to some extent depends on. In the following we discuss two aspects of why these frameworks may be misleading.

(1) The first two concepts rely heavily on how shared interpretations around a certain technology arise and affect interaction with that technology. They tend to downplay the material and structural aspects of interacting with technology.[9] They implicitly recognize technical structures as a social or cultural construction. *However technology-induced impact on organization structure and work design is a fact.* Even ICTs that incorporate a lot of loosely bundled capabilities still consist of a definite set of features and constrain application possibilities. In this way features control social interaction.[10]

(2) It is the goal of human centred system design to find a match between the organization of work and the technology. The concepts generally accommodate a technology and its context of use at the time of the implementation. If changes are necessary, they will be covered by routine maintenance or continuous improvements. But people, tasks, and at least the informal organization structure change in response to market demands. The increasing innovation rate in technology is well known, nevertheless *the human centred system designs do not systematically consider the impact of technological and organzational change.*

So the relationship between technology and organization is much more fluid than these concepts suggest. This is true for IT, but is exceedingly valid for ICT: The flexibility and the multifunctionality of ICT implies that multiple forms of structures and work organization can be supported.

A balanced view of the technology-organizational relationship avoids overemphasis on one dimension to the exclusion of the other. It promotes a perspective where neither technology nor organization are treated holistically or as a 'black box'. A framework that recognizes the complexities of each dimension could be the technology structuration concept.

[9]Karlene H. Roberts, Martha Grabowski: Organizations, Technology and Structuring. In S. Clegg, C. Hardy, W. R. Nord (eds.): Handbook of Organization Studies, London Thousand Oaks, New Dehli, 1996, pp. 409-423

[10]Gerardine DeSanctis, Marshall Scott Poole: Capturing Complexity in Advanced Technology Use: Adaptive Structuration Theory. Organization Science 5, No. 2, 121-147 (1994)

3 Technology Structuration and Women's Work

3.1 Technology Structuration

The concept of technology structuration depends on the more general structuration theory by Giddens.[11] In this theory structures are viewed as a result of previous human interaction and a basis for enabling and constraining agents to interact. Shulman (1996) summarizes the structuration theory as followed: „Within an agency view, human interaction is concerned with the communication of meaning. To accomplish this, interpretative schemes must be used by the actors to interact in a sense-making manner with the world. Through the use of one's interpretative scheme and communication, the structures of signification are created which represent rules that inform and define interaction (...). The rules however are not 'fixed'. Having been created by actors who are both knowledgeable and reflexive, the rules can be challenged or reaffirmed. The actors can potentially change the existing structure, but the extent or type of change cannot be predicted with complete accuracy, in part because of attention to the notion of 'unintended consequences of action'."[12]

Because structuration theory understands structure as a duality that is open to interpretative flexibility it is very useful to be applied to the study of ICT. Because ICT can be more than other technologies put to varied uses and is therefore more open to reinterpretation, the duality of structure and the interpretative flexibility helps to describe and analyse uses and impact of ICT more precisely. Now technology can be seen to be a product of human action, while it simultaneously presents a tangible constraint on action.

From the perspective of the structuring of technology the 'duality of structure' refers to the process through which users manipulate their technology to accomplish their work. And it refers to the ways in which such actions draw on and reproduce, as well as sometimes change, the particular social context within which they work. While working with ICT the user is influenced by his or her interpretation of work, the organization, and this technology ('interpretative flexibility'). The access to organizational and technological resources and the normative rules that guide action in the social contexts are also of crucial importance.

Orlikowski (1992) shows that just like technology organization can be viewed as a structuration. How do technological and organizational structuration interplay? Users draw on existing properties of their organziation (e. g. division of labour and work procedures) to use the technological features available to them. In using technology to accomplish some tasks, users appropriate technological features and enact a set of social practices, which reinforce, adjust, or change the already existing organizational properties. This influence of individuals' technology use on the organizational properties is often unintended and unnoticed, just as the influence of the organizational properties on technology use is often unacknowledged.[13]

---

[11]Anthony Giddens: The Constitution of Society: Outline of the Theory of Structure. Berkeley, CA: University Press 1984

[12]Arthur D. Shulman: Putting Group Information Technology in its Place: Communication and Good Work Group Performance. In: Clegg et. al. (eds.) op. cit., pp. 358-374, (1996, 365)

[13]Wanda J. Orlikowski: The Duality of Technology: Rethinking the Concept of Technology in Organizations. Organizations Science, 3, 398-426 (1992)

3.2 Technology Structuration and Gender: Issues for Research

In the last chapter we have presented a new possible framework to interrogate the relationship between organization and ICT. This framework seems to be quite useful to describe and analyse the impact of ICT on organization. But this does not mean the technology structuration concept is also applicable in research seeking to examine the impact of ICT on womens work and on their prospective job opportunities. There is however some plausibility that this concept besides a better understanding of ICT has at least two advantages:

(1) The structuration theory can not only be applied to the use of technology or to the development of organization. The idea of the dualities of structure is also suitable for *understanding aspects of gender and gendering*. Gender constrains the interaction of women and men on the one hand and is established und reaffirmed through their genderspecific behaviour on the other hand.[14] Like Orlikowski (1992) demonstrated the interplay of technological and organizational structuration this modell could be modified by integrating the perspective of gender structuration. Then the gendering of social practices, the interpretation of task and access to technology can be examined. The result of this research will reveal how the ICT effects the gender segregation in the workplace.[15]

(2) The structuration theory views the agents as knowledgeable, reflexive and able to challenge and reinforce existing rules. A 'gender and technology' approach based on the theoretical framework of Giddens might therefore be useful for *developing strategies to improve the working conditions and job opportunities for women*.

A starting point for the creation of improvement strategies may be interpretative flexibility. Here the relation between the social interaction with ICT and its features can be reflected from a gender perspective. Recent research has shown that interpretative flexibility partly depends on metastructuring of expert users (a) and appears in an episodic manner (b). The spirit of a specific ICT limits to some extent the interpretative flexibility (c).

(a) *Metastructuring* contents of a set of activities that are deliberate, ongoing, and organizationally-sanctioned intervention within the context of use.[16] These activities help to adapt a new ICT to a context or modifies the context so that it is appropriate for using a given ICT. In this way they facilitates the ongoing effectiveness of the technology use over time. A particular type of metastructuring is technology-use mediation. It is a powerful mechanism in the context of dynamic organizations, because it enables rapid and customized adaptions of the technology and its use to changes in circumstances, organizational forms, and work practices. The actors of technology-use mediation are not authorized support staff or trainers, but expert users. They use ICT proficiently and share their software customizations and innovations with less proficient colleagues, but they rarely play an ongoing role in metastructuring. From a gender perspective of ICT could examine how metastructuring and techno-

[14]Candace West, Don H. Zimmermann: Doing Gender. In: Judith Lorber, Susan Farell (eds.): The Social Construction of Gender. Newbury Park, London, New Dehli 1991, pp. 13-37

[15]op. cit.

[16]Wanda J. Orlikowski, JoAnne Yates, Kazuo Okamura, Masayo Fujimoto: Shaping Electronic Communication: The Metastructuring of Technology in the Context of Use. Organization Science, 6, No. 4, 423-444 (1995)

logy-use mediation take part in creating a more or less sex segregated workplace. The role of the expert users can be cruical to understand this issue.

(b) Tyre and Orlikowski (1994) studied ICT adapted to social contextes in an *episodic manner*.[17] After examining the timing of ICT adaptation activities in three organizations, they concluded that the patterns of adaptation are distinctly discontinuous, or episodic. While the full integration of a new ICT may take several years, adaptation attention and effort are not applied constantly over the period. Adaptation activities are concentrated in short spurts during the period. The initial episode of adaptation seems to be very important. Decisions and directions taken in this period determines to a large extent how the ICT will be used over a longer term. Indeed, it appears that further adaptation is rare unless some sort of unusual event and discovery triggers subsequent adaptive activity. The initial period is called a window of opportunity. It is a window in the sense that, for a time users can view the new technology as a distinct artefact, and they can take part in negotiation which establishes the social interactions with that technology. Interruptions are another possibilities for the emergence of a window of opportunity. Here actors can be triggered to review and revise their procedures and challenge them to create new ways of balancing ICT and organization. The episodic manner of change is of special interest for the development and implementation of strategies that want to improve the working conditions for women. Windows of opportunity seem to be short periods when changes easier take place. Therefore they should be used for restructuring the working organizations that fits the needs of the women.

(c) The *spirit* of a technology provides a normative frame which forms the behaviour that is regarded to be appropriate in the social context of a specific ICT.[18] Spirit refers to the general intent as well as to the values and goals underlying a given set of features. Although spirit is a property of technology, it is not identical with the designer's intention or with the interpretation of its users. DeSanctis and Poole suggest that a spirit of an ICT can be identified by treating this technology as a 'text' and by developing a reading of its philosophy. Objects of this deconstruction may be for example the design metaphor underlying the ICT system, or the features the ICT incorporates, and the way in which they are named and presented. From a gender perspective it would be interesting to explore, if the spirit of a ICT can be gendered at all and how the gendering of the spirit might effect the sex segregation in the workplace. Suitable theoretical frameworks for this explorations could derive from feminist epistomologies.[19]

4 Conclusions

The progressive use of ICT brings about a lot of risks for women's work. In this paper we suggest a theoretical framework - the technology structuration, which might be of

[17]Marcie J. Tyre, Wanda J. Orlikowski: Windows of Opportunities: Temporal Patterns of Technological Adaption in Organzations. Organization Science, 5, No. 1, 98-118 (1994)

[18]Gerardine DeSanctis, Marshall Scott Poole: Capturing Complexity in Advanced Technology Use: Adaptive Structuration Theory. Organization Science 5, No. 2, 121-147 (1994)

[19]see for example: Susan Aiken et al. (eds.): Changing our Minds: Feminist Transformation of Knowledge. Albany, N. Y. 1988

special interest to study the impact of ICT on the workplace as well as the labourposition of women. It can also be used to develop strategies that improve their working conditions. Therefore the technology structuration perspective has to be integrated in action research. Then it can help to build efficient and innovative organization structures that integrate the specific skills and capacities of women.

Making Other Futures: Professional Women and their I.T. at Work

Zena Cumberpatch

School of Business, Nene College of Higher Education
Moulton Park, Norhampton NN2 7AL, England
Tel: 44 1604 735500, Fax: 44 1604 711214
email: zena.cumberpatch@nene.ac.uk

Setting the Scene

The following discussion notes are from ongoing doctoral research, looking at women in three professions : Law, Academia and Librarianship. The critical statements below come out of preliminary research results collected up to March 1997.

The research question asks:
What are the personal consequences of the triadic interrelationship of the woman, her I.T. and the profession she's in?

The results show:

- IT is being driven into 'solicitors' work by government practices
- Librarians may lose their jobs because of end user access
- Academics have individualistic preferences for IT
- Hierarchical work practices influence IT usage in all three professions

Remarks

It is suggested that IT has emancipatory possibilities for individual women, for example the librarian who has her own Web pages where she can transcend the difficulties and frustrations of daily work.

More examples of individual sites of agency for women will be given. Wider related issues of policy and practice for the professions involved will also be put forward.

Accepted Papers and Discussion Notes

Topic 4: Labour and Living: Apart or Together?

Part 4: Technological Innovations and Gendered Experiences

New Technology and Its Impact on the Female Labour Force in Russia

Dr Vitalina Koval

Institute of Political Sciences and Labour Problems
of Russian Academy of Sciences
Moscow, Center, Kolpachney pereulok, 9A

Abstract. The impact of new technology is different for men and for women. It has positive and negative sides for female labour. The introduction of new technology leads to a reduction of the number of workers. Women are the first victims. They are laid off first of all. There are many specialists among them. As a result the general professional level of the female labour force becomes lower and the gap between men's and women's professional skill increases. In many cases new technology negatively affects worker's health. On the positive side there is the reduction of the number of women in manual jobs, the increased opportunity to enter new, more interesting professions, to increase levels of qualification, to improve their skill, to earn more for their work and to improve labour conditions. The facts and figures testify to the gender character of using of new technology in Russia and about discrimination of women in this sphere. Estimating all positive and negative sides of technological innovations and their impact on female labour, we stress that the technical modernization of all economic branches provides wide opportunities that, with a correct approach could make women noticeably better off and could progressively change the professional and industrial structures of women's labour and improve their standard of living in general.

1 Introduction

The main aim of this paper was to retrace the positive and negative sides of technological innovations for men and women, to investigate who gained more - men or women from the introduction of new technology, to show how this process influences the structure of the labour force, its labour conditions, what are the links between new technology and gender relations at the macro and micro level. It was also important to show who made decisions concerning the introduction of new technology in different branches of industry - men or women.

The author used socio-economic methods of the research, using the official statistics and documents, results of sociological questionnaires, which were used by the author in Moscow manufacturing enterprises in 1991-1992 and material from scientific onferences.

The impact of new technology on the development of human society is widely known. In the Soviet literature we had no lack of studies of this subject (1). From the 1960s onwards the economic, political and social correlates of technological change in the former Soviet Union have been an important research theme. But the problem of the impact of technological changes on gender and female labour force is a relatively new one for Russian researchers. It became the theme of my research within the framework of the International Project (1991-1993) carried out by the Vienna Centre for Coordination and Information in the Social Sciences. Thus I was stepping into unexplored terrain.

2 What Does "New Technology" Mean?

Technology in our analysis the author understands as implementation of advanced technical knowledge in all fields of human activity for the satisfaction of people's needs in all spheres of their life. Each society has its own level of technical achievements at a certain stage of its development and its specificity. The specific features of using new technologies in the former Soviet Union was the implementation of advanced technology in the branches of industries connected with the production of weapons and a concentration of the best technical specialists in the military complex.

In pre-perestroyka times the characteristic feature of the economy (except the military complex) was the shortage of technical equipment - Xerox machines, printers, computers. To use personal computer was prohibited without special permission from the authorities. It was impossible to obtain personal computers in the country. All personal computers, printers and Xerox machines were under the strict control of the security services. The latest technological achievements, including information systems, were widely used by the military complex and by the administration of Soviet Ministries. The changes have taken place since the end of the 1980s when all restrictions were lifted and people were then free to make wide use of personal computers, electronic and microelectronic technic and information systems. A computer revolution is on-going in the country today.

3 The Discriminating Nature of Technological Innovations in Russia

The introduction of new technologies, essential for economic development, affects men and women in different ways. Their abilities to develop new technology in their own interests differ for a number of reasons. These are rooted in historically based differences in the forms and spheres of the male and female labour. The most widely spread cultural stereotypes, strong patriarchal traditions in the society, the overwelming prevalence of men in all echelons of power, especially at the top, have resulted in weaker ties between women and the technological employment, on the one hand, and prejudices in respect of the application of new technology in the economy. We may trace discrimination against working women in the process of the introduction of technological innovations both at the macro and micro levels.

At the macro level we may see the direct connection between authoritative structures and the way new technology was used in the interests of certain social groups - these groups often being determined by sex. Until recently all enterprises belonged to the State. The bureaucratic authoritative administration in command decided what kind of new technology should be introduced and where. Women have been largely absent from high-level decision-making positions in the State planning departments that have determined levels of investment in technology and the kind of technologies for both industrial production and individual consumption that society required.

Female labour is concentrated mainly in such traditional "female" branches of economy as textile, shoe, garment and food industries and also in all social services, medicine, education, culture and trade. Between 60 and 90 percent of the labour force in these branches are women. The shortage of technology in "female" branches has resulted in the widespread employment of women in manual jobs. More than 40% of work in these industries has been done manually by women for low wages - the lowest in the country. The immediate replacement of out-dated equipment with the latest technology is badly needed. However, management at the decision-making level (practically all men) do not seems to be in a hurry to invest in these branches of employment. It is more profitable to use cheap female labour instead of expensive equipment.

According to the official statistics more than 4 million women are engaged in the most dirty, harmful and hazardous jobs. Their labour conditions do not comply with labour protection norms or rules and medical standards. Women's health and ability to bear children are adversely affected by this. Around 90 thousand women are injured annually in industry, around 500 with fatal results. The reproductive health of working women worsened during last decade. The number of babies born with different defects increased 22-fold during the last 12 years according to the International Centre for Law Research. In 1994 every fourth child was born with some defect.

Thus, there is a situation in which scientific and technological progress finds extensive application in "male" industries and only slightly affects the industries where women's labour prevails. Technological progress therefore has had little effect on the number of women employed in hard manual jobs, nor has it positively affected their labour activities or conditions. Even where new technology is used in the design of new equipment, women's needs are not considered. New machinery is designed exclusively to be used by men. As a result, women are forced to suffer, working in uncomfortable positions throughout the working day. This leads to a loss of productivity and efficiency of work by 13-20%. In spite of equal rights, there exists a contradiction between the formal economic equality of women and men in relation to production tools and their unequal opportunities to exercise this right. The introduction of new technology is often used by the administration against the interests of women and leads to a rise in unemployment amongst women. It is extremely difficult for women with low-grade skills and who were laid off because of the new technology to find new jobs. Looking at this from another angle, 70% of unemployed women have higher education. There are many engineers among them. This implies that high professional qualifications and higher education do not guarantee jobs for women. A significant reduction in the number of specialists with higher and secondary education has had its a negative impact on the level of qualification of the female labour force. Highly qualified women - specialists in different fields - very often take alternatve jobs which do not correspond to their profession nor to their education. As a result their social status is lowered.

4 New Technology and Its Impact on Women's Professional Lives

In modern Russia women make up 53% of the population (78,5 mln.), they numbered 48% in the labour force (34 mln.) and 90% of able-bodied women are involved in public production. Mass involvement of women in the production sphere began at the end of 1920s. Many million of people, including women, moved from the villages to the cities. Unskilled and non-professional female labour occupied the most unprestigious, mainly auxiliary jobs. Historically, women have always done the most dirty and difficult work in the home.

Attitudes towards women are based on the old patriarchal traditions where women are considered to be second rate persons. The position and role of women in society is underestimated, though many of them achieved great success in their professional fields. The industralisation of the economy demanded an educated and professional labour force. The former Soviet Goverment's policies aimed at involving women in public production, making secondary education complusory for all citizens and thus providing equal access to education has led to impressive results; it has changed the level of women's educational and professional standards. At the end of the 80's women made up 61% of specialists with higher and specialised secondary education. Among them women made up 58% engineers, 87% economists, 67% doctors, 89% bookkeepers, 91% bibliographers. Noticeable growth in educational and professional fields has enabled many women to do well in such complex and untraditional fields as management - about 26% of leaders in the national economy are women. They are directors of enterprises, production or scientific-production associations and other different kinds of small enterprises.

While analysing conditions to enable women to master new technologies, two factors should be taking into account. One is that women specialists with specialised secondary education, whose activity is based on a relatively small volume of scientific and technical knowledge, make up more than half of women specialists. They comprise 12.6 million of 20.7 million of these women specialists, or 60%. The second fact is that women are prevalent in jobs involving people: teachers, medical workers, planners, economists, trade workers etc.

Development of new technology in the "male" branches of industry where women employed mainly in subsidiary technical jobs affects the female work force in a different way. Along with the introduction of technological innovations, an increase in number of highly qualified women is observed. Recently the number of such women - specialists has doubled in the engineering, radio and electronic industries and in electronic and automatic machine manufacturing as well. The other side of this process is the creation of a great number of subsidiary unskilled jobs for women. For example, in the precision instruments and radio industry women workers make up 67-70%. They occupy jobs mainly connected with auxiliary operations, such as assembling, which demand a great deal of precision, attention, accuracy-qualities more inherent in women than men. These jobs are rather tiresome and monotonous and men do this work reluctantly.

The introduction of new technology and technological processes require highly professional workers with new professional levels of knowledge, who may use computers, electronic and microelectronic equipment. Unfortunately, it was discovered recently that the professional skills of the vast majority of engineers and technicians, especially among women, had become outdated because, for a long time, they had been working with old equipment or in administration. As a result, a new problem appeared - non-competitiveness of female labour force in the labour market.

In order to solve this problem it is necessary to create a broad system on the State level for the training and retraining of women personnel for new professions. It is necessary to pay special attention to the demands of the labour market and to professional knowledge and working experience of those who express the desire to be trained. Unfortunately, very often after training and increasing their qualifications, women still don't get any advantages in their career or any increases in pay. Indeed their social status appears to be even one step lower.

Few obstacles still exist wich prevent women entering new professions - inadequate training or re-training programmes although the majority of women are not trying to improve their qualifications. Women are extremely busy doing many jobs simultaneously. About 70% of married women do nothing to increase their qualifications, arguing that they do not profit from it.

Remarkable changes in social and economic spheres in the period of new reforms led to the change in the structure of female labour force. Today, now that there is a private sector there are new alternatives and choices for women's activities and employment. From one side, the reduction of female labour force in the traditional women's branches of industry is taking place. From the other side, along with the creation of various kinds of private, cooperative, and joint-venture companies and other commercial structures, the female work force, is in a state of flux in the non-state sectors of the economy. In the private sector, flexible forms and part-time women's employment have become more widespread. These may help women to solve the serious problem inherent in combining their work outside their homes with their domestic activities. Women prefer to work in the private sector because the wages there are two or three times higher than thea are in the state sector. First, new technology is widely used in the private sector of the economy. All offices and banks are supplied with computers, and other electronic systems. As a result of this process new professions have appeared who provide new technical services; among these women make up more than 80% of the workforce. In the manufacture of radio and precision instruments where electronic technology is used, women are now around two-thirds of the work-force. However the vast majority of them are busy in routine assembly work seen as calling for women's qualities of accuracy and attention. This work is unpopular with men. It is not only macro factors that influence the changing structure of the female labour. In the sociological research which the author conducted at a Moscow manufacturing enterprise she showed how the introduction of new technological innovations influenced female labour at the micro level.

5 New Production Technology in the Hosiery Industry

For our case study of technological innovation we carried out research in an enterprise producing one of those consumer goods so badly needed by women: panty-hose (tights) for themselves and their children, socks for the family. We were afforded access to the Tushinskaya stocking factory, an old Moscow branch of this sector of light, female industry. Panty-hose now constitutes just over half its output, 70% for children, 30% for women. There were 1750 employees at the time of a study, 80% of them women - it was characteristic of the female sector.

This was still a state interprise, not yet privatized. As a half-measure, however, the administration was technically now renting the plant and building from the state. The collective of workers controlled such matters as the distribution of bonuses and investment in the social fund. The Tushinskaya hosiery plant had been modernized four years previously by the replacement of its old knitting machinery with automatic, computer controlled production equipment - the main focus of our interest.

The research had three phases. First, a questionnaire (69 questions) was distributed to 250 workers, the entire labour force of one particular shop that was operating the new technology. Two hundred usable replies were received, 180 from women; 20 from men, questions sought information on the social relations within the factory in general. Second, a selection of 77 employees was made from the original 250. There were 43 women and 34 men who had been working in the factory before, as well as since, the technological innovation. All answered the second questionnaire which aimed to explore their feelings about the consequence of new technology for their lives and in particular for gender relations. Third, the opinions of decision-makers were felt to be particulary significant, so ten people (five men, five women) in mid-level managerial posts were approached with the questionnaire and were also interviewed in depth. In all cases the information sought included questions about the subject's home life and consumption, from which, together with the information about production, we have attempted to develop a rounded picture of the gender relations during technological change.

First, the educational level of the employees at Tushinskaya was found to be high. Among the general sample, no less than 83% had achieved 10 years of secondary education, some with compensatory or additional vocational, specialized or higher education; only 17% had incomplete secondary education without further vocational, specialized or higher education. Among the second sample, those who had experienced technological change, the educational standard was even higher. Of these who were mainly in the age band 35-50 years and who were trusted long-serving employees, only 6% of men and 2% of women had failed to complete secondary education. There was, besides a striking gender difference in educational standard. 40% of women in the general sample, against only 26,5% of men had higher education. In the Tushinskaya factory women, as well as being the great majority of employees, did also have a substantial presence in supervisory and management posts. The overall director of the factory was a women, as were two out of three deputy directors. Three of the five shop forepersons were female, together with a majority of brigade leaders. (An exception was the knitting shops where most of these supervisory posts were filled by men.) It appears however that this presence of women in supervision and management does not, significant as it is, reflect the leadership role women feel their education merits. Only 70% of women, against 88% of men, felt their job matched their educational achievements. As we shall see this feeling arose partly from women's inability to benefit from the new opportunities deriving from the technological change. It is a finding that reflects a widespread awareness among women of an undervaluation of women endemic in Russian society, a failure to use and reward their considerable abilities.

New technology had, it seemed, been a mixed blessing at Tushinskaya. Drawing on the questionnaire given to those who had lived throught technological change at the factory, we found that the most people's experience was broadly positive (67% rated it so). It should be noted at the outset that one important factor in worker's current satisfaction with the enterprise's, may have been that soon after the technological innovation, at the time of reform of the price mechanism, the enterprise social fund increased and the administration began spending more on subsidising of facilities such as the canteen, day nursery, the rest home and the sauna and sports complex. In connection with the introduction of new technology itself, in addition, most respondents reported that labour conditions had improved. Wages for both sexes had risen.

Women were even more positive than men (76% as against 59%). They reported a number of gains resulting from the new technology. They felt it had afforded them greater responsibility and called for greater skill (61% of women,45% of men). More than half these women workers had been retrained, acquired a new occupation or advanced their qualifications in the course of the technological innovation. In the case of men it was less than half (due however to the fact more men than women had had appropriate qualifications beforehand.) Against this must be set a number of factors. Two-thirds of all respondents, women and men alike, felt new technology had increased stress and adversely affected their health - though it was difficult, we felt, to be sure this effect was one of new technology rather than a general decline in nutritional standards in Russia, a deterioration in the environment and increases in stress in the society in general in this period. The wage increases due to new technology had been largely eaten up by inflation, and 70% of women and 65% of men felt anxiety about their financial situation. The inequalities in pay between women and men (women earning 70% of the male wage on average) had not been improved. While new technology, for instance, had led to an increase in pay for both the female and male managers we interviewed, and the gender difference at this level was only 5-10%, nonetheless it was men who had gained most.

More importantly, there had been no relaxation of the technological sexual division of labour. In fact, sex segregation had been exacerbated by the change. In the days of the old technology, women and men engineers had done similar jobs in the plant. In the new technological regime, men acquired the controlling jobs and it was particularly young male graduates who entered the leading positions generated by the electronic and computer revolution. 53% of forepersons and assistant forepersons were men and men were particularly the ones in charge of the new electronic equipment. Among the five male managers we interviewed, all were in engineer/technologist posts and three had been appointed to management for the first time in their lives after the introduction of new technology.

Of the five women managers, only one was fully technical while, of the others, three were engineer/economists and one was the enterprise accountant.In general the roles women in the factory had entered in connection with the new technologies were subordinate roles: those of programmer, operator, perforator. Even when they received special training - as was the case with a batch of 50 young women - it was only for routine work of this kind.

Some older employees nearing retirement age were made redundant, particularly those whose knowledge was considered obsolete - and these were mostly women. Many other women chose to move from production into more social or service roles. Women were thus consolidated in departments and jobs involving distribution, finance and administration. Women were in a majority amongst economists, accountants and brigade leaders. Overall, women felt a technological dependence on men, who were so frequently their technical superiors, the ones familiar with electronic techniques and control systems.

It is not surprising if our study at the micro level finds that the experiences of workers and managers in the Tushinskaya hosiery factory confirm trends observable in the country as a whole. We saw the undoubted benefits new production technology had brought to the plant and its people. Despite increased pressure of work and some reported deterioration in health there was general satisfaction with the outcome: fewer harmful manual tasks, more interesting work and more responsibility, new job opportunities, higher wages. Increased revenue had enabled the provision of more amenities through the social fund. These gains were reported by women as well as men. Yet the changes associated with new technology had not narrowed and in some cases had widened the gap between women and men. The gender wage differential remained unchanged. The sexual division of labour, with men in skilled and responsible posts in new technology and women in subordinate, less skilled and routine occupations, had increased with new technology. We found possibilities for career advancement were only feebly and ineffectually used by women. The professional standing of the sexes overall had diverged further. Women, particularly older women whom it was felt were unlikely to adapt to the computer and electronics, were experiencing more technological redundancy - exemplifying a trend observable in Russia as a whole.

The effects of technological innovation at Tushinskaya do not stop here of course. We saw that increased labour productivity and an improved product had enabled the factory to become competitive in price and quality with foreign manufacturers of panty-hose. Tights, a commodity long desired by women, were now widely available on the market. The Tushinskaya development is in many ways a model of what women might wish for from any industrial capital investment policy. It could be a model for the diversion of production capacity from military to civilian - even domestic- products.

However, the full gain will not be experienced by women unless technological change is accompanied by a deliberate and conscious policy to end patriarchal attitudes and the disadvantages of women that these entail. Research should be carried to aid the development of a technology strategy for women, for example, on factors determining women's occupational choice and on the correlation between women's qualifications and career achievements. Women should be equally involved with men in decision-making concerning new technology, in trade unions, enterprise managment and state bodies. Equal rights should be accompanied by equal opportunities for women. The solution for women's issues in Russia is a part of the solution of economic, social and political problems in the transition period to a market economy. Once these problems have been solved a well grounded situation will be created to solving women's issues.

Notes

There are some research reports by Russian authors on automation, women's working conditions and women's professional qualifications. Among the authors are Drs. L. Rzanitsina, Z. Hotkina, N. Pozdniakova, L. Sadovichia, N. Zacharova and Prof. N. Shischan.

References

1. Berg A.-G. The Smart House as a Gendered Socio-Technical Construction. IFIM, Trondheim, 1991.
2. Cockburn C., Ormrod S. Gender and Technology in the Making. London, 1993.
3. Conception of Women's Employment. Institute of Economics of Russian Academy of Sciences. Moscow, 1994.
4. Family and Family policy. Moscow,1991.
5. Francis A., Grootings P. New Technologies and Work: Capitalists and Socialists Perspectives. London, N.-Y., 1989.
6. Gender: Reproduction, Employment and Household Problems. By Kalabichina I. Moscow, 1995.
7. Goscomstat USSR (1988-1991) Women in the USSR. Statistical materials.
8. Grusdeva E., Chertichina E. Soviet Women at Work and at Home. Moscow, 1983.
9. Job, Family and Home Life of Soviet Women. Moscow, 1990.
10. Krevnevitch V. Automation and Satisfaction with Work. Moscow, 1987.
11. Labour, Family and Life of Soviet Women. Moscow, 1990.
12. National Platform of Actions to Improve the Situation of Women. Moscow, 1994.
13. National Report for IV World Congress. Moscow, 1995.
14. Problems od Work Security and Health of Women Today and Ways Towards their Solution. Thesis of the reports at the all Union Practical Scientific Conference. Ivanovo, 1988.
15. Schineleva L. Women and Society. Moscow, 1990.
16. Sergeeva G. Women's professional employment. Moscow, 1987.
17. Silverstone R., Hirsch E., Morley D. Information and Communical Technologies and the Moral Economy of Household, 1992.
18. Social Security of Women: Modern Problems. Ivanovo, 1994.
19. The Population of Russia over 70 years. Moscow, 1988.
20. Wajcman J. Feminism Confronts Technology. Pennsylvania State University Press, 1991.
21. Women in Contemporary Russia. Ed. by Vitalina Koval. Oxford-Providence, 1995.
22. Women in Modern World. Moscow, 1989.
23. Women in Society: Reality, Problems, Prognosis. Moscow, 1991.
24. Women of Russia - Yesterday, Today, Tomorrow. Moscow, 1994.

Notes on Gendered Experiences in Fieldwork Related to a Teleradiology Experiment

Helena Karasti

Department of Information Processing Science
University of Oulu, Linnanmaa, FIN-90570 Oulu, Finland
email: helena@rieska.oulu.fi

Abstract. This paper discusses experiences of how gender mattered in fieldwork carried out in relation to an experimental teleradiology project. The purpose was to study emerging teleradiology work practice in order to provide information for redesigning the system. The paper starts with selected notes on gendered experiences as encountered during the fieldwork and proceeds to describe how these affected further involvement and intervention in the provision of redesign information. It concludes with a brief discussion of the achievements.

1 Introduction

The 'turn to the social' in systems design has drawn more attention to the social context of computer use. In systems design for work settings this has meant focusing interest on work practice. Furthermore, the paradigmatic change has given increased prominence to social research methods. The number of field studies, for example, has multiplied greatly within the systems design community. Not surprisingly, gendered field issues have not been discussed within the Information Systems community at large. This follows the tendency noted by Green et al. for new approaches to fail to take gender-specific aspects into account in systems design [3]. Field studies have been carried out within feminist information system development projects (see [7]), but the articles have not specifically discussed gender issues from the point of view of women fieldworkers. The purpose of this paper is to share some of the experiences gained from our work, as it seems likely that female systems designers in similar projects will be faced with similar issues in challenging situations.

The fieldwork was carried out in connection with an experimental teleradiology project organised by the Department of Diagnostic Radiology at Oulu University Hospital and at Kuusamo Health Centre. The aim of the project was to develop a PC-based, low-cost teleradiology system for exchanging requests and reports and transferring images and to implement it for daily clinical use over a period of six months. This goal was met quite successfully. Our object of interest in the fieldwork was to gain a better understanding of the relationship between the emerging teleradiology work practice and technology and to see how this understanding could be used to provide information for redesigning the technology. Gender issues were not specifically to the fore in the first instance, but they emerged upon commencement of the process of studying the new teleradiology system and related work practice from the point of view of the participants.

The first part of this paper discusses some of the experiences gained by systems designers as fieldworkers aware of gender problems while carrying out the field study of technologically mediated work in a hospital environment. Although the fieldwork phase was comparatively short some of the experiences recorded are similar to those recounted in the anthropological and sociological literature on gender issues in fieldwork [11, 13]. The rest of the paper describes how these experiences shaped our reading of the work practice and further design concerns. The aim is to give an idea of how attempts were made to take gender issues into account by organising the workshops in the form of gender-aware interventions in the design process. An example is presented to illustrate what was discussed in the workshops. The paper concludes with a brief discussion of the achievements of the gender-aware orientation that was adopted.

2 The Teleradiology Experiment

Upon returning to Oulu University Hospital, the author was reminded of the first phase of fieldwork that had taken place one and half years earlier. The group had then been engaged in studying work practice in four departments of radiology, focusing on cooperative image interpretation. Walking through the public corridors, we became aware of the hospital atmosphere: sterile smells, subdued colours, restrained voices and composed behaviour. The door to the staff area of one of the departments of radiology opened onto another kind of hospital environment. The constant hum of various technical devices - alternators, imaging equipment, printers and computers - reminded the observers of the technology-intensive character of radiology. Piles of patient folders and stacks of films were to be seen everywhere. Images were laid out on light screens. Momentary glimpses were caught of patients in spatially segregated examination areas. The staff wore badges denoting their name and occupation on their differently coloured uniforms. People were working in close proximity, talking and negotiating, occasionally forming cooperative teams to solve a problem, and then disbanding again to take up their individual, occupationally differentiated tasks. Attendants were rushing in and out of doors, carrying patient folders, nurses were preparing patients for their examinations and helping radiologists in carrying out the examinations, assistants were arranging images on the light screens of alternators, radiologists in front of the alternators were interpreting the images and dictating reports, students and junior radiologists were consulting seniors about their work, physicists occasionally stepped in to be consulted on technical matters, and secretaries at their computer terminals were typing out the dictated reports.

Our initial impression of teleradiology was quite superficial, having been formed through the somewhat elitist viewpoint of the chief radiologists with whom the fieldwork had been discussed. Teleradiology is one of the more diffuse applications of telemedicine, the idea being to transfer images for the attention of expert radiologists regardless of geographical distance. This means that a hospital without a radiologist can transmit images to a radiologist at an associated hospital. The films are scanned and the images are transmitted electronically along with a request for consultation.

The radiologist interprets the images, provides a diagnosis and sends a report to the doctor attending to the case.

The fieldwork began with interviews with members of the staff who had been involved in the process of designing the teleradiology system. The design team had consisted of radiologists and physicists from the University Hospital and designers from the two hardware and software companies involved, in addition to whom the chief physician and head nurse in radiology at the Kuusamo Health Centre had participated in video conference meetings on a couple of occasions.

We gradually gained an understanding of the experiment as our early formulations were continuously revised and new observations challenged the old ones. The amount of supporting work and staff required in the experiment was one surprising aspect. The supporting staff had not been included in the design of the system, but their cooperation was taken for granted in the daily practice of using it.

After some renegotiations on the extent of the fieldwork, it was allowed to continue in a more extensive form. The next stage was observation of teleradiology-related working activities in clinical practice and in situ interviews with staff at both the University Hospital and the Kuusamo Health Centre. Actual occasions of using the system were videotaped, and stimulated recall interviews were carried out with the people whose work had been recorded. The interviewees and researchers watched the tapes together, questioning, commenting on and explaining the events recorded.

We, the fieldworkers, would get together after a day in the field to share our interpretations of the incidents, to talk about and comment on our tentative and partial formulations of what was going on and to reflect on our evolving understanding of the situations we were encountering. As fieldwork can be quite exhausting another important function of these sessions was to allow us to 'unwind' and to cope with our emotions and the difficulties or problems that we had encountered. It was during these sessions that we also started to talk and reflect about the gender issues intertwined in the fieldwork.

2.1 Gendered Fieldwork Relationships and Encounters

The present fieldwork was less intensive in its involvement with the 'native community' by comparison with the established anthropological and ethnographic traditions. The assignment was merely to observe the daily clinical use of a novel form of experimental technology for a relatively short period. The nature of the fieldwork, however, namely that it was carried out in and through social encounters, involved extensive contacts with the staff of the institutions concerned and required intimate personal involvement with these people. Although we were aware that "since gender is a key organising device in all cultures, male and female researchers will always be treated differently by those they study" (van Maanen et al. in [11]), it still came as a surprise how much gender mattered in these encounters. Every interactional encounter required adjustment to one's interlocutor and a search for a new approach in an attempt to create an atmosphere in which communication would be most congenial for all concerned.

Information meetings were held to give everyone in the departments an idea of the nature of the fieldwork, our background and research interests because we had learned during the previous fieldwork phase that the staff in the radiological departments are not used to being studied, as they are normally the ones who examine the patients. Most of the people already knew the team from previous fieldwork and were happy to see the same people back. Some still found the reversed setting of being studied too unfamiliar and it was deemed diplomatic not to bother them any further. Furthermore, some radiologists felt strongly about and questioned the qualitative approach of the research and fieldwork, which did not match their ideas of quantitative research in medicine.

At first the staff seemed to hold the research team in cautious esteem because we represented the field of computers. Computers occupy a somewhat unique position in this work community. Senior radiologists show varying degrees of reluctance towards the whole idea of computerisation, and especially towards using computers in their own work, whereas junior radiologists are more computer-literate and more willing to use them. Nurses and secretaries are the only occupational groups in the radiology departments that are required to use computers in their daily work, a mainframe radiology information system that they call 'the dinosaur'. Gradually the staff realized, however, that we were not only concerned with what we obviously should have been concerned with, computers. Instead they saw us carrying video equipment, observing them working and talking with them about their work - all matters that they could not relate to computers. On the other hand, it was easy to sense their puzzlement at the equation which they were presented with: two young female researchers from the field of computers making their observations by 'hanging around', watching them work and taking videos of the teleradiology system in use. The staff of the departments of radiology nevertheless tried hard to grasp who the fieldworkers were and to fit us into their own social and cultural worlds.

We were acutely conscious of the issue of power and equality between informants and researchers from the start, as it was realised that the investigation would be dealing with staff at all hierarchical levels in the two hospitals, with varying relationships of status, seniority, occupational background and gender. It was obviously not possible in all instances to create non-hierarchical relationships between the fieldworkers and the interviewees (as suggested by [8], for example). We were nevertheless prepared to invest our own personalities in an attempt to build up relationships of mutual trust.

The frequently aired assumption that women workers and women system designers would easily be able create non-hierarchical relationships of trust simply because of their subordination to men in society in general proved highly problematical in this case. It seemed to be the background differences and our status as researchers that set us apart from the female staff. In any case, we became clearly aware of the privileged position granted to us by our higher education and expertise in information systems. This meant, in the first place, that the nurses, secretaries and primary care assistants played down and belittled their own views, as they seemed unused to having any value or importance attached to their knowledge and experience in the workplace. However, after finding out that we were truly interested in them, they willingly offered their views. The two sides thus ended up sharing the same interests, but it required an effort to overcome the boundaries.

A mutual understanding and good working relations were also established eventually with another key informant, but the road to it was quite different. Participation of this senior radiologist was of essential importance for the daily use of the teleradiology system, and we spent quite a lot of time observing his work and talking with him. He in fact put us through a series of challenging situations as we tried to find a common way of communicating. He kept trying out and offering different ways of interacting, and it seemed that our relationship with him was constantly having to be renegotiated. He started in a flirtatious manner, and even asked us to go out for a beer with him after work. Another tactic that he tried was to be fatherly and educative, offering suggestions and advice on how the work could be continued, where to go and what to observe. Yet another ploy was to demonstrate his seniority by giving instructions on how to conduct the research or what changes should be made in the topic. It seemed that he was ready to try out a new approach at every encounter. This certainly made the meetings interesting, but also challenging and consuming in terms of time end energy. It also led us to reflect how much one has to adapt one's principles and compromise on one's ways of dealing in different kinds of gendered fieldwork situations.

2.2 Participant Observation and Involvement of the Action Research Type

Participant observation is a complex skill requiring continuous reflection on the process. The observer has a double role to play: "her primary attitude is that of a novice who tries to become a part of the life of the community; at the same time she needs to maintain enough distance to record her observations and reflect on her evolving understanding of the situations she encounters" [6]. There are several ways of conducting observations, ranging from the proverbial unobtrusive 'fly on the wall' to a field worker who becomes a full participant in the activities being studied.

The plan in this case had been to adopt something closer to the first approach, but this had to be re-evaluated in the course of the fieldwork. One reason for this was that we were constantly being asked for advice in our capacity as computer experts, there being many situations in which the staff would try to solve problems by trial and error on account of the superficiality of their training. These instances made us feel most uncomfortable just sitting there, not helping and were naturally quite unnerving for the staff as well. After some consideration, it was decided that a more participative approach should be adopted with the supporting staff, trying to help them where possible, after first noting what the problem was, why and where it had occurred and how the person had first tried to solve the problem herself. The adoption of a second role of teacher or consultant in addition to that of an observer entailed some uncertainty at first, but it turned out that the workers seemed comfortable about asking for advice and accepting help in solving their problems. The nurses, secretaries and primary care assistants, both at the University Hospital and in Kuusamo, explained that this was part of their work practice and that they had a tradition of learning from each other and training each other on the job. We were also satisfied as we could be of direct help.

2.3 Situated, Partial Views and Power-Related Discourses

It became quite clear during the fieldwork that the participant categories would not form a single coherent *emic* entity but rather represented situated, partial views (*sensu* [4]) of the teleradiology system and the work practice emerging around it. The participants had their own, different and at times contradictory views of the system, its use and related working activities. These views were gendered, as they were based on the participants' particular occupational standpoints, educational backgrounds and fields of expertise, their positions within the organisational hierarchies and their participation in, interest in and experiences with the teleradiology system.

The design group took a planning view of the system, being concerned with how it should work. Since there were plenty of technical questions to deal with, less consideration was afforded to other matters during the design phase. After the busy implementation period most of the members of this group had little to do with the daily running of the system. Some physicists were occasionally called upon to solve software or telecommunications problems. The research radiologist in charge of organising the experiment focused his follow-up survey on diagnostic accuracy and efficiency issues, as it is these that lie within the area of interest of medical teleradiology research.

The staff who worked with the system formed their own views according to what they experienced during the experiment, i.e. based on the part of the teleradiology system and process that was visible to them in their own tasks. It would have been difficult for those involved in the everyday work of the experiment to gain an overall understanding of it, as they were so immersed in their own aspect. Also, the new, distributed nature of the work made understanding of the whole teleradiology process more difficult, as it reduced people's awareness of what was happening at the other end of the teleradiology link.

We, the researchers, formed our own views in the course of the fieldwork. We gained an overall but also situated understanding of the work practice centred around the new teleradiology system by observing and talking to all the occupational groups involved and synthesizing the different, partial experiences of the various participants. The view obtained was definitely that of an outsider, however, and although some understanding had been gained of traditional ways of working in radiology during the earlier fieldwork and this had been deepened through the detailed analyses of work practice in connection with teleradiology, we still lacked the medical, institutional, historical and contextual knowledge and understanding of the staff.

2.4 Attachment and Ethical Accountability

Our triple role as observers, participants and teacher/consultants, with the additional role of 'agent for change in gender awareness' with respect to the redesigning of the system, aroused some reflection on the particular ethical problems entailed in further actions related to our responsibility for the welfare of the participants.

As Van Maanen writes: "ethnographers frequently identify with the interests of those studied ... the fieldworker not only represents but takes the side of the studied" [10], there is no problem in taking sides when the fieldworker is liable for just one community and can take sides with it. Fieldworkers in any workplace research should value the trust that builds up between them and the employees. Blomberg et al. noted, however, that "those involved in linking ethnography and design must be aware of their role as 'change agents'. This raises the question, as it does for anthropologists who act as change agents in more traditional settings: 'In whose interest does one operate?'" [2]. What happens when there are several groups with conflicting interests - a familiar problem in participatory systems design? What does a fieldworker do when the interests of the various participants conflict? Whose interest in and view of teleradiology should be considered legitimate and relevant for design purposes?

Furthermore, some feminist writers have warned about situations in which making womens' work visible without an understanding of the dynamics of their jobs may simply damage them, because the invisible aspects of women's work may be the only aspects over which they retain control [12]. This point of view is in stark contradiction to the need to make the views of workers and the work practice visible for design purposes. Should we then try to reveal the knowledge and experience embodied in women's work practice in spite of the potential harm? Writers discussing this set of problems call for "dynamic, situation-contingent discourse" [9] and "practices alert to the varying contexts and dynamics of women's work" [12].

In this case we could foresee that some of the views held by the participants might apparently arouse more attention in the redesign process and might be considered more legitimate than others. These views would not be those of the women workers positioned low in the organisational hierarchies and excluded from the design group. After careful consideration, it was decided here to try to encourage the participation of women workers and to describe the whole body of teleradiological work practice, including the supporting work carried out by women as it was thought that in this case the women would benefit more from exposure of their work than from continued omission from the design process.

2.5 Multiparty Workshops for Work Practice Analysis and System Redesign

Planning of the intervention in the design of the teleradiology system was commenced in the spirit of Henwood's argument that we need analyses aimed at interventions into the technology design process itself which are informed by feminist theories and in the service of positive changes in the practical conditions under which women work and live [5]. Likewise the feminist literature emphasizes that simply involving women workers in conventional decision-making processes regarding technological design and change is quite inadequate for ensuring that the concerns of women are addressed. Instead, it seems necessary to create arenas in which these concerns can be explored, articulated, recognised as legitimate, and fed into the decision-making process [12]. The following questions were felt to be particularly puzzling: How can the hidden knowledge, experience and practices of the women's supportive work be articulated and integrated into the redesigning of the system? How can an understanding of the use of the teleradiology system and associated work practice that includes an awareness of gender be communicated to the community at large? How can the dominant notions of relevant expertise and views be challenged in a sufficiently discrete manner to avoid rejection by the dominant groups?

It was decided to intervene in the design process by means of workshops planned in a gender-aware manner. Participation of all occupational groups was insisted upon, in order to bring together their multiple partial views. The idea would be to undertake a collaborative analysis of the videotaped instances of work practice and use of the system. A video collage was created of selected fieldwork recordings to cover the whole work process associated with the teleradiology link and to reveal the work carried out by the supporting staff. The workshops were invited to pay special attention to giving women a legitimate voice by encouraging as informal and appreciative an atmosphere as possible in the discussion, the research team's role being to mediate and facilitate shifts in perspective between practice, analysis and design. The progress of the workshops may be illustrated with the following example of image-related articulation work that came to light during the experiment.

At the University Hospital all patient images are in current practice printed out on films and interpreted using alternator light screens although increasing numbers of images are being produced by digitized modalities. The teleradiology experiment was the first occasion on which radiologists were called upon to carry out clinical interpretations using only digitized images on computer screens. Having dealt with the initial problems of getting used to having images displayed on a computer screen, the teleradiologists became increasingly annoyed with having to move, turn and rotate many images on the screen before and during the process of interpretation.

In terms of current work practice, radiologists are used to taking an overall glance at all the images at the beginning of a session in order to gain a general understanding of the case. As they proceed with the diagnosis they need to concentrate on the image interpretation work as they go through the preorganised images - and do not have to handle the films themselves. They may make some minor changes to the layout of films, but the idea is that all the image-related articulation work: retrieval of films, organisation and layout, should be carried out prior to the interpretation session. The task is carried out at the University Hospital by a special, all female, occupational group regarded as one of the lowest in the department hierarchy. Part of these people's job is to arrange the films on the alternator light screens prior to the interpretation session so as to ensure an efficient flow of interpretation work.

This problem and the circumstances that had led to it were discussed in the workshops. Comparison of traditional work practice with the new teleradiological way of working indicated that tasks corresponding to the articulation work carried out by the 'image handlers' at the University Hospital was dispersed into four aspects of the teleradiology system: 1) how the scanning of films and transmission of images in Kuusamo affects the images displayed on the teleradiologist's screen in Oulu, 2) how the image display system lays out the images on the teleradiologist's screen, 3) how the radiologist arranges the images on the computer screen at the beginning of a session in order to obtain an overall view of the case, and 4) continuous image handling by the radiologist during the interpretation process.

Some of the causes of the problem experienced by the teleradiologists could be traced to the scanning and transmission stages at the other end for, unlike the situation in Oulu, where the division of labour and the content of working tasks had remained the same, the novel teleradiology system had introduced entirely new tasks and working procedures in Kuusamo, and further new ways of working emerged during the experiment as more experience was gained with the system and its use. The head nurse in radiology had volunteered to look after the teleradiology work in addition to her regular duties, and when she could no longer continue with the project, the work was delegated to primary care assistants, who collectively took responsibility for running the system. However, these people lacked the expertise necessary in scanning and transmitting the images which resulted in the problems experienced by teleradiologists with image layout and organisation on their screens.

Little attention had been paid to the issue of image organisation during the initial phase of teleradiology system design, the design team having addressed it only as a technical matter. As no easy algorithm was found for arranging the images on the screen it was decided that they would be displayed in random order. The workshops took up the issue of tacit knowledge related to the image articulation work. Watching and analysing the tapes and listening to the workers recount their experiences revealed this previously hidden work practice to the participants, and it was appreciated that the job of finding, selecting, arranging and laying out the relevant images on the light panels is a laborious process of going through a stack of new and old films in the patient folder and comparing them with various written documents. Selecting and organising the images requires a knowledge of their function as radiological representations, of their technical quality, of their relevance to the request and to the specific case, of the rules, norms and traditions of radiological image reading and even of the personal preferences of the radiologist making the interpretation, to name but a few items of tacit knowledge used in the task.

The workshops were the first occasion in the experimental teleradiology project on which the entire work practice of the teleradiology service, including the supporting part, were exposed, and they succeeded in providing a forum in which women's work, knowledge and expertise were brought forward as legitimate and consequential and articulated as an important design issue worthy of discussion.

3 A Brief Discussion of a Small Step

The attempts made to bring about a qualitative, gender-aware change in the teleradiology experiment by combining a field study of work practices with workshops aimed at contributing to the redesigning of the system, clearly fall beyond the scope of institutional and organisational gender politics affecting technological development, and merely add up to a small step at the level of work and systems design in the present setting. It may be regarded as an important step in several ways, however.

In the first place, it provided the participants with an example of an alternative approach to redesigning the system. It also succeeded in investing women with power at the local level, in their actual work situations, through using the system and attending the workshops aimed at redesigning it. The field study was focused on explaining the whole process of teleradiology, and took into account the practical conditions under which the women were working. The result was that the workers could be given some help in the settings created by use of the new technology and in the emerging work practice associated with the system.

Without the design intervention the redesigning process could have continued to be quite one-sided in its interests and focus. The workshops exposed the entire sequence of teleradiological work practice. The comparison of traditional and emerging work practices helped to point to some of the omissions regarding women's knowledge, expertise and practices that had been made in previous design process, in that these aspects were given a legitimate voice by highlighting the women's supporting work via video recordings and facilitating open discourse in the workshop, where different voices would be appreciated. Furthermore, important issues were raised in the workshops which were clearly of relevance to womens' work practice and could be used to generate information for use in redesigning the system so as to recognise the need for training in connection with the implementation of new technology and the need to develop working procedures in relation to the design of systems.

4 Acknowledgements

Special thanks are expressed to Sari Tuovila for sharing the fieldwork and to Kari Kuutti for cooperatively organising and facilitating the workshops. Thanks also go to the staff of the departments of radiology at Oulu University Hospital and the Kuusamo Health Centre for contributing to the investigation. Marjo Favorin, Tonja Molin-Juustila and Tuomo Tuikka are thanked for comments on an earlier draft of this paper.

5 References

1. Bell, D, Caplan, P, and Karim W.J. (Eds.): Gendered Fields, Women, Men and Ethnography, Routledge, London, 1993
2. Blomberg, J. Giagomi, J. Mosher, A. and P. Swenton-Wall (1993) Ethnographic Field Methods and Their Relation to Design. In Participatory Design: Principles and Practices. Schuler, D. and A. Namioka (Eds). Lawrence Erlbaum Associates, Hillsdale, NJ
3. Green, E, Owen, J. and Pain, D. (Eds.): Gendered by Design? Information Technology and Office Systems, Taylor & Francis, Basingstoke, 1993
4. Haraway, D: Situated Knowledges: The Science Question in Feminism and the Privilege of Partial Perspective, Feminist Studies 14, no. 3, pp. 575-599 (Fall 1988)
5. Henwood, F: Establishing Gender Perspectives on Information Technology: Problems, Issues and Oppertunities, in Green, E, Owen, J. and Pain, D. (Eds.): Gendered by Design? Information Technology and Office Systems, Taylor & Francis, Basingstoke, 1993
6. Jordan, B: Ethnographic Workplace Studies and CSCW, in Shapiro, D, Tauber, M. Traunmuller, R (eds.): The Design of Computer Supported Cooperative Work and Groupware Systems, Elsevier Science B.V, 1996
7. Karasti, H: What's Different in Gender Oriented ISD? Identifying Gender Oriented Information Systems Development Approach, in Adam, A. Owen, J. (Eds.): Proceedings of the 5th IFIP International Conference on Women, Work and Computerization, Breaking Old Boundaries - Building New Forms, Manchester, July 2-5, 1994
8. Oakley, A: Interviewing Women; A Contradiction in Terms, in Roberts, H. (ed.): Doing Feminist Research, Routledge, London, 1990
9. Rogers, Y: Reconfiguring the Social Scientist: Shifting from Prescription to Proactive Research, in Bowker et al (eds.): Social Science, Technical Systems and Cooperative Work (forthcoming)
10. Van Maanen, J: Tales from the field, University of Chicago Press, Chicago, 1988
11. Warren, C: Gender Issues in Field Research, Qualitative Research Methods, Vol. 9, Sage Publications Inc, 1988

12. Webster, J: Shaping Women's Work: Gender, Employment and Information Technology, forthcoming
13. Whitehead, T.L. & Conaway, M.E: Self, Sex and Gender in Cross-Cultural Fieldwork, University of Illinois Press, Urbana and Chicago, 1986

Introducing Point of Sale Technology in a Retail Chain Store: Voices from the Checkout Counter

Martha L. Nangalama and Andrew Clement

Faculty of Information Studies, University of Toronto
Toronto, Canada M5S 3G6

Abstract. Retail check-out work is one of the major areas of women's work which has been significantly transformed in the past decade through computerization and related managerial rationalisation initiatives. This paper reports on a case study of a retail store which sought to examine the implications of POS technology for checkout clerk jobs and to learn how the cashiers themselves experienced the changes in their work. Based on participant observation and interviews with cashiers and their managers, the study found that while some of the claimed benefits of POS in enhancing accuracy and productivity were valid, such gains were achieved through intensifying rather than simply automating work. Whereas POS had been adopted in the name of improving customer service, the result was often the opposite, due largely to staffing reductions in the pursuit of cost cutting. The cashiers reported they were having to work harder, with diminished opportunity to talk with and help customers. They felt more watched and less trusted. As the number of their co-workers dwindled, the security of their own hours and hence income was undermined.

1 Introduction

Let's go shopping for a moment in a 'typical' modern store. We are faced with shelves overflowing with goods, but finding a person to help is too often an exercise in frustration. Only when we have a purchase in hand and are headed out the door do we encounter a store employee, positioned to take our money. Retailing hasn't always been like this. What has happened to the store personnel and the work they used to do?

An enduring irony surrounding much of 'women's work' is that while so much part of everyday life, often even conducted in public view, it is yet so routinely overlooked. Perhaps nowhere is this more the case than with retail checkout work. However, its commonplace character should not lead us to overlook its significance. Cashier work simultaneously represents one of the largest female predominated occupations and the scene of dramatic transformation related to computerisation.

Increasing global and domestic competition has pressured many retailers to seek greater efficiencies. A principal strategy for this has been to expand and intensify the use of information technologies notably at the checkout counter. Point of Sale systems (or POS) have now been widely adopted in North America and Europe, both to improve revenues and to reduce costs involved in delivering products to customers. A key element of the technological shift is the use of optical scanning and computerised cash registers to capture product sales information; which in turn is used for marketing or sales functions, inventory control, forecasting, bookkeeping, etc. Proponents claim that the benefits that retail stores can gain from POS include improved checkout speed and accuracy, simplified training, and enhanced performance evaluation [4].

While the growing adoption of POS is a testimony to its attractiveness to management, there have so far been few studies of what switching to POS means for employees and customers. To begin such an investigation, it is useful to draw upon studies of clerical work informed by labour process perspectives. Where managers have computerized large pools of low status, 'women's work', researchers have often found that management has gained greater control over work and worker, the tasks become more routinized and speeded up, details of work performance are automatically recorded for surveillance, workers experience greater stress, and jobs are lost [2,3,6,11].

These findings are mainly derived from research conducted in administrative office settings. A similar pattern emerges from studies of retail work in the fast food industry, which brings in the added dimension of direct service to customers [9,10]. The studies of bank tellers by King and Randall [8] reported at the last Women, Work and Computerization Conference (1994), usefully highlight the importance of 'demeanour work', and the obstacles that computerization can put in the way of smooth interaction with customers.

These changes in service work are taking place against a disturbing backdrop of labour market trends. The number and proportion of temporary and part time workers in North America has been steadily increasing. Unemployment and partial employment figures reported by Statistics Canada and the US. Bureau of Labour Statistics [7] indicate a prolonged erosion of steady, full time employment towards contingent labour that is characteristic of checkout work. This reflects longstanding patterns of labour market stratification, that puts female predominated occupations in a weak strategic position *vis-a-vis* managerially led computerization drives. Consequently, many women, particularly in service industries, are finding their jobs and skills under a growing threat [1].

To gain insight into this complex and widespread phenomenon, involving the interplay of a host of technological, managerial, and social dimensions, this paper adopts the perspective of the workers themselves as they experience the changes in their working lives. The paper reports on a participant observer case study which paid close attention to the ways in which computerization had affected a group of store front personnel in the retail industry. In particular, the aim was to learn from the cashiers and other employees at a large chain drugstore how check out work had been transformed in recent years through the introduction of POS technologies. We used the various management and labour process claims mentioned above to structure the account. The principal guiding research questions were: what was the nature of a cashier's job, why do retail stores adopt POS, does POS increase cashier accuracy and productivity; how does POS affect cashier skills, does POS lead to labour reduction, is control over cashier work increased by POS, and how does POS affect customer service?

2 The 'Goodcare' Site Drugstore

This study was conducted at the "Goodcare" drugstore in a small Ontario city. The field researcher, Martha Nangalama, had been shopping at the store for several years and got to know some of the staff. Curious about the introduction of POS technologies, her subsequent postgraduate studies provided the opportunity to investigate this more systematically. The formal study was conducted over a period of nineteen weeks from January to June 1995. She spent spent from three to six hours a week at the store working on the floor. This involved shelving, observing the activities in the store, and talking with the cashiers and receivers about their work. Altogether, the researcher spent 69 hours of participant observation, and formally interviewed nine cashiers and five managers.

At the time of this study, Goodcare had twenty seven employees, four males (the associate, merchandise manager and two receivers/stockers) and twenty three females. All cashiers working at Goodcare were women with education levels ranging from high school graduates to some with university education. The university graduates indicated that they were working at Goodcare because of failure to find suitable jobs in their areas of study. Six cashiers had worked at Goodcare for one to three years while the other three cashiers had worked at Goodcare over ten years. Three of the newer cashiers had been employed elsewhere as cashiers and were able to compare their past experiences to their work at Goodcare. All managers had worked at Goodcare for ten to twenty-seven years.

Goodcare is one of 800 DrugCo stores across Canada which together in 1994 employed approximately 30,000 people. Many of these stores were equipped with computerised cash registers with POS capabilities at its checkout stations. Goodcare had six, with a lone non-computerised cash register at the postal outlet. To understand how Goodcare used this technology, the researcher worked with cashiers at several cash registers and noticed significant differences in how the postal outlet and computerised checkout stations functioned. Furthermore, the manner in which cashiers were supervised varied. In this respect, Goodcare provides a snapshot of traditional cashier work versus modern cashier work. Whereas the front checkout counters had a steady flow of customers (and cashier/customer interaction was shorter and appeared more controlled), the postal outlet area had fewer customers and a more relaxed atmosphere. Two of the cashiers who had previously worked at non-computerised stores, indicated that the postal outlet looked like their former places of work.

All Goodcare products had prices encoded into the computer system except postal outlet items. Lack of computerisation meant that postal clerks had to manually process more information than other store cashiers. Clerks entered the price of the item and pressed the corresponding button (e.g., parcel). One of the cashiers noted that when the register malfunctioned, cashiers just pulled out the till, placed it in a cupboard and used a price list to continue handling customer purchases. While the postal outlet was able to continue conducting business even when the cash register was broken the computerised cash registers could not be used in case of a malfunction and business had to be interrupted. Furthermore, at the postal outlet, customers took more liberty talking to cashiers. For example, in two hours spent with one of the cashiers, only 18 customers were served. This was far fewer than the front checkout where there was at least one customer every minute and cashiers hardly had time to do anything else. On one occasion at the postal outlet, a woman from a neighbouring bank chatted with the cashier for two minutes and purchased only one stamp. Another customer spent half an hour talking to the cashier and purchased nothing.

Relaxed interchanges between customers and cashiers seemed to be a quality that had been lost at the front checkouts. Although front cashiers talked to customers, conversations were brief. One cashier suggested that front checkout conversations were fairly mechanical:

> I think it [scanning] makes cashiers ... more industrialised - like you are just like a machine. You check them [customers] through, you just take their money and check them through. I think it is mostly depersonalising the service, like before you could nicely talk to the customer but now you just ring them through and have a conversation which is more mechanical... You don't even look at customers anymore....

Observation of the front cashiers at work confirmed the above description. Their work gave the impression that they were extensions of scanners and computerised cash registers. One day the researcher watched Darlene, a cashier, working at the checkout. A customer placed her purchase on the counter. Darlene briefly greeted the customer and within a matter of seconds had scanned the item, put it into a bag, collected cash, made change and turned to the next customer.

To achieve this smooth operation, the cashier had to work quickly and accurately, paying close attention to the purchase items and the screen display. For instance, before scanning the product, the cashier had to check for the location of the UPC code, the small set of black stripes and numbers attached to each product for identification. This didn't always work, and the process would have to be carried out again, or the code input manually. When cash registers failed to identify the product, the register screen displayed "Item Not Found in the System". The merchandise manager or the woman who operated the Pricing System Manager was then paged to provide a price for the product. This delayed the checkout process. All the cashiers pointed out that these unnecessary delays were the biggest problem they had experienced with the new technology.

3 Introducing POS

Reasons cited for the adoption of POS varied among the people interviewed. While cashiers indicated that speed and accuracy may have inspired the adoption of POS, Goodcare managers cited information control and increased accountability as factors contributing to POS adoption. The POS coordinator from head office suggested that DrugCo management were concerned about the level of customer service stores were providing. As a result, DrugCo felt that stores had to be given a means to provide excellent customer service without sacrificing the chain's financial performance. She indicated that repetitive tasks such as attaching prices to each individual product would be automated, leaving employees with more free time to attend to customer inquiries. Despite official head office desire to help local stores improve customer service, most cashiers were sceptical; one woman pointed out that customer service had deteriorated since the adoption of POS.

> Since they got this new system they [DrugCo management] keep cutting hours and cutting hours. And we keep saying, 'how do you expect us to keep providing superior customer service if we don't have the bodies to do it with?'... But [they] say everybody should be thinking customer service and we really can't think that way when you have four customers in line and need to leave your station to help another customer ...

Goodcare was busy at lunch time. During this time, customer inquiries were at their peak but cashiers were least likely to leave their counters and show customers where a product was located. Worse still, since employee work hours were reduced, customer service deteriorated. During the course of this project, the researcher and two high school students (all unpaid) often worked on the floor stocking shelves and answering customer inquiries. Although POS had been implemented almost three years earlier, there was no sign that Goodcare employees provided more customer service on the floor, as expected. Only the merchandise manager spent much time on the shop floor.

Although all Goodcare managers and the POS coordinator indicated that POS was introduced to improve store efficiency, their feelings regarding how increased efficiency would be achieved varied. For example, the store accountant who seemed satisfied with POS, said that:

> Point of Sale ... was introduced to make everything more efficient. To make checkouts faster [and to minimize product] categories when it was input manually. This way [a purchase] can't possibly go in the wrong category. [Before POS] the girls had to memorise all the categories.

The cashier manager, on the other hand, expressed fears that this system may have been introduced in order to eliminate jobs. After twelve years at Goodcare, she had seen many changes and firmly believed that the new technology would even eliminate some middle management jobs in time:

> I think POS was introduced to reduce the costs to DrugCo. And you know what those costs are? People. For example, POS can make you scan things faster, when everything is working. So the first reaction is, you do not need as many cashiers as before. You lay them off. Oh, but DrugCo won't do that. So you do not replace the ones who quit, you basically get rid of shifts, you end up with fewer cashiers. Then, you don't want anyone to lose their job, you cut a few hours here and there. The whole point ends up being you are reducing your labour cost. But ... I think DrugCo is now moving onto the managers.

At the time this project was conducted, no managers or cashiers had lost their jobs. However, the cashier manager's fears of job loss as a result of the new technology were supported; as discussed later, some cashier work hours were eliminated.

4 Accuracy and Speed

Prior to POS, Goodcare used to have the "DATA 2000" type of cash register. This type of register did not have scanners but products had codes. Entering the code into the register automatically provided the price, department, total purchase with tax and the change for the customer. Several cashiers mentioned that it was easy to enter the wrong code for a product on the Data 2000. All of them agreed that accuracy in checkout had been improved since the introduction of POS and that scanning technology reduced errors by automating the entry of product codes. Furthermore, since POS technology allows stores to preset prices, undercharging or overcharging customers is avoided. Nevertheless, there were several ways in which price discrepancies arose, causing service disruption, extra work for cashiers and frustration or embarrassment for customers. Inaccuracy occurred when the information provided by a centralised POS system differed from that entered at the local store. When prices were down loaded from head office to be edited by local stores, editing errors caused down loaded prices to differ from prices usually charged at the store. This discrepancy would be caught at the cash register - if a customer complained or the cashier noticed the mistake.

Such incidents reduced accuracy and created delays if cashiers had to leave their checkout stands to solve problems. One cashier suggested that some problems arose when customers misread labels; in order for POS to fully benefit the retail store, customers were required to contribute to the process. Since customers were often not socialised for this requirement, Goodcare employees had to do extra work whenever customers misread labels. This implies that the POS system was designed without adequately taking customers into consideration. Customers had to adjust from reading the price label on the product to reading the price label on the shelves, matching the UPC code on the product to the one on the shelf. Given the small size of the UPC code digits, reading and matching them is a hard task. Many cashiers at Goodcare indicated that scanning resulted in increased speed at the checkout, since cashiers could process more customer purchases. Not having to remember when a product was on sale meant that cashiers did not have to consult price lists as often as before introduction of POS. One cashier said:

> you can go a lot faster than the old cash registers and there is less opportunity for human error ... you don't have to worry about counting money. Like at my former place of work we had to memorize all the different departments, we had to know what was on sale to ring it through properly and that was every week. If we had to do it now with Goodcare, we would just, poof! ...

One can conclude that POS technology had increased work speed at the checkout. Nevertheless, despite increased speed, since the second phase of the POS project was introduced (MMS II in October 1994) the scanner and cashier manager's computers performed at a much slower rate than before. This decrease in speed caused unnecessary delays for cashiers and some managers. Two cashiers mentioned that slower computer speed for reports caused cashiers to spend a longer time in the office after their shift, waiting to be rung off. Worse still, on many occasions the computers or cash registers would break down - at least once a week during the research period. When this happened, some customers became so frustrated that they left the store without purchasing anything.

5 Cashier Skills and Reduction of Labour

Point of Sale technology malfunctions were not the only concerns at Goodcare. In a surprising revelation, one cashier indicated that POS technology had eroded her skills, since she could work faster than the POS system allowed. This cashier had worked with the semi-computerised cash register - DATA 2000- which had no scanning technology and had required her to key in product codes. She pointed out that the older system allowed experienced cashiers to work faster than POS. This indicates that POS was designed with little consideration for the experienced cashier, whose past knowledge was not put to use.

Cashiers' skills were affected in other ways too. By not requiring memorisation of prices and departments, POS de-skilled the cashier. By providing change for the cashiers, minimal arithmetic skills were required. If the cashier could recognise a twenty dollar bill and input that amount into the register, change would be provided and the cashier was only required to count. In addition, the trend towards debit cards for purchases is eliminating this counting aspect in cashiers' jobs, further reducing the need for cashiers.

At Goodcare, cashier labour was reduced via attrition in several ways. Many cashiers were students who returned to school in September or moved to another city to attend college or university. When store managers needed to eliminate hours, the staff who were leaving were not replaced. On other occasions, when managers needed to reduce employee hours - the hours of departing cashiers were reallocated to people who would otherwise have their work hours reduced.

According to the cashier manager, before POS was introduced, Goodcare had 12 to 15 cashiers; at the time of this study, there were only eight cashiers left in the store. The other staff had also experienced indirect labour cuts. For example, a woman who used to work full time in receiving and stocking the shelves retired in 1994 and was never replaced. Another employee who used to work on the floor full time, was moved to the postal outlet when it opened in 1994, while also working part time in receiving. As a result, the floor staff was reduced from four full time staff to two full time and one half timer in 1994.

Reductions in cashier work hours and floor staff affected everyone in the store. Whereas in the past when there were price discrepancies at the checkout counter, a cashier would have paged a floor person for a price check, she now has to go to the floor to verify prices;. Furthermore, due to the decreased number of floor staff, customers came to the checkouts for help more, but often could not be helped because the cashiers were busy scanning purchases. Several cashiers predicted that this situation would worsen if employee hours were further reduced, mentioning that management had reduced hours without fully considering the employees' work. A cashier who had lost four hours a week (the other two lost two hours each) noted that:

> [The associate] doesn't know what goes on so when he cuts hours, ... that really puts pressure on everyone to do more ....

Three managers suggested that the implementation of POS did not necessarily cause reduced hours; rather head office was attempting to reduce its costs. One manager's opinion, however, was that labour was being reduced because head office expected increased speed and reduced workload as a result of introducing POS. She said:

> What they [head office] tell you, it will save in the long run, it doesn't. Now, your computer experts will say 'oh that is because you are not following the proper procedures'. Okay, human error - which is true, but ... customers are human, staff are human ... And staff say, 'well we used to have so many people working on the floor' whatever and now we are short staffed. And they say 'no, according to the new system, we are not short staffed, you have to work harder, faster and more accurate.'

In order for Goodcare to increase productivity and accuracy in POS, the employees were expected to work harder. Hence it is unclear how much productivity increase resulted from the new technology and what resulted from making store employees work harder and faster. At the very least, this supports Dunlop and Kling's (1991) argument that organisations often uncritically assume that technology will lead to increased productivity [5].

6 Controlling Work and Informing the Boss

Point of Sale technologies allow an organisation to measure productivity and control processes by various means. At Goodcare, all computerised cash registers automatically shut off if no cashier used them for two minutes displaying "THIS LINE IS NOW SECURED". This control feature reduced the need for a supervisor's presence and discouraged cashiers from leaving their cash registers unattended. For example, while Denise - a cashier - was working at the cosmetics counter, she was not scanning products as often as the front cashiers. As a result, she had to log onto the register more frequently. Forcing the cashiers to log onto the cash register before using it produced a record for management of who was using a cash register at any time. Every cashier left a trace of her activities in the computer system and this information allowed management to easily pinpoint the performance, mistakes, and 'balancing record' of each cashier.

Subsequent investigation revealed that not only could store managers determine a cashier's performance by looking at the information generated by POS, but managers could also observe a cashier at work via the computers in their offices. One manager said that electronic monitoring was only carried out if there were grounds to suspect that a cashier was being dishonest; for example if she had too many voids on her journal tape or never 'balanced'. Other managers said that they did not have the extra time that monitoring would require. Yet another manager felt that it was unethical, preferring to talk to an employee rather than "snooping" via the computer screen.

By knowing all the sales and staff activity in the store, DrugCo management could more easily control cash operations. One cashier compared DrugCo to her former place of work, concluding that DrugCo had far more controls. She pointed that if mistakes on the product code aren't noticed until after the transaction, DrugCo cashiers are prevented by the POS system from carrying out a cash register void on their own, and must wait for a supervisor, thereby causing longer line ups and frustrated customers..

In spite of the overall increase in work controls at Goodcare since introduction of POS technologies, the cashiers visibly worked as a team and trusted each other. This was observed, for example, one day when Nadia (cashier) went for lunch. She pulled out her cash drawer and placed it underneath the counter. The other cashiers watched her 'till' while she was on her lunch break. In other ways too, Goodcare still relied on employee honesty for its day to day operations. In any case, this pattern of close control contradicted DrugCo literature claiming to treat its employees as members of "one big family". In reality, the employees were treated like troublesome people who had to be monitored in everything they did.

There were other signs of solidarity among some of the cashiers in the face of subordination within the managerial and technological regime of the drug store franchise. For example, one cashier observed that, "We cashiers do the hardest work around here, but we are paid the least". Interestingly, there is little sign that they related this to the clearly gendered division of labour. Cashiers never spontaneously brought up gender in the interviews or conversations. However, when the cashier supervisor was asked why all the cashiers were women, she replied "Because they can take a lot more BS [from customers] than men."

While there appears to be little gender consciousness among these cashiers and a pattern of compliance in the face of mistreatment by managers or customers, there has been at least one recent attempt at collective action. When the POS technologies were first introduced in 1993, Goodcare cashiers expressed strong interest in joining a union, prompting a visit by head office managers. This "calmed things down" sufficiently that the drive faltered and no subsequent attempts at organizing have been made. Ironically the very aspects of the work that unionizing might help remedy - the insecure, part-time nature of the job - also make organizing in settings like this especially difficult.

7 Conclusion

In summary, DrugCo adopted POS to: provide better information tracking for management; provide better control over the retail chain store's operations; and reduce labour costs. Although some managers suggested that the technology was introduced to simplify work and allow store employees to provide better customer service, this study has shown ways in which customer service deteriorated after POS was adopted. This poor customer service is attributable to fewer employees and minimal training for users of the new technology. Therefore, the Goodcare case demonstrates that even if DrugCo prided itself on "exemplary" customer service, local store employees were not in a position to attend to customer needs. If DrugCo seriously wished to improve customer service, its local stores like Goodcare would have to stop reducing employee hours.

This study has revealed that great differences existed between working in computerised and more traditional non-computerised environments. At Goodcare, postal outlet cashiers could check out purchases manually and process requests even when the cash register was broken. Front cashiers, on the other hand, could not process purchases manually when the computerised cash register broke down. Although non-computerised cash registers provided little control over cashier work, computerised cash registers allowed management to effectively monitor cashiers' activities whenever desired. Overall, management control over cashier work at Goodcare increased with the introduction of POS, contradicting DrugCo literature claims that employees were treated like family, in a 'caring and supportive' way.

One cannot deny that POS technology improved accuracy and increased checkout speed. Nevertheless, we cannot ignore the circumstances which counteracted these benefits. Accuracy was sometimes undermined by price discrepancies in the computer system, by lack of customer adaptation, and by system malfunctions. While POS simplified cashier work, the workload for cashiers and some immediate supervisors was actually increased. But here again, the effect is mainly due to management choices over staffing levels rather than inherent technological requirements. Although no Goodcare employees were laid off, company management achieved net labour reduction via attrition, hour redistribution, and hour reduction. These managerial practices account for the 'hollowing out' of store operations and the disappearance of floor personnel.

While some of the changes can clearly be attributed solely to the shift from manual to computerized cash registers, the effects on check out work derived much more from deeper 'systemic' shifts in the management of retail operations. The adoption of POS technologies in this case was only part, albeit a major and highly visible part, of a wider strategy of reducing costs and centralizing effective control. In other words, this depressingly familiar trajectory of degraded service, subordinated employees and routinized interactions between people is due not so much to intrinsic characteristics of the computing technology, but to choices about implementation made by the lead actors. Reversing this dismal trend will likely require that service personnel better recognize their collective interests both as women and as workers, make their work more visible to others, and voice their concerns more loudly. At the same time, it would help if customers insisted on real human service - as well as showing appreciation when given. By linking such approaches, cashiers and customers alike can find some common cause. Going shopping could then become much more an activity for social exchange and rewarding work.

Acknowledgements

We are grateful to the staff at Goodcare for so generously sharing their experiences and views. Martin Dowding and Lucy Suchman contributed valuable editorial assistance. SSHRC provided research funding.

References

1. Appelbaum, E.(1993) New Technology and Work Organization: The Role of Gender Relations, B. Probert & B. Wilson (eds.), *Pick Collar Blues*, Melbourne.
2. Braverman, H.(1974). *Labour and Monopoly Capital: The Degradation of Work in the Twentieth Century*. New York: Monthly Review Press.
3. Clement, A. (1992). Electronic Workplace Surveillance: Sweat Shops and fishbowls. *The Canadian Journal of Information Science*, 17(4). p.18-45.
4. Duncan, J. (1991). The Essentialities of Productivity in Information Services. *The Information Society 8*. pp.77-82.
5. Dunlop, C. & Kling, R. (eds.) (1991). *Computerisation and Controversy: Value Conflicts and Social Change*. Boston: Academic Press.
6. Garson, B. (1988). *The Electronic Sweat Shop: How Computers are Transforming the office of the Future into the Factory of the Past*. New York: Simon & Schuster.
7. Greenbaum, J. (1994). Windows on the Workplace: The Temporisation of Work. *Proceedings of the 5th IFIP International Conference on Women, Work and Computerisation*. Adam, A. & Owen, J. (eds.)..

8. King, V. & Randall, D.(1994). Just Trying To Keep The Customers Satisfied ... Information Technology and Clerical Work in a Financial Institution. *Proceedings of the 5th IFIP International Conference on Women, Work and Computerisation.* Adam, A. & Owen, J., (eds.), pp.345-359.
9. Leidner, R.(1993). *Fast Food, Fast Talk: Service Work and the Routinization of Everyday Life.* Berkeley: University of California Press.
10. Reiter, E. (1991). *Making Fast Food: From the frying pan into the fryer.* Montreal: McGill-Queen's University Press
11. Rule, J. & Brantley, P. (1992). The Computerised Supervisor: A New Meaning to 'Personal Computing'. *IFIP Transactions, Managing Information Technology's Organisational Impact, II.* Clarke, R., & Cameron, J. (eds.), Amsterdam: Elsevier Science, pp. 287–297

Accepted Papers and Discussion Notes

Topic 5: Education

Part 1: From School to Informatics: Inclusion or Exclusion?

Why has Female Participation in German Informatics Decreased?

Prof. Britta Schinzel

Institute for Informatics and Society
University of Freiburg, Friedrichstr. 50, D-79098 Freiburg, Germany

Abstract. The deplorable decrease of women in German informatics is due to a number of specific causes unhappily interacting. The effects appear mainly in high school[1]. The structure of the German school system with its coeducational element and the continuous shifts in contents and technical resources in the subject of computer science negatively influence female participation. This effect is augmented by the typical German association of science and engineering with masculinity. The context-dependency of coeducation is apparent. For example, coeducation does not lead to the same consequences in Romanic or Slavic countries[2]. This paper explains why and how within the context of the coeducational system in Germany the computer has developed into an instrument to keep girls away from informatics. It also shows some effects of the structure of the university curriculum which create a problematic environment for women within the field[3]. However the situation seems to be changing, therefore, we will indicate circumstances which might be improving the position of women in computer education.

Motivation for the Investigation

The decrease of female participation in the school-subject informatics does not only keep women away from the relevant professions. Knowledge of computer use and programming will form a critical filter for a wide variety of skilled professions. In Europe, we expect a substantial and competent use of computers in more than 60% of all jobs in the year 2000. If women stay away from the computer it will considerably decrease their options in choosing academic education (e.g. in science and engineering) and impair their future career chances. A deeper gender-based segregation in the job market will be the consequence.

[1] these are results found in a joint project with Dr. Christiane Funken and Prof. Dr. Kurt Hammerich on "Female and Male Pupils in the Subject Informatics", an investigation of 1128 pupils in the 11th schoolyear from 18 out of the 24 gymnasiums in the region of Aachen in 1990. This was the biggest sample ever tested on the theme in German speaking countries. (Funken, Hammerich, Schinzel, 1996)

[2] see for example (Durndell 1991)

[3] these are results found in our current project about "The Situation of Students in Informatics" (SSI) by C. Freyer, C. Funken and B. Schinzel. In 1994 all informatics students in the first, fourth and eighth semester in Germany have received a standardized questionnaire, fourty percent of whom returned it filled in.

Moreover, female reluctance to participate in the university subject computer science, in software development and application programming will find its reflection in the software itself: deficits caused by the lack of female competence in these areas will harm not only female but also male computer users.

Introduction

Since 1983 the participation of women in academic studies of informatics in Germany has decreased from more than 20% to between 11-9%. From 1991 to 1994, the percentage of female newcomers amounted to only 5 - 7%. These considerable cuts can be traced back to the introduction of PCs into households, and the reunion of East and West Germany. In 1986 50% of students of informatics in East Germany were women.As of today these universities are down to the same level as in West Germany. Fortunately the numbers are rising again: in 1995 there were over 9,5% newcomers and female participation as a whole was 8,7% [4]. But again there is some evidence that this is due to the rising participation of foreign students: our investigation into "The Situation of Students in Informatics" (SSI) showed for example that in 1994/95 11% of the female informatics students came from foreign countries while only 6% of the male students were foreigners. This means that among the German students the females constitute on even a smaller percentage than 8,7%.

At first sight, the hesitation to choose a new and promising field seems paradoxical, if we take into account that women are not biologically determined to be less capable or interested in the subject. Girls and women have equal opportunities and access to education and choice of subjects. Why should women restrict themselves to interests less beneficial in terms of further career and even job hunting? This cannot be a conscious decision or plan.

Causes in the German School System

In their choice of subjects, distinctive tendencies have been noticed for boys and girls. And partially it is due to the fact that the choice of subjects is highly optional in German high school. In senior grades (from age 16) no subjects are mandatory, restrictions only apply to the combination of subjects. Whereas boys mostly choose subjects from the complex of sciences, engineering and mathematics, girls keep away from these subject. This trend has been on the increase since 1980. Metz-Göckel and various coauthors (1988, 1989, 1992) see the reasons in the increase of coeducational secondary schools in this period. Girls who have not chosen such a subject as “optional/mandatory subject” by the ninth school year will not choose it as an “in-depth subject” in the eleventh or later. So the German “course choice system” imposes the professional course on the eighth graders at the age of thirteen (Roloff 1989, Kreienbaum, Metz-Göckel 1992). This is the age of adolescent problems, when girls have an insecure female identity and are therefore likely to hold on to traditional role models promising better security. With respect to education, these roles imply that

[4] according to the Fakultätentag Informatik 1995

competence in science and engineering is strictly a male domain, an attitude heavily confirmed by the boys in the same classroom for the corresponding reasons.

A further reason for the girls' preferences can be seen in the choice offered by the course system, which seems to be adapted more to boys' interests. It was found that while the interests of the boys as a group tend to indicate more homogeneity in the choice of subjects throughout the high school years, girls' interests vary, and this is reflected in the combinations they choose. But the course system favours certain combinations and inhibits the girls' free choice (Kreienbaum, Metz-Göckel, 1992). For example the research already mentioned, showed that the combination of religion and computer science was not possible, but desired by a number of girls who consequently only chose religion. No boys wished to choose this combination.

As a whole the choice system is opposed to typical girls' interests such as getting an overview, or obtaining a holistic picture of the connection between the subjects and knowledge in general. In any case the point at which the course of education is selected is too early to allow for awareness of the professional implications of subject choice. At the age of fourteen girls do not consciously decide on their future professional life, as they know far too little about their opportunities and inclinations. But unfortunately, unwillingly they restrict their future choices. As a consequence they end up in social or service areas or they receive education in humanities or social sciences, where jobs are rare and by far less well-paid than in science and engineering.

On the other hand according to our SSI investigation, the relevance of the school subject informatics to the decision to major in informatics is questionable: most of our informatics students considered it to be of low importance. As for the female students, especially the younger ones, hardly any of them had chosen the subject at school.As a consequence female students start their university studies in informatics with very little computer and programming experience. We will examine the implications of these facts later in the paper.

Computing Occupations

Up to the early eighties access to computers was reserved for adults. Interest in computer science was mainly driven by interests in (non-numeric applications of) Mathematics. With the penetration of PCs into households computers were made accessible to children. It was mostly boys who took advantage of this and they used them mainly for games or as a hacking medium to outwit restrictions such as access boundaries etc. According to our investigations, not only twice as many boys as girls have access to a computer, but frequently boys also have their own PCs, whereas girls, at best, are allowed to use their father's or brother's PC. German parents seem to resist their daughters' ambitions to own their own PCs. It appears that parents in Romanic or Slavic countries do not share this attitude. Girls in single sex schools are slightly better equipped with computer resources.[5]. Also no decrease of interest in the subject computer science has been observed in these schools.

Consequently the situation for computer science in schools is characterized by the advantage of some boys in relation to their familiarity with computer, often setting the

[5] as they are mostly eldest children in the family their wishes seem to be taken more seriously.

pace and the priorities in the classroom. As a result, the remaining students are excluded. No wonder computer science is the school subject with the largest decrease of interest. In particular girls´ participation shrinks continuously from an initial 40% in the eleventh class to 1% in the thirteenth (Sander 1986).

The SSI investigation shows that, in contrast to the boys, 78% of the female students had no access to a computer during school time. Accordingly only the male students expressed interest in computer work as a reason for their choice of the subject. The females on the other hand made their decision in spite of their lack of experience in programming. Also our SSI investigation implies that the decision to go to university and the choice of the subject informatics is made at an older age by female students than by male students. Also in the case of the female students this decision is directed more by job and future work considerations than by an intrinsic interest in the subject, unlike to the male students. In a context with the gender based partition of labour and of professional content, this is a remarkable finding. Normally intrinsic interests are attributed to female students while extrinsic motivations are attributed to the male students.

Shifts in the Subject´s Identity

There has been a shift in the identification of computer science from discrete applications of mathematics to an orientation towards applied and engineering sciences. It is well known, that the participation of women in mathematics is much higher than in engineering. On one hand this paradigm shift presumably is a consequence of the similarity between computer science and engineering with respect to the requirement of resources to build the artifacts. On the other hand it is also the outcome of continuing problems with software quality and its assumed alleviation by engineering methods. Although these methods are to a large extent derived from organizational and social sciences, the mere notion of engineering gives a flair to the subject, attributing in the German context[6] to the male identification and at the same time discriminating against female competence. In cooperation with gender role models this shift from mathematics to engineering is one of the major causes for ruling women out of computer science in Germany. This phenomenon does not seem to hold with equal strength in the United States. There engineering sciences which encompass software engineering, have connected with social sciences and humanities (Martin, (Martin D. et al, 1996).

Consequently the SSI investigation revealed that for the existing female students (the few survivors) in informatics neither the identification with engineering, nor the computer as a working tool had any relevance, they chose the subject in spite of these gender odds. Taken this we believe that the percentage of female informatics students would increase dramatically if there were less identification with engineering and if girls were familiarized with computers during school as much as boys. Anyway for male students the interest in computers has been of far higher importance for the decision to study informatics than for females. As only a few female students have had

---

[6] not in Bulgaria or other countres of the former Soviet Union, nor in most countries of the third world like Egypt or South America.

experience with computers it is clear that this is not a motive for women to study informatics. Unlike the male students they don´t mention talents and abilities as reasons for their choice of subject, but job expectations and future professional considerations. With such a rational utilitarian approach they are inverting the assumed gender-based motives for choice of subject: females have intrinsic motivations and male students follow extrinsic ones. Another finding of the SSI was that both female and male students in informatics equally expect interesting work in their future jobs and - females more than males - a good scientific training in their university courses.

Recently a further shift in the scope and contents of the discipline has started. This shift is caused by the new possibilities in networking. The use of computers is moving from a production, workplace and organization supporting tool to a medium supporting communication and providing information and knowledge. Thereby new skills of computer scientists are needed to push the subject closer to the social sciences and humanities. As communication is the major competence of the female gender role this should have a strong impact on the self definition of the subject and a positive effect on the participation of women in the field. Unfortunately these new aspects have not yet been incorporated into German school and university curricula. The presentation of informatics might still be based on a very technical and formal view of the subject with the consequences for the female students that have already been mentioned. In the United States we already find curricular alterations encompassing knowledge from social sciences and humanities as necessary for the new needs and paradigms.

Other Causes

In this part I will refer mainly to the literature (Dick 1987, 1988, 1990, Enders-Dragässer 1989, Faulstich-Wieland 1987 and 1989, Hofmann 1987, Horstkemper 1990, Schiersmann 1987, Volmerg 1991,Wagner 1982) for the well known reasons inhibiting girls from getting involved with information processing techniques. Of course all of the following findings do not hold for every single student or adult person, but they do show tendencies and frequencies. Also these studies show the constitution of the general social processes connected with the new medium of computers and the subject computer science.

Here causes lie in

- the less beneficial family situation of girls for gaining experience and self confidence in mathematical, technical and scientific contexts,
- the unequal distribution of resources (like playing and learning materials and parents´ interests) among boys and girls, the gender stereotypes carried within these materials;
- the consequences of the stereotypical capabilities of each gender with respect to science and engineering, like social discrimination, discouragement and demotivation in everyday school life, especially in the coeducational situation;
- the strong influence, or even pressure, of (male and female) friends, to fulfill the role models of the peer group, which are extremely conservative in respect of gender roles in Germany;

- unequal crediting of the different (socially created) gender - based interests in the classroom, in teachers' consciousness and in the curricula (i.e. the girls´ are more reason-oriented motivations, the boys´ more play-oriented motivations);
- teachers and parents do not point out to girls the usefulness of technical and scientific subjects for their future professions (if they accept the gender-based job market), whereas this is made transparent for the boys;
- in particular in coeducational situations boys are treated as being more competent, they are given more attention, are asked questions more frequently and more is demanded of them ; implicit assumptions are made about their higher competence, although this does not comply with reality. As a consequence girls attribute themselves less and boys more competence - as do the boys - than is justified by reality.
- Boys are well aware of the better or equal competence of girls in the classroom even though higher expectations are put on boys. This leads them to think they were discriminated against by teachers, and often makes them extremely aggressive towards girls, especially in computer courses. (Barz 1984)
- Boys also tend to lay claim to an expert status, and sometimes pursue strategies to hold this status even if it is unjustified. This they achieve by throwing around acronyms, keeping good solutions to themselves, not answering questions, confusing girls under the pretence of help, bluffing, etc. (Kreienbaum et al 1992). Boys enjoy demonstrating knowledge but they do not want to share it. The explanation for this behaviour lies in the importance of the computer and technical competence in the constitution of male identity in German speaking countries.
- Another cause may be seen in the different choice of sources of information about informatics in university: according to our investigation (SSI) female students gain their knowledge from people of their social context (friends, family) while male students refer to more "objective sources" (professional consulting, teachers). Our female informatics students were lucky, as they were supported by parents and friends in their choice of subject. But if women in general tend to rely more on information from their social context, then the socially imparted role images will be transported together with the advice.

Coeducation

The social processes described lead girls to socially generated likes and dislikes, reducing self confidence within technical areas. If the opponent is missing (girls in single sex schools: GS) the segregation of interests (as found for girls in coeducational schools: GK) disappears. For boys, who are considered here in coeducational schools only (B) this holds as well (Funken et al 1996). The following table gives the percentage of answers from (about 600) students, once having chosen the subject computer science, to the question "which subject do you prefer, e.g. German or computer science?".

	GS	GK	B
German *vs.*	43	71	32
Computer science	57	30	68
English *vs.*	49	77	48
Computer Science	51	23	52
Arts *vs.*	43	66	29
Computer Science	57	34	72
Social Sciences *vs.*	40	52	31
Computer Science	60	48	69
History *vs.*	42	69	51
Computer Science	58	31	49
Physics *vs.*	20	27	50
Computer Science	80	73!	51
Biology *vs.*	56	77	41
Computer Science	44	23	59
Mathematics *vs.*	48	73	68
Computer Science	52	27	32

Tab 1. Subjects´ Interests compared with Informatics´ Interests (in %)

Analogous findings hold for the distribution of self-esteem within the respective subjects. Moreover, we found a correlation between segregation of interests and self confidence and the percentage of boys in the classroom!

Strangely it has been observed, that girls (not boys) alter their social behaviour (Kreienbaum et al,1992) in gender-mixed situations, whereas in women-only groups they show the same variety of social behaviour as boys, i.e. from cooperative to aggressive and destructive. In mixed groups they are uniquely cooperative, and adopt the inferior "secretary" role (Kauermann et al 1988, 1989) also without pressure from the boys.

Furthermore our investigations showed that the students have conceptions of skills and properties required for professions centered around computers, which coincide with their conceptions of male skills and properties. Especially boys believe, that males have the better professional skills, and are more assertive, persevering and cooperative, but this belief is shared by the girls.

Also the role-ideals were investigated by asking for desirable skills of prospective sons and daughters. Subject skills were much less favoured for daughters than for sons. Summing up the findings: sons should be equipped equally with good professional and private skills and properties, whereas for daughters, skills for coping with their private lives were expected. This means most students believe that informatics is a male profession, and that they find traditional role models desirable. Consequently women in informatics are bound to be outsiders, either they are competent or they fulfil their gender role; doing both together is a very difficult act of balance, especially in adolescence.

We also asked about life planning. Male students expect and wish to have a contented partner and family, whereas female pupils center on their personal needs.

Obviously they anticipate the difficulties within family life in fulfilling their own professional wishes. This is consistent with their more critical attitude towards marriage found in our investigation. German girls do not expect to be able to remain in a job when they have children. We found that the girls´ anticipated private and public roles are extremely contradictory. Still the girls do not rebel against the role models, but share them and want to pass them on to their own children. Although girls claim equal chances and abilities for themselves personally, they do not believe in them for their own gender. Obviously this discrepancy between role self-comprehension and role guidance has important consequences in this context.

Although the percentage of female students coming in single sex schools is between one and two percent, these girls make up for up 13% of the female students in informatics. But the single sex schools are vanishing from the educational scene. Also our empirical study on the "Situation of Students in Informatics"(SSI) also shows that with growing youth the fraction of female students with offspring from a single sex school is decreasing to 9% in the first semester.

Reasons for Studying Informatics at University (According to the SSI Investigation)

Expectations about the contents of informatics are wrong: 69% of the students believe that the informatics curriculum focuses on programming. These false expectations are shared equally by male and female students, but bear differently on the two genders. Male students may become uninterested in the subject when they find their expectations not fulfilled, and may halt their studies. As the females are less acquainted with programming their self confidence in respect of the subject is lower: as pointed out above, female students choose the subject in spite of their lack of programming experience and in the expectation that they might overcome these expected deficiencies after some amount of work at the beginning of their studies.

In line with their expectations of the contents the expectations of necessary skills for studying informatics are also wrong: skills required for studying informatics are widely identified with programming skills. Therefore especially the hackers and freaks are disappointed with the different emphasis of the university subject. In the introductory courses they sometimes loudly express their frustration and try to influence the curriculum. The image of computer freaks and hackers widely determines the image of students in informatics, although three quarters of the students in this subject do not wish to become hackers. But the hacker model keeps a lot more females away from the subject than males, and also among students in informatics females disapprove of this model more strongly than male students (SSI).

After this necessary correction of expectations a number of possibly justified disappointments in the curriculum need to be overcome: both genders are heavily interested in practical problems and applications. Male students are more interested in system development, female students tend slightly more to applications and are significantly more interested in theoretical informatics than men. Both genders complain about the lack of examples of applications, the delayed revelation of the practical value of the curricular contents, the lack of coherence between the courses, and the failure to point out any links with social interaction. In summary they complain about the abstractness and the distance from real working life of a computer scientist. For both genders this is consistent with their answers in respect of the necessary skills and capabilties for the working life of a computer scientist.

A further reason for discontent is the fact that the students see group work of the most efficient way of conducting their investigations - in particular the females (68% against 54% of the men) prefer this form of learning - , in computing examples, in project and seminar work, but also in individual studying. In contrast to these students' preferences most teaching is given in form of lectures. The students consider group working as successful, when there is an atmosphere of sympathy, when the group stay together, if the level of knowledge is comparable and if there is mutual willingness to perform within the group.

The pretest for our investigation showed the importance of some of the socio-cultural behaviour amongst colleagues: the chatting and conversation between the courses mostly evolve around current hardware and commercially oriented computer techniques and computer games. This rules out the female students, because they are more concerned about the content of the courses as well as political and cultural subjects. Especially at the start females get the impression they are not learning the right things, because the conversations deal with acronyms and themes not taught within the courses, but obviously belonging to the field. As they are not experienced in those conversational topics, women easily feel incompetent. They are astonished when they find out that in spite of their own feeling of incompetence they are performing well on the courses and examinations. Very often women therefore claim that they must have a very high level of self confidence and courage to be able to compare themselves with the male students.

Information Technology at Work

In contrast to the school findings, on computer courses women show greatest interest and success (Brandes, Schiersmann 1986). Women and men at work share the same interest in computers (Brosius, Haug 1987), while non-working married women have a greater distance from engineering and technical issues in general. Moreover a correlation has been found between the age of the husband and animosity towards computers on the part of the wife (Brosius, Haug 1987). The same study brought forth the more distinct opinion of younger men in Germany, that women are incapable of technical thinking: This favours the assumption that the competition in the jobmarket has far a stronger influence on prejudices about gender capabilities than has been realized.

Still jobs with computers are kept by women as well as by men, but there the gender hierarchy of work and income is reproduced again.

Also the findings about critical or enthusiastic attitudes towards information technology, their dangers and their values vary to the point where they are contra-dictory, i.e. they show great context dependencies (Schelhowe 1988). This, among other reasons, supports the denial of gender typologies as manifest talents or invariants. This variability in attitude and opinion gives us hope that there is a potential for change in Germany.

The Role of Computers in Negotiations about Gender Roles

From the above it is obvious that girls' choices are not driven by a deficient socialization of women, leading them to disinterest and incompetence in the subjects considered. Rather it stems from male dominance inhibiting girls and women from exercising certain capabilities and from the cultural embedding of that training. Moreover in informatics it can be observed how masculinization not only determines the environment, but increasingly also the subject matter and didactics.

Already in childhood boys play with aggressive computer games, disliked by girls. Since programming has become an important economic factor, these jobs have migrated from women to men (programming had been a women's job until the fifties), since informatics is an important academic subject, curricula have been disregarding female interests, and the self-definition of the subject migrates from mathematics to engineering. Men create the aggressive computer games, catching the attention of boys by transporting a certain image of masculinity; boys push the school subject matter in direction of equipment opposed to the holistic interests of girls, computer journals and -clubs carry myths of qualifications not matching the real requirements of university study nor of the profession, but coinciding with the male interests. By dominating the development of technology and by excluding women from the computer environment, men cut women off from informal knowledge, from implicit learning, from learning by doing.

This all shows that informatics and computing is not neutral with respect to social processes. As soon as a new medium like computing arrives, negotiations start about definitions and the distribution of resources around it. The relation between genders is enclosed in this process. As far as the computer is concerned these negotiations with respect to gender have clearly moved the subject into the male domain. Distance from or affinity towards computers are part of and the result of these gender combats. Engineering and computers therefore are also employed to maintain the (seemingly natural) distribution of work and resources between the genders.

We have seen how intensively school is unconsciously setting the pace in this process. In school not only is knowledge transmitted, it is also a field for communication and negotiations. In coeducational schools these negotiations also contribute to the definition of the future gender roles and the gender-driven distribution of resources. The computer has become an influential resource for these negotiations with respect to gender identity, at least in German speaking countries. Thus genderdependent domains of knowledge are constituted defining normative interests and achievements. The respective peer groups hold and enforce these norms, because parental influence decreases when the youth's identity is established. With the distance from home the influence of friends and peer group increases. Individualization against these groups is achievable only at the cost of isolation. For occupations with computers boys win social respect, girls the contrary.

From the outset, the difference in confidence, interests and personal role understanding between girls from coeducational and single sex schools can be understood. For students from single sex schools, the confrontation with the contradiction between individualization through unconventional professional goals and prevailing gender roles is much weaker than in coeducational schools. The confrontation with the male world is postponed until the time the girls enter the hetero-world: university, professional training or a job. The advantage of this postponement is that by the time this confrontation does happen, the girls are much better prepared for it. Self-identity, self-confidence and life planning one better developed and more stable. For girls in coeducational schools it is not possible to live with the controversy between claim and possibility. The early confrontation with male pretensions hardly allows them to follow the contradictory aims, their scope of action by role and life- expectation is highly restricted. Not even interest and good school performance in science or informatics help in convincing them, that choosing a related profession will lead to a worthwhile occupation for women.

The Exceptions - and Positive Trends: Women in Informatics and Computing

In the former GDR the stronger representation of girls and women can be explained by the different school system: also girls gained experience in technical matters via the polytechnic courses. Children experienced their mothers working and not only at home, a fact that may also influence the difference in participation of women in science, engineering and informatics within economically less developed countries than Germany, like Italy, Spain, Greece, or the Slavic countries. Also the identification of technology with masculinity is not found to the same extent as in Germany.

But all the findings or assumptions made in (West) Germany do not resolve the question, why some girls and women (not only those from single sex schools, which hardly exist any more) still find their way to informatics, science and engineering.

Some girls and women build their self confidence and identity from an oppositional attitude: towards role models, parents and/or teachers.

Whereas in the seventies and early eighties the support of the fathers (mostly of the eldest child) helped girls to find identification with these subjects, today this no longer holds: today the support of the mothers is also given, as younger children gain more freedom from role expectations.

Female expertise also often exists without being noticed: the secret female experts at school are detected only in written exams or by chance (Roloff 89, Kreienbaum 92).

It is not yet possible to interpret the rising female participation of newcomers in informatics in Germany. There is some evidence that the increased rate stems from foreign students: in Stuttgart for example [7] the percentage of German female newcomers is 7%, whereas the rate of foreign female newcomers is 25%, raising the entire rate of female newcomers in informatics. But there is also hope that improvement has taken place in German education.

Recapitulating the causes for women's draw back from informatics I would like to give some conjectures for today's improvement:

- children's situation has changed: computers are more often also available for girls, parents are starting to realize the value of computer competence for girls
- the number of computer games available on the market now has grown enormously, among them also didactically very good and non-aggressive ones;

[7] Private information by Prof. Dr. Volker Claus

- there is also a great variety of educational and training software available. Children and parents are conscious of this and support training on good games and software also for girls. All this might have influence on peer groups with regard to the computer being employed as an instrument for the constitution of role models.

The findings about coeducational problems in the early eighties have won a great deal of public attention. This may have created teachers' awareness of the problem, a first step towards the solution. Numerous school experiments with partially single sex training in science and informatics have been very successful.

This may explain a good part of the growing numbers of female newcomers in informatics today.

The German Society of Informatics (GI FB 7) as well as professional school units (Landesinsitut Soest 1993, DIFF in Niederdrenk-Felgner 1993) have edited recommendations (Schulz-Zander 1993) for school curricula, which in part have been realized. Thereby the girls' motives and interests with respect to meaning, orientation and holistic as well as critical views are better met.

For the university curricula such changes are still outstanding in Germany. As mentioned before in the U.S. there already exist curricular proposals with balanced indepth in social content as in the mathematical-technical content (Martin 96).

Also according to our SSI investigation there is evidence that the rating of the importance of a school course in informatics is decreasing. Of the female students only 26% were interested in the subject during their school years (males 43%) and only 19% of the female informatics students were motivated by a school course to study informatics. Therefore to support women in the decision to study informatics it might be more effective to

focus on future workplaces than on trying to make women more enthusiastic about programming: programming is not the main occupation of computer scientists, but it is communication! It is well known that not only for the work with the new communication and information media but also for classical software development three quarters of the time is spent in communication - and this is an aptitude typical of women.

I would like to thank the referees for their constructive comments and Gila Jasper and MashaMakowski for their help in polishing my English.

References

1. Barz, Monika: Was Schülerinnen und Schülern während des Unterrichts durch den Kopf geht und wie sich ihr Denken dabei verknotet. In: Wagner, Angelika: Bewußtseinskonflikte im Schulalltag, Weinheim 1984.
2. Brandes, Uta und Schiersmann, Christiane (Institut Frau und Gesellschaft): Frauen, Männer und Computer. Eine repräsentative Untersuchung über die Einstellung von Frauen und Männern in der Bundesrepublik Deutschland zum Thema Computer. Hamburg: Gruner und Jahr Verlag 1986.
3. Brosius, Gerd und Haug, Frigga: Frauen, Männer, Computer. Argument Sonderband 151, Berlin 1987.

4. Dick, Anneliese: Mädchenbildung und neue Technologien. Computer in der Schule: Benachteilligung für Schülerinnen oder Chance zur Kompetenzerweiterung, Hessisches Institut für Bildungsplanung und Schulentwicklung, Wiesbaden 1987.
5. Dick, Anneliese: Koedukation in der Schule: Benachteiligte Schülerinnen? Der heimliche Lehrplan der Geschlechtererziehung und seine Folgen. In: Erziehungswissenschaft und Beruf 2/90, S. 107-119.
6. Dick, Anneliese und Hannelore Faulstich-Wieland: Der hessische Modellversuch. Mädchenbildung und Neue Technologien, in: Login, 1, 1988, S. 20-24.
7. Durndell, Alan: Paradox and Practice: Gender in Computing and Engineering in Eastern Europe. In: Lovegrove, G./Segal, B., a.a.O.
8. Enders-Dragässer, Uta und Claudia Fuchs: Interaktionen der Geschlechter. Sexismusstrukturen in der Schule; eine Untersuchung an hessischen Schulen. Weinheim (Juventa) 1989.
9. Faulstich-Wieland, Hannelore: Mädchenbildung und Neue Technologien, Institut Frau und Gesellschaft (Hrsg.): Frauenforschung. Frauen und neue Technologien, Heft 1 + 2, 1987.
10. Faulstich-Wieland, Hannelore und Anneliese Dick: Mädchenbildung und Neue Technologien, Abschlußbericht der wissenschafltichen Begleitung zum hessischen Vorhaben. Hessisches Institut für Bildungsplanung und Schulentwicklung (HIBS), Wiesbaden 1989, Sonderreihe Heft 29.
11. Freyer, Catrin: Alles nur Bluff? - Programmieren als ein Bestandteil der Fachkultur Informatik, in Funken Ch., Schinzel B.: Frauen in Mathematik und Informatik, Tagungsbericht Dagstuhl 1993, S 60-64.
12. Funken, Christiane/Hammerich, Kurt/Schinzel,Britta: Geschlecht, Informatik und Schule. Oder: wie die Ungleichheit der Geschlechter durch Koedukation neu organisiert wird. Köln, 1996.
13. Heppner, Gisela/Osterhoff, Julia/Schiersmann, Christiane/Schmidt, Christiane: Computer? "Interessieren tät's mich schon, aber..". Wie sich Mädchen in der Schule mit Neuen Technologien auseinandersetzen. Theorie und Praxis der Frauenforschung, Bd. 13. Bielefeld 1990.
14. Hoffmann, Ute: Computerfrauen, München (Rainer Hampp Verlag) 1987.
15. Horstkemper, Marianne: Schule, Geschlecht und Selbstvertrauen. Eine Längsschnittstudie über Mädchensozialisation in der Schule. Weinheim (Juventa) 1990.
16. Kauermann-Walter, Jacqueline und Sigrid Metz-Göckel: Geschlechterverhältnis und Computerbildung, Ergebnisse aus einem Forschungsprojekt. In: Kreienbaum, Anna Maria (Hrsg): Frauen bilden Macht, Dortmund 1989.
17. Kauermann-Walter, Jacqueline/Kreienbaum, Maria Anna/Metz-Göckel, Sigrid: Formale Gleichheit und diskrete Diskriminierung. Forschungsergebnisse zur Koedukation. In: Rolff, H.-G. u.a. (Hrsg.): Jahrbuch der Schulentwicklung, Band 5, 1988, S. 157-188.
18. Kreienbaum, Anna Maria (Hrsg): Frauen bilden Macht, Dortmund 1989.
19. Kreienbaum, Anna Maria und Metz-Göckel, Sigrid: Koedukation und Technikkompetenz von Mädchen, Juventa Verlag, Weinheim 1992.

20. Landesinstitut für Schule und Weiterbildung (Hrsg.): Mädchen und Neue Technologien. Ein Leitfaden für Lehrerinnen und Lehrer. Soest 1993
21. Lovegrove, Gillian und Barbara Segal (Hrsg.): Women into Computing. Selected Papers 1988-1990, London Berlin Heidelberg (Springer) 1991.
22. Martin, Dianne C., Huff, Chuck, Gotterbarn Donald, Miller, Keith: Implementing a Tenth Strand in the CS Curriculum, Communications of the ACM 39, 12, 1996.
23. Niederdrenk-Felgner C. et al. (Hrsg.): Studienbrief: Mädchen und Computer, Computer im koedukativen Unterricht; Deutsches Institut für Fernstudien, Konrad Adenauerstr. 40, 72072 Tübingen, 1993.
24. Roloff, Christine: Von der Schmiegsamkeit zur Einmischung. Professionalisierung von Chemikerinnen und Informatikerinnen. Pfaffenweiler 1989.
25. Sander, Wolfgang: Schüler und Computer. Eine Untersuchung zum Informatikunterricht an Münsteraner Gymnasien, Institut für Pädagogische Lernfeld- und Berufsfeldforschung der Universität Münster 1986.
26. Schelhowe, Heidi: Frauenspezifische Zugänge zur und Umgangsweisen mit der Computertechnologie. Bericht im Rahmen des Projekts Persönlichkeit und Computer des SoTech-Programmes, NRW 1988.
27. Schiersmann, Ch.: Computerkultur und weiblicher Lebenszusammenhang. Hrsg. BMBW Nr.49, Bonn 1987.
28. Schulz-Zander, R. et al. (Arbeitskreis "Informatik in der Schule" der GI): Veränderte Sichtweisen für den Informatikunterricht. GI-Empfehungen für das Fach Informatik in der Sekundarstufe II allgemeinbildender Schulen. In: Informatik-Spektrum (1993) 16, S. 349-356.
29. Volmerg, Birgit/Creutz, Annemarie/Reinhardt, Margarete: Sag mir, wo die Mädchen sind? Geschlechtersozialisation und soziale Herkunft in ihrer Bedeutung für Lernchancen und Lernhindernisse im Informatikunterricht der gymnasialen Oberstufe. Universität Bremen 1991.
30. Wagner, Angelika: Auf Jungen achtet man einfach mehr. Lehrerverhalten. Betrifft: Erziehung 15(7-8) 1982. (Ergebnisse des Projekts: Unterrichtsstrategien und ihre Auswirkungen auf Schülerverhalten).

Girls and Computer Science: "It's not me. I'm not Interested in Sitting Behind a Machine all day."

Bente Rasmussen

Department of Sociology and Political Science, University of Trondheim, NTNU, N-7055 DRAGVOLL, Norway.

Abstract. The low recruitment of women to computer science has been explained by women's fear of computers and mathematics. This presumed fear explains the lack of interest in computers for girls in schools as well. A study of girls in secondary school showed that mathematics and natural sciences were among the more popular subjects among the girls. They were also not afraid of computers or the computerization of society. The reason they gave for not choosing to study computer science was that it was not interesting. They were more interested in a profession where they could work with people. These findings were supported by interviews with 14 and 15 year old girls who used computers in school. The image of the nerd fascinated by the machine seems to be a powerful image of computer scientists.

1 Introduction

The level of women in higher computer science education and among computer professionals is very low and has been declining steadily of the last 10 years. The importance of involving women as producers and advanced users of new information technology is not just motivated by a policy of equal opportunity for women and men in the area of computers. Women may also contribute with different ideas and interests to the development and use of computer technology (Kvande and Rasmussen 1989, Avner & Gunnarsson 1992). Womens' interests and qualifications in the use and social organization of information technology may be an important resource in developing usable and effective systems. When women are wanted and needed, why do they not choose computer science?

The official policy in Norway has been to encourage girls to take technical education and to go into male- dominated professions. In the 80s, Norway saw a noticable increase in women in male-dominated education and professions. Before 1979 the rate of women graduating from the Norwegian Technical University never exceeded 5% (Kvande 1987). In the period 1985-1993 the rate has been 25-27% which is sensational on a world scale. How can the very low rate of women in computer science be explained, a rate that has declined and now stabilized below 10%?

The efforts to increase the proportion of women in computer science are mainly directed towards informing and motivating individual women to choose non-traditional careers. They are built upon the idea that it is women's fear of computers, fear of mathematics and lack of self-confidence that form the main obstacles. Girls and women are compared with young men who are fascinated with the computer and teach themselves to master the new technology. What is wrong with girls and women that they are not likewise fascinated?

A research project on women and computer science at university level in the Scandinavian countries found great variations in the proportion of female students between the different types of education. The figures from Denmark illustrate this clearly:

Institution	Position women	Proportion of
Århus University Copenhagen University Ålborg University Center	Mathematics Department Computer Department Dept. of Electronic Systems	approx. 1/6 women
Roskilde University Danish School of Business Administration & Economics	Administrative Data Processing	approx. 1/3 women
Århus University Ålborg University Center	Information and Media Science Dept. of Communication	approx 1/2 women

(Håpnes & Rasmussen 1991).

Fig. 1. The proportion of women in Computer Science at universities in Denmark.

The same variation is found in Norway where Information Science at the University of Bergen located in the department of social sciences had an even distribution of men and women. Informatics at the University of Oslo located in the department of mathematics had 15-20% female students and computer Science at the Norwegian Technical University located in the department of electronics had 5-10% female students (Håpnes & Rasmussen 1991). The proportion of women declined when computer science was related to technical subjects. This suggests that women are not afraid of computer science. Women are represented in computer science, but the content and institutional setting as well as the application area of computer science are important for whether women apply or not (Kvande & Rasmussen 1989).

In all the three different studies of computer science in Norway we found that the women students had chosen computer science because they liked the subject and were interested in and fascinated by computers and how you could use them. They had chosen a variety of specializations within their study of computer science: systems development, cybernetics, telematics and technical control systems. What they had in common, was that they chose *applications* of computer science; the use of computers and computer systems to solve problems in industry and society. They were not interested in the working of the computer as a machine or in operating systems (Håpnes & Rasmussen 1991).

Their choices, however, did not have the same status in the three studies of computer science. Computer technology at The Norwegian Institute of Technology (NTH) is the subject with the lowest participation of women and the subject where the women experienced themselves as being different from how students of computer technology are supposed to be. They described their "difference" in reaction to what they saw as the dominant male culture in the study. They rejected this culture of men who sat all day and night before the screen pressing the keys of the computer (Rasmussen & Håpnes 1991).

The female students had chosen to study computer science both because they were interested in the subject and because the profession offered good career opportunities. However, with their choices of specializations in the field of "applications" of the technology they felt "on the periphery" of computer technology. Typical computer people, they felt, sit in front of a terminal and are fascinated by what's inside the computers.

The professional identity of the women was tied to other aspects of computing than the machine or the technical possibilities. They feel that the most exciting thing about computer science is all the different things you can make, and the problems that you manage to solve. They do not find it especially interesting to make a million numbers go through a machine one millisecond faster. Even if their choices lay well within the main areas of the discipline, they felt that they were not "real" computer scientists (Rasmussen & Håpnes 1991).

This strong image of the computer scientist fascinated by the machine and using all "his" time behind the computer screen, is a powerful popular image. American studies have paid attention to the hacker culture as a freakish computer culture among men (Weizenbaum 1976, Levy 1984, Turkle 1984 and 1988), but this marginal group is not representative for the majority of students or the discipline as such. Still it seems to be reinforced by the experience in schools as well as in higher education among girls and women. The students at the Norwegian Institute of Technology saw no difference between the hackers and other groups of dedicated men who worked late at night: they were for them compulsive computer students (Rasmussen & Håpnes 1991).

Is this popular image of the compulsive computer nerd an important factor in deciding the plans of young girls towards computer science? Are the girls afraid of computers and do they dislike mathematics? What are their future plans, and do they consider choosing computers as a career?

2 Method

This paper is based on data on the interests and plans of young girls at secondary school that were in the process of choosing their subjects for specialization. The data were collected through a survey among two generations of students from 6 different schools in Trondheim. This data will be supplemented with data from an ongoing project on young girls and information technology. In this project we observed 14 and 15 year old pupils using computers in school and interviewed them about their interests in the use of computers in school and at home.

In this article I will first look into some of the myths about girls' orientations and interests. We will see how girls in secondary school choose and evaluate their subjects. In the last section we will discuss the interests and disinterests of girls in computers.

3 Girls and Science

A popular belief, especially strong among computer scienctists and educational institutions that have few female students, is that girls - or women- are afraid of science and computers. Are girls afraid of science or prejudiced against computer science?

Girls in secondary school who were about to choose their subjects for specialization were asked about their preferences and plans and about how they saw computer science. Only a small minority said that they planned to graduate as computer scientists:

No, probably not	36
Yes, higher education	6
Yes, as part of an education	53
No answer	15
N= 191	

Table 1. Do you plan to study of computer science after secondary school? Percentage.

Table 1 does not indicate a fear of computer science as more than half of the girls said that they would take computer science as part of their professional education, even if they did not want to be computer scientists.

Another popular belief is that girls are not very good at mathematics and natural science and therefore shy away from any education where these subjects are central. Girls are thought to opt for social sciences, arts and languages. We therefore asked the girls about their most popular subjects:

Foreign Languages	68
Natural science	49
Gymnastics	47
Mathematics	43
Norwegian litterature	36
Social science	21
Arts	17
N=191	

Table 2. The three most popular subjects in school among the girls, percentage.

The table shows that natural science and mathematics scored highly as the most popular subjects among the girls. Nearly half of the girls mentioned one or both of these subjects. Only foreign languages scored higher. It seems that dislike of natural science or mathematics cannot account for the lack of women within computer science education.

Instead of looking at the school-subjects and their popularity, another approach to choice of education would be to look at the use of an education. What can you do with the education, and is that something that you would want to do? How do the girls view the use of computers in society, and can prejudice against the use of computers explain their reluctance to be computer scientists?

We do not find widespread prejudices and negative views on the use of computers in our society in our material:

The girls disagree with the following opinions:	
Computer scientists are only interested in technical matters:	88% disagree
Computer science is especially well-suited for men:	60% disagree
Computers make society cold and inhuman:	47% disagree, 28% don't know
Many problems in society are caused by computerization:	47% disagree, 34% don't know
They agree with the following opinions:	
Most people will profit from using computers at work:	85% agree
Computers make work easier:	83% agree
Computers are important for the development of the country:	83% agree
Most professions will demand a knowledge of computers in the future:	82% agree
Computers are important in solving the problems of daily life:	59% agree.
People who understand computers manage better in society:	49% agree

Table 3. Statements about computers. N= 191.

This table does not show any of the "common" prejudices that one might find in their parents' generation. The girls in secondary school are positive about the use of computers in society.

International studies of girls and boys and natural science have found that they see scientists as very boring and strange people, not creative and not very social. The girls and boys see themselves as creative and social and their image of the scientist colludes with their image of themselves (Sjøberg 1986). Computer scientists are also often thought to be weird and asocial (Turkle 1984), and we therefore presented the girls with different opinions of computer scientists.

Intelligent:	94%
Conscientious:	93%
Industrious:	85%
Strong willed:	77%
Politically engaged:	50%
Creative:	52% yes or in some degree
Helps other people:	36% yes and 48% don't know
Sporty:	32% said no and 50% don't know.

Table 4. What do the girls think is a typical computer scientist? N= 191.

If we compare these results with what the girls say about themselves, we find the following picture:

Intelligent:	61%
Conscientious:	70%
Industrious:	55%
Strong willed:	78%
Politically engaged:	52% said no
Creative:	61%
Helps other people:	54%
Sporty:	70%

Table 5. The girls' view on themselves. N= 191.

There are no incompatible differences between the characteristics of the computer scientists and the girls themselves. If the problem does not lie with the girls and their fears or prejudices, an alternative angle is to ask what is the problem with the subject since women shy away from it.

4 Not Fear but Lack of Interest

The data from the survey could help us unmask some popular myths about girls and computers. However, it could not explain why they do not choose computer science as a career. At the end of our survey we asked them to comment upon their own future plans. The girls' comments ran like this:

> "I don't think computer science is very interesting. I'm more interested in working with people", or

> "I would not like to sit behind the computer all day. I'm more interested in other subjects."

In our current research we observed the use of computers in school and interviewed young girls. We found that teachers often believe that the girls are afraid of the computer. "They are hiding their hands behind their backs because they are afraid to press the keys", one of them said to us. When we interviewed some of these girls, they told us that they were not afraid of the computer at all. They told us that they often played with the computer and pressed the keys to see what happens. That's how they use computers at home. What they did at school was different and depended upon what the were supposed to use the computer for. If they liked the subject, it was interesting to use the computer. Some of them were not interested in mathematics, one of the subjects where they were to learn to use a computer program:

> "I think math is boring and uninteresting. Math is even more boring when we use the computer. It is complicated to find out what to do, and when I don't like doing it in an ordinary lesson, it is not fun to try to find out how to do it on the computer."

This girl preferred to use the computer to write a text:

> "I find the letters along the way, so I manage. As soon as I find the rythm I can write a text. That's OK."

The ones who liked math, thought using the computer was fun, and they learnt to use the program fast. Because they understood math, they soon overtook some of the computer nerds. The girls wanted to use the machine to do something useful, or for fun. Useful things could be text, or information collection in relation to projects that they had. At another school they used multimedia and the Internet to collect information, and the girls found that interesting.

The Internet was popular because they could find pictures and texts about their pop-idols. They could also write to pen-pals in other countries and chat in a group. They wanted to use the computer by themselves, without the teacher hanging over them to see if they did it "the right way". They did not want to be pressured to achieve. Computers, and especially the Internet, were for them play and time-off, not something to have to learn and achieve marks. They did not want to use computers for their work in the future. When asked about their future plans, nearly all the girls said that they wanted to help people. Even if they could help more people by using computers, they said that they hoped that they did not have to sit behind a computer at work.

Not all of the girls were interested in playing with computers. One of them said:

> "I can't stand sitting pressing these keys. To me that is an asocial sport and indicates a lack of things to do outside school. I want to do things with my friends, talk with them and have fun."

Often the families showed a genderd pattern of computer use. Few of the mothers used computers outside their work:

> "My mother is more like me, I think. She does not care for playing with the computer. We want to sit in the living room talking and having a nice time while my father and brother play with the computer in our home-office."

When the girls are not playing with the computer, it is not because they are afraid or find it too difficult. They are simply not interested and want to do other things; talk with their friends and family. They want to have a futrue where they do work "to help people"; they do not want to sit behind a machine.

5 Conclusions

Computers and information technology has been associated with numbers, calculations, engineering and programming. These associations have shaped the recruitment into higher education. The media and its preoccupation with girls "lacking" the fascination with the machine, has probably not helped. We end up with an image of the computer scientist being "someone else - different from us". This image helps reproduce a certain computer scientist, the compulsive programmer or the computer nerd. The low recruitment of women into higher education in computer science and the general diffusion of the image of the computer nerd in popular media may indicate that the selection of this kind of students for computer science may be worse than it was 10 years ago. At that time it was fairly normal that the students of computer science or computer technology did not know anything about computers or programming beforehand. Very few of the women we interviewed in the 80s knew anything about computers when they started their study at the university. Now there is a strong image of the student of computer science as somebody who already knows the workings of the computer. One of the current female students of computer technology at the technical university said:

> "The youth of today have always had some "supernerds" in their class who know "everything" about computers, boys who started with computer games and went on to program and the newest and hottest stuff. When you have had them in your class, you think when you're 18, they're studying computers, I'm not."

However information technology is now becoming communication technology with less emphasis on numbers and calculations and more on communication networks. Machines and standard packages can be bought, and computer professionals need to develop solutions with technology and organizational structures to suit their customers. The growth is within consultancies rather than producers of technology or in-house services. The application of technology and its use is more important, and it seems that different computer scientists than the technology-fascinated nerd will be needed in the future. Women may be recruited to computer science when we stop asking what is wrong with women and start asking what are the interests of women in computer technology. In order to recruit women from their interest, computer science would have to work on a new image for itself.

Computer science would need a change according to the computer industry: there is a serious need for more interest in the users, the complex reality of computers and their applications, the work organization and individual users. Women in computer science might be an important *resource* in initiating such a change.

References

1. Avner, E. & E. Gunnarsson: I människans tjänst. Copenhagen: Nordisk Ministerråd 1992:531.
2. Håpnes, T. og B. Rasmussen: The Production of Male Power in Computer Science. In: I. Eriksson, B. Kitchenham & K. Tijdens (eds.): Women, Work and Computerization. Proceedings from the 4th IFIP Conference in Helsinki. Amsterdam: North-Holland 1991.
3. Kvande, E.: Barriers and Coping Strategies Among Female Students at the Technical University of Norway. International Journal of Science Education, vol. 9. (1987).
4. Kvande, E. & B. Rasmussen: Men, Women and Data Systems. European Journal of Engineering Education, vol. 14, no 4 (1989).
5. Levy, S.: Hackers: Heroes of the Computer Revolution, Bantam Doubleday Dell Publ. Group, New York 1984.
6. Rasmussen, B. & T. Håpnes: Excluding Women From the Technologies of the Future? Futures, Vol.23, no. 10, 1107-1120 (1991).
7. Sjøberg, S.: Elever of lærere sier sin mening. Report from the SISS-project<. The Second Onternational Study. Oslo: Universitetsforlaget 1986.
8. Turkle, S.: The Second Self. Computers and the Human Spirit. London: Granada 1984.
9. Turkle, S.: Computational Reticence: Why Women Fear the Intimate Machine. In: Kramarae, C. (ed.): Technology and Women's Voices. Keeping in Touch. London: Routledge and Kegan Paul 1988.
10. Weizenbaum, J.: Computer Power and Human Reason. San Fransisco: Freeman 1976.

Australian Women in IT Education: Multiple Meanings and Multiculturalism

A. Greenhill[2], L. von Hellens[1], S. Nielsen[1], R. Pringle[2]

[1] School of Computing and Information Technology,
[2] Faculty of Humanities, Griffith University, Brisbane, 4111 Qld, Australia

Abstract. Information technology (IT) education continues to be male dominated and fewer women are entering computing courses at the university level. Earlier research by authors of this paper (Greenhill, von Hellens, Nielsen and Pringle, 1996a; 1996b) indicates that despite the masculine computer culture, women of Asian extraction outweigh other ethnic groups in IT education in Australia, suggesting that these women have challenged dominant meanings of both gender and computing, and have developed strategies to cope with the hostility of computing culture. This paper reports the results of interviews with female high school students in Brisbane, which sought to identify factors particular to Asian women that affect their entry into and successful completion of IT studies at university. The paper considers these results in relation to the construction of new meanings of IT which may empower women and considers the implications in relation to multiculturalism in Australia.

1 Introduction

In its inception information technology (IT) was suggested to be the first area where men and women would be equally represented. However despite the satisfactory gender balance in the past it now has a decreasing proportion of female graduates [3, 10].

The research for this paper builds upon a pilot study into the situation of female students in the School of Computing and Information Technology (CIT) at Griffith University in South East Queensland, Australia [5, 6]. The gender imbalance at CIT follows the unsatisfactory trend identified elsewhere: in 1995 only 17% of all 270 first year students (including repeating students) were female. In 1996 19.9% of all 191 starting their IT studies at CIT were female. When considering the ethnic background of the students it was noticed that in 1995 one fifth of all IT students - male and female - were of Asian extraction although Asians comprise less than 5% of the Australian population. In 1996 the percentage was 30.9%. The rest of the students are mostly of Anglo-Celtic and European background. Students of Asian background represented half of all female students in 1995. In 1996 the percentage of Non-English speaking background students increased to: 31 % of all students and 37% of all females.

This paper continues our research into this aspect of multiculturalism in Australian IT education by interviewing female high school students to identify factors particular to Asian women that affect their entry into and successful completion of IT studies at the university level. A long term question is understanding how the Asian women have overcome the apparent hostility of the international computer culture, how they have challenged the dominant meanings of both gender and IT, and what is the significance of their example for IT educators. Our research provides some preliminary answers to this question and suggests directions for future research. This research is a part of a larger study which aims to demonstrate that both computing and gender are open to multiple meanings. Bringing alternative meanings to the fore may open up strategies for achieving gender balance and equal opportunity in IT education. The practical objectives of the larger study are to improve recruitment practices and to identify factors that are within the control of the university departments to enhance curricula and teaching methods to nurture the observed success strategies. Ultimately, we aim to develop a conceptual model of cultural factors affecting female participation in IT education.

There is now substantial literature on the low proportion of women in computing science [3, 15]. With few exceptions, women are treated as an undifferentiated category and research focuses on the psychological characteristics [2, 19, 20], cultural stereotypes and social relations which restrict them. However this paper argues that there are cultural differences amongst female IT students from different national and ethnic backgrounds that affect their participation and success in IT education. The focus in this paper is how IT is understood by high school students, as an area of study and as a profession. This understanding is discussed in relation to the new potentially feminine meanings of IT provided by the Internet and the idea of cyberspace as well as the changing meanings of IT as a field of study and work which contrast to the traditional, male constructed view of computing and IT. The problem of the construction of new meanings of IT for women is also considered from the multicultural viewpoint, especially the potential conflict between the dominant national culture and minority/individual cultures. Issues of empowerment were identified but need further exploration.

This study has particular significance in the Australian context, where 23% of the population is overseas born and almost 40% are migrants or children of migrants. Although Australia has one of the most ethnically diverse population in the world, the findings of this study may have applicability to any country which has significant ethnic minorities and which is concerned with equity of access to and participation in the IT industry and IT education.

2 Research Strategy

This paper reports the findings of research carried out among female high schools students in Brisbane. It discusses some of the factors that seem to be important when female students formulate their perceptions on computing studies at the university and the subsequent career options. The research builds upon the findings of a pilot study of Asian female students in an IT degree at Griffith University in 1995. [5, 6]

Our research problem addresses cultural factors and contextual influences affecting female participation and success in IT education. Due to the exploratory nature of the research a variety of methods was applied in order to capture all potential factors affecting the phenomenon under investigation. An interpretive approach to the research is thus warranted. Surveys among female students in IT education and secondary schools included open questions and were complemented by focus group interviews.

Given the multi disciplinary nature of the research behind this paper, it is important that we have the different fields - computing and IT as well as humanities - represented in our project to assure the credibility of the research. Because of the very different backgrounds and skills of the authors the research has involved extensive collective discussion and planning. The focus group interviews have been recorded and the transcripts have been read by each of the authors who all have contributed to the analysis and interpretation of the data from the perspective of their research discipline.

2.1 High School Surveys

In this paper we discuss the research investigations in three High Schools in Brisbane during July-August 1996. Surveys provide background statistics of the proportion of non-English speaking females in the schools included in the study as well as specific details about their access and exposure to computing facilities. The focus group interviews were used since they can reveal "wild card" type of issues that flow from free group discussion [14] which would help identify the emerging cultural factors that are influencing the career choices of high school students. There is a need for qualitative research to support surveys in order to understand the influence of cultural factors on career orientations within the IT field [9] to better understand the complexity of the situation and influences.

The High Schools included in the study were chosen because of the high proportion of Asian students enrolled. They comprised two private (fee paying) schools - one girls' school and one coeducational school, and one state (free) coeducational school close to a suburb which has relatively high Asian population. All three schools are located in suburban areas, within 20 kilometres of the Brisbane city centre. All students doing the mathematics course that is the entry requirement to university level IT courses were surveyed (224 students in total, see table below for the survey audience). The questionnaire included questions about the general background (age, gender, country of origin, native tongue, number of years spent in Australia), previous computer training at school and elsewhere, computer usage outside the school and opinions on tertiary studies (including preferred university courses).

Two researchers carried out the focus group interviews in July-August 1996 among female students in the three High Schools. The interview questions focused on their opinions about tertiary education in general and the courses they were considering. The questions aimed at finding out why computing courses were or were not preferred and what are the students' perceptions of IT education: the course content, the skills and personal characteristic required, and the type of occupation that a person graduating with an IT degree would enter. Students were also asked from where the students received advice and information about IT courses and how accurate it was (eg. open days organised by university, school's career adviser), and lastly whether they felt that women could be equally successful in an IT profession as men.

Schools	Focus groups Interviews with female students in groups of 3 to 4	Survey audience Female Asian	 Non-Asian	 Male
School 1 all girls, private school	11 girls, each group was a mixture of Asian and Non-Asian students	51	109	na.
School 2 coeducational, private school	12 female students, all were Non-Asian	2	17	18
School 3 coeducational, state school	8 female students, all were Non-Asian	1	9	17
Total	6 Asian, 25 Non-Asian	54	135	35

Table: Focus Groups and Survey Audience in High Schools

3 Meanings of Computing and Gender

Interpretation of the focus group interviews has been attempted in relation to the new meanings of computing and IT as a field of study and work which emerged from the initial analysis of the data from the surveys and focus group interviews in the three Brisbane High Schools.

The dominant meanings of computers for women have been drawn from an existing sexual division of labour in which women are thought to be disinterested in and uncomfortable with technology [13: p429]. The characterisation of IT as masculine and the permeation of these meanings through society have made women feel marginalised, and limited their participation in the construction of new types of work and social relationships [16: p8]. Since IT is a relatively new technology and its applications are changing rapidly, its past and current meanings need to be challenged, and hence destabilised to allow other more egalitarian meanings to come to the fore. The notion of multiple meanings is explored further in this paper by considering the meanings afforded by new developments in communication technology and emerging meanings relating to IT studies and work.

3.1 Power and Control in Virtual Environments

With women's use of the telephone as an analogy, Jennifer Light [12] has argued that computer mediated communication technologies can cut across the grain of traditional power lines. The use of new communication technologies affords an opportunity to establish new meanings of IT which can compete with and complement the traditional and dominant meanings of IT. These new meanings open up new possibilities for rethinking current perceptions of IT and its social uses. However, increased use of these new technologies necessitates the step towards fuller participation [12: p137, 18]. If women are not involved in the development of the larger infrastructures upon which the working arrangements of any information technology is dependent (such as the Internet), they will inevitably be shaped in ways that are disempowering. In this study the promise of internet as a medium which reduces the significance of culture and gender is not confirmed by the reactions of the female students interviewed. The internet is not always made freely available through the school. It was not used since "someone is watching" and students who use it indicate that is slow and often boring, as the following quotations illustrate.

> "Actually we just have one computer going into the Internet, and its is pretty restrictive cause you have to ask the librarian, and you have to give the librarian a reason why you are using it, and a couple sit right next to you while you are using it just to make sure that you are not checking out pornography"

> "... it took 10 minutes even before you can get into Griffith because there is so much traffic."

The issue of power and control needs to be explored in detail as it seems to limit female students' ability to discover that the implications of information technologies in fact extend to all areas of human activity, including those which traditionally appeal to females. IT professionals need to be able to create not only new systems and applications but also new uses of technology. The better the understanding of the uses of systems, the better the systems that are developed. The production and use of systems are interlinked and dependent on each other. The distinction between the use of computers and the creation or production of computer artefacts emerged during this research. Although the authors have not had time to investigate this issue in detail, the survey seems to indicate that the blurring of the boundaries between these two areas is changing the perceptions and motivations of students entering the IT field.

3.2 Skills Required for Professional IT Work

According to Kling and Sacchi [11: p47] computers are not merely tools in the workplace but resources in "webs" of technological, political and social commitments, produced by a network or "lattice" of producers and consumers. Successful implementation of information systems involves the participation of users, which in turn entails skills that, in other contexts, are associated with women. These skills are being explicitly required by employers in the IT industry. As one young female IT manager has put it "...women now moving into the network, telecommunications and systems management areas have much to offer because of their 'non-threatening' negotiating skills, particularly the inherent ability to bridge the communication gap in all areas of their work". [22: p12]

Information technology graduates in Queensland, Australia, are most likely to work in small and medium sized organisations with fewer than 20 employees and $1 million operating profit. The small and medium sized enterprises (SME) are by far and large the most prolific group in every industry sector in Australia, and in the IT and communication industry even more so. [1] In such organisations, graduates need both technical skills and the ability to understand and work effectively with customers, particularly in team environment. Despite the requirements for 'feminine' people-centred skills, IT education continues to be constructed and represented in a way that both discourages girls and means that all students come in with a false set of expectations both about the course and about future job opportunities. The female students in our research characterised an IT professional as someone who likes to work alone, with no communication skills. They don't have to have "people" skills as they are only working with computers. Computing and IT in High Schools has an image of being "boring" and computer professionals are seen as unsociable personalities who like to work alone, which does not appeal to girls in High Schools. The computing profession is seen as being programming, of which most girls had very bad experiences, as the exercises in the Information Technology and Processing course which several had done were too difficult and cumbersome

The problem solving skills were emphasised, as was competence in mathematics. However, since problem solving was not seen as necessary in doing studies such as economics or law, students' perceptions and understanding of intellectual skills such as problem solving need to be explored further. The perceptions of the computing profession as well as the skills required seem to be equally inaccurate in the IT education and industry. More research needs to be done on where and how to provide more useful perspectives and to implement these in recruitment and teaching practices.

3.3 Perceptions of Female Participation

Another "false" perception of IT emerging from this study is that gradually the participation of women will improve. The students interviewed considered computing to be a relatively new area and gave that as one of the reasons why women were not equally represented, but they also expected a gradual change to this situation. There was no indication that they knew that female participation has actually declined as the following comments indicate.

> " I think in a couple of years women will start doing it [computing courses]"

> "... in the 80's more males did computers, whereas in the 90's it's getting to be an equal share. So they are sort of coming out of the 80's movies like that and so ... that's their job and women are still getting up to that stage"

> " Yeah, I think that women will catch up to men though, I think men will always have a higher proportion in computing, but I think you'll get more women in a few years"

> " I think in a couple of years women will start doing it. I think some people think that computers are a relatively new thing too. No matter how fast they are moving in the technology it's still new"

The reason given for this view was because women generally are entering more courses and more options are becoming available to them. This perception probably relates more to the discourse of equal employment opportunity, exemplified by such slogans as "girls can do anything", which are frequently seen in the media and in employment and careers centres, than it does to any real life experience that the girls may have. It may also be reinforced through the media - for example, the use of a female star in the film "The Net". No examples were given of female friends or relatives working in non traditional areas. This false perception of more women entering IT was the only positive image of computing as an area of study and work gained from the interviews, except for the two girls who intended to study computing who described it thus: "But when you get to secondary it´s like we are having fun now it's so different" In this case the student was pushed into studying computing by her mother, and "... I'm glad she did because I am thoroughly enjoying it now". These two girls also had a wider idea of the opportunities in education and work: "A lot of girls don't want a job in that area. I don't think they realise that it is so wide". The positive image of computing as a profession expressed by these girls was strikingly different from any other girls interviewed. The reason for this could have been the female teacher who was highly regarded by the girls doing computing ("... she is so smart, she knows everything"). The girls also expected the computing class to become bigger as the female teacher had started only this year.

However, the main impression conveyed by these interviews is that girls perceive computing study and work as boring, hard, requiring primarily logic and maths skills, and involving little contact with other people. There was also a strong impression that women preferred different types of work and particularly those which involved communication. Interestingly, one of the girls intending to study computing, said that women would be better than men because they communicate better. Notions such as "boring" and "communication", need to be explored further to ascertain how the students relate them to study and work.

3.4 Culture and Gender

In this survey the female students in high school expected boys to be more interested in computers than girls were. Doing computing seems to them to be a power thing. Boys like games more than girls, and they show off how good they are. It has to be different type of woman who does information technology, it wouldn't attract women in general because of the low number of women in the IT courses.

As was mentioned earlier, the research into the gender imbalance has tended to emphasise the psychological characteristics of males and females [2, 19] in relation to the modes of thought required for IT study. Computing is perceived as a masculine arena. However, the work by Edwards suggests that the culture of engineering and IT involves the "deeply entangled institutions of military service and of masculinity as a political identity in an age of high technology war - connections that provide a bridge between the masculinity of war and the different but related masculinity of the world inside the computer." [4: p102] Ewards also indicates that this perspective is intended to apply only to the United States, where "high technology and military power have been profoundly linked since World War II". He speculates that other national experiences may indicate other possibilities, as yet unexplored for the "articulation of gender identity around computing machines" [4: p102]. This reinforces our perspective that gender and culture are interwoven in the construction of new meanings of IT. A number of studies into national culture are therefore considered relevant to the current study to determine the national and cultural differences as well as gender differences in the construction of multiple meanings of computing.

Masculinity/femininity has been identified as a dimension of national culture (7, 8). "Dominant values associated with the feminine role include not showing off, putting relationships with people before money, minding the quality of life and helping others." [9: p5] The study by Igbaria and McClosky of MIS employees in Taiwan indicates that Taiwanese culture varies greatly from North American culture on three out of the four dimensions of culture, including a marked difference on the masculinity scale. Another dimension which is relevant to the present study is that of certainty. Igbaria & McClosky [9] also found that the Taiwanese culture is higher in uncertainty avoidance.

There was no notable difference between the perceptions of IT education and profession between Asian and other students interviewed. The question then remains of why Asian female students continue to participate at much higher levels. Apparently negative factors such as lack of computer knowledge, difficulty, lack of interest and male domination of IT studies do not inhibit their participation. Not many girls had taken a computing courses outside the school, however the proportion of Asian females was slightly higher than for Non-Asians (7% as opposed to 3%). The survey also indicated that Asian females were more inclined to choose computing and

IT subjects at school (27% said "yes" as opposed to only 10% of non-Asian female students). Of all students - male and female - about a 30% are taking IT subjects.

Asian females indicated more often than their non-Asian counterparts that IT will be their *first* preference (18% as opposed to 8%), and only a third would not consider IT courses, whereas two thirds of non-Asian female students were "not interested" or "don't like computers". The survey showed that both groups - Asian and non-Asian females - had very similar views about the type of work and IT professional would do, programming and software testing being predominantly seen as the main activity in that profession. Positive factors identified in this study - the usefulness of computing and the likelihood of getting a job may be much stronger motivating factors for female Asian students than for other female students. This is confirmed by research which indicates that Asian women are "less likely to choose computing because it interests them" [20]. The study by Igbaria & McClosky [9] also indicates that the career orientation of Taiwanese employees is most closely associated with security, service and challenge rather than autonomy, independence and entrepreneurial creativity.

4 Multiculturalism and Multiple Meanings

Moving beyond the traditional research into the psychological characteristics of gender preferences, we can see that the construction of multiple meanings of IT is complicated by cultural and national differences. Within the Australian context of multiculturalism we can also see that the concerns of female participation in IT may be related to the general concerns underlying the idea of multiculturalism. These include notions such as equity – women and minority groups have the right to succeed in the male dominant culture of computing – and diversity; the dominant culture of computing can benefit from the diversity of views of different groups. According to these principles, computing like society would gradually be transformed to better serve the multiple interests of participants. There is some tension between these principles and the idea of social cohesion where some diversity is tolerated as long as it does not threaten the unique culture which already exists.

The notion of multiculturalism may be criticised in relation to the second point above - that is that the views of the different groups need to be subordinate to those of the dominant group. In this way the relationship between female students and the dominant images of computing may be likened to those between the dominant Australian culture (Anglo-Celtic) and minority ethnic groups. The latter are expected to adapt to, be assimilated by and "benefit" from the dominant culture [21: p85]. For example, upward mobility, formal education and social "improvement" are identified as appropriate indicators of minority success.

During the course of this study, the authors have attempted to understand the causes of low female participation, with a view to improving recruitment, educational practices, and course content. The higher participation of Asian students indicated that the barriers inhibiting female participation could be overcome and that useful lessons could be learnt and perhaps transformed into practice. However, the relationship between student perception of the IT education and industry amongst different cultural groups is complicated by misconceptions and by motivations which may be culturally incompatible. The challenge of increasing the participation of women in the IT area may face similar obstacles to those facing the development of a multicultural society.

In order to avoid trivialising the issue, we may need to accept that different approaches may need to be used for female students of differing ethnic/cultural backgrounds, without assuming the superiority/inferiority of one or other groups determination to enter or ignore computing as field of study and work. We also need to consider the implications for the IT industry of the construction of new meanings of IT. Considering the high participation of Asian women in IT education, we need to explore the characteristics of Asian culture in relation to IT education and industry.

5 Conclusion

For reasons of equity, we consider that female access to education should not be inhibited by factors irrelevant to either women or to the industry for which the education is a preparation. There is evidence that women in computing make a significant contribution to the industry and that they find their careers satisfying and worthwhile. Secondly, there are also concerns in the industry (such as software quality, and communication between IT professionals and IT end users) which may be alleviated by the application of skills which women are traditionally thought to possess (eg interpersonal skills). Thirdly, we do not assume that IT education will necessarily increase the power of women in that arena. We accept the argument that indispensability should not be confused with power [17: p152]. However we would argue that the nature of the IT discipline and the products which are generated through IT research, although ultimately determined by power brokers, are shaped by the interests and expertise of the IT research and academic community. At present this community is dominated by a view of computing and its applications, developed primarily by men. To change this situation, female participation in the information society should not be limited to active use of technologies such as the Internet, or to general familiarity with computers. Higher level participation is needed.

Our research so far has been a kind of snapshot of reasons female students choose or reject IT education with some emphasis on the reasons why they choose to remain in IT and on study practices and success strategies. This paper suggests that culture is as important as gender in this choice and that findings relating to Asian students may not be applied in a simplistic fashion to female students with other cultural backgrounds. Our plan is to continue the study in a longitudinal fashion focusing on the performance of Asian women in the later years of their IT study and to compare this study with students from other backgrounds. In parallel to this research we will also attempt to develop an understanding of the implications of cultural factors for the construction of new meanings of IT within the context of Australian multiculturalism and to compare our findings with similar studies of other nationalities and cultural groups.

Acknowledgments

The authors thank all students who kindly agreed to participate in this research and the High Schools for allowing us to interview the students in their final year of secondary education. Vicki Ross did an enormous job in interviewing the students. Kim Taylor from the computing support group in Griffith University deserve special thanks. She has helped us mount the questionnaire on the Web and analyse the survey statistics.

The authors also gratefully acknowledge the financial support from the URIS scheme in Griffith University.

References

1. ASTEC (1995) The Science and Engineering Base for Development of Australia's Information Technology and Communication Sector, A discussion paper by Australian Science and Technology Council, September 1995
2. Brosnan, M. J. and Davidson, M. J. (1996), Psychological gender issues in computing, Gender, Work and Organization, Vol. 3, No. 1, January 1996: 13-25
3. Cottrell, J. (1992), I'm a stranger here myself: A Consideration of Women in Computing, Proceedings of ACM SIGUCCS User Services Conference, Cleveland, 8-11 November 1992
4. Edwards, P. (1990) The Army and the Microworld, Journal of Women in Culture and Society, 16, 1990: 102-127
5. Greenhill, A., von Hellens. L., Nielsen, S. and Pringle, R. (1996a), Asian Women in IT Education. An Australian Examination, Proceedings of the First Australian Conference on Computer Science Education (ACSE-96), Sydney, 2-4 July 1996: 171-176
6. Greenhill, A., von Hellens. L., Nielsen, S. and Pringle, R. (1996b), Larrikin Cultures and Women in IT Education, Proceedings of the 19th Information Systems Research Seminar in Scandinavia (IRIS-19), Gothenburg, Sweden, 10-13 August 1996: 13-28
7. Hofstede, G. (1980), Motivation, Leadership and Organization: Do American Theories Apply Abroad? Organizational Dynamics, Summer 1980: 42-63
8. Hofstede, G. (1994), Management Scientists are Human, Management Science 40, 1994: 4-13
9. Igbaria, M. and McClosky, D.W. (1996), Career Orientations of MIS Employees in Taiwan, Computer Personnel, A Quarterly Publication of the SIGCPR, ACM Press, Vol.17, No. 2, April 1996: 3-24
10. Klawe, M. and Levenson, N. (1995), Women in Computing: Where Are We Now? Communications of the ACM, January 1995, 38(1): 29-44
11. Kling, R. and Sacchi, W. (1982), The Web of Computing: Computing Technology as Social Organisation, Advances in Computers 21, 1982: 3-85
12. Light, Jennifer S. (1995) The Digital Landscape: New Space for Women, Gender, Place, and Culture, Vol. 2, No. 2, 1995: 133-146
13. Lie, M. (1991), Technology and Gender: Identity and Symbolism, Proceedings of the Conference on Women, Work and Computerization, Helsinki, Finland, June 30-July 2, 1991: 425-446
14. Malhotra, N.K. (1993), Marketing Research: an Applied Orientation, Englewood Cliffs, New Jersey: Prentice-Hall, 1993
15. Pearl, A., Pollack, M.E., Riskin, E., Thomas, B., Wolf, E. and Wu, A. (1990), Becoming a Computer Scientist: a report by the ACM committee on the status of women in computing science, Communications of the ACM, Vol. 33, No. 11, November 1990: 47-58
16. Poster, M. (1990) The Mode of Information: Post Structuralism and Social Context, Cambridge, Polity Press, 1990

17. Robins, K. and Webster, F. (1987), Dangers of Information Technology, in R.Finnegan, et al. (eds), Information Technology: Social Issues, A Reader, London, 1987
18. Spender, D. (1995) Nattering the Net; Women, Power and Cyberspace, Spinifex Press, North Melbourne, 1995
19. Teague, G.J. and Clarke, V.A. (1994), A Psychological Perspective on Gender Differences in Computing Participation, Phoenix, Arizona: SIGSCE Conference Proceedings, 1994: 258-262
20. Teague, G.J. and Clarke, V.A. (1996), Improving Gender Equity in Computing Programmes: Some Suggestions for Increasing Female Participation and Retention Rates, Proceedings of the First Australian Conference on Computer Science Education (ACSE-96), Sydney, 2-4 July 1996: 164-170
21. Tsolidis, G. (1989), Ethnic Minority Women: Reassessing the Assumed., in S. Taylor and M. Henery (eds), Battlers and Bluestocking, Women's place in Australian Education, Canberra: Australian College of Education, 1989
22. Weekend Australian (1995), "No 'attitude' needed: top achievers", The Weekend Australian, March 11-12, 1995: 12

Accepted Papers and Discussion Notes

Topic 5: Education

Part 2: Quality of Education with IT

Use of Quality Function Deployment to Develop a Women's Studies Strategy

Ita Richardson

Department of Computer Science and Information Systems
and
National Centre for Quality Management
University of Limerick, Ireland
email: ita.richardson@ul.ie

Abstract. Quality Function Deployment (QFD) is a quality tool which has been used within manufacturing since its development in the early 1970's. In recent years it has also been used as part of the software development requirements engineering process. This author has been involved in projects using QFD as a requirements engineering tool, and her current research is based on the application of QFD to the process improvement strategy of small Software Development organisations. To illustrate how QFD can be used to elicit and prioritise an improvement strategy, the study in this paper discusses the generating of ideas and strategies for developing Women's Studies within the University of Limerick.

1 Introduction

Quality Function Deployment (QFD), a method of including quality into the design and production of products, was developed by Yoji Akao in Japanese shipyards during the 1970's. Its use spread to the automobile industry in Japan, and in the mid-1980's was introduced to the car industry in the United States. Since then, it has been used in various types of manufacturing industry, in providing services, and in software development. The purpose of QFD is to ensure that the customer is satisfied with the product.

2 Customer Satisfaction

Let us consider the question of what makes satisfies the customer. While discussed and debated at length, quality is not the only dimension that is important to the software customer - on-time delivery and cost are also important. Companies are in business to make profit. To do so, customers must purchase the finished product. To have an impact on market share, an organisation's productivity must be improved. This ultimately means that quality, cost and time-to-market must improve. If an organisation can match a competitor's product in any two of quality, cost and time-to-market, and better them in the third, then it can be argued that the rational customer will buy from that organisation. (Calloway and Chadwell, 1990). In the case of development for internal use, where the customer has no choice but to deal with the internal department, a reduction of development costs and on-time delivery will help the reduction of overall costs within the organisation, and consequently will have an effect on the cost of the company's product.

However, because the question of product quality is often debated at length, it is appropriate to discuss the subject of quality in relation to software. During the software development process, measurements are often taken as an indicator of whether a software system is a 'quality product' or not. These are often statistically based. An example is the metric for measuring quality of software code:

$$\frac{\text{Number of defects discovered in the code}}{\text{Number of lines of code}}$$

which has "become almost an industry standard" (Fenton et al., 1995). Using measurements such as these, there is a failure to consider if the working product, while conforming to software and test specifications, will fulfil the requirement of the customer. In reality, customers are not interested in metrics indicating the number of defects discovered during testing, which may in fact be a measure of how stringent test procedures are within the organisation. In fact, they are particularly interested in receiving a product that works reliably, and is delivered on time at as low a cost as possible. Similarly, "...customers do not want to be involved in legalistic nitpicking about whether specifications have been met. They expect their needs to be satisfied even when those are imperfectly defined." (Kenny, 1988).

To produce a quality software product, therefore, the software developer must be more interested in producing a product so that it contains " 'every good thing the product can be' from the point of view of both product producer and product user." (Walsh, 1990). The software user is most important, as it is they who will purchase and pay for upgrades to the software. If they are dissatisfied, the developer will not have a customer.

The users' perspective of quality must be uppermost in the mind of the developer. Eight dimensions of quality from a customer viewpoint have been provided by Garvin (1984). These are: Performance, Features, Reliability, Conformance, Durability, Serviceability, Aesthetics, and Perceived quality.

3 What is QFD?

> "QFD is a systematic means of ensuring that customer or marketplace demands (requirements, needs, wants) are accurately translated into relevant technical requirements and actions throughout each stage of product development" and it "helps companies design more competitive products, in less time, at lower cost, and higher quality." (Fortuna, 1988).

Emphasis is placed on collecting the voice of the customer using various methods, and then maintaining this voice throughout the product life-cycle. For this purpose, QFD uses a set of matrices which are used to convert the customer's voice into a final product. A number of different models are available for use, and are usually adapted to suit the process as required by individual companies. The original Japanese model consists of over 70 matrices. GOAL/QPC in the U.S.A., promotes a model consisting of 32 matrices. For software development, Richard Zultner (1990) has modified the matrix set to include 14 matrices. The model currently being used by the National

Centre for Quality Management at the University of Limerick, has been adapted by the American Standards Institute (ASI) and contains 4 matrices as illustrated in Figure 1. Although QFD consists of many matrices, it is often the first house, known as the house of quality that is focused upon. This alone can have a significant effect (Fortuna, 1988).

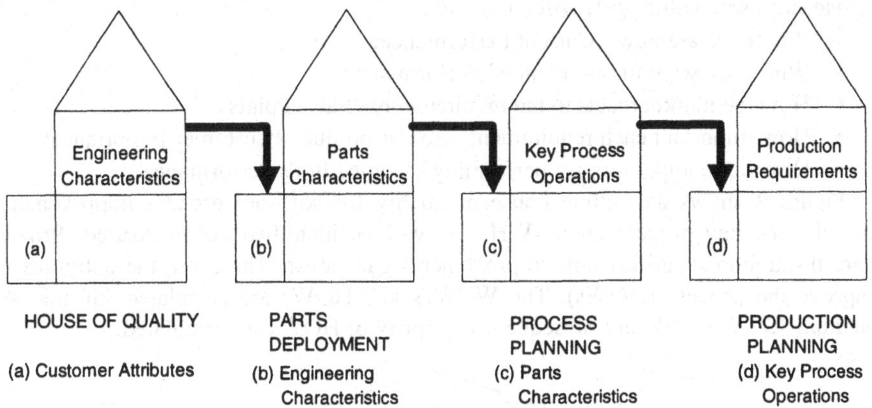

Fig. 1. QFD Matrices

In the House of Quality, customers' requirements (WHATs) are listed, the importance of WHATs are measured and their priority calculated. Matrices are used to visually represent the relationship of the WHATs with the means by which these requirements can be satisfied (HOWs). HOWs are prioritised. It is also easier to identify conflicting HOWs, and those that complement each other.

3.1 QFD for Requirements Engineering

Requirements Engineering is concerned with the elicitation of requirements from the software user and including those requirements in the product being developed. QFD has been used successfully as a requirements engineering tool. For example, Karlsson (1995) explains that when QFD was evaluated in an industrial project, it "helps developers to focus more clearly on the customer's needs and in managing non-functional requirements." At the National Centre for Quality Management, QFD was used on a project during the development of a database system. This system is for use by small companies, and requirements were prioritised using the house of quality.

3.2 Technique for Process Improvement Strategy

This author's main interest is in the investigation of Quality Function Deployment as a technique to help small software companies successfully implement a process improvement strategy for software development. One of the difficulties which has been presented by practitioners when discussing the use of QFD in small companies (which are prevalent in Ireland), is that it can take an unjustified amount of time, particularly in collecting customer requirements and in building the matrices.

Therefore, the research aims to provide a generic model from which small software companies can develop a Software Process Improvement (SPI) strategy.

In developing the QFD/SPI technique, the WHATs must be presented. These would normally reflect the voice of the customer. In the case of Software Process Improvement, the customers' voice is the measured key process areas within the organisation. These become the individual WHATs.

Metrics used within QFD will consist of :

- Where we are now - Current Performance;
- Where we want to be - Planned Performance;
- How the market reacts to the requirements - Sales Points;
- How important each requirement is to our product - Customer Importance;
- How our competitors are performing - Competitor's Performance.

Figure 2 shows an outline house of quality for software process improvement. Initially, the key process areas (WHATs) will be identified and measured. Project team discussion identifies how improvements can occur. These are the activities to improve the process (HOWs). The WHATs and HOWs are correlated (Strong '●', Medium 'O', Weak 's') and subsequently, priority of HOWs are calculated.

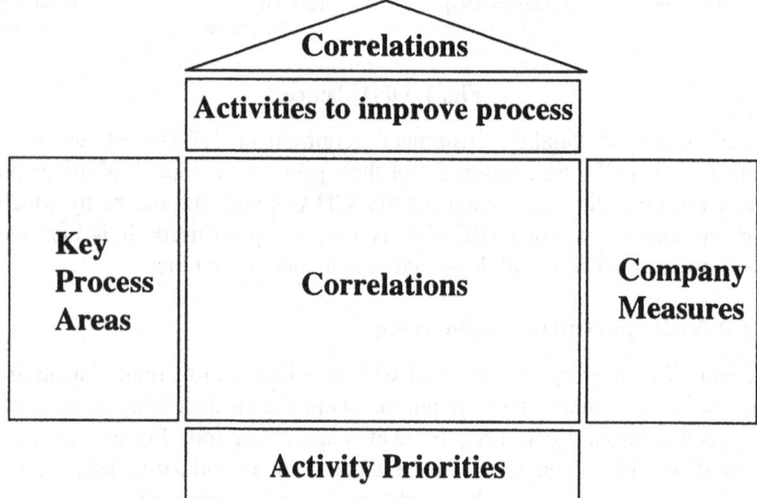

Fig. 2. Outline QFD House of Quality for Software Process Improvement

4 Contribution to Women's Studies

To date, the author has become familiar with Quality Function Deployment, investigating and working with Irish companies who have been using QFD for various purposes. One of the QFD projects which has been completed as part of this research was to generate ideas and strategies for developing Women's Studies within the University of Limerick.

Initially, the Women's Studies course board conducted a brain-storming session, which 42 people, all of whom have an interest in the development of Women's

Studies, attended. These consisted of faculty, students and other interested parties. During this session, 112 ideas were written down as ideals that were important to the people attending, and what should be done about them. The course board was then faced with prioritising these ideas. The author, having attended the initial meeting, conducted a QFD analysis of the information gathered.

Following the Women's Studies group meeting, two categories were created:

- WHAT should be done with the money (ideals) - for example "Develop consciousness among Humanities students"
- HOW these ideals should be implemented (practical) - for example "Produce a newsletter".

There were 30 WHATs and 82 HOWs identified from the Women's Studies forum.

To establish the importance of each WHAT the original group involved was surveyed. All WHATs were collected into a voice of customer questionnaire. On this questionnaire, the participants were expected to indicate how important each WHAT was, and how well the Women's Studies group were performing at that time. Eighty-two percent of participants returned the questionnaire.

For example, participants were asked: *How important is it to profile Women in non-Traditional Careers?* They could give one of five answers, value for each is bracketed: Not important (1), A Little important (2), Fairly important (3), Very important (4) or Extremely important (5).

They were also asked: *How well or badly do we profile Women in non-Traditional Careers?* Answers available here were Extremely badly (1), Very badly (2), Fairly well (3), Very well (4) and Extremely well (5).

For each question, the rates given were averaged. Examples of questions with average rates are given in Figure 3. The Women's Studies team then decided what their Planned Performance should be on a scale of 1 - 5 (1 - Low priority; 5 - High Priority) for each of the categories. Improvement Factor was then calculated as a ratio of Planned Performance to Company Performance. (See Figure 3).

Comment	(a)	(b)	(c)	(d)	(e)	Rank
Profile Women in non-Traditional Careers	4.0	2.5	3.0	1.2	4.8	24
Develop consciousness amongst Eng/Sc/Computing Students	4.3	1.5	3.5	2.3	10.1	1
Profile Women's Studies M.A. Thesis	3.9	2.7	4.5	1.7	6.6	11

(a) Importance to Participants (b) Women's Studies Performance
(c) Planned Performance (d) Improvement Factor (e) Overall Improvement

Fig. 3. Rating WHATs

From this data, overall importance of each requirement was calculated as:

*Importance to Participant * Improvement Factor.*

From this information, the percentage importance of each WHAT was calculated, and the WHATs ranked from one to thirty in order of importance. Rows completed for a selection of customer requirements (WHATs) can be seen in the Figure 3.

The top 10 WHATs, listed in ascending order are:

1. Develop consciousness of Women's Studies among Engineering / Science / Computing Students.
2. Develop consciousness of Women's Studies among Senior Administrators / Management.
3. Profile post-graduate career paths.
4. Develop consciousness of Women's Studies among other students (non-Humanities/Engineering/Science/Computing).
5. Promoting equality within the University.
6. Profile Monograph series.
7. Develop consciousness of Women's Studies among Engineering / Science / Computing Staff.
8. Develop consciousness of Women's Studies among other staff (non-Humanities/Engineering/Science/Computing).
9. Links with teachers including Career Guidance.
10. Profile new initiatives.

The course team continued the QFD process by correlating the ways in which they could provide their service (HOWs) with WHAT was required. In this particular case, the HOWs had been collected during the initial brainstorming session. For example, one HOW was to 'Produce a Newsletter'. During discussion, the team then decided where there was a correlation between each HOW and each WHAT, and whether this correlation was strong, medium, or weak. This resulted in a correlation table of HOWs vs WHATs. For example, the HOW 'Produce a Newsletter' is correlated strongly with 'Develop Consciousness among Engineering / Science / Computing Students', correlated medium with 'Develop Consciousness among Engineering / Science / Computing Staff' and weakly with 'Develop Consciousness among Senior Administrators / Management'. For visual purposes these correlations are marked on the matrix as l (strong), m (medium), and Δ (weak). They are given values 9, 3, and 1 respectively. A subset of the final House of Quality is displayed in Figure 4. This figure shows how the 10 most important WHATs have been deemed by the course team to correlate with 10 HOWs.

WHATs vs. HOWs Legend		
Strong	●	9
Moderate	O	3
Weak	Δ	1

	Prize for atricles by students on Women's Studies in An Focal	UL societies and clubs to hold competitions - prizes sponsored	Auto/Biography workshops for students	Technology Workshops with women from WITS etc.	Postgraduate/staff conference	Publish proceedings from Postgrad/Staff Conference	Lectures / Seminars on women's literature and art	Student Debate on Gender	Seminars on awareness/information in Gender/Women's Studies	Produce a Newsletter
Develop consciousness among Eng/Sc/Computing Students	O	O	●	●	Δ	●		●	●	●
Develop consciousness among other Students	O	O	●		●	●	O	●	●	●
Develop consciousness among Eng/Sc/Computing Staff		O	●	●	●	●		O	O	O
Develop consciousness among Senior Admin/Management			●		●	●	O		Δ	Δ
Develop consciousness among Other (Bus/Ed) Staff		O	●		●	●		O	O	O
Profile Monograph series			●		●	●	O			O
Profile Post-Graduate Career Paths			O		●	●			O	●
Profile New Initiatives			●		●	●				
Promoting Equality within the University	O		●		●	●	Δ		Δ	Δ
Links with Teachers including Career Guidance										O

Fig. 4. Subset of the completed House of Quality

Using the values of the correlations, the Importance of each HOW was calculated. These were ranked in order of importance, showing that the 'Autobiography workshops for students' was the most important HOW to proceed with.

The following 10 HOWs showed up as being the most important:

1. Autobiography workshops for students.
2. Postgraduate/staff conference.
3. Publish proceedings from postgraduate/staff conference.
4. Publish monograph series.
5. Media attention from postgraduate/staff conference.
6. Form equality group.
7. Liaise with National agencies.
8. Produce a newsletter.
9. Liaise with International agencies.
10. Support Women in Technology and Science Role model day.

5 Conclusion

The Women's Studies course board has successfully implemented a strategy to develop Women's Studies within the University of Limerick. This strategy is based on the priorities developed during the Quality Function Deployment exercise, and many of the HOWs have been implemented. The advantages of this approach are that input can be taken from all members of faculty and students, and the outcome prioritised.

Other work with Quality Function Deployment continues within the University of Limerick. In particular, the author continues her work with small software development companies using QFD as a tool to develop a software process improvement strategy.

Acknowledgements

The author wishes to acknowledge Dr Pat O'Connor, Women's Studies Course Leader, who initiated the Women's Studies developmental project within the Department of Government and Society at the University of Limerick. The Women's Studies developmental project was funded by the Higher Education Authority, Ireland.

References

1. Dave Calloway, Dave and Brian Chadwell: Manufacturing Strategic Plan - QFD and the Winchester Gear Transfer. Transactions from the 2nd Symposium on QFD, June, Michigan, U.S.A, pp. 370-380 (1990)
2. Norman Fenton, Robin Whitty, and Yoshinori Iizuka, Editors: Software Quality Assurance and Measurement - A Worldwide Perspective. International Thomson Computer Press, U.K. (1995)
3. Robert M. Fortuna: Beyond Quality: Taking SPC Upstream. Quality Progress. June, pp 23- 28 (1988)
4. D.A. Garvin: What Does "Product Quality" Really MSean?. Sloan Management Review. Fall Issue, pp. 25-43 (1984)
5. Alan C. Gillies: Software Quality, Theory and Management. Chapman & Hall, U.K. (1992)
6. Mike Goodland and Caroline Slater: SSADM A Practical Approach. McGraw-Hill Book Company, London, England (1995)
7. Eugene Stephen Haag: A field study of the use of Quality Function Deployment as applied to Software Development. PhD Thesis, University of Texas at Arlington (1992)
8. Watts S. Humphrey: Managing the Software Process. Presentation to SPI 95 - The European Conference on Software Process Improvement, The European Experience in a World Context. 30th Nov-1st Dec, Barcelona, Spain (1995)
9. Joachim Karlsson: Towards a Strategy for Software Requirements Selection. Thesis no. 513, Department of Computer and Information Science, School of Engineering, Linkoping University, Sweden (1995)

10. Andrew A. Kenny: A New Paradigm for Quality Assurance. Quality Progress. June, pp. 30-32 (1988)
11. Steve Neupauer: Improving the Software Process. Presentation to CEEDA 96, 3rd International Conference on Concurrent Engineering and Electronic Design Automation. 18-9th January, Poole, U.K. (1996)
12. Mark C. Paulk: The Evolution of the SEI's Capability Maturity Model for Software. Software Process - Improvement and Practice, Volume I, Pilot Issue, August, pp. 3-15 (1995)
13. Bill Peterson: Transitioning the CMM into Practice. Proceedings of SPI 95 - The European Conference on Software Process Improvement, The European Experience in a World Context. 30th Nov-1st Dec, Barcelona, Spain, pp. 103-123 (1995)
14. William J. Walsh: Get the Whole Organisation behind new Product Development. Quality Progress. Nov-Dec, pp. 32-36 (1990)
15. Richard E. Zultner: Software Quality [Function] Deployment - Applying QFD to software. Transactions from the 2nd Symposium on Quality Function Deployment. June, Michigan, U.S.A., pp144-149 (1990)

Do the Promises Made by the New Technologies Fulfil Women's Educational and Employment Needs?

Mrs D.M. Thompson and Dr G. Homer

School of Computing and Information Technology, University of Wolverhampton, WV1 1SB, UK.

Abstract. The impact of modern technology on the education/training and employment of women is examined. The role of the superhighway in the context of Higher Education is discussed, with specific reference to the Wolverhampton "Broadnet" project - a pilot programme utilising wide-bandwidth fibre-optic cable communications to support the remote delivery of education and training materials. The paper puts forward the hypothesis that the blossoming Internet and Multimedia technologies represent employment opportunities for women who possess the necessary aptitudes.

1 Introduction

This paper examines the changes that modern technology has brought about in two main areas of women's lives, namely education/training and employment patterns. In most institutions it is the Information Technology or Computing Departments who have been the first to seize upon the changing methods for delivering training and education. It is perhaps appropriate to examine these departments to find examples of practice that will illustrate possible ways forward for the future of women's education, training and employment. It is necessary firstly to consider "What is modern technology?" and to define such terms as multimedia, internet etc.

Multimedia - the use of a high specification PC to display, store, retrieve and manipulate content which could include any combination of; conventional text, numeric data, high resolution - full colour still images and pictures, high quality animated graphics/images, video and multichannel sound.

The equipment required often includes CD-ROM drives, additional plug-in video and audio processor cards, amplifiers and speakers, Magneto-optical drives, scanners and so on. The software tools used include graphics image processing tools (Adobe Paintshop, 3D Studio, Asymetrix Toolbook etc.) as well as tools to process video sequences.

The Internet has grown rapidly in recent years [1]. It started life in the early seventies as a method of minimising the vulnerability of the US and NATO network of strategic computer systems to an air-detonated nuclear blast. In effect, tens of thousands of computer systems around the world are interconnected via telecommunication systems. Each computer system can have enormous quantities of information (text, pictures, video etc.), an enormous information repository.

Software tools (many of them free or low-cost) allow the vast store of material to be searched and examined. Other tools allow people to hold (text-based) conversations in real-time, provide electronic mail (e-mail) facility that ignores geographical and political borders. The Internet is not owned or controlled by any one organisation or group, this is both its strength, and its weakness.

2 Education and Training - The Traditional Scene

Women's education has traditionally begun at school up to the age of 16. An increasing number of women have then entered a traditional university to obtain a HND or degree, while other women have gone straight into employment. These patterns are of course, not particular to women. The divergence of education and training for men and women often becomes apparent later in life [2]. A significant number of women have traditionally been less concerned with on the job training or indeed any education later in life [3]. With new employment trends it is obviously necessary for on the job training and education to take place and also perhaps training away from the job environment.

Many institutions of Further Education and Higher Education have realised the needs of "women returners" to return to the job market after bringing up a family or other enforced career break. Courses have been developed for women who wish to return to their original area of work and require an update as well as those women who desire a career change [4].

Although these courses have attempted to meet the needs of women returners i.e. by providing child care facilities on site and often free, and by providing courses between the hours of 10.00 am - 3.00 p.m. the question remains can modern technology help such women and provide a more flexible form of learning? Perhaps equally importantly, are there drawbacks to this form of learning that particularly affect women?

Focusing on a particular case study of education and training for women returners will highlight the important issues. This case study is taken from the field of Computer Education.

The School of Computing at the University of Wolverhampton has for many years run a series of courses for women returners. The programme has involved three day taster courses, six week courses and an MSc Conversion Course in Information Systems Engineering. All these courses have been provided free using funding from the ESF. They have all involved attendance at the University between 10.00 am and 3.00 p.m. Childcare has been provided at the University's nursery. Many women have benefited from these courses and have obtained HND's, degrees and MSc's. Although the courses have been successful it was felt that modern technology could be used to make the courses even more accessible.

Three years ago it was decided that some of the modules that comprise the MSc should be delivered by distance learning. This involved the students borrowing a computer and software from the University and providing links to the university from their home via a modem. This meant that attendance for one term was on a very limited basis. It was discovered that a tremendous amount of technical support is necessary if students are to set up computer equipment reliably in their own homes. They become extremely frustrated when they can't get immediate help with their problems. The other, perhaps more surprising, problem was that they missed the companionship of other women which they had experienced when they attended college. Although they were in communication with other members of the course, they missed the daily dialogue and camaraderie.

However there were advantages. Each student could work when she was able to, to fit in with family commitments. Childcare problems were minimised and if any family crisis did occur, the time could be made up at a later date. Travel was obviously reduced which meant that women from a wider geographical area could access these modules.

This early, simple excursion into electronic remote course delivery, although far from a complete success, raised interest in the role of technological support for remote course delivery amongst both staff and students.

3 The Role of the Superhighway at Higher Education Institutions

Examination of the literature relevant to the role of the Internet and similar technologies in supporting remote or distance learning initiatives at educational and other institutions reveals a plethora of examples and case-studies. Most are relevant to the needs of women although not designed exclusively for them.

Much of the reported work has taken place in USA. The 'Knowledge Integration Environment' (KIE) project based at the University of California [5] resulted in the development of a number of software tools (for example, 'SpeakEasy' - a discussion tool) designed to support remote instruction and delivery. Berge and Collins [6] summarise what they feel should comprise 'Computer-Mediated-Communication'. Whilst these authors fully support the concept of remote delivery and interaction they note the steep learning curve for both students and educators in using the technology effectively. They also believe the lack of social cues and face-to-face interaction increases the sense of isolation for people using this medium.

In the UK, the Open University have announced several courses designed for Internet delivery. These include postgraduate courses at Masters level in Open and Distance Education and in Computing. The first, 'User Interface Design and Development', is scheduled for a November 1996 start. [7] Similarly, the Open University based at Orlando, USA, also advocate the use of Internet as an ideal mechanism for certain sections of the population. [8] They suggest that mature women with a family and career are likely to benefit from such a delivery and support system. In addition, they feel that the 'isolation' resulting from this mode of delivery could be an advantage for mature students, removing the competition from the younger students.

Returning to the UK, several universities have begun to experiment with remote delivery and support, these include Heriot Watt University [9], and Southampton [10]. Henley Management College [11,12] offer an MBA supported heavily via Internet.

The private sector has also not been slow in recognising the potential afforded by the Internet for education and training. 'On-Line Education Ltd' in Hong Kong provide courses for working professionals in Hong Kong, the courses are accredited by the University of Paisley [13]. The Oxford Computer Group recently announced their 'On Line College Oxford' which will be available under the umbrella of

Microsoft On-line Institute (MOLI). This will ..."allow busy, employed professionals to study for Microsoft's Certified Professional Examinations..." [14].

The vast majority of these have been initiatives that have commenced within the last three years or so. Clearly, there has been an explosion of interest and activity. However, a careful examination of these reported cases often reveals a picture of uncoordinated and piece-meal development. There are many examples of good practice but examples of the potential of this new delivery/interaction medium being exploited to the full are scarce.

4 The Developing Scene

In the longer term, as the bandwidth of the technology improves and as the Internet establishes itself as a serious business tool (a process that is currently taking place at an astounding rate), then the full technological features could be harnessed.

The education and training opportunities afforded by the blossoming technology might include;

Access to course notes, assessments, case studies, contact names/'addresses' to include;

- Video clips
- Audio
- Animated Graphics sequences (e.g. a computer program 'executing', a machine operating etc.)
- Static Graphics/Hi-res colour images
- VIP lectures via Internet (Sound only, Sound+Video)
- Access to external information sources/reference material via Internet

Student-to-Student-to-Tutor dialogues

- Video Conferencing
- Telephone
- E-Mail
- Fax-Back
- Voice Mail
- Bulletin Boards/Conference Groups

Submission of work/assignments/tutorial solutions

- Including dynamic solutions (e.g. answers with a temporal
- or time-base element to them....data flows, program logic etc.)

Return of work, marked

- Annotated with
  - Text
  - Audio
  - Animated sequences
  - Video
- Computer marked

Participation in group work

- Business games
- 'Electronic' presentations (e.g. inc. use of Powerpoint-type tools etc.)
- Work requiring several contributors, shared activities
- Use of data from Employing Company, i.e. real-world 'personalised' data/information.

5 The Wolverhampton Broadnet Project

Although the Internet represents a tremendous resource, one that is expanding and maturing at a tremendous rate, there is currently a problem. Most people access the Internet via a modem and a dial-up telephone line to a service provider. The telephone line can only carry a limited amount of data per unit time, it has a limited bandwidth. This in turn limits the speed at which data can be fed to the clients PC, resulting in large, multicoloured graphical images taking several seconds to load and significantly limiting the effective use of video and sound.

A project at the University of Wolverhampton, the 'Broadnet Project', is attempting to develop a pilot programme that should overcome the bandwidth limitations of telephone lines and instead will use a high bandwidth fibre-optic cable channel to carry true multimedia material, offering video, audio, high-resolution still and animated colour images.

A large file server (64 G.bytes) sited at Wolverhampton Science Park is connected to several selected SME's (Small to Medium sized Enterprises/Companies) via the existing cable TV/Telephony network installed by TeleWest Communications PLC in the Industrial Midlands and Shropshire areas of the UK. During this pilot programme, education and training materials, making full use of multimedia techniques (video, sound etc.), will be accessed by these trial companies and, over the next twelve months, their effectiveness will be rigorously evaluated. These training materials, currently under construction, employ various techniques and tools - Powerpoint supported by streamed audio, Asymetrix "Toolbook" and conventional HTML.

In a second phase of the project, these training materials will be made available to a wider audience. Basically, an enhanced set-top box (similar to existing cable TV set-top boxes, but with a significant amount of micro processing power built into them) will allow customer to access these training materials, in addition to several other information services supplied by other third party information providers. (Currently these are subject to commercial confidentiality agreements and will not be discussed further in this paper)

Clearly, the advent of this home-based broadnet service will particularly benefit the 'house-bound' community, of which the biggest proportion are women. Thus, the project will offer this community the opportunity of improving their education and employment potential via this home-based study mechanism. The presence of high quality video content (for example, an interview with a VIP expert in the field of study) will be supported by video conferencing allowing the student to interact with Tutors in real time. This will enhance the learning experience - particularly for women who might otherwise feel isolated or alienated by this remote form of study. (Currently the university is using an ISDN video conferencing link between certain colleges of Further Education and the University Education and Careers Service).

6 Enhanced Employment Prospects

Experience over six years of running Women into Computing courses at the University of Wolverhampton has shown that even after a one year MSc Course, few women go into the "hard" side of computing. The majority of mature women combine their previous skills (either learnt in the workplace or at home) with newly acquired skills in modern technology. A breakdown of the jobs/courses followed by women leaving the Wolverhampton courses in 1996 revealed the following destinations.

Receptionist at a Veterinary Surgery
Further business courses
Administrative assistants
Maths course with Open University
Business Administration courses
Setting up own business
Business/Computing courses
Teacher Training courses
Foundation Course in Art and Design
Computing courses

These destinations are typical of previous years. A more rigorous national analysis indicated a similar pattern. Frances Grundy states that only approximately 8% of University computer technicians are male [15].

The rapid development of the Internet as a robust, business tool supported by the equally rapid developments, (and applications) of multimedia technology raise the prospect of significant employment opportunities arising as a result. Further, due to the very nature of the Internet and the type of skills likely to be required by these new jobs, it is possible that these job opportunities will be suited to women, particularly women with family or similar commitments that limit their mobility.

Let us examine these new employment opportunities. The Internet represents a massive, and freely available information source. Many business and commercial organisations have the need to search and organise information to support their business activities. Most companies already possess Internet access. What they often lack is a) employees with the *specific* Internet searching skills and b) the *staff time* to perform such time consuming searches.

There maybe a role for a home-based information researcher using the Internet from a modest-specification PC, working from home, at a time to suit the worker's personal circumstances and constraints. The researcher would need only a modest outlay for capital equipment (PC, printer, modem, software etc.) and would work on a commissioned-based for the business commissioning the information.

A second example of the potential employment opportunities arising as a result of the developing technologies is in the area of multimedia design.

More and more organisations are beginning to realise the business advantages afforded by well designed, attractive visual applications. A well designed, visually attractive Web page can enhance the image of an organisation and represents a marketing 'plus' (the reverse is also true). Similarly, a Building Society may wish to offer its customers an interactive, touch screen information service - providing the customer with information regarding pensions, insurance, mortgages etc. - all presented in a professional, visual (and audio) fashion that makes a statement regarding the corporate image. The application of multimedia technology is virtually endless.

The skills required to produce such professional multimedia applications are diverse, ranging from the technical (ability to use sophisticated software tools; 3D Studio, Adobe Paint Shop etc.) to the aesthetic (an appreciation of the use of colour, image, layout etc.)

People with these skills are currently in short supply. Graduates of university Schools of Computing are often too focused on the technological issues and possess few, if any, aesthetic skills. Similarly, people coming out of Art Schools are often completely lacking in any significant appreciation of the vast technical knowledge and skills required to implement their graphical artistry on a PC.

Universities are beginning to address this gap but currently there may be an opportunity for women to get into this new employment area at the very birth. Often women are at an advantage over the majority of men in respect of their ability to design attractive and effective images (whether it is a room design, selection of soft furnishings or skills in water-colours). Such women will need to acquire sufficient technical skills and knowledge to transfer their aesthetic ideas and concepts to a machine-based environment (use of software tools, HTML, principles and practices of the Internet etc.) However, it is far easier to acquire these skills than for a technocrat to acquire skills in graphic artistry etc.

Again, this is a job that could be undertaken as a 'home worker'. A word of caution. Currently the software packages required to support these activities are expensive and the PC hardware required to run this software is far more sophisticated, and hence, expensive.

7 Conclusions/Analysis

Women can benefit from modern technology both in the field of education and in enhanced employment opportunities. In the computing field, great strides have been made in developing "distance learning" materials that will assist women returners access courses that they would otherwise be inaccessible to them. These materials do however, have their drawbacks, namely the lack of person to person interaction and the inevitable technical problems. The advantages in saved travelling time, reduced child-care problems etc. can in many cases outweigh these disadvantages. The way forward looks extremely promising. Many new developments via Internet and Broadnet will make distance learning more exciting, effective, and perhaps equally importantly, more accessible for women.

There are many new employment opportunities developing as a result of the new technology. The opportunity is there for women to grasp these challenges *before* the hierarchies have been established in the newly developing internet/multimedia applications industry. After all, the proportion of women computer programmers when 'programming' was a 'new' career, was far higher compared to what it is currently. Women's skills and abilities may be particularly suited to the development of multimedia packages, if they are prepared to invest the necessary time and money.

References

1. Mintel, Leisure: Multimedia - The Domestic Market, November (1995)
2. Sears E., Encouraging Women Returners into Computing Courses in Higher Education, Women into Computing - Selected Papers 1985-1990, Springer Verlag (1991)
3. Platt, Attracting Women Returners to Computing, Women into Computing - Selected Papers 1985-1990, Springer Verlag (1991)
4. Thompson D, Positive Action to Encourage Women Returners to follow Higher Education Courses in Computing: A Case Study, Proc. Conf. Gender,Science and Technology, Eidenhoven, (1992)
5. http://www.kie.berkeley.edu/KIE.html (Knowledge Integration Project, University of California)
6. Berge Z and Collins M, //sunsite.unc.edu/cmc/mag/1995/feb/berge.html
7. http://cszx.open.ac.uk/zx
8. http://www.openu.edu/intro.html
9. http://info.mcc.ac.uk/cgu/SIMA/WWW/teach.html
10. http://ilc.ecs.soton.ac.uk
11. http://www.henleymc.ac.uk/classrm/lotusno.htm
12. Bickerstaffe G. When a screen takes the place of a classroom. The Times, 29th January 1996, p5
13. http://www.online.edu/online/online.html
14. Oxford Computer Training Newsletter, Issue 13, Feb 1996
15. F Grundy: Women and Computers. Intellect 1996, pp51 - 52

(All Internet/www locations as at 1/4/96)

Changing Perceptions through a one day Introduction to Information Technology for Secondary School Girls

Annemieke Craig, Julie Fisher, Angela Scollary

Victoria University of Technology, Melbourne, Australia

1 Introduction

Current literature suggests that girls have a perception that computers are for men and all computing is about mathematics or engineering. In 1992 Victoria University of Technology hosted its inaugural *Girls in Computing Day.* In subsequent years between sixty and eighty 15 to 16 year old girls participated annually in the day with a range of 'hands-on' activities highlighting different aspects of computing. The principal motivation for organising such a day is to present girls with a broader picture in the hope that we may encourage more to consider a career in Information Technology. The purpose of the panel will be to encourage discussion on organising such a day, the benefits and to explore what activities might be offered.

2 Organisation

Local schools are invited to participate giving the University greater local exposure. The girls are organised into groups and rotate through activities. The activities are specifically designed to be different from those the girls would normally encounter and where possible to allow for active participation. Workshop leaders are generally female academic staff or enthusiastic female graduate students. The schools are very keen to participate and we have no difficulty getting the numbers. Evaluation sheets completed by the girls and staff at the end of the day indicate the day is interesting and thought provoking and has widened their horizons.

3 Pre and Post Survey Results 1995

Since 1995, the girls have been asked to complete a pre and post survey on their attitudes towards the computing profession. The purpose of the surveys is to determine whether or not the girls' attitudes change as a result of the activities they participate in during that day. The girls are presented with a series of statements and asked to indicate their opinion of the statement on a five point leichart scale. The results of the surveys have been interesting. They indicate that the girls did change their perceptions in a number of ways. For example in the pre survey most girls saw computing as a solitary occupation, primarily involving computer programming and with little opportunity to be creative. In the post test the girls' attitudes had shifted away from these perceptions. In terms of whether or not women in general or they themselves could become computing professionals, again attitudes shifted over the day with more girls strongly agreeing with these statements in the post test. The conclusion therefore is that, at least in the short term, the perceptions girls have of computing can be changed if they are presented with appropriate examples and activities.

Accepted Papers and Discussion Notes

Topic 6: History – Herstory

The Construction of the von Neumann-Concept as Constituent for Technical and Organic Computers

Heike Stach

Interdisciplinary Research Project "Social History of Computer Science"
Technical University of Berlin.

Abstract. In 1945 von Neumann wrote the "First Draft of a Report on the EDVAC", the first paper to develop the concept of the modern stored program computer. The "device" described in this paper is constructed as a counterpart of man, who in a society of war was seen as a kind of soldier-like input-output mechanism, an image of man virulent in different scientific discourses. Arguing in a mathematical way von Neumann creates his device as a structure that seems to underly all technical as well as organical realizations of the function "to carry out instructions to perform calculations". As von Neumann also discussed the material construction of his device, it obtains a hermaphrodite character being on the one hand material and on the other hand a mental object. He thus introduced patterns of orientation into the discussion concerning computing technology that are important to the woman-computer relation too.

1 Introduction

The electronic computer as we know it today came into being during the Second World War. The computers of that time - mostly women equipped with an electronically driven desk calculator and working together in large computing offices - had to struggle hard to handle the masses of calculations required for ballistic tables, the development of the atomic bomb, and other wartime military operations. By early 1943 the production of ballistic tables had fallen so far behind schedule that the US-Army Ordnance Department Ballistic Research Laboratory at the Arberdeen Proving Ground in Maryland, USA, decided to support two young engineers, J. Presper Eckert and John Mauchly from the Moore School of Electrical Engineering of the University of Pennsylvania, to realize their plans for an electronic calculator, later called the ENIAC. In need of large-scale calculating help in the solution of a difficult series of problems concerning the construction of the atomic bomb, von Neumann came into contact with these efforts. He promptly took a deep and lasting interest in the project and became a regular visitor to the Moore-School. As a result of his discussions with the ENIAC-group he wrote the "First Draft of a Report on the EDVAC" in summer of 1945.

On the ENIAC, the programming had to be done by hand in a long and laborious process: by setting mechanical switches and plugging hundreds of cables. On the EDVAC - in contrast - the program could be stored and modified electronicallly, as we know it today. Program as well as data were read into the memory at electronic speed before the program was carried out. The control of the device now was located inside the machine. What was to be done, the task the machine had to carry out, was invisible from the outside. The concept described in the "First Draft" later was referred to as "von Neumann architecture" and today is regarded as fundamental to the construction of most of the modern computers. At the end of the paper von Neumann derives from the construction of the device a "list of orders which control the device, i.e. [...] the code used in the device" (14.1). Thus the "First Draft" can also be seen as a starting point for the development of the later so called "programming languages".

In the following I would like to point out that not was the "First Draft" important in a pure technical sense to the development of the later computing machines and their programming but that it was also significant for how computing technologies were later perceived and interpreted. Underlying the First Draft are patterns of orientation that gave a certain meaning to the new technology and to programming and along with this shaped the development of later technologies, theories and of informatics and computer science as scientific disciplines. These patterns of orientation can also give hints as to why for women it is in general less tempting to deal and work with computers[1].

Underlying von Neumann´s considerations is an epistemological image that is based on the idea of man as a kind of self-steering mechanism to which the rules and the end of behaviour are always given in advance. This image of man was virulent in different biological, psychological, mathematical and engineering discourses of the time von Neumann as an exposed scientist participated in. These discourses confirmed each other as to the image of man underlying the "First Draft" that on the background of the Second World War gained even more imaginational power. Von Neumann translated this image of man into the description of a "device" that internalizes instructions and - according to technically built-in rules - carries them out automatically.

It is interesting to note that the "First Draft" is not, as the title seems to indicate, a design plan for a specific machine, the EDVAC. While it is true that von Neumann attaches importance to typical engineering topics and to the technical realizability of his explanations, he actually describes a "system" or a "structure" that has the character of a law of nature concerning all technical as well as organical realizations of the function "to carry out instrucions to perfom calculations of a considerable order of complexity". He thus creates an object that on the one hand seems to be a material machine and that on the other hand is an immaterial structure and laid a foundation for a world of hermaphrodite objects that later was regarded to be the specific sphere of e.g. German informatics. When Friedrich Bauer, one of the main driving forces in the institutionalization of informatics at German universities, wrote in 1974 that informatics is both a science of engineering and a humane discipline (german: eine "Geistes-Ingenieurwissenschaft") and at the same time characterized von Neumann as the founder of informatics this last but not least is an expression of the fact that von Neumann established those patterns of orientation that were part of the way German informatics saw and defined itself.

---

[1]The concept of "patterns of orientation" and its usefulness to research on the genesis of science and technology is outlined in (Stach 1996).

I will now describe in more detail the different mentioned discourses and how they acted in combination.

2 Neurophysiology

The device that von Neumann described in the "First Draft" at first glance seems to be a physical machine whose constituents are vaccuum tubes. Von Neumann discussed how many vaccuum tubes are necessary and how they must be combined to make possible the realization of a high speed memory of the desired size, and he briefly goes into the construction of vaccuum tubes. Comparing the First Draft with engineering papers of the time[2] it is striking that it also developed ideas quite unusual in an engineering context. E.g. von Neumann introduced vaccuum tubes as a special case of digital elements in general that according to him can be mechanical devices as well as human neurons. In chapter 4: "Elements, Synchronism Neuron Analogy" von Neumann explicitly compares the human nervous system and his device. The neurons of the higher animals were, as he put it here, digital elements like relays or vaccuum tubes: "4.2 It is worth mentioning that the neurons of the higher animals are definitely elements in the above sense". As vaccuum tubes have the shortest "reaction time" of all these elements - shorter than the human neuron, too, as he adds - he favours them as contituents of his device.

Von Neumann postulated that electronic elements function principally the same way as the human neuron. Though he knew that neuron functioning was in fact more complicated, the analogy between neurons and "relay-like elements" seems to have been so comprehensible for him and maybe attractive that he never did fundamentally doubt it. To him the human brain and nervous system and his device seemed to be constructed in a similiar way - an assumption he expanded on in later papers dealing with what he called the theory of automata[3].

The idea that his device and the human nervous system and thus the technical and the biological are very similiar pervades the whole terminology of the "First Draft". For example the device described has "specialized organs" for addition, substraction, multiplication, division, "general control organs", a "memory organ", and so on. These organs are composed of suborgans or neural networks. It is interesting to note that his metaphor does not allude to mental processes as functions, and this very often was, and is, the case when later people described a computer, but it explicitly refers to the physical construction of the nervous system the brain was regarded to be a part of. Thus he argues that the instructions (data and code) must be given to the device "in some form which the device can sense" (1.2) - by means of suitable "input organs" - and the output must be stored in such a way that it can be "sensed more or less directly by human organs." (2.6). The "sensing" by the organs of the device thus was treated as equivalent to sensing by human organs.

Von Neumann had adopted this idea of the human neuron from the paper "A Logical Calculus of the Ideas Immanent in Nervous Activity", which had been

[2]E.g. (Mauchly 1942) and (Goldstine and Goldstine 1946)

[3]E.g. "The General and Logical Theory of Automata" from 1948 or "The Computer and the Brain" written from 1955 till 1957.

published in the "Bulletin of Mathematical Biophysics" in 1943. Warren McCulloch, a neurophysiologist from the Laboratory for Basic Research of the Department of Psychiatry at the University of Illinois and Walter Pitts, an 18-year old mathematician and logician, in this paper described the functioning of the human nervous system as a network of connections between neurons. As in simple threshold logic they assumed neurons to have two states - active and inactive. Given the state of neurophysiology in 1943 this proposition - though not uncontested at that time - was more supportable than it is today, as neuron-functioning has since turned out to be a much more complicated affair. On the basis of their assumptions it was possible for them to describe what the nervous system was supposed to be doing, by means of propositional logic: "Because of the 'all-or-none' character of nervous activity, neural events and the relationships among them can be treated by means of propositional logic", as they put it in their first sentence.

The central result of the paper was that any finite logical expression can be realized by McCulloch-Pitts neurons. This seemed to show that the brain was potentially a powerful logic and computational device. According to this exciting result McCulloch and Pitts did not hesitate to draw far-reaching conclusions concerning human thinking in general at the end of their paper, for example that "in psychology, introspective, behaviouristic or physiological, the fundamental relations are those of two-valued logic." (p. 25)

Von Neumann adopted his idea of the neuron from a paper that declared the human nervous system and brain to be a computing device, and then drew the reverse conclusion: If the nervous system is essentially a computing device then you can describe computing devices by means of the same elements -hence neurons - in the form of neural networks, too: "The analogs of human neurons [...] seem to provide elements of just the kind postulated at the end of 6. 1 [they are hypothetical elements which can be discussed as an isolated entities without going into detailed radio engineering questions]. We propose to use them [...] as the constituent elements of the device [...]." (6. 2)

3 Engineering

During and after the Second World War many scientists working in the USA were dedicated to the question of analogies between machines and living organisms. Besides von Neumann, McCulloch and Pitts these were especially Norbert Wiener, Julian Bigelow and Arturo Rosenbluth. In 1945, when von Neumann wrote the "First Draft", he and Wiener had been in contact for several years and had discussed their work and ideas quite often. That is why in the following I will consider in more detail the paper "Behaviour, Purpose and Teleology" that Wiener, Rosenbluth and Bigelow wrote in 1942, and discuss the impact it had on the "First Draft".

The main problem American scientists had to face during the war was - apart from the construction of the atomic bomb, a task von Neumann was devoted to - the improvement of air defense. As bombers were the most effective German weapons in attacking European cities, and the anti-aircraft of the time was quite ineffective against these quick and well-targetted aims, a "Radiation Laboratory" was established at the MIT to develop better anti-aircraft systems. Here Norbert Wiener, already a well-known mathematician, and the young engineer Julian Bigelow worked together on a mathematical theory that should help to determine the future course of an aeroplane from its location and the speed and direction of its movement.

One of the characteristics of the anti-aircraft system to be developed was to make use of feed-back loops: First on the basis of radar-data a gun directed towards a moving aim (e. g. a plane) and its alignment was examined. The results were then used to correct the alignment of the gun, and so on. If the necessary computations were carried out automatically - this was the crucial insight of Wiener and Bigelow - this would be a self-steering mechanism comparable to a human carrying a glass of water from the table to the mouth or picking up a pencil. They asked a physiologist and friend of Wiener, Arturo Rosenbluth, to discuss with them these analogies between machines and living organisms, and published the results in the paper "Behaviour, Purpose and Teleology" in the journal "Philosophy of Science" in 1943.

Like Pitts and McCulloch, Wiener, Bigelow and Rosenbluth here draw far-reaching conclusions concerning the relationship between man and machine, the functioning of the human brain, and human behaviour in general. For example they stress "that a uniform behaviouristic analysis is applicable to both machines and living organisms, regardless of the complexity of behaviour." According to this they state: "Such qualitative differences [between characteristics of living organisms and machines] have not appeared so far. The broad classes of behaviour are the same in machines and in living organisms." (p. 22) The assumption that qualitative differences between the behaviour of man and machine do not exist made it possible for them to make use of experiences with feed-back mechanisms to explain the functioning of the human brain and to "suggest that the main function of the cerebellum is the control of the feed-back nervous mechanisms involved in purposeful motor activity." (p. 20).

It is striking that Rosenbluth, Wiener and Bigelow and McCulloch and Pitts as well as von Neumann were concerned with the same segment of behaviour - the execution of an action according to certain rules the actor has already internalized and serving a purpose that is taken for granted. Although they only deal with this small part of human behaviour, they do not hesitate to draw conclusions concerning the functioning of the human nervous system and human behaviour in general:

- The whole terminology of Rosenbluth, Wiener and Bigelow is pervaded by the problem Wiener and Bigelow were dealing with at that time, the self-aiming of a gun towards a given target: Their "behaviouristic study of natural events [...] consists in the examination of the output of the object and of the relations of this output to the input" (p. 18), hence it reflects the idea of self-aiming by means of feed-back processes. "Behaviour" to them is "any change of an entity with respect to its surroundings" (p. 18), hence is characterized by its relation to the outer world as the success of the alignment of a gun is dependent on the relation of the gun and its target. And, last but not least, they make use of a very reduced notion of the term "purpose": "The term purposeful is meant to denote that the act or behaviour may be interpreted as directed to the attainment of a goal - i. e. to a final condition in which the behaving object reaches a definite correlation in time or in space with respect to another object or event." (p. 18). Hence purpose only relates to the attainment of a goal, the question of how the origin of the purpose has emerged is not discussed - as this would be very unusual for an anti-aircraft system. This restriction to a very special form of behaviour does not prevent them from stating that there are no essential qualitative differences between machines and living organisms.

- McCulloch and Pitts, too, excluded the question of how a certain goal or purpose emerges. Following their theory, the future states of the nervous system can be computed from a given state, therefore are determinded by the given state, whereas one cannot completely determine the preceeding states. Behaviour thus is determined by rules incorporated in the neural network, the purpose of behaviour is mirrored by the structure of the net itself. As they do not deal with the genesis of the net, they do not deal with the genesis of the purpose of behaviour either. In spite of this restriction they draw the much more general conclusion that in psychology the fundamental relations are those of two-valued logic.

- For von Neumann the central question was how his device could automatically carry out the orders it received and internalized in the memory: "Once these instructions are given to the device, it must be able to carry them out without the need for further intelligent human intervention." (1.2) Hence he was interested in how one could build a machine copying the described segment of behaviour - the automatic execution of an action governed by detailed rules. Like the authors of both the other papers who drew far-reaching conclusions concerning human thinking and behaviour in general, von Neumann assumed neurons and vacuum tubes, as well as his device and the human nervous system, to function similarly if not identically.

4 Behaviourism

As they did not seem to attach any importance to other aspects of human behaviour we can conclude that the authors of the three papers mentioned were guided by the assumption that man is basically a kind of self-steering mechanism acting according to given rules and to a given purpose. Since the main goal of Rosenbluth, Wiener and Bigelow was to define a "behaviouristic study of natural events" it seems reasonable to suspect that behaviouristic ideas that were quite popular in the USA before the war, had a significant impact on this way of thinking.

Before the scientists mentioned could ignore the boundary between man and machine, the behaviourists had blurred the differences between man and animal and had made "behaviour" the central category of psychology. Behaviourism can be seen as a "psychology of organisms, where man and animal [and whole societies] are regarded to be equal in so far as they behave according to the same rules." (Sonntag 1988, p. 58; my translation) Processes of consciousness were declared to be unimportant or even non existent. Instead organisms were supposed to transform a stimulus into a reaction through "reflexes" in the muscular and the nervous system. According to this theory a reflex is congenital and can be changed gradually by means of conditioning. The purpose of behaviour thus, according to behaviouristic theories, is incorporated in the system of reflexes, and hence is given in advance. An action is ruled by the structure of the reflexes. These are roughly the assumptions governing the papers discussed above. As it was normal that behaviourists gave far-reaching explanations not only for human behaviour, the authors of the papers in question did the same, when drawing far-reaching conclusions concerning their mechanical or biological "organisms".

5 Military Practice

It seems reasonable to assume that during a technological war the blurring of the boundary between man and machine was a quite obvious thing to do. In "Männerphantasien" Klaus Theweleit described, that with the technization of the army during the First World War, soldiers began to feel like a part of a formation whose members were men as well as machines. Similiarly (Galison 1994) points out that during the Second World War the enemy which the scientists and especially Wiener dealt with was kept distant by a wall of strategy, velocity and metal. The pilot and his machine were seen as one system. The emerging theories blurred the boundary between man and machine. To scientists like von Neumann, Wiener and Bigelow who during and after the Second World War were working on the construction of military weapons it might have been a natural thing to use the technological fighters as a defining model for man, especially, as in the military context, "man" foremost means "soldier" who was already supposed to function like a machine. The "organisms" Rosenbluth, Wiener, Bigelow and von Neumann describe show exactly the kind of behaviour a soldier is obliged to engage in to shoot at a given target, or to internalize instructions and carry them out according to the drill without doubting the given purpose.

Seen in this way that the Second World War was not only the condition for financing certain developments in science and technology. It also played a role as a social practice coining the feelings, experiences, and ways of thinking of people and scientists in a society of war. The fact that von Neumann described his "code" by means of a military metaphor may be regarded as an expression of this influence. For example he introduced the word "code" as follows: "It is therefore our immediate task to provide a list of orders which control the device, i.e. to describe the code used in the device" (14.1). The orders controling the device were given from the memory to the "general control organs" which like a good soldier were supposed to execute - and this is what von Neumann emphasizes - any order: "... the general control organs which see to it that these instructions - no matter what they are - are carried out." (2.3). In contrast to e.g. Turing 1936, von Neumann stressed the aspect of control, while Turing emphasized the aspect of description.

Not only von Neumann's terminology, but also the structure of his device mirrors the military background. The construction of the EDVAC was strictly hierarchical. One of the central design decisions was to introduce a "central control organ" as superior to the arithmetic organs and the memory organs, and to assign the "logical control" to it. According to von Neumann this hierachical organization was the most efficient possibility to realize the device: "2.3 Second: The logical control of the device, that is the proper sequencing of its operations, can be most efficiently carried out by a central control organ." Thus for von Neumann the efficiency of the logical control was associated with a hierarchical structure, an assumption he didn't feel necessary to argue about. Incorporated in his device thus is the idea that optimal efficiency is achieved by hierarchical structures. To him this was an everyday-experience: During the Second World War because of the close coupling of military and scientific research the US- economy gained a productivity unknown before, a process that went along with the establishment of more and more complex hierarchical stuctures.

6 Mathematics

Now I come to the last discourse I want to allude to. The structure of the mathematical way of thinking von Neuman, as a modern mathematician, had studied reserved a significant place for the soldier accepting orders and carrying them out automatically. In "Moderne-Sprache-Mathematik" (Modern Age - Language - Mathematics) Mehrtens characterizes modern mathematical thinking as follows: "The language of mathematics is a language of irrevocable orders to the signs. If the master says 'Let M be a set', then M is a set, and has to follow the rules ascribed to a set. The 'ideal subject' is the ideal servant, because he has incorporated the rules of his behaviour." (Mehrtens 1990, p. 514, my translation) What is the difference between the soldier carrying out his orders according to the military drill and this "ideal servant"? Neurophysiological and behaviouristic ideas, military practice and mathematical thinking reinforce each other as to this point. Man mechanically carrying out orders, that was von Neumann's model for a device that - as a servant or as a soldier - carries out its orders according to built-in rules like reflexes.

The mathematical way of thinking did not only go well with a quasi-military image of man, but it also allowed to von Neumann to construct his "device" as a kind of law of nature concerning organic as well as machine-realizations of the function "to carry out instructions to perform calculations of a considerable order of complexity". Already the outer appearance of the First Draft indicates it to be written by a mathematician. Von Neumann subdivided the paper into small, numbered paragraphs. This reminds of the structure of a mathematical paper consisting of definition, theorem, proof. In the beginning he defined: "1.2 An *automatic computing system* is a (usually highly composite) device, which can carry out instructions to perform calculations of a considerable order of complexity". Qua definitionem he seems to create the "automatic computing system" at this moment, the efforts at the Moore School in building the forerunner of the EDVAC, the ENIAC, and thus the context in which von Neumann´s ideas arose is not mentioned at all. Von Neumann who in 1929 and 1930 studied at the University of Göttingen where Hilbert was teaching and who intensively worked on Hilbert's program of proof theory here shows that he was a modern mathematician in Hilbert's tradition. To make this plausible I would like to follow Mehrten's considerations concerning the axiomatics of Hilbert: "Hilbert's axiomatic is exactly such creation pretending to be a creation out of the nothingness. The signs, names, rules, everything is created as a world the creator is the master of." (Mehrtens 1990, S. 124) In the "First Draft" von Neumann takes the attitude of a demiurge to create an "automatic computing system" that seems to exist beyond history.

Having created the central object von Neumann analyses its functioning: "2.1 In analyzing the functioning of the contemplated device, certain classificatory distinctions suggest themselves immediately." 2.2 to 2.9 then expose the basic construction of the device consisting of a "**C**entral **A**rithmetic", a "**C**entral **C**ontrol", a "**M**emory", an "Outside **R**ecording Medium", the "**I**nput" and the "**O**utput". Why von Neumann's analysis of the functioning of the device leads to this and no other construction depending on the unity is not justified, or it seems to be a consequence of the properties given in the definition, or it appears to be a result of the structural identity between the device and the human nervous system: "2.6 The three specific parts CA, CC, (together C), and M corrrespond to the *associative* neurons in the human nervous system. It remains to discuss the equivalents of the *sensory* or *afferent* and the *motor* or *efferent* neurons. These are the *input* and the *output* organs of the device". Later von Neumann deduces from the construction of the device the appearantly naturally given structure of the code necessary to control the device: "The orders which CC receives fall naturally into four classes" (14.1). Central design decisions like the basic construction of the device an its code thus appear to be evident: following von Neumann they derive in a logically unavoidable way from the definition of the device or from its equivalence to a natural object, the human nervous system.

7 Conclusions

Von Neumann constructed his device as a counterpart of man, who in a society of war was seen as a kind of soldier-like input-output mechanism, an image of man that was grounded in different scientific discourses, e. g. in behaviourism and neurophysiology. Arguing in a mathematical way von Neumann creates his device as a structure that seems to underly all technical as well as organic realizations of the function "to carry out instructions to perform calculations of a considerable order of complexity". As von Neumann also discussed the material construction of his device, it acquires a hermaphrodite character being on the one hand material and on the other hand a mental object. In the institutionalization of informatics as a scientific discipline this hermaphrodite character later should play an important role. E. g. Zemanek, one of the founders of Austrian informatics, wrote in his paper: "What is informatics?": "The computer scientist according to his training and attidude of mind has to become an engineer - but an engineer of a completly new kind. [...] The computer scientist constructs, but what he constructs are abstract objects." (my translation).

It is worth mentioning that in computer science the mental, the structure, has the tendency to occupy the material world; e. g. connotated as "objects" these structures seem to be capable of replacing the material. This became particularly obvious in Artificial Intelligence, where programs like the "**G**eneral **P**roblem **S**olver" of Newell, Shaw and Simon on the one hand were regarded to be a theory on human thinking. On the other hand the GPS should replace the human problem solver - hence be a kind of human problem solver itself. The difference between theory and its object tends to disappear. In the discussion on "cyberspace" today this hermaphrodite, mental-material character is expressesd in an impressive way. Following the common terminology here a whole world comes into being that is, though connotated materially, non-physical. In this hermaphrodite world the language of mathematics, Mehrtens characterizes as a language of orders to the signs, becomes a language of orders to hermaphrodite objects. If a programmer in a MUD says "Let M be a monster" then M is a monster and has to follow the rules ascribed to an object of the class monster. M is an ideal subject, because it consists of nothing but the rules it is obliged to follow.

To me it is an open and interesting question, if the tendency of the objects of computer science to occupy the material world has to be seen in connection with the fact that women - symbolically more closely associated with material[4] - in general are less interested in computers than men. Also in another respect the patterns of orientation underlying the "First Draft" seem to be of importance to the women-computer relation. The body of the computer von Neumann described reminds one of the soldier carrying out his orders in a predictable way. We are not told by von Neumann who is the one giving the orders. In the "First Draft" he wrote about "the instructions which govern a complicated problem" (2. 4) - hence to him the orders seem to given by the problem to be solved itself. Reading von Neumann's paper "The General and Logical Theory of Automata" from 1948 this propsition becomes more comprehensible. For von Neumann nature was the master builder constructing the world according to rational rules and giving instructions in the form of the gene. Accordingly to him there "is no doubt that any special phase of any conceivable form of behaviour can be described 'completely an unambigously' in words" (von Neumann 1948, p. 310). The world, as von Neumann described it was completly controllable by means of instructions. The programmer in this world is making out the orders imposed by a certain situation and translating them to the machine, the obedient soldier or servant. The programmer thus is situated somewhere in the middle of a hierarchy having a connotation of a military - hence a male-sphere. He is one factor in a hierarchy of control, he is ruled and has to rule over his inferior. As for example (Fox-Keller 1985) or (Wagner 1986) pointed out, in our culture this logic of power and control for most women is a source of ambivalent feelings, while for men it goes well with their sexual identity. Thus programming a computer for women does not have the same fascination as it has for most men.

References

1. Bauer, Friedrich L.: Was heißt und was ist Informatik? Merkmale zur Orientierung über eine neue wissenschaftliche Disziplin. In: IBM-Nachrichten 24, Heft 223, 1974
2. Fox Keller, Evelyn: Reflections on Gender and Science. New-Haven London, 1985
3. Galison,Peter: The Ontlogy of the Enemy. In: Critical Inqury 21, 1994
4. Goldstine, Adele, Goldstine Herman H.: The Electronic Numerical Integrator and Computer (ENIAC). In: Randell, Brian: The Origins of Digital Computers. Selected Papers. Berlin, Heidelberg, New York 1982 (orig. 1946)
5. Mauchly, John. W.: The Use of High Speed Vaccuum Tube Devices for Calculating. In: Randell, Brian: The Origins of Digital Computers. Selected Papers. Berlin, Heidelberg, New York 1982 (orig. 1942).
6. McCulloch, Warren S., Pitts, Walter: A Logical Calculus of the Ideas Immanent in Nervous Activity. In: Anderson, James A., Rosenfeld, Edward: Neurocomputing. Massachusetts Institute of Technology 1988 (orig. 1943).

[4]E.g. the history of the conception of "intelligence" shows how the male god and later men were regarded as having intelligence, whereas women were thought to be closely connected with the subordinate material world and thus were less able to raise their spirits to the sphere of intelligence (see Stach, in press).

7. Mehrtens, Herbert: Moderne - Sprache - Mathematik: eine Geschichte des Streits um die Grundlagen der Disziplin und des Subjekts formaler Systeme. Frankfurt am Main 1990.
8. Neumann, John von: First Darft of a Report on the EDVAC. In: Aspray, William, Burks, Arthur (Hg.): Papers of John von Neumann on Computig and Computer Theory. Charles Babbage Institute Reprint Series for the History of Computing. Cambridge, Massachusetts, 1987 (orig. 1945).
9. Neumann, John von: The General and Logical Theory of Automata. In: Taub, A. H. (Hg.): John von Neumann. Collected Works. Vol. V. Oxford 1963 (org. 1948).
10. Neumann, John von: "The Computer and the Brain". New Haven 1958. Dtsch: "Die Rechenmaschine und das Gehirn". München 1960 (orig. 1958).
11. Rosenbluth, Arturo, Wiener, Norbert, Bigelow, Julian: Behaviour, Purpose and Teleology. In: Beiheft zu Band 8 der Grundlagenstudien aus Kybernetik und Geisteswissenschaft, 1967 (orig. 1943).
12. Sonntag, Michael: Die Seele als Politikum. Psychologie und Produktion des Individuums. Berlin 1988.
13. Stach, Heike: Orientierungsmuster - ein methodischer Ansatz für eine Sozialgeschichte von Wissenschaft und Technik. In: Wechselwirkung, Oktober 1996
14. Stach, Heike: Schöpfermythos "Künstliche Intelligenz". In: Ritter, Martina (Hg.): Denken über Technik - Handeln in Technik, in press
15. Turing, Alan: On Computable Numbers with an Application to the Entscheidungsproblem. In: Proceedings of the London Mathematical Society. London, 1936.
16. Wagner, Ina: Das Erfolsmodell der Naturwissenschaften. Ambivalenzerfahrungen von Frauen. In: Hausen, Karin, Nowotny, Helga (Ed.): Wie männlich ist die Wissenschaft? Frankfurt a. M. ,1986
17. Zemanek, Heintz: Was ist Informatik? In: Elektronische Rechenanlagen, 13, Heft 4, !971

Gender and Expertise in Retrospect: Pioneers of Computing in Finland

Marja Vehviläinen

Work Research Centre, University of Tampere, P.O. Box 607
33101 Tampere, Finland

Abstract. This paper examines the historical construction of gender in information technology by studying autobiographies of male computer pioneers as well as archives of the national Computer Association in Finland.

1 Introduction

Information technology is used by women and men, but it has a clear label of the male domain (cf. Wajcman 1991). In all Western countries, the developers of information technology are mostly men and the interconnection between information technology expertise and masculinity is still strengthening during the 1990's (Klawe & Leveson 1995, Oechtering & Behnke 1995).

The gendering of information technology, however, shows up in a variety of forms, and for example in Finland gets its shape in a peculiarly divided manner. It turns out to be "worlds without women" (Noble 1992). There are extremely few women among information technology students in technical universities (Koulutus 1993:9, 1994:9). At the same time, women make up one third of the information technology developers (Membership Register of the Finnish Association of Information Technology 1995). In many universities and colleges half, or nearly half, of the information technology students during the 1980's and 1990's have been women (Koulutus 1990:18, 1993:9). On the one hand, information technology has had room for women but, on the other, it has had an exceptionally exclusive character, especially as regards entrance into technical education. In this paper, I explore the social and historical shaping of gender in information technology by using the history of Finnish information technology from the latter half of the 1950's as a starting point.

Information technology is seen as a textuality (cf. Smith 1990) which consists of texts - artefacts, computers, programs, but also of discourses of information technology in the records of computing associations, in books and journals - as well as the processes of producing and interpreting texts. The interpretation and the production processes involve knowledge of information technology. Texts, knowledge and the social order intertwine, and it is through the socially organised activities that gender intervenes in the textuality - texts, knowledge and social practices - of information technology.

Gender is examined from the point of view of the social and textual order. Gendering of information technology takes place in local activity and practices, when people concretely use and develop information technology in organisations and in various groups, but also in information technology organisations and institutions, in national cultures and in multinational practices and artefacts (Scarbrough & Corbett 1992). Gender is shaped through the divisions and hierarchies between the sexes, and gender intervenes in the textuality - e.g. methods, journals - of information technology when women and men produce and interpret information technology from the starting point of their own lives (cf. Acker 1992).

Secondly, the gendering of information technology is examined through the activity (e.g. definitions of information technology) of a subject. Gender relations and textuality frame people's activities within information technology, but people also take part in them and produce them (Smith 1990). A subject's definitions show the shaping of gender and subjectivity as a process where the bodily and historical experiences of the subject meet the social and textual reality (e.g. of information technology) (Haraway 1991). People are not entities with borders but there is - also technical - textuality built into them. Furthermore, desires and experiences cannot always be articulated at a political and conscious level (Braidotti 1994). Information technology relates to images of male expertise (Wajcman 1991) which leave little room for women.

I study the gendering of information technology, the shaping of expertise, by exploring the culture of the early computer pioneers in administrative data processing in Finland. I read autobiographical accounts - from the early years of computing - written by the male pioneers (edited by Tienari 1993) and especially Otto Karttunen (1986), the first director of the State Computing Centre. At the same time, I examine the minutes and publications of the professional association of information technology[1]. I then go on to discuss women's space in the information technology professions and textuality.

2 Computer Pioneers' "Worlds Without Women"

2.1 Punched Card Men

The first computers were developed for the calculation problems of the Second World War. Finland had its own computer project at the latter half of the 1950's - ESKO was built along the lines of the German G1 computer. The first IBM computer was installed in 1958 in the Post Bank of Finland, and after five years there were 48 computers (Varsila 1968).

The first computer based systems were designed for administrative data processing, rather than for calculation problems[2], and were based on punched card

[1]Reikäkorttiyhdistys: The Punched Card Association 1953 - 1960, Tietokoneyhdistys: The Computer Association 1960 - 1971, later called Tietojenkäsittelyliitto: The Association of Data Processing (1972 - 1983) and Tietotekniikan liitto: The Association of Information Technology (1984 -). Journals: Reikäkortti: Punched Card 1955 - 1960, Tietokone: Computer 1961 - 1966, Luuppi 1966, ATK-Tietosanomat: ADP Datanews 1967 - 1970, Tietosanomat: Datanews 1970 - 1971.

[2]Within Nokia there was a group which during the 1960's provided alternatives to IBM computer systems, worked with mathematical applications and "educated" many of the first

systems. Many organisations, e.g. insurance companies and banks, had used punched card systems from the 1920's. The Punched Card Association and its journal Punched Card prepared its members for the arrival of "the electronic brains" by giving lectures, publishing informative articles and by arranging visits to the suppliers and other organisations that had experiences with computers. The association changed its name to the Computer Association in 1960.

The first managerial level computer experts were often former "punched card men". The (Finnish) Computer 2/1961 lists the data processing professions: department manager, programmer, operator, keypunch operator, technical assistant, mathematician, and office designer. The only new profession compared to the punched card systems was programmer. Women made up 7.6 per cent of the programmers, 9.6 per cent of the office designers and three per cent of the department managers. Keypunch operators were all women, and women made up 18 - 48 per cent of the various groups of operators. In the Computer Association, women's numbers were low similar to the figures of department managers. The executive committee of the Computer Association as well as the writers of the Finnish Computer journal were all men.

The field of computing inherited the typical and clear gender hierarchy of the technical fields of the 1950's (Anttalainen 1980) from the punched card systems: men took care of the managing and expert jobs as well as the development of expertise, and women worked - in large numbers - in the keypunch and operator jobs, at the bottom of the hierarchy.

2.2 Otto Karttunen and ADP Club: Brotherhood and Progress

One of the pioneers of the Finnish Computing was Otto Karttunen. He started his career as a Second World War artillery officer, and later - after completing a Masters degree in political and managerial sciences - worked for the Statistical Bureau of Finland, with punch card systems, and for the city of Helsinki, where he for the first time took part in the establishment of a computing centre in 1960. He worked also as the first EDP expert in the Ministry of Finance and as the first director of the State Computing Centre.

He tells that he had already in 1957 made a proposal for installing a computer in the Statistical Bureau, "when the first information about the so-called computers or 'electronic brains' arrived" (ibid 37), one year before the first Finnish computer was installed, but in the Statistical Bureau "there was no possibility for that" (ibid 37). There were "fears that were felt towards EDP or electronic data processing" (ibid 43). The computers were expensive, they caused "a huge increase in costs" (ibid 43). "Enterprises were tied to the punch card systems and it was hard to get rid of the old thinking" (ibid 39). There was little experience of computers and the only education available in the home country was provided by the computer manufacturers. "The State Computing Centre practically needed to be improvised from nothing. Education and work went side by side. Sometimes they meant the same. Afterwards I felt that here - if somewhere - we made the impossible possible - from nothing" (ibid 97 - 98).

---

professors in Computer Science. Here I , however, will focus on administrative data processing, the major trend in Finnish computing.

In this situation, Otto Karttunen together with a dozen other men established the ADP club in 1961. The club aimed to "advance its members' professional expertise in the use of automated computers in commercial and administrative applications" (ibid 51), and it supported a wider and more accessible education (Karttunen 1986, 99), for example the start of ADP education in universities (ibid 186 - 190). In 1967 Karttunen made a proposal for founding a special institute of ADP education (ibid 182 - 184, minutes of the Computing Association).

The ADP club was a small "secret society". The club membership was limited to "management and planning personnel of commercial and administrative data processing" (ibid 52). The club had frequent, sometimes weekly, meetings. It aimed to develop data processing for the whole country (cf. Huusko 1993). The computer pioneers did the development work "as a service for their ideals" (Karttunen 1986, 79). "Otto Karttunen also evoked the future of the nation in his talks" (ibid 74). Yet, Otto Karttunen warned against the "trick art" of programming which in his opinion had sometimes become a goal of its own. Technical progress was necessary but it should not be given an inherent value. In Otto Karttunen's and his colleagues' minds the country needed computers. In the ADP club they, in a small group, among brothers (their letters started with "my good brother") figured out the preconditions of computing and also tried to arrange these prerequisites for "our country". The pioneering period of Finnish computing, if anything, was a project of national progress.

During the 1960's, the "computer men" of the Punched Card and the Computer Association, and the ADP club created - or managed the creation of - the foundations of Finnish computing: the computer departments for big organizations, the computer centres of the state and cities, the ADP educational programmes as well as the practices and methods of information systems work. The members of the ADP club and the working groups of the Computer Association, writers of the Finnish Computer journal as well as the public speakers in the association meetings were all still men.

2.3 The Multinational IBM

One of the most important actors in the development of Western commercial data processing has been IBM, International Business Machines, and it was the most significant computer supplier in Finland, too, especially during the 1960's (Varsila 1968). IBM training courses were almost the only source of computer education at the end of the 1950's and in the early 1960's (cf. Karttunen 1963). The first computers in both Helsinki City and the State Computing Centre were ordered from IBM. Otto Karttunen as a director of those, however, required good service of IBM. "I sent IBM a sharply worded letter in which I demanded them to give more resources to put the machine in a proper working order" (Karttunen 1986, 114). There were frequent breakdowns in the machines. It was only with hot-tempered letters that Otto Karttunen was able to both defend the national interest and co-operate with a multinational computer supplier.

IBM training and testing were developed in the North American culture, but there was no discussion about the cultural differences between Finland and the United States in the journal of the Computer Association. It seems that there was a belief that the US training and testing could be applied in Finland as easily as the computer machines. IBM is known as an especially male dominated company, the organization of which - regardless of its equal opportunity goal set in 1975 - has remained very male also in Finland even during the period when women made up one third of the computer professionals in the country (Norrmark 1985). The strong connection of the computing field to IBM has certainly not shaken the male label of computing expertise.

2.4 Brothers-in-Arms

Maybe the "hot-tempered letters" were easier for Otto Karttunen to write because the head of the Finnish IBM was one of his fellow artillery men: "don't you think that we old artillery men can find means to solve the situation?" (Karttunen 1986, 115). The head of IBM was ready to "look for help around Europe including Paris and supplied the materials that we had asked for" (ibid 48). Otto Karttunen mentions the head of IBM as one of the artillery men friends with whom he reminisced about the war and the artillery. He "was an irreplaceable help in crisis situations which always grew when we had urgent tasks. It is true that sometimes we went out together in the evening, but then we would not be discussing professional issues but only the war and artillery" (ibid 32).

Otto Karttunen's autobiography includes ten, twenty remarks of his acquaintances from the artillery and other officers, in the governmental and city bureaux, in universities and elsewhere on the upper levels of the Finnish society. The discussions and the consultations with the army acquaintances helped Otto Karttunen to manage the conflicts (cf. Seppälä 1993). Otto Karttunen tells that he was known as "Major" both in the labour union negotiations (Karttunen 1986, 227) and in the international IBM (ibid 217). After the Second World War former army officials and even whole research groups within the defence forces (Lovio 1989, 55) started to work in significant positions in Finnish working life.

2.5 The Computer Association Defines Gender

The Punched Card / Computer Association aimed to promote professional development to study and develop the use of methods especially in the domains of commercial and industrial life and science. The rules of the Association contain information about the social and gender orders of the computer culture. Firstly, computers were big, rare and expensive. They were managed by "the computer men" who developed professional competence in a small association. The number of the association members was consciously limited, and membership was given only to experts who either had long experience or who worked at managerial levels in the business member associations (cf. Huusko 1993).

The early 1970's a change of rules opened the association to wide groups of computing professionals and among them large numbers of women. Women were able to participate in professional clubs and discuss the everyday practices of professional work. The Computer Association and its journal remained, however, very male dominated up to the 1970's. The first women appeared in the Finnish Computer journal at the end of the 1960's. They were mentioned as members of working groups - but none of them wrote articles or were described as possessing an individual role in the public development of computing. The association allowed women's membership, but did not publicly create room for women as developers or holders of professional computing qualifications. Similarly, only few token women have been invited to join the executive committee of the Association which - as Risto Vehviläinen (1993, 434) reports - "has in practice invited its members itself and this principle has not been changed in the new organization of the 1980's." After the Association as a whole was no longer organized as a brothers' club, "the world without women" was kept alive among the leadership of the association.

2.6 The Legacy of the Pioneer Culture

What kind of influence did the computer men's and artillery officials' brotherly consensus have on the Finnish computing culture? It was in their time that the major part of the practices and institutions of the Finnish information technology were built.

First of all, the consensus among brothers made possible the rapid implementation of computers. In the early 1960's, Finland was clearly behind Sweden and many Western countries in computerization (e.g. Computer 1/1961), but already in the latter half of the 1960's the Finnish Computer journal reported that Finland was becoming one of the forerunners in computerization. The first Nordic professorship in Computer Science was established in Tampere, Finland, in 1965 (Kurki-Suonio 1993). Without this consensus the rapid computerization might not have been possible.

On the other hand, the consensus shows up as a scarcity of public discussion and especially of critical discussion. In the Computer journal the first critical evaluations of ADP practices, education and methods appeared only at the very end of the 1960's, at the point when computers had been used for ten years. Computerization did not proceed through grass root evaluation or critical discourse but was directed by the managers from above. The 1960's pioneers worked for the national interest and aimed to manage the implementation processes wisely from a perspective which took the whole country into account. In this spirit Otto Karttunen was allowed to become the "big data emperor whose word was the law" (ibid 175). Although, for example, the university professors (cf. Kurki-Suonio 1969) did not always agree with Karttunen on questions of national interest, the mathematically and technically oriented university staff never established their own association - as happened in Sweden (EDP-historik 1989) - but on the public level everyone maintained the unified front.

The pioneer culture influenced gendering in two ways. On the one hand, the project of national interest supported the start of public information technology education and services. In principle, both sexes and all social classes were able to study computing in Finland - and women used this opportunity. On the other hand, the practice of management from above and lack of critical discussions gave rise to a closed culture in which differences were neither discussed nor appreciated. Gender differences faded away in the pioneer culture, and the male gender became the only gender in the field. In the legacy of the brothers-in-arms and the ADP club the "world without women" got a legitimate space in Finnish information technology.

3 Gendering in Two Lines

The new computer based systems created new professional practices of systems development. The NordSAM data processing conferences (organized from 1959,

EDP-historik 1989) soon raised the issue of information systems development as distinct from programming and the expertise provided by IBM (cf. Karttunen 1963). In Otto Karttunen's opinion, "it was only systems design in its full width that formed the basis for the real changes in the 1960's" (Karttunen 1986, 269). Eero Kostamo, the author of the first Finnish systems design book from 1965, tells: "The systems analyst profession was not at all known in the United States in the 1960's. We did not get models for systems design, but had to develop the theory and methodology ourselves" (Risto Vehviläinen 1993). The Finnish pioneers relatively early created development practices which not only took into account the technical progress but also the organisational activity as a whole, and thus gave a strong start to a new professional group of system analysts or systems designers.

During the 1960's, women's share of the programmers' jobs had increased to 33 per cent while it was only 12 per cent among the analysts. The programmers were often selected and trained on the basis of tests. Otto Karttunen (1986, 32) tells that he had all his workers tested, mostly in the Institute of Occupational Health. At the end of the 1960's, women commonly participated in the labour force (Anttalainen 1980), and had (twelve-year) high school diplomas more often than men (Lahelma 1992, 84), and through the tests women also gained access to the programming professions. The expertise of women - as programmers - was, however, considered as a "low in the hierarchy" expertise which did not provide possibilities for career advancement. The data processing experts were seen for a long time, until the end of the 1960's, solely as "computer men" (cf. Computer 1/1969). The situation changed essentially during the 1970's after computing education started. Women's share of computer science students and degrees grew first to 20 and soon to 30 per cent (Statistics Finland, Degree file).

In Finland women came to systems design through formal education whereas in Holland and Great Britain the start of formal education - together with women's low participation in information technology education - has lowered women's numbers in information technology professions (Kirkup 1992, Oost 1991). Finnish women studied from 1960 almost as commonly as men (Koulutus ja tutkimus 1988:7) and completed academic degrees that were required for analysts' work.

Formal education opened the doors for women who became multi-skilled experts in information technology. In the 1980 Census women made up 28 per cent of computing professionals in general and 26 per cent of systems analysts. During the 1980's women's share still grew being a good third within systems analysis and the education related to it (Members' file of the Association of Information Technology, September 1995, Koulutus 1987:21, 1988:16, 1990:18). In the Finnish information technology culture that emphasised systems design, and in the Finnish society where women already before computing participated in the labour market and education in great numbers, women gained space as experts and project leaders in practical information technology work.

On the other hand, technical universities and colleges have been very male dominated similar to the other Western countries (Frenkel 1990, Blomqvist et al. 1994). During the 1980's, women's share of technical university information technology students was around 8 - 10 per cent (Koulutus 1990:4). From the early 1990's information technology has become more male in Finland - similar to almost all Western countries (cf. Thomborson 1993, Oechtering & Behnke 1995). Women's numbers amongst the new information technology students in universities have declined generally (Statistics Finland, Tieto & Kone 8.3.1996) and especially in technical universities.

There have been two distinct trends in information technology from the perspective of gender. The borderline is drawn between the management, the publicity and the technically oriented education and the other areas of information technology, most importantly systems design. There are still very few women among information technology managers, women are still in a minority - also relatively - in professional publications and executive committees, and women are not entering technical education. Finnish women's large participation in the professional computer education and development work has not been able to prevent the rise and reproduction of male fortresses inside information technology.

Many of the female information technology experts have been able to act in workplaces and educational institutions in which women have made at least one third or even half of the information technology professionals (Vehviläinen et al. 1986). However, there have been very male dominated educational schemes and workplaces, and women have had token jobs especially in managerial positions. There have not been any systematic studies of the female computer professionals in Finland but women in corresponding white collar token positions report more than other women that their work has been undervalued (Kauppinen et al. 1989). Women in the token positions need to develop specific coping strategies in order to be able to act as experts. They need to avoid the label of being "attractive but not understandable". Women's definitions of their own femininity and womanhood intertwines with the understandings of womanhood in male cultures (cf. Cockburn 1991, 69). Nevertheless women engineers give birth to children and start families similarly to other women in their social class (Hertzberg 1989, Kauppinen et al. 1989) and that seems to be the case also among information technology professionals according to a survey conducted in 1985 (see Vehviläinen et al. 1986). Finnish womanhood is built on work and the family, and women information technology professionals share the general pattern rather than make an exception.

4 Women's Space in Information Technology Textuality

Is there any room for the textualities created by women and feminists in Finnish information technology? A woman can work as an expert. Still she might not be able to develop texts - e.g. information systems methods - that fit both her own experience and the mainstream textualities in the field.

The first systems design methods were step-by-step - or phase - models in which the systems work was split into work phases that followed each other in a linear order. Otto Karttunen (1986, 103 - 104) tells that the phase model - developed under his supervision in the State Computing Centre - aimed to make "order and control more general in the design work" and to weed out "the unnecessary growths from the very beginning". These thoughts fit into the principles of Scientific Management - which were well known in the editorials of the Punched Card journal at the end of the 1950's - but Karttunen's words have an especially strong emphasis on management from above. It is from the above that one can see which growths can be weeded out as unnecessary and it is from the above that they are cut away. Karttunen's army experience is quite likely to have strengthened the application of Scientific Management ideas in the Finnish systems design practices.

The principle of managing from above lived on in the practices of Finnish information technology as the phase model was the dominant systems design method until the 1980's. There has been little space for the standpoints of citizens and workers - or women - in the development models. Not even questions around the responsibility and the participation in the information technology development were taken up in labour unions or in grass root activities as was done in the other Nordic countries (Ehn 1988). There have been no movements around race, ethnical groups or disability in Finnish information technology. Where the feminist movement as a whole has been weaker in Finland than in many Western countries there has been practically no women's movement in information technology (or in the other technologies or sciences). This is different to the strong women's movement countries, e.g. Denmark, the Netherlands, and Great Britain (Cockburn 1991, 172, writes about the mutual support of the political movements). The question of the characteristics of women and women's work, and even less the possibility to take them into account and support them has not even been raised. This has meant that the understanding of objective truth and objective information common in the main stream information technology discourse (Vehviläinen 1994) has not been challenged in any essential manner in the Finnish debate. Instead, the perspective of managers and experts - within Scientific Management computer systems were developed from their perspective - was legitimized as "objective truth".

New approaches are nevertheless possible. Eeva Piispanen and Katriina Pallas (1991) have created an information systems development method, based on organizational games, in which the workers, the participants of the game, present their own daily work in a play which covers one of the work processes in their organization. The method gives room for the different worker groups to express their views and their ways of working in the work process, distinct from the mainstream understanding of objective knowledge.

Information technology developers can build new everyday practices in their own workplaces. They are aware of the professional textuality but still use their own experience - born through living in female and male bodies and facing the social relations of their societies. In current societies women often live in quite a different world than men: in female bodies, in the lower ends of the segregated working life, by taking care of the greater part of the domestic work load (cf. Rantalaiho & Heiskanen 1997). These different worlds of lives might make a starting point for different textualities, including information technologies (Gunnarsson & Mörtberg 1994). Finnish women systems developers have built numerous systems that have been used in the everyday work situations of organizations, systems that have been used by other women. However, since women's everyday practices are seldom discussed publicly, the knowledge is not transmitted from one woman to another. The method based on organizational games relates to Eeva Piispanen's experience in a voiceless position within - gendered - hierarchy, but the method could be developed only after Eeva Piispanen had also done research projects in between her development work. Within information technology, there is no women's textuality to refer to. Everybody still needs to refer to the mainstream textuality, produced by men, legitimizing the perspective of managers and experts as objective truth - or, should look for the alternatives from outside as Eeva Piispanen did. The experiences seldom speak for themselves but need "textual help" to become a source to be elaborated in the development of new texts and practices. For this reason, Finnish society, Finnish women and men, have lost (too) much of the potential for innovation and variation that it had in a relatively large number of women computing professionals.

5 Unbalanced Lines

Gendering of information technology is shaped in the orders of the particular societies as well as in the activities and identities of women and men. In the case of Finland, information technology professions were born during the 1960's and expanded only in the 1970's, during a period when women participated in the labour force almost as often as men and during a period when women's participation in professional education had grown above men's participation. The information technology professions could have become balanced in terms of gender divisions. This did not happen, however, and instead of becoming a gender balanced field, information technology split into areas in which women have room and areas that are totally in men's hands. The computer pioneers kept alive the strong gender divisions and hierarchies of the 1950's, ideas of Scientific Management, managerial and other practices of the army and even patriotism. These were embedded in the methods, practices and textuality of information technology for decades. However, Finnish women's large participation in the labour market and the professional education also intervened in the gendering of information technology. High numbers of women work as experts in information technology similar to other areas of the Finnish society.

Finnish information technology has carried within itself "worlds without women" throughout its history. The pioneers who established the information technology institutions and practices during the 1950's and 1960's were all men. The pioneers considered computerization as a national project - between men. Information technology in technical universities has remained very male in all Western countries and Finland is no exception. However, the Finnish figures that approach zero are more extreme than the figures elsewhere. Women's exclusion from information technology management has also taken extremely strong forms. In addition women have not - except for maybe a few token women - come out as subjects or starting points for discussions in journals or in the association activities, in the public terrain of information technology, where the professionalism and the practices are defined and where the concepts, metaphors and images of the field are created. This has happened in spite of the fact that most women in information technology have had long educational backgrounds and certainly would have had the ability to participate in the public discussion.

On the other hand women have had room especially in the domain of information systems design and development. Women's representation amongst information technology professionals has been high compared to the other Western countries. Women have been active subjects and have done significant expert work. They have participated in the formation of knowledge and social order in information technology in concrete work situations. This information technology defined by women means a real possibility for change in terms of technology, in terms of gendered subjectivity and in terms of gender.

"The world without women" and the women's space, the two trends in Finnish information technology, intertwine and overlap but are very unbalanced. The pioneers in their "world without women" created professional practices, for example systems development methods and association practices, which intervened in the activities of both men and women until the 1980's. This has made it difficult for the women - in spite of their relatively high number - to consciously produce textualities of their own. The pioneer culture intertwined with women's space. Women were able to devise alternative methods or practices only by relating them to the methods already created by the male pioneers. Subjects in the second, in the women's trend, always have to refer to the first trend, but subjects from the first trend seldom refer to "the other".

References

1. Acker, Joan (1992) Gendering Organizational Theory. In Albert J. Mills & Peta Tancred (eds), Gendering Organizational Analysis. SAGE, London, 248 - 260.
2. Anttalainen, Marja-Liisa (1980) Naisten työt - Miesten työt (Women's work - men's work, in Finnish). Valtioneuvoston kanslian julkaisuja 1980:1, Valtion painatuskeskus, Helsinki.
3. Blomqvist, Martha & Mackinnon Alison & Vehviläinen, Marja (1994) Exploring the Gender and Technology Boundaries: An International Perspective.In Tina Eberhart & Christina Wächter (eds), Proceedings of the 2nd European Feminist Research Conference, Feminist Perspectives on Technology, Work and Ecology, July 5-9, Graz, Austria, 101 - 108.
4. Braidotti, Rosi (1994) Nomadic Subjects. Embodiment and Sexual Difference in Contemporary Feminist Theory. Columbia University Press, New York.
5. Cockburn, Cynthia (1991) In the Way of Women: Men's Resistance to Sex Equality in Organizations. Macmillan, London.
6. EDP-historik - i nordisk perspektiv (EDP history - Nordic perspective, in Swedish) (1989). Erik Bruhn (red.), DATA aktieselskabet af 2. april 1971.
7. Ehn, Pelle (1988) Work-Oriented Design of Computer Artifacts. Arbetslivscentrum, Stockholm.
8. Frenkel, Karen A. (1990) Women & Computing. Communications of the ACM, 33: 11, November, 35 - 46.
9. Gunnarsson, Ewa & Mörtberg, Christina (1994) Systemutveckling i förändring: Nya livsmönster och kvalifikationer i ett könsperspektiv (Changing patterns of systems development: new forms of life and qualifications from gender perspective, in Swedish). Forskningsrapport 1994: 11, Tekniska högskolan i Luleå, Luleå.
10. Haraway, Donna (1991) Simians, Cyborgs, and Women: The Reinventions of Nature. Free Associations Books, London.

11. Hertzberg, Veronica (1989) Kvinnliga diplomingenjörers väg till yrkesliv (Women engineers' way to labour market, in Swedish). In Harriet Silius (ed), Kvinnor i mansdominerade yrken: Läkare, ingenjörer, jurister. Institutet för kvinnoforskning vid Åbo Akademi, Åbo, 53 - 89.
12. Huusko, Juha (1993) Reikäkorttiyhdistyksestä Tietotekniikan liitoksi (From the Punched Card Association to the Association of Information Technology, in Finnish). In Tienari, Martti (ed), 406 - 429.
13. Karttunen, Otto (1963) Tietokonealan koulutuksesta (On education in computing field, in Finnish). Tietokone 1/1963, 17.
14. Karttunen, Otto (1986) Avainpaikalla tietotekniikan kehityksessä (In a key position in the information technology development, in Finnish). Suomen atkkustannus Oy, Helsinki.
15. Kauppinen, Kaisa & Haavio-Mannila, Elina & Kandolin, Irja (1989) Who Benefits from Working in Non-Traditional Workroles: Interaction Patterns and Quality of Worklife. Acta Sociologica, 32: 4, 389 - 403.
16. Kirkup, Gill (1992) The Social Construction of Computers: Hammers or Harpsichords? Teokessa Gill Kirkup & Laurie Smith Keller (eds.), Inventing Women, Science, Technology and Gender. Polity Press, Cambridge, 267 - 281.
17. Klawe, Maria & Leveson, Nancy (1995) Women in Computing. Where are We Now? Communications of the ACM, 38: 1, January, 29 - 44.
18. Kostamo, Eero (1965) ATK-systeemien suunnittelun perusteista (On foundations of ADP systems design, in Finnish). Tietokoneyhdistys, Helsinki.
19. Koulutus ja tutkimus. Tilastoja Suomen korkeakouluista vuosilta (Statistics of Finnish Universities) 1980 - 1994: 1987:21, 1988: 7, 1988:16, 1990:4, 1990:18, 1993:9, 1994:9. Tilastokeskus, Helsinki.
20. Kurki-Suonio, Reino (1969) Tietojenkäsittely yliopistossa (Data processing in a university, in Finnish), Suomalainen Suomi Valvoja, 4/1969.
21. Kurki-Suonio, Reino (1993) Tietojenkäsittelyopin korkeakouluopetuksen käynnistyminen (The start of the university education in Computer Science, in Finnish). In Tienari, Martti (ed), 24 - 47.
22. Lahelma, Elina (1992) Sukupuolten eriytyminen peruskoulun opetusohjelmassa (The differentiation of the sexes in school programmes, in Finnish). Yliopistopaino, Helsinki.
23. Lovio, Raimo (1989) Suomalainen menestystarina: Tietoteollisen verkostotalouden läpimurto (The Finnish success story: the outbreak of the network economy of information industries, in Finnish). Hanki ja jää, Helsinki.
24. Noble, David (1992) A World Without Women, The Christian Clerical Culture of Western Science. Alfred A. Knopf, New York.
25. Norrmark, Britta (1985) Women in Finnish IBM. Presentation, Nordisk seminar om likestilling i databransjen, Oslo 16-18.10.1985.
26. Oechtering, Veronika & Behnke, Roswitha (1995) Situations and Advancement Measures in Germany. Communications of the ACM, 38: 1, January, 75 - 82.
27. Oost, Ellen van (1991) The Process of Sex-typing of Computer Occupations. In I.V. Eriksson et al. (eds.), Women, Work and Computerization. Elsevier, Amsterdam, 407 - 421.

28. Piispanen, Eeva & Pallas, Katriina (1991) TOTO. Tietotekniikalla tulosta hallintotyöhön (Information Technology Gives Profits to Administrative Work, in Finnish). VAPK-kustannus, Helsinki.
29. Rantalaiho, Liisa & Heiskanen, Tuula (eds) (1997) Gendered Practices of Working Life. Macmillan, London.
30. Scarbrough, Harry & Corbett, J. Martin (1992) Technology and Organization. Power, Meaning and Design. Routledge, London and New York.
31. Seppälä, Yrjö (1993) Moottoriajoneuvorekisteri uranuurtajana valtionhallinossa (The register of motor vehicles as a pioneer in the state government, in Finnish). In Tienari, Martti (ed), 243 - 270.
32. Smith, Dorothy E. (1990) Texts, Facts and Femininity: Exploring the Relations of Ruling. Routledge, London and New York.
33. Thomborson, Clark (1993) Why Are Fewer Females Obtaining Bachelor's Degrees in Computer Science? ACM SIGACT News 24:3, October, 114 - 116.
34. Tienari, Martti (ed) (1993) Tietotekniikan alkuvuodet Suomessa (The first years of information technology in Finland, in Finnish). Suomen Atk-kustannus, Helsinki.
35. Wajcman, Judy (1991) Feminism Confronts Technology. Polity Press, Cambridge.
36. Varsila, Kari (1968) Tilastotietoja Suomen tietokonekannasta (Statistics of the Finnish Computers, in Finnish). Tietokone 5/1968, 13 - 16.
37. Vehviläinen, Marja (1994) Reading Computing Professionals' Codes of Ethics - A Standpoint of Finnish Office Workers. In Ewa Gunnarsson & Lena Trojer (eds), Feminist Voices on Gender, Technology and Ethics. Centre for Women's Studies, Luleå University of Technology, Luleå, Sweden, 145 - 161.
38. Vehviläinen, Marja & Laine Pirjo & Norrmark, Britta (1986) Rapport från Finland: ADB-kvinnor - en finländsk pilotstudie (A report from Finland: ADP women - a Finnish pilot study, in Swedish). Nordisk DATAnytt, Nr. 1, 27. januar, 18.
39. Vehviläinen, Risto (1993) Tietotekniikan liitto - monipuolinen vaikuttaja (The association of information technology - influencing many areas, in Finnish). In Tienari, Martti (ed), 430 - 451.

Gender Segregation in IT Occupations

Kea G. Tijdens

Department of Economics, University of Amsterdam,
Roetersstraat 11, 1018 WB Amsterdam, The Netherlands
E-mail KEA@BUTLER.FEE.UVA.NL

Abstract. The explanatory power of four theories about gender segregation is tested for IT-occupations in the Netherlands, which are studied for a period of four decades. Theories on occupational choices explain women's low participation in computer science, allthough entry requirements changed tremendously. Theories about employers' hiring practices explain the post-war recruitment of men in the female-dominated programmer's occupation, but not that employers went beyond gender boundaries because of labor shortage. Theories about the segregation code explain hierarchical gender relations. Yet, these have changed because of women's inroads into IT-occupations and because of the high proportion of women among non-professional users. Social closure theories explain why the professional community tries to keep a male image. Female computer professionals pay for their inroads into the high status and skilled male-dominated occupations by adapting to the male pattern of working hours and the male-dominated attitudes and by postponing maternity.

1 Introduction

Women's and men's paid work is highly segregated by occupation. In various disciplines occupational segregation has been studied. Long term approaches of desegregation and resegregation processes over time are probably the most promising analyses in this field. In general, findings indicate a strong tendency towards segregation between the sexes, and towards establishing hierarchical relationships between male and female occupations. In order to understand the segregation processes in one occupational group fully, in this paper four groups of theories that apply to segregation processes in occupations will be explored for their explanatory potential. These are theories about women's occupational choices, theories about employers' hiring practices, theories about male employees' segregation codes, and professionalization theories concerning closure strategies of professional communities. Each theory has its own particular view of who is the main actor involved in the segregation processes.

The similarities between these theories are that each is focusing on one actor in the gender segregation processes. A complex interrelationship exists between the main actors, e.g. employers, predominantly male as well as the organizations they are heading, male employees and their organizations, either trade unions or professional bodies, and female employees and their organizations, all of them operating in a social environment. Moreover, these theories reveal conflicting interests in the segregation processes among and between the actors. Whereas it is usually suggested that all actors persist in continuous segregation, the theories show very dynamic processes.

In this paper we will test four theories for their explanatory power. The economic theories on employers' hiring behavior and employees' searching behavior explain the impact of supply and demand factors. The organizational theories focus on either personnel policies, male and female attitudes in organizations or group behavior. The psychological theories study occupational choices and socialization. The sociological theories usually are used to analyze professionalization and the exclusionary strategies of professional associations. These four theories are applied to the long term segregation processes in the field of Information Technology (IT) over five decades in the Netherlands. The IT occupations are chosen for several reasons: 1) the percentage of female workers changed over time backwards and forwards; 2) the occupations continuously had a masculine image; 3) the number of workers has grown tremendously; 4) entry requirements changed greatly; 5) organizational settings changed; 6) the occupations went into a process of professionalization. Gender segregation can be divided into hierarchical and occupational segregation, sometimes also called vertical and horizontal segregation. Hierarchical segregation refers to the unequal distribution of women and men across job levels, whereas occupational segregation refers to the unequal distribution over occupations. Here the focus is on occupational segregation, but when applicable hierarchical segregation will be discussed too.

2 Theories Explaining Occupational Segregation

One of the *theories on employers' hiring practices* is the statistical discrimination theory, stating that women are supposed to be more costly to employers than men due to higher turnover or absence rates because of motherhood. Because employers do not have any specific information about an applicant other than their sex, they will treat individuals on the basis of their group's average behavior (Arrow 1973). However, looking at wage costs, one would predict that employers would prefer women, because women's wages are on average far below men's. Bergmann (1989) specifies the statistical discrimination theory by arguing that employers do not prefer women for male-dominated occupations and men for female-dominated occupations, because this would undermine the existing labor relations and status quo and this would be costly to employers. Thus, the theories on employers' hiring practices are not unanimous, they predict that employers prefer either male employees to female employees, female employees to male employees or men for male-dominated occupations and women for female-dominated occupations.

As far as segregation processes are concerned, employers' behavior is characterized by conflicting rationalism. If they prefer women due to lower wage cost, this would imply gender-based wage and employment competition, but occupational boundaries impede this general competition. If for wage policy reasons employers intend to substitute men's labor with women's labor, these occupational boundaries need to be broken down. However, male workers will organize themselves to resist substitution by strengthening occupational lines. On the other hand, female workers can organize themselves and demand equal pay for equal work by breaking down occupational boundaries. Thus, by reinforcing segregation, employers avoid vulnerability to labor unrest among male workers or client dissatisfaction, but at the same time this limits their possibilities of replacement and they would not meet female workers' demands. Therefore, it is most likely that employer's hiring strategies are in accordance with gender segregation. Because our study focuses on a male-dominated occupational group, we predict that employers will hire men for these occupations. Moreover, we predict that in the event of shortage of labor employers will go beyond gender boundaries.

Theories of professionalization offer an explanation to understand the process by which occupational groups define occupational boundaries. Processes of professionalization involve guidelines for recruitment and training, formal organization and informal relations among colleagues, and codes of conduct (Mok 1977). In two ways these process also include a gender identity. Professions will try to keep a male identity by exclusion strategies, and female-dominated occupations will not be defined as professions, following Etzioni (1969: vi) ".. the normative principles and cultural values of professions, organizations and female employment are not compatible". Usually the skilled female-dominated occupations are classified as semi-professionals, i.e. nurses, teachers. The theory of social closure has been elaborated by Parkin (1979). He distinguishes two groups in the process of social closure, both following their own strategies. The privileged group follows a strategy of exclusion to keep their position by subordinating the groups they want to exclude. The subordinated group follows a strategy to appropriate some privileges of the former group. According to Witz (1986, 1992), these closure strategies include the establishment or maintenance of the exclusively male character of the professional community to protect the qualification structures.

Theories on the informal segregation codes focus on workplaces. The codes state that women should not exercise authority over men (Bergmann 1986). The segregation coding process includes two elements. The first refers to the code that supervising relationships at work should be in accordance with the hierarchical relationship between genders at home as well as in society: women should not exercise authority over men. The second element is that women as a group, in contrast to men, are perceived as non-hierarchical: men can exercise authority over men, women cannot over women. Workers, male and female, are likely to enforce these codes. Probably, they coincide with the code that young people should not exercise power over middle-aged people. Control over the sex-typing of tasks is instrumental in maintaining gender-related hierarchical structures in the division of labor within the occupational field (Kanter 1977, Cockburn 1983).

Economic and psychological *theories on occupational choices* focus mainly on female employees-to-be, and anticipating their behavior. Women, the economic argument goes, seek occupations in which the effects on their income will be low in case of a career break, whereas men do not seek these occupations (Polachek 1979). Therefore, women will have jobs with flat age-wage profiles (Jusenius 1976). Psychological gender-role socialization theories state that women due to their primary socialization choose occupations that are in accordance with their sex roles (Ireson 1978). Socialization is a process by which families, peers, schools and the media teach society's expectations to girls and boys. Thus, women are primarily oriented towards their families rather than their careers. In this sense, gender-role socialization explains occupational segregation because it focuses on gender-related occupational choices in childhood. This might explain why girls in contrast to boys do not choose occupations that might require mathematics or technical qualifications, whereas boys do not choose occupations in which caring is an important element. Thus, there would be hardly any women found in IT occupations, because these occupations do have steep age-wage profiles, they do require mathematical or technical skills and they don't include caring tasks. Moreover, one might expect girls to avoid occupational choices related to subjects in the IT field, and that, as a consequence, women will not enter these occupational groups. In case qualifications change towards less technical or mathematical skills, desegregation processes will take place slowly, because girls need to become aware of these changes before they can change their occupational choice.

When analyzing gender segregation processes over time, four variables are examined in section 3: employer's hiring strategies, processes of professionalization, the use of segregation codes and finally women's occupational choices. In section 4 conclusions are drawn about the complex interrelationship between employers, male and female employees and the professional associations in IT occupations.

3 Segregation in the History of IT Occupations

In order to study gender segregation, IT occupations are defined using the International Standard Classification of Occupations (ISCO), which is meant to provide a structure for the classification of all jobs in the labor force, i.e. to group all jobs into successively broader categories. We consider four groups in four occupational groups as belonging to the IT occupations: the *system analysts* (ISCO code 083), the *programmers and other computer professionals not counted earlier* (084), the *card- and tape-punching machine operators* (322), which we will call key-entry operators, and the fourth occupational group, i.e. the *automatic data-processing machine operators* (342). Managerial occupations in the IT field were not classified as such.

3.1 The Late Forties and the Fifties: The Switch of Sex-typing

It was not until the end of WWII that scientists, all of them male, invented the electronic computer. This happened more or less at the same time in the US, the UK, France and Germany. The first computers in the world were mainly used for calculations for military purposes. The calculating work traditionally was done by mathematically skilled women, being a female-dominated occupation in a men's world (Hoffmann 1987, Shurkin 1984). Some of these women changed to programming, because they were the only ones who knew the structure of the calculations. Moreover, ENIAC, the first electronic computer in the US, was programmed by a female mathematician: Adèle Goldstine, and COBOL, the first programming language was written by a female physicist: Grace Hopper.

Programming was the first occupation in the IT field and it was a female-dominated job, although the work environment in the computer labs used to be male-dominated. When men returned from the war and women withdrew from the labor market because of marriage, men took over the programming jobs, as they did in quite a number of other occupations as well. Presumably this job was taken over (and others were not), because this one existed in an all male environment. Anyhow, in the fifties, the sex-typing of programmers' jobs had changed completely, although a few women still could be found in computer programming (Kraft 1979, Hoffmann 1987). Comparable processes were found in the Netherlands (Romeny & Van Vaalen 1988). To summarize the four criteria: along with their changing tools the female calculators changed jobs to programming computers quite naturally. As conditions changed, i.e. male labor became abundant and women withdrew from the labor market, employers' hiring strategies changed, probably because the sex-typing of the job was adapted to the sex-typing of the work environment. Neither processes of professionalization, nor occupational choices, nor segregation coding, had yet started, because the occupation was so new.

3.2 The Sixties: Division of Labor

In the sixties, computers, mostly the IBM 360 series, were introduced in the Netherlands (see for a historical overview Kerf 1977, Tijdens 1989). Companies did not require complex calculations, but used these first computers mainly for repetitive calculations and to store data. Therefore, in companies the programming jobs were not a continuation of the calculating jobs as had been the case in the computer labs, but they made up a rather new job category. Moreover, for data storing purposes, data had to be entered for processing transactions. This was done by key entry operators, being a continuation of the card punch operating jobs. Diversification in the occupational field went further and a third IT occupation arose, because computer operating was separated from the programmers' job. Thus, the development of computer equipment was accompanied by a process of division of labor within the field of IT jobs. The number of workers rose, although at the end of the sixties there were still neither many programmers nor computer operators, but there were some key entry operators. Training for these first two occupations was usually provided by the equipment supplier. This division of labor could also be seen in the US and in other countries (Greenbaum 1976, Kraft 1979, Game & Pringle 1983).

In the sixties, the new occupations were pretty soon sex-typed. Van Oost (1994) has analyzed the process of sex-typing in one firm in detail. This firm's first computer application was expensive, risky and huge. It should not fail. The combination of the male image of IBM, which supplied the hardware, and the negative attitude to women's capacities in managerial jobs led to the selection of men for the programming jobs. It is harder to understand the male sex-typing for the operator's job. Van Oost (1994) suggests that operators were recruited in two shifts, because for reasons of efficiency it was decided that the computer had to be used day and night. Female applicants were excluded because they were forbidden to work at night by law. Another explanation is that the operator's job was defined being an attractive job. The operators were recruited from the department that dealt with the work flow before computerization, probably including card punch operators, and the operator's job was obviously seen as a promotion. Van Oost's study shows that male employees especially were promotion chasers and the women who wanted to be considered for the operator's job faced stiff competition from them. Obviously, employers' hiring strategies were mostly focused on the internal labor market. At the end of this decade, the programmer's and the computer operator's occupations were male-dominated, whereas the key entry typists used to be women.

The process of professionalization of the IT occupations started as the professional association was set up. As programming languages were developed independently from the computer equipment, they set up programming courses for workers in the IT field independently from the suppliers. A chain of certificates would ensure qualifications. Access to this vocational training system was limited to employees already having an IT job. Thus, these courses were not imbedded in the educational system.

3.3 The Seventies: Increasing Numbers of Workers in IT Occupations

In the seventies, computerization expanded tremendously: the number of mainframe computers multiplied by a thousand or more and so did the number of terminals. Because of this growth, the number of workers in IT occupations multiplied many times, especially among programmers and key entry typists. At the same time, the IT occupations underwent further diversification. The programming job required an increasing knowledge of information systems. In the late seventies, the systems analyst's job had to be distinguished from the programming job.

In the early seventies, many companies set up computer centers including IT departments, sometimes isolated from the rest of the company. Employers' hiring strategies changed towards the external labor market. Now, programmers usually were recruited among boys, leaving high school, but because of shortage of labor girls were sometimes recruited as well. Once recruited, the school leaver would become a qualified programmer by passing through a number of vocational training courses after which certificates of progressive advancement were granted. The systems analysts' jobs were a career step for programmers, if they had passed subsequent training courses. Key entry operators were also recruited externally, usually among young and medium skilled women, but due to labor shortage, employers were forced to recruit among middle-aged reentering women with outdated qualifications.

The sex-typing of the IT occupations did not change in the seventies. The programmers job remained a male dominated job, although women sometimes were recruited. The systems analysts were men, because only qualified programmers, usually men, could enter. The computer operating job was male dominated and the key entry job was female dominated. However, the gender segregation processes continued, now by setting up distinct organizational settings. As soon as data communication technology enabled separation of computer equipment and key entry terminals, the key entry centers were separated from the computer centers, for example in banking and insurance. Due to these distinct organizational settings the promotion chain from key entry typist to computer operator was broken. Moreover, due to the shortages in the labor market, the key entry centers were moved to regions with a larger labor supply. Thus, the male-dominated jobs were separated from the female-dominated jobs. At the end of this decade, 5.4% of the systems analysts were female, 7.9% of the programmers, 25.5% of the computer operators and 98.0% for key-entry operators (Tijdens 1996).

In the seventies, the professional association grew to maturity. It was involved in setting up certificates for the vocational training courses. Moreover, it defined its professional domain, as professional organizations usually do, by explicitly excluding key entry typists. By doing so the professionals kept their domain male-dominated and they defined their domain as skilled. They could have excluded the computer operators as well, defining them as manual work, but they did not.

3.4 The Eighties: Reaching into Higher Hierarchical Levels

During the eighties information technology spread rapidly and irrevocably in the business world. In the first half of the eighties, computerization was a continuation of the seventies, whereas its nature started to change in the second half of the eighties, when the dominance of centralized information systems using mainframe computers with terminals declined in favor of decentralized local information systems on microcomputers. As technology progressed, computer operating became easier and key entry tasks were taken over by optical character reading, by data entry by clients, by data entry at counters, etc. The number of mainframe computers demonstrated low growth, whereas in the first half of this decade the number of terminals increased very fast and in the second half the increase of microcomputers dominated growth figures. The number of IT workers multiplied, while unemployment was very low.

In this decade, the employment structure in IT occupations changed profoundly. Whereas the number of systems analysts multiplied by more than five times and the number of programmers by four, the number of key entry typists decreased slightly and the number of computer operators was at least halved. The increased number of computers and the increasing data to store did not counterbalance the decreasing need for computer operators and key entry typists. The expanding occupations underwent further diversification. The systems designer had to be distinguished from the systems analyst and programming was divided into application programming and operating system programming.

In the early eighties, full-time education in programming and computer science was set up at secondary, tertiary and university level. Moreover, because of high unemployment rates during the recession and the expanding number of employees in IT occupations, the government set up training courses in IT subjects for unemployed graduates. Thus, from the mid-eighties the labor market showed an increase in the supply of highly qualified people. The demand side responded by changing entry requirements from general secondary level qualifications into full-time secondary or university level business-oriented qualifications. As a consequence, qualification structures in IT occupations diversified. Moreover, the job ladder between the programming job and the systems analyst job was increasingly interrupted, because entry for the latter was limited to those having higher education. As the value of the stored information as well as the financial risks related to computerization increased, managerial levels in the IT field moved higher into the firm's hierarchy. At the end of the decade, in large companies the board of directors usually included someone responsible for computer issues.

The sex-typing of the declining key entry occupation remained female, whereas women's share among the declining computer operator occupation decreased. Both occupations became low status groups in the companies. The sex-typing of the high status and fast expanding programmers' and systems analysts' occupations became slightly less male dominated. In 1987, 5.6% of the systems analysts and 10.3% of the programmers were female. This cannot be explained by girls' educational choices, because these remained low. Labor supply showed an increased percentage of women, because the courses for unemployed adults were a result of positive action and IT courses for reentering women were successfully set up (Van Hoek 1989, Biemans & Tijdens 1989). These women have taken advantage of the changes on the demand side of labor, as they did in all EU countries (Social Europe 1993). However, there are still only a few women at the managerial levels.

Professionalization went on as the occupational community defined the job titles in detail in 1986 in order to define their professional domain and the tasks within the domain. Increasingly, the systems analysts, the systems designers and the programmers could be characterized as a professionalized occupational group, whereas the computer operators were increasingly seen as a marginalized and non-professional group within the IT field. The key entry operators were already categorized as a non professional group. The professional community defined the qualification level of the IT occupations higher than ever before and stressed full-time availability within the occupations (Tijdens 1991). Obviously, this was not sufficient to keep women out of the occupational group. The women that entered the occupational group were young, they had no children and on average they were working nearly as many hours as men did, usually forty hours or more. The long working hours indicate that they had to make difficult choices when they wanted to have children. In the Netherlands during the eigthies it became common for women not to withdraw from the labor force, but to request for a reduction in working hours in their job. The female IT professionals were fully aware of these limited possibilities of working part-time (De Olde & Van Doorne-Huiskes 1991). They either had to withdraw from their jobs facing hard times in case of those re-entering or they had to negotiate individually with their employer for him to accept part-time work.

Employer's hiring strategies have been studied in detail in one insurance company (Tijdens 1991). Based on personnel data from 1981 to 1987, the figures show that with increasing computerization the company recruited more well-educated systems analysts and programmers. Their numbers as well as their educational levels at entry rose during the eighties. Quite obviously, the employers' hiring strategy was not limited to the recruitment of men, because also well-educated women entered the department, breaking through segregated occupations. In 1981, the IT department was a fully segregated department with female key entry typists, male computer operators, male programmers and male systems analysts. Six years later the department was less segregated, because the female entry typists and some of the male computer operators had left and a number of female programmers as well as female systems analysts had entered, changing the sex-typing of these two occupations slightly towards desegregation. As the IT department faced high turnover rates for women and low rates for men, we suggest that the gender differences in occupational careers will limit women's promotion prospects because of tenure-based requirements, but provide them with more opportunities to enter, especially when personnel composition for occupations changes. Thus, the female work force can react faster to changing qualification demands than the male work force, because a higher percentage of them is recruited per year. However, the progressive desegregation did not close fully the gender gap between the female and the male workforce in the EDP department. The gap in working hours has nearly disappeared, because women's working hours approach those of men, just as in the field of IT as a whole. The gender gap in wage groups decreased considerably, but the wage gap itself decreased only slightly. The gender gap in ages and tenure hardly changed during the eighties. In this respect, the employer did not break the segregation code.

3.5 The Early Nineties: Blurring Occupational Boundaries

From the end of the eighties, computerization became integrated in the companies' business because of end-user computing. The isolated organizational settings of the computer centers and the key entry centers were broken down in several respects. Key entry partly disappeared. Programming was partly contracted out, as can be seen from the growth of software houses as well as from the availability of packages that could be bought off-the-shelf. The isolated computer centers were partly replaced by information centers, which in many companies were established providing support to end-users. Computer operating changed in favor of help desk tasks and intermediary jobs. Entry requirements shifted away from mathematical and technical skills, and away from company-related requirements towards more business-oriented qualifications with additional knowledge of information systems. Moreover, internal recruitment systems were replaced by external recruitment on all levels.

The occupational group was submitted to further changes. The distinction between professional users and non-professional end-users became blurred and so did their hierarchical relationship. Moreover, the category of non-professional end-users increased more than a thousand times from the end of the seventies to the beginning of the nineties, and became much larger than the occupational group (Tijdens 1994). Due to these changes, labor market demands shifted from computer science based qualifications towards business-oriented qualifications, for example, in areas where computer professions and business administration coincide. Moreover, the male-dominated computer science qualifications in the skilled IT occupations, as well as the male-dominated technical qualifications in the poorly skilled computer operators are no longer the only entry qualifications. In 1993, the percentage of females had grown to 8.9% among systems analysts and to 13.0% among programmers.

The nature of gender segregation in IT occupations is now changing. Among the non-professional users, the proportion of women is much higher -aproximately 50%- than among the professional users, and therefore women quite naturally enter the field of IT. Moreover, the changing entry qualifications are opening up opportunities for women to enter the IT professions. As women's share in computer science and engineering remained unchanged at low levels, their share in business subjects was considerable. This might be due to the fact that managerial jobs require years of experience, and women are still at an entry level of the career ladder, whereas men already had years of experience, enabling them to fulfill the requirements for managerial positions. On the other hand, research shows that here women face the same glass ceiling as they do in other occupations (De Olde & Van Doorne-Huiskes 1991). Nevertheless, as the latter research shows, female IT professionals seem to deny that in the IT field male-dominated attitudes prevail. Moreover, women with children are underrepresented, therefore we can expect that conflicts will arise as the women in the IT professions will grow older and potential care obligations will intervene more persistently with their careers. Because they are not able to solve these conflicts at the moment, women in these occupations probably postpone maternity. Moreover, female IT professionals face a male-dominated culture and they adapt this culture in order to stay in the occupational group.

As the number of job titles in the IT field continued to increase and became blurred, the occupational community had defined the job titles in detail again in 1993. They had to redefine their occupational domain, now allowing job titles that did not cover the computer science only, and thus opening up the domain for women. Moreover, they were starting to loosen the factor binding together the occupational group, as declining membership shows. Professional identity became so diversified, that the association lost ist grip, and therefore was not able to define the occupational group as having a male identity.

4 Conclusions

Now conclusions are drawn about the explanatory power of the four theories as far as the segregation processes within the one occupational group is concerned. Before doing so, we will summarize the history of gender segregation in the IT occupations in the Netherlands.

Computer professional occupations have not been male-dominated occupations from the beginning. In the forties, the programmer's job, the origin of all IT occupations, was a female dominated occupation. It turned into a male dominated occupation in the fifties. From the sixties onwards the occupational group diversified. The female-dominated key entry operators and the male-dominated computer operators were split off from the programmer's job. In the eighties, the same happened to the male-dominated systems analysts' and designers' jobs. In the nineties, managerial levels in IT reached into highest organizational hierarchy. Moreover, from the eighties onwards, the isolated organizational settings were broken down. In the eighties and in the nineties, the job titles were defined by the professional community, and by doing so the professional domain was defined.

In the eighties and nineties, the two skilled IT occupations became professions, whereas the two low-skilled IT occupations, one being an all-female area in computing, were marginalized. One could expect women to be increasingly over represented in the marginalized occupations, but this is not the case. Moreover, women entered into the two skilled occupations, due to characteristics of labor demand favoring women. Within this time frame, women's share in computer science and engineering subjects in higher education remained stable, indicating that women's educational choices did not change. Thus, they cannot be taken fully as an indicator for women's share in occupations. Research has indicated that women pay for these inroads into the high status and skilled male-dominated area's by adapting to men's pattern of working hours, by denying the male-dominated attitudes and by postponing maternity.

As far as the *theories on employers' hiring practices* concerned, it was predicted that employers will hire men for the male dominated IT occupations, but in case of shortage of labor they will go beyond gender boundaries. Our historical research has shown, though, that employers were likely to recruit male employees for the female-dominated programmers occupation because of labor supply factors after WWII. In the late forties, employers' hiring strategies included recruitment for programmers among men, probably mainly due to supply factors. In the fifties and sixties, internal recruitment prevailed, and the sex-typing of IT occupations was established. In the seventies, employers' hiring practices included recruitment among non-traditional groups, i.e. women, for the male-dominated programmer's job, because of labor shortage among men. However, as shortage waned, men were recruited only, and the number of women in the occupations was not enough to 'survive'. In the eighties, women were recruited for the male dominated occupations because of a increasing labor supply, that included women, directed into these occupations. In the nineties, women were recruited for the male dominated occupations because they fitted the changing entry qualifications. Thus, supply factors influence employers' labor demand as far as recruitment according to sex typing is concerned. Due to changing entry qualifications women were sufficiently educated to fulfill this labor demand.

As far as the *theories on professionalization* are concerned, the community of Dutch computer professionals showed that it tried to maintain the occupation's male image in two ways. The strategy to control occupational boundaries as part of the social closure theory was confirmed as the community very clearly stated that the key entry tasks did not belong to the occupational field, which they mainly did in the seventies. By doing so they excluded the key entry typists, being an occupational group with mainly female, poorly qualified workers in the IT field. Another low status IT occupation, the computer operators, was not excluded as explicitly as the key entry operators were. Therefore, this can not be interpreted as an attempt to remain a high status occupational group, it is an attempt to maintain the occupation's male image. Secondly, in the eighties the community stressed several times that the workers in the profession must be available full-time. Thus, the community does not exclude women, but it excludes groups in which women are the majority, either being key entry typists or part-time workers.

Looking at the *theories on the segregation code*, our study of the IT department shows that although the employer recruited women he did not break the segregation code because the men in the department were on average older and had more years of service than the women. The F/M rate hardly changed in this respect. Thus, the segregation code theory seems to be useful for jobs that are part of company's hierarchical lines, but it does not serve for professional occupations. For the IT professions this mechanism is revealed by the fact that women are able to enter the professional field, but are rarely to be found at higher managerial levels. Nevertheless, something can be said on gender relations in the IT field in general. In the seventies the terminal was the most extensively used piece of computer equipment. Male workers in skilled jobs used terminals mainly for systems analysis or programming and they designed and controlled the computerized information systems, whereas female workers used terminals for key entry processing and were regarded as marginal users in unskilled jobs (Bird 1980). Therefore, gender relations within the field of information technology were extremely hierarchical. By the nineties, the gender relations in this field had changed. They are no longer as hierarchical and male-dominated as they used to be, partly because of women's inroads into the IT professions, partly because of the considerable proportion of women in the hugely increased category of non-professional end-users.

As far as the *theories on women's occupational choices* are concerned, the theory that women seek jobs in which a career break does not affect their income might explain that women are underrepresented in the computer professions, because these professions have steep age-wage profiles. However, in the Netherlands women's attitudes towards paid work have changed since the late seventies, because increasingly they decide to have a working career instead of a home making career, and therefore will seek occupations with a steep are-wage profile as men do. This also might explain the rising proportion of women in IT occupations. As argued, women's share in computer science and engineering subjects remained stable, indicating that women's educational choices did not change. Therefore, women's participation rates in computer science and technical subjects will only partly predict their participation rates in IT occupations. It is quite reasonable that women's share in IT occupations has increased while this was not the case with their share in computer science. Theories on women's occupational choices hardly are able to explain sex segregation processes in such fast changing occupations as, for example, the IT field. The theory can explain women's low participation in computer science, but since this is not the appropriate subject as it used to be, the theory does not fully explain women's share in the occupations.

To conclude, the dynamics in the occupational IT field are expressed in the rise and fall of employment figures, the diversification of the occupational groups, the shifts in entry requirements, the shift from internal to external recruitment, and the segmentation processes as far as promotion chains are involved. Labor supply and demand were found as relevant factors for explaining resegregation and desegregation processes. Women's educational choices were found not to be fully indicative for women's share in occupations as entry requirements changed. Mature women are obviously less reluctant for gender-role socialization as girls are. Women's very low share in the increasing managerial level of the IT occupations could be explained by the segregation code theory, but this theory does not apply to the profession as such. Social closure theory seems to be adequate to explain the masculine image of the occupational group, because the professional community defines the profession as having male characteristics. This strategy did not lead to a total exclusion of women, but to adaptation of the male-dominated culture on the part of the female IT professionals.

5 References

1. Arrow, K.J. 1973. The Theory of Discrimination. In O. Ashenfelter & A. Rees (eds), *Discrimination in labor markets.* Princeton: Princeton University Press
2. Bergmann, B. 1986. *The Economic Emergence of Women.* New York, Basic Books Inc. Publishers
3. Bergmann, B. 1989. Does the Market for Women's Labor Need Fixing? *Journal of Economic Perspetives*, 79, 294-313
4. Bird, E. 1980. *Information Technology in the Office: TheImpact on Women's Jobs.* London, Equal Opportunities Commission.
5. Cockburn, C. 1985. *Machinery of Dominace.* London, Pluto Press

6. Etzioni, A. (ed.). 1969. *The Semi-professions and their Organization - Teachers, Nurses, Social Workers.* New York, The Free Press
7. Game, A. & R. Pringle. 1983. *Gender at Work.* London, Pluto Press
8. Greenbaum, J. 1976. Division of Labor in the Computer Field. *Monthly Review*, 28: 40-55
9. Hakim, C. 1993. Segregated and Integrated Occupations: A New Approach to Analysing Social Change. *European Sociological Review*, 9: 289-314
10. Hakim, C. 1994. A Century of Change in Occupational Segregation 1891-1991. *Journal of Historical Sociology*, 7: 435-454
11. Hoek, S. van & E. Rienstra. 1989. Strategies and Education. Pp 191-198 in*Women, Work and Computerization,* edited by K. Tijdens et al. Amsterdam, Elseviers Science Publishers
12. Hoffman, U. 1987. *Computerfrauen.* Rainer Hampp Verlag, München
13. Ireson, C. 1978. Girls' Socialization for Work. Pp. 177-189 in *Women Working*, edited by A. Stromberg & S. Harkess. Palo Alto, CA, Mayfield
14. Jusenius, C.L. 1976. Economics. In *Signs*, Autumn 1976
15. Kanter, R.M. 1977. *Men and Women of the Corporation.* New York
16. Kerf, J. de 1977. De geschiedenis van de automatische digitale rekenmachine: van abacus naar computer. *Informatie*, 19/10: 582-595
17. Kraft, Philip. 1979. The Routinization of Computer Programming. *Sociology of Work and Occupations*, 6: 139-155
18. Mok, A.L. 1977. Professionalisering als maatschappelijk verschijnsel. *M&O*, 31/4: 219-231
19. Olde, C. de & A. Van Doorne-Huiskes. 1991. Positions of Women in Information Technology in The Netherlands. Pp 347-362 in *Women, Work and Computerization*, edited by I. Eriksson, B. Kitchenham & K. Tijdens Amsterdam, North Holland
20. Oost, E.C.J. van. 1994. *Nieuwe functies, nieuwe verschillen: Gender processen in de constructie van de nieuew automatiseringsfuncties 1955-1970.* Enschede: Technical University Twente
21. Parkin, F. 1979. *Marxism and Class Theory: A Bourgeois Critique.* London, Tavistock Publications
22. Polachek, S. 1979. Occupational Segregation among Women: Theory, Evidence, and Prognosis. Pp. 137 - 157 in *Women in the Labor Market*, edited by C. Lloyd et al. New York, Columbia University Press
23. Shurkin, J. 1984. *Engines of the Mind: A History of the Computer.* New York, W.W. Norton & Co
24. Tijdens, K.G. 1989. Automatisering en vrouwenarbeid. Utrecht, Jan van Arkel
25. Tijdens, K.G. 1991. Women in EDP Departments. Pp. 377-391 in *Women, work and computerization*, edited by I. Eriksson, B. Kitchenham & K. Tijdens. Amsterdam, North Holland
26. Tijdens, K.G. 1994. Behind the Screens: The Foreseen and Unforeseen Impact of Computerization on Female Office Worker's Jobs. Pp. 132-139 in *Proceedings of the 2nd European Feminist Research Conference*, edited by T. Eberhart & C. Wächter. Graz, Austria, Technical University

27. Tijdens, K.G. 1996. Segregation Processes by Gender: the Case of Electronic Data Processing Occupations. In P. Beckmann (ed.): *Gender Specific Occupational Segregation*. Nürnberg, Institut für Arbeitsmarkt- und Berufsforschung der Bundesanstalt für Arbeid, BeitrAB 188, pp. 106-131
28. Witz, A. 1986. Patriarchy and the Labour Market: Occupational Control Strategies and the Medical Division of Labour. Pp. 14-35 in *Gender and the labour process*, edited by D. Knights & H. Willmott. Aldershot/ Brookfield, Gower
29. Witz, Anne. 1992. *Professions and patriarchy*. London/New York: Routledge

Biographical note. Kea Tijdens is a sociologist and senior research fellow at the University of Amsterdam. She has published articles and books on IT-professions, developments in office technology, technology in the banking sector, occupational segregation, and impact of new technology on secretaries.

Posters

Project WEBIN – Women's Electronic Business Incubator Network

Natalya Babich[1], Steffi Engert[2], Renate Fries[3], Ann-Margreth Göranson[4], Clem Hermann[5], Helga Heumann[6], Maggie McPherson[7]

[1] Zhenski Innovatsionni Fond Vostok-Zapad (ZhIF), Moscow
[2] SOKOM GmbH, Köln
[3] PID, Köln
[4] Agendum, Svenstavik
[5] Women's Electronic Village Hall, Manchester
[6] Super Nofa, Munich
[7] DACE, University of Sheffield

Goal and Target Grou

The poster will present the network "Women's Electronic Business Incubator Networks", which was founded as a result of the project "Business Incubators - Model(s) for Women in the Electronic Age". This project was co-funded by the Directorate General XXIII of the European Commission.

The members of WEBIN are using and investigating the potential of new information technologies for business creation by women and networking of business women. First findings have been collected in an expert paper, submitted to the European Commission and available to the interested public.

The poster will show the main results from the expert paper and the current work of WEBIN.

The presentation is aimed at the general public at the conference.

Mediums and Materials Used

Poster and hand-outs.

Duration

Presentation 10 minutes, presence of poster all through the conference.

The Coming of the 3rd Industrial Revolution: Will Women Again be Relegated to Service Positions?

Renee Blake[1] and Sigrid Mueller[2]

[1] 110 Bleecker Nr. 4F, New York, NY 10012, USA
Tel. 212 998 7947 (office), 212 673 9839 (home), blake@turing.stanford.edu

[2] 2756 Golden Gate Avenue, Apt. A, San Francisco, CA 94118
Tel. 415 752 5696, sigrid@turing.stanford.edu

Within popular discourse, journalists, economists, and other social scientists are discussing the coming of the 3rd industrial revolution, a 'revolution' through microelectronics. Although the discourse of an industrial revolution implies the availability of jobs to women other than those of support staff, today, women are still concentrated in stereotypically female positions in high technology. We identify the patriarchal belief systems existing within high technology, and the kinds of social and cultural presuppositions generated by such a system, in an attempt to understand the dynamics that limit the advancement fo women, and relegate them a narrow set of occupations.

Drawing from the work of Mueller and Fuchs (1993) and Mueller (f.c.), we analyze the discourse in several genres such as advertisements, movies, and office documents to determine the degree of gender biases within advanded technology. In this study, we are primarily concerned with how women are publicly presented in terms of technology, and demonstrate that women continue to be publicly misrepresented in high technology, usually to their detriment.

One way we unveil cultural stereotypes is by anlayzing advertisements for computers and software and determining how women are visually and lingustically portrayed as employees, as well as targeted as perspective consumers. For example, in several business journals men are depicted as the masters of high technology, be it with their laptops in a restaurant, on a remote island, or on a fishing boat. On the other hand, in professional settings women are usually presented in support positions, i.e., administrative staff, with a minimized relationship to the surrounding technology, which we show is even more minimal outside of the professional arena. While we focus on women in general, we investigate the extent to which gender biases are further exacerbated when race is also considered.

References

1. Mueller, Sigrid and Fuchs, Claudia. 1993 Handbook on How to Avoid Sexism in Public Texts. Frankfurt am Main; Fischer-Verlag.
2. Mueller, Sigrid, forthcoming. Language, Gender and Bureaucracy. Ph.D. dissertation, University of Frankfurt am Main.

Women and Education in Information Technology

Daisy C. Jiang

Department of Management Information Systems, University of Arizona, Tucson, AZ. 85721
Hughes Missile Systems Company, Tucson, AZ. 85706

Current forms of information technologies provide potential for women to eventually overcome gender inequalities in technical areas. Education is proving to be the most important factor in determining the level of access to IT and the resulting experience with IT. Women in developing nations struggle with attaining basic education, although IT is providing increased educational opportunities and hands-on technical experience. Women in industrialized countries fare better in basic education, but are not yet trained and educated in sufficient numbers to substantially eliminate the gender gap in technical capability and experience.

Multimedia-assisted education can complement traditional schooling and training programs and may potentially become a viable alternative to conventional education in poor and remote areas. Primary levels of education, especially, can benefit from long-distance education through radio, TV, telephone, or the Internet. The development of community-based media and rural radio will be the key to spreading education to areas that are too poor for other forms of IT support. Women are proving to be very important to the design and success of these programs. Radio technology in the future will be enhanced by projects like the Washington D.C. based WorldSpace, which will launch three digital satellites in 1988, each capable of 288 high quality radio channels that will be broadcast to digital radio sets. The satellites will be aimed, one each, at Africa, South America, and Asia, with expected operation by the end of the century. Women in industrialized nations suffer a notable loss of interest in technical fields when choosing undergraduate majors and feel less secure in computer science graduate programs. Between 1975-1982, the percentage of women receiving bachelorís degrees in computer science doubled to 35 percent in the US and remained steady throughout the late 1980s. Universities have begun reporting, however, dramatic decreases in the percentage of women majoring in computer science rivaling early 1970s levels without correspondingly severe drops in other technical majors. The level of women receiving PhD's in computer science has remained at a steady 12-13 percent since 1980, while all other fields of science, math, and engineering have experienced increases of women earning PhD's. ITs have provided the most promising tools thus far for eliminating the pattern of male dominance in technology, but women, because of their limited education, experience, and influence, have yet to realize the sort of profound and lasting benefits possible with recent innovations in IT.

Tutorials

Qualifying Female Computer Users - Luxury or Necessity?

Angelika R. Rudolph
Computer Centre of the Hamburg University
Schlüterstrasse 70, D-20146 Hamburg

Nowadays, computers play a more and more important role in all parts of the professional life. Throught this, more and more women are forced to work with computers. And they need special qualifications to use it in a sophisticated way.

In this tutorial we want to discuss amongst others what 'qualification' especially of computer users means. Is it e.g. enough to learn how to use a text processing program like the usage of a typewriter? Or do modern application programs and IT services require a more differentiated education? In particular, the topics of the tutorial and the questions to examine are:

- What means 'qualification of computers users'?
- What about the current training situation? Are there differences in different countries? Have employees in big companies more easily the chance to get a solid education than those in smaller companies or in public services?
- Are there differences between men and women in their access to computers? What are the consequences for the qualification process?
- We will become aquainted with different methods to qualify computer users, like tutorials, on-line help, manuals, CBT, tranining on the job or local experts. And we want to discuss the pros and cons of these methods.
- Finally the consequences and costs of non qualified female computer users will be examined, on the women themselves, the work quality and business effectivity.

Two selected goals of the Tutorial

- Receiving aid to decision-making for the best qualification method in dependenco fo the professional environment.
- Learning why qualifying female computer users will bring profit not only to the women but also their employers and even to the society.

Duration of the Tutorial

1 Full Day

Target Group of the Tutorial

- Personal Managers
- Trainers
- People interested in qualification methods

Information Technology Management for Women

Maggie McPherson, MSc.[1] and Steffi Engert, M. A.[2]

[1] Course Director at Division of Adult Continuing Education, University of Sheffield
[2] General Manager of SOKOM GmbH, Köln

Goal and Target Group

The tutorial is going to introduce a teaching program on informationtechnology-management and telematics as relevant for women. The background to this is the postgraduate distance education course taught at Sheffield University and its adaptation to other cultural and teaching environments, namely its transformation into a requalification program for women returners in Germany.

On the basis of this, the tutorial will

- enter into a discussion of telematics as a subject and a delivery method and
- look at how this is to benefit women, in order to re-enforce their position in the information society
- discuss with the participants the wider issues in the Information Society considering the gender dimension as well as utopias and dystopias.

The tutorial is aimed at teachers and trainers in adult continuing education and vocational training. But also to business women, faced with the practical implications of telematics in their work. But specialist from other areas of IT should not feel deterred, if they are interested.

Mediums and Materials Used

Samples from the course material from our work will be used. The telematics delivery, e-mail and the world wide web, will be either online or in a simulated offline version (projected from the computer by video-beamer).

Duration

The tutorial will take half a day.

Women and Intelligent Networks: Experience in a Leading-Edge Technological Project

Tiziana Margaria[1], Viola Kriete[2], Barbara Massion[2], Cornelia Molic[2], Jutta Schütt[2], Karl-Friedrich Bruhns[2]

[1]Universität Passau (Germany)
[2] Siemens AG, Munich (Germany)

Over the last three years the authors were involved in the development of a new generation solution for Intelligent Networks, as part of a telecommunication project that involved large firms like Siemens but also software houses, consulting firms, and academia.

The importance of the project (it is now the leading-edge product in a highly strategic and innovative area of telecommunications and winner of the 1996 'Information Technology European Award') and the relevance of the roles played throughout the phases of the project by the many involved women in technical, scientific, managerial, and marketing areas, moved us to propose our experience as a topic for dicussion in this conference. It is our explicit wish to start a discussion with experts of the social sciences: this will contribute a real-life case study and bring insights in the collocation of this experience in a general picture. The goal of the tutorial is twofold:

- To introduce Intelligent Networks as a key technology of future telecommunication networks.
  IN services will soon allow the combination of telephone, multimedia, as well as internet features, bringing another generational revolution into our information technology capabilities.
- To present our experience as contributors to this project, with a particular regard to the gender issue.
  As a basis for a discussion with the audience we present our personal experiences, complemented by those of the other women involved in the project. In addition their contributions, in form of short position statements, will be part of the tutorial material.

Covered topics

1. Intelligent networks, presenting global principles and the innovative technical aspects,
2. Social Benefits, discussing how the innovative approach impacts the economy and the societey, e.g. throgh flexibilization of the working life and of jobs. This constitutes a major chance towards real equal opportunities for both genders.
3. Reflections in discussion with the audience, based on the experiences in the project and on first summary of lessons learned.

Telework: The First Step to the Virtual Company. Consequences for the Employment of Women and their Life

Birgit Godehardt, Cornelia Brandt, Illeana Hamburg, Hans-Ulrich List, Christina Oteri, Francesca Sbordone

TA Telearbeit, Geilenkirchen, Germany

Based on the increasing progress of the information technology (IT), new ways of organising the workplace and working times are possible. Telework is one of these innovations, which opens new opportunities for both women in the area of management and in specialisms. In this context telework can be defined as a flexible work, which entail working remotly from an employer, wheras the use of IT is essential for the employers' activities.

Based on the negative experiences in the 80s (the isolated telework was especially introduced in jobs on a lower level of qualification), telework today is predominantly practiced as part time telework. This form of telework combines the advantages of flexible coordination of working time and workplace with maintaining the contacts to colleages and superiors on the basis of regularly meetings in the office.

In many cases the initiative is taken by women who want to stay in the business world during the time of child education in order to retain their skills. As it makes it possible to better arrange private and job-related interests (i.e. arrange the working time with the timetalbe of the children), telework is an interesting alternative especially for this group of staff. Although there remains the necessity for child care, the advantage of telework is shown in a flexible reaction to unexpected events (i.e. illness of the child, stay away of the nanny). In addition the time savings caused by the reduced commuting can also spent for managing private tasks.

The importance of agreeing with the wishes of the staff (considering more flexible time and improved possibilities to unite the family and the job) becomes also a significant aspect in the companies considerations. Thus not only cost savings but also the high motivation of teleworkers convince the companies to put telework into practice. This aspect get its strong meaning as the importance of investments in the staff increases and should be maintained.

Telework as an alternative to the classic paperwork is already practiced in credit banks, assurances, service companies, commerce and industry als well as partly in public authorities and public organizations. The diversity of activities which are basically suitable for telework comprises both professionals, i.e. financial analysts, computer programmers, systems analysts or managers and clerical, i.e. telephone enquiry agent or secretaries.

Although the advantages of teleworking are obvious, there still remains the necessity to establish a positive framework. Insofar, the economy, the policy as well as the society are asked in support of remotly working in order to get a fast breakthrough of telework.

Working Towards the Integration of Women: New Forms of Work and the Use of New Information and Communication technologies in Production

Eileen Green[1], Alison Adam[2], Peter Brodner[3], Ileana Hamburg[3], Julia Kuark[4], Kea Tijdens[5]

[1] School of Social Sciences, University of Teesside, UK
[2] Dept. of Computation, UMIST, UK
[3] Institut Arbeit und Technik, Gelsenkirchen, Germany
[4] Work and Organizational Psychology Unit, ETH, Zurich, Switzerland
[5] University of Amsterdam, The Netherlands

Abstract. This tutorial explores new opportunities for women in the world of labour, especially where these arise from the introduction of modern production systems using information and communication technologies. trategies for women to break down obsolete barriers are examined, drawn from the experiences of projects at IAT in Germany, ETH in Switzerland and the European WITCHES project involving partners from UK, Netherlands, Ireland, Norway, Greece and Spain.

1. Aspects of Integrated Company Renewal. From cases of best practice and change proesses a number of generic guidelines and design principles can be derived including systematic human integration as a strategic investment strategy and ICTs as tools for increasing worker productivity.

2. The Integration of Women in Modern Organizational Structures. This section describes a research project launched at the Work and Organizational Psychology Unit of the Swiss Federal Institute of Technology (ETH) to promote the Integration of Women in Modern Organizational Structures in Production (™ - CIM 1). Male employees in production systems usually hold skilled positions while most women do unskilled work with little opportunity for learning and developing new skills. With the aid of training and reorganization programmess embedded in a participative approach, the participating women and men can develop their social skills through interaction as equal partners, as well as widening their scope of action by influencing the structure and content of their work environments.

3. Ongoing projects in Germany. This section describes a number of projects including a study on "Consequences of new information and communication technologies on the employment situation of women", a new EU project on multimedia and its role in the integration of women into new production systems, a project developing models of tele-work, and a study analyzing female qualifications in the electrical, metal working and textile industries.

4. The WITCHES project. This project is engaged in constructing an interdisciplinary network to carry out a comparative project with two major aspects. (1) a focus upon women's progression within European IT industries, (2) an exploration of the effects of women's under-representation on the design and implementation of IT in industrial contexts. Key questions for discussion include: How can we develop methodologies to explore gendered perceptions of and relationships with IT? What impact might the inclusion of more women designers have upon the practice and outcomes of the design process?

Software-Demonstrations

SEAMLESS: Knowledge-based Evolutionary Software Synthesis

Jutta Eusterbrock

eusterbr@darmstadt.gmd.de
http://www.darmstadt.gmd.de/eusterbr/seamless.html

The objective of deductive program synthesis is to offer automated methods for the development of correct and maintainable software. In particular, programs and software systems which meet declarative specifications and further constraints, as complexity bounds, are extracted from constructive proofs by instantiating templates and composing re-usable procedures or software components from libraries.

Within the logic-based SEAMLESS framework interactive synthesis is perceived as a non-linear, incremental knowledge acquisition process rather than being performed from scratch by a mechanized one-step procedure, reflecting that one of the major problems in software engineering is specifying in advance the requirements in a non-ambiguous, complete, correct and adequate way. The process is divided into the phases **S**pecification, **E**xample Solution, **A**bstraction, **M**odification, **L**earning, **E**xtraction for **S**oftware **S**ynthesis (SEAMLESS).

A multi-layer architecture is used for structuring and representation of heterogenous kinds of synthesis artifacts and synthesis knowledge on different abstraction layers within a declarative framework. Synthesis knowledge includes domain specific and meta knowledge as software components, domain knowledge, complexity bounds, strategies, generic methods for construction, program optimisation and theory formation. The interaction between object layers and metalayers is realized by dynamically linked "viewpoints," which connect abstract concepts with concrete realizations, eg.\ declarative descriptions with software components. The multi-layer architecture provides a flexible, easy extensible system, composed of re-usable, independent knowledge units on different abstraction layers.

The SEAMLESS prototype is implemented in Prolog and integrated into a client-server architecture, using SchedCom, a tool for the management of the communication between parallel processes and embedding CoGLay. The system provides a generic World-Wide Web user interface for invocation of methods and presentation of synthesis results. CoGLay is used to visualize proofs at different levels of abstraction in a composite way. Complex problems are solved by an incremental process. Knowledge is automatically derived from failed as well as sucessful reasoning processes, maintained in a knowledge-base, may be interactively refined and re-used furtheron.

The practical applicability of SEAMLESS in a non-trivial domain was shown by the discovery of a previously unknown sophisticated algorithm. Search complexities were tackled by strategic knowledge, which was implemented as annotated expert knowledge and automatically augmented at runtime. One of the future goals is to extend the WWW user-interface so that end-users can develop domain theories and software incrementally on a globally distributed network.

MultiMedia Forum – An Interactive Online Journal

Ingrid Gabel-Becker
Marlies Ockenfeld

Institut für Integrierte Publikations- und Informationssysteme
GMD - Forschungszentrum Informationstechnik GmbH
Dolivostraße 15, D-64293 Darmstadt

The Need for Multimedia Information in Modern Enterprises

Today, success and survival of geographically dispersed enterprises, working groups, project teams, and associations largely depends on the internal and external information and communication. In view of the developments of telecommunication and the vision of tele-working with selfdefined working hours, the importance of multimedia online information and communication will increase dramatically. The dialogue with the employees in order to promote loyality and motivation and to keep up corporate identity is just as important as the dialogue between the partners and clients in order to arrive at a lasting relationship and to foster the confidence of the client in the competency of the enterprise.

The GMD Prototype Online Multimedia Journal

To meet this demand for multimedia information and communication instruments are needed, to produce a concept for attractive enterprise media which are tailored to specific user groups with pretentious layout standard, which are professionally produced and managed, which are delivered at the right time, which can be used interactively, and which are apt to spread one's message internally and externally.

Since the beginning of 1993 the GMD has been running a field experiment gaining experience with the production and acceptance of a multimedia electronic online journal and a media archive. We have not only elaborated the concept and developed the prototypes, but we have also been systematically evaluating the tests.

The MultiMedia Forum (MMF) is a multimedia online information service with periodic issues for the employees and for external partners of the GMD and with a searchable archive pool. It is available via the GMD intranet and on the Internet and it combines text, image sound and digital video. All documents are highly structured and stored in a single database. A common SGML (international standard for electronic publishing) Document Type Definition determines the structure for all contributions. In contrast to many other electronic newsletters and forums, the MultiMedia Forum is produced by an editorial team. The editorial system – unlike desktop publishing systems – does not aim at concentrating all tasks in the hand of one person. It is rather aimed in providing the various experts involved in the publishing process with the tools best suited for their task and through integration making sure that they cooperate consistently.

SCUA - Secure Conferencing User Agent

Elfriede Hinsch (hinsch@gmd.de)
Anne Jaegemann (jaegemann@gmd.de)
Lan Wang (lan.wang@gmd.de)
http://www.darmstadt.gmd.de/TKT/PROJEKTE/MERCI.html

In the context of the EU project MERCI, technologies are investigated and provided which allow somebody to run confidential conferences between authenticated participants. The tools available for audio, video and data communication described in *[ftp://cs.ucl.ac.uk/mice/videoconference]* are working with the Mbone and they are being enhanced in that way that the data-streams exchanged may be DES encrypted. The objective of our work was to make provision for tools which allow the preparation, announcement, invitation and opening of secure conferences. So GMD has implemented the SCUA, which is an E-mail based approach analogous to the conventional way of announcing and inviting participants to conferences.

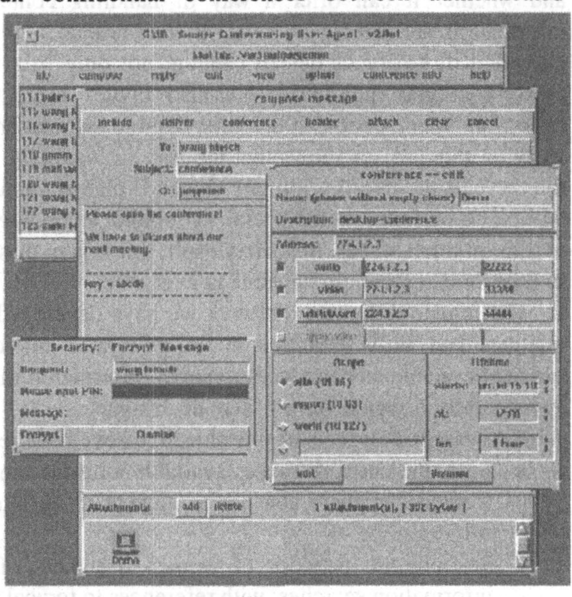

SCUA is based on the MIME standard and has the following features:

- Exchange of encrypted messages between participants who are strongly authenticated by their certified public/private RSA key pairs. The security infrastructure is based on SECUDE, a software package developed by GMD and available on the Internet. Mail encryption is currently based on PEM (Privacy Enhanced Mail, RFC 1113-1115) and will be adapted to more recent standards such as S/MIME.
- Easy inclusion of specific conference data, such as conference name, tools used, multicast addresses etc.
- Easy joining conference by a single click directly from the E-mail.
- Reminder call (tone) for a user, when the starting time of a conference has come.

To achieve cross-platform support and interoperability with existing mailtools, work has been done to enhance existing mailtools with secure conferencing functionality. So far a demonstration prototype with Netscape has been realized.

International Designers´ Network

Petra Luiza Klapper, Melanie Völker
causa formalis • informationdesign, cologne/germany
online: http://www.ds.fh-koeln.de/iwd

For those who see design as something more than simply creating colorful buttons, amusing jingles or deciding how large or small the font should be, it is worth investigating what design can contribute to promoting communications via networks, and whether it can offer a way of handling contents that is appropriate to the information and media at hand. It was crucial to create a space which, unlike a classified directory or design catalog, not only lists new design products and their creators around the world, but also invites users to engage in interdisciplinary reflection. While people at one time liked to distinguish between form and content, the work on this project shows that the two are mutually dependent on one another, and thus reveals the interdisciplinary demands placed upon design. This means that design work is to be found in the social, economic, technological and cultural aspects of our world –in other words, in society itself. For it is in these contexts that design solutions will be rendered comprehensible to everyone.

The female designers´ network we have developed has the goal of conveying the qualities and skills involved in design-related interdisciplinary thought and work processes. Achieving this goal requires information that, in particular, focuses on the conceptually-oriented work of female designers.

Two essential aspects of this objective have been realized:

- First, the network makes available a discussion and issue-related forum which women designers can use to engage in an interdisciplinary discourse on the subject.
- Second, the network of women designers offers user assistance in global information searches, with references to topical issues.

designers´ talk

Every three month a new interdisciplinary issue will be published in the designers´ talk. The forum is open to design theory, sociological and philosophical topics, for those, who see design-related aspects in her own work.

The designers´ talk provides a new discussion and issue related forum. Designers and other persons can use to engage in an interdisciplinary discourse on the subject.

Everbody is invited to propose new topics. The integrated program of Hypernews offers the possibility to read the written dialogs continously and to start the discussion at any point you like without leaving the International Designers´ Network.

resources

resources offers access to detail information about worldwide design-related disciplines. For example, ínteresting exhibitions, scientific and research information. Every person with concrete proposals for the designers´ talk will be represented within the webpages in the "resource collection."

BÜCHERSCHATZ – A Children's OPAC

Ute Külper, Hamburg.

In 1995, the prototype BÜCHERSCHATZ (Book Treasure) was developed as an interdisciplinary project between Ursula Schulz, professor of the Department of Library and Information Studies at the Fachhochschule Hamburg, ten of her students, the designer Manfred Krüger, and two former computer science students Ute Külper and Gabriela Will of Hamburg University. BÜCHERSCHATZ is an online public access catalogue (OPAC) designed to help children aged 8 to 10 find books appropriate to their age and interests and to help them identify the contents of books.

When developing BÜCHERSCHATZ, we followed a model of software development called STEPS (**S**oftware **te**chnique for evolutionary **p**articipatory **s**oftware development). In STEPS, future users of the system participate in the process of software development as much and as early as possible. Evolutionary system development implies that the development is cyclical and software versions are founded in each other. From the outset our intention was to emphasize methodical aspects rather than develop a software fit for commercial use. We therefore focussed on the process of prototyping while letting users participate in software development.

As seen above, BÜCHERSCHATZ has an attractive graphical user interface. It is mouse-driven, uses a metaphor which arouses children's curiosity (treasure hunt), and presents topics of children's books as a limited number of search categories tested with children. These categories are a result of discussions with children and librarians, the study of literature and the collections of children's topics in the children's libraries. BÜCHERSCHATZ also encourages children to read through book descriptions appropriate for children.

Travelling to book descriptions is made simple. Instead of having to type in search statements, the classification is a journey of three decisions (for three levels in the hierarchy) to the book description, each potentially hosting a further 100 classifications on two levels.

Speech Generation in Information Retrieval Dialogues: The SPEAK! Prototype

Adelheit Stein

GMD-IPSI
GMD -- German National Research Center for Information Technology
Integrated Publication and Information Systems Institute
Dolivostr. 15, D-64293 Darmstadt
e-mail: stein@darmstadt.gmd.de

Text-to-speech synthesizers (TTS) commercially available today produce speech which sounds unnatural and is hard to listen to. To sound acceptable to humans high quality synthesized speech requires the assignment of appropriate intonation contours. The effective control of intonation, however, requires synthesizing from meanings, rather than word sequences, and understanding of the functions of intonation in dialogue. The communicative context of the actual dialogue between user and system must be considered for generating appropriate linguistic output and constraining intonation selection. To be able to do this, sophisticated dialogue systems need to maintain models of the dialogue, their users, and the users' communicative goals.

As an alternative to existing text-to-speech and concept-to-speech approaches, the SPEAK! project (Copernicus Programme of the European Union, Project No. 10393) has developed a context-to-speech approach to automatic speech production. The project was conducted from 1994 to 1996 as a cooperation between the technical universities of Budapest and Darmstadt in collaboration with GMD-IPSI.

The SPEAK! prototype is a generic dialogue-based interface to information retrieval systems (the current version provides access to a large text database in the domain of art and art history). The system is able to generate appropriately intonated spoken output to guide users through their interaction with the retrieval system. Integrating dialogue modeling, text generation and speech synthesis paradigms, the overall architecture of the SPEAK! prototype combines a knowledge-based dialogue manager (using the COR model), a text generation system (KOMET-PENMAN), and the speech synthesizer (MULTIVOX, developed by the Speech Research Technology Laboratory of the TU Budapest).

The integrated system features multimodal interaction combining graphical user input (for querying and inspecting the retrieved information items) with spoken output (meta-comments of the system addressing the current dialogue situation). Based on the communicative context/the dialogue history, the system automatically generates utterances with intonation markings, which are interpreted by the speech synthesizer. As the spoken channel is reserved for meta-communication, users can concentrate on the visual channel for information presentation and navigation in the information space.

Information on IFIP, GI, and GMD

International Federation for Information Processing

The International Federation for Information Processing (IFIP), a non-governmental, non-profit umbrella organization for national societies working in the field of information processing, was established in 1960 under the auspices of UNESCO as an aftermath of the first World Computer Congress held in Paris in 1959. Today, IFIP has several types of members and maintains friendly connections to specialized agencies of the UN system and non-governmental organizations. Technical work, which is the heart of IFIP's activity, is managed by a series of Technical Committees. Each of these committees has two major types of activities - Events and Publications.

IFIP's Mission Statement

IFIP's mission is to be the leading, truly international, apolitical organisation which encourages and assists in the development, exploitation and application of Information Technology for the benefit of all people.

Principal Elements

1. To stimulate, encourage and participate in research, development and application of Information Technology (IT) and to foster international co-operation in these activities.
2. To provide a meeting place where national IT Societies can discuss and plan courses of action on issues in our field which are of international significance and thereby to forge increasingly strong links between them and with IFIP.
3. To promote international co-operation directly and through national IT Societies in a free environment between individuals, national and international governmental bodies and kindred scientific and professional organisations.
4. To pay special attention to the needs of developing countries and to assist them in appropriate ways to secure the optimum benefit from the application of IT.
5. To promote professionalism, incorporating high standards of ethics and conduct, among all IT practitioners.
6. To provide a forum for assessing the social consequences of IT applications; to campaign for the safe and beneficial development and use of IT and the protection of people from abuse through its improper application.
7. To foster and facilitate co-operation between academics, the IT industry and governmental bodies and to seek to represent the interest of users.
8. To provide a vehicle for work on the international aspects of IT development and application including the necessary preparatory work for the generation of international standards.
9. To contribute to the formulation of the education and training needed by IT practitioners, users and the public at large.

Address: IFIP Secretariat, Hofstraße 3, A-2361 Laxenburg (Austria),
Phone: +43-2236 -73616 , Fax: +43-2236) 73616 9,
Email: ifip@ifip.or.at, URL: http.//www.ifip.or.at/

Gesellschaft für Informatik e.V.

The Gesellschaft für Informatik e.V. (GI), the German Association of Informatics, was founded in 1969 in Bonn to promote informatics. The 20.000 individual and more than 300 corporate members come from informatics-research, -education, -industry and -applications and also students in informatics.

Scientific work within the GI is done by more than 200 Expert Committees, Special Interest Groups and Working Groups. These Committees and Groups are divided into nine Divisions: Foundations of Informatics, Artificial Intelligence, Software Technology and Information Systems, Telematics and Computer Architecture, Information Technology and Technological Applications, Business Informatics, Informatics in Law and Public Administration, Informatics in Education and Profession, Informatics and Society.

Twenty seven regional groups look after the interests of members and other interested people as far as professional and regional matters are concerned.

The Deutsche Informatik Akademie GmbH (DIA), located in Bonn, initiated and mainly supported by the GI, offers an advanced program of continuing education for professionals in informatics throughout Germany.

In 1990 the International Conference and Research Center for Computer Science (IBFI) was opened at Dagstuhl Castle. It is jointly supported by the GI and seven universities. Financial support comes from the Saarland and Rheinland-Palatinate.

The GI and the GMD not only arrange the Informatics Olympiad but they are also responsible for the "Bundeswettbewerb Informatik", a competition in informatics, which is supported by the Federal Ministry for Science, Education, Research and Technology, backed by the Federal Conference of States Ministries for Education and under the patronage of the Federal President.

The GI has a seat on the council of the Werner-von-Siemens-Ring foundation and is a member of the "Deutscher Verband Technisch-Wissenschaftlicher Vereine" (DVT), which comprises all technological associations in Germany.

Every two years the GI awards the Konrad-Zuse-Medaille (Konrad-Zuse-Award) for outstanding contributions to Computer Science.

The GI is a member of the Council of European Professional Informatics Societies (CEPIS) and of the International Federation for Information Processing (IFIP).

The organ of the GI is the scientific journal "Informatik-Spektrum", which is published bimonthly by Springer-Verlag.

Address:
Gesellschaft für Informatik e.V., Wissenschaftszentrum, Ahrstr. 45, D-53175 Bonn, Tel.: +49-228-302145, Fax.:+49-228-302167, Email: gibonn@gmd.de

Fachausschuß 8.1 "Frauenarbeit und Informatik" in der Gesellschaft für Informatik e.V. (GI)

"Women's Work and Informatics" is the name of a Special Interest Group founded in 1986 under the auspices of the German Society for Informatics (Gesellschaft für Informatik). Today the group has about 450 members and is a forum for female computer professionals to exchange experiences in the discipline and in their various work situations. Together with members of other professions they investigate the historical, social, and educational circumstances of women in computing; interdisciplinary cooperation occurs as a matter of course. About 40 women meet twice a year for workshops that last a whole weekend. In September 1996 the group celebrated its 10th anniversary with a symposium.

Nine local and thematic working groups and a biannual journal promote the general aim, which is to increase the influence of women on the design and application of information technology. Some examples of specific activities are:

- *Women's Research*: In 1989 the group held an interdisciplinary conference on women and informatics [see: Schelhowe, H. (Ed.): Frauenwelt - Computerräume. Proceedings of GI-Tagung der Fachgruppe Frauenarbeit und Informatik. Informatik-Fachberichte 221, Springer-Verlag, Berlin 1989]. A continuing cooperation among scientists resulted from this.
- *Motivation and encouragement of young women*: In 1993 a 50-page brochure for female students was developed and distributed in all high schools.
- *Political demand*: Since 1993 the group has been a member of the National Council of German Women's Organizations to represent the interests of female technicians in the political environment.
- *Integration of women's issues in the professional organization*: Within the "Gesellschaft für Informatik (GI)" the group has been represented on several committees and working groups to increase sensitivity to women's issues. One visible result is the new statutes passed in 1996 that set up a women's representative as a regular member of the presiding committee and declared the promotion of women as an explicit aim of the GI.
- *Network of experts on women in computing*: The group is developing a database to meet the increasing demand for experts to give courses, lectures, reports, interviews, expert opinions and conference contributions.

Address:
Gesellschaft für Informatik e.V., Wissenschaftszentrum, Ahrstr. 45, D-53175 Bonn
Tel.: +49-228-302145, Fax.:+49-228-302167, Email: gibonn@gmd.de

Women´s group at the GMD

GMD, german´s national research center for information technology, conducts research in informatics, communication and media. While in former years GMD was mainly concentrated on basic research, recently it has become more strongly oriented to partnership with industry.

Two years ago, some female researchers at the GMD set up a group to improve the situation of female scientists in this institute. Motivated by the fact, that there a still only a few female scientists in computer science, this group analyses the working conditions of women to gain some insight in possible reasons. The main objective is to increase the proportion of women in research and scientific management by offering better qualification and further education, by looking for more flexible time managment of work and a better integration of both familiar and professional obligations. At the first hand, this group has decided upon a plan of action to promote women of the GMD in different ways. Furthermore, this group supports women by giving advice concerning various aspects of their professional life.

Address:
GMD – Forschungszentrum Informationstechnik GmbH, D-53754 Sankt Augustin
Tel.: +49 - 2241 - 14-0, Fax.: +49 - 2241 - 14-2618, URL: http://www.gmd.de

Printing: Saladruck, Berlin
Binding: Buchbinderei Lüderitz & Bauer, Berlin